Modern
Transportation

MODERN TRANSPORTATION
Selected Readings

Second Edition

Edited by

MARTIN T. FARRIS

Arizona State University

PAUL T. McELHINEY

California State University, Los Angeles

HOUGHTON MIFFLIN COMPANY · BOSTON

Atlanta · Dallas · Geneva, Illinois
Hopewell, New Jersey · Palo Alto

Credit: Photograph of cargo vessel courtesy of Farrell Lines, Inc.

Preface

New to this second edition of *Modern Transportation: Selected Readings* are such subjects as AMTRAK, the U.S. Department of Transportation, and the debate over our national transportation policy. In the first edition, we brought together the first comprehensive collection of transportation readings. Now, in keeping pace with American transportation—via railroads, trucks, jets, freight forwarders, pipelines, inland waterways—we add new readings, subtract older ones, and retain classic ones.

As we wrote in the preface to the first edition, no textbook can cover all aspects of transportation but, with limited space, must concentrate on the general principles of transportation economics, management, regulation, and public policy. Here, we continue to illustrate and to supplement such principles, with articles that range from the "macrocosm" of business logistics to the "microcosm" of the motor bus.

The basic format of the first edition is retained. The four parts cover "The Carriers," "Industrial Traffic and Distribution Management," "Transportation Rates and Costs," "Transportation Problems and Issues." A full introduction to each part sets the stage for the selections that follow; indeed, in sum, the introductions give the student an overview of the whole field of transportation. A headnote precedes each selection, thereby outlining its significance.

The compilation of the selections and the writing of the introductions and headnotes has been a joint endeavor of the two editors: neither of us has served as a "junior" or "senior" editor, nor failed to participate in each step. We wish to express our appreciation to our colleagues in transportation education, who have encouraged us in our task. Our special thanks go to Professors H. David Bess, University of Hawaii; Douglas L. Cochran and Robert E. Swindle, Arizona State University; Grant M. Davis, University of Arkansas; and Roy J. Sampson, University of Oregon—all of whom evaluated for us, in specific ways, their experiences in using the first edition at their various universities. Further, our gratitude goes to the many students who have "pre-tested" the selections by reading them from their viewpoint. When all is said and done, we, of course, accept full responsibility for the compilation of the selections and for the writing of the text.

Martin T. Farris   **Paul T. McElhiney**
Arizona State University   *California State University*
Los Angeles

Contents

PART TWO: INDUSTRIAL TRAFFIC AND DISTRIBUTION MANAGEMENT

PART THREE: TRANSPORTATION RATES AND COSTS

PART FOUR: TRANSPORTATION PROBLEMS AND ISSUES

Modern
Transportation

Part One

The Carriers

Introduction

Transportation always has been a dramatic subject. Past and present song and film writers tend to play on the movement of things and of people, for instance, in "The Wabash Cannonball" and "They Drive by Night," in "By the Time I Get to Phoenix" and "Easy Rider." All in all, transportation's carriers or suppliers convey not only things and people but also transportation's image.

Transportation is a gigantic (as well as a dramatic) subject, in terms of Transportation Association of America estimates of per cent of Gross National Product, capitalization, and manpower. Of our total GNP, some 20 per cent is spent on transportation. We may be surprised, for at least two reasons, to learn that one out of every five dollars goes for transportation. First, many, many trips—expensive ones—are made by goods as they progress from raw materials through the various stages of processing through the channels of distribution (such as brokering, wholesaling, and retailing) and, finally, enter our homes. Second, our direct expenses for transportation are apt to be paid out in small, regular amounts, for bus fares, gasoline, car payments, and so forth.

When we look at capital invested in transportation, we find that in 1966 private industry invested some $192 billion in equipment, terminals, tracks. Additionally, government invests large sums in streets, roadways, airways, waterways—in 1969, $19.8 billion. Of course, transportation and transportation related firms pay large taxes as well—in 1969, 18 per cent of all federal taxes and 30 per cent of all state taxes.

As of 1970, manpower employed directly in transportation numbered 2.6 million people. Many times that number were involved in manufacturing, servicing, operating, and regulating transportation equipment. If these groups are added to the employees furnishing for-hire transportation, the 1970 total comes to over 10 million people or 13 per cent of the labor force.

In this section of the book, we will concentrate on the business function of transportation as supplied by the carriers and give scant attention to the movement of passengers. In later sections, we will introduce more of the problems associated with "people transportation." Now, then, it is meaningful to point out that for many years all of the freight bills added up by all of the shippers in the United States have come, for freight only, to some 9 per cent of the GNP—in 1970 to upwards of $92 billion.

When we look at the carriers, we find that each group of carriers is in itself a separate industry, with distinctive characteristics and specialized functions.

Thus, the railroads engage in long-haul transportation of heavy commodities which sometimes are of small value per unit in carload traffic. Trucks excel in door-to-door, less-than-truckload traffic, with emphasis on the short haul. Air transportation undertakes long-haul, high-value goods in need of quick delivery. Inland water transportation has an advantage in hauling bulk goods of low value which can stand slow transportation and bulk handling and motion. Pipelines allow for liquid goods which flow in one direction at a fair rate of speed and in a continuous stream. Finally, freight forwarders offer speedy and personal handling of less-than-carload and less-than-truckload lots.

Of course, there is some "overlap" among these modes. That is, more than one mode often can do the same job and competition among modes exists. The technological changes that constantly are taking place increase the area of "overlapping" and competition. Of course, some shippers may need one mode of transportation at one time; another, at another time. All in all, transportation is, to a considerable extent, a competitive industry—among modes, as well as among firms within the same mode.

Since different types of transportation are supplied by different modes, we can compare them only in terms of a common denominator. One readily attainable and understandable denominator is "ton-miles"; another is revenues generated. Ton-miles mean just what it says—a ton moved a mile. A ton-mile measurement will give emphasis to heavy goods and to goods moved long distance. If we were to measure by revenues generated, instead of by ton-miles, emphasis would be given to high-value goods and high rates. Thus, it is possible to find various measurements and to end up with various emphases. This fact is illustrated in the following table:

Relative Shares of the Supply of Transportation

	Per cent of ton-miles	Per cent of revenues
Railroads	40.1	35.2
Trucks	21.4	41.5
Pipelines	22.4	3.2
Inland water	15.9	1.3
Air	0.2	18.8

These relative shares have not been constant over time. Previously, railroads were almost the only mode of transportation over land and, as late as World War II, they carried upward of 60 per cent of total ton-miles. While today all modes carry more ton-miles than the total carried pre-World War II, the relative shares have changed. Or, to put the matter another way, much of the increase in ton-miles has gone to the newer modes of transportation, particularly to the motor carriers.

We must realize that, by economic standards, all carriers are not equally healthy. Some of the economic problems appear to be short term (for instance, those of air transportation). Others may be long term and fundamental (say, those of the railroads). A few of the causes of these problems will be analyzed in selections on particular modes.

Finally, we must not overlook the various social and ecological ramifications of the carriers' operations. We must confront the perplexing questions of airport noise, highway safety, adequacy of the railroads for both passengers and shippers.

As we proceed, in the following selections, to consider the carriers, we will use the familiar breakdown by modes of transportation—railroads, motor carriers, air transportation, freight forwarders, pipelines, and inland water transportation.

A.

Railroad

Transportation

Appropriately, our readings about transportation carriers begin with railroads. Since the early 1800's, railroads have been the backbone of the American transportation system. At one time they carried nearly all of the freight and passengers bound for substantial distances. As competitive transport technologies have developed, the relative volume carried by rail has been declining. This is particularly obvious in the movement of passengers. The decline in market share of freight is misleading, however: in absolute terms, the volume of goods hauled by the railroads is as great as ever.

Because of their geographical coverage, and the nature and volume of goods which they carry, railroads are essential to the smooth functioning of our economy. Over 200,000 miles of railroad line in the United States form one of the most comprehensive rail networks in the world and reach into every city and town of importance in the nation. Since the companies are common carriers and are required by law to form connecting routes, this complete network is open for use to everyone in the country. On it, about 27,000 locomotives pull 1.76 million freight cars and a few thousand passenger cars; employees number over 660,000.

Much of this plant and equipment is reasonably up-to-date and well maintained. In the last few decades railroads have increased productivity more than any other American industry. Thus, it is a paradox that they do not operate with a high enough rate of profit to attract necessary private investment for extensive modernization.

The first five articles in this section were written in 1969 to celebrate the first one hundred years of the Pacific railroad. They present a good description of what railroading involves and illustrate well the technological improvement which has occurred in the last century. The balance of the selections discuss some of the most important aspects of the general problems of low profit and low investment which these essential carriers face.

1   Roadway to
the Future
Merwin H. Dick

The main distinguishing feature of a transportation mode is the medium or roadway it traverses. The railroad was an invention which made possible the movement of heavy steam engines over soft ground at a time when the science of highway building was unknown. This article compares the crude hand methods which created the marginal railroad of 100 years ago with the techniques which produced the super railroad of today.

The foundation of tomorrow's transportation is in place today. Made of steel and wood and concrete and crushed rock, it's the guideway called railroad track, two steel rails 56½ inches apart, linking together all parts of a nation and providing a steel channel for the nation's commerce.

To look back at yesterday's railroad—the railroad of Promontory days—is, in fact, to look ahead. To look back to the changes which turned yesterday into today is, perhaps, to get some gauge on the kind of change railroads can be capable of in coming decades.

A railroad civil engineer today, contemplating the methods used to build railroads a hundred years ago, must feel at least a twinge of pity for his counterparts of that era. This would apply all the way down in the organization to the point where the operator of a modern rail-laying machine, sitting comfortably at his control station, is confronted with a picture of the sweating, straining rail handlers in the track-laying gang of a century ago.

It was raw, human muscle that built the first transcontinental line. Horse-drawn scrapers, crude winches and black powder were the only "power-driven" aids, except for the steam locomotive, that human ingenuity had been able to contrive at that time. The main tools of track-laying crews were the shovel, the spike maul, the hand wrench, the claw bar, the lining bar, the hand adz and rail tongs. Even rail tongs were not always available—there is photographic evidence that rails, at least some of the time, were carried forward in the bare hands of the workers.

"Caught up in the spirit
of a great enterprise"

But any feeling of pity for these early track-builders would almost certainly be wasted. A driving desire to get the job done was a force that the men at the top were able to communicate to the entire organization. Sure, the laborers were

From "The Second Revolution in Transportation," *Railway Age,* May 10, 1969. Used by permission.

working for a wage, but that wasn't all. There had to be something else. Why else would a crew of Chinese laborers on the Central Pacific drive itself to rack up a record of 10 miles of track laid in a day, from sunup to sundown? Why, when the average daily output of track built was one to three miles?

The answer lies partly in the fact that the Chinese had a bit of competition going with the predominantly Irish crews that were building the Union Pacific. And the Irish, who could achieve only 8½ miles of track in a single day, are reputed to have cried "foul," perhaps because the Chinese had craftily done considerable preparatory work in advance.

The spirit of competition was part of it, of course. But published reports of those early railroad builders picture them as being a brawling, hardy breed, caught up in the spirit of a great enterprise. They as individuals identified themselves with an organization that was building the first transcontinental railroad. And all the hardships imaginable—heat, cold, snow, primitive living conditions, hostile Indians and a terrain that sometimes was almost impossible— were simply nothing more than part of the day's work. The ultimate goal—the closure at Promontory or at whatever point—was the big thing. Pity indeed!

Are not the seeds of a similar spirit present today as the railroads, having shaken off the past, look forward to the next hundred years? Could they not set for themselves a goal that would rival in significance and importance the goal they pursued with such single-mindedness a century ago? Is not that new goal logically the creation of a vast new multi-modal transportation complex built around a railroad industry that has justified its claim to a keystone position by having converted itself into the world's most efficient transportation machine?

Attainment of the goal won't be easy any more than construction of the first transcontinental rail line was easy. But with the help of the same spirit that motivated the early railroad builders, the fabricators of a new integrated transportation industry would find their goal within reach—and long before another century has passed.

It's technology, at least in large part, that is giving the railroads the muscle they will need for their new role in the transportation picture. And no better illustration of that muscle is available than through a comparison of modern track and track-building practices with those in use when the first transcontinental line was being built. What makes the comparison a striking one is not that the early builders were inept. Far from it. They were superbly skilled in the use of the tools available to them. It's just that the tools available today are so much more advanced than they were in those days.

These advances include the tools used in locating new railroad lines. The early locating engineers, travelling by foot or on horseback, painstakingly sought out the most promising route. But their main tools were the surveyors' chain, the transit, the rod and the level. If these same engineers had the tools that are available today, they would have gone into the field only after the location had been established through aerial photography and the science of photogrammetry, which relieves the field parties of everything except setting the final grade and line stakes.

If a line from Omaha to Sacramento were being located and constructed today, it's certain that the builders would use "super-railroad" specifications. The crude, costly and slow methods of grading in use a century ago required that the lines be built with a minimum of grading. No such limitation would apply, or could be tolerated, today. Modern earth-moving equipment, and more efficient and precise methods of blasting out rock cuts or constructing tunnels, have taken care of that.

Freed of the old limitations, designing engineers could set their sights on a line having (except possibly in mountain districts) ruling grades of 0.5% and maximum curvature of 30 minutes. Fills would be higher, and cuts would be deeper, but economically they could be justified. And who knows but what nuclear explosions would be used to blast cuts straight through mountain ranges?

The changes that have taken place in the economic relationship between embankments and bridges would certainly result in fewer or shorter bridges being built, in favor of earth fills. And certainly the spindly-looking timber trestles of the original lines would be replaced either with embankments or with modern concrete or steel bridges.

In designing the track itself, the engineers would keep in mind several requirements. One, of course, would be the need for track capable of carrying modern loads at high speeds. Another, equally important, would be the need for a structure capable of holding its line and surface for a long period of time, thereby reducing maintenance costs.

With about 1,700 miles of line to be built, the engineers would certainly select their track specifications with the greatest of care. As Japanese engineers did with the New Tokaido Line, the American engineers might even elect, after extensive laboratory work and field testing, to adopt a type of track support entirely different from that in common use today. Possibly it would have concrete slabs or longitudinal beams under the rails. Or the ties might be of concrete, using one or more of the types available today.

Today: heavier rail
that is smoothly welded

However, if the line were built in accordance with specifications in common use today, it would have rail weighing at least 115 pounds per yard, supported with double-shoulder tie plates on creosoted hardwood crossties embedded in crushed-stone ballast. For riding qualities and economical maintenance, the rail would most certainly be welded into continuous lengths, probably a quarter-mile long, before being placed in the track. The rail would doubtless be fully-spiked on curves and anchorage would be sufficient to restrain it from longitudinal movement. The long strings would be joined by field butt welds so that the lengths of continuous stretches of rail would be limited only by the presence of insulated joints or switches.

Such construction would be a far cry indeed from the track that was built a century ago. Its main characteristics were 50-pound or 56-pound iron rail in 30-foot lengths, crossties that appear in some cases to be merely parts of logs with the bark still in place, and dirt "ballast." Such refinements as tie plates and stone ballast were still years away.

The contrast between the methods of track construction used a century ago and those that are finding favor today are striking. Accounts of early track-laying work depict scenes of feverish activity with hordes of men participating. All told, a track-laying gang of that time might include 1,000 men and 100 teams of horses, some used to push cars loaded with rails and other track materials. Foremen frequently directed the work from horseback. The tamping crew made up the largest single unit in the track-laying force. Four-hundred strong, the tampers did their work with shovels and tamping bars.

By comparison, the methods in use today for building new new track, being highly mechanized, require only a handful of men. For distributing the ties on the subgrade ahead of the rail-laying operation, today's organization might employ a self-propelled machine, called the Tiematic, which the Southern Pacific developed for use in the construction of a cut-off line 78 miles long. This machine, manned by an operator and two men, takes crossties from bundles, applies two tie plates to each tie, drives a single spike through each tie plate into the tie, and deposits the ties on the subgrade at the correct line and spacing.

The lengths of welded rail would be delivered to the rail head by the trainload, each load comprised of at least 40 strings—sufficient rails to build five miles of track. A rubber-tired crane, straddling the ties on the subgrade, would grab the ends of two rail lengths at a time and pull them off the train onto special rollers placed on the ties. When the two rail lengths are resting on the rollers for their full length the rollers would be removed and taken ahead for the next pair of rails.

Behind the rail train the track would be fully spiked and anchored, again using highly mechanized units. Ballast would be unloaded to permit the track to be raised and tamped in successive lifts by one-man automated machines possibly tamping two or even three ties at once. The last of these machines, equipped with an automatic lining device, would put the track in final line and surface.

Total manpower requirements for the track laying, ballasting, raising, tamping and lining would come to not more than 80 men, and the daily output of finished track would approach three miles. That's with machines and techniques available now. And who knows what the next big breakthrough might be?

So there is a prescription for the success of the railroad industry in the coming century: Take the technological know-how of 1969, and combine with it a liberal portion of the spirit and drive of 1869. Are there any obstacles that could not be overcome by this combination?

The Job Doesn't
Change, the Cars Do

Fred N. Houser ·

The vehicles which each transportation mode employs are adapted, of course, to fit the mode's roadway. The characteristics, which include lack of friction, of a railway make possible the movement of enormously heavy vehicles at high speeds. Since the inception of American railroads, improvements in roadway construction have been matched by improvements in vehicles. Today, all of the cars on our railroads are operationally standard and compatible but many specialized types are available to accommodate different types of freight.

Phrases like "multi-modal" and "multi-level" are fully as significant to the coming century's transportation patterns as were "trans-Missouri" and "trans-continental" a century ago. In 1869 it was the railroads' fixed plant that was undergoing dramatic expansion in order that the nation's far-flung territories could be united and served. In 1969 it is the mobile property—the cars and the locomotives—which are undergoing the rapid transformation that can bring a new cohesiveness to America's diverse transport modes.

Actually 1969's multi-modal concept which can see 1800 new automobiles or upwards of 200 trailers and containers moving in a single freight train is not new. Even the line-haul segment of the journey of a nineteenth-century prairie schooner was often performed most efficiently when it was done by rail. But do the freight car and locomotive have a role in an era when the competition is not the horse-drawn wagon but the supersonic jet, the double-bottom highway hauler and the "Big Inch" pipeline?

The inherent advantage of the rail mode is the guided movement that gives railroads the ability to outproduce their transport counterparts by almost unbelievable ratios. To move 100,000 tons of freight between New York and San Francisco takes 43,417 man-days by highway, 11,158 man-days by water, and only 3,320 man-days by rail. The actual surface contact of a steel wheel on a steel rail is only about the size of a dime. By contrast, the flexing of a rubber tire as it flattens over a broader area is such that it takes 7½ times as much force to move a comparably-loaded rubber-tired truck on a highway as it does to move a steel-wheeled railroad car on steel rails. It even takes four times more force to move a hull of comparable capacity through water. A century ago the spread between the railroad and its overland competitors was even more favorable.

The "long" (33 ft.) car of a century
ago could carry 18,000 pounds of lading

The freight cars which had borne Union Pacific and Central Pacific construction materials to the rapidly advancing railheads in the late 1860s were of designs

From "The Second Revolution in Transportation," *Railway Age*, May 10, 1969. Used by permission.

which had been in existence for over 20 years. A few years earlier the superintendent of an Eastern line had reported: "Whether the present plan of construction of cars is the best adapted for the cheap and safe transportation of freight is very questionable. A long—or eight-wheel—car is 28 to 33 feet in length, weighs, including the trucks, 16,000 pounds, and is permitted to carry 18,000 pounds of lading. This load, in addition to the weight of the box, is carried by two bolsters, each resting on a center bearing or pivot. The weight being so great upon these two points renders it difficult to construct bolsters sufficiently strong to carry the weight without bending." Car department officers can take a modicum of comfort in the fact that bolsters and center plates were already in trouble 114 years ago! And while the unfavorable tare-to-payload ratio in the 1855 wooden box car had discouraged its operator, attempts to produce the first iron cars during the Civil War resulted in even poorer ratios. It was five years after Promontory that steel in the form of channels for sills and bolsters was introduced to carbuilding.

Twenty-five years later, the first steel cars

By then the effects of larger locomotives and power braking were resulting in longer trains which necessitated greater longitudinal strength in cars. By the late 1870s, the result was an unchanged payload ratio with box and cattle cars of 20,000-pound capacity weighing 18,000 pounds empty. The wooden eight-wheel coal cars of this period weighed 13,400 pounds and carried 22,400 pounds. About 1880, a pioneer iron hopper car was developed which weighed 12,800 pounds and had a capacity of 26,000 pounds. It was exactly a quarter of a century after Promontory that Carnegie Steel Co. built six steel flat cars. In 1897 the first order for 40-ton steel hopper cars was placed.

When steel cars came into existence, the cast-iron wheels of the period proved inadequate and shortly thereafter the forged steel wheel went into production. The evolution of car components, and even of complete car designs, was carefully guided by the Master Car Builders (MCB) Association, first industry organization to appreciate the problems involved in operating the early American railway network as a system. From its founding in 1867 through its evolution into today's Mechanical Division of the Association of American Railroads, there has been a unifying influence on matters concerned with car construction and car repair.

Soon after its founding it was sponsoring development of the automatic knuckle coupler, pushing application of the automatic air brake, and standardizing car parts so that, for instance, 58 different axle designs were cut to five standard types. Only a dozen years after Promontory, the head of MCB was warning members that "the rapid increase in cars with the large variety of parts used in their constructions shows a want of harmony in the ideas of master car builders as to what constitutes the most economical mode of construction and leads to many evils with no end of annoyance, delay and expense."

Growing standardization was accompanied by a steady upward trend in capacity. Through the first two decades of the twentieth century the American freight fleet increased by 54% to 2.4 million cars while its aggregate capacity went up 250%. The following years were then marked by the first major acquisitions of 70-ton cars; the 1930s saw the 90-ton car enter general interchange service.

For 75 years after Promontory, during which railroads performed virtually all overland freight transportation, America's shipping requirements were met with a minimum of basic car types. In such a period, the subtleties of payload ratio, density/cube relationship, and maximized utilization were not the make-or-break factors into which they have since developed. Transportation had not been confronted with what has lately become known as "environmental control" which encompasses, along with shock and vibration protection, such things as temperature, humidity and atmospheric regulation.

In those good old days, customers weren't cranky

Upward traffic trends and the low-cost cars of that period meant that railway equipment did not have to be utilized efficiently to assure railroads a reasonable level of economic return. Railway customers of that less sophisticated period were not overly concerned with the costs of loading and unloading, the costs of bracing loads for shipment, and the expense of inventory in transit. Loss and damage were an accepted factor in the movement of goods. Railroads could concentrate on efficient ton-mile production, often to the detriment of the service they offered.

One observer of the transportation scene has recently predicted that the role of the rails in the coming decades could be primarily the movement of the products of the mines and forests—mainly the raw materials of our economy. Certainly the carriers are developing techniques to do this job more effectively—jumbo tank cars, Big John covered hoppers, the unit train. For such traffic in volume, the concept of the individual car seems destined to evolve into an articulated train, incapable of being divided into individual units for handling to multiple origins and destinations. What is inevitable in almost any event, will be a relaxing of the design restraints involved in complete car-fleet compatibility. At some sacrifice in today's complete interchangeability, there may be dual standards in the industry.

Today, cars are tailored to the exacting needs of a particular shipper

Already there are two levels of longitudinal protection—traditional draft gears for rugged ladings and elaborate cushioning systems for fragile freight. The industry may soon have to adopt two types of running gear—one style for operation at low speeds and a new and more sophisticated arrangement for the higher freight-train speeds which are inevitable. The industry's automatic coupler is now being examined with the assignment of making it compatible with a new era of railroading, possibly at some sacrifice of complete compatibility.

Like car components, cars themselves are being increasingly tailored to do specific transportation jobs. Even the lowly flat car, once the epitome of the general service vehicle, has lost this role as, in special configurations, it transports containers, trailers, automobiles, farm machinery, wall board, coil steel, airplane parts, and rocket propellants. These hardware advances, combined with "software" improvements such as Automatic Car Identification and computerized maintenance records, can preserve the railroads' ability to be competitive across the entire transportation spectrum. Increasingly this will not mean meeting, or beating, the competition, but evolving systems which make rail and other modes partners—truly multi-modal transport.

---

3   **Power to Speed**
                               Tomorrow's Commerce
                               Fred N. Houser

By the end of the Civil War, nearly all of our railroads were using a rugged little steam engine called the "American" type. The American had four wheels on the leading truck, four drive wheels, and no wheels at all under the cab. It was a standard engine suited to all railroad tasks. As technology progressed, the American gave way to other types with other wheel arrangements, each designed for a particular job. The steam engine, however, produced too much heat and light and too little tractive energy. Modern railroads turned, as a result, to the diesel-electric engine which has high thermal efficiency—and which, like the old American, is becoming standardized.

A century ago it was power and speed unrivaled in other transport modes that characterized the American railroad. In the century ahead there is the potential for using the nation's increasingly scarce natural and manpower resources more effectively than is possible in any other form of transportation. Whether tomorrow's traction be in the form of locomotives, as it has for 140 years, or in the configuration of individually-powered vehicles (the electric Metroliners are a prime example), there is a fuel economy about the rail mode that is tough to match.

While the ceremony at Promontory a century ago marked the beginning of a new railroad era, the locomotives pulling the two trains essentially represented an era of motive power that was ending—not beginning. Already on the American scene were a growing number of specialized locomotives which shortly

From "The Second Revolution in Transportation," *Railway Age*, May 10, 1969. Used by permission.

were to displace the general service American (or 4-4-0) type from many of its traditional assignments.

This trend was predictable—more power, more specialization. It was happening a hundred years ago; it is happening today; it can be expected to continue to happen. While the general concepts of the relatively new 4-4-0 Central Pacific "Jupiter" and 4-4-0 Union Pacific "119" (both built by Alco predecessor companies in 1868) were destined to be duplicated (in declining numbers) for three more decades, Angus Sinclair sets 1870 as the peak of popularity of the American type with 85% of U.S. motive power then of this wheel arrangement. What was ending was the idea that a single type of locomotive was adequate for the passenger trains, freights and switching assignments of a growing nation where each of these operations was being transformed into something very specialized.

From its development 30 years earlier, the 4-4-0 locomotive had been well suited for all services. Its flexible suspension enabled it to operate well over uneven track. The locomotive had relatively few, easy-to-repair parts and was low in first cost while being relatively powerful. Smithsonian Institution's John H. White, Jr., has identified it as "the national engine, a machine without peer in this country because it answered every need."

Then: conservatism and resistance to change

Initially American railways had relied on the pioneer, but sophisticated, steam locomotives turned out by British builders—units which were designed for the carefully engineered and well constructed railways that were being put down in Britain. Conditions in America, including a shortage of investment capital, demanded a less sophisticated engine of greater power, durability and stability. Soon the 4-4-0 emerged as the motive power which could best be operated successfully on the poor track of that time and operated despite the poor maintenance facilities, untreated water and incompetent engine-men of those early years.

Domestic builders were soon producing these flexible, cheap machines in volume. White cites the requirements of U.S. locomotives in the mid-nineteenth century in order of importance: Flexibility, simplicity, power, low initial cost, and ease of maintenance. Fuel economy was definitely a secondary consideration, although the transition from wood to the more efficient coal was already under way in 1869.

Commercial locomotive builders, from the beginning, were responsible for most of the significant American design reforms. Generally, however, nineteenth century locomotive building was characterized by conservatism and resistance to novel designs. Until 1900 it was possible to increase locomotive capacity satisfactorily simply by increasing boiler and cylinder size, or by raising steam pressure. This simple, straight-line development reached its limit about 1900 when the era of the superheater, booster and stoker began.

From its earliest days, with the benefit of respectable track, the American locomotive had been capable of speeds up to 60 mph. Within 25 years after the Golden Spike ceremony, one would attain a speed of 112.5 mph.

Half a continent back of UP 119 that May 1869 morning was evolving the mechanism which was to have as profound an effect on railroading as designers' attempts to increase locomotive output. Just a month prior to the Promontory ceremony, a young Pittsburgh, Pa., inventor had received the world's first patent for the air brake.

George Westinghouse's invention climaxed 40 years of attempts by engineers and inventors to stop trains by means other than muscle power; its principle continues in use today. While Westinghouse had seized upon the transmission of compressed air (after reading of the powering of rock drills in an Italian tunnel), the railroad industry had really been introduced to the transmission of power and control signals from a remote point to all the units making up a train. By 1880 it was current for electric traction; by the 1890s it was electric signals for multiple-unit control; by the 1920s it was inductive signals for train protection; in the 1930s it was radio for train communication. The groundwork had been laid for railway automation.

The most serious shortcoming of the 1869 straight air brake was the loss of braking power and control when a train separation occurred. This was recognized early and led to the development of the Westinghouse automatic air brake system in 1872. The expression "fail safe" had become a railway industry by-word. The air brake immediately made possible the operation of longer, heavier and faster trains. That trend has continued to the present; with the continuing refinement in control techniques it, if anything, will accelerate in the years ahead.

While their immediate effects on railroading were minor, the two most significant motive power developments of the century after 1869 took place within less than 30 years following the driving of the Golden Spike. By 1880 Thomas Edison was pushing his pioneer work in electric traction; by 1897 Dr. Rudolph Diesel had built his first successful compression-ignition internal combustion engine in Germany. It would be 1925 before there was a real marriage of these American and German technical developments, resulting in the first commercially successful diesel-electric locomotive. In the meantime, the technology of the straight electric locomotive was being refined.

Now: experiments with new types of power

There was a stage in dieselization of the American railways when the 1500-hp, four-motor unit constituted a breed of locomotive almost as numerous, relatively, as the steam 4-4-0s had been at the time the Jupiter and 119 met in Utah. This new American type, however, was destined for a much shorter period of supremacy. Soon the motive power evolution shoved single-engine unit ratings to 1800, 2000, 2500, 2750, 3000, 3300 and 3600 horsepower. By early next year there is to be a single-engine, 4000-hp unit operating in North America . . . and more are in prospect.

Although the dual-engine diesel unit emerged in the earliest days as a solution to the need for high power, it has had relatively few advocates except in passenger service. Union Pacific has been the principal proponent of the highest-power-per-unit possible and its 6600-horsepower Centennial model is the latest (and largest) dual-engine design for freight service. For nearly 20 years this railroad fostered development of the gas-turbine-electric locomotive as a solution to the quandary of attaining power ratings approximating those of its final 4-6-6-4 and 4-8-8-4 steam locomotives. The rising cost of low-grade liquid fuels has recently acted to make UP's big turbines as uneconomical as their oil-fired steam predecessors and all American attention is again focused on the diesel.

The fuel economy of the diesel engine in freight service seems to render it invulnerable to inroads of other prime moves . . . with one possible exception. Faced with the same rising fuel-cost trend which has already side-tracked the gas turbine, railways are showing increasing interest in (but so far no commitment to) full electrification. In decades ahead when national policy may establish the patterns for consumption of energy and control of atmospheric pollution, railroads could emerge as the consumers of central-station-generated electric power distributed by catenary to completely smokeless motive power units. The consumption of fossil fuels would be left to the air and highway modes which seem far less capable of utilizing energy produced by nuclear power stations. The major investment represented in the catenary for railway electrification is a quandary which so far goes unresolved.

Fully as significant as the fuel economy of the diesel-electric locomotive have been the changes in operating, maintenance and servicing practices which accompanied its introduction. The electric transmission and multiple-unit concept make it possible for a single engineman to regulate the development of virtually any tractive effort which is needed, thus eliminating many traditional steam practices such as double-heading and helper districts for surmounting grades. Completely gone is the once-complex problem of locomotive water supply, particularly troublesome in arid territories such as that where the Golden Spike driving occurred.

Pulling the railroads
into the 21st century

Locomotive manufacturing and maintenance facilities have been transformed from job shops to full scale production lines. Component replacement and unit exchange have completely altered the philosophy of locomotive repair. Currently locomotive maintenance is undergoing a transition which might be described as "having the maintenance program manage the engine, rather than having the engine manage the program."

Spectrographic analysis of crankcase oils, radioactive analysis of engine component wear, automated diagnostic testing, and computerized locomotive component records are giving motive power managers the real power to manage. These tools promise to go far in depriving the locomotive of its "prima donna" status in railroading. What is emerging is the predictable, productive power source necessary to pull the railroads through their next century.

---

4   **Communications for**
                            Space Age Railroading
                            Robert W. McKnight

Railroads always have had a communications advantage over other forms of transportation in that stations along the line could communicate with a train as it progressed. The telegraph made it possible, very early, to string the stations together and provide central control of a whole system. In water, truck and air transport, vehicles are not tied to a company right-of-way; in these modes central control of large systems had to wait for the invention of the radio. Today, railroads, too, benefit from radio communications and use many electronic aids to data transmission. Further, they retain their basic communications advantage: coaxial cables can be buried along their self-controlled right-of-way—to provide enormous private communications capacity.

What a difference a century makes.

Back in 1869, telegraph was the one means of fast communications. The agent-telegrapher, no matter how far out along the line, could always be in quick—and in those days almost instant—contact with headquarters, the division offices and usually the dispatcher. Telegraph did a fine job then; it does now, although by using a typewriter keyboard, messages can be sent much faster than using the old key and sounder method. And the old-time telegrapher probably wouldn't believe some of the other communications tools now serving the industry.

Railroads have progressed much in the 100 years since the nation was linked by rails on that May 10, 1869. One of the evidences of the years of progress: Development of the digital computer—a machine that just sits, hums and does literally millions of routine, repetitive jobs without complaint. Its one drawback: It works only when told to and does only what it is told. It can't think. So, in the 100 years since the Golden Spike was driven, that agent-telegrapher—now he may be an agent or agent-operator—has had a many-fold increase in his ability to communicate. He can now have literally the entire railroad at his fingertips. The vast storage capacity plus the almost instantaneous information-retrieval

From "The Second Revolution in Transportation," *Railway Age*, May 10, 1969. Used by permission.

capabilities of the computer enable this agent out on the line to get almost any information he needs or wants.

With only the telegraph, the agent was really an order-taker. He took orders from customers and from headquarters—dispatchers and superintendents. Now he is a manager. At his instant grasp via today's tremendous communications capability are the facts with which he can intelligently manage his area of activity.

The next 100 years of railroading will truly see a revolution in the way things get done, in how railroads operate, in what people can do. The tools of this managerial revolution are here, right now . . .

There will be some breakthroughs and undoubtedly some startling developments not now foreseen. But the basic tools are here. Computers will no doubt increase in capacity to calculate, compare, sort, tabulate and correlate data. With the increase in calculating ability will come a similar marked increase in storage capacity and a great shortening of time required to calculate and retrieve information. Techniques in miniaturization will make it possible for the truly desk-size computer to become a standard device for a manager's office.

Communications links will be expanded in capacity and speed so that from the desk-size computer to the large-scale mammoth in the general office, there can be direct links. Computer-to-computer communications will be commonplace. Also, the man-to-machine links will be greatly expanded.

Railroad managers at all levels—from the agent or supervisor along the line to the supervisor or department head in the general office—will be better able to manage because of the computer communications links including the man-machine links drawing all together into a unified whole.

Quality control requires information interchange

Railroads are now well along the road toward unified control of their operations. But most of the progress is spotty, with no one really to a point for resting on laurels. In general, the control picture is good, but there is much to be done. Consider the communications area: While several railroads have system-wide microwave networks, there are others just starting to install this bulk-communications facility. Until all roads have the bulk-communications capability, individual roads will be compartmentalized or fragmented. Communications between railroads must be as easily obtainable as freight cars are in moving from one road to another. True quality-control of operations will require nothing less.

To achieve such control, the amount of communications in terms of equipment and facilities will be staggering. Right now, outside of the military and the telephone and telegraph companies, railroads are the largest communications users. Communications usage in the next 100 years will border on the truly fantastic. For man-to-man, there will be the telephone and radio for voice communications. But these will be supplemented by various types of graphic systems enabling a man in his office to write or draw pictures for his listener on the other end of the line. Data transmission will include today's techniques with refinements which will make the terminal equipment smaller, easier to maintain and more reliable.

For the bulk-communications facilities required for man-to-man, man-to-computer and computer-to-computer contact, microwave is the present-day work-horse. However, cable communications is to the point of economic justification in many areas. Because cable can be buried along the right-of-way, it is immune to weather and electrical disturbances of high-voltage power lines. In congested metropolitan areas, cable communications might well be the answer—it does not use spectrum space which requires Federal Communications Commission licensing. Also, cable communications is now technically able to provide the circuit of microwave.

In addition to hardware that can provide greater circuit capacity, improved microwave and cable systems, improved coding techniques and bandwidth compression make it possible to cram more circuits or communications paths into a given electrical space, often called spectrum.

Whether it be basic communications equipment or improved coding techniques, bandwidth compression, or whatever, one thing is clear: Technology will provide the railroads with all the communications facilities they will require, now and for the next 100 years.

This tremendous communications capability will enable the railroads to have true centralized control at their headquarters. Even now, railroads can have operations control centers, and some do. The extensive use of visual displays, plus on-line, real-time computing back-up for information processing and retrieval make such a control center possible.

---

5   It's Men Who
Make Revolutions
Gus Welty

This selection stresses the need for cooperation between railroad labor and management in order to continue railroad progress. At the same time, it introduces the reader to conflicts between the two groups. Yesterday's railroad was operated by men who repaired the tracks, ran the trains, and manned the stations. Tomorrow's railroad could be fully automated with men acting only as managers. Today's railroad is in transition. In the past 20 years, railroad employment has decreased from some 1.5 million men to 660,000. Ton-miles carried, however, have increased in the same period from 577 billion to 770 billion.

From "The Second Revolution in Transportation," *Railway Age*, May 10, 1969. Used by permission.

Men built the Pacific Railroad—men armed with little more than blasting powder, picks, shovels and spike mauls. Men—the Irish, the German, Crocker's Chinese—created that first land-transportation revolution a century ago.

Now, men will create a new, all-transportation revolution—and these men will be drawing on a well-stocked arsenal of weapons designed to prevent transport chaos and to provide transport capability undreamed of just a few years ago.

Railroads have come a long way, in the 100 years since May 10, 1869. Other forms of transportation—motor carriers and airlines, especially—have also come a long way, and in a much shorter time-span. How far railroads can go in the next 100 years—and how well all transportation can be welded into a true service "industry"—will depend upon many factors. But no single factor will weigh more heavily than that of manpower quality.

In this context, there's much to be said for IBM's advertising slogan: "Machines should work. People should think." Today, in the front office and out in the field, there's a kind of man/machine competition—and the question of "who's master?" is sometimes in doubt. Railroads—all transportation, in fact—will move much more smoothly into the future when that competition gives way to a coordination of the work/think processes.

In any far-flung enterprise—and transportation is certainly that—this man/machine coordination will place extreme demands upon management quality and upon management's ability to motivate and to communicate its goals.

The machines are here, now. Between today's highly efficient communications systems and today's computer complexes, today's managers have the tools for timely and accurate decision-making. This is true in the front office, where the big decisions are made. It's also true, to an increasing extent, out in the field, where the minute-by-minute operating decisions must be made.

But one job remains to be done: Men must learn to be more comfortable in the presence of machines, if the machines—and the men—are ever to do the work they're capable of doing.

All of this takes on added importance, with a study of the demands which are likely to be placed upon transportation. Certain conclusions might be drawn: First, the projected growth of the economy will produce a steadily rising market not just for more transportation but for more efficient transportation; second, this demand for efficiency in distribution systems may be too much for any one mode to cope with; third, industry and government alike then may be forced to think in terms of integrated or multi-modal transportation; and fourth, the railroads' across-the-board transport capability should place them in a keystone position when total-transportation arches are built.

Super-transportation should be the result. But again, it can be only as "super" as the quality of its managers and operators permits.

What about the quality of transportation management today? Generally, it is better than critics will admit. If there are failings, in a broad sense, they lie in lack of flexibility and narrowness of vision. And not all of these failings can be blamed on the current generation.

Certain types of management can be identified. In trucking and among the airlines, both relatively young businesses, there's still an element of founder-management. But the airlines, blessed with glamor and growth, have had a steady feed of new blood into the enterprise. Even in trucking—where legend revolves around the iron-fisted pioneer who built an empire from a one-truck start—top people talk proudly of their improving record in recruiting college-trained and business-oriented talent. Railroading presents a somewhat different picture—dictated by history. Railroading's managers are successor-managers—blessed with certain advantages created by their predecessors but also cursed with most of the disadvantages, the bad and the shortsighted decisions that a company or an industry can pile up in 100 years or more.

New generation of college graduates
rediscovers the railroad as a career

Age itself has been a handicap in railroading. Any hundred-year-old industry has a problem in generating a positive, forward-looking image. Many railroad men looked apprehensively at the whole Golden Spike celebration buildup, for instance, out of concern that press and public would dwell only on the past—looking misty-eyed at the nostalgic and refusing to turn an eye to today and tomorrow.

Railroads have been cut, deeply and bloodily, by history. The industry's well-publicized labor problems, its difficulties with the passenger train, its chronic revenue/income/investment problems all have their roots in history.

One result has been that until recently railroads have had a tough time competing for talent on the open market. A rigid seniority system seemed to prevail, in management just as much as in unionized jobs. Young men knew, coming in, that it might be years before they could amass enough time-in-grade to move up into responsible—and better paying—positions. Many of them simply elected not to come in. The airlines got them, or IBM, or the aerospace industry, or somebody else.

This is changing. There is more mobility within the industry. Case in point: One midwestern road, at last count, had nine officers of vice-president rank or better who came in from the outside. Movement like this was unheard-of just a few years ago. At the same time, better opportunities are opening up for young men straight off the campus—and more and more railroads are reporting better and better results from their campus-recruiting campaigns. For one reason or another, the current generation of graduates is rediscovering the railroad career. Perhaps, as one observer puts it, "the kids are a step ahead of us—in looking at a transportation system with the railroad at the center of it."

Unfortunately, this same brand of success is less noticeable where general railroad employment is concerned. With employment declining and with labor problems everywhere, working on the railroad doesn't hold the attraction it once held for the youngster straight out of high school—even if his father and grandfather before him were career railroad men.

One of the major rail labor organizations surveyed its membership a few years ago—and the results indicated the scope of the problem. Most employees regarded their own jobs as interesting. But most also regarded their chances of advancement as poor—and a great majority indicated they would not recommend a railroad career to a young man searching around for career opportunity.

If railroads are to have the future that's hoped for, this situation has to change. But it won't, most observers would probably agree, until the entire personnel structure—top to bottom—has the understanding of what has to be done, why it has to be done, and why it's important in the context of each individual's contribution.

This is where motivation and communication come in. This is where history has to be forgotten—with management and the labor organizations trying to make a fresh start.

Top management and labor are finding that their interests are the same

It would, perhaps, be far easier to abolish railroads and begin all over. Restrictions and inflexible rules built up over the years—like barnacles on a ship's hull—would be scraped off; manpower utilization could be geared to the here and now, not to the past.

This, however, isn't today's answer. As matters stand, railroads and the labor organizations must live with precedent—and only hope that it can be modified before it becomes an instrument for self-destruction.

Again by reason of age, the railroad industry has transportation's toughest labor problem. It has a morale problem. It must contend with a multiplicity of labor organizations, each struggling to survive as total employment has dropped. It has a more subtle problem in an apparent lack of understanding, on the part of union people, of what must be done to make changing times work to the benefit of the industry and its employees. It has, in short, both an anachronistic union structure and one not now capable of assessing the opportunities that tomorrow's transport demands will present.

Still, there are signs of progress in the rail labor movement. Consolidation of operating unions has reduced their number from five to two. The biggest of the non-operating organizations has had a degree of success in promoting merger.

Some representatives of management are skeptical, or fearful, of the results of this movement. There is a concern about concentration of power. At the same time, union consolidation makes a great deal of economic sense. It should result in an upgrading of union leadership, at all levels. It should produce organizations which are more capable of adjusting to change—organizations with a greater measure of stability.

Now, top management people and top union people are meeting, at more-or-less regular intervals, to try to reach agreement on matters of mutual interest. Hopefully, positive programs will come out of these meetings. But even under the best of top-level conditions, positive programs won't work unless those people who execute the programs—management and rank-and-file personnel alike—know not just what is being done but why it is being done.

Other forms of transportation don't lack for management-labor difficulties. The maritime industry is cursed with problems rivaling those of the railroads. The airlines have their own version of the railroads' locomotive-manning controversy, along with serious problems with maintenance personnel. Motor carriers don't find it easy to bargain with their drivers, even though the operators' union gets generally high marks for its desire to grow in strength by helping the industry to grow.

Still, railroads seem to have the toughest of problems—in trying to improve manpower utilization without always being able to show, in concrete terms, the benefits which will be realized.

This is one factor in the rail unions' lack of support for railroad expansion into other forms of transportation. And it's an ironic thing, in view of the lack of support found for these proposals in other quarters: Outsiders seem convinced that railroad desires for transport expansion are based on an intent to put all the traffic on rails and dry up non-rail traffic; rail union people fear that multi-modal expansion will lead to rail management's throwing the business elsewhere and further cutting down on rail operations and rail jobs.

A program for managing change—rather then being managed by it

There are, in short, several major goals which must be achieved if the railroad is to play the role envisioned for it. The list is not especially long—but it contains no unimportant targets:

—To an even greater extent, the educational community must be made aware of the opportunities that exist in railroad and transport management.

—Management itself must improve its ability to translate objectives, in meaningful terms, to all levels of supervision and, in fact, to all levels of employment.

—Common interests must be developed and pursued by industry's management and by the labor organizations' management, working together.

—Those men who plot the course for organized labor must recognize a need for change; they must have the capability for understanding change and they must be given, by management, both the surface and the underlying reasons for new proposals.

—New channels of communications must be opened up, top to bottom and bottom to top, in management and in labor and between the two.

—Realization must come, that the enterprise cannot succeed if the work force reacts negatively or even passively to proposals for improvement; and realization must come in the labor movement that both union and individual employee can win no long-range gains from an enterprise that isn't in good competitive and financial health.

Finally, there is this point to be made: In no business today is progress a unilateral thing. Management has its responsibilities, organized labor has its. But the big responsibility—that of ensuring success—rests upon both.

---

6   The Railroads Are Running Scared
Gilbert Burck

Soon after this analytical article was written, the federal government took over passenger train operation, a new labor contract revised outmoded work rules, and the Penn Central went bankrupt. Although these major happenings change the article's slant, its author's explanation of the productivity and investment situations in the railroad industry is lucid and helpful. Of particular interest is his observation that railroads are private businesses which are not allowed to solve their own problems.

Testifying before the Senate subcommittee on surface transportation last year, Professor George W. Hilton, chairman of the President's 1964 Task Force on Transportation, discharged a shocker. The U.S. railroads, Hilton declared flatly, are in a long-term decline that is essentially irreversible. Some may judge Hilton's statement as a kind of grim joke, but those familiar with the railroad industry find it all too credible. The railroads are in deep trouble. Between 1961 and 1966 they enjoyed a lustrum of vigor that inspired optimists to predict they would be a growth industry again. But in 1967 and 1968 everything seemed to go wrong, as it often had before:

In both years the whole industry earned less in constant dollars than it did in 1932, the worst year in the history of private enterprise. The eastern carriers, which make up roughly 40 percent of the whole industry, ended up with less actual net operating income than in 1932. It began to look as if the carriers' low earning power, which has kept them chronically starved for capital, might be an incurable disease.

In 1967 and 1968 the railroads' share of intercity freight traffic, which for several years had held steady at about 43 percent, dropped to around 41 percent. The American Trucking Association smugly predicted that by 1980 the share would slide to 34 percent.

In 1968 operating losses of passenger trains soared to a new high, past the $170-million mark—even as congressional and Interstate Commerce Commission resistance to eliminating trains also reached a new high.

In 1968 the carriers lost many of the gains they achieved in their famous

Reprinted from the June 1969 issue of *Fortune* magazine by special permission; © 1969 Time Inc.

1959-64 featherbedding campaign against the unions. This year they may lose them all.

The merger movement, which was calculated to rescue many roads from their special troubles, has run into horrendous troubles of its own, because the merger architects failed to anticipate all the pitfalls of consolidation.

About the only bright page in the current record, ironically, is provided by the carriers' investments in nonrailroad enterprises. About a decade ago railroads began to grasp the advantages of becoming what are now known as conglomerates; some had large tax or investment credits, and all could realize additional tax credits by selling fixed assets at less than book value or abandoning them altogether. So many began buying into unrelated activities. The Kansas City Southern Railway became Kansas City Southern Industries. The Chicago & North Western became Northwest Industries, which owns two chemical companies and is trying to buy B. F. Goodrich. The Illinois Central became Illinois Central Industries, which last year doubled its revenues by buying Abex, a manufacturer of specialized controls. The Penn Central's total investment in hotel, real-estate, pipeline, and other subsidiary operations amounts to perhaps $1.5 billion, and last year it brought the P.C. more than $200 million.

An important question is whether all this investment, no matter how much it may boost corporate earnings, will help or hurt rail transportation. Advocates of diversification argue that it will provide railroads with capital they could not otherwise raise. But some are very skeptical. Just as the carriers' investment in more profitable enterprises represents a flight of scarce capital from railroading, so the chances are that the money generated by these enterprises will not be reinvested in railroads if it can be put to work more profitably elsewhere. These conglomerates, the argument goes, may find themselves forgoing investment in railroads to the point where their properties deteriorate. Then the government would have to step in and take them over.

Fortunately for the nation, this is very unlikely. The Interstate Commerce Commission could and probably would seek the power to prevent rail properties from deteriorating. Last fall Henry C. Darmstadter, an ICC examiner, questioned President Ben Heineman of Northwest Industries sharply and at length about his willingness to keep on investing in a marginal rail operation. Heineman admitted that a determined management could starve a property, but he observed that doing so would be foolish because the railroad would end up in bankruptcy, "and one would lose one's total investment." Others point out that although railroad investment as a whole earns a low return, the carriers are full of internal opportunities that can, if properly exploited, earn a handsome return. All in all, it looks as if railroadmen were stuck with the problems of railroading.

Is 6 percent really necessary?

The industry's basic, ruling, and all-pervasive problem is that it can't make money. Not since the boom days of World War II has it come close to earning the 6 percent on depreciated investment the ICC has considered fair and proper. Its best postwar achievement was in 1948, when it earned 4.3 percent; and much of the time since its earning trend has been level or downward. In both 1967 and 1968, when good corporate bonds fetched more than 7 percent, it earned only around 2.5 percent. Although the earning power of the seventy-five Class 1 railroads (grossing more than $5 million) varies widely and a few show handsome profits, even the most prosperous share a common decline in earning power and a common inability to raise it. Since 1960 the Southern Pacific, probably the most progressive U.S. carrier, has expanded freight traffic by about 50 percent. Last year its net railway operating income came to $102 million. Yet that rather decent sum, after income taxes, represented a mean 3.4 percent on its depreciated railroad investment. About 40 percent of the S.P.'s consolidated net before taxes came from other-than-railroad investments.

Just why railroads should earn 6 or even 5 percent on their investment has given pause to some. Although the carriers have earned that fair and proper return only once in the memory of most men, they have managed to stay in business and serve the nation, often remarkably well. Is 6 percent really necessary? Or to put it another way, is the railroad investment overvalued?

On balance, it is not. Railroads value their depreciated investment at about $28 billion, of which roughly 60 percent is accounted for by fixed plant, mainly track and bridges and buildings, and the other 40 percent by locomotives and cars. The carriers probably deliberately overvalued fixed plant seventy years ago, when they were still expanding and issuing a lot of debt. And the largest single item of fixed plant is accounted for by track, which is not depreciated at all. But at today's replacement prices, fixed plant is probably enormously undervalued. There are 210,000 miles of main line in the U.S. To replace only half of them would probably cost far more than the book value of the entire railroad investment.

Even if their investment were worth only $20 billion, railroads need barrels of money to improve their performance and become more competitive. As Chairman William B. Johnson of the Illinois Central remarks, it takes a lot of capital to reduce costs, and it takes a lot more capital to grow. The crux of the matter is this: the carriers' earning power is low, and their credit standing is therefore generally low. Equity financing, for practically all of them, is out of the question. Rolling stock, however, is easy to come by. Since locomotives and cars can be repossessed, financing them is almost risk-free. They can be financed either with equipment trust certificates, which generally call for a 20 percent down payment and carry close to the prime interest rate, or with so-called conditional sales contracts, which take no down payment and carry a slightly higher interest rate. So during the past decade the carriers spent an average of more than $900 million a year on locomotives and cars. But other investment, such as new yards and line revisions, had to come largely out of cash flow, and amounted only to $300 million a year. Total annual outlays have accordingly averaged only $1.2 billion. William Johnson, who believes railroads will grow with the economy, reckons they should be investing at least $3 billion a year, and some estimates run higher. To raise that kind of money, railroads have got to earn at least 5 percent, or $1.4 billion, on their $28-billion investment. But in 1967 and 1968 their net operating income averaged less than $700 million.

"All they want to talk about is passenger trains"

An ordinary business, confronted with a huge earnings decline, turns a sharp eye on its products, operations, pricing, salesmanship, and management. If some of its products are unattractive or obsolete, it changes them or drops them and develops new ones. If its operations are fat and inefficient, it sweats them down and reorganizes them. If its prices don't sell the goods, it restructures them. As the Communists in East Europe and even the Soviet Union have discovered, there is nothing in the world like the profit motive to increase efficiency.

The fact is that enterprises in Yugoslavia enjoy more freedom in striving for profitability than U.S. railroads do. For eighty-two years now the carriers have been regulated by the Interstate Commerce Commission, and for nearly as long they have been a favorite target for the extortions of special interests, labor monopolists, tax collectors, and national, state, and local lawmakers. Almost everywhere they turn, they are hauled up by regulations, rulings, politics, court decisions, and so-called arbitration and mediation. Today they find themselves with problems whose solution is inherently possible, and could save them as much as $800 million a year. But they alone are not free to solve many of these problems easily because solving them is not their prerogative.

A good example is the passenger business, which in the past two years has been running up dangerous losses. According to the old ICC system of accounting for passenger service, which assesses each train a proportionate share of overhead costs, the passenger trains have been losing, on the average, more than $400 million a year for more than a decade. But nearly everybody agrees that the old ICC formula is arbitrary. Some say it overestimates passenger costs; a lot of money charged against passenger service by that formula, such as for maintenance of bridges and track, would be spent even if passenger trains were abandoned. Others, by contrast, argue it often underestimates passenger costs. President Benjamin Franklin Biaggini of the Southern Pacific points out that the formula takes no account of the fact that a passenger train demands money, executive time, and track space all out of proportion to its importance. The average S.P. passenger train grosses about $4 a mile, while its average freight train grosses about $22. The economic principle of "opportunity cost," which even the Soviet Union is belatedly discovering, says it is bad management to lavish scarce resources on an activity that does not use them as efficiently as alternative projects.

But everybody agrees that a train *is* losing money when it is not grossing enough to pay "out-of-pocket" costs or bare operating expenses plus equipment rentals and taxes. Until fairly recently the industry's out-of-pocket losses have been relatively small—between $5 million and $50 million. But in 1967 patronage of long-distance trains fell off more precipitously than ever. Late that year the Post Office Department began to shift first-class mail from Railway Post Office cars to trucks and planes, and forced the carriers to haul storage or bulk mail in freight trains. Mail revenues, which contributed greatly to passenger-train revenues, dropped from $304 million in 1966 to less than $200 million last year, and are now disappearing. So out-of-pocket losses on passenger trains shot up from about $50 million in 1965 to nearly $140 million in 1967, to $170 million in 1968, and they will be much higher this year. Hit hardest was the Penn Central, which does more than 30 percent of the U.S. passenger business. Last year the P.C. lost $100 million on passenger traffic by the old ICC formula, and perhaps $50 million out-of-pocket.

Until two years ago the ICC regarded unprofitable passenger trains as a burden on the industry and its shippers, and gave a sympathetic ear to companies that could prove they were a burden. Then, just about the time many trains were becoming indisputably unprofitable, the commission changed its tack. What had happened was that the passenger train had become a Congressional Cause. Concerned citizens as well as railroad buffs, suddenly aware that the long-distance passenger train was disappearing, began to bombard their Congressmen with protests. Senators and Congressmen, always grateful for a cause that will offend nobody and please everybody, became passenger-train conscious. "I have interviewed 150 Senators and Congressmen about railroad problems," laments one rail lobbyist, "and all they want to talk about is passenger trains."

Although the ICC is supposed to be above congressional pressure, it suddenly took an avuncular attitude toward long-distance trains. In July, 1968, the commission refused for the second time to allow the Western Pacific to discontinue the California Zephyr between Salt Lake City and San Francisco. This great train, like the cable cars in San Francisco, has been described by an ICC examiner as a national asset. But it is no longer patronized by business travelers, and the airlines' youth fares have emptied its coaches. Only in summer months does it run to capacity. It is grossing, on the average, about $3 a mile, against out-of-pocket expenses of nearly twice as much, and so is losing $4 million a year out-of-pocket. Furthermore, it is twenty years old, and needs $8 million worth of repairs, or must be replaced at a cost of $30 million.

Manifestly, nothing is more important than a formula for determining passenger-train costs fairly. At the request of Congress, the ICC is accordingly trying to frame a new measure of passenger-train profitability based on "avoidable" costs, or the amount that could be saved if a train were pulled off. Since out-of-pocket losses already exceed $170 million a year, losses on an avoidable cost basis will probably come to at least $200 million. The Association of American Railroads, facing such a deficit, has finally cried Uncle Sam. Against the better judgment of some of its members, who felt they were already too much mixed up with government, it has proposed that the government assume the deficits of money-losing trains, and that the Department of Transportation buy replacement equipment and rent it to the railroads.

Such an arrangement, as a matter of fact, would not be new. The commuter problem around Philadelphia and in northern New Jersey has been satisfactorily solved by joint railroad-government deals, and it is only a matter of time before it will be solved elsewhere in the same way. Large government outlays will be necessary for high-speed trains in heavily populated "corridor" areas. The Penn Central's Metroliners, now averaging as much as ninety miles an hour between New York City and Washington, were developed with the help of $13 million in public money, and will need vast amounts to realize their full potential.

The Department of Transportation is not very cordial to the notion of subsidizing old-fashioned long-distance passenger trains because it frankly regards them as done for. Any money for trains, it feels, should go into "creative" projects like the Metroliners. Yet the cost of running old-fashioned long-distance trains is mounting as steeply as their patronage is declining. The government simply must come to terms with the verdict of the market. If enough American people won't use long-distance trains and pay high enough fares to enable the trains to break even, then by definition operating them is not in the public interest. If the government wants to operate these trains in the interests of a special few, then it should absorb their losses. Or it should allow the railroads to discontinue them.

Payrolls are still too high

Government arbitration and legislation have been largely responsible for the carriers' inability to keep close control of their wage costs, which claim more than two-thirds of all their operating expenses. Under the circumstances the roads have done astonishingly well. Thanks to both competition and technology, they have improved productivity, or output per man-hour, during the past twenty years by an average of more than 5 percent a year—against only 3 percent for all manufacturing. Since the carriers haven't been growing very much, their rising productivity has necessarily ended up mainly as fewer jobs. Rail employment fell from 1,300,000 in 1948 to 590,000 at the end of 1968.

The great defect of this impressive record is that it has done the industry itself no good. Despite the painful reduction in the work force, the percentage of operating revenues going to labor costs has actually risen over the years—from 48.5 percent in 1929 to 53 percent in 1949 to around 54 percent today. "Improvement in labor utilization," concludes Paul H. Banner, assistant vice president of the Southern Railway, in a scholarly paper entitled *Capital and Output in the Railroad Industry*, "has all been passed along in the form of higher wages, with an insufficient proportion retained for investment. Labor has used the argument that productivity has been high and increasing, and the industry should share the benefits of this increase. The data indicate that the industry has been profligate . . . If wage rates at the current level are to be justified, increases in output per man-hour will have to be even higher than they have been."

The noble "victory"

One reason output per man-hour increases haven't been higher is that management has succumbed to the pressure of union representatives for train and engine and yard-service men, who account for 29 percent of the industry's labor force and more than 35 percent of its payroll. Back in 1959 the carriers made their first concerted assault on the make-work or featherbedding rules. Their case was devastating, and several fact-finding boards endorsed it. In 1963 they won the right to reduce some train and yard crews by one man, and gradually to ease 90 percent of freight and yard diesel firemen out of their jobs. But the proposal to revise the mileage-pay system, which would have saved up to $200 million, was mediated in the White House in 1964 by President Johnson, who "persuaded" the carriers to drop their demands in return for small concessions. The total settlement was officially described by a few railroad men as a victory, but it really amounted to a sellout to the unions.

The savings the industry did gain, furthermore, may be ephemeral. The firemen's pact has expired, and Henry Gilbert, president of the Brotherhood of Locomotive Firemen and Enginemen, has demanded the restoration of 18,000 firemen's jobs at an annual cost of some $200 million. If the union rejects arbitration by the National Mediation Board, the case will probably wind up in Congress. The trainmen's union, in return for not opposing the repeal of certain state full-crew laws, got the eastern railroads to restore some of the jobs eliminated in the 1963 agreement. But then it demanded the same concessions from other lines, and began striking them one at a time. The trainmen's strategy, upheld by the Supreme Court, has worked successfully enough to restore jobs of some 4,000 men earning $40 million to the rosters of the railroads. The railroads, in short, not only gained less than half as much as they asked for in 1959, they have given a lot of it back and may yet be forced to give it all back.

The trainmen's agreement, however, expires next year. Railroad management, confronted with the absolute necessity to raise output per man-hour still more, will be derelict in its duty if it does not ask for everything it asked for back in 1959, including revision of make-work mileage rules. If this means trouble, and it probably does, much of the trouble can be blamed on the noble "victory" President Johnson forced upon the carriers in 1964.

Until about a decade ago, ICC regulations made it hard if not impossible for railroadmen to price their product to maximize profits. For this they had themselves, or more precisely their fathers and grandfathers, to blame. As Professor Hilton remarks, the ICC may be an incubus, but it is the railroads' own incubus. For they helped powerfully to establish the ICC in 1887, and later aided and abetted the passage of acts of Congress that gave the ICC power to set rates and to control exit and entry into the business. The railroads, in other words, became a cartel, and the ICC became the cartel administrator.

How the cartel worked

Together they developed a rate structure based not on costs but on maximizing business by charging according to the "value of the service" or "what the traffic will bear." Heavy, low-value freight like coal moved at low ton-mile rates, while valuable merchandise like dresses and tobacco moved at high ton-mile rates. This rate structure, like all rigged pricing systems, proved enormously vulnerable to new competition, particularly trucks. Although the average cost of moving a ton by truck is roughly five times as much as moving it by rail, the trucks were under no obligation to behave like true common carriers and compete for everything the rails hauled. Both by cutting rates and by giving better service, they ran off with the high-rated stuff.

The cartel, originally set up to shelter the railroads from the exigencies of the market, now began to hurt them. For the ICC, directed by Congress in 1935 to preserve the "inherent" advantages of each form of transportation, took other forms of regulated transportation into the cartel, and made rates that allowed *all* regulated carriers to share in the business, regardless of costs. Thus is irony defined. The railroads, painfully aware that their inherent advantages were great, now began to talk like free enterprisers, pointing out accurately enough that if all American business had to price its products as they did, economic progress would have long since been stifled. An inordinately large percentage of rail costs, they argued, are fixed and therefore the cost of handling additional tonnage is low; they should be allowed to reduce rates to get the additional tonnage, so long as they did not actually lose money out-of-pocket.

Their complaints were finally rewarded by the Transportation Act of 1958, which gave them considerable if not very specific freedom in making rates. But last year their cause suffered a setback when the Supreme Court upheld an ICC decision that denied the Penn Central and Louisville & Nashville the right to base rates for ingot molds on out-of-pocket rather than "fully distributed" costs, i.e., containing a proportionate share of all overhead costs. The commission had decided that a combination of truck and barge service provided an "inherently" lower-cost service.

Meantime, however, the railroads had taken enough advantage of their rate-making freedom to practice "creative" pricing. They published trainload, unit-train, and other incentive rates, some of which did not cover fully allocated costs. They developed jumbo cars, and gave shippers special discounts for loading them to capacity. They brought along piggybacking to the point where it accounts for 4.7 percent of all carloadings. Some set up marketing departments to analyze costs closely, to study shippers' needs, and to spot new business possibilities.

All these seemed to work very well indeed. Between 1961 and 1966 . . . the carriers cut average rates by 8.5 percent, increased ton-miles by 31 percent, and at the same time kept costs well enough in hand to lift net operating income by nearly 100 percent. It looked at last as if they had hit upon the right formula for success. But in 1967, rising expenses and a slight dip in traffic drove down net operating income by 35 percent—below its 1932 level, measured in constant dollars. In 1968, despite two successive across-the-board rate increases and a traffic increase of 3.5 percent, net rose only slightly.

It is possible that the across-the-board rate increases were not large enough, and that larger ones might have increased net without losing traffic. But it is also possible that the railroads had cut prices a little more in 1958-66 than their cost structure warranted. Their revenue for hauling the average ton a mile dropped from 1.46 cents in 1958 to 1.26 in 1966, or by 14 percent—while most other costs were rising much more than 14 percent. If their 1967 freight had moved at the same average rate they got in 1958, they would have grossed $1.4 billion more than they did, and they would have earned close to $2 billion, or no less than 7 percent on their investment. If they had not cut rates, to be sure, they probably would not have achieved the volume they did. But they failed to show the earnings they should have shown to offset stiff wage increases and a slight traffic dip in 1967. Between 1961 and 1967, significantly, their share of the intercity freight *dollars* fell by 12 percent, while the regulated truckers' share was rising 10 percent—i.e., the truckers on balance did not have to cut rates to get business. The railroads, it seems plain, have got to reduce costs still more. At the same time, they have got to improve the quality of their service so that they can try to get more for it.

Keep those cars rolling

At least one of the industry's biggest potential sources of cost reduction lies in improving measurably the utilization of its $10-billion fleet of freight cars. The average railroad-owned freight car rolls only about 20,000 miles a year, against 35,000 miles for shipper-owned cars and perhaps 70,000 miles for highway trucks. Paul Banner of the Southern explains why this is more serious than it seems to be. Cars are accounting for a larger and larger part of railroad investment, partly because they are easily financed and partly because the carriers have so little capital for fixed plant and such activities as research. The new equipment, particularly automobile, appliance, and other such special-purpose cars, has reduced costs and enabled the carriers to make competitive rates. But the cost of the cars is rising much faster than revenues, and this, of course, tends to offset the operating savings the cars generate. Unless railroads use these new cars more efficiently, they will have to buy so many more cars to handle future traffic increases that their rate of return will drop further still.

One reason cars don't roll more of the time is that the demand for them varies both seasonally and geographically; having enough cars to meet peak demands necessarily means having idle cars at other times. Another reason is that turnaround time is excessive. Shippers are not obliged to pay demurrage fees until two weekdays have elapsed, both before loading and unloading, and thus shippers tend to use cars as warehouses. Banner notes that the Indian State Railway, which is also cursed with an inadequate supply of capital, allows only five hours of free time at either end of the trip, but of course the Indian system is a government-owned monopoly that doesn't have to cater to the whims of shippers. Yet some progress may be made in reducing U.S. turnaround time.

Still another reason cars roll so little of the time is that until the advent of computer technology there was no cheap way of knowing precisely where each car was all the time. Now a new electronic intelligence system, known as Automatic Car Identification, is being installed. By the end of 1969 all cars will be equipped with reflecting weatherproof labels that will be read automatically by scanners strategically located throughout the nation; the scanners will be connected by wire or microwave to local or distant teletype machines. Eventually they will be hooked up with the railroads' computer systems. If A.C.I. increases car utilization by only 10 percent, which many think is a conservative estimate, it will reduce costs by about $200 million a year.

Made-to-order mini-trains

The biggest potential of such information systems cannot be measured in dollars and cents saved. What they obviously will do is help provide better service. Some experts, indeed, argue that the carriers have more to gain by improving service than by cutting rates. One example of how service can pay off is the so-called mini-train concept. Three years ago the deficit-ridden Reading Railroad decided to try to recapture short-haul, high-rated traffic. It proposed to move cars to the customers' order, and persuaded the unions to drop restrictions on crew size and divisional sovereignty. Now, as soon as a shipper calls up for service, the Reading sends an engine to his siding and promptly rolls as few as five or as many as twenty cars to any destination on the system without stopping. The Reading says its scheme has been successful and profitable beyond expectations; several other roads, including the Illinois Central and Penn Central, are considering it.

Some railroadmen also talk of improving service by diversifying into highway and waterway transportation, and so offering shippers the cheapest and most expeditious of the three, or a combination of the three. This will probably require an act of Congress, for the Supreme Court has generally interpreted the Interstate Commerce Act as forbidding railroads to get into other kinds of transportation. The experience of a few companies that did so when doing so was clearly legal has been edifying. One of them, the Southern Pacific, last year realized some $29 million net from its trucking, pipeline, and other nonrail transportation subsidiaries.

The consolidation blues

Mergers offer the carriers the only real hope of abandoning or downgrading thousands of miles of redundant or marginal lines that cannot possibly make money as they are now operated. The process of merging, however, is long and difficult. Although the ICC has made a policy of expediting consolidation, the Justice Department, driven by a misguided concept of inter-railroad competition, has seen fit to challenge many mergers and delay them interminably. Other intervenors, including railroads that want concessions for real or fancied potential damage to their interests, have done all they can to slow the grinding of the merger mills. And once approved by the government cartel, a merger is just starting on overcoming its troubles. Under the best and luckiest of circumstances, it takes years to eliminate all the differences as well as the duplications in previously competitive companies, whose operating practices are at odds and whose staffs are dominated by seniority and working rules.

Some recent mergers have run into appalling difficulties. The Atlantic Coast

Line and Seaboard Air Line, which became the Seaboard Coast Line nearly two years ago, thought they had anticipated most consolidation costs. But seniority prevented the expeditious transfer of employees; more men had to be relocated at company expense or given severance pay than the merger architects had reckoned on. And the unions insisted that the S.C.L. observe the deal on job protection that they had on the Penn Central: nobody would be fired because of the merger.

Because both predecessor S.C.L. companies had been prosperous and growing, they had little excessive plant. In order to abandon one facility, the new company had to enlarge another one; and owing to rising construction costs, this came to more than expected. Since most, if not all, these costs were charged to operating expenses, the S.C.L.'s 1968 net income dropped steeply. Investors and speculators who had been led to expect results too soon promptly panicked. Despite all this, there is no doubt the merger will eventually pay off handsomely. S.C.L. President W. Thomas Rice describes the consolidation expenses as money in the bank.

The major difficulty in the Penn Central union appears to have been the Pennsylvania Railroad itself. Accountants classified the Pennsylvania—New York Central union as a true marriage, but it really amounted to a take-over by the Pennsylvania, which controlled a majority of the stock and board members. And the Pennsylvania's income from real estate and other nonrailroad ventures accounted for most of the combination's 1967 net income (before extraordinary charges). The P.R.R. once described itself, not extravagantly, as the Standard Railroad of the World. Unfortunately, its plant and operating techniques at the time of the merger were years behind the New York Central's, and the rather simple Pennsylvania computer system was not compatible with the more sophisticated New York Central system.

"If P.C. doesn't work out, we're all sunk"

On top of that, nobody took the trouble to make sure yardmasters on connecting roads designated the precise destinations of cars bound for the Penn Central. Cars that should have been routed through the Pennsylvania yard in Chicago or Cleveland, for example, found their way into the New York Central yard in Chicago and Cleveland. Some got lost for days, and the P.C. lost millions of dollars' worth of business to competing roads and truckers. Last winter, piggyback traffic arriving in Chicago from the West and bound eastward via the P.C. was being taken off flatcars and rolled eastward on the highways. Other lines did all they could to help the floundering giant. "If the Penn Central doesn't work out," was the common reaction, "we're all sunk." P.C. service is improving, and the two organizations are gradually meshing. But it will take at least two more years to begin to realize benefits from the union.

About the best thing that can be said about such examples of the art of merger is that they will teach valuable lessons to other merger candidates. There is no basic reason why two big railroads cannot be put together successfully. The almost 22,000-mile Penn Central has few if any more operating problems than the 14,000-mile Southern Pacific. The Soviet Union's railroad network, which handles much more traffic than the whole U.S. industry, is operated as a single, integrated system. Since 1950, according to a recent study by Holland Hunter of Haverford College, the Soviet system has more than tripled its output without using very much more manpower. Granted that the Soviet system's *level* of productivity was and still is low. But if American railroadmen cannot match their Soviet counterparts in improving performance, they all should resign.

7	The Utilization and

The Utilization and
Adequacy of the
Freight Car Fleet
John Richard Felton
University of Nebraska

More than 500 American railroads connect to form a vast network, with over 200,000 miles of line. To expedite shipping, cars are sent straight through from origin to destination, regardless of what company owns them. The roads use a system of per diem (by the day) interchange to account for the cars and to bill each other for their use. Because of regional differences in demand at different seasons, even a total fleet of 1.8 million cars is sometimes insufficient and localized car shortages develop. This selection discusses the problem and proposes a solution.

The persistence of the problem of freight car supply certainly does not stem from lack of attention on the part of Congress and the Interstate Commerce Commission.[1] As early as 1907 the Commission held extensive hearings on freight car shortages, receiving testimony from shippers of grain, coal and lumber on their inability to obtain freight cars in sufficient number and at the times requested.[2] At frequent intervals ever since, Congress and the Commission have addressed themselves with considerable vigor, but with meager results, to the issue of the utilization and adequacy of the freight car fleet.

While the relationship of the car rental, or per diem rate to the allocation of existing cars and the acquisition of new ones has long been recognized, the late Yehuda Grunfeld pointed out the effect of the per diem rate on freight car supply with a precision and a completeness not previously achieved. Specifically, he noted that (a) a per diem rate which was less than prospective daily ownership costs of a new freight car would lead to an over-all deficiency in freight car ownership; (b) a single per diem rate would discourage the purchase

From John Richard Felton, "The Utilization of the Freight Car Fleet," *Land Economics,* August 1971, pp. 267-273. Used by permission.

of the more expensive freight cars with their greater annual depreciation expense; and (c) a seasonally inflexible per diem rate would fail to equate freight car demand with opportunity costs during peak and off-peak periods.[3] The present study integrates the analysis of per diem rates with other devices employed to influence car supply and proposes a general solution in the form of a car rental system.

The measurement of freight car supply

The supply of freight cars cannot be determined merely by the process of enumeration. Freight cars are not homogeneous as to type and capacity, and intertemporal comparisons must take into consideration changes in car capacity, in fleet composition, and in the percentage of serviceable cars. Thus, in the decade from 1960 through 1969, while the total number of freight-carrying cars owned by Class I railroads declined by 13.5 per cent, the capacity of serviceable cars increased by 6.2 per cent.[4]

While effective capacity of the freight car fleet conditions freight car supply, it is no more a measure of freight car supply than the capacity of a manufacturing establishment is a measure of its output. Therefore, the supply of freight cars over any short time-period is a function not only of aggregate capacity but also of the percentage relationship between average carload weight and average car capacity, the time required for loading and unloading operations, the time spent in classification yards, and on sidings, train speed, and distance. The net result of all of these factors can be ascertained by comparing the revenue ton-miles in 1960 with those in 1969. Revenue ton-miles increased from 572 billion in 1960 to 768 billion in 1969, or by 34.2 per cent.[5] Thus, while the freight car fleet decreased by 13.5 per cent during the decade, the ton-miles per freight car day increased from 954 to 1,426, or by 49.8 per cent, so that the productivity of the aggregate fleet increased by more than one-third.[6]

The system of freight car allocation

Efficiency in the transportation of commodities beyond the lines of the originating railroad requires the movement of freight cars "off-line" rather than the transfer of commodities from the cars of the originating line to connecting or terminating lines. As a consequence, however, two problems arise: (one) the compensation of the owning road for the use of its equipment and (two) the principles which are to govern the subsequent movement of freight cars once they have left the home road.

In 1902 the American Railway System, the predecessor of the present Association of American Railroads, adopted a per diem system of freight car rental charges.[7] These rates have been adjusted from time to time by agreement among the Association's members, one of the more significant modifications occurring in 1964 when a "multi-level" system in which the per diem rate varied with the depreciated original cost of the freight car was adopted.[8] In 1968 the Interstate Commerce Commission promulgated a new car rental system which combined per diem and mileage charges.[9] The car rental rates devised by the Commission did not represent any change in the rationale of the rental system, viz., that the payments should cover the historical costs of car ownership, but rather it constituted an attempt at a more precise allocation of cost on the basis of depreciated original cost of the equipment plus the additional costs to the owning railroad associated with the use of cars by a foreign line.[10]

While the rental charge may be a deterrent to the holding of idle foreign cars, railroads have not relied primarily upon such payments to govern car allocation. The Association of American Railroads (hereinafter referred to as AAR) has developed a comprehensive body of regulations, known as "car service rules," to control car movement.

The underlying principle of these rules, as Eugene W. Coughlin has observed, is that "a railroad buying cars to serve its shippers is entitled to a reasonably prompt return of the cars after they have moved beyond the owner's rails, but that this return should, to the greatest practicable extent, be under load, to keep empty car haulage to a minimum, and even though this process of loading might involve some delay and circuity in returning the cars to the owner."[11] More specifically, the AAR's rules provide that "foreign cars shall be loaded to the fullest extent possible to, toward or via the owning road, and system (home) cars shall not be loaded off owner's rails when the use of foreign cars, properly applicable under these rules, is practicable."[12]

Whatever the merit of the principle embodied in rules, and this will be examined later, the rules themselves suffer two basic shortcomings: they are not enforceable and they are regularly superseded during periods of heavy shipper demand by "car service orders." Such orders typically require Eastern roads to effect certain reductions in the number of freight cars of a particular kind or kinds to specified railroads at particular junctions within a given period of time without regard to ownership.[13] While AAR car service orders, like AAR car service rules, are not enforceable, the Interstate Commerce Commission has authority to issue binding orders, violation of which will subject the violator to substantial penalties.[14]

The per diem system and the adequacy of the freight car fleet

Whether the so-called "freight car shortage" is the product of the maldistribution of freight cars or an inadequacy in their numbers is dependent, in part, upon an answer to the question: Do railroads, as a group, have the incentive to invest in freight cars up to the point that the expected future earnings of such equipment equal the cost of capital? The answer is that it all depends upon the relationship of the per diem rate to expected daily ownership costs to the home road. Even though per diem payments cancel out for the railroad system, as a whole, they play a crucial role in the investment decision process.

If the per diem rate is insufficient to defray expected daily ownership costs of newly-acquired cars, then railroads will need to anticipate earnings for home-line use in excess of the cost of capital before undertaking such investment. By the same token, if the per diem rate is more than sufficient to defray expected daily ownership costs of new freight cars, then an anticipated rate of return for home-line use of less than the cost of capital will still induce new car purchases.

The next question is: Has the per diem rate generally been of sufficient magnitude to cover prospective daily ownership costs of new equipment? The answer, it would appear, is "no." Secular inflation and rising interest rates have tended to raise the expected daily ownership costs of newly-acquired freight cars above the historical daily ownership costs of the existing fleet.

Studies by Yehuda Grunfeld[15] and Robert J. Tosterud[16] have demonstrated that the rate of return to railroads for the off-line use of freight cars has probably not exceeded 3 per cent. While the most recent system of freight car-rental payments is designed to yield a 6 per cent rate of return on depreciated original cost,[17] such a return would scarcely be regarded as adequate to compensate an owner who must borrow at 8½ per cent or more.

Pursuant to Public Law 89-430 of May 26, 1966, Congress conferred authority upon the Interstate Commerce Commission to impose so-called "incentive" per diem charges over and above the ownership costs of freight cars.[18] In Ex Parte No. 252 (Sub. No. 1), the Interstate Commerce Commission did adopt a schedule of incentive per diem charges for general service unequipped boxcars. The incentive charges in effect from September through February of each year would yield the owners of boxcars of foreign lines an 18 per cent return during these months, or an average annual return of 12 per cent.[19] While the higher per diem rates during the peak period of boxcar freight loadings may promote the return of such cars to owning roads and provide an incentive to the acquisition of additional boxcars, it is not obvious that we shall be any closer to achieving an optimum fleet size or to improving upon the efficiency of its utilization. This follows from the fact that the freight car is not necessarily of greater value to the home road than having possession of the car and that any "shortage" in the over-all supply of freight cars is relative to a given level of effectiveness in the utilization of existing equipment. Thus, an improvement in car utilization could easily transform the shortage into a surplus by depressing the anticipated earnings of further additions to the fleet. From this it can be concluded that a solution to the problem of an adequate freight car supply necessitates a simultaneous attack upon car utilization and the size of the fleet itself.

A critique of freight car utilization

The average freight car moves only about 55 1/3 miles a day which, at an average train speed of about 20 miles an hour, it can accomplish in about two hours and forty-five minutes.[20] The remainder of the time it is being held by shippers, consignees or the railroad itself in terminals, classification yards, repair shops, etc. The present practice of allowing "free time" of 1 or 2 working days for loading and unloading operations without the payment of demurrage provides no incentive for loading or unloading prior to the end of this period.

The portion of the year which the average freight car is in the possession of shippers and consignees is greatly exceeded by the time it is held idle by the railroads themselves.[21] A primary reason for the existence of unused freight car capacity at various periods would appear to be seasonal fluctuations in demand coupled with the simultaneity of production and consumption of transport service. In 1969 freight car loadings in the week of October 25th, the 1969 peak, exceeded those of the week of December 27th, the 1969 low, by 57.5 per cent, those of the week of January 4th by 45.4 per cent and those of the average week by 10.5 per cent.[22] The failure of freight rates to vary in accordance with seasonal fluctuations in the demand for transportation service most certainly contributes to the poor utilization of the freight car fleet.

The earning capacity of a car is a reflection of freight rates and the extent of car utilization. Therefore, the demand of railroads for freight cars will exhibit the same seasonal pattern as the demand of shippers for transport service. During periods of greater than normal shipper demand, a railroad in possession of foreign cars finds it profitable to divert such cars to its own use and pay the per diem charge rather than to return the cars to the home road. Conversely, in periods of less than normal demand, foreign cars tend to be returned to the home road to avoid per diem charges. Thus empty car mileage rises at such times as cars are transferred from one location where they are in surplus to another place where they are equally likely to lie idle.[23]

The seasonal inflexibility of per diem rates not only tends to increase the ratio of empty to loaded car miles, but also to militate against optimum utilization. The value of a foreign freight car to a railroad having the car in its possession need only be equal to the per diem charge; the car may have far more value to some other railroad. An inflexible per diem system, however, provides no opportunity for the expression of such demands.

In the interest of the owning railroads, car service rules and orders, as already noted, have been employed to supplement inflexible and inadequate per diem rates. Thus, it seems appropriate to characterize railroad freight car allocation in the United States as based on the ownership principle, modified by notions of efficiency in car utilization, and overlaid by authoritative determinations as to shipper needs. As a consequence, car allocation, at least during periods of heavy demand, is reminiscent of the decision-making process in a centrally-planned socialist system. It should, therefore, occasion no surprise that car allocation has been the subject of unceasing controversy for decades, that much unnecessary empty car movement takes place and that the distribution of cars probably bears slight resemblance to one governed by market principles.

Some proposed solutions

The elimination of "free time" for loading and unloading operations should serve to reduce such delays. Either demurrage which would begin as soon as the car came into the possession of the shipper or consignee or, alternatively, a refund of a portion of the transportation charge for the return of the car before the termination of the "free" period, would provide an incentive for speedier loading and unloading operations.[24]

An obvious method of improving freight car utilization would be through the institution of seasonally variable freight rates. More than fifteen years ago George H. Borts pointed out: "If the present [railway] pricing system were replaced by one under which customers were charged more for service during peak periods, they would have an incentive to even out their demand over time."[25]

While seasonally variable freight rates would be a novelty in railroad transportation, they are a familiar characteristic of the exempt sector of highway transportation. The Marketing Economics Division of the United States Department of Agriculture, in a survey of truck brokers of agricultural commodities, found seasonal fluctuations of 27 to 40 per cent in the rates for the transportation of produce and grain.[26]

The corollary of seasonally variable freight rates would be seasonally variable per diem rates. More than 60 years ago the Interstate Commerce Commission itself gave serious consideration to the adoption of variable per diem rates. The commission suggested that 50¢ might well be regarded as a minimum per diem rate and that a rate as high as $2 a day could be established during the period of greatest demand in the latter half of the year.[27]

The institution of truly flexible freight rates would require the dismantling of the present elaborate system of rate regulation, especially the requirement that rates be published well in advance of any changes therein. Nevertheless, regulation does not preclude peak and off-peak pricing policies, as is evident from the evening, night and holiday rates of the American Telephone and Telegraph Company.[28]

While any proposal for extensive deregulation of freight rates is likely to be dismissed as politically infeasible, any proposal for utilizing the market mechanism to establish the rental charge for freight cars is subject to the objection that connecting and terminating carriers of interline shipments are involuntary renters of freight cars. How can the rental charge be determined by the forces of the market when one of the parties, the railroad receiving a foreign car, cannot refuse to enter into the transaction?

While the involuntary nature of the existing car-rental system would appear to preclude a market for the allocation of freight cars, the creation of a market in which prospective renters and owners would be free to participate or refrain from participating is, nonetheless, a distinct possibility. Insofar as the initial movement of a freight car to an off-line destination is involved, the participating railroads are free to negotiate a division of the joint rate, taking into consideration the rental value of the freight cars employed in transporting goods from origin to destination. Furthermore, whatever the constraints on freedom of negotiation in the initial off-line movement, they are absent for any subsequent movements of the freight car on foreign lines.

Once a foreign car completed its original off-line journey, its disposition could then be determined by a process of bidding for its use. Per diem rates would be established by the competition of railroads and shippers for cars and the proceeds would be paid to the owning railroad or private car company after the deduction of a broker's fee. Cars would presumably be rented on a delivered basis, and a mileage payment would be made to any carrier participating in the movement of the car to the location designated by the renter. Under such a system, cars would be classified by size and type and graded by quality, whenever relevant. Car rental charges would be a function of these variables, as well as of the season of the year and of the distance which the freight car must travel to reach the shipper.

The Car Service Division of the AAR, or some newly-established organization, could undertake the creation and operation of a freight car rental exchange. The Automatic Car Identification (ACI) system and the TeleRail Automated Information Network (TRAIN), which are soon to be in operation,[29] should be invaluable in the assembly of the information necessary to operate such a market.

There would appear to be a number of advantages to be derived from the adoption of a market system of freight car rentals: (1) The existing car fleet would be allocated on the basis of economic considerations of productivity rather than legal considerations of ownership and administrative determinations of relative shipper need. Specifically: (a) empty car mileage should be greatly reduced through the elimination of rules designed to move cars, whether loaded or empty, in the direction of the home road; (b) owners could always assume possession of their own cars merely by making a mileage payment to one of their own junctions; and (c) per diem rates would fluctuate with seasonal variations in the intensity of demand. (2) Carriers which might not have participated to any great extent, if at all, in the movement of a particular carload of goods would no longer be charged for the privilege of transporting empty cars to or toward an owner's lines.[30] The rental system suggested here would provide such compensation for all empty-haul transport. (3) Whenever, despite improvements in car utilization, the anticipated proceeds from freight car rental rose above prospective ownership costs, railroads would be induced to add to the existing fleet. Thus, a freight car-rental exchange system would contribute to the simultaneous solution of the long-run as well as the short-run problem of freight car supply.

NOTES

1. Senator Vance Hartke, Chairman of the Senate Subcommittee on Surface Transportation, opened the 1969 hearing with the observation that the "problem of freight car supply, or lack thereof, has been with us for several years and even decades." "Opening Statement by the Chairman," *Freight Car Supply,* Hearing before the Subcommittee on Surface Transportation of the Committee on Commerce, United States Senate, 91st Congress, 1st sess., May 23, 1969 (Washington, 1969), p. 1.
2. *In the Matter of Freight Car Shortage and Other Insufficient Transportation Facilities,* 12 ICC 561, 568-9 (1907).
3. Yehuda Grunfeld, "The Effect of the Per Diem Rate on the Efficiency and Size of the American Railroad Freight Car Fleet," *Journal of Business,* January 1959, pp. 56-7. Grunfeld's article did, apparently, exert some influence on subsequent car rental policy. The Association of American Railroads instituted a system of multi-level per diem rates on January 1, 1964, the rates varying with the original cost, less depreciation, of the

freight cars, and, in 1966, Congress passed Public Law 89-430 authorizing the Interstate Commerce Commission to establish per diem rates in excess of the historical daily ownership cost of existing equipment in order to provide an incentive for the acquisition of new freight cars.

4. *Statistics of Railroads of Class I in the United States, Years 1959 to 1969* (Washington, D.C.: Association of American Railroads, August 1970), p. 9; *Yearbook of Railroad Facts* (Washington, D.C.: Association of American Railroads, April 1970), p. 58.

5. *Yearbook of Railroad Facts,* p. 35.

6. *Ibid.,* p. 56.

7. E. W. Coughlin, *Freight Car Distribution and Car Handling in the United States* (Washington, D.C.: Association of American Railroads, 1956), pp. 268-9.

8. *Code of Car Service Rules, Code of Per Diem Rules,* Circular OT-10-B (Washington, D.C.: Association of American Railroads, 1968), p. 6.

9. Chicago, Burlington and Quincy Railroad Co. *et al. v.* New York, Susquehanna and Western Railroad Co., *et al.,* 332 ICC 176, 242-3 (1968).

10. *Ibid.,* pp. 213 and 230.

11. Coughlin, *op. cit.,* p. 5.

12. *Ibid.,* p. 9.

13. *Ibid.,* p. 211-2.

14. The authority of the Interstate Commerce Commission to fix per diem rates, promulgate car service rules, issue car allocation orders and impose penalties for violation was established by the Car Service Act of 1917, *United States Statutes at Large,* Part I, pp. 101-2. In 1969 the ICC collected fines totaling $315,700 for violations of its car service orders. See, *Freight Car Shortages,* Hearings before the Special Freight Car Shortage Subcommittee of the Committee on Commerce, United States Senate, 91st Cong., 2nd sess., March 24, 25, and April 1, 1970 (Washington, D.C., 1970), p. 35.

15. Grunfeld, *op. cit.,* pp. 62-3.

16. Robert J. Tosterud, *Economics of the Boxcar Supply* (Unpublished M.S. thesis; Fargo, North Dakota: North Dakota State University, 1969), p. 136.

17. 332 ICC 176, 213 (1968).

18. 80 Stat. 168 (1966).

19. The net credit balance accruing to any railroad from these incentive charges is to be employed only for the purpose of acquiring boxcars over and above such railroad's average additions in the preceding 5 years. ICC, Ex Parte No. 252 (Sub. No. 1), decided April 28, 1970, Appendix B, pp. 3-4.

20. *Yearbook of Railroad Facts,* p. 55.

21. In 1967 inactive car days, including car repair, accounted for 38 per cent of the time of the average freight car while only 18 per cent of the time was devoted to loading and unloading operations. Patrick P. Boles and John O. Gerald, "Demurrage and the Freight Car Situation," *Marketing and Transportation Situation,* MTS 174 (Washington, D.C.: United States Department of Agriculture, August 1969), p. 34.

22. Cars of Revenue Freight Loaded, 1969, CS 54-B (Washington, D.C.: Association of American Railroads, January 23, 1970), p. 4.

23. *Cf.,* Burton H. Weisbrod, "The Per Diem Freight Car Rate and Railroad Efficiency—The Short-Run Problem," *Journal of Business,* October 1959, p. 383.

24. *Cf.,* John G. Kneiling, "How Not to Solve the Freight Car Problem," *Trains,* April 1968, p. 37.

25. George H. Borts, "Increasing Returns in the Railway Industry," *Journal of Political Economy,* August 1954, p. 328. See also, George W. Wilson, *Essays on Some Unsettled Questions in the Economics of Transportation* (Bloomington, Indiana: Foundation for Economic and Business Studies, Indiana University, 1962), pp. 74-5.

26. Marketing Economics Division, ERS, *The Role of Truck Brokers in the Movement of Exempt Agricultural Commodities,* Marketing Research Report No. 525 (Washington, D.C.: U.S. Department of Agriculture, 1962), pp. 25-7.

27. 12 ICC 561, 573 (1907). The AAR did experiment with seasonally variable per diem rates for foreign freight cars during the years from 1910 to 1913. The difference between the March to July rate and the August to February rate was so small, 30¢ and 35¢, respectively, that its effect could not have been pronounced. Lenor F. Loree, *Railroad Freight Transportation* (New York: D. Appleton and Co., 1922), p. 389.
28. See also, William G. Shepherd, "Marginal Cost Pricing in American Utilities," *Southern Economic Journal*, August 1966, pp. 64-5.
29. Gilbert Burck, "The Railroads Are Running Scared," *Fortune*, June 1969, p. 191.
30. As the Vice President of Operations, Pennsylvania Railroad Company remarked in the 1965 hearings on the freight car shortage: "In view of the short haul we receive in the loaded movement, we should not only be relieved of per diem but actually compensated by the owner for moving the car empty in long haul." David E. Smucker, "Statement," *Freight Car Shortages*, Hearings before the Freight Car Shortage Subcommittee on the Committee on Commerce, United States Senate, 89th Cong., 1st sess., on S. 179 and S. 1098, Sec. 89-23 (Washington, D.C., 1965), pp. 100-1.

---

8   Unit Trains: A Decade of Progress

Frank E. Shaffer

Productivity, investment, and car supply have been emphasized in the foregoing selections. The "unit train" is an innovation which deals boldly with all three matters; in addition, it makes possible the most efficient railroad service. The permanently coupled train, often composed of cars belonging to the customer, moves directly and quickly from origin to destination without passing through any yards or switching operations. This article assesses the present status and success of the unit train after ten years of trial by major railroads.

The unit train—marketing magic with a shuttle—is weaving a pattern of new railroad service in what promises to be the basic design of the future.

Railroading's brightest tool for holding bulk traffic and winning new business was born in the dark aftermath of an unsuccessful fight to block a coal pipeline from northern West Virginia to New York City. The job that lobbying failed to accomplish was done by ratemakers and operating men: they cut rates and transit time, thus washing out any economic advantages the slurry pipeline might have had to offer.

After a slow start in the early sixties, the unit train idea began to expand. As the second decade begins for the shuttle concept, there appear to be no limits to its future growth. Using coal as a base, unit trains have expanded into other commodities: iron ore, taconite, steel, sulphuric acid, phosphate and automobiles.

From Frank E. Shaffer, "Unit Trains: A Decade of Progress," *Modern Railroads*, June 1970, pp. 46-49. Used by permission.

Despite the new products being won to unit train movements, coal and other minerals are by far the most important. The future looks bright, even dazzling, for more and more longer and faster coal trains with larger and more sophisticated cars.

"Long distance trains will become more commonplace," one industry observer stated, "as utilities reach out for low-sulphur coal to meet pollution problems at existing generating stations." Coal has never been important to the Union Pacific but it has completed a partial inventory of its low-sulphur fuel and filed trainload rates for movement to Chicago.

The Pennsylvania Power and Light Co. claims to have been the first utility to own its own cars. Starting with two 74-car trains in 1963, it has doubled operations to four trains and is planning a fifth for service in late 1971. Coal originates at five points near Tunnelton, Pennsylvania, and moves over the Penn Central to generating stations near Harrisburg and Easton (see *Modern Railroads*, August 1964, p. 48).

Chicago's Commonwealth Edison in 1964 became another large user of its own equipment in unit train operation. Its fleet of 400-plus Thrall cars is being augmented this year by 300 new cars. Long-distance service will bring low-sulphur coal to Chicago from the Dakotas and Wyoming. "Service has been far above our fondest expectations," a Commonwealth spokesman told Modern Railroads.

Coal producers have accentuated the trend to privately-owned equipment. Consolidation Coal Co., Pittsburgh, has a fleet of more than 600 cars leased from Greenville Steel Car Co. for service on seven unit trains; Peabody has 244.

One of the nation's most refined unit train operations will go into operation later this year. No announcement has been made by the owner but cars are under construction and details of operation are generally known: A train of 180 125-ton aluminum gondolas will operate as a single unit over all but the final few miles of its journey. Mid-train power enables the train to be split into two 90-car sections, each to a different mine.

Aluminum cars are not uncommon in unit train service; neither are 125-ton cars. This, however, is the first application of cars of that metal and capacity. And it's the first time a utility has purchased its own locomotives.

Car ownership by utilities will become more common in the future. The belief is that utilities can better afford the capital expense because their rates are regulated according to investment.

Pipelines prodded progress

Coal operators made no secret of their displeasure with rail rates in the fifties. Railroads were completing dieselization to hold down costs, but found solvency possible only with rate increases.

One of the protest leaders, Consolidation Coal Co., was attracted by potential cost reduction offered by a slurry pipeline. In 1957 it began operation of a 10-inch line 108 miles between Cadiz, Ohio, and Cleveland. Before rail cuts could regain the business, the pipe handled 6.5 million tons in six years.

Encouraged by the success of the pipe as a carrier and an effective rate tool, Consol moved on two new fronts in late 1961. With the Texas Eastern Transmission Co., a $100 million line was planned to New York City from West Virginia; with Commonwealth Edison, Chicago, a line was projected northward from downstate.

Jervis Langdon had become president of the B&O shortly before the storm broke. The battlefield was to be the January 1962 session of the West Virginia Legislature, as pipelines sought the right of eminent domain. Although the railroads fought the proposal through the state association, Mr. Langdon did not take part. As he recalled the incident recently:

"I decided that, if the pipeline proved it could be economic, there would be no beating it. I did not testify because B&O service was so poor, with a bad car supply, that I didn't see what solid grounds I had."

Mr. Langdon took action of another sort. He set the B&O on an immediate program of improvements and experiments. Cost and rate experts sifted the evidence to determine how much of a rate cut could be offered. The answer: $1 a ton.

The B&O reduction was topped by a $1.25 cut by the N&W. That was beaten by the PRR's $1.50 a ton slash. The B&O met both cuts. "It did so with some bitterness," the *New York Times* reported, "feeling that its own invention had been spoiled."

West Virginia approved the pipeline but Consol lost in Virginia. Rate reductions, in effect, defeated the pipeline in Illinois and West Virginia. The pipe's major backer, Consol, has found lower rates and unit trains so attractive it is now one of the leading operators of private cars.

Of his own role as a unit train pioneer, a role in which some large coal producers have cast him, Mr. Langdon says:

"Oh, no, the B&O was not the first. The Southern had some unit coal trains run by Bill Brosnan for the TVA. You'd better check that before you write the article."

He was right. The Southern was the nation's first. January 21, 1960, marked the inauguration of service with 85 Silverside gondolas on a 132-mile route from Parrish to Yellowleaf, Alabama. Two trains on a 48-hour turn handle 2.6 million tons of coal annually for Southern Electric Generating Co. The Southern freely admits that the pipeline was a threat which spurred its unit train development.

The pipeline in Ohio was moth-balled; the one from West Virginia was never built; but the concept of slurry transmission remains a threat. There are two schools of thought.

One consulting engineer says: "By and large a railroad line already in existence can turn in a better economic performance than a new pipeline. This is true even if the existing rail line is a branch which must be upgraded to handle 100-ton cars."

Peabody Coal Co. provides a different illustration of transportation economics. Its Black Mesa mine in Arizona uses a 273-mile pipe to handle 5 million tons per year to one power plant. An 80-mile railroad will be built in 1974, and by 1976 will be handling 7.8 million tons to another plant.

A longer slurry pipeline was recently described by Robert Roberts in *Modern Railroads* (March 1970, page 80):

"Cascade Pipeline Ltd., a wholly-owned subsidiary of Canadian Pacific, has just announced its intention to apply for a permit to build a 490-mile coal slurry pipeline to move coal from South-eastern British Columbia mines to Roberts bank. Although seemingly in competition with itself, the pipeline venture may be instrumental in holding off development of other coal pipelines."

The battle, clearly, has not been won by railroads to date.

The grain train

The Illinois Central is responsible for what is probably the most famous of all unit trains. Its Rent-A-Train is now in its second year hauling grain from Central Illinois to Gulf Coast ports for Cargill, Inc. IC's marketing vice president and originator of the concept, John W. Ingram, is happy with Cargill's renewal.

"The concept is sound," he says, "and the economics are right for both the shipper and the railroad. Our performance—when you get past the goofs, derailments and strikes—was precisely what Cargill needs for overall capacity and scheduling efficiencies.

"Equipment shortages would have been much more severe if Cargill's Rent-a-Train hadn't been steadily reducing the size of the pile of grain that needed to be moved in central Illinois."

Sound as it is, Rent-a-Train isn't home free. The ICC has announced it still must consider the matter as a subject of "general transportation importance." And Cargill's W. B. Saunders, vice president grain division, seemed to add a word of caution:

"Renewal for another 12 months doesn't mean the train will run forever. It's still in the experimental stage so far as Cargill is concerned."

Saunders said two factors adversely affect long range objectives and add to the cost of moving corn from Illinois for export: fleet maintenance, and the switching operation needed to move the train from the IC yards to the export terminal in Port Allen, Louisiana.

"Nevertheless," he added, "the single train delivered more than 6500 carloads of grain and appreciably relieved the chronic boxcar shortage in the grain belt of central Illinois."

While Rent-a-Train was the first grain movement in a true unit train concept, other railroads have operated irregularly scheduled service. A Soo-PRR movement started in 1964 to handle grain in 95-car trains from Duluth to Buffalo. In 1969, the Soo handled 26 such trains. The N&W moved 41 trains of grain last year and the Milwaukee 27.

What, exactly, is a unit train? The best definition came in an ICC hearing (Docket 34822) last August in testimony of Harold F. Egan, assistant director of coal supply for the Consumers Power Co., a Michigan utility.

Mr. Egan told the ICC there are four categories of rates for coal: 1-single car, 2-volume, 3-trainload, and 4-unit, or shuttle. Unit train rates were defined as "rates applicable on a specific minimum tonnage in a solid train of dedicated cars operated and managed as a single unit from one specified loading point to one receiver at one specified destination and return."

Management of a unit train system is an exact science. Even though the concept is relatively new, a how-to-do-it textbook, *Integral Train Systems*, has been written by a consulting engineer, John C. Kneiling.

"Integral train technology starts with some almost painfully obvious but neglected concepts," Kneiling writes. "They amount to a strictly commercial plan to run each train as if it were intended solely to produce low-cost—low total cost—transportation. The train needs accessories to load and unload, service, fuel and maintain it. These accessories are essential to the economic operation of the train. The entire system is an integral train system."

Classifications vary

Because a wide range of problems affects the engineering of a unit train system, *Modern Railroads* has found it difficult to arrange them in convenient categories. Only a few of the trains are alike in all aspects of loading, movement, and unloading. The Santa Fe's liquid sulphur trains at Rustler Springs, Texas, enter a loop to reach loading facilities. Each train returns intact with its empty cars to complete an 1860-mile round trip. Canadian Industries, Ltd. operates three 36-car unit trains of sulphuric acid weekly from Copper Cliff, Ontario: one over the CP to Hamilton, two to Courtright via CP-C&O. The return movement is on regular trains. Alcoa's 50-car train of alumina to Messena, New York, has two routes and two styles of operation: on alternate weeks it is handled between Mobile and East St. Louis as a unit train by the Gulf, Mobile & Ohio and the St. Louis-San Francisco. The weekly movement east of East St. Louis on the Penn Central is in a regular train.

The D&RGW has a unit train fleet of three trains operating daily five days a week from two different mines. On Saturdays and Sundays, the three trains become two longer trains to serve a third mine.

In any study of unit train operations, one category must be established for railroads constructed from the ground up for this sole purpose.

Oro Dam Contractors used a portion of a former Western Pacific main line in California, plus new trackage (*Modern Railroads*, November 1964, p. 118) for a 12-mile railroad to move almost 925,000 tons of earth fill weekly. Four 42-car trains operated around the clock because engineers found rail movement more economical than a conveyor belt.

Ohio Power Co. constructed a 15-mile electrified and automated railroad near Zanesville, Ohio (*Modern Railroads*, September 1969, p. 75), to move 4.6 million tons of coal annually.

In 1955 the Reserve Mining Co. opened a 47-mile line in Minnesota to move 30 million tons of taconite annually in eight 160-car loaded trains daily.

A year earlier, the Quebec, North Shore and Labrador opened a new 356-mile railroad to handle 100-car trains of ore (*Modern Railroads*, December 1954, p. 55).

Decision before 1975

Can unit trains torpedo the fleet of Great Lakes ore boats?

"Yes," says one consulting engineer with emphasis. "They'll have a golden opportunity within the next five years. The majority of the ore fleet is about to reach the economic age where replacement must be considered."

If rail haul is to become the way of life, he goes on, management must start its planning immediately. Rates and schedules must be studied. Steel mills can be sold but it will take "real salesmanship backed up by real engineering and imagination."

Ore now begins and ends in a rail car. Expensive facilities are needed to load and unload lake boats. These could be eliminated by an all-rail journey.

"I do not think there is a real problem on rates," the consultant said. "The only problem is the division between the connecting carriers at Chicago."

Bypassing the lakes is not new: it happens almost every winter as steel mills top off their stock-piles to replace tonnage lost by a shortened lake season or for other reasons. The Burlington Northern operated a 105-car train every four days during the past winter to Burns Harbor, Indiana, from Nashwauk, Minnesota.

"It's going to take a lot of persuasion beyond mere economics," the engineer insisted. "The very thought of getting along without lake boats will shake some steel men to their heels. And there's that obviously human factor of inertia to new ideas as well as the desire to protect individual 'kingdoms.' "

There is no time to lose. If contracts are signed for new lake boats, the steel companies will be locked in on long-term arrangements and the potentially heavy volume will be lost.

A look at the future

When the "ultimate" unit train goes into service, the shape of U.S. railroading will be altered forever. Such a train was designed in a 1961 PRR-sponsored study by Kauffield Engineering Co. Although the train wasn't built, the concepts it developed became standards for the first generation of unit trains.

The Kauffield engineers saw the train of the future as made up of several 3000-ton sections. A power package between each section would have two power units and a tank holding a week's fuel supply. Control cars at each end of the 8, 10 or 12-section train would eliminate need for turning. Electrically heated cars would eliminate winter delays in running through heating sheds.

With its annual production of 5 to 6 million tons, an integral train could replace thousands of cars and hundreds of locomotives, reducing track occupancy, the need for signalling systems, and yard congestion.

The key to efficient use is fast loading and unloading. Kauffield's study targeted 10,000 tons per hour as the ideal loading speed. So far as we have been able to discover, only one of today's operations has that speed: Kaiser Steel's D&RGW train at Sunnyside, Utah.

Most trains today are unloaded in rotary dumpers because utility plants are often equipped with these facilities. Unloading speeds of 3,000 tons per hour are being engineered. CP Rail is unloading its Kaiser train from Sparwood, B.C., at that rate in Roberts Bank, B.C. Pennsylvania Power and Light will achieve 4000 tons at Strawberry Ridge in 1971.

The road to the future for unit trains is bright but will be marked by low joints and high spots:

Anti-pollution forces are protesting the use of coal and demanding a switch to other fuels.

Prices for residual oil and natural gas are climbing in response to the demand. Natural gas is in short supply but moves are underway to import it in a liquified state, a new threat to coal.

Demand for all coal is so great that mines are hard pressed to meet their contracts. Tonnage in the first half of this year will be about 2 percent below 1969.

Export demand is adding firmness to prices and is delaying cars at tidewater far beyond usual limits. Japanese interests are putting up funds to open their own mine and are paying a premium price for coking coal.

Despite the obstacles, the unit train is here to stay. It is one of the finest marketing tools ever devised by the nation's railroads.

---

9   National Railroad Passenger Corporation: Requiem or Renaissance?

Edwin P. Patton
University of Tennessee

While the following article was being written, the National Railroad Passenger Corporation, or "Rail Pax" as it was then called, was in the planning stage. On May 1, 1971, under the name of "Amtrak," it took over the operation of most of our intercity passenger trains. ("Am" stands for American, "tr" for travel, "ak" for track.) NRPC is an independent but government-owned corporation which hires the railroads to run the passenger trains for it. The corporation has purchased 1200 cars from the roads; has selected specific routes over which trains will run; pays the affected railroads cost plus 5 per cent. Initial funding of the corporation was $337 million. Forty million came from government subsidy and $100 million from guaranteed loans. Another $197 million was to be paid in over a span of 26 months by the railroads in consideration for the $460 million-a-year loss of which the government relieved them. This selection presents the new

From Edwin P. Patton, "National Railroad Passenger Corporation: Requiem or Renaissance?" *High Speed Ground Transportation Journal*, Vol. 5, Winter-Spring 1971, pp. 83-93. Used by permission.

corporation's necessary goals and possible achievements, and raises the question
of whether we want to subsidize a third travel alternative in the passenger train.

The November signing by President Nixon of legislation creating a federally-sponsored enterprise to operate intercity passenger trains means different things to different people. To inveterate railroad adherents it saves their friend the passenger train from extinction and heralds possible re-establishment of rail passenger services that have been terminated abortively, to their way of thinking, by narrow-minded rail managements. To others, it represents another wasteful government project to support a service that society no longer patronizes nor requires but nonetheless remembers fondly from past years and feels should be preserved in the event it might want to utilize it.

Those not taking either extreme position but who are concerned with the degree of mobility of the American people and the cost of this mobility view the event with mixed feelings. On the one hand there appears to be a limit to which our society can be dependent upon the automobile. The question arises: Is there room for the development of an alternative form of surface transport to compete effectively with highway transport? On the other hand, the rapid growth of air transportation means greater mobility through greater speed but at the same time promises higher bills for the taxpayer in terms of airways, airports, navigation aids, and, perhaps, outright subsidy for some of the carriers. Introduction of the air bus type aircraft is producing excess capacity for most of the airlines. Is this the time to consider seriously a for-hire competitor for air transport?

Even though one may not favor an attempt to redevelop rail passenger transportation, anyone interested in the future of intercity travel in this country should be concerned with the new legislation. It commits up to $340 million to provide intercity rail service and introduces governmental operation and control to a large segment of rail transportation. Secretary Volpe should have presented his prescription for a basic rail passenger network by the time this article is published. After other interested parties have presented their arguments for modification of this network, the initiation of federally-sponsored intercity passenger service will be a reality.

Determination of goals

What should society demand of this new Corporation? How should it evaluate the effectiveness of the National Railroad Passenger Corporation (NRPC)?

It is argued that the Corporation must have a single all-encompassing goal: to carry people in large numbers. It must arrest the decline in rail patronage and create the framework for an effective alternative to highway and air transport. What must be proven is that the traveling public will utilize train transportation. If it refuses to desert the automobile and/or jetliner in significant numbers, the pessimists are correct and the sooner the Corporation becomes history the better.

Profitability should be only a secondary consideration, despite the fact that the Corporation is planned to be a profit-making enterprise. If patronage is assured, profits should be realized eventually, though this cannot be guaranteed.

What is required to assure patronage? One answer appears obvious. The Corporation must offer reliable, fast (compared to highway transport) train schedules at convenient hours, with comfortable, clean accommodations and adequate food and lounge facilities—all at a competitive price. The question then becomes, if the Corporation offers such services and merchandizes them aggressively, will increased patronage be assured and the success of the Corporation guaranteed? The object of this article is to offer an answer to this question. Through an analysis of the rail passenger experience of recent years, the study offers predictions as to the degree of success of the new enterprise together with recommendations as to the actions that will have to be taken by the Corporation to achieve this success.

These predictions and recommendations are the result of a three step study. First, what is required in the way of service to achieve passenger acceptance of rail transport? Second, a sample of carriers is developed and studied over the period 1955-1965 in terms of service provided versus patronage and compared with equivalent results for the United States as a whole and the Southern District. Third, the 1960's experiments of the Canadian National are reviewed and evaluated in terms of possible lessons to be gleaned by the NRPC as it begins operations.

The study is exploratory. It does not pretend to have all the answers but represents a starting point for serious discussion of a new and potentially significant concept in American transportation.

The relationship between service and patronage

To determine what relationship exists between service and patronage, several correlation coefficients are computed employing data published by the Interstate Commerce Commission for the period 1947-1965. The objective is a twenty year study of passenger service following World War II; however, 1946 results are not used due to the obvious influence of the conflict on the variables.

In addition to studying data generated for the country as a whole, the operating results of the carriers composing the Southern Territory are included in the analysis. The latter group is employed in an effort to narrow the study to intercity transportation. Many U.S. rail passenger statistics combine commute and intercity services. Conclusions regarding strictly intercity service may be invalid when based on data generated by both services.

None of the Southern Territory carriers maintain commuter operations with the notable exception of the Illinois Central. The data for this carrier, thus, is subtracted out of the Southern Territory statistics in all calculations. The Pocahontas District carriers are included in the Southern Territory figures.

Table 1 reveals that there is a very strong relationship between passenger-miles, the measure of patronage employed, and railroad service, as measured by (1) train-miles, (2) first-class plus diner and lounge car-miles, and (3) the percentage of these car-miles to total passenger-carrying car-miles. The correlation co-efficients computed range from +.9771 (U.S. train-miles *and* passenger-miles) to +.5589 (percentage of pullman-diner service to total passenger service in the South *and* equivalent passenger-miles). Such strong relationships may allow us to predict ridership given a particular level of service; however, caution must be observed in determining and using these forecasts.

It is an obvious fact that rail passenger service, as reflected by train-mile, passenger-mile, and car-mile statistics, has declined since the end of World War II. As such, one would expect strong correlations between the variables since there is a common trend approaching zero out-put. Also, while decreasing service may result in decreased patronage, an increase in service may not assure an increase in riders. One can pull a string but not push it. The potential weakness in the comparisons is revealed by observing the relationship between average miles-per-hour of U.S. and Southern Territory trains and patronage. The coefficients are .9549 and .9609, respectively, but they are negative. Thus, as speed increases, patronage declines!

TABLE 1

The Relationship Between Patronage (In Passenger-Miles) and
Railroad Service for the Period 1947-1965.

Independent Variable (X): [Dependent Variable in all correlations: Revenue Passenger-miles (in billions) for U. S. or Southern Territory, as indicated]	Coefficient of Correlation	Regression Equation:	
		Slope	Y Intercept
1) Train-miles, a) United States	+.9771	+·.0982	− .111
b) Southern Territory	+.9770	+ .0928	− .633
2) First-class + Diner-lounge Car-miles			
(FC+DL), a) United States	+.9536	+ .0235	+ 3.219
b) Southern Territory	+.9376	+ .0244	+ .039
3) (FC+DL) to total Passenger Car-miles,			
a) United States	+.8418	+1.6101	− 56.228
b) Southern Territory	+.5589	+ .2444	− 9.604
4) Average Miles- a) United States	−.9549	−4.7078	+213.03
per-hour, b) Southern Territory	−.9609	− .4534	+ 20.869
5) United States Primary Highway Mileage	−.9703	− .0908	+ 68.179
6) Southeastern U.S. Primary Highway Mileage	−.9571	− .0324	+ 7.437
7) Average Miles-per-hour; United States Domestic Scheduled Air Carriers	−.8896	− .1539	+ 57.195

Sources: Interstate Commerce Commission. *Transport Statistics in the United States;* U.S. Bureau of Public Roads, *Highway Statistics 1968;* Civil Aeronautics Board, *Handbook of Airline Statistics.*

Other not surprising relationships exist between patronage decline and increases in primary highway mileage and the average speed of air transportation. As in the other determinations, the coefficients are high but of questionable usefulness.

A more significant comparison

Despite potentially inconclusive findings from correlating certain measures of service and patronage, some interesting results are obtained from comparing the data of a group of carriers operating from 1955-65 with data generated for the same period by U.S. and Southern Territory carriers as a whole. The sample is not selected randomly but consists of carriers in different parts of the country, which, in the author's opinion, operated some of the highest quality passenger service ever available to the U.S. traveling public. Carriers offering commuter service were excluded since passenger statistics published by the I.C.C. include both intercity and commute operations. The sample is limited to ten carriers, all of which, with one exception, operated for the entire period. The carriers composing the sample are: Santa Fe, Atlantic Coast Line, Chesapeake & Ohio, Delaware & Hudson, Florida East Coast (passenger operation through 1963), Great Northern, Missouri Pacific, Seaboard, Texas & Pacific, and Union Pacific.

The ten year period, 1955-65, represents a time when many rail managements had decided that passenger service could never be a profit-making venture. To many, the handwriting was on the wall when, in 1958, Commissioner Hosmer made his now-famous prediction that in a "decade or so" the passenger coach would join the stage-coach and sidewheeler in the historical museum.

The sample of ten carriers is compared with all U.S. carriers and the carriers in the Southern Territory in terms of patronage loss and changes in service during this period. The results are shown in Table 2 and tend to support the thesis that patronage is a function of good service.

In terms of patronage, U.S. carriers as a whole sustained a 43.9 percent loss in passenger-miles during the period. The Southern Territory carriers sustained a 34.4 percent loss and the sample carriers a 25.0 percent decline in patronage. A review of the service standards of the sample railroads reveals, perhaps, why their decline was the least of the three groups of carriers.

In terms of speed, the sample carriers operated their best trains at about 47.5 miles per hour while the other lines never exceeded 41.3 m.p.h. One word should be said relative to the sample carrier figures. Whereas the U.S. and Southern carrier figures were taken from official I.C.C. statistics, the sample carrier figures were computed using the *Official Guide of the Railways* schedules employing only the best train services offered by each line. These included any service on which diner-lounge and/or pullman service was offered. It is argued that the trains offering such services would be the ones primarily patronized. A lower figure might have resulted using I.C.C. data which presumably includes all passenger services operated.

The next measure of comparison involves daily passenger train-miles operated at 65 miles-per-hour or faster. This data is obtained from Donald Steffee's excellent annual speed survey effort for *Trains* magazine.[1] Steffee's survey does not consider origin to destination times of the trains, perhaps a weakness, but fastest point-to-point times recorded between points between origin and destination. Though the majority is not aware of these tables and the survey, *changes* in these point-to-point figures do reflect management's approach to operating quality passenger service.

The changes in daily train-miles at 65 m.p.h. indicate a reduction of 19.7 percent for both the U.S. and the sample carriers. The Southern Territory carriers, on the other hand, show an increase of 31.9 percent. The next section compares total daily train-miles with daily train miles at 65 m.p.h. The figures show that the sample firms operated the highest percentage of 65 m.p.h. operation to the total but had the lowest percentage increase relative to the other two groups. The South led in the latter category with an increase of 81.0 percent.

As far as the change in car-mile operation of pullman-diner-lounge service, the sample carriers had the smallest decline relative to the other two groups, 42.8 percent compared to 45.7 percent for the South and 57.9 percent for the coun-

TABLE 2

Comparison of United States, Southern Territory, and Sample
Carriers in Terms of Service and Patronage for the Period 1955-1965.

Measure of Service and Patronage		United States Carriers	Southern Territory Carriers	Sample Carriers
1) Passenger-miles (billions):	a) 1955	23.7	3.2	6.0
	b) 1965	13.3	2.1	4.5
Percentage Change 1955-1965		−43.9	−34.4	−25.0
2) Average Miles-per-hour:	a) 1955	39.8	39.1	47.5
	b) 1965	41.3	41.2	47.6
Percentage Change 1955-1965		+ 3.8	+ 5.4	+ .2
3) Daily Train-miles at 65 m. p. h.:	a) 1955	. 73.7	4.7	24.9
(thousands)	b) 1965	58.2	6.2	20.0
Percentage Change 1955-1965		−19.7	+31.9	−19.7
4) Percent Miles at 65 mph to total	a) 1955	9.0	4.2	13.3
Daily train-miles:	a) 1965	12.3	7.6	15.7
Percentage Change 1955-1965		+36.7	+81.0	+18.0
5) First-Class + Diner-Lounge Total	a) 1955	931	140	271
Car-miles (thousands):	b) 1965	392	76	155
Percentage Change 1955-1965		−57.9	−45.7	−42.8
6) Percent First-Class + Diner-Lounge Car-				
miles to Total Passenger	a) 1955	50.7	54.0	57.2
Car-miles:	b) 1965	44.5	47.5	49.6
Percentage Change 1955-1965		−12.2	−12.0	−13.3

Sources: Interstate Commerce Commission, *Transport Statistics in the United States; Official Guide of the Railways* December 1955 and January 1966; *Trains* Magazine May 1956 and June 1966.

try as a whole. It is remembered that the sample carriers constitute part of the nationwide total.

The final comparison involves relating the car-miles of pullman-diner-lounge operation to total passenger-carrying car-miles of service. In this category the sample carriers operated the highest percentage of the three groups in all years of the survey. In 1955, 57.2 percent of sample carrier passenger car-miles consisted of first-class and diner-lounge service compared to 54.0 percent for the Southern carriers and 50.7 percent for the country as a whole. 1965 equivalent figures were 49.6 percent for the sample firms, 47.5 percent for the South, and 44.5 percent for all U.S. carriers. In terms of the decline in these percentages, the sample carriers' decrease was highest, 13.3 percent, compared to 12.2 percent for the country, 12.0 percent for the Southern carriers.

In summarizing the 1955-1965 survey, the sample carriers maintained the highest standard of service, with the Southern carriers placing second, relative to all U.S. carriers treated collectively. It is to be expected that the sample firms would sustain the smallest decrease in patronage over the period and that is what occurred. In fact, as a point of reference comparing the three groups of carriers, a simple linear regression line was computed for each group for the study period utilizing the least-squares method. The resulting regression equations developed were, for the sample $Yc = 5.3 - .14x$, for the South $Yc = 2.5 - .11x$, and for the U.S. $Yc = 17.7 - 1.05x$. In using these equations to predict the length, in years, of continued patronage of the three carrier groups (solving where $Yc = 0$), the U.S. carriers should be patronized for 16.9 more years, the Southern carriers for 22.7 years, and the sample carriers for 37.9 additional years, over twice the U.S. total. Patronage appears to be a function of good service.

The Canadian National experience

Many U.S. rail travelers look to our northern neighbor as an example of how to operate passenger trains for which there will be an effective demand. In the early 1960's, this publicly-owned enterprise reversed the familiar negative stance toward passengers so popular in this country and held also by Canadian National (CN) management during the 1950's and sought actively to win people back to CN service.

The railroad attacked its passenger service problems on all fronts. Not only were existing cars refurbished but additional ones purchased, both new and from U.S. carriers who no longer had need for them. Schedules were accelerated and in some areas new trains introduced. New equipment and several schedule speed-ups were tried in this country, of course, after the war, but whereas most U.S. carriers ended their improvements at this point the Canadian firm went further. CN revamped its fare schedule, modernized stations, dressed their employees in new uniforms and their equipment in a new paint scheme, offered new services such as transportation for the family car, and advertized aggressively. In short, CN sought to create an entirely new image for rail passenger service.

The policy has, and continues, to produce positive and negative results. In discussing the positive side first, we can argue that the Canadian National experience shows that, under certain circumstances, people still will patronize rail service. Table 3 indicates that passenger revenues and passenger-miles climbed each year during the period 1962-1967. In 1962 revenues amounted to $34.3 million and passenger-miles totaled 1.044 billion. In 1967 the carrier received $83.9 million for providing 2.495 billion passenger-miles of rail transport. The exceptional 1967 increase over 1966 figures is attributable to the 1967 Expo World's Fair. Though 1968 results were down from the previous year's, they still exceeded the totals for 1966.

There are those who argue that the Canadian experience is not applicable to the United States due to differences in affluence, availability of good highways, and the stage of development of air transportation. Yet in 1960, 85.5 percent of intercity Canadian travel was done by car compared to 90.1 percent in this country.[2] By 1964 these percentages were 85.1 and 89.5 respectively.[3] For-hire air transportation has grown in Canada just as it has in this country. Air's share of the Canadian market climbed from 4.4 to 5.3 percent during the 1960-64 period whereas it climbed from 4.0 to 5.1 percent in this country for the same period.[4] A recent examination of air service between Montreal-Toronto compared to Chicago-St. Louis showed 44 schedules available between the former pair of cities to 48 available between the U.S. points.[5] The postwar tendency to forsake rail transport appears little different in Canada than in the United States. Before initiation of the CN program, rail's share of the Canadian travel market dropped from 14.1 percent in 1949 to 3.8 percent in 1962, a decline of 73.5 percent.[6] In this country the rail share of the travel market slipped from 7.5 to 2.5 percent for the same years, a decline of 67 percent.[7] In the following two years, however, the Canadian rail market share increased to 4.6 percent while the U.S. equivalent dropped to 2.1 percent.[8] Since CN's only rail competitor, privately-owned Canadian Pacific, was following a rail passenger policy of retrenchment during these years, it is apparent that the former carrier's new passenger policy certainly dampened, perhaps reversed indefinitely, the trend away from rail to other modes of transportation.

TABLE 3

Canadian National Railways Passenger Revenues and Passenger-Miles for the Period 1962-1968.

Year	Passenger Revenues (In Millions)	Passenger-Miles (In Billions)
1962	$ 34.3	$ 1.044
1963	44.4	1.189
1964	51.8	1.613
1965	58.3	1.782
1966	67.5	1.995
1967	83.9	2.495
1968	70.6	2.046

Source: *Annual Reports*, Canadian National Railways, 1962-1968.

Table 4, which shows some of the improvements carried out by Canadian National between 1961 and 1970 in terms of overall train speed and the introduction of new fare plans, illustrates again that patronage is a function of service. In terms of speed, origin to destination mile-per-hour figures improved on all routes shown, more notably on the relatively short, corridor-type services (Montreal-Quebec-Ottawa-Toronto-Windsor) than the longer overnight to 3-day services (Montreal-Halifax-Vancouver). Most significant improvements are on the Montreal-Toronto run. In 1960 three trains operating in conjunction with the Canadian Pacific averaged 45.0 m.p.h. over the 335-mile route. In July 1970, seven Canadian National-operated trains covered the distance at an overall aver-

TABLE 4

Canadian National Improvements in Train Speeds and Revisions
in Fares, Selected Years, for the Years 1960, 1965 and 1970.

Measure of Service		1960	1965	1970
1) Overall Speed-Origin to Destination:				
(Number of Schedules in Parentheses)				
a) Montreal to Vancouver	[2924 miles]	41.9(1)	43.0(1)	42.4(1)
b) Montreal to Halifax	[840 miles]	36.5(2)	39.1(2)	40.5(2)
c) Montreal to Quebec	[167 miles]	40.9(3)	46.3(3)	55.7(2)
d) Montreal to Ottawa	[118 miles]	51.8(3)	54.5(3)	54.4(4)
e) Montreal to Toronto	[335 miles]	45.0(3)	52.5(4)	62.5(7)
*Consists of *Turbo & Rapido* runs.				73.4(4)*
#Consists of *Turbo* runs only.				82.0(2)#
f) Toronto to Windsor	[228 miles]	36.0(3)	52.6(3)	52.6(4)
g) Toronto to Sarnia	[174 miles]	42.7(4)	45.0(4)	43.1(3)
h) Toronto to Chicago	[511 miles]	42.9(3)	43.8(3)	44.1(1)
	TOTAL	41.1(22)	46.8(23)	47.6(24)
2) Fares: Coach and Single Roomette				
or Club Car Seat:				
a) Montreal to Vancouver:	Coach-Lowest Fare	$ 98.72	$43.00	$ 47.00
	Coach-Standard Fare	98.72	52.00	61.00
	Roomette-Lowest Fare	152.46	81.00	102.00
	Roomette-Standard Fare	152.46	90.00	116.00
b) Montreal to Halifax:	Coach-Lowest Fare	$ 29.35	$15.00	$ 15.50
	Coach-Standard Fare	29.35	20.00	21.00
	Roomette-Lowest Fare	44.90	30.00	29.50
	Roomette-Standard Fare	44.90	35.00	35.00
c) Montreal to Toronto:	Coach-Lowest Fare	$ 12.80	$ 8.00	$ 8.90
	Coach-Standard Fare	12.80	11.10	12.90
	Club Seat-Lowest Fare	18.30	15.00	15.90
	Club Seat-Standard Fare	18.30	18.10	19.90
d) Toronto to Windsor:	Coach-Lowest Fare	$ 8.55	$ 5.20	$ 5.90
	Coach-Standard Fare	8.55	7.20	8.70
	Club Seat-Lowest Fare	12.35	10.20	10.90
	Club Seat-Standard Fare	12.35	12.20	13.70

Sources: Canadian National Railways Timetables effective 10/30/60, 4/25/65, and 4/27/69;
Official Guide of the Railways July 1970.

age speed of 62.5 m.p.h. The new *Turbo* and more-established *Rapido* trains averaged 73.4 m.p.h. over this route in 1970, with the *Turbos* themselves covering the distance at an average speed of 82.0 miles-per-hour. As a point of comparison, Penn Central's *Metroliners* operating between New York and Washington average 75.3 m.p.h. on their 226-mile run.

Other noteworthy speedups include the Montreal-Quebec run, 40.9 to 55.7 m.p.h., 1960 to 1970, for 167 miles, and Toronto-Windsor, 36.0 to 52.6 m.p.h., for 228 miles, over the same period.[9] A look at Steffee's speed survey again shows the concern with speed exhibited by Canadian National management. In 1961, CN and its subsidiary Grand Trunk operated a total of 577 daily train-miles at better than 65 but no higher than 70 miles-per-hour. By 1964 this figure had climbed to 1396 miles of 65 m.p.h. operation, 439 miles of which included over 70 m.p.h. operation. By 1968, 2639 daily miles were operated at better than 70 m.p.h., including 1317 miles at better than 80 m.p.h. (the influence of the *Turbo*).[10]

Canadian National did not stop at just refurbished equipment and higher speeds. In an attempt to increase patronage generally and level out the peaks and troughs associated with passenger travel, the company introduced three levels of fares, the level applicable being dependent upon the month and day of the year the train trip commenced. First-class and coach differentiation was eliminated, with the basic fare applicable to coach travel plus an additional charge for parlor car (renamed club car) or room accommodations. Meals became complimentary with the purchase of club car or room space.

Table 4 shows how these changes affected fares on some of the railroad's major routes. The Montreal-Vancouver 1960 coach fare, good any day of the year, was $98.72, with a roomette costing $152.46. In 1965, however, a coach seat on a low travel day sold for $43, on a high travel day for $52. A roomette, which included meals, went for $81 on a "red" (off season) day, $90 on a "blue" (most heavily traveled) day. In 1969, the highest fares between the two cities, $61 for coach and $116 for roomette, still were below the 1960 charges. On the Montreal-Toronto route, coach passengers paid $12.80 and parlor car seats sold for $18.30 in 1960. Nine years later, coach fares between these points varied from $8.90 to $12.90 and club car fares from $15.90 to $19.90 (meals included), depending upon the date of travel.

In this country, a coach seat between New York and Los Angeles cost $167.95 in 1960 and $186.93 in 1969. A roomette between these cities could be purchased for $300.75 in 1960, $367.96 nine years later. These fares applied regardless of travel date. In the so-called corridor between New York and Washington, the one-way 1960 coach fare was $9.68, the parlor car rate $18.15. In 1969 the coach fare was $11.75 on regular trains. $15.75 by *Metroliner*. A parlor car accommodation cost $21.65 by either regular train or *Metroliner*, meals not included.[11]

To summarize the positive aspects of the Canadian National approach—passengers will patronize rail service if it is convenient, comfortable, and price competitive. The question now must be considered, what of the costs involved, and the consequent profit potential, of providing such a rail product.

The negative aspects of Canadian National's experience

The major problem with the CN's program, from the point-of-view of U.S. rail management at least, is that it has yet to produce a profit carrying passengers and no profit date appears in sight at the present time. Originally the road predicted a break-even operation by the early 1970's but its experience has been that rising costs have kept close pace with rising revenues. For the period 1961 through 1965, the road lost over $40 million annually on passenger service, ranging from a low of $41.7 million in 1962 to a high of $47.4 million in 1961. The 1968 expected loss was $45 million.[12] No privately operated firm can sustain such annual losses and remain solvent for many years. Perhaps even a publicly-backed enterprise cannot afford to provide such an unprofitable product indefinitely.

Despite the growth in patronage referred to earlier, it was reported in December 1969 that CN held out little hope profitwise for its transcontinental runs (Montreal-Toronto-Vancouver) or its maritime Provinces schedules (Montreal-Halifax) and in November 1970 the company officially requested that the Canadian Transport Commission subsidize the losses incurred in providing these services.[13] The road feels that its major fiscal hopes lie in its Corridor services (Montreal-Quebec-Toronto-Ottawa) provided it can re-equip the trains on these routes.[14] This has been accomplished partially with the initiation of the *Turbos* between Montreal-Toronto and the *Tempo* trains between Toronto-Windsor-Sarnia.

Thus, it remains to be seen whether CN's own "great experiment" can be profitable, in whole or in part. The results of its policies and actions, however, do contain guidelines for this country's National Railroad Passenger Corporation and a criterion upon which the public can evaluate NRPC's performance.

The critics speak

Professor Hilton writes that the new NRPC legislation will provide us with "some 5 years to find that a subsidy won't do the job either. A subsidy can't reduce the value of people's time enough to get them out of airplanes, or make trains run from door to door to get them out of automobiles."[15] An example shows the nature of Hilton's first point. Assume a point-to-point distance of 300 miles. Average air travel time is one hour (300 m.p.h. average), rail is five hours (60 m.p.h. average). If the air cost is 5¢ per mile and rail is 3¢ per mile, air price will total $15 while the rail price will be $9. However, if the earning power of the individual is $5 per hour, an additional cost of $5 is added to the air fare, an additional $25 to the railroad fare. Thus, air transport costs less, 6 2/3¢ compared to rail's 11 1/3¢ per mile. Yet CN's *Rapido*, which covers 335 miles in 5 hours, often operates at full capacity.

Does the door-to-door convenience of the automobile eliminate all possibility of another surface travel alternative? A survey of highway travel in the early 1970's, taking into account the completed portions of the Interstate System and the planning of its completion by 1976, reflects increases in congestion, even in many rural areas, pollution of the environment, highway deaths and injuries, together with property damage. A new concern for the sociological aspects of building roads has slowed construction in many areas and increased costs of further highway development. Can the automobile operator be enticed out of his car but continue to remain on the ground? To find out we must provide him with such an opportunity. Rail transport can provide that alternative.

What of the profit problem? Experience indicates that at least many services show no potential for even break-even results. How can a profit-oriented enterprise operate permanently at a loss? Perhaps we should consider a revised criterion for evaluating rail passenger service, at least in the short run. The criterion would involve comparing the net cost of providing certain rail services with savings realized through reduced highway and air expenditures, those savings attributable to people's abandonment of road and air transport in favor of rail.

A million dollar rail deficit is better if it means *more* than a million dollars *not* spent on new roads and roadway maintenance, bigger airports, or installation of more refined air navigation aids. Some governmental agencies, such as Ontario's (Toronto's GO Transit), are beginning to realize this. Canadian National's frustrating search for profits still may have been "profitable" in the big picture if the services provided by the carrier reduced the need for more highways and air facilities. The Association of American Railroads makes a great to-do over European passenger train losses but one should compare these losses with what it would cost to provide equivalent road and air facilities for those forced to use these means of travel were rail services abandoned.

This justification for money-losing services muddies the picture because it is hoped that the National Railroad Passenger Corporation will be a profit-making enterprise. Would the Corporation become "profitable" only because of government subsidy? It is possible and not unprecedented by any means. In 1970, the profitability of several local air carriers and U.S.-flag international steamship lines still hinges on direct government subsidy.

The question for our society

In view of the post-World War II decline of rail passenger service and its present physical and mental state, it is obvious that a large injection of government aid will be essential if it is to become the third travel alternative. Society must ask itself how much it is willing to gamble on creating this alternative for it may take several years to attract sufficient patronage and support to justify its existence, especially on a short to even long run money-losing basis. The sum of $340 million may represent only a "drop in the bucket." It is, after all, little more than our annual outpouring on the development of the Supersonic Transport.

The new Corporation will have to operate just as the CN operated to create an entirely new rail image. Refurbished equipment must be provided in the short run, but more comfortable, faster, and more productive rolling stock has to be developed and introduced extensively in the next few years. Abandonment of almost all existing terminals and stations for more appropriate facilities, phasing out of most employees in favor of younger, more appealing and productive personnel, creating of realistic pricing systems, development of attractive food and lounge services at competitive prices, are only some of the areas which have to be resolved to evoke an enthusiastic public response.

With NRPC, however, we have the opportunity to elicit this response. The creation of a single agency, whether privately or publicly-operated, has been long overdue. Only a single agency can mount an effective attack upon all the problem areas in a coordinated manner.[16] No single railroad could reverse the trend away from rail travel, no matter how much it spent upon the project. But the new Corporation will need money to succeed. It may be forced to operate money-losing services in an effort to maintain a truly nationwide, coordinated passenger rail network. It will be confronted with the same 1919 work rules to which labor clings defiantly and probably political pressure to maintain some services not justified under any circumstances. The required cost and effort to resolve these areas may be more than we are willing to pay.

This article has indicated that rail patronage is a function of good service. Although it cannot be proven until tried, there are indications that restoration of attractive railroad passenger service would achieve the goal of the National Railroad Passenger Corporation—to transport persons in sufficient quantity such that we no longer are dependent upon automobile and air transportation. What society must decide in the 1970's is how much, in view of its previous commitment to highway and air transport, it is willing to spend on the possibility of such a development's becoming a reality.

NOTES

1. These surveys appear in the May or June issue of *Trains*. The issues employed in Table 2 are May 1956 (Vol. 16; No. 7) at p. 40, and June 1966 (Vol. 26; No. 8) at p. 40.
2. Dominion Bureau of Statistics, *Canada One-hundred 1867-1967* (Ottawa: Queen's Printer, 1967), p. 224, and Transportation Association of America, *Transportation Facts & Trends, Seventh Edition* (Washington: Transportation Association of America, 1970), p. 16.
3. *Loc. cit.*
4. *Loc. cit.*
5. *Official Airline Guide, Quick Reference North American Edition*, Vol. 14, No. 6, June 1970.
6. *Canada One-hundred 1867-1967, op. cit.*, p. 224.
7. *Transportation Facts & Trends, op. cit.*, p. 16.
8. Referring to footnotes 6 and 7, *Loc. cit.*
9. Table 4 reveals, however, that the Toronto-Windsor acceleration was accomplished by 1965 *and* that during the period 1965-1970 there has been a slight decline in overall speed on the Toronto-Sarnia and Montreal-Ottawa runs.
10. Donald M. Steffee, "Annual Speed Survey" (Different Titles), *Trains*, Vol. 22: No. 8, p. 52 (June 1962); Vol. 25: No. 8, p. 30 (June 1965); Vol. 29: No. 8, p. 27 (June 1969).
11. Union Pacific Railroad Timetable effective 9/25/60 and 5/15/69 (Revised 6/22/69); Pennsylvania Railroad New York-Washington Timetable effective 10/30/60; Penn Cen-

tral New York-Washington Timetable effective 10/26/69; National Railway Publication Company, *Official Guide of the Railways-July 1970 Edition* (New York: National Railway Publication Company, 1970), p. 82.

12. Nancy Ford, "CN's Passenger Revenues Boom, Deficit Narrows," *Modern Railroads,* 22:110-117, April 1967; David Morgan, "Bless Me! This Is Unpleasant Riding on the Rail," *Trains,* 28:4, October 1968.

13. Association of American Railroads, *Information Letter,* No. 1940, November 11, 1970.

14. David Morgan, "Not Out of the Farebox," *Trains,* 30:6-7, December 1969.

15. George Hilton, "Ralph in the Roundhouse," *Trains,* 30:47, November 1970.

16. See: Edwin P. Patton, "A Plan to Save the Passenger Train," *Business Horizons,* 12:5-15, February 1969.

B.

Motor
Transportation

Motor transportation is a vital part of the domestic transportation system of the United States. Many, many cities have no other means of transportation. A part of almost all shipments go by trucks and some industries depend entirely on trucks for transportation.

Motor transportation of both property and people is a relatively recent phenomenon. Only with the provision of improved highways in the last 40 to 50 years has it been possible for the trucking industry to exist.

The motor transportation industry is characterized by a multiplicity of firms. There are approximately 15,000 for-hire motor carriers of property in interstate commerce today. Compare this with the few hundred railroads discussed in Section A and with the few dozen air carriers to be discussed in Section C.

The motor carrier industry has many types of carriers. While all railroads are "common carriers" and hold themselves ready to serve all comers, in the motor carrier industry many firms are specialized. Therefore, we must note the existence of a well-developed "contract carrier" system, and an "exempt carrier" group, as well as the dominant "common carrier" system. Further, many carriers, even though they are common carriers, specialize by type of service. Thus, the household goods carriers, heavy haulers, newspaper carriers, film carriers, frozen food carriers, liquid goods carriers, and others, are separate sub-industry groups.

Motor carriers are also classified according to revenue. Class I motor carriers are those with gross revenues of $1 million per year or more (there are approximately 1500 of these). Class II carriers have gross revenues of from $300,000 to $1 million (there are some 2000 of these). The remaining 11,700 carriers are classified as Class III and have gross revenues of less than $300,000 annually.

The typical or average Class I intercity motor carrier operates 135 power units and 210 trailers, represents an investment of $850,000, carries average loads of 12 tons for average hauls of about 260 miles, and earns approximately 6.9 cents per ton-mile. This typical carrier employs approximately 370 people and brings in gross operating revenues of over $3.8 million annually. Of course, many carriers in the Class I group are larger and many more are smaller. Like all averages, these figures are deceiving.

There is considerable concentration in the motor carrier industry with sizable firms. For instance, in 1965, under 2 per cent of the 6000 carriers of general commodities, earning over $10 million annually, grossed over 58 per cent of all operating revenues of the group. At the other end of the scale, over 23 per cent of the general commodity carriers, earning under $25,000 annually, grossed only 0.2 per cent of all revenues.

Finally, motor carriers operate on a very small margin. The industry is competitive in many ways and entry is easy if regulatory permission can be gained. It is not uncommon for motor carriers to expend 96 per cent of all revenues in expenses of operation. The amount left for profit is extremely small and it can be a negative figure for considerable periods.

This section is designed to acquaint the reader with the characteristics of the trucking industry, the importance of highways, and some of the current developments and regulatory problems in the motor carrier field. Some selections will deal with all of these subjects; others, with only one.

---

10 **The Available Alternatives: Motor Carriers**
Paul T. McElhiney
California State University, Los Angeles

Charles L. Hilton
Tri-State College

This selection, a chapter from a book written from the shippers' point of view, organizes and outlines the alternatives in motor carriers available to the shipper. It provides thereby an overview of the motor transportation industry.

Although the trucking industry is organized differently from the railroad industry, the range of services offered is approximately the same. The geographical availability of trucks is greater than that of any other mode. Also, a truck frequently performs at least a part of the service provided by other types of carriers. This, of course, is because the highway virtually begins at the shipper's door and there are more miles of it than of any other transport way. There are about three and one-half million miles of roads and streets in the United States. Much of this mileage provides the service of providing access to farms and to residential property so that, of the total, approximately 570,000 miles can be considered as providing a basic intercity transportation system. Over this network, more than 16,000 interstate, for-hire trucking companies now carry more than 140 billion ton-miles of freight annually. In addition, twice this amount is carried by intrastate, nonregulated and private truckers. The extent of intrastate

From Paul T. McElhiney and Charles L. Hilton, *Introduction to Logistics and Traffic Management*, Dubuque: Wm. C. Brown Co., Publishers, 1968, pp. 105-119. Used by permission.

trucking operators who do business only within a particular state is surprisingly large. Research experience indicates that California, for instance, has about fifteen thousand intrastate trucking permits in force in any given year; many less extensive states generally have between one thousand and three thousand local companies in operation. The American truck fleet is correspondingly large. Approximately twelve million truck-type vehicles are presently registered in the various states. Over half of these, however, are light vehicles having gross weights of less than 10,000 pounds. About one million trucks are operated by the for-hire carriers.

Motor carriers are much harder to classify by their service availability than are railroads, because a large proportion of them do not offer a general and diversified service to the public. There are several limitations which need to be emphasized in this regard.

First, motor freight carriers are restricted in the amount of territory which they may serve. Grants of authority from regulatory bodies set forth the cities they may connect and the highways over which they may pass. Although there are several true transcontinental trucklines, most operate on fairly restricted routes, and the average length of haul for major intercity carriers in recent years has been about 235 miles.

Second, trucking companies are restricted by regulation as to the commodities they may carry. In a proceeding known as *Ex Parte MC 10*, the Interstate Commerce Commission set forth a listing of seventeen commodity groups for which motor carriers would be granted operating rights. These are as follows:

1. General Freight
2. Household Goods
3. Heavy Machinery
4. Liquid Petroleum Products
5. Refrigerated Liquid Products
6. Refrigerated Solid Products
7. Dump Trucking
8. Agricultural Commodities
9. Motor Vehicles
10. Armored Truck Service
11. Building Materials
12. Film and Associated Commodities
13. Forest Products
14. Mine Ores (not Coal)
15. Retail Store Delivery Service
16. Explosives and Dangerous Articles
17. Specific Commodities not Subgrouped

The operating authorities which the Commission issues to motor carriers may specify one or a combination of the above listed commodity rights.

Third, not all motor carriers are common carriers who hold themselves out to the whole public. Much tonnage is carried by *contract carriers* who are allowed to serve under long-term contracts, only a few customers each. . . .

Fourth, many truck companies are relatively small undertakings. More than thirteen thousand of the approximately sixteen thousand interstate, for-hire carriers are Class III carriers which earn gross revenues of less than $200,000 per year. Considering that the average truckline pays out about ninety-five per cent of its revenue in expenses, this may not leave the small trucker much profit.

General freight carriers

Best known to the public are the common carriers of general freight who operate regular schedules over regular routes. The names of the large motor freight lines in this category are familiar trademarks. Examples of such major lines found throughout the country are the following: Consolidated Freightways, Inc.; Denver Chicago Trucking Company, Inc.; Eastern Express, Inc.; McLean Trucking Company; Pacific Intermountain Express Company. Such carriers are available between all cities on the basic 570,000 mile intercity highway network. Interstate commerce regulation does not require them to form through routes and joint rates as it does the railroads, but virtually all motor lines participate in through-movements with interlining companies so that all points in the nation are effectively connected. Mergers and business changes cause the total number of general freight lines to vary from year to year. The total number of active companies is about two thousand, and the listings in the *Official Motor Carrier Directory* are typical of carriers in this category.

As indicated above, the general freight lines are common carriers who serve all the public and who accept each shipment on a bill of lading as do the railroads. In the 1920s there was a trend toward combined passenger and freight operation by motor carriers. Today, however, the individual lines specialize and are not combination carriers. Many certificates of public convenience and necessity have been issued to passenger bus operators as well as to trucklines. The major bus companies are welded through association, merger and holding arrangements into two great national bus systems. These lines, of course, specialize in passenger carrying but also offer a package express service.

Age and development

Motor carriers constitute a young industry which began during and subsequent to World War I when both highways and vehicles became truly usable. As these two transport devices improved, the industry grew. The earliest companies were regular route, regularly scheduled carriers of general commodities and passengers. By 1928 thirty-three states had recognized this sort of operation and were regulating the companies. By 1935 it had become apparent that opportunities in the motor carrier industry were not limited to regular, general freight service. Many sporadic and itinerant operations had developed and were engaging in cutthroat competition which had adverse effects on the whole transport industry. Consequently, for the first time the federal government recognized the trucking industry and brought the interstate carriers under the jurisdiction of the Interstate Commerce Commission.

Basic services

For the types of commodities which they handle, motor carriers of general freight provide service and rate structures quite similar to those of the railroads. *LTL,* or less-than-truckload and *volume* services are offered. Technically, the large-lot service is referred to as *volume* rather than *TL,* or truckload; although in practice the terms are used synonomously. In rail service the concept of the *carload* rate is essentially restricted to the physical vehicle. In other words, a carload of freight taking the carload rate is expected to move in one vehicle. In trucking, however, the minimum weight needed to gain the lower freight rate may exceed the capacity of one truck. As in rail service, the rates for *LTL* movement are appreciably higher than those for volume, or *TL* movement. Minimum charges for shipments of less than one hundred pounds are often deliberately set very high to discourage the movement of unnecessarily small lots. Unlike the railroad practice, pickup and delivery service is generally accorded to all shipments. In recent years some trucklines have published commodity rates which are lower when the shipper loads and the consignee unloads the freight.

Quality relative to other carriers

Unlike railroads, the quality of service for both *LTL* and *TL* lots is good in truckline movement. Because the equipment is flexible, and there is no need for switching moves, less-than-truckload shipments move through junction points almost as fast as truckloads. For large lots, many motor carriers exchange the fully loaded and sealed trailer so that equipment moves straight through from origin to destination. For short moves, truck is ordinarily faster than rail. On hauls of 300 miles, for instance, general freight carriers give overnight service, while railroads often deliver only by the second morning. Transcontinentally, the customer may depend on the same time-in-transit by truck as by rail carload service, that is, seventh morning from New York to Los Angeles and fifth morning from Chicago. Frequently, faster service is given; although, it is not yet generally guaranteed. Trucking industry periodicals recently carried a story reporting the test run of a major motor freight line from Newark, New Jersey, to Los Angeles, which took sixty-one hours.

For commodities on which the two are competitive, motor carrier rates often approximate those of the railroads. In some areas *LTL* rates are slightly higher than rail *LCL* rates; in some they are slightly lower. Volume rates for straight truckload shipments are also often closely competitive. The result is that the service difference may change the decision of which alternative to use. For instance, a recent investigation by a traffic consultant disclosed that truckload rates on certain types of steel-bar stock are slightly higher from Gary and Chicago to Denver than are comparable rail rates. Such steel products are used in quantity by small machinery manufacturers, but several such plants in the Denver area are not located on rail trackage. This necessitated the unloading of rail cars on a public team track and a trucking operation for delivery to the users. When the costs of these terminal operations were added to the rail rate, the traffic managers found that the common carrier truck rate was actually cheapest for them. The various manufacturing firms began pooling their steel orders into truckload lots and securing split deliveries directly to the fabricating plants.

When railroad freight and motor carrier revenues are compared, a different impression is gained, however. It was reported earlier that the average railroad revenue per ton-mile (average railroad cost per ton-mile to the customer) is 1.27 cents. The average revenue per ton-mile of major motor carrier companies, on the other hand, is 6.80 cents, or about five cents higher than the rail cost to the customer. This is because there are some rail-hauled products for which the trucks do not compete. Railroads carry immense quantities of coal and other bulk goods at extremely low rates. This dilutes the average of their revenues per ton-mile and creates the impression that rail rates in general are much lower than motor carrier rates. On general merchandise movements, the rates of both modes should be carefully analyzed by the traffic department.

Special services

Generally, common carrier general freight motor lines offer the same extra services as do railroads. The shipper may usually expect to obtain the same privileges for a competitive extra charge; however, there are some minor differences which are worth noting.

1. Special Equipment: General freight haulers do not provide as many varieties of special equipment for the customer as do the railroads. This is partly due to the use of the term *general freight* in their operating authorities. A rule of thumb is that *general freight,* or *dry freight* as it is sometimes called, is any type of ordinary merchandise which can be loaded into the usual van type of trailer used by general freight carriers. Specialized vehicles such as tank trailers, hoppers or livestock equipment are often provided by irregular route, contract, exempt product or other specialized haulers.

2. Piggyback: The use of piggyback service by trucklines might be termed the "other side of the coin" from rail use of this arrangement. Essentially, motor freight lines use trailer-on-flat-car service as an underlying carrier in place of highway travel. To them it is not a competitive weapon and the truck rate to the customer is usually the same whether the truck is carried by train or is pulled over the road. Major motor lines often use piggyback service to "deadhead" empty trailers to places where they are needed for peak, outbound traffics.

3. Protective Service: Heating and refrigeration of commodities in transit are performed by truck carriers much the same as by railroads. Insulated trailers are utilized and the heating or cooling device is usually a mechanical one. Dry ice is used extensively, but water ice is infrequently seen. An extra charge, of course, is made for such service, although some carriers include it in the line-haul rate.

4. Passing Reports and Tracing: Reporting on location of shipments is not as good throughout the trucking industry as are the carload passing reports of the rail lines. Small carriers seldom provide this courtesy because hauls are so short as to make it impractical. The billing systems of major lines, on the other hand, frequently are designed to reveal the exact progress and location of both TL and LTL shipments at all times.

5. Diversion and Reconsignment: These extra privileges are also available to the user of freight motor carriers. Again, because the average haul is short, there is little call for them.

6. Transit Privileges: Generally such privileges as stopping in transit, milling in transit and fabrication in transit can also be found in motor carrier practice. Perhaps the one which can have the greatest competitive impact, however, is the stop-in-transit to complete loading or to partially unload a volume shipment. Virtually all railroads who give this privilege, limit it to two stops in addition to the origin and destination. That is, a stop-in-transit shipment may effectively have three origins and then move through to one destination. Or it may, effectively, have one origin and be stopped twice for partial unloading before it reaches final destination. Some motor carrier transit tariffs are also as restrictive as this; however, some will allow stops-in-transit for both completion of loading and for unloading. The number of stops also may be allowed to exceed two. One carrier in the Pacific Northwest allowed unlimited stops to load or to unload. A shipment requiring three loading stops for assembly and ten partial unloadings on the way to final destination can produce much carrier revenue when the charge per stop is approximately fifteen dollars.

    Since the motor freight concept of volume movement is not tied to the physical truckload, stop-in-transit lots do not all move in the same vehicle. In rail practice the same freight car usually must be switched out of and back into the train at each stop; this is very time-consuming. Motor lines, however, load partials of such shipments on separate vehicles. Thus, it is theoretically possible that all part loadings are being made at the same instant, and that later, all part unloadings are made simultaneously. The variety of practices followed and the divergence from railroad custom indicate that truck stop-in-transit service is worthy of careful examination by the prospective shipper.

7. Other Services: The basic flexibility of the motor truck is again seen in two other special services, both of which relate to pickup and delivery. Since the semitractor with its detachable trailer has come into wide use, some carriers

have found it possible to leave trailers with the customer for loading at his convenience or as goods come off the production line. When the vehicles are loaded, the tractors pull them out and leave others. Under such circumstances freight rates can be lowered as the shipper does the loading, and the carrier may use its driver labor more efficiently.

A unique feature of trucking operations is the "split" pickup or the "split" delivery. Similar to the stop-in-transit concept, this type of collection and distribution is limited to the prescribed-delivery limits of the origin or of the destination city. The carrier picks up and delivers once as part of the regular truckload-rated service accorded the individual shipment. Then he performs a number of additional pickups or deliveries as specified by the customer on the bill of lading. A small additional charge per hundred pounds is assessed; usually, the "split" is allowed only at one end of the journey. This is particularly useful for a shipper such as a large cannery which makes one daily truckload shipment of food products to serve ten large grocery outlets in another city.

General freight motor-truck service is thus seen to be broadly similar to railroad service. Categorically, however, the similarity does not continue in our examination, for no other types of carriers have been derived from this basic sort of motor freight line. Indirect carriers such as REA Express and freight forwarders developed to use railroads as underlying carriers. These same operations, including Parcel Post, also use trucking as an underlying service, but they did not grow out of it. With the exception of bus express, treated next, other trucking activities are variations of basic common carrier trucking rather than derivations from it.

Bus express

Express service is a derivative of motor carrier passenger transport as railway express is of railway passenger service. Bus express, or bus package delivery service is a relatively new operation in the motor carrier field. This has made remarkable strides since World War II. Since buslines blanket the United States, the transport of packages on an express basis is a useful means of transport which fills a gap in the transport system. This sort of express is not related to REA Express but is, to some degree, competitive with it and is operated by the buslines themselves. A convenient feature is that in major cities packages are received at the bus stations during the entire day and night, including Saturdays and Sundays. Pickup and delivery service is not performed and package size is limited to one hundred pounds apiece. Another advantage is that, with few exceptions, franchise rights or company policy require that outlying bus terminals be open when the bus arrives. This means that the package will be put in a safe place regardless of the time of arrival or that the consignee may take it immediately. Coupled with the frequent schedules of many bus companies, these features make the service extremely useful for emergency shipments.

Irregular carriers

The supply of motor transportation available to modern industry is by no means limited to regular route, regularly scheduled carriers of general freight. The operating authorities of many truck operators do not require them to operate a daily service between fixed terminals or to carry any and all commodities. There are at least two broad categories of what might be termed irregular carriers. These are not nearly as well known to the public as the companies already described. Also, they do not maintain large enough sales forces to call on all customers; therefore, the traffic manager may find it necessary to make himself aware of their existence in his community and to seek them out.

Some common carriers are limited to operation over *irregular routes* on a *radial* basis. Essentially, this means the company may haul between a fixed base and points in a designated surrounding territory. Often, such carriers are limited to the carriage of one or a few commodities. Major motor lines sometimes own a subsidiary with rights specializing in the tank-truck hauling of liquid petroleum products.

Perhaps greater in number are common carriers with *irregular route, nonradial* operating authorities. These operators usually can haul a few categories of goods such as heavy machinery or building materials. They are permitted to use the necessary highways between specified cities or groups of communities. Some carriers are allowed to operate over territories which may include several states. Colloquially known as call and demand operators, they carry only full truckload consignments, preferably of a reasonably regular traffic. They have almost no terminal cost and can offer an attractive scale of rates to shippers who can use them. Although carriers of this sort were originally intended to be common carriers of only specific commodities, they are tending to expand their operating rights. They do this by applying for additional authorities to haul heavy one commodity traffics which they discover. These are often granted because the request to haul one commodity does not appear to threaten the market of the general commodities carriers. Also the specialized irregular carriers tend to follow or establish routes different from those of general freight haulers.

Other motor transport alternatives

When they operate in interstate commerce, the types of motor carriers discussed are within the regulatory jurisdiction of the Interstate Commerce Commission. The Motor Carrier Act of 1935, later made Part II of the Interstate Commerce Act, provides that a person who hauls property for other people, for-hire in a motor truck in interstate commerce, must obtain a *certificate,* or *permit* to do so. This certificate, or permit is evidence of the Interstate Commerce Commissioner's control over the commodities carried, the routes traveled, the areas served and the rates charged. Regulation of such matters is usually referred to as economic regulation. For common carriers, economic regulation of rates means that all rates must be published and that the same prices must be charged all like customers. There are, however, at least four types of motor service in which the amount paid depends on the arrangement the user can make with the carrier. These include Local Cartage, Exempt Carriers, Contract Carriers and Private Carriage. Technically, the first two of these are common carriers which are held out to any who can use them. Historically, the latter two are private arrangements, although today the contract motor carrier has a statutory for-hire status. The traffic departments of different business firms use these types of carriers in varying degree, so they must be considered as shipping alternatives.

Local cartage

Even the smallest cities in the United States domicile truck operators who specialize in performing hauling and delivery within the immediate area of the municipality. Large cities usually have many of these firms which are referred to as *transfer* companies, or as *transfer and storage* companies. Many such cartage operators had their inception years ago as *draymen,* who performed pickup and delivery of rail freight and baggage before the advent of competitive motor carrier pickup and delivery service. They were the *teamsters* who went with horse and wagon to the *team* tracks of the railway lines to load and unload the freight of their customers. Today, they include among their services the operation of public warehouses and often act as agents for household-goods motor carriers. The industrial firm which does not have its own fleet of local delivery vehicles may find their services convenient indeed. Since the Interstate Commerce Commission has not exercised its power to regulate the thousands of carriers in this category, rates for their services often may be negotiated. In many cities, however, local cartage rates are closely regulated by the state, and tariffs are published which apply to all alike.

Exempt carriers

Certain interstate trucking activities are exempt from the economic control of the Interstate Commerce Commission. This means that rates for their services are completely open to negotiation between carrier and customer. Altogether, there are eleven categories, or classes of exempt carriers, among which are the following:

1. A person (or company) may carry his own goods in his own truck in interstate commerce.
2. An agricultural cooperative association (or federation of such associations) may engage in interstate, for-hire carriage of property between its suppliers, warehouses and outlets.
3. Motor vehicles used in carrying property consisting of ordinary livestock, fish or nonmanufactured agricultural or horticultural commodities on a for-hire basis in interstate commerce are wholly exempt from economic regulation.
4. Any person not engaged in motor transport as a primary business may perform casual, occasional or reciprocal for-hire interstate transport for others.

Probably, the exemption which most frequently comes to notice is the third point. This is the general agricultural exemption relating to vehicles used for carriage of nonmanufactured agricultural goods. The Interstate Commerce Commission often has recommended that this exemption be interpreted or modified to cover transportation only from point of production to the primary market. Congress has never incorporated this recommendation into the Act, however. Thus, it is possible for a for-hire trucking company to operate exclusively in interstate commerce between any part of the marketing chain as an exempt carrier of property for others. It is safe to say that in establishing agricultural exemptions it was not the original intent of Congress to create this type of for-hire carrier. The probable intent was to allow only a farmer or agricultural dealer to haul the products of others as well as his own and to gain some sort of reimbursement for the service.

In addition to this carriage of exempt commodities by carriers not subject to economic regulation, transportation of agricultural goods may be performed by regulated common or contract for-hire carriers as long as they do not place them in the same vehicle with regulated goods. In effect, exempt commodities become nonexempt when carried in a mixed load with commodities subject to regulations.

Definition of Exempt Commodities. There has been a good deal of controversy as to what constitutes a nonmanufactured agricultural commodity. Exempt carriers have sought to increase—and regulated carriers to restrict—the number of products which might fall into this category. The litigation generally has questioned the extent to which an agricultural commodity may be processed or modified and still remain a nonmanufactured agricultural product. A series of cases before the Interstate Commerce Commission and the federal courts began the development of a list of commodities which might be processed by drying, dehydrating, powdering, freezing, curing, cooking, salt curing and so forth, and still remain in the exempt category.

By 1958 the list had become so long and complex that the Interstate Commerce Commission issued an administrative ruling to clarify the status of various commodities in relation to the agricultural exemption. Known as the Commodity List in *Administrative Ruling Number 107*, this document indicates whether each of a group of over three hundred agricultural products is exempt or nonexempt. The *Transportation Act of 1958* gave the force of law to *Administrative Ruling Number 107* by incorporating the Commodity List into Section 203 of the *Interstate Commerce Act*. Thus, the Act now includes a substantial list of specific items which are designated as exempt or nonexempt. But because the listing is not all inclusive, the Interstate Commerce Commission and the courts can still decide whether or not nonincluded products fall within the exemption.

Contract carriers

In railroad transportation the average shipper has no alternative but to deal with a public carrier which is open to everyone, in other words, a common carrier. In trucking, however, there are two other possibilities. The shipper may haul his own goods in his own trucks which is referred to as *private carriage,* or he may make a long-term contract with someone else who has a truck to do his trucking for him. The latter is now known as *contract carriage* and has led to the development of a special type of trucking company which serves only a limited number of customers and does not hold itself out to the general public. To prevent such companies from hauling for everyone and competing unfairly with common carriers, they are subject to regulation by the Interstate Commerce Commission (and by most state regulatory commissions). Thus, a contract carrier must obtain a *permit* from the I.C.C. before he can do interstate business. Although he is allowed to discriminate among customers and charge them different amounts, a schedule of the lowest actual rates he charges as well as a copy of each of his contracts must be on file with the I.C.C. There are more than two thousand six hundred operators which presently hold interstate contract carrier permits and many more which operate wholly within individual states. Because no terminal facilities are maintained and because a steady traffic is assured, contract carrier rates are often lower than those of common carriers serving the same area. Also, due to his continuing relationship with the customer, the contract trucker's service can be somewhat special. Drivers do not need to be instructed continually in such matters as where to find the goods; service such as moving freight into the warehouse and stacking it may be performed in addition to transportation. The contract carrier is a useful alternative for the traffic manager, although he is not as easy to locate as the common carrier. Also, the operating authority and regulatory status of the carrier should be checked carefully by the new customer since the management of some of these carriers is not performed by experts.

Private carriage

For the landlocked shipper, the shipping arrangements discussed so far constitute most of the alternatives in surface carriage. In most localities several of these services will be available. The shipper with a reasonably regular or heavy traffic will find that competition between different modes or different carriers of the same mode will usually produce a service reasonably well fitted to his needs. At times, however, a shipper will be so isolated or handle a product so specialized that there is very little carrier competition for his patronage. Many a flourishing firm of moderate size constitutes the major industry of the small town in which it is located. Such towns often enjoy the service of only one railroad. The shipper finds that his carloads are switched into the slow "local" freight train rather than the high-speed "manifest" train which does not stop there. Because the cost of serving him is high, the carrier shows little interest in his rate problems. Motor carrier service may not be much better for the same reasons. Under such circumstances the customer must create his own transport competition. There is still a very useful transport alternative by which he may do it, and this is private carriage.

Under the American system of regulation a person is entitled to carry his own goods in his own vehicle in interstate commerce so long as he respects the motor vehicle and highway regulations of the states and the safety rules of the federal government. Thus, the entire highway network of the country is open to the shipper who wishes to provide his own motor transportation. Many shippers take advantage of this opportunity and probably as many private trucks are operated in this sort of competition to for-hire carriers as are operated by the common and contract carrier trucklines themselves. There are approximately eleven million private trucks registered in the United States; however, due to peculiarities of the registration procedure perhaps ninety per cent are light vehicles, small pickup trucks and even some station wagons. Only about one million are large enough to be considered regular freight vehicle types.

Cost and convenience are the two main advantages of private truck operation. Volume of traffic is not necessarily a limiting factor since the first cost of a vehicle is relatively low, and the key to success is sufficient traffic to keep each vehicle full regardless of whether there are two or a hundred in the fleet. Since carriage is only incidental to his primary business, the person who transports his own goods need not make a profit on their transportation. In addition, he has no terminal costs, and many functions such as maintenance and accounting may be performed by other departments of his company. Because of these things, the thirty-five to forty cents per vehicle-mile cost, which some traffic managers estimate, is realistic. It is also very close to the line-haul cost (excluding all other expenses and profit) of the for-hire carrier. The traffic manager who visualizes using this alternative should study it carefully in advance of recommending it to management. Precise estimate of cost per vehicle-mile should be made. This estimate should be calculated with the estimated average load and the estimated average length of haul to produce a cost in cents per hundredweight. This cost then can be compared readily with the published rates of for-hire carriers.

The American Management Association estimates that savings over common carrier rates can run as high as twenty per cent. One traffic manager warns that costing must be done for each individual haul contemplated. On the New York to Chicago haul, for instance, common carrier rates are so low that they make private trucking impractical. Other traffic managers feel that the ability to schedule their own transport by itself represents an advantage.

There are, of course, some disadvantages to "do it yourself" motor transportation, and the prospective user must be prepared to establish an effective supervisory system to cope with them. The investment problem is paramount. A modern tractor and trailer combination costs in excess of twenty thousand dollars. The firm may be reluctant to invest such an amount in what may seem to be an experimental operation. This may lead to the acquisition of vehicles through leasing rather than purchasing. The Interstate Commerce Commission has issued strict regulations regarding leasing to prevent the leasing companies from operating as illegal for-hire carriers. The traffic manager should ascertain that he is leasing the equipment in a manner that will insure his complete direction and domination of the operation in order to comply with these rules.

Next in importance is the problem of backhaul. Every type of carrier except the pipeline is faced with the dilemma of filling his vehicle in both directions of its travel. If the private carrier cannot do this, he must double the cost per mile estimate which he has made for his operation. Some industrial firms are successful in loading their own products in both directions. A major producer of automobile tires, for instance, delivers its finished products to seaboard cities in its own trucks; it then picks up imported crude rubber at steamship terminals and hauls it back to the inland tire factories. Other companies act as exempt for-hire carriers on the return trip, carrying fruits and vegetables from growing areas to market. The backhaul problem often creates a strong temptation for the traffic manager. His suppliers or his customers may consider it a favor if he will haul their goods on a for-hire basis at less than the going rate; with the exception of agricultural products, however, this constitutes illegal carriage and must be avoided entirely.

Thus, the private truck operator has a two-fold problem: how to obtain the equipment at the least expense and how to keep it fully occupied. Obtaining trucks through rental or renting out owned equipment to others are both strictly regulated by the Interstate Commerce Commission. The purpose of the Commission's leasing rules is to prevent private truck owners from acting as for-hire carriers without a certificate or permit to do so. Important leasing rules may be summarized as follows:

1. The equipment must be leased by the shipper to perform only his own trucking operation.
2. It must be in his exclusive possession.
3. It must be operated by his employees under his direction and control.
4. Equipment may not be "trip" leased to a for-hire carrier in lieu of private backhaul movement.
5. Equipment may not be rented to other shippers to attempt full utilization.
6. It cannot be leased by two shippers who will use it in opposite directions.

Private carrier management must also face the licensing and fee problem. Each state has different requirements for truck registration and taxation. The proper permits and plates must be obtained and proper bonds posted for each state through which the operator passes. Finally, in similar vein, the safety regulations of the states and the federal government must be ascertained and met.

---

11   Highways to 1985
American Trucking Associations, Inc.

In the mid-1950's, the United States launched a massive program of highway building—the "System of Interstate and Defense Highways," more popularly known as the "Interstate System." This program was intended to be a "crash" one and to be completed in 16 years, but in fact it has had to be extended beyond 1972. Hailed originally as an economic boon and as the method of solving the

From American Trucking Associations, Inc., Department of Research and Transport Economics, Washington, D.C., for the ATA Foundation. Used by permission.

highway needs of the nation, the whole concept of the Interstate System has come into controversy and criticism. Much of the criticism has revolved around the general needs for urban transportation and the particular ecological-sociological effects of the Interstate System.

As the Interstate System draws nearer to completion, the question of "what next?" is asked increasingly. This selection presents the American Trucking Association's review of highway policy and tries to answer, in part, "what next?"

In 1956 when the Federal government, acting upon the recommendations of a distinguished committee headed by General Lucius D. Clay, embarked upon an expanded highway program designed to provide the nation with a system of interstate and defense highways adequate to meet the needs of commerce and defense for the foreseeable future, it was thought of as essentially a catch-up program. Road building, which even before the war lagged behind demand, was virtually abandoned during World War II. Even routine maintenance was neglected so that we emerged from the conflict with our roads in sorry shape indeed.

In 1955 the nation's highway needs for the next 10 years were estimated by the Clay Committee at $101 billion, with the National System of Interstate and Defense Highways to cost $27 billion—or more than one quarter of this amount. After years of "catching up," the nation's highway needs for the period following the Interstate program—the period 1973 through 1985—are estimated at $225 billion, or more than twice as much as the estimate for the previous 10 years. And this estimate anticipates the National System of Interstate and Defense Highways will be completed before the new program gets underway.

There is a sort of limbo in the transition from one period to the next because the cost estimate for the new program is based upon taking off where the present program ends. The problem is, no one knows when the present program will end. Estimates range from 1974 to a hopefully realistic 1975, and no one expects the program to be completed by the target date of 1972 nor even 1973.

Although these new cost estimates may come as a shock to some, nobody close to the scene was taken by surprise. The fact is that everyone familiar with the direction of growth of our nation in recent years has known for some time that the current highway program was only a beginning.

Concern over the future highway needs of our nation was expressed in Current Report, No. 5, *Highways—The Years Beyond 1972*, February 1965. At that time we said: "And it is becoming increasingly apparent that the nation may not have solved all of its highway problems by the magical year 1972. While the National System of Interstate and Defense Highways is propelling the country headlong into the future, the way is not always smooth."

The Congress in August 1965, in anticipation of completion of the Interstate System in 1972, adopted legislation directing the Secretary of Commerce (this duty has since been transferred to the Secretary of Transportation) to report every two years, beginning in 1968, estimates of the future highway needs of the nation. The first of these reports, "1968 National Highway Needs Report," is now at hand. While it contains no specific recommendations for the future highway program, it does report needs as estimated by the states and suggests the possible direction of any future Federal highway program. The Transportation Secretary's report, together with hearings in February 1968 by the Roads Subcommittee of the Committee on Public Works of the House of Representatives pretty well point the way.

One thing appears certain. That is, any future Federal highway program is going to be much more city oriented than have been past programs. This is already evident in the increased urban funds provided for in the 1968 ABC Federal-Aid Act. In this respect we seem to have come fully about. Early Federal-aid highway programs forbade spending of Federal money in cities. This ban was modified in the middle 1930's to permit the expenditure of Federal monies on urban extensions of rural highways. In 1944, Federal highway-aid was further broadened and urban areas were given additional consideration. Federal funds authorized for the so-called ABC roads, excluding the Interstate System, were divided 45% for the (A) primary system, 30% for the (B) secondary system, and 25% for the (C) urban projects.

The Federal Aid Highway Act of 1956, which expanded the Federal Highway Program and provided for completion of the National System of Interstate and Defense Highways on a basis of 90% Federal and 10% state funds, also continued the ABC program with the 50% Federal and 50% state matching funds.

Authorizations for these road systems were gradually increased over the years until they reached $1 billion in fiscal year 1966. New authorizations for fiscal 1970 and 1971 provide $1.42 billion for each of these years. Authorization for the Interstate System included urban extensions, by-passes, and circumferential roads around cities. In all, 16.2% of the total miles and 46.7% of the money is to be spent on urban portions of the interstate system as now designated.

Battle over Interstate extension likely

Another thing that appears certain from the report and the testimony before the House Roads Subcommittee, is that there will be a battle over extension of the Interstate System and matching ratios for future Federal-aid projects. There has been heavy pressure over the years to expand it by designating new routes between major points as parts of the System, eligible for 90-10 matching money. This pressure has been resisted, but there have been implications that the program would be expanded upon completion. The 1968 Federal Highway Act added 1,500 miles of Interstate—over the protests of the Department of Transportation. Sentiment to discontinue the program upon completion has been growing, however, and a battle looms. Included in this battle will be the question of matching ratios. There is talk of placing the entire program on the same basis, but whether this should be 50-50, 60-40 or 90-10 has not been officially put forth by any responsible group.

The Department of Transportation and The American Association of State Highway Officials appear to be strongly in favor of discontinuance while a number of members of the House Roads Subcommittee appear anxious to extend the System perhaps by as much as 10,000 miles.

The problems of urban highway congestion and the impact of highway location and construction in the cities have brought pressures for alternate solutions to the task of moving people in our cities and these alternatives will undoubtedly be explored thoroughly before any new program is adopted. The Transportation Secretary's Needs Report places the matter of future highway programs in perspective as follows:

The scale and impact of today's highway programs are of such magnitude that Federal policy must continue to stress the planning of highways in coordination with other transport modes and also to preserve or improve the quality of the environment they affect. Particularly in urban areas, Federal policy will need to place even greater stress—by program requirements and incentives—to help achieve coordination and unity of responsibility and action by the multiplicity of local governmental units and the state highway departments toward the solution of transportation problems. Because of the growth of urban areas and the size and complexity of today's urban transportation problems, continued and enlarged Federal assistance toward the solution of urban transportation problems appears highly desirable.

Judging from the experience of the past and the expected trends of the future the general direction of desirable Federal highway policy seems to be as follows:

1. Continuing assistance to the states for improving the efficiency and safety of the highway system in both rural and urban areas, particularly where traffic growth is expected. Studies will be necessary to redefine the Federal-aid systems and enable sound economic analyses to reveal how and where the investment of Federal funds would be most beneficial in terms of national objectives, general economic and social benefits, and transportation service to people and commerce. Additional urban and safety funds provided in the 1968 Act take a large step in this direction.

2. Greater stress than in the past on the improvement of urban transportation and the development of transportation plans calculated to raise the quality and satisfactions of urban life.

3. Additional emphasis on the coordination of highways with other modes of transport, both intra- and inter-urban, to insure the optimum provision of the best features of all modes.

4. Continuing emphasis on making the highway a salutary influence on the environment both in rural and urban areas.

Justification of needs

In justification of the needs requirements of $225 billion—and it must be kept in mind that this figure is based upon the improvement of the national highway plant to a given level of adequacy—the Department of Transportation cites the growing dependence of the American economy upon highway transport. It says:

The nation's transportation requirements are served by railway, waterway, highway, airway, and pipeline. It is estimated [*Transportation Facts and Trends*, Transportation Association of America, Washington, D.C., April 1967] that the nation's transport costs (costs of the travel way, the conveyance medium, and the costs of their operation) in 1965 amounted to nearly $141 billion, or 20 per cent of the gross national product of $681 billion. Of the total cost, $78 billion (55 per cent) was for passenger transportation, of which automobiles and buses accounted for 91 per cent; and nearly $63 billion was spent for freight movement, of which highways and trucks accounted for 73 per cent. All highway vehicles combined were responsible for 83 per cent of total transportation costs. Highway passenger transportation by automobiles and buses accounted for 61 per cent of total highway transport expenditure, trucks for the remainder.

Comparison of the 1950 and 1965 passenger and freight shares of intercity transport by mode . . . evidences the changes that have taken place in the past 15 years. In passenger service, travel has nearly doubled from 446 to 843 billion passenger-miles. The highway has held its dominant position, while air travel has made inroads on rail travel. In freight transport, although total movement increased 55 per cent from 1.1 to 1.7 trillion ton-miles, the railroads' share declined from 57 to 44 per cent. In ton-miles moved, pipelines, highways, and waterways showed increases of 140, 120 and 57 per cent, respectively, in the 15 years, while rail tonnage rose only 19 per cent.

And, after discussing the various assumptions utilized in arriving at its projection for the future, concludes:

The growth of highway travel in the 1965-85 period, therefore, is expected to take place within a range of 60 to 100 per cent over that existing in 1965. The most likely projection, based on moderate levels of growth in the economy and in other factors influencing travel, is 71 per cent, an average annual rate of 2.7 per cent.

Effects of technological change

The Needs Report discusses current research and development projects designed to promote more efficient and attractive mass transportation. These projects include the several high-speed ground transport studies in the North east Corridor. What may be the impact of these projects on future highway needs?

The Report points out that only 6 per cent of the estimated highway needs are for intercity highways in the Corridor: "And most, if not all, of those intercity route improvements will still be required whether or not high-speed transportation is installed." The same general conclusion resulted from the analysis of urban transportation needs: ". . . while improved mass transportation facilities are needed in both intra-urban and intercity high-density corridors, there will continue to be in the same corridors a need for continuing attention to improving the street and highway systems."

Future urban highways

Whereas current and past Federal highway programs have included urban highways only when they connected rural highways, it appears that in the future Federal highway funds may be spent for purely local streets. The Secretary's Report indicates that urban highway needs during the post Interstate period covered will be $98 billion. More than half of this amount, $57 billion, would be for urban streets off the Federal-aid systems. If the Federal government is to assist in improving urban mobility, it appears certain that Federal-aid will have to be extended to the major urban arterial streets not now on existing systems.

The magnitude of this problem is shown by the fact that the Bureau of Public Roads now estimates that there are 51,000 miles of urban roads and streets presently on Federal-aid systems. It further estimates that there are an additional 26,000 miles of urban arterial streets.

That there will be strong pressure for Federal-aid for urban streets was shown by the testimony of Patrick Healy, executive director of the National League of Cities, and Bernard Hillenbrand, executive director of the National Association of Counties, before the Roads Subcommittee of the House of Representatives on February 20, 1968. Both called for a greater concentration of Federal funds in the metropolitan areas of our nation.

Future Federal-aid to rural highways

As indicated earlier, the direction of our future rural highway programs will be hotly debated in the Congress. The Transportation Secretary's Needs Report describes a study by the Bureau of Public Roads of a possible intermediate highway network. Routes selected for the study network, which was called the "intermediate system," were considered to be next in importance to those in the Interstate System. About 66,000 miles of highways were taken as possible candidates for the intermediate system. This total was further divided into three "increments" of decreasing priority of importance.

Increment 1, comprising about 10,000 miles, serves about one-sixth as much rural travel as the present Interstate System on about one-fourth as much mileage. Its routes generally provide additional connections between centers served by the Interstate System and extend service to all places of over 125,000 population.

Increment 2, with about 22,000 miles, would serve only 17 per cent more travel than Increment 1, but would extend service to include all places with more than 50,000 people.

Increment 3, with about 34,000 miles, would serve only 25 per cent more travel than Increment 2, but would extend service to all places of more than 25,000 population and most places of 15,000.

The intermediate system tends to be made up of relatively short routes, most in one or two states, connecting the Interstate System and important points off that system.

The Bureau of Public Roads notes that the study network was deemed useful for exploring the general subject of future highways, but specific routes for an actual system would require much more elaborate analysis in cooperation with the states. However, the intermediate system study suggests the nature and perhaps the extent of intercity routes on which priority seems logical, according to the Department of Transportation. Some of the routes already have been improved to high standards by the states, including a number to freeway status, and others have been given high priority in state planning.

Results of the study, the Department says in its report, suggest the desirability of more exploration of a special program to encourage and assist the states in constructing an intermediate, supplementary highway system. Although the level of Federal financing provided for the Interstate System may not be warranted, some Federal incentives would be appropriate to encourage the states to give precedence to an intermediate system over routes at a lower level, the Department adds. One idea is to allow use of regular primary highway system funds for intermediate system projects but at a higher matching ratio than for primary system projects. Another idea is to authorize special funds earmarked for intermediate system purposes.

In a recent statement to the Subcommittee on Roads of the House Public Works Committee, Ross G. Stapp, chief administrative officer of the Wyoming State Highway Department and first vice president of the American Association of State Highway Officials, reminded the subcommittee that when the Interstate System program began there already existed a pile-up of ABC needs, and that these needs, which have been held in abeyance, have grown.

In 1956, the highest priority highway need of the nation was an interstate freeway network. To get that monumental task going and keep it going as close to schedule as physical impediments and skyrocketing costs will permit, the major portion of Federal-aid funds has been allotted to it.

For the state highway departments, ABC requirements will take top priority with the completion of the Interstate System, Mr. Stapp said. And he added:

The state highway administrators are unanimous in their hopes that we can finish the 41,000-mile Interstate network and not add to that mileage, either now or later, for to do so will continue to put off the day when we can turn our financial resources to modernizing our primary system, which includes the replacement of a number of substandard bridges, and address our attention to taking care of urban problems. In upgrading the primary system, those routes qualifying will be built to freeway standards. Others will be expressways or vastly improved two-lane facilities.

The Interstate System
—what of the future?

As mentioned before, the future of the Interstate System is of primary importance in the development of any future Federal highway program. All who have been heard from so far in the current Congressional inquiry have side-stepped the issue or have come out flatly for discontinuance of the interstate concept, upon completion of the presently designated system. No one seems to question the need for additional highways of the interstate type, but those who oppose extension of the present system do so on the grounds that the present matching ratio for the System puts too great a stress on these particular highways which results in neglect of other needed segments of the highway plant.

On the other hand, many who have waited in hopes that the admitted gaps in the system could be filled in once the present system is completed, have expressed strong support for its extension. Examples of the gaps in the presently designated Interstate System include the southwestern coast of Florida, from the Tampa-St. Petersburg area to Miami, and the area between I-70 at Salina, Kansas, and important points in central Nebraska, North and South Dakota.

Cost estimates of concern

Of major concern to the trucking industry is the constantly spiraling cost of building highways and the growing tendency to finance all highway expenditures from highway user funds. The cost estimates contained in the Secretary's report show average annual needs for capital expenditures, maintenance and administration of all roads and streets during the period under study in the amount of $31 billion. The report also estimates income available for highways at current rates at an average of $18 billion during this period. Thus there is a projected annual shortage between projected costs and income of $13 billion per year. This is equal to total highway income at the present time.

It must be kept in mind that the current highway cost estimates are in 1965 dollars at 1965 prices. Experience with past projections of this type indicate that these will be extremely conservative. For example, the 1956 estimate of completing the Interstate System was $27 billion. This estimate has been revised upward at regular intervals. The latest estimate for completing this system puts the cost at $56.5 billion, an increase of more than 100 per cent.

No matter how the many complex problems facing the future of the highway program are resolved, it is apparent that Congress will hold extensive hearings and all sides will be heard from. When the issues are finally decided we will be in a better position to analyze the impact of these new programs upon the industry.

One thing is certain, however, regardless of the program selected. Highway transportation will continue to dominate our domestic scene for many years to come. Highways and highway transport with their stimulating appetites for raw materials, finished goods, machinery and manpower will remain a mainstay of our economy.

12 Danger Rides with Big Rigs

August Gribbon

Are the big trucks safe? Is the public needlessly endangered by competitive pressures on the carriers? Are safety regulations really enforced? What is the public responsibility of the motor carriers? This selection gives some of the flavor of the national debate which centers on these questions.

You may drive superbly—like an Al Unser of the sedan set. But skill avails little when a passing tractor-trailer heaves a wall of water from a wet road and drowns out your vision, or when a 70,000-pound van follows too closely down a steep hill and there's no way to elude it. Then you trust to luck.

In fact, motorists unwittingly test their luck on untold other occasions just by mingling the family car with the big rigs on the highway.

There is evidence that significantly large numbers of long-distance truck drivers take amphetamines and drink while driving. Many pilot seriously defective machines. Many force themselves to stay at the wheel after fatigue has made them dangerous. This despite industry concern and sometimes lavish spending on safety.

Accident rates deceive

Similar past allegations have had small impact, largely because they lacked proof. Many motorists recoil at such reports, for they've come to regard big-rig truckers as the best, most-courteous drivers on the road. Truckers change flat tires for elderly ladies and help other distressed motorists. Besides, it obviously takes skill just to maneuver a giant truck.

Truck companies and the American Trucking Associations Inc. (ATA), the industry's trade organization and lobbyist, explain—correctly—that trucks' accident rate is lower than cars'. They say the rate keeps dropping even though more trucks take the road each year. The rate for all trucks is 14.6 accidents per million miles driven, according to ATA figures; later National Safety Council statistics put it at 12.6. The rate for cars is 27.7.

Yet the small Bureau of Motor Carrier Safety, the Department of Transportation's truck-safety policeman, has intensified and expanded its accident investigating and reporting in recent months. Its files now abound with illustrations of the threats big rigs pose.

Examples?

In early morning on U.S. Highway 70 outside Roswell, N.M., a tractor-trailer

From August Gribbon, "Danger Rides with Big Rigs," *The National Observer*, Vol. 10, No. 23, June 7, 1971. Used by permission.

eased onto the wrong side of the road toward an onrushing Buick, which defensively swerved far onto the road shoulder. Still the truck rammed it, killing its four occupants.

Federal officials blamed the trucker, terming him "negligent, . . . inattentive, dozing, or very possibly disoriented" because a "psychological or physical disorder" made him unable to stay awake while driving in darkness.

A truck lugging bombs over U.S. 75, which meanders through Coalgate, Okla., tried to make a right turn in the town. The rig flipped. The bombs didn't detonate, but two persons suffered injuries; property damage totaled $10,000. Official finding: The truck's improperly secured load shifted, tipping the trailer.

Near Rockland, Fla., a tractor-trailer hauling grapefruit roared up behind a line of five cars pausing at a traffic light on U.S. 1. It didn't stop. Three persons died; six were hurt. Federal officials said the driver "had amphetamines in his possession."

One year's toll: 1,953 dead

Outside Ashton, Idaho, a runaway tractor-trailer hit a herd of cattle on a bridge, then bounded to a river bank below. The driver died. Federal officials said the truck's brakes were "almost nonfunctional and so badly neglected that [the truck] obviously had been in a dangerous condition for a relatively long period of time."

Investigators said the trucker had not kept the mandatory driving log properly, lacked a valid medical certificate, and apparently had not slept more than 2½ hours in the 29 hours preceding the crash. Among his effects was an empty whisky bottle with a partially dissolved tranquilizer in it.

Freakish, isolated incidents? Not at all.

Bureau of Motor Carrier Safety (BMCS) files contain reports of 47,877 big-rig smashups that killed 1,953 persons, injured 24,106, and caused $102,051,590 in property damage in 1969. The BMCS hasn't completed its 1970 tally yet, so *The National Observer* hand-counted 1970 reports of the six largest—and purportedly the most safety-conscious—trucking companies.

Those six carriers alone had at least 4,317 accidents in which 36 persons died and 96 others were injured seriously. The totals are conservative, because some carriers' files spanned only eight months.

Roadway Express Inc., Akron, Ohio, the nation's third-biggest carrier by ATA reckoning, topped the list with an 11-month record of 790 accidents, killing 10 persons and seriously injuring 21. R. R. Johnstone, Roadway vice-president, refused to converse about "such a sensitive subject as safety" over the phone.

Asked again, by telegram, to comment and to reply to a Roadway driver's criticism of Roadway's safety program, he wired: "Suggest you review steady improvement in safety performance before accepting criticism of one driver as fact." In 1969 Roadway reported 869 crashes that took 29 lives and hurt 427 persons. How many were seriously injured isn't known. The bureau's 1969 figures don't show the degree of injury.

The file of the nation's biggest carrier, United Parcel Service, New York City, lacked a month's accounting from an Ohio subsidiary. Otherwise it reported 629 accidents, 10 fatalities, and 13 serious injuries. A company spokesman remarks: "Unfortunately we are all the victims of human folly—if not ours, then someone else's."

Figures don't tell all

The nation's second-largest carrier, Consolidated Freightways, Inc., Menlo Park, Calif., reported 1,093 crashes that killed 26 persons and injured 492 in 1969. Consolidated's 1970 file shows 460 wrecks causing five fatalities and 13 serious injuries in eight months.

O. H. Fraley, Consolidated's executive vice-president, comments: "We don't like to talk in terms of the number of accidents. No other company does. The number of accidents is relative to the number of miles driven. The number might look large, but the frequency rate of truck accidents is going down. Our road-accident frequency in 1970 was 16 per cent lower than in 1969."

Not even the BMCS contends that its statistics realistically portray the state of big-truck safety. Its figures are far too conservative, for they cover only a fraction of U.S. trucks.

Arthur MacAndrew, chief of the bureau's compliance division, explains: "Some 18,000,000 U.S. vehicles carry truck-license tags. Of those only 5,000,000 are the medium and heavy trucks we're concerned with. About half of those big rigs engage in interstate commerce and thus come under our jurisdiction. Really we deal with and get our data from roughly 10 per cent of the nation's truck fleet."

Besides, bureau officials have discovered that at times companies don't report accidents. All mishaps causing $250 property damage, personal injury, or a fatality must be reported.

But last fall, for example, the bureau alleged that Thunderbird Freight Lines, Inc., of Phoenix failed to report accidents. For that and other reasons Thunderbird was fined $3,000.

Moody Suter, Thunderbird's vice-president for safety, comments: "They charged us with 15 counts of failure to file [reports of accidents causing $16,600 in property damages]. We got that cut to about six charges that we didn't contest."

Evidence of big-rig safety problems comes from other sources too:

The National Safety Council has compiled information from 23 states and tallied 725,000 big-rig crashes in 1969. They killed 4,700 persons.

The New Jersey Turnpike Authority says large trucks constitute 12 per cent of its road's traffic. But they're involved in 31.1 per cent of all accidents and in 61.8 per cent of all fatal accidents.

The University of Michigan's Highway Safety Research Institute found large trucks "overinvolved in accidents" in Oakland County, Michigan, which is traversed by main roads connecting Detroit with Flint and Saginaw. The discovery is based on one of the first applications of a formula that considers known accident-causing factors and comes up with "accident norms" for various kinds of vehicles.

John Reed, a former governor of Maine who heads the National Transportation Safety Board, declares: "I say the big trucks do pose a significant safety problem. The generally strict Federal regulations apply only to 10 per cent of the trucking industry. States' rules cover all trucks, but the states' rules aren't now good enough to get bad drivers off the roads. We need an upgrading of those regulations."

Cowcatchers and better brakes

After analyzing a truck-caused New Jersey Turnpike pile-up that took six lives and involved six trucks plus 23 other vehicles, Mr. Reed's board recently recommended installing special bumpers on trucks. They would function like cowcatchers on locomotives and streetcars, preventing the high-riding trucks from shearing the tops off cars they hit—or that hit them.

The board suggested occasionally segregating trucks into special lanes, forbidding "overtaking and passing by heavy vehicles," and creating standards that would make trucks less prone to tip over. It also called for tougher truck-brake standards.

According to the Bureau of Public Roads, the average passenger car traveling 50 m.p.h. needs 122 feet for stopping; the average three- or four-axle truck needs 445 feet.

Dr. William Haddon, the physician who heads the Insurance Institute for Highway Safety and formerly ran the nation's traffic and highway safety programs, declares: "It's obvious that mixing small, fast-stopping vehicles with ponderous, slower-braking ones would create a problem. And it does. It's an inherent safety hazard."

The Department of Transportation has faced the problem. Its National Highway Traffic Safety Administration ruled in March that trucks built after Jan. 1, 1973, must be able to stop almost as quickly as automobiles.

"We agree there should be improvement in current truck-brake performance," volunteers Kevin Smith, manager of product reliability for the International Harvester Co., Ford, and other truck makers agree.

Yet manufacturers, trucking companies, and some Government officials consider the Transportation Department's braking specifications and deadlines unrealistic. They want the rule modified and delayed. A BMCS engineer estimates that the proposed new brake systems would add $2,200 to the cost of an 11-axle truck.

The ATA "seriously doubts" the new system can be developed by 1973. It frets that truck makers may be unable to warrant that trucks with the new brakes will function with existing trailers. Loss of this "compatibility" would cost trucker and shipper time and money.

Even if opponents fail to delay implementation, the brake rule's impact will

come slowly. Just 150,000 new replacement trucks enter the long-haul fleet yearly. At that rate, it conceivably could take 33 years before the entire fleet had presumably better brakes.

The fender dilemma

The reason: Trucks, unlike cars, live on and on. They are routinely rebuilt piecemeal as parts wear out. A truck that looks sparkling new may be just a new cab fitted onto an aged, overhauled diesel engine and chassis.

Other aspects of safety are being scrutinized too. Anticipating Federal regulation, truck makers are studying the feasibility of fenders to reduce spray from trucks on wet roads.

"It's a horrendous problem," says Gale Beardsley, Ford's chief heavy-truck engineer. He and others say that fenders big enough to permit the wheels' considerable vertical and horizontal movement would cause trucks to exceed width limits. They say fenders would necessitate major trailer modifications, cause maneuvering troubles, and inhibit the air flow that cools brakes.

Truck makers deny there's a hazard in the air blitzing that passing trucks give cars. About the alleged tendency of some tall trucks to flip over, International Harvester's Kevin Smith volunteers:

"There are no Federal standards governing this. But auxiliary stabilizing devices are available now." Ford's Mr. Beardsley adds: "Trucks tend to sit on the road. Their current stability characteristics are quite acceptable if drivers drive them with reasonable intelligence."

The motor-carrier bureau also has set new driver-qualification regulations. It has found "a marked increase" in accidents involving "unqualified," "reckless," "accident prone," "mentally and physically ill," "emotionally unstable," and "drunk drivers." So for the first time it has provided for "removal from service" of drivers convicted of "motor-vehicle crime involving drug or alcohol abuse or of fleeing the scene of a fatal or injury-producing accident."

"Of course, we have to rely mainly on voluntary compliance with rules," comments Kenneth L. Pierson, BMCS deputy director. "To police this industry, surveying company and driver records and examining all trucks, we'd need tens of thousands of inspectors." The bureau has 203 employes; 103 are inspectors.

States make few checks

The bureau's unarmed inspectors work with state police. They check trucks at weighing stations and other public facilities, crawling over and under rigs, looking for such things as bad brakes, malfunctioning lights, and faulty trailer connections.

In many states sporadic BMCS road checks and inspections of company files provide the only effective policing. Bureau officials say this. So do drivers.

Dale Crum, a trucker from Lemoyne, Pa., with 15 years and a million miles of driving experience, says: "Yes, I've had my outfits checked. Twice.

Ronald Perry of Dillsburg, Pa., another veteran driver, declares: "I've heard more about inspections than I've seen 'em. But the times the state police checked me they ambled around with their clipboards. Anybody could see they didn't know what to look for. They waved me through when my truck was fallin' apart."

A Department of Transportation official comments: "Relatively few states have tough regulations for police to enforce. The quality of regulation runs the gamut. For all intents and purposes Louisiana has no rules and no enforcement; Arizona has the best."

Seventeen states have adopted all of the Government's model motor-carrier strictures, which are the toughest; 14 have adopted a few. Except for California, whose laws are considered rigid, the remaining 18 states have weak laws or none.

The inspection debate

Bureau inspectors checked 46,731 tractor-trailer units in 1969. They found 10,781 vehicles—23.1 per cent—so unsafe that they had to be immediately barred from the highway until repairs were made. Some 8,400 of those vehicles had dangerously faulty brakes. The number of defective vehicles spotted was up 8 per cent over 1968.

"Those figures make us look bad," admits Will Johns, director of the trucking associations' safety operations. "But remember, the Transportation Department inspects only the dogs, the trucks that look and sound bad. You would expect it to detect a higher number of faults that way than it would if it checked all trucks."

Drivers confirm that Federal inspectors tend to be selective. But some contest Mr. Johns' conclusion. Mr. Crum says: "I feel that they [the inspectors] never touch the big companies. They see you're with a big outfit and they wave you by. They get the small carriers and the private individuals. But a lot of times the private individuals' equipment is as good if not better than we drive."

One veteran driver alleges he has had to drive with no brakes after his company told him to take the truck to a garage; it would not send a mechanic to him. He alleges seeing trucks "pass" company safety inspections and take the road with "brake drums completely broken off a wheel, and with broken fifth wheels."

The "fifth wheel" isn't really a wheel, but a heavy metal plate attached to the platform just behind the tractor cab. It holds the trailer coupler and lets it pivot during turns. A weakened fifth wheel could cause the trailer to break loose.

Mr. Perry, who quit trucking late last year to become a preacher, asserts: "I know companies let safety flaws go by. They let tires get down pretty slick. Brakes may be bad; the company figures it will get to fixing them next week. Some companies figure a truck's okay if it will make the next run."

Drivers concede that company higher-ups occasionally do order garage men not to let a truck with a single safety fault reach the road. But in the next breath the executives badger dispatchers to move urgently needed cargoes, the truckers say. "That's where everything falls apart: They feel they've got to keep the trucks rolling," says Mr. Perry.

"I drove for a small carrier once," a veteran driver relates. "Went across the

Pennsylvania Turnpike from Ellwood City, Pa., clear through the Blue Mountain tunnel [roughly 130 miles], wiping snow from the windshield with a wrench because the wiper motor had been broken for some time. Here I was with two gear shifts to handle, plus a steering wheel and a wrench. When I told the guy [the truck owner] I wanted the wipers fixed, he said I was 'ridiculous,' and to 'get going.' "

Big bark, little bite

Both driver and owner thereby broke the law. Federal regulations prohibit drivers from driving, and owners from letting them drive, unsafe trucks. Each safety violation carries a possible $100 to $500 penalty, applicable alike to $12,000-a-year drivers and to carriers like Consolidated Freight, whose 1970 revenues totaled $397,246,000. The BMCS can revoke a driver's license or ask the Interstate Commerce Commission to rescind a carrier's operating certificate in serious cases.

But prosecution is light. "We prosecute more than zero and less than 1,000 cases a year. We keep the laws; we haven't time to keep the statistics," declares Dave Benkin, the Federal Highway Administration's assistant chief counsel for motor-vehicle law. Mr. Pierson, BMCS deputy director, estimates the bureau prosecutes 500 cases a year.

The BMCS can levy fines for records-keeping violations, or it may turn these and other cases over to the Federal courts. "Commonly the courts impose minimum fines," says Mr. Benkin. "We get the impression the courts do not regard motor carrier violations as serious. We have had judges excoriating attorneys for 'making a traffic court of our court.' "

The bureau may use its administrative muscle as it did last year against Associated Transport, Inc., the country's seventh-ranked hauler in terms of revenues grossed.

The BMCS alleged that the company violated safety regulations 5,000 times within three years by operating unsafe, improperly equipped trucks; "having drivers drive more than 10 hours in one day"; "filing false [driver] logs"; and failing "to keep vehicle condition reports." The agency ordered Associated to begin a thorough safety program and dictated how the program must run. It levied no fine.

A survey's allegations

Thomas L. Mainwaring, an Associated executive vice-president, says, "We're co-operating fully and will continue to co-operate fully in carrying out this comprehensive safety program."

But BMCS actions leave some analysts unimpressed. Robert C. Fellmeth of Ralph Nader's Center for the Study of Responsive Law suggests in his book, *The Interstate Commerce Omission,* that the bureau does too little.

Mr. Fellmeth points to an analysis of 1,700 replies to a safety poll of 50,000 long-haul drivers. Eighty per cent of the respondents said they drove at times with inadequate brakes; 73 per cent said exhaust fumes seeped into their trucks' cabs; 70 per cent said their equipment had weak or broken springs; 56 per cent drove tractors with broken fifth wheels; 60 per cent said they drove on treadless tires; and 64 per cent assertedly piloted rigs with faulty lighting systems.

Moreover, 51 per cent of the drivers alleged that it was "fairly common" for drivers to exceed Federal driving-time limits; 61 per cent said "bennies" or "pep pills" were commonly used. Drivers complained of too little time off between duty stretches; of being forced to drive under hazardous conditions; and of being encouraged at times to mark their required log books inaccurately—and thus illegally.

The Government requires drivers to keep logs, to ensure compliance with work limits. No driver may legally drive more than 10 hours in a 15-hour "on-duty" period, which may include driving, waiting for repairs, loading or unloading, and the like. After that he must have eight hours off. He may legally work no more than 70 hours within eight consecutive days.

There's a reason why drivers push themselves illegally to the point of using pep pills. Big companies pay drivers 13 to 14 cents per mile, depending on the size of the truck. These truckers make $12,000 to $20,000 a year. A few make $25,000.

Pressures on drivers

Men working for small companies or driving their own "gypsy" rigs, usually heavily mortgaged, are paid by the load. The more loads they deliver, the more they earn. So they stay on the road, and they hustle.

One small-company driver relates:

"Once I drove five days straight. I was havin' trouble with the truck. Oil leaks. I repaired them as I went. I loaded and unloaded. And drove. My wife caught me and hugged me when I finally climbed from the cab. I don't remember anything from then until I woke up in bed some time later.

"Believe me," this driver urges, "there are companies whose dispatchers say, 'Don't worry about that book [the log]. You're a good man. You can do it. Keep going.' "

Much of what these drivers say is "absolutely untrue," argues Warren Ambler, general safety manager of Ringsby United, a large Colorado freight mover. He particularly denies that his company or others ever knowingly permit defective vehicles on the road.

Lloyd Rizer, vice-president of Navajo Freight Lines, another big Denver hauler, adds: "When you have a $30,000 piece of equipment and valuable cargo besides, you're just not going to question a driver or mechanic and risk breakdowns. You can't afford to turn a truck over or burn it up. You've got to be safety-conscious."

The ATA asserts that most companies, especially those under Federal jurisdiction, are sticklers for safety. They hold safety seminars for drivers and reward truckers driving the most accident-free miles.

Many companies have safety directors who patrol the roads to spot company drivers violating regulations. The directors may place letters of reprimand in offenders' personnel files. They may fine, suspend, or even fire drivers for grievous offenses.

Still, trucking executives say they have relatively little direct control over drivers. They say men sometimes feign fatigue or illness in the name of safety and slow deliveries of tens of tons of cargo. The shipping public "always wants its freight before breakfast," one executive says. "And if one company can't deliver it, its competitor can."

"Safety face" vs. "safety farce"

The company's ability to avoid mishaps and to deliver the goods on time depends too on the uncontrollable: tangled traffic, foul weather, poorly designed highways, and "wild" motorists. In the light of this, the regulated carriers are proud of their accident records.

Pacific Intermountain Express (PIE) of Oakland, Calif., is considered one of trucking's most safety-conscious companies. Its extensive safety program and low accident rate have won PIE the trucking industry's highest safety award 10 times. It won in 1969 with an accident rate of 3.1 accidents per million miles. (The 1970 winner has not been announced.)

Ken Beadle, PIE's vice-president for safety, says: "As of the first quarter of 1971 we're ahead of that winning record. But safety is more than a business thing with all of us. It means dollars, but it also represents civic duty. We care about the motorists."

The ATA, whose members are the 50 states' motor-carrier-safety associations, rates safety high. It supplies books, driver manuals, films and slides, speeches, and other safety campaign materials to its member groups.

Some 42 state members have safety councils made up of trucking-company executives. They sponsor auto rodeos for teen-agers, defensive-driving courses, and exhibits. Some run brief safety seminars at truck stops on major trucking routes.

But during a 9½-hour, shouted conversation above the growls of a tractor pulling 32,000 pounds of potentially dangerous chemicals, a driver yells: "The bosses call safety programs our 'safety face.' They're our 'safety farce.' "

This trucker has driven nearly a decade for top companies. He alleges that in the name of safety executives gig drivers for speeding over some routes but ignore offenders who must race over other routes simply to meet company-imposed schedules. He says safety directors clamp down on incorrect log entries made by drivers plying some routes and blink at persistent infractions by drivers who must work overtime to meet schedules on others.

"You say you're bushed and can't take an assigned trip, and you're forced to take 15 hours off, or maybe 24," the driver continues. "Your name goes to the bottom of the board [the assignment-rotation list]. You needed a few hours rest, but you wind up with a day or two off, a smaller pay check, and a reputation as a crybaby. Your union chapel chairman just may or may not back you up if you stand pat. So you take the load. That's the system. Think it's safe?"

---

13   Rationale:
The Regulation
of Motor Carriers
Martin T. Farris
Arizona State University

The motor carrier industry involves economics, management, and public regulation. Economics stresses the cost of operation and the provision of the "roadway"; management stresses personnel and financial administration and overall control of the firm; regulation stresses the institutional framework within which the industry functions. In the motor carrier industry, regulation applies to entry into the business (certificates of public convenience and necessity), to price (control of rates), to service (route and commodity limitations), and to highways.

The federal government regulates, to some degree, all interstate modes of transportation—and has regulated the motor carrier industry since 1935. In this selection, the author explains why he feels regulations are necessary and how they are implemented and interconnected.

In recent times there has been a great deal of interest shown in regulation—by the press, the state legislature, the carriers themselves, and the general public. Much of this interest has been concerned with the personalities and practices of regulatory authorities. Some of the press interest borders on sensationalism and plays upon emotion. However, emotionalism and personality scrutiny obscures the real issue. The fundamental question involved is the "rationale of regulation." The basic question which must be asked is "Why do we regulate?" This article is aimed at discussing the rationale of regulation and the fundamental question of "Why regulate?"

The background of regulation

Many services and professions are regulated. These include, among others, undertakers, plumbers, power companies, contractors, gas companies, beauty shops, communication systems, doctors, barbers, druggists, and, of course, motor carriers. Others undoubtedly could be added and the above list is in no way com-

From Martin T. Farris, "Rationale: The Regulation of Motor Carriers," *Arizona Roadrunner*, December 1970, pp. 16-17. Used by permission.

plete. But the point is, motor carriers are but one type of firm, one type of service which is regulated. In no way are they alone as a regulated industry.

The firms and individuals regulated have many types of economic characteristics. Some are large absolute monopolies granted exclusive service areas such as power, gas, and communication service companies. Some are highly competitive and small—such as barbers, beauty shop operators, and druggists. Many are neither small nor large but are middle sized firms with varying degrees of competition. The motor carriers often fall in this group.

The type of competition also varies among firms regulated. In some cases it is intramodal or between firms in the same line of commerce. Certainly this is the case in barber shops, drug stores, and beauty parlors. In some cases, it is intermodal or between businesses in varying lines of commerce. This certainly is the case between power and gas companies where both sell energy even though each has its exclusive service area. And in some cases, competition is both intramodal and intermodal. This is certainly the case in motor carriers where they compete with one another while at the same time competing with the railroads.

Irrespective of the structure of the industry involved or type of competition involved, regulation has but a single aim. That aim is to protect the public. The public may need protection from the exploitive tendencies of the legally monopolistic firm. But the public may also require protection because firms are too highly competitive. While competition is generally accepted as desirable public policy, it can also lead to undesirable ends in some instances. Regardless of whether the public regulates against the excesses of either monopoly or competition, the general aim is always the same: To protect the public.

The devices of regulation

Basically there are three devices used to regulate. These are regulations over service, price and entry. Some public regulation involves the use of all three devices, some regulation utilizes less. However, all regulation rests upon these three devices.

1. Service regulation involves the public, acting through a board or commission, imposing some standard of service. This standard is typically in terms of a minimum. With the utilities (as well as the common carriers), this standard of service comes out of our heritage in the common law. Basically, this common law standard can be conceptualized as the duty to (a) serve all comers, (b) serve at a reasonable price, and (c) serve without undue discrimination. Certainly holding one's self out to serve all comers without undue discrimination (a & c) constitutes a service standard.

These obligations of a common carrier, or a "common calling," to use the common law term, are necessary irrespective of the existence of a regulatory body or a commission. These obligations have existed, to quote the U.S. Supreme Court in Munn v. Illinois (1877), "from time immemoriam." Incidentally, to illustrate that regulation is not a new thing and that, under our system of laws inherited from medieval England, society has always regulated the common callings, one needs to but note that the Supreme Court was here quoting a treatise written by Lord Hale in 1670. Or, to put it another way, Lord Hale said in 1670 that the common callings had been regulated as long as anyone could remember.

Minimum standards of service are imposed on a number of professions and services. Many, such as the barber, beauty operator, and plumber, must physically demonstrate their degree of skill in order to be licensed. Others, such as the doctor, dentist, mortician, druggist, must pass an examination and file proof of certain training or educational attainment in order to practice. While these may seem (and are) entry restrictions, they likewise impose a minimum standard of service as well.

The motor carrier must show financial responsibility, live up to standards of frequency of service and move over specified routes with specified commodities. These are likewise minimum (and sometimes maximum) service standards. In a very real sense they are no different from the barber's demonstration of skill or the druggist's attainment on an examination. All are ways in which society prescribes minimums of service.

2. Price regulation likewise involves both the public's representatives via boards and commissions and the common law. Again, one of the obligations under the common law is to serve at a reasonable price. Who determines what is reasonable? In medieval times it was often the king or the sovereign who determined what was a reasonable price. During the Middle Ages and Dark Ages it was the universal church with its concept of "just price." The writings of St. Thomas Aquinas and others of the Scholasticism group of the 13th century give us proof of this. During more recent times, it has been the courts acting under the common law and, during modern times, commissions and boards acting for the sovereign (conceptualized by the legislature and/or the people). In practically all regulation the power to determine "just and reasonable rates" has resided with the duly appointed or elected commissions. It is felt that generally this keeps rates from being abnormally high.

Price regulation means earnings regulation since the common carriers have an obligation to serve. Thus, this type of price regulation is more than merely placing a ceiling upon the ability of a business to take advantage of its common carrier status. This brings up the whole interesting but confusing area of rate control.

Our constitution requires that a person, whether common carrier or not, may not have his property seized without due process of law. Thus it is clear that a level of rates may be too low as well as too high. When they are too low, it is commonly said they are confiscatory, i.e., they confiscate or seize property without due process (condemnation). But who is to determine what constitutes confiscation? Here is the rub. Again the courts have been used (and are used) to establish when rates are confiscatory. Yet the courts are busy and cannot spend all of their time determining rate levels and earnings levels. Hence, this job is delegated to the various commissions, with the courts retaining the right to review and the right to make the ultimate determination in case of dispute.

But the point is even deeper than merely guarding against arbitrary action on the part of commissions in establishing confiscatory rates. Rate level and earnings control is closely connected to service standards. If minimum service standards are required in the public interest, these must be paid for. In common carriers particularly, earnings high enough to provide a minimum service standard are important. Experience has proven that the public is better served by a financially healthy carrier than one who is so involved with the competitive struggle that his service standard depreciates. This was recognized in railroad transportation in the Transportation Act of 1920 and has generally been recognized in other forms of transportation as well. Earnings levels must be adequate enough to allow the carrier to earn enough to be financially stable and to maintain the required service standard that the public expects. Finally, price regulation affects public safety. If the competitive struggle is allowed to ensue and follow its natural course, some firms will go bankrupt. This is the natural process our competitive system uses to adjust the supply to the demand, to weed out the inefficient, to allocate the available resources to the needs of the public. Generally this is a very good and desirable device which serves the public's needs. However, when this process of failure, of bankruptcy, of reallocating resources involves the public safety, the process is not necessarily desirable. In the competitive struggle, the process of bankruptcy means cutting costs, operating with a minimum of "extras," with a "barebones" type of service. When the public is directly involved (such as when they are passengers or shippers) or indirectly involved (as when the carrier's vehicles use the roadways or the skyways), the firm's competitive struggle may endanger others.

The public expects a safe service to be rendered. Passengers must be protected, freight must reach its destination, innocent co-users of the facilities must not be endangered. But a safe service is not always the cheapest service—indeed it rarely is the least costly service. Safety costs money. Hence rate regulation cannot set rates so low as to endanger safety or cause the carrier to endanger others. Commissions in determining rates must not only keep in mind that earnings must be high enough to establish financial responsibility and a minimum service standard but also that earnings must be high enough to allow a safe service to be provided.

3. Entry regulation brings us back to our beginning where we noted that the number of persons or firms in an undertaking is often limited in one way or another. But also entry requirements are an integral part of providing minimum service standards and price regulation. It could be said that by limiting the number of firms, adequate and safe service minimums are more readily possible. By limiting the number of firms, adequate earnings are possible. Indeed, entry requirements or limitations are the *device* used to impose standards of service and the *device* used to guarantee adequacy of earnings and the *device* used to assure public safety . . .

Limiting competition by imposing entry requirements is very much in the philosophy of regulation. When a single seller serves best (such as a utility), this may well be a monopoly. But more often than not, it means th existence of several (though a limited number) of sellers—perhaps a duopoly (two sellers) or oligopoly (few sellers). The point here is that entry should be limited so that the sellers provide a safe, adequate service with adequate earnings and at reasonable prices. The problem, of course, is determining how many firms to allow in the market in order to attain these goals.

Irrespective of this interesting problem of how many firms are needed to meet these goals, the point is that entry must be limited. Typically this limitation in the common carrier industry takes the form of certificates of public convenience and necessity. The applicant must convince the public (acting through its appointed or elected commission) that a necessity exists and that the public convenience will be served. Also typically, the carrier must show that he is "fit, willing and able" to carry on this service. Again the requirements of service, safety, reliability and financial responsibility are embodied in "fit, willing and able." Or to repeat, entry requirements are the device the public uses to secure the standards it demands.

Viewed in this light, the limiting of competition (or "monopoly law" if you insist) has a completely different connotation from that often given to it by popular usage when it is equated to "a license to rob." Limiting competition via certificates is the public's *device* to attain its desired standards and not the granting of privilege to a lucky few to do business protected from the rigors of competition.

The goals of regulation of motor carriers

Basically the goals of public regulation of motor carriers can be summarized in one statement. The public expects, indeed demands, (1) an adequate service of its needs readily available when it is needed; (2) rendered by financially adequate firms who are trustworthy and financially responsible; (3) in a reliable manner which cannot only be counted upon to deliver the goods but to do so with regard to public safety; and (4) all at a reasonable and just price. These four goals are all interdependent and rest upon the three devices noted above (regulation of service, price, and entry).

Conclusion

That one can argue that these goals are not efficiently accomplished is beyond doubt. All the devices may not be fairly or justly administered in motor carrier operations. Regulatory practice and personalities may not be as we might like them to be. But this is not the fault of regulation and does not detract from the goals of regulation.

All the recent public interest in regulation is good. The more attention and concern the better. But too much of this interest has centered upon the personalities and practices of the regulatory commissions. Carriers have a vested interest in effective regulation and should welcome discussion. But carriers also have a responsibility to call attention to the goals of regulation, to explain the rationale of regulation and to answer the question "Why do we regulate?" After all of the emotionalism has cleared, after personality problems have passed, after discussion of the practices of regulation has ceased, we are still faced with the fundamental bed-rock issue of the rationale of regulation. We regulate to attempt to meet society's goals and the ultimate rationale of why we regulate is to protect the public.

---

14   Regulatory Requirements
        for Motor Transport
        Dudley F. Pegrum
        University of California, Los Angeles

From the point of view of economic theory, a convincing argument could be made for the elimination of economic regulation of motor freight companies. The argument would run as follows. The trucking industry approaches, in many ways, the economists' ideal of pure competition or, at least, of workable competition. Entering or leaving the industry is, in terms of dollars and cents, relatively easy; and the number of operators is relatively large. Price and service competition among firms ought to lead to self-regulation of the market. That is, since an alternative is always available to the customer, trucking firms are not in a position to use their economic power in ways inimical to the public interest and thus it is not necessary for the government to regulate them.

The following selection, in contrast with the previous one, argues strongly against government regulation of motor carriers and suggests a limited form of economic regulation only.

The need for the regulation of motor transport rests on one of the two following conditions, or perhaps on both: (1) the necessity of regulation in order to assure consumer protection and (2) the necessity of regulation in order to prevent motor transport from subjecting the other agencies to destructive competition. The first of these two questions may be examined on the assumption that no other media of transport are in existence.

Is regulation necessary to protect consumers?

The need for regulation to protect consumers against exploitation arises from deficiencies of competition. If an industry is competitive by virtue of its economic structure, the role of public policy is that of maintaining the environmen-

From Dudley F. Pegrum, "Regulatory Requirements for Motor Transport," *Public Regulation of Business*, Rev. ed., Homewood, Ill.: Richard D. Irwin, Inc., 1965, pp. 619-623. Used by permission.

tal conditions of competition against predatory attempts to destroy them and against pressure groups seeking special privilege designed to accord these groups advantages which they cannot acquire under the rigors of competition. Consumer protection, where competition obtains, does not require limitation of supply, the fixing of prices, or the control of profits. It rests on a different set of assumptions, which does not relate to the public control of prices or limitation of output. The consumer is interested in the lowest economic cost; this is what the competitive standard means and what competition will give him. The precise details of the regulation which is necessary under competition will vary from industry to industry. It may involve standards of quality, standards of service, financial responsibility, price discrimination, and so forth; but it does not require the fixing of relative prices or the control of profits. If the latter are included in a program of control, the advantages of competition are lost.

For an industry to be competitive, it is necessary that resources be both legally and economically mobile. To be legally mobile, it must be possible for them, as far as the law is concerned, to be free to move from one use to another and from one market to another. There must be freedom to move the physical facilities according to the wishes of the producers, or to convert them or divert them to other uses. Similarly, the decision for investment or disinvestment must be left to the enterprisers. In other words, what is called freedom of entry, which also carries with it freedom of exit, is one of the fundamental requirements of a truly competitive structure. If this is denied by law, special privilege is accorded to an entrant into an industry or to an existing producer, which protects him to the extent that freedom of entry is limited against the pressures of competition. He is no longer faced with the threat of an alternative supplier of similar services who may wish to risk his resources in the belief that his venture may be successful.

In industries that possess a high degree of legal and economic mobility, little difficulty of relative over- or undersupply of facilities will occur, because inducements to ready response to changing conditions are always present. If, at any time, more services are available than can be disposed of at the prices which will take them off the market, losses will be suffered until contraction takes place. By the same token, however, undersupply will lead to higher prices until the needed additional facilities are made available. It is the function of competitive forces to maintain the balance. If they are prevented from doing so by private action, the evils of monopoly appear. If they are prevented from doing so by public policy, then the government is deliberately creating a monopoly situation. In such a case, either the monopolist will enjoy the advantages of the privileges thus bestowed, or governmental action designed to provide a substitute for the competition it has eliminated will have to be invoked. If competitive forces are restrained in their action by such a policy and the structure and conditions of the industry are primarily competitive, then the government is trying to play at competition with the necessary ingredients missing. The results are bound to be unsatisfactory, especially to the consumer.

As was pointed out earlier, the economic structure of motor transport is that of a highly competitive industry. It possesses a ready adaptability of plant and facilities to changing market conditions, a high degree of geographic flexibility of plant and facilities, easily accessible alternative sources of supply of services to consumers, and an absence of economic characteristics that make competition a destructive force leading to the elimination of competitors and the emergence of monopoly. Competition can thrive if given the opportunity to do so by public policy which gives full weight to the economic characteristics of the industry. The consumer of motor transport services has alternatives that are not available in other forms of transportation and that are more closely related in type to ordinary commodities than to railroad or public utility services. The consumer, in the absence of public restrictions, can make his choice among a number of competitors. He may contract for services, hire equipment, or supply his own. These alternatives afford him protection against exploitation such as he enjoys in the area of competitive business. As far as the economics of motor transport is concerned, there seems to be no more foundation for the type of regulation that has been applied to railroads than there is for its application to business in general. Consumer protection and public policy do not require rate regulation so as to insure reasonable rates or stability of rates, nor do they require regulation of security issues in order to safeguard the financial stability of carriers. Restrictions on freedom of entry and rigid prescriptions of routes are likewise unnecessary. The only purpose they can serve is to protect existing carriers against competition and to aid them in maintaining possession of the field they have been afforded by public sanction.

It is an assumption of public policy today that a common carrier is entitled to some degree of protection against competition because of the obligations it assumes and is required to maintain, and that this protection should even limit the amount of competition which other common carriers should be permitted to offer. Because motor transport embraces a large number of suppliers who do not fall into the category of common carriers, it is necessary to draw a distinction between the latter and the former, so that those who are not common carriers are prevented from offering common carrier service. This, however, is not a sufficient reason for limiting the number of common carriers who wish to compete with each other. If a carrier wishes to offer common carrier service, presumably it thinks the business is worth-while and wants to compete for it. There is no apparent reason why this should be denied when the structure of the industry is competitive; certainly, consumer protection is not furthered by a policy which imposes limitations on such competition. Nor is it necessary to restrict the competition of contract carriers if the objective of the policy is public interest or consumer protection. By the same token, present moves to reduce the role of exempt carriers seem to serve no useful public purpose. There is little evidence of protest from those who use these services. In fact, the avowed purpose of limiting the exemptions is to protect the regulated carriers. The economic justification for this warrants more careful study than it has received to date.

Is regulation necessary to protect interagency competition?

The second major question—namely, whether there is the necessity of regulating motor transport in order to prevent motors from subjecting other agencies to destructive competition—can be dealt with very briefly. If there is no threat of destructive or ruinous competition, then public policy in the interest of further-ing an economical transport system should not impose limitations on motor carrier opportunities to participate in interagency competition. The need for protection of the other agencies against motor competition rests on the assump-tion that motor transport, by virtue of its economic structure, possesses some kind of advantage that makes it possible for it to resort to tactics designed to and able to kill off its rivals. If motor competition is not destructive within itself, however, it cannot be destructive to the other agencies. The relation of motor carrier costs to output precludes this, and so does competition among the motor carriers themselves. It is possible that motor carrier competition with railroads may be unfair because of the inadequacy of the charges imposed upon motor carriers for the use of the streets and the highways, but this is another matter. It is a problem of administration, not regulation, and it cannot be resolved by the latter. Motor carrier transport, therefore, does not need to be regulated because of its impact on interagency competition.

Limited need for regulation

In view of the nature of motor transport, it seems to be clear that the role of positive regulation is very limited. In fact, the requirements, in some respects, are less than those which the Federal Trade Commission faces in its administra-tion of antitrust, because there is little threat of monopoly or monopoly prob-lems in motor transportation. Nevertheless, regulation by an agency established to deal with transport seems to be in order because of the distinctive functions and obligations assumed by the suppliers of transport services. However, this regulation should be administered in the setting of a thoroughly competitive industry. This does not characterize public policy or its administration today.

The administrative aspects of motor carrier control are much more important than the regulatory. Highway investment, construction, finance, and the way that the costs arising from these should be met as a whole and assessed upon various users, are administrative, not regulatory, matters. Conditions imposed upon the privilege of using the highways, weights and loads for vehicles, safety measures, and so forth are also administrative details. The regulatory commission is not competent, by the nature of its organization or as the result of the major responsibilities which it must discharge, to handle these questions. The formula-tion and administration of national transport policy today needs to take full cog-nizance of this fact.

15   The Case for Unregulated Truck Transportation

Richard N. Farmer
Indiana University

One of the long-term and interesting problems of transportation policy is the exempt motor carrier. The regulated common and contract motor carriers are required by law to provide service, within their capabilities, to all comers. They are regulated as to charges, routes, and commodities hauled. The exempt carrier is regulated only as to safety.

Some groups, particularly farming groups, are most interested in continuing and extending motor carrier exemptions. This selection states strongly their case and outlines the policy considerations it raises.

Interstate agricultural trucking has never been controlled in the typical public utility style of other forms of American common carrier transportation. While common and contract carriers in interstate commerce are subject to the key economic controls on rates and entry associated with federal regulation, agricultural truckers were made specifically exempt from such controls under the Motor Carrier Act of 1935, which first placed motor carriers under federal regulation. [1] Exempt carriers are also not required to report their operating statistics, and relatively little is known about the economic characteristics of agricultural trucking. One result has been that most attention in transportation has been paid to firms whose operating characteristics are known, and whose actions are subject to regulatory procedures and policy. However, the agriculture truckers are critically important to agriculture, as well as being interesting as a rare example of unregulated for-hire transportation in the United States.

The absence of traditional transportation regulation in agricultural trucking means that the firms in this sector are generally subject to standard business law, rather than special transportation law. Carriers are free to enter the business if they choose, or to withdraw if profits are not up to expectations. Firms are not bound to routes granted by regulatory commissions, and if demand is inadequate in one area, they are free to shift to more promising territories. The prices charged shippers for their services can rise or fall freely as buyers and sellers bargain for advantage. Redress for injured customers follows traditional legal procedures, rather than the complaint system developed for regulated transportation companies.

If the controlled segment of motor trucking shows significantly better or worse economic results than the unregulated sector, policy implications would

From Richard N. Farmer, "The Case for Unregulated Truck Transportation," *Journal of Farm Economics*, May 1964, pp. 398-409. Used by permission.

immediately follow. The question of proper American transportation policy is now under intensive debate and review,[2] and evidence drawn from a presently unregulated sector could suggest the course of future control practice. Hence, the purpose of this paper is to examine some of the differences in performance between exempt and regulated carriers, and to assess the implications for public transportation policy.

Background of the regulatory problem

Regulatory policy in United States transportation historically regarded this industry as a monopoly oriented public utility subject to close government control. This philosophy, which began in 1887 with the passage of the first Act to Regulate Interstate Commerce, carried forward in the railroad era until 1920, when railroads were made subject to minimum rate control and exit and entry control. Farmers led the fight for effective railroad control, charging that railroads were rapacious monopolies whose prime interest was in exploiting all shippers unmercifully.[3] There was ample evidence in the period 1860 to 1900 to demonstrate that this view was substantially correct.

The controlling theory was that transportation was a public utility, with an obligation of service to the general public at reasonable prices. Hence services could not be started or discontinued without commission approval, nor could rates be raised or lowered without similar sanction. During the period 1887-1920, a running regulatory battle was fought between the railroads, shippers, the Interstate Commerce Commission, and the Congress, with the eventual result being a complete railroad defeat. The Transportation Act of 1920 marked the complete public acceptance of the theory that transportation companies, mainly railroads, formed a market structure which required close public control to function in the public interest.

Just as the railroad regulatory battle was resolved, motor trucking began to assume considerable economic importance. The technology was in its infancy in 1920, but it grew rapidly through the 1920's, until it offered substantial competition to the railroads by the early 1930's. As early as 1917, some states had begun to regulate intrastate trucking,[4] seeing in this new competition a potential threat to the services offered by railroads, and pressure for federal regulation continued through the early 1930's. One problem was that motor trucking was an atomistic, rather than a monopolistic industry. Any person could buy a secondhand truck and begin to compete with the largest railroads. All freight transportation firms sell the same product, ton miles, and while this output can be differentiated somewhat in quality terms, such as in quality of service rendered, prompt payment of damage claims, and similar factors, it is quite difficult to maintain product differentials over long periods of time. With easy entry and relatively homogeneous outputs created by firms representing a fraction of 1 per cent of the output of most submarkets, the trucking industry rapidly became an example of intensive competition between relatively small firms.

Atomistic industries in the depressed 1930's suffered from excessive entry and cutthroat price competition, and motor trucking was no exception. The destructive competition of that underemployed era resulted in losses for trucking firms, below cost rates, and substantial diversions of traffic from railroads. Hence in 1935, the first federal Motor Carrier Act was passed to regulate motor trucking.

The act was basically designed to bring order from chaos in motor trucking by attempting to restrict competition to some extent. An atomistic industry was to be restored to economic health. The technique of control was analogous to those used in other transportation sectors—maximum and minimum rate controls, entry and exit controls on firms, and safety and financial controls designed to provide a firm economic base for future policy.

However, some groups were disposed toward competition and avoiding regulation designed to protect carriers, and they succeeded in having exemptions from control placed in the act. The most notable of these were exemptions on agricultural products. Since the act was clearly designed to get trucking rates up, not down, and since the intent was to protect carriers, not shippers, farmers were opposed to it. This led to agricultural exemptions in the 1935 act which continue to this day with only relatively minor modifications.

The result has been that there are two different types of for-hire interstate motor trucking operations in the United States today. One group, consisting of regulated common and contract motor carriers, operates in a manner analogous to other controlled groups in railroading, airline operations, and domestic water transportation. With relatively few exceptions, this group must obtain commission approval for route changes or extensions, rate changes to shippers, and some types of financial operations. They are subject to the general common carrier requirement that as public utilities they must serve the public generally, within limits prescribed by the relevant commission.[5]

Rate making in this group of controlled motor firms also follows the system used by other types of common carriers. Rate associations, comprised of representatives of the carriers, meet to set prices appropriate to all, and prices determined are published by rate bureaus and sent to the Interstate Commerce Commission for approval. Public protection lies in the ability of the Interstate Commerce Commission, any shipper, or any competitor to protest charges considered exorbitant.[6]

The exempt carriers have a completely different type of economic organization. In this sector, no federal economic controls exist to force the carriers into a public utility mold. Rates are set by the play of market forces, and any competitor is free to compete in the market. Freight brokers serve an important function of general rate quotation and of bringing together buyers and sellers. The market resembles more a securities or commodity exchange than the familiar regulated transportation market.

The two trucking markets are linked by their technology, since both sectors use the same general types of equipment and produce similar outputs, ton miles. They also are linked economically, in that it is legal for a regulated firm to utilize equipment in agricultural hauling, and also in that agricultural truckers can trip lease their equipment to regulated carriers for single hauls. A further potential supply source in the agricultural trucking market is the use of trucks engaged in private hauling. Such equipment is normally used to carry only the goods of the truck owner, but it can be used in agricultural work if it becomes profitable to do so. Hence, there is considerable supply flexibility in the market, although both groups of for-hire carriers tend to remain mainly in their major segments. The agricultural carriers cannot legally enter the regulated market as firms without first obtaining a certificate of convenience and necessity from the Interstate Commerce Commission—which is typically a lengthy, time consuming, expensive, and often impractical process.[7]

The atomistic status of both types of carriers is shown by estimates that 17,586 common and contract carriers, with 721,508 vehicles were in interstate operation in 1960. This group represents the controlled carriers in interstate commerce only, as an additional 30,700 operators with 170,000 vehicles operated in the exempt sector.[8]

Costs and revenues

The Department of Agriculture has collected data on 25 exempt carriers in the Washington, D.C., region, which forms a preliminary basis for comparison with various types of for-hire carriers operating in the same area, for which Interstate Commerce Commission data are available. Table 1 shows roughly comparable operating costs and revenues for various types of carriers in this region. Exempt agricultural carriers have operating costs and revenues which are substantially below those of any type of regulated carrier, and the average load per trip is also higher. No group of carriers was able to make large profits per unit of output, the maximum being the two mills per ton mile recorded for the agricultural carriers. Not only were revenues substantially higher for the regulated carriers, but costs also were much higher.

The comparative data shown in Table 1 must necessarily be used with caution, since the statistical compilation differs considerably. The Department of Agriculture's data on agricultural carriers are a sample from the tri-state region surrounding Washington, while the Interstate Commerce Commission data cover a much larger area. Except for the fact that the various firms use about the same type of line haul equipment, their operations may differ sharply. Interstate Commerce Commission data also include only direct expenses assignable to vehicles, while the Department of Agriculture data include all costs. Such data should be regarded as suggestive, rather than definitive, given problems of comparability.

An examination of this fragmentary data suggests that the farmers were right in 1935. The effect of regulations is to raise, not lower, average rates in the trucking industry. If true, this is a serious indictment of regulation. Conceived as a shipper protest against exploitative railroads, and carried over into other transportation technologies, the effect of regulation is to protect competitors, not shippers.

When suggestions are made to narrow the list of exempt commodities, agricultural shippers typically protest and request that the exemption be maintained or extended. When frozen poultry and other semiprocessed agricultural commodities were being considered for nonexemption in 1958, many shippers pointed out that prices of regulated carriage were too high, while trucking services were poorer than those offered in the exempt sector.[9] Frozen poultry was in a curious regulatory position, in that until 1953, it was a regulated commodity. In that year a Supreme Court decision held that it was exempt, and from 1953 to 1958 the nonregulated carriers handled the product without interference from the Interstate Commerce Commission. In 1956-57, prices for motor carriage of frozen poultry were a third less than in 1953, although transport prices in general had risen substantially in the same period.[10] Shippers were understandably not in favor of being returned to regulation, foreseeing sharp price increases for transportation if this were done.

The lower costs and revenues of carriers of exempt traffic have not led to substantial instability of firms. It has been alleged by the regulated carriers that the exempt group consists of fly-by-night operators who drift in and out of business constantly, operating at below cost levels because of cutthroat competition in the exempt sector. However, an extensive sample of exempt carriers studied suggests that the firms are in fact quite stable and long-lived. Three-quarters of the firms surveyed had been in business over 5 years, 60 per cent over 10 years, 40 per cent for 15 years, and 8 per cent had actually been in business for 30 years—which goes back to the dawn of the highway era in most sections of the United States.[11] These figures compare favorably with survival rates in many more concentrated economic areas, and they do not suggest that competition in this sector has the effect of forcing prices below cost for long periods.

Agricultural hauling rates do vary depending on supply and demand conditions in agricultural areas. Typical variations range from 10 to 20 per cent from highs to lows, with most variations probably occurring at the beginning and end of a harvest season.[12] More extreme variations are unusual, because truckers will normally refuse to haul at rates below their direct operating costs, while sharp increases in rates will attract vehicles from both the regulated and the private trucking sectors. Since entry in the exempt area is completely free, such carriers are able to increase supply and force prices down in periods of peak demand. The flexibility of motor trucks is an asset here as well, since submarkets cannot get out of line with general demand for carriage. Such deviations would quickly cause a shift of vehicles out of the lower priced market into the higher priced.

Explanations for cost and rate differentials

Available evidence indicates that regulated carriers have higher prices and costs than exempt carriers. Services provided by regulated carriers may be more comprehensive, explaining in part the higher costs, but careful examination of the level of motor carrier costs is relevant.

While shippers required to use regulated trucking can expect to pay higher charges than users of exempt vehicles, the regulated carriers definitely cannot charge significantly higher than cost prices. Exorbitant prices could cause shipper protest to the Interstate Commerce Commission, and rates could be reduced. More importantly, the option of private carriage is legally open to every shipper, and if rates are greater than twice the one-way cost of truck operation for a given haul, shippers will undoubtedly use their own private trucks.

However, "cost" in motor trucking is a slippery concept, since one would expect some range of both fixed and operating costs in an industry composed of thousands of firms. Efforts to calculate costs for given types of operations by government agencies must necessarily be averages, and if the dispersion around the average is large, there will be ample opportunity for clever operators to make large profits at prices approximating the average cost level for the industry.[13] A rate approved on this average basis by the Interstate Commerce Commission has the advantage (for controlled firms) that it cannot be undercut by brash competitors. In a similar situation in exempt trucking, rates would tend to fall if the more efficient firms chose to expand their operations, or if rate pressure forced less efficient operators to improve their performance. Unfortunately, there are no data, except for the suggestive statistics noted in Table 1, to prove or disprove this contention.

The nature of operations under regulation suggests reasons why regulated carriers have higher costs. One is the inflexibility of operations under Interstate Commerce Commission control. Trucking companies are restricted to given routes and stated commodities. Hence a firm authorized to carry canned goods may not be able to ship canned beer. The result can be higher operating costs, particularly if such commodity restrictions result in empty backhauling because the firm cannot legally carry an available commodity.

One example of such narrow interpretation of commodities and routes authorized is now before the Supreme Court. The Willis Shaw Frozen Express, Inc.,

TABLE 1

Costs and Revenues of Motor Trucking Firms

	(25)[a] Exempt Agricultural	(117)[a] Common Carriers General Freight	(14)[a] Contract Carriers	(40)[a] Common Carriers Special Freight
Revenue per intercity ton mile	$.0344	$.08126	$ .0942	$ .05784
Costs per intercity ton mile	.0324	.08094	.1018	.05956
Net revenue per ton mile	$.002	$.00032	$(.0076)	$(.00172)
Average tons per load	14.8	10.47	5.66	8.43

[a]Numbers refer to total carriers in each sample.
Sources: USDA, "Costs of Operating Exempt For-Hire Motor Carriers of Agricultural Commodities, A Pilot Study in Delaware, Maryland, and Virginia," Washington, D.C., USDA, 1963, p. 16; and ICC, *Transport Statistics in the United States for the Year Ended December 31, 1960, Part 7: Motor Carriers*, Washington, D.C., ICC, 1961, pp. 84-85. Cost data is for regulated carriers in the Middle Atlantic region.

had carried frozen fruits, berries, and vegetables in exempt status until 1958, when these commodities were made subject to regulated trucking. The 1958 act provided that grandfather rights be given to all firms previously exempt who had carried these commodities earlier, and Shaw was granted a certificate of convenience and necessity in 1961 covering such transportation. However, the Interstate Commerce Commission held that Shaw could only handle these commodities in exactly the same proportions and routes on which the firm operated before 1958. Hence the construction of a new frozen food plant a few miles off a 1958 route could not be serviced by this firm, even though the company had the necessary specialized equipment, was willing to serve the firm, and might be the only trucker able to give satisfactory service. Similarly, if frozen vegetables were offered on a route where only frozen fruits had been shipped before 1958, the firm could not handle the commodity legally. Shaw has contended that such restrictions in fact have resulted in an "injurious diminution of business," although it has already lost its case in the lower courts.[14] This type of narrow operating authority leads to higher operating costs and transportation rates than in exempt transportation, where firms can send trucks to any point where demand justifies the activity.

Regulated firms are often obligated by the terms of their operating authority to accept business, even though costs may be high. A major type of high cost business in trucking consists of less than truckload lot shipments, where the carriers must maintain expensive collection systems and terminals in cities on their routes. This type of business is extensive for most common carriers, as shown in Table 2. Table 3 shows that the exempt carriers have small terminal costs compared to regulated class 1 carriers. Much of the variation in classes of expenses is in this area. Since an exempt carrier is not obligated to handle any traffic or shipment which might prove unprofitable, such a carrier can avoid costs associated with unprofitable business, while a regulated carrier may not be able to do so. Since shipments of 149 pounds or less have a terminal cost of $54.32 per ton, while shipments of 20,000 pounds have a terminal cost of $1.70 per ton,[15] the ability to avoid small shipments can reduce costs substantially. The bulk of the cost increase for smaller shipments is for pickup and delivery, which is normally done in lightweight city trucks with high ton mile operating costs.

What may be happening here is that the larger, truckload lot shippers by

TABLE 2

Truckload and Less than Truckload Shipments in Regulated Truckings:
Middle Atlantic Region (class 1 carriers)

	Tons of Intercity Freight	Number of Shipments
Truckload	8,671,435	728,170
Less than truckload	7,637,474	26,808,710

Source: ICC, *Transport Statistics in the United States for the Year Ended December 31, 1960, Part 7: Motor Carriers,* Washington, D.C., ICC, 1961, pp. 40-41.

regulated firms are subsidizing small lot shippers in some cases. Costs by truck-load lot are computed at much lower figures than less than truckload lots, and rate differentials for various classes of traffic may not reflect cost spreads.[16] There should not be significant cost differentials between truckload lots of machinery loaded at a factory dock and delivered directly in the same truck to the consignee's loading platform and a similar shipment of exempt agricultural products handled in precisely the same manner—yet rate differentials persist.

Another reason for lower costs in exempt carriage may be that in some cases there are diseconomies of scale in motor trucking. Studies on economies of scale in this industry suggest that at least no economies of scale exist, in the sense that large carriers have no clear-cut cost advantages over smaller carriers. A small firm has about the same costs as a large one.[17] It has also been suggested that the economies of scale in the industry stem more from effective utilization of routes, in terms of tons per route mile per year, than in the absolute size of the firm.[18] Hence a one-truck operator able to use his route pattern efficiently, in the sense of getting maximum vehicle utilization per year, can be as efficient as a 100-truck operator doing the same thing. But a firm of any size which is unable to get efficient routes will likely have high costs.

Exempt carriers surveyed by the Department of Agriculture average only 1.2 straight trucks and 2.2 tractors per firm in the United States,[19] yet their oper-ating costs remain consistently low. Regulated carriers, on the other hand, have tended to merge for years under Interstate Commerce Commission control, re-flecting the attitude that both regulatory efficiency and economies of scale can be realized in this manner. However, the nature of route and commodity restric-tions in regulated trucking may cause firms to serve areas whose traffic potential is now uneconomic. There is no reason to expect that any regulatory body,

TABLE 3

Comparisons of Costs in Various Categories:
Exempt and Common Carriers

Item	Exempt Carriers	Common Carriers
	(Percent)	
Maintenance	18.6	12.8
Transportation	75.0	50.4
Terminal	2.4	20.3
Traffic	2.0	4.2
Insurance and safety	2.0	4.9
Adm. and general		7.4
	100.0	100.0

Sources: USDA, "Costs of Operating Exempt For-Hire Motor Carriers of Agricultural Com-modities, A Pilot Study in Delaware, Maryland, and Virginia," Washington, D.C., USDA, 1963, p. 16, and ICC, *Transport Statistics in the United States for the Year Ended Decem-ber 31, 1960, Part 7: Motor Carriers,* Washington, D.C., ICC, 1961, pp. 28-29. ICC data is for the Middle Atlantic region.

however able and efficient, can follow closely the myriad of shifts of transportation demand which may occur constantly in a growing economy. Evidence such as the Shaw case cited above suggests that the granting of restrictive route and commodity rights may lead to substantial increases in costs—for which the shippers must eventually pay.

Exempt carriers can also reduce costs by trip leasing their vehicles to common carriers for return hauls, or for longer periods over 30 days. Since it costs almost as much to return empty as to carry a load, this type of haulage has the advantage of covering some of the operating costs of a complete trip, while increasing revenues. The exempt firm does not need a certificate to participate in such business, as the regulated carrier can use its operating authority for this purpose.

The burden of proof for better performance rests on the regulated carriers and the regulators in the trucking case. Evidence available about exempt carriage suggests that these carriers are more efficient, in that both costs and revenues are significantly below those in the regulated sector. When the regulated truckers or the commissions suggest that additional traffic be brought into the regulated sector, shippers are prompt to protest, arguing that the exempt carriers are more flexible, cheaper, and offer substantially better alternatives than the regulated firms. To regulate for the sake of regulation, or to tidy up what seems to be a confusing, chaotic free market seems unsound, but persistent pressure is exerted both by the regulated and the regulators to extend the control net. Unless some substantial benefits can be demonstrated for a control system, it is difficult to see why such regulation should be extended.

Conclusion

Transportation regulation in the United States has followed the pattern of forcing all of the new transportation technologies into the railroad regulatory pattern, without much thought as to whether or not the economics of other types of carriers would lead to efficient operations. The modern result is curious. When regulation is proposed, the shippers object, claiming advantages from lack of regulation; most carriers not regulated seem to prefer to remain that way; and the result of new regulation is to increase transportation costs. Those favoring new and extended regulation are the regulatory commissions and the presently regulated truckers who see economic difficulties in new competition if regulation is relaxed. Carriers such as railroads, who see in less regulation a potential competitive advantage, also generally favor less control. Apparently the notion of transportation public utility regulation has been perverted from a situation where the public was protected to a situation where the carriers are protected and the regulatory bureaucracy tries to expand its control perpetually. It is hard to see what advantages regulation may have when such economic results are forthcoming.

Railroad fervor for deregulation also stems from possible gains to be achieved by lowering their rates—given the intense competition in transportation today, few firms see significant rate increases as a certain method of gaining additional revenues. Only in situations where marginal costs presently exceed marginal revenues are rate increases proposed, and then more to drive away unwanted traffic than to gain revenue.

Agricultural attitudes towards transportation have come full circle. From fighting bitterly in the 1870's and 1880's against rapacious railroad monopolies, farmers now fight bitterly against rapacious regulatory commissions, originally established by farmer pressure to hold the common carriers at bay. The perversion of the regulatory motive is perhaps now complete, brought about by rapidly changing technology and shifting market structure.

Much is made of the argument that a common carrier does have an obligation of service to all customers, and that deregulation would imply that at least some shippers would not be served properly. With easy entry in trucking a persistent possibility, it would seem to be safe to predict that any lack of service would quickly be rectified by new entry, if the unserved customer was willing to pay any price above cost for service. There is a suggestion here of internal subsidy if in fact a group of shippers can only obtain service through carrier regulation. While such internal subsidies may be justified by noneconomic arguments, it is difficult to see why some shippers must overpay for service to benefit others.

Rapid development of motor trucking as an economic force in transportation has overturned many traditional attitudes toward transportation. The industry, characterized by small firms, easy entry, and potentially competitive markets, does not resemble the older model of railroad economics, with its large firms, difficult or impossible entry, and highly concentrated market structures. But the regulatory commissions are now well institutionalized and respected, and the procedures laboriously developed in a different economic context are maintained even though there may be little reason for their present existence. There seems to be ample evidence that the result is higher than necessary transportation prices for many consumers.

NOTES

1. Provisions of the Motor Carrier Act of 1935 are fully covered in D. Phillip Locklin, *Economics of Transportation*, 5th Edition, Homewood, Ill., Richard D. Irwin, Inc., 1960, pp. 667-673.
2. See, for example, President Kennedy's 1962 Transportation Message to Congress (reproduced in its entirety in D. F. Pegrum, *Transportation: Economics and Public Policy*, Homewood, Ill., Richard D. Irwin, Inc., 1963, pp. 585-600), as one example of recent proposals.
3. Emory Troxel, *Economics of Transport*, New York, Rinehart & Company, Inc., 1955, pp. 358-362.
4. California began to regulate common carrier trucking in 1917. This state also regulates agricultural trucking, as do a few other states. See Public Utilities Commission, *Annual Report: 1961-62 Fiscal Year*, Sacramento, PUC, 1962, p. 17.

5. These general requirements vary somewhat between transportation modes. Transporta-tion regulation in the United States has substantial inconsistencies, reflecting both the fact that various regulatory laws were passed at different times by different congresses, and that under the American Constitution, intrastate traffic is the prerogative of the states. See M. L. Fair and E. W. Williams, *Economics of Transportation*, New York, Harper, 1959, Chapters 22, 23, 24, and 26 for a detailed discussion of existing transpor-tation law.

6. C. A. Taff, *Commercial Motor Transportation*, 3rd Edition, Homewood, Ill., Richard D. Irwin, Inc., 1961, pp. 458-468.

7. J. R. Meyer, M. J. Peck, J. Stevanson, and C. Zwick, *The Economics of Competition in the Transportation Industries*, Cambridge, Harvard University Press, 1960, p. 213.

8. Taff, *op. cit.*, p. 513. The interstate trucking markets are also linked to various intrastate markets in many cases, adding further potential supply.

9. *Hearings before the Subcommittee of the Committee on Interstate and Foreign Com-merce, U.S. Senate, Eighty-Fifth Congress, Second Session, on Problems of the Rail-roads, Part 4*, Washington, D.C., U.S. Govt. Printing Office, 1958, pp. 2094-2101; pp. 2121-2338. These hearings contain many nonquantitative references by shippers to the much lower motor trucking rate in exempt sectors, as compared to regulated com-panies.

10. *Ibid.*, pp. 2109-2114.

11. Mildred R. DeWolfe, *For-Hire Motor Carriers Hauling Exempt Agriculural Commodi-ties: Nature and Extent of Operations*, Washington, D.C., USDA, Marketing Economics Division, ERS, Marketing Research Report No. 585, p. 5.

12. J. H. Hunter, Jr., *The Role of Truck Brokers in the Movement of Exempt Agricultural Commodities*, Washington, D.C., USDA, Marketing Economics Division, ERS, Market-ing Research Report No. 525, pp. 20-27.

13. Thus costs computed by the Interstate Commerce Commission for rate making pur-poses in the Middle Atlantic region were taken from data provided by 134 carriers, each grossing over $500,000 per year. See ICC, *Cost of Transporting Freight by Class I and Class II Motor Carrier Common Carriers of General Commodities: Middle Atlantic Region, 1960*, Washington, D.C., U.S. Govt. Printing Office, 1962, p. 1. Some statistical adjustments are made for obvious large deviations from standard operating situations, but costs found by this method must clearly remain general average rather than reflec-tions of specific cases.

14. "Supreme Court to Review ICC's Licensing Frozen Food Truckers," *The Wall Street Journal*, October 22, 1963, p. 8.

15. Meyer, *op. cit.*, p. 89.

16. *Ibid.*, pp. 89-94.

17. The more important studies of scale economies in motor trucking are: W. Adams and J. B. Hendy, *Trucking Mergers, Consolidations and Small Business: An Analysis of Interstate Commerce Commission Policy*, Washington, D.C., U.S. Govt. Printing Office, 1957; Robert A. Nelson, *New England Governor's Committee on Public Transporta-tion: Motor Freight Transportation for New England; A Report to the New England Governor's Conference*, Boston, Report No. 5, October 1956; M. J. Roberts, "Some Aspects of Motor Carrier Costs: Firm Size, Efficiency, and Economic Health," *Land Economics*, Vol. 32, August 1956, pp. 228-238; Edward W. Smykay, "An Appraisal of the Economics of Scale in the Motor Carrier Industry," *Land Economics*, Vol. 34, May 1958, pp. 143-148; Robert A. Nelson, "The Economies of Scale in the Motor Carrier Industry: A Reply," *Land Economics*, Vol. 35, May 1958, pp. 180-185. The general consensus (Smykay partially excepted) is that visible economies of scale in this industry are either very small or nonexistent.

18. Meyer, *op. cit.*, pp. 88-89.

19. DeWolfe, *op. cit.*, pp. 5-9.

16   Getting the
Gray Out
Gary Klein

One of the major problems of motor transportation is illegal carriage. The variety of types of operations (noted earlier), plus the fact that some carriers are exempt from all but safety regulation, encourage what is known as the "gray area" of motor transport—in which carriers operate outside the regulatory laws.

The majority of the exempt and private carriers operate, of course, within the laws. However, because the highway is furnished by the public and the costs of entry are low, almost anyone can operate a truck. To survive, many of these marginal operators conveniently avoid federal and state regulations. The key to the problem lies with the shipper. This selection is directed toward him and makes a plea to him to use only legal operators.

Gray area transportation, simply stated, is an outlaw. It is an illegal operation used openly by a number of shippers trying to cut costs and corners, and by some carriers robbing their contemporaries of freight.

Few people are aware and not enough care about this outlaw and the problems it causes, the contribution it makes to increasing PDM costs across the board.

The majority of gray area transportation operations falls into one or more of the following categories:

- A shipper leasing one or more vehicles and drivers from one source, or from separate sources, in unlawful consort with the shipper.
- A trucker, or his customer, purchasing goods at origin, transporting the goods to and selling at destination while claiming private carrier operations. This is actually a buy and sell operation for transport purposes.
- A regulated carrier conducting operations beyond a territorial or commodity scope of authority.
- An exempt agricultural trucker hauling non-exempt goods. Similarly, an exempt farm co-op hauling non-farm related goods not incidental to the co-op's primary function.
- A broker arranging for-hire transport without proper authority.
- A gypsy for-hire operator carrying commodities without a permit or certificate of authority.
- An exempt local cartage agent operating beyond a specific metropolitan area.

Trucking associations, the ICC, state governments, and a dedicated group, the Committee on Transportation Practices, are working hard to catch and confine this outlaw. But they need your help, in the final analysis you are the one who can provide the most pressure to clean the gray spot from the transport segment of your physical distribution management.

In 1965 Congress passed public law 89-170. The purpose of the law was to strengthen Federal and state officials' powers. This law was a culmination of years of effort by those agencies and organizations most concerned about the spread of illegal transportation. In part, PL89-170 authorized—

1. States to require ICC-regulated motor carriers to register with the states.

2. ICC to enter into cooperative agreements with the states to enforce highway laws. Prior to this the ICC was prohibited from doing so.

3. ICC to obtain service of process in court cases against unlawful operators, and to enjoin other parties regardless of where operators reside.

During the calender year 1968, states with active enforcement programs made over 26,000 arrests for unauthorized interstate and intrastate operations. Arrests for these illegal movements resulted in excess of $1.25 million in fines or bonds posted. That $1.25 million is not only paid by the carrier but by the shipper who tries to cut costs and corners by using gray area carriers. Even more surprising is the fact that the figures for 1969 reflect new arrests and fines but are relatively the same as 1968.

In 1969 there were over 25,000 arrests, resulting in fines and bonds exceeding $1 million. What is the reason for this continuing high rate of arrests and fines paid? The fact is as more states increase their enforcement of intra- and interstate registration, the gray suddenly becomes very clear. It's like an iceberg, less than 30% can be seen, the large part remains hidden.

How much regulated common carrier revenue is siphoned off by this gray area of transportation? Estimates run from $600 million to $5 billion per year. It is not unreasonable to suggest $2 billion-a-year to be a close estimate. Even at the $600 million figure, the revenue loss by the regulated carriers is staggering. The continued erosion of revenues by the outlaw carrier can only result in:

• curtailed common carrier service
• increases in common carrier rates

This hurts the carrier industry but also the majority of the shipping public, who rely upon a stable and healthy common carrier system.

An example of gray area transportation, and what specifically is tried by these illegal carriers and the shippers who insist in using their service is as follows: A truck was stopped by a state enforcement officer who asked the driver for his paperwork. The bill of lading presented to the officer stated that the carrier was transporting 40 barrels of salt fish in brine, which is exempt when moved in interstate commerce. Upon investigating the trailer contents, the officer discovered the following cargo:

• 388 cartons of shampoo
• 386 cases of bath oil
• 143 cases of baking goods

- 85 cases of cookies
- 43 crates of steel hinges
- 6 cases of candy

Not only did the carrier lose but the shipper also, jeopardizing rapid delivery, monetary loss if the products would have been damaged, plus the fact that both had to pay a fine for breaking the law. Unfortunately this is not an isolated case but one of many which happen every day.

The ICC and COTP are fighting the battle to end gray area transportation but in the end it must the people who keep supporting this illegal form of transportation to cease to use it and therefore starve it out.

COTP is the single active force that directs the light of the law upon the gray area activities. The main factor in the success of COTP is its executive secretary, Don Lawrence. Lawrence, a lawyer, has more than twenty years of experience in the transportation field, and particularly in the area of law enforcement. His credits include work in the trucking industry, in and with state transportation commissions, and in transportation education.

"COTP," Lawrence says, "has one purpose, that is to eliminate illegal transportation by whatever legitimate avenues that are available to us. To do this, we need the help of all shippers and carriers. Shippers, particularly, should know their state enforcement officials who are fighting illegal transportation."

Key elements which affect any physical distribution program are increasing costs and reduction in services. Any shipper who hears and reads about gray area transportation, and does nothing about it, is in effect approving of the thing which can hurt him.

How can you help to eliminate this illegal form of transportation? Hopefully you will support the ICC and COTP and stand behind the laws that help these state and federal agencies to do their job more effectively. More, you can refuse to become a party to involvement in this illegal transportation. There are ways to overcome this problem. Get to know your carriers, their operations and services. Develop a check list for your transportation department, the shipping and receiving areas and all who come in contact with outside services.

Gray area transportation has been a problem in physical distribution for many years, and because not enough people care, the problem remains. The trucking industry is trying to solve its problem and they have help from the ICC and COTP, but in the end it will take you, the shipper, to help clean this gray spot from the transportation industry.

C.

Air
Transportation

Of all vehicles, perhaps the most fascinating is the airplane. Modern flight comes close to achieving one of the ideal goals of transportation—the easy conquest of obstacles to man's progress across the surface of the earth. No longer are mountains, canyons, or even storms impediments to movement. The jet plane ignores virtually all of them.

The history of flight can be traced back at least to Leonardo da Vinci who conceived of the helicopter and the parachute and very nearly invented the glider. Man has been flying in balloons since the time of the American Revolution. Heavier-than-air flying machines are a more recent development, however; they began with the Wright Brothers and led, through the early air mail, to the many carriers serving us today. Only since World War II has air transportation's greatest attribute—speed—become remarkable.

The modern day airplane is a marvelous complex of shiny metal and mid-twentieth century technology. It is a major investment, often costing in excess of $20 million—surely the most expensive single vehicle used in transportation.

It is operated by a crew of technicians and operators who are perhaps the most highly trained and paid of all transportation employees. They are supported by a multitude of on-the-ground technicians whose skills, prior to take-off and during the flight, make speed and safety possible.

The airlines are specialists in transportation—principally in the transportation of people. They operate in a very efficient manner and at a price which is competitive enough so that they can seize the majority of the for-hire passenger market. Although the private automobile continues supreme as the major mover of passengers, in the for-hire portion of this market, air transportation in the late 1950's beat out its nearest rival.

Air transportation also has a very important freight market. For goods with such characteristics as high value, the need for speed, and perishability, air transportation is a major means of shipping. As technology progresses and as rates are lowered, more and more firms find air transportation an alternative means of moving their goods (as we will see in the following selections).

Finally, air transportation is the most romantic of the modes of transportation. The thrill of man's flying through the air is greater by far than that of any other means of movement. The early pilot struggled against the unknown, against the elements, and against his natural fear, struggles which wove a colorful and romantic history of flight.

This section contains nine articles which deal with various aspects of air transportation, including not only the economics of scheduled airlines but also some of the inherent social problems of airports and the regulation of the air transportation industry.

---

17   The DC-3
Nathaniel Benchley

This personal recollection of the venerable DC-3 evolves some sense of early flying. The noted author recalls some of the adventure and romance which may be missing in the all-jet age of today, with its coast-to-coast, nonstop flights.

The island where I live is serviced in the off-season by small, STOL* DeHavilland Twin Otter airplanes. They are neat and efficient and as their designation implies, they almost literally jump into the air. On a recent trip to the mainland I was talking with the pilot, a youth who may or may not have reached thirty, and he mentioned that the line was going to put two DC-3s into service this summer to increase the payload. "They tell me they're as easy to fly as these Otters," he said, "but I just don't see how that could be." He had the voice of a yachtsman who'd been told to take over the Santa Maria.

Looking down the tiny, crowded aisle of the Otter, I thought back on how large and luxurious the DC-3s had seemed when every summer—starting in 1939 and continuing up to the war—my wife and I took them from New York to California. They carried twenty-one people, featured a so-called Sky Room compartment for honeymoon and other friendly couples and even provided upper and lower berths on the port side, with small windows to view the stars. In daytime, berths folded away like those in a Pullman. It was luxury of the highest order, and the flight was scheduled to take only seventeen-and-a-half hours. It usually wound up more like nineteen, and for all the next day your head rang with the noise of the Cyclone engines. It was almost a point of pride to see whose head kept ringing longer.

My vacation always began on Sundays, so Sunday evenings we'd go out to La Guardia (the first time, it was Newark) and board the Flagship sleeper. The port-side seats were like a train compartment—you sat facing one another with a table between you for your meals and gin rummy. Shortly after takeoff while the plane still climbed toward the sunset, supper was served by a stewardess who was invariably beautiful and, by regulations, a Registered Nurse.

Washington's old Hoover Airport was the first stop. It consisted of a single

*Short Take Off (and) Landing.

From Nathaniel Benchley, "The DC-3," *The American Way*, September 1971, pp. 15-16. Used by permission.

strip, one end of which stopped in the Potomac River and the other in a railroad track, and overhead wires. If the wind was right, there was no particular sweat getting in or out; for takeoff, the pilot simply trundled toward the river, swung around and put his tail wheel as close to the water as he could, then set the brakes and opened the throttles wide. The whole plane quivered and strained, then leaped forward as he released the brakes, while the passengers rested their foreheads on the windows and watched the railroad tracks grow bigger and bigger and drop suddenly away below. If the wind was wrong, the pilot went to another airport.

The next stop was Nashville, generally around ten o'clock at night. On Sundays, the people of Nashville used to come out to the airport to watch the planes come in, much as I—at a younger age—used to watch the trains at Crestwood station. It was a heady experience to step, like a person from distant space, out of the plane and into the glare of the floodlights and dimly see the Nashvillians peering at you from the other side of a chain-wire fence. Some of them even waved, which you acknowledged with a casual flick of the hand. Then back aboard, and off into the nighttime sky.

The stewardess then made up the bunks for those who wanted to turn in and the plane took on the muted, softly-lighted aspect of a nighttime Pullman. There was a washroom aft, where you could just about brush your teeth without hitting your elbow on the wall, and where those who insisted on a full change into nightclothes could do so standing up. For those who simply peeled down to the underwear, it was simpler behind the curtains in the berth. The bedding was soft, the safety belt lay loosely across the blanket and the only impediment to sleep was the drone of the engines, which was transmitted through the pillow and into your skull if you lay with one ear down. Even this proved soporific, except for habitual engine-noise-listeners. The stewardess was handy with sleeping pills for anyone who needed them.

Dallas and Ft. Worth came in the dead middle of the night and, so it seemed, simultaneously. The two cities are so close together that the plane barely gets up from one before it's on its way down to the other in something of a long, soaring broad jump. The only explanation for two stops so contiguous is the fierce rivalry between the cities, which must have twisted arms in high scheduling circles. (This is admittedly a guess, but I can think of no other.) At any rate, window-watching passengers got a good chance to study the gleaming white arc of propellers, reflecting the beam of wing-mounted landing lights, and on take-off, to watch the blue border lights race past the window. From higher in the Texas sky, they looked down on the flickering oil-well fires, and sometimes saw flashes of lightning darting through clouds.

It was at Ft. Worth, at 1:30 in the morning, that we made an unscheduled change of planes that is probably still remembered by those Texans who saw it. We had completed the stop; the door thudded closed and the engines started and as we trundled away from the apron, there was a *bang* like a rifle-shot, and the plane came to a halt. The engines slowed, wheezed and stopped with a sound of weary invective. A buzzer sounded and we could hear the stewardess go up into the cockpit. She returned shortly and passed the word: "I'm sorry, but we've blown a tire and will have to change planes. Don't bother to get dressed; just come as you are." We got up, and out, and there followed the ludicrous sight of twenty-one people trooping across the floodlit airport: some were in dressing gowns, some in pajamas and some in hastily-donned trousers and sockless shoes —all clutching bits of clothing and toilet articles, and one woman carrying a loudly protesting baby. Hair standing on end or falling in the eyes, eyelids squinted against the glare of the lights, neckties dragging and trousers slipping, we looked like the victims of some demented fraternity initiation as we straggled behind the man leading us to a standby airplane. Other ground personnel transferred our luggage, and the last thing to cross the tarmac was a pink Toidy-Seat, encircling the arm of a mortified attendant.

Somehow in the reshuffling of places my wife and I got the Sky Room compartment, along with a large and noisy fly that refused to get off. The plane was oven-temperature—it had been standing in the Texas heat for several hours—and since the night was pretty well shot, we declined the stewardess' offer to make up the bunks. We said we'd sit up, thank you, and rough it the rest of the way. The idea of going back to bed seemed somewhat of an anticlimax. It was then that we found out—as we should have guessed before—that the privacy of the Sky Room was incomplete; any crew member going from the cockpit to the rear of the plane passed through the room. It was still a nice idea, and gave an added air of *"luxe"* to an already plush situation.

Then came the long part of the trip: across northern Texas, southern New Mexico, and Arizona—to Phoenix. Cruising altitude was nine-thousand feet— little more than takeoff height these days—and while it was generally smooth flying at night, in daylight hours the desert heat made conditions somewhat choppy. (Once, on the eastbound flight, we unbelievably ran into a hailstorm over Arizona, which gave the unsettling impression that the roof of the plane was being torn away.) It was on the Texas-to-Arizona section of the run that the engine noise finally established itself as a part of daily life, and you knew that your head was going to hum forever. I discovered an interesting phenomenon, however; when your ears become a part of the engines, and your brain accepts noise as a way of life, then your thoughts become audible; if you think, for instance, of a tune, you can actually hear it in your head. And I mean *hear* it. As a discovery, this is unlikely to make me a great deal of money, but it's something the medicine men might kick around when they're not busy.

After Phoenix—and breakfast—came the climb toward the San Bernardino pass, leaving the desert and passing between mountains that looked so close you could almost count the trees; after that, came the slow descent to Burbank airport and the smogless California sunshine. You felt like a combination of Charles Lindbergh and Meriwether Clark, and to anyone who would listen you gave as detailed an account of your trip as a golfer replaying a tournament round—and generally just about as dull. Watching people's eyes glaze over as you talked, you finally came to realize that your excitement was something that couldn't be communicated in words; it had to be lived.

The DC-3 was a friendly aircraft. Developed in 1935 as a lure to the luxury sleeper trade, it was fast (180 mph), forgiving of pilot error and, to quote C. R. Smith, president of American Airlines, "the first airplane that could make money just by hauling passengers." By 1938 it was carrying 95 percent of all commercial traffic in the United States, and by 1939 it had 90 percent of the world's airline business. It was an aircraft on which both the passengers and crew could feel relaxed and at home, and there was a cheerful informality that is necessarily missing in the battleship-sized, mass-transit planes. On one trip, for instance, when we went by way of Denver, most of the passengers deplaned at Cheyenne, after which the stewardess joined us for breakfast in our compartment; then I went into the cockpit and took pictures over the co-pilot's shoulder as we came in for our Denver landing.

But probably the most cheerful trip on record was experienced by two friends of ours who were married in El Paso and then came East by sleeper plane. The agent who booked their passage told the airline of their newly-married status and they were, therefore, plunked in the honeymooners' Sky Room, where they received all sorts of special attention plus the extreme delicacy of a knock on the door before any of the crew passed through. The word was even communicated to the ground crews, and when, at one stop, the plane was being refueled, the men walking on the wing outside the Sky Room made hugging and kissing gestures through the window and offered all sorts of advice that fortunately went unheard. When, finally, they arrived in New York, they were convinced someone must have tied old shoes and tin cans and ribbons onto the plane's tail wheel—and, since it was a DC-3, such festooning wouldn't have hurt its flying qualities in the least. A DC-3 could fly itself, and often did.

---

18 **DC-10:**
The Good Neighbor Airplane
Glen Walker

New equipment always calls for comparison with the old. This selection, like the previous one, discusses the older equipment and its importance in the development of the airline industry. It deals too with the newest planes and their functions.

The flappers were out and the Great Depression was in. Franklin D. Roosevelt had just been elected to his second term as President and the New Deal was in full swing. Across the Atlantic, the Prince of Wales was soon to take the throne

From Glen Walker, "DC-10: The Good Neighbor Airplane," *The American Way*, September 1971, pp. 17-20. Used by permission.

and then abdicate to marry a Baltimore divorcee. Everyone traveled by train or car and only the adventurous flew, despite such airline inducements as "Fly with the Air Mail" and "No More Husbandless Nights—He'll Be Home Tonight by Air."

Everyone knew the airlines were the growth industry of the decade, but no one was certain just how they'd make it. Airplanes carried mail and made money. They barnstormed at county fairs and made more money. But there was no airplane built that could make money by carrying people. The most modern transport of the era was the DC-2, which carried fourteen passengers and— without a revenue-producing load of mail—lost money every mile of the way.

That's what made historic a telephone call that C. R. Smith in Chicago made to Donald Douglas on the West Coast in 1935. Smith, the new president of American Airlines, had won a cross-country air mail contract and he and his chief engineer William Littlewood wanted the Douglas Aircraft Co. to enlarge the DC-2 so that it could profitably carry people at the same time it carried mail. The plans that Littlewood had in mind called for a 50 percent increase in passenger space. That meant a bigger fuselage and a bigger wingspan. He envisioned an airplane that would be 85 percent DC-2 and 15 percent "new."

The final version of the Douglas plane turned out to be 85 percent "new," so it was called the DC-3 (World War II flyers would know it as the C-47 or the R4D or, more commonly, the "gooney bird.") Because of its twenty-one seats and low operating costs, the DC-3 made money carrying people. Because of its reliability, it helped make air transportation an accepted way to travel.

"The DC-3 freed the airlines from complete dependency on Government mail pay," said C. R. Smith. "It was the first airplane that could make money just by hauling passengers. With the previous planes, if you multiplied the number of seats by the fares being charged, you couldn't break even, not even with a 100 percent load."

It also made the passenger king. To woo and win recalcitrant travelers, airlines began hiring and training registered nurses to serve as stewardesses aboard each flight. To compete with trains, airlines abandoned box lunches and introduced hot meals on longer flights.

"By the time I first flew the DC-3 in 1939, it was the established aircraft of the time, carrying about 90 percent of the world's air travelers," recalls Franklin W. Kolk, then an aeronautical engineering student and now head of American Airlines' development engineering department. "I remember looking at the stewardess and thinking it was a shame that such an attractive girl had to wear such thick stockings and such a military uniform—though I suppose it was reassuring to other first-time flyers. The airplane, even with twenty-one seats, wasn't as big as I had imagined. But once in the air, with a cup of hot coffee in my hand, looking out the porthole window, whizzing along at 180 miles an hour, I also remember thinking, 'This sure beats the hell out of going any other way than by plane.' "

Frank Kolk's recollection of the DC-3—the workhorse airplane of the late 1930s and early '40s—is noteworthy because he as much as any man is credited with development of another aircraft that industry observers believe will be the workhorse of the '70s. At one point, in fact, the engineering specs that Kolk and his team developed for manufacturers were identified simply as "the Kolk machine." Today, the product of those plans is called the wide-body trijet, or intermediate jumbo jet. One version made its debut in August as the McDonnell Douglas DC-10. Another scheduled for service next year is the Lockheed L-1011.

When American introduced the DC-3 in 1936, the country was still struggling through a Depression. Now, with American's D-10 LuxuryLiner just introduced, the country is struggling out of a recession and airlines are trying to recover from a period of no traffic growth and record financial losses. Whether the workhorse trijets can accomplish for the industry what the DC-3 did three decades ago is a question many people are asking.

The outlook is bright. The DC-10 and L-1011 represent the most advanced and most comfortable airplanes ever built. Their flexibility will permit them to operate economically over segments as short as 300 miles or on routes as long as 3,000 miles. Because of their passenger capacity, they can take the place of two or even three smaller jets, thus relieving air congestion and delays. And their economy of operation permits airlines to offer more capacity to the traveling public without a proportionate increase in costs.

For the passenger, the trijets feature the smooth, comfortable ride common to wide-body aircraft. American has utilized the extra space of its DC-10 Luxury-Liner to provide first class and coach lounges, complete with stand-up bars and plenty of room to socialize. In first class, only six seats are placed across the width of the cabin, which accommodates just thirty-four passengers. In the 172-passenger coach section, seats are arranged in four pairs across the cabin, so that no passenger is more than one seat from an aisle. All seats are equipped with an individually operated lower-back support, and coach comfort is further enhanced by a full 36-inch spread between rows. There's a broad, eight-foot ceiling, overhead storage compartments instead of racks, a food preparation center on a deck below the cabin floor, and this aircraft offers 30 percent more window area in proportion to total size than any other jetliner.

To an extent unprecedented in airplane design, McDonnell Douglas set as an objective in the development of the DC-10 the reduction of engine noise to levels acceptable to airport communities—a "good neighbor" policy that's now a happy reality. Advanced powerplant technology by General Electric has produced a DC-10 engine twice as powerful as those on smaller jets yet much quieter. Sound reduction is achieved through the basic design of the engine, which derives most of its thrust from a large fan rather than a primary turbine. A breakthrough in sound suppression materials enabled G.E. to equip its CF6-6D engine with a material that not only absorbs sound but also tunes out specific pure tones that psychoacoustic research showed were most grating to people on the ground. Furthermore, virtually no *smoke* is created by the engine.

Frank Kolk is convinced that this combination of advantages—increased size, flexibility, operating economy, and a smoother, more comfortable ride—make the wide-body trijet the universal airplane of the future. He speaks of a time when the DC-10, like the DC-3 before it, will serve virtually all of American Airlines' routes. Its big cousin, the 305-passenger Boeing 747 LuxuryLiner, will continue to ply the high-volume transcontinental routes for which it was designed. And the 92-passenger 727 Astrojet will continue to serve low-volume short-haul routes. But for everything in-between, the DC-10 LuxuryLiner will be the workhorse airplane, the ultimate in passenger comfort and airline economy: the good neighbor airplane.

---

19   Air Transport Facts & Figures
Air Transport Association of America

The year 1970 was one of record losses for the scheduled airlines of the nation. By now, the air transportation industry is doing better financially. A year of losses has at least one advantage: it makes both firms and industry take a very close look at costs, demand, operations—undertake self-examination.

This selection from the annual report of the Air Transport Association of America is a part of such self-examination. From it, the reader can gain an insight into the economics of the scheduled airlines—in terms of pressures, costs, demand.

1970 in review

Inflationary pressures, combined with poor traffic growth, resulted in the heaviest losses ever for the airlines.

Powerful economic forces both within and without the industry combined in 1970 to give the scheduled airlines the worst financial results in their history. But the sting of their heavy losses was lessened, at least in part, by some bright spots—most notably an outstanding safety record and the very successful introduction of the Boeing 747, the first of the new wide-bodied, advanced technology jets.

Total scheduled airline traffic, as measured by overall revenue ton miles flown in all services, gained only 1.0 per cent in 1970, compared with an average growth rate in the sixties of 16.6 per cent, and airline financial statements this year show in 1970 the largest losses ever for the industry—$179 million. These losses caused the rate of return on investment to fall to its lowest level in history—1.5 per cent—certainly nowhere near the 12.0 per cent the Civil Aero-

From Air Transport Association of America, *Air Transport Facts & Figures,* Annual Report of the Scheduled Airline Industry, pp. 6-19. Used by permission.

nautics Board (CAB) has said to be fair and reasonable. And, so far in 1971, these trends seem to be deepening: traffic on domestic routes is declining and the 12 major carriers have reported losses of over $100 million for the first quarter of 1971.

There are a number of significant trends that went into these results. These include:

Traffic Decline. The national economic recession that began last year and is continuing into this year slowed domestic passenger traffic growth almost to a halt in 1970. In fact, beginning in August, passenger traffic on the domestic trunk carriers has actually declined each month from the level of the same month in the previous year. This trend has continued throughout the first quarter of this year, with domestic trunk traffic showing a decline of 2.4 per cent from the first quarter of 1970.

Inflationary Pressures. Inflation continued to plague the airline industry at a rate of about 9 per cent in 1970 over 1969, almost double the national rate of inflation. The major portion of this inflationary pressure came from labor settlements which increased airline wages by some 15 per cent in 1970.

Inadequate Fares. Airline fares have not kept pace with the rising cost of offering service to the public. The average yield, or revenue per revenue passenger mile, in 1970 increased only 1.8 per cent over 1969 and was 5.9 per cent lower than it was 10 years earlier in 1960. In the fourth quarter of 1970, the yield was lower than in the fourth quarter of 1969 despite some selective fare increases.

On April 12, 1971, the CAB released its decision in the passenger fare phase of the Domestic Passenger Fare Investigation, granting an immediate across-the-board 6.0 per cent increase in domestic fares and a possible additional 3.0 per cent rise to come later. This increase, while welcome, is still well below the increases sought by the carriers.

Competition. Increased competition from other classes of carriers has eroded the traffic of the scheduled carriers to the point where they are no longer able to make a profit on many of their most lucrative routes to support service on losing routes that must be served in the public interest. This is especially true in international service where the supplemental airlines have taken the lion's share of the peak season traffic on a number of peak routes with no obligation to provide regular, dependable service.

Extensive cost cutting measures

In response to these adverse forces, the industry initiated early last year, and is still continuing, a number of steps to improve its economic situation. Some of the most important ones include:

Schedule Reductions. Many carriers are cutting flight schedules to eliminate unprofitable flights and reduce uneconomic competition. This began in the second half of 1970 on a unilateral basis and by May, 1971, there were 5.2 per cent fewer domestic flights scheduled than there were in May, 1970, meaning that some 700 daily flights have been eliminated. In March of this year, the CAB agreed to permit the carriers to meet and discuss reducing flights on mutually acceptable routes. The first meeting was held in late March and 21 routes were agreed upon and submitted to the CAB for approval. If the CAB approves the discussion of these routes, the carriers serving them will meet to plan actual capacity reductions on them.

Equipment Order Reductions and Delays. Another step towards curbing capacity has been the cancelling and stretching out of orders for new flight equipment by some carriers. These airlines have found that it is more economical to forfeit some penalty payments and cancel a new aircraft than to take delivery of and operate one that current traffic trends indicate will not be needed.

Employee Layoffs. Extensive layoffs of airline employees have resulted in industry employment actually being reduced in 1970 from 1969 levels for the first time in 10 years. So far, 12,000 employees have been furloughed and more cuts are expected.

Elimination of "Frills." Many carriers are now cutting down on some of the "extras" to which airline passengers have become accustomed. Gone now on many flights are such amenities as cocktail snacks, meals at off-mealtime hours and movies on morning flights.

Best year ever in safety

Early this year, the Chairman of the National Transportation Safety Board, John H. Reed, said: "By almost any statistical yardstick, 1970 was a truly remarkable year in aviation safety." The scheduled airlines in 1970 had a safety rate of .001, marking the first time that the rate was below .01. In scheduled domestic service, there were no passenger fatalities and in all operations there was only one fatal passenger accident and two passenger fatalities.

There are a number of reasons for this outstanding safety performance by the carriers. One of the most important is the sustained major effort the airlines have made over the years to improve the quality of flight crew training, especially the use of simulators with visual attachments for most hazardous maneuvers. Also, the latest in educational practices and theories have been applied to airline training techniques and the ground school for 747 training, in particular, incorporated the most sophisticated refinements in training.

Another important contribution to airline safety has been the effort to measure, improve and control runway friction to reduce aircraft skidding and hydroplaning. Runway grooving has been the most visible of these efforts but other improvements have included the setting up of snow and ice committees at airports to measure accumulation on the runway and decide if it should be shut down, experimentation with urea to prevent ice formation and the use of devices on runways that can collect data on braking action.

Also contributing to the excellent airline safety record is the engine reliability program—a process whereby measurements are made, in flight, on the temperature, speed and other performance characteristics of an engine. This enables a constant monitoring of the health of the engine and gives airline engineers the ability to predict where problems are going to occur and stop them before they happen, even before the flight crew is aware of them.

It is notable that this outstanding safety year coincided with the year of the introduction of the Boeing 747 into passenger service. This aircraft turned in such an excellent performance in its first year of service that the National Aeronautics Association awarded its manufacturer and the airline that first put it into service the coveted Collier Trophy. This trophy is the single award of the aviation and aerospace community for "the great achievement in aeronautics or astronautics in America with respect to improving the performance, efficiency or safety of air or space vehicles, the value of which has been thoroughly demonstrated by actual use during the preceding year."

Progress in reducing jet pollution

Although the airline contribution to air pollution is relatively small, about 1.2 per cent of all emissions nationwide, the industry initiated, in 1965, a program to reduce and eliminate even that small amount. There are two different approaches to the problem. The first is the phasing into airlines fleets of the virtually smoke-free advanced technology jets—the 747, DC-10 and L-1011. The reduction of smoke was designed right into the engines of these aircraft and the airline investment of $5.5 billion in this kind of aircraft is an investment in a cleaner environment.

The other approach has been to retrofit the engines on aircraft already in the fleet. Presently, the program is focused on the JT8D engine which powers the DC-9, B-727 and B-737 aircraft. These aircraft account for more than one-half of the airline fleet and, because they are short- and medium-range aircraft, make many more takeoffs and landings than do the long-range B-707 and DC-8. Due to these factors, the JT8D engine accounts for about 70 per cent of all jet engine smoke, according to an estimate by the National Air Pollution Control Administration.

A modified combustion chamber for the engine was developed by its manufacturer, Pratt and Whitney, and after extensive testing by the Federal Aviation Administration and the airlines for safety and efficiency was certificated for scheduled service. In January, 1970, the airlines agreed to begin retrofitting their JT8D engines with the combustors and to have the program "substantially complete" by late 1972. At the end of the first quarter of 1971, the airlines had already retrofitted approximately one-third of the JT8D engines in their fleets.

Fuel venting

Another pollution problem the industry confronted during the year was that of fuel venting. This involves a small amount of unburned fuel that collects in reservoirs inside the engine cowling when an engine is shut down. The fuel remains there until takeoff when it is automatically expelled at about 2,000 feet and 200 knots airspeed. The amount of fuel for each engine varies from one to three pints and studies have shown that fuel dumped in flight at speeds above 100 knots will be fully evaporated within 200 feet below the aircraft.

In order to eliminate this small amount of pollution, the carriers are now evaluating a system whereby a drain valve is capped and the fuel remains in the engine instead of draining into the reservoir. The program began in February, 1971, and evaluation should be finished in September of this year. In the meantime, the airlines have instructed the manufacturers to continue research on other ways of disposing of the fuel in the reservoir in case the fuel drain method does not work out in testing.

Airports and airways

Another significant event for the industry in 1970 was the passage of the Airports and Airways Development Act of 1970 which was signed into law last May. The act created the Airports/Airways Trust Fund which collects taxes from the users of the aviation system—primarily airline passengers and shippers—through ticket and waybill taxes. The fund is expected to generate $600 million in its first year—funds which are to be spent for "catch-up" airports and airways facilities.

Now, however, this fund is being threatened from two different sides. First, the $280 million that the Congress, in passing the bill, had intended would be spent for airport development, has not been appropriated. Instead only $124 million has been appropriated for that purpose so far this fiscal year. But, an even more serious threat to the needed development of an adequate aviation system is the Administration's transportation revenue sharing proposal that would distribute to the states and localities all of the money in the Aviation Trust Fund and all other transportation trust funds, except those for the completion of the Interstate Highway System. This money would be earmarked for transportation facilities but with no provision that any of it be used for aviation facilities.

Airline re-equipment program

In January, 1970, the age of the wide-bodied jet began when the airlines introduced the Boeing 747 into scheduled service. By the end of the year, the airlines had taken delivery of 78 of these aircraft. 1971 will see the delivery of most of the remainder of the airlines' orders of 747s—17 more will come into service later this year, leaving only 6 to be delivered in later years.

Just as 1970 was the year of the 747, 1971 will be the year of the McDonnell Douglas DC-10. This new trijet will join its wide-bodied companion in scheduled service sometime in the fourth quarter of this year with 12 expected for delivery. The other entry in the wide-bodied jet market, the Lockheed L-1011, is expected to begin service sometime in 1972, somewhat later than originally expected, due to the bankruptcy in February, 1971, of Rolls Royce, the manufacturer of the engines for the aircraft.

All of these new aircraft represent an investment of $3.5 billion in the years 1971 through 1974 in flight and ground equipment. It is interesting that of a total of 202 aircraft on order by the carriers, 97 per cent of them are for the wide-bodied jets and after the end of this year, the airlines will have no smaller, first generation jets on order.

Aircraft delivered during 1970 totaled 128, including 74 747s and in the first 5 months of 1971, the airlines have taken delivery of 29 more new aircraft. The total value of these aircraft delivered in the past 17 months was $2.0 billion.

In addition to these subsonic aircraft on firm order, the airlines also have placed orders for 38 British-French supersonic Concordes which have an approximate value of $760 million. Thus, the airline industry investment in subsonic and supersonic aircraft totals more than $4.0 billion.

An interesting aspect of the airline re-equipment program is the dwindling of the number of different types of aircraft, both on order and in the fleet. This means that the airlines are gradually standardizing their fleets to just a few types of aircraft. This standardization allows an airline far greater efficiency in almost all areas of its operation—crew training, supplies of spare parts, ground facilities and maintenance.

Airline costs—a mounting problem

The inflation rate for airline costs in 1970 was 9.0 per cent, almost twice the overall national rate.

In 1970, the scheduled airline industry lost a total of $179 million, marking only the third year since the end of World War II that the industry did not turn a profit. The rate of return on total investment fell to its lowest level ever—1.5 per cent which is nowhere near the 12 per cent rate of return that the CAB has said is "fair and reasonable."

This year's poor financial results represent the coming together of a number of trends in airline economics that began as far back as 1967 when industry profits began to drop off from their 1966 all-time high of $427 million. The basic problem is that airline costs have, despite stringent cost-cutting, continued to be very difficult to control. These costs, and the industry's poor traffic growth, were primarily responsible for such heavy losses.

An indication of the extent and severity of the industry's financial problems is contained in a survey in the April, 1971, issue of the First National City Bank's Monthly Economic Letter. In it, the earnings of 64 industries were listed and the airline industry was the only one, out of all 64, to show a net loss for the year as an industry group.

Unit costs

One measure of an industry's financial health is the trend of profits per unit of production—in the airlines' case, per available ton mile (ATM) flown. In 1970, the airline industry posted a profit margin per available ton mile of less than two-tenths of a cent—the lowest ever.

This came about because operating revenues per ATM, despite some modest

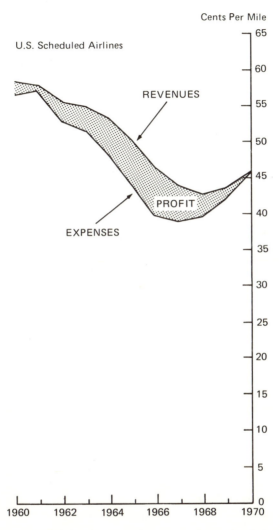

Unit Revenues, Expenses and Operating
Profit Per Revenue Ton

Cents Per Mile

U.S. Scheduled Airlines

REVENUES

PROFIT

EXPENSES

65
60
55
50
45
40
35
30
25
20
15
10
5
0

1960   1962   1964   1966   1968   1970

increases in passenger and freight rates, have stayed at a level that is far below that of 5 and even 10 years ago. This drop in revenue per ATM had been steady until 1969 when it reached its lowest level in over 20 years. In 1970, it rose only slightly.

At the same time, the expense per revenue ton mile dropped sharply from 1959 to 1967 when it bottomed out and for the next few years stayed at approximately the same level. In 1969, it began for the first time in 10 years to rise. The reason for this bottoming out and then rise in unit costs was that the carriers, by 1967, were almost fully jet equipped with aircraft in a range of sizes, each best suited to the needs of the route it served. This substitution of less efficient piston and jetprop aircraft with the more efficient jet aircraft had, throughout the sixties, allowed the carriers to reduce unit operating costs substantially. However, once this re-equipment program was pretty well completed, the carriers could no longer enjoy the same rate of savings and cost reductions to offset inflationary pressures. Consequently expenses per ATM flattened out and then began to rise.

These increasing unit costs have now come so close to unit revenues that the industry's operating profit is now only a small fraction of a cent.

Labor costs

Just about one-half of the airline expense dollar goes for wages, salaries and employee benefits. Not only are these costs increasing faster than most other airlines costs, they are increasing faster than the average national growth rate in employee costs.

In 1970, the average rate of inflation of all costs for the 12 major airlines was about 9 per cent. This 9 per cent represents an average between a 15 per cent rate of increase in wages and salaries, including fringe benefits, and a 5 per cent rate of increase in all other cash operating expenses.

The average annual wage of an airline employee in 1970 was $12,300, some $4,800 above the average annual wage of employees in all private industry. Even taking out management and pilots, the average airline employee last year earned more than $9,500, still over $2,000 per year more than the national average for all employees.

Not only are airline employees paid more than those in private industry, but their wages have been increasing and still are increasing at a faster rate. Between 1965 and 1970, airline employees' salaries increased at an annual rate of 8.1 per cent, while their counterparts in private industry got annual increases of 5.6 per cent. And these kinds of wage pressures on the airlines are going to accelerate in the future, rather than lessen, if the major contracts negotiated in 1970 with some of the most important unions representing airline employees can serve as any kind of indicator. These settlements looked like this:

Average Annual Wage Increase Over Life of Agreement
Major Contracts Negotiated in 1970

Classification	Number of Carriers	Annual Average Increase-Weighted Average
Clerical/ Agent	5	12.5%
Dispatcher	4	8.7
Mechanic	7	11.4
Stewardess	8	8.8

Other airline costs

There are other factors along with labor costs which have had an adverse effect on airline cost trends. While these are often difficult to measure, it is possible to get some indication of how rapidly these other costs have been rising.

Jet Fuel. Fuel is, of course, a very basic cost to the airline industry and accounts for one of the largest single operating cost items after labor costs. In late 1970, the price of jet fuel was raised by 6.2 per cent per gallon, an increase that will add about $50 million per year to the airlines' fuel costs. And this latest increase has come on top of earlier increases that have raised the price of jet fuel by as much as 12.0 per cent, depending on the type of aircraft.

Cost of Capital. As the airlines are constantly re-equipping themselves with new and more advanced technology aircraft, a very important expense item for them is the cost of obtaining capital to finance these new equipment purchases. Because of this, interest expense has been one of the industry's fastest growing expenses. In 1970, it totaled $384 million, a 35.5 per cent increase from 1969 and almost five times the level of 1960.

Another way of raising capital, of course, is equity financing. It has been, however, over the past couple of years, for most large airlines, very difficult for them to raise money in the equity market because of the low prices of airline stocks which would make a stock issue not very attractive or profitable and at the same time dilute the value of stock already held by the company's stockholders.

Because of this, the airlines have been almost forced to borrow money to finance new equipment purchases. The only other alternative has been to lease aircraft from financing companies; this has become more and more prevalent and now some $1.5 billion worth of aircraft are actually owned by and leased from another company. However, with the elimination of the Investment Tax Credit, this form of investment is becoming less and less attractive to the financing companies.

The airlines, over the past five years, have spent about $11 billion for flight and ground support equipment and much of this has been raised by borrowing at higher and higher interest rates. A sampling of the interest rates that some carriers have paid for capital gives some idea of just how much this expense has been rising for the industry.

This high level of borrowing has had an additional effect, besides causing heavy interest payments, of raising the industry's debt/equity ratio to 66/34 in 1970. This compares to 54/46 in 1965 and is the highest ever.

Airport Costs. The use of airport space for landings and for passenger handling has also become a more and more expensive item for the airlines. Landing fees paid by the carriers have more than quadrupled over the past 10 years and in 1970 totaled almost $185 million. This increase has not been due entirely to the use of heavier aircraft and a higher volume of traffic. The cost per landing has gone up rapidly also, even in years when the type of jets used by the carriers stayed basically the same. In 1960, the domestic trunk and local service carriers paid an average landing fee per landing of $6.20. By 1965 this had more than doubled to $12.54 per landing. And in 1970, when the number of scheduled airline operations showed a net decline, the average landing fee was $25.69, up 19.5 per cent from 1969 and 104.9 per cent from 1965.

On top of landing fees the carriers also pay for rental of space in the airport for passenger terminals, maintenance and overhaul facilities and cargo handling areas. At many airports these rentals are imposed on top of the cost incurred by the carriers themselves for the actual construction of the facilities.

Airline cost cutting

To trim their budgets airlines have been cutting flights, laying off employees and taking many other steps aimed at more efficient operations.

Any company or industry that finds itself with heavy losses, continually rising expenses and almost no growth in sales has to take drastic steps to cut everywhere it can to keep costs down. The airlines have been for the past year or so looking more and more closely for ways to cut unnecessary expenses without seriously reducing their level and quality of service to the traveling public. The major steps have been employee layoffs, flight schedule reductions, and the delaying and cancelling of flight equipment orders. Some less visible steps have taken the form of not quite so many services to their passengers and other behind-the-scenes cost cutting.

Equipment cuts

While the airlines are bringing the new generation of advanced technology aircraft into service, they are offering for sale many of their older, first generation jets. This has come about because of the depressed passenger traffic market brought on by the national economic recession which could not have been foreseen three or four years ago when the carriers were making their plans for the seventies. At that time, traffic was growing at annual rates up to and above 20 per cent per year and the national economy was in a seemingly endless boom.

To handle the growth that everyone was sure was on the way with rising incomes, increasing business activity and more leisure time, the carriers ordered many new and more efficient aircraft that would be able to carry this new traffic without causing any more congestion at airports and in the airways. But, in 1970, this traffic simply did not materialize. Declining corporate profits made businessmen cut back on their out-of-town trips and fears of unemployment and inflation made pleasure and personal travelers put off their flying vacation to another, more prosperous year.

Because of this, airline managements found they had flight equipment on order and flights scheduled that would not be needed in light of current passenger and freight loads. Thus, some carriers have found it more expedient to cancel or "stretch-out" their equipment orders rather than take delivery of unneeded aircraft, as well as to sell their older jets.

Schedule cutbacks

But most carriers are taking delivery of their new flight equipment and reducing flight frequencies to cut capacity. This has resulted in an unprecedented spate of schedule cutting and a request to the CAB for multi-lateral talks among the carriers to cut competition on key routes.

A close monitoring of flight schedules in the Official Airline Guide gives a clear picture of the impact these cutbacks have had on airline service. Comparing each month from January through May, 1971, with the schedules for the same month of the previous year shows that in each of those five months fewer flights are being offered than were being offered a year earlier.

These cuts have been building until the months of April and May showed decreases of 5.2 per cent in total flights. This trend can be expected to continue, as many carriers have announced that they will not build up their schedules for the summer season as they have in the past. This is because traffic trends so far in 1971 show domestic traffic declines to be deepening and the growth in international traffic to be lessening from last year. Also, advance bookings for 1971 summer travel indicate that traffic could continue this decline throughout the summer.

Employment reductions

Another cost cutting step taken by the airline industry in 1970 was the large-scale furloughing of employees. In all, a total of 12,000 employees were laid off during the year and more have had to be furloughed in 1971. Due to the fact that some carriers were still hiring in some areas, while others were affected by strikes, the actual net decline in total employment was from 312,000 in 1969 to 297,374 in 1970. This figure is low and does not reflect actual total employment because one local service carrier was on strike at the end of the year and one trunk carrier was still in the process of recalling employees after a lengthy strike. However, the remaining carriers showed a net decline in employment of 1.4 per cent.

In addition to furloughing, the carriers have found a number of other ways to keep their employment costs down. Some are hiring part-time or temporary extra help to handle increased summer traffic rather than take on full-time people. Bonuses have been eliminated and merit raises for management personnel sharply curtailed at some airlines. At least one carrier has cut top executives' salaries by as much as 15 per cent. Several airlines have taken the rather novel step of giving any employee who will take leave without pay a free ticket to anywhere on its system.

But these employment cuts have not affected the quality of airline service and the main reason for this has been the airline employees themselves. Most of them have pitched in and helped out—by working a little bit of extra overtime, by putting out a bit extra on the job and in many other small but very important ways.

Other cost savings

The airline industry is, of course, an extremely competitive one, and because of this the airlines have always been reluctant to cut costs in the area of service to their passengers. But, in looking over their budgets they have found ways in which they could make savings that would not substantially affect the overall quality of the service to the passenger.

Some of these service cuts have included such items as no more fresh flowers on aircraft, fewer snacks with cocktails, reduction in the number of flights receiving meal service, taking movies off morning flights and many other minor changes in passenger and other services.

Cost cutting is also showing up in such areas as advertising, more austere annual reports and employee publications and the consolidation of sales offices and other facilities for greater efficiency.

The scheduled air system—
A valuable national asset threatened

"Scheduled services are of vital importance to air transportation and offer services to the public which are not provided by charter services. Only scheduled services are expected to offer regular and dependably frequent schedules, provide extensive flexibility in length of stay, and maintain worldwide routes, including routes to areas of low traffic volume. Substantial impairment of scheduled services could result in travelers and shippers losing the ability to obtain these benefits. Accordingly, in any instances where a substantial impairment of scheduled services appears likely, it would be appropriate, where necessary to avoid prejudice to the public interest, to take steps to prevent such impairment" [Statement of International Transportation Policy of the United States, June 22, 1970].

Despite the importance placed on the preservation of the scheduled air transport system by this policy statement, recent experience has shown that the scheduled system is being substantially impaired by the inroads of the supplemental airlines into the pleasure travel market to Europe and other parts of the world. These carriers, who have no obligation to provide regular service are supposed, by their very definition, to supplement the scheduled air system.

However, in a growing number of the peak travel markets, especially during the high summer season, these airlines have done much more than supplement the scheduled system. For example, during the 1969 summer season, the supplementals' penetration of some peak markets looked like this:

New York-Rome	39.7%
California-Europe	63.7
New York-Amsterdam	67.4
New York-Frankfurt	68.2

One expert has predicted that in the California-Europe market, the supplementals will carry 90 per cent of the 1971 summer traffic.

A survey of charter flight passengers by Louis Harris in the summer of 1969 demonstrates that the supplementals are carrying many passengers that would otherwise be on a scheduled airline, not adding to the air travel market.

∘ The demographics of these passengers were almost identical to those on scheduled flights in terms of income, education and profession.
• They were relatively experienced air travelers. Almost all had flown before,

more than half had used the scheduled airlines for their previous foreign trips.

- • 35 per cent of them would have "certainly" and another 22 per cent would have "probably" taken a scheduled flight if they had not been able to get a charter flight.
- ◦ Over 80 per cent planned to travel individually in Europe rather than with a group.

These results are quite contrary to the supplementals' assertion that they are developing a whole new market of travelers who like to travel in groups with their friends and who cannot afford the scheduled airlines. They are actually raiding passenger markets developed over many years by the scheduled carriers with low promotional and discount fares.

An estimate of the diversion of passenger traffic was made based on the assumption that at least one-half of the passengers carried by the airlines would have used the scheduled airlines if a charter flight had not been available—a fairly safe assumption in light of the Louis Harris survey results. Based on that figure, the two U.S. scheduled trans-Atlantic carriers lost more than $50 million in revenues in the 12 months ended June 30, 1970, due to diversion by the supplementals.

The fact is that the supplementals are skimming the cream off of the scheduled systems' traffic. The scheduled airlines must have good loads and heavy traffic on the peak routes in peak seasons to support their low season and low volume services which, as the policy statement made clear, they are expected to provide. The effect of the erosion of the scheduled system by the supplementals is to take away the profit from these routes that make possible the provision of the unprofitable services, throwing off the balance of the whole scheduled system built up through the years.

Air fares—still a consumer bargain

Despite some recent increases, airline rates still lag far behind other consumer prices and have helped hold down the cost of travel.

As the cost of just about everything the consumer buys goes up and up, air travel remains one of the best bargains in the consumer's market basket. And because it is such a bargain, it has helped keep down the cost of travel by counterbalancing the rising costs of all other elements in the travel market—hotel costs, restaurant costs, local transportation fares and many tourist attraction admissions.

In 1970, the average fare paid by a passenger on a U.S. scheduled airline per mile, or the average revenue per revenue passenger mile, was actually 5.9 per cent lower than it was in 1960. This happened because, although the basic fare for a coach or first class ticket has gone up, more and more people have been taking advantage of the many discount fares offered by the airlines—such fares as Discover America, Family, Excursion, Youth and Military Standby and Visit

Airline Fares and Consumer Prices

Index: 1957-59 = 100

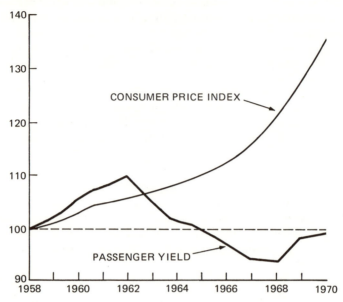

Quarterly Passenger Yield

Cents Per Mile

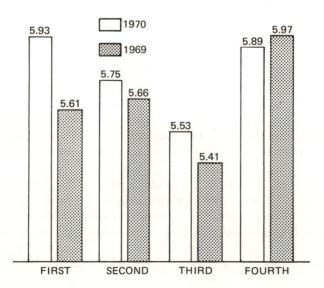

USA (for foreigners) fares. The use of these fares has become so widespread that, during peak travel seasons, almost one-half of all airline passengers are flying on some kind of discount fare, and paying, on the average, 35 per cent less than the full-fare passengers.

Another way of showing what a bargain air travel is, is to compare the trend of air fares with the Consumer Price Index. Using the average passenger yield for the 1957-1959 period, exactly as the CPI is constructed, shows that while consumer prices have risen 35.8 per cent since then, the average passenger yield is at just about exactly the same level as it was in 1957-1959.

While it is too early to gauge the effects of the recent selective fare increases in congested markets and the overall 6.0 per cent increase granted recently by the CAB, it is known that the effect on passenger yield is not as great as the amount of the fare increase. This is because, as fares increase, people often tend to change to a less expensive class of travel. For example, a first class passenger might decide to switch to coach or a coach passenger might decide to stay a few extra (or fewer) days in order to take advantage of some kind of discount or excursion fare. Factors such as these tend to change the "mix" of the air travel market and, therefore, dilute the yield that would have been realized if everyone retained their former travel habits after a fare increase takes effect.

An example of this effect is the fact that, despite some selective fare increases that were already in effect in the fourth quarter of 1970 and, therefore, basic fares were slightly higher than they were in 1969, the passenger yield in the fourth quarter of 1970 actually was lower than in the fourth quarter of 1969. For October through December, 1970, the average yield was 5.89 cents per mile; in the same period of 1969 it was 5.97 cents—1.3 per cent higher.

Because of this fact—that airline passengers are paying less for an airline ticket, on the average, than they were 10 years ago—the cost of taking a trip by air has been held down to a level far below what it would have been had air fares gone up at the same rate as everything else in the travel package. For example the average trip to Europe by a U.S. citizen in 1970 cost about $836. But if air fares had gone up at the same rate as hotel rooms and restaurant meals in Europe, that same trip would have cost, instead of $836, almost $1700, or twice the actual cost.

Another measure of the role of air fares in holding down the cost of trips by air is the fact that between 1958 and 1970, the per cent of air fare as part of the total cost of a trip to Europe declined from just over three-quarters to just under one-half. Within the U.S. the story is the same—air fares have decreased as a per cent of the total travel package. Since 1958, the air fare has declined from 31.6 per cent of the total package to 18.7 per cent.

The Business of Airports
James H. Winchester

The airport is of pivotal importance to the airline. Most of the airports are owned and operated by municipal or other governmental agencies and so their design, adequacy, and service become a part of public finance and operation. The airlines, of course, pay landing fees, rentals, and other charges for the use of the facilities and thus are vitally interested in airport improvement and operation. Finally, the federal government is also involved in airport improvement and financing.

This selection, a series of three articles, provides a survey of airport finances and the related problems of the design and impact of airports.

U.S. AIRPORTS FLY BIG-BUSINESS TAG

For millions of people, young or old, air travelers are just plain sight-seers, airports are the most fascinating show on earth. They are also one of the nation's biggest industries.

No exact over-all figure of the total value of all airport assets in the United States exists, but there are plenty of authoritative signposts.

Recently, for example, 39 airports with commercial-airline service, representing large, medium, and small-sized cities, provided balance sheets to the Airport Operators Council, a trade group with headquarters in Washington, D.C. For each of the airports in the survey boarding more than two million passengers a year, the average value of assets was $12,194,310, with the top one reporting assets of $406,978,637.

Among the cities reporting between 500,000 and 2 million passenger boardings a year, the average airport value was $22,497,358; and for those cities with less than 500,000 passengers boarding annually, the average airport assets were $8,573,919.

Based on such figures as these and others, reliable authorities estimate the value of the nation's airport system at between $7 billion and $8 billion.

The vast majority of the 9,500 airports in the United States today, however, are without paved runways, have only primitive ground facilities or none at all, and are largely suitable only for small planes and weekend pilots. There are, however, 540 airports with scheduled airline service and two or three times that many others geared to multiengined charter, taxi, and corporate planes.

From James H. Winchester, "U.S. Airports Fly Big-Business Tag," April 21, 1971; "Revenue Bonds 'Fuel' Airports," April 22, 1971; " 'Build a Whole Area, Not Just an Airport,' " April 24, 1971. Reprinted by permission from *The Christian Science Monitor* ©1971. The Christian Science Publishing Society. All rights reserved.

Expenditures ahead

As a big business getting bigger, more than $800 million is being spent in 1971 alone by local and federal governments on U.S. airport construction and improvements, according to the Airport Operators Council. At just those airports offering scheduled airline service in the United States an estimated $4.9 billion will be spent for expansion and improvements before the end of the 1970's, and this is hardly half of an estimated $8.7 billion which the airlines say is needed to really modernize the system by 1975.

At O'Hare Airport in Chicago, where 27 million people were handled last year—making it the nation's busiest air terminal—a $200-million expansion program now is under way to accommodate the 40 million passengers expected there by 1975.

In the New York-New Jersey area, the New York Port Authority, which runs the airports, has a five-year plan to spend well over $650 million to expand and improve John F. Kennedy, LaGuardia, and Newark, and is meanwhile seeking a site for one more all-jet airport.

In addition, other great sums will also be spent in the 1970's for expansion and improvements to the several thousand general aviation and private-plane airfields in the nation which are not served by scheduled airlines.

Not included in these general airport spending figures—where the money is coming from public funds or is being raised in other ways—is another estimated $2.5 billion which the country's 18 scheduled airlines plan to spend themselves as private money to expand and improve their own facilities at U.S. airports during the 1970's, according to an Air Transport Association of America survey covering the 1968-75 period.

Typical examples: At just three airports—Houston, Kansas City, and Dallas—Braniff plans to spend $14,700,000 for new work. Delta has planned construction costing $119,720,000 for its own improvements and facilities at the 67 cities it serves. Trans World Airlines, at just New York's Kennedy and at Kansas City, is planning to spend $71,500,000.

Taking advantage of this giant-sized airport building boom are dozens of construction and engineering companies, some small but many quite large, who now specialize in airport planning and building. Among the more active ones are the king-sized Ralph M. Parsons Company in Los Angeles; Metcalf & Eddy in Boston; the Airways Engineering Corporation in Washington, D.C.; and New York City's Transplan, Inc.

Big revenue produced

Big-city airports, in particular, are big spenders, but they are also enormous revenue producers, with income totals soaring. In addition to their private investment in facilities, the scheduled airlines estimate they will pay an additional $3.3 billion for the period between 1969 and 1975 to the nation's airports just in the form of fees, rentals, and other charges, according to the Air Transport Association of America.

As centers of economic gravity within their communities, the airports, of course, stimulate general business and commerce by providing scheduled air-passenger service. At the same time they generate great spending and payrolls themselves in the actual operation of the airport complexes.

The three New York City airports, for instance, create more jobs than there are in a city the size of New Haven, Conn. John F. Kennedy Airport alone has 44,865 employees. Five hundred of them, for instance, are used only in refueling operations, feeding more than 95 million gallons of jet fuel—costing an estimated $12 1/2 million—into 16,000 aircraft every month.

More than 30,000 people are employed at San Francisco International Airport. Others: Washington National, 8,400, with an annual payroll of $70 million; Chicago's O'Hare, 17,000; Louisville, Ky., 2,380; Lambert Field, St. Louis, 5,740; Portland, Ore., 2,145.

Employment involved

Pittsburgh says that 49,938 local people are employed directly or indirectly at its airport and in related businesses, such as hotels and restaurants, and the economic impact of the airport on the area was an estimated $228 million in 1970, with more than $3 million being paid in state and local taxes.

As another economic indicator, a modern airport greatly increases the value of real estate around it. Chicago, for example, acquired its O'Hare site for as low as $400 an acre. Today the price of land in the immediate vicinity of the airport is estimated to be as high as $50,000 an acre. In 1965, large tracts of land in the Dulles airport area near Washington, D.C., were available at less than $3,000 an acre. Now land in the same vicinity is going for about $20,000 an acre.

As the economic importance of airports to their communities continues to grow, airport building, expansion, and improvement must also boom. "Airport planning, investment, and development during the 1960's did not keep pace with aeronautical demands," says Philip J. Steece, chief of the System Planning Division, Airport Service of the Federal Aviation Administration. "The result is a backlog of urgent airport-development requirements compounded by rapidly advancing aircraft technology and increasing public use of air transportation."

REVENUE BONDS "FUEL" AIRPORTS

The principal sources of funds supporting the estimated $8 billion investment in this nation's airports are revenue-bond issues of local municipalities or authorities. Federal grants-in-aid help the larger-airline airports, and federal and state grants-in-aid, bank loans, operational funds, and tax levies assist at the smaller fields.

Until the late 1950's and early 1960's, the bulk of the local-airport bonds issued, even at major hub airports such as Los Angeles and Atlanta, were general obligations, secured by the full faith and credit of the issuing municipality. Their maturity dates run typically from 10 to 14 years.

With the switchover from piston to jet planes in the 1960's, and the big jump in airline traffic, general-obligation bonds have been largely replaced by revenue bonds as the preferred method of capital financing at most major hub airports.

At five big-city airports recently surveyed, with a combined funded debt of $649 million, all but $8 million was in revenue bonds. Today, about one-third of all U.S. airport debt is in the form of general-obligation bonds and the remaining two-thirds is taken up by revenue bonds.

In mid-February, for instance, investors fully subscribed a two-part $75 million revenue issue of the new Dallas-Fort Worth Regional Airport in Texas, with serial bonds priced to yield 5 percent for the 1979 maturities to 6 percent for those due in 1986.

Financing traced

To get $25 million for a two-year construction improvement program now under way at the New Orleans International Airport, $17 million in revenue bonds were sold, backed by firm airline contracts with the New Orleans Aviation Board, which runs the field. The rest of the money came from cash reserves built up in recent years. No public funds are involved in this current construction program.

Revenue bonds have the advantage of being secured solely by the future revenues of the airport without recourse to the resources and taxing powers of the community, most of which are badly pressed for general operating money today. The bulk of major airport investment now rests largely and solidly on what the air centers generate in income themselves.

At airports with scheduled air service, the airlines contribute heavily as they pay landing fees, hangar and terminal-space rentals, ramp tiedowns, and other charges: an estimated $3.3 billion over the next five years alone.

Concessions, in all forms, are also big earners at major airports today, contributing an estimated 60 percent of airport income. The major concession producers are auto-parking lots, car rentals, and food and beverage outlets. Flight-insurance counters, as well as stores such as newsstands, also pay off big. Coin-operated devices are another bonanza, contributing an average of $116,069 in fees every year to the average large hub U.S. airport.

At Cleveland's Hopkins Airport, in a recent year, the parking lot alone returned $1,055,580 to the airport, which was almost as much as the $1,690,990 the 10 airlines serving the field paid all together. In the same year, three car-rental concessionaires paid the Cleveland airport $375,130; the restaurant and bar fees were $345,290.

Gross revenue from car-rental concessions at all U.S. airports now tops $325 million a year, and the airports collect a heavy share. In 1971, for instance, Hertz alone expects to pay about $17 million in fees to the nation's airports.

Matching grants asked

However, there are some dark clouds on the horizon. The financially hard-pressed airlines say they can't continue to prop up local airport-revenue bonds to the extent they have in the past.

During the last 10 years, the airlines, in nearly every instance of airport construction and improvement, have been required to at least partially "guarantee" local revenue bonds. This has been largely accomplished by individual airports requiring the airlines to execute long-term "user agreements"—some of them up to 40 years.

Surveys show that 74 percent of the scheduled airlines will experience difficulty during the next few years in meeting such guarantees in the way they have in the past. At the same time, says the Air Transport Association, 75 percent of the airports plan to increase their charges and assessments on the airlines in order to pay for future improvements.

For a number of years now, the federal government, through the Federal Aids to Airports Program, has been providing about $75 million a year to help out on airport construction, provided that the states and local governments receiving grants matched them.

Last year everyone agreed that these federal funds were not enough for the needed job, so Congress—with the administration's support—passed the Airport and Airways Development Act of 1970. This called for new taxes on airport users, including an increase in the existing tax on domestic tickets from 5 percent to 8 percent.

Many funds diverted

This tax program, which went into effect in mid-1970, is expected to bring in about $612.5 million in the first year. At the time the act was passed, with strong support from the aviation community, Congress declared as policy that no less than $280 million of the annual income from these new user taxes would be available each year for new airport construction, along with a similar amount to help modernize the nation's air-navigation system.

Now the airlines and the aviation community generally are crying "Foul!" The administration has chosen to divert large portions of these funds to other uses, mainly to cover administrative costs for the Federal Aviation Administration.

So far, Congress has balked at this all-out switch, but—at the same time—the administration has released only about $170 million of the promised $280 million a year for new airport construction in fiscal 1971. So far this year, there have been 562 requests from communities for airport projects, totaling $437 million.

Another point of contention with the airport operators and the airlines is that none of the old federal funds—or the promised new ones under the users' tax plan—allow for any money to be spent on the terminal area; only on the runways and associated facilities.

No funds, for example, are available for the improvement and modernization of passenger and baggage areas, cargo areas, parking lots, and other airport areas where most of the congestion problems now exist.

"Over the next five years," the Air Transport Association of America points out, "some 80 percent of the total financial needs at the nation's largest airports will be in the terminal area."

"BUILD A WHOLE AREA, NOT JUST AN AIRPORT!"

With the limited amount of funds which will be available, new ideas are going to be vital as this nation's airports get ready for annual handling of 450 million airline passengers and 18 million tons of air cargo within the next decade.

"Closer cooperation between architects, airport planners, and airlines is going to be necessary," says Stuart Tipton, president of the Air Transport Association of America. "Don't just build an airport, build a whole area. For too long a time, airports have been viewed as entities outside the community master plan, when they should have been an integral part of such planning processes.

"Compatible land-use planning is essential if the community and the airlines are to live together harmoniously. Too often, we have seen an airport built in what has been rolling farmland only to discover the real-estate developers came right behind, building homes right up to the airport fence.

Executive comments

"Everything has to be in balance. The ability of runways, taxi strips, and aircraft parking areas to handle enough takeoffs and landings, without delays, must be at least as high as the capacity of the terminal and its associated facilities, such as parking lots, to handle passengers.

"The whole complex must be served by an adequate and direct system of convenient roads, not only from downtown but from the entire metropolitan area served by the airport. To provide real economy and efficiency, all of these factors have to complement each other."

Furthermore, there is growing opinion that construction of unnecessarily grandiose and elaborate terminal buildings must stop. Says Robert F. Six, outspoken president of Continental Airlines:

"Cities throughout the country are building monuments that are concrete wastelands. It's costing a fortune, and we can't afford it. What people really want is fast check-in and better baggage handling. They're disgusted with the miserably long hike between airport ticket counters and debarkation point."

What many regard as the first fully planned airport community in the world is the new $350 million Dallas-Fort Worth Regional Airport, whose first runways and passenger terminals are scheduled to be opened in 1975.

Automation, too

Located on an 18,000-acre site straddling the line between Dallas County and Fort Worth's Tarrant County, the new air city, when fully completed, will be by far the world's largest commercial airport, able to handle more than 50 million passengers a year and more cargo than any seaport anywhere. More than $35 million in construction is already under way at the new air complex, but it will still be growing at the turn of the century.

Planning calls for an eventual 13 passenger terminals, located on both sides of a central-spine roadway that will guide surface transportation from the surrounding interstate and regional highway system into the airport. More than 200 jumbo-sized 747's, or similar-sized airliners, will be able to load and unload at the same time, and there will be convenient, covered parking for 40,000 cars.

Two fully automated air-cargo-terminal centers, each able to handle 100 giant-sized freight planes at a time, will flank the ends of the passenger-terminal complex. Completely separate STOL (short takeoff and landing) and executive aviation airfields and terminals are planned. They will operate independently of the central-airline passenger and cargo terminals.

The new airport is designed to be completely self-contained. Several hotels, with acoustically treated sleeping rooms and convention facilities, and a world trade center are planned. For airport employees, whose working hours preclude them from the convenient use of services in their own neighborhoods, there will be a special area with around-the-clock supermarkets, shops and stores, laundries, automobile service centers, barber shops, and banks.

Series of terminals

Dallas-Fort Worth is already the seventh largest commercial air center in the nation—more than 800 daily airline flights in and out—with passenger growth expanding at an annual rate of 16 percent in recent years.

One major key to coping with this flow and load is an automated, computer-controlled transit system that will enable a person to go from his parked car to an airplane with less walking than it now takes just to reach the check-in counter at most airports.

"First of all," reports Continental Airlines, one of the airlines involved in the planning of the new airport, "there will be no long terminal building. Instead there will be a series of horseshoe-shaped terminals, set on either side of a highway, with each one having its own parking areas and boarding gates for planes."

These parking areas will be connected to the terminals by automatic cars—probably running on an overhead rail of some sort. Passengers will enter these capsules and push a button indicating which terminal they want to use, and the electric-powered car will go there immediately. Other automatic equipment will shuttle baggage between parking areas, terminals, and planes.

In solving the nation's pressing airport problems, federal and state governments are going to get increased pressure to lend a stronger hand in financial aid, helping to relieve the airlines of some of the too-high cost burden they now are called upon to meet. Costs are also going to have to be at least partially controlled through more functional, less elaborate designs.

"Every community must have an airport," says the Air Transport Association of America, "if it is to have a share in the rapidly expanding commerce of the skies. It needs an airport today for exactly the same reason that it first needed a railroad station 60 or 70 years ago. And if the aviation industry is unable to handle the heavy burden of furnishing ground facilities which cannot be expected to pay for themselves in the immediate future, then governments at various levels must assume the responsibility."

---

21 The Dilemma of Aircraft Noise at Major Airports

Donald V. Harper
University of Minnesota

In recent times, there has been an increasing concern with the "quality of life." Airports are inherently noisy—a fact which, for those living nearby, diminishes that quality. As airports expand or relocate, noise becomes a fiercely debated issue.

In this article, the author discusses, in depth, the problem of airport noise: its legal aspects, its sources, its regulatory aspects, and some of its possible solutions.

Aircraft noise is an increasing problem

In the past ten years it has become clear that air transportation, like other forms of transportation, is cursed by a major nuisance factor. The factor is aircraft noise. Although there is also an air pollution problem associated with the emissions from jet aircraft engines, and there is aircraft-caused interference with radio and television reception, and there is the fear of airport neighbors that aircraft will crash into their dwellings, it is noise that has received the most attention as an undesirable by-product of air transportation. "What was once merely a major nuisance has . . . grown into a roaring calamity for millions of people living near airports. Jet noise stops conversation dead; it keeps people awake at night; it terrifies children; it can damage buildings and can lower property values."[1]

Complaints about aircraft noise are usually directed at the large jet aircraft

From the *Transportation Journal,* Spring 1971, a quarterly publication of the American Society of Traffic and Transportation, Inc. Used by permission.

operated by commercial airlines, although business-owned jets and turboprop aircraft have also drawn some criticism.[2] The main sources of jet aircraft engine noise are the roar of the jet exhaust and the whine of the compressor and fan. The roar of the jet exhaust is of concern primarily during the takeoff phase. The whine of the compressor and fan is of concern primarily during the landing approach,[3] particularly from a point some five miles from touchdown.

The severity of the noise problem on the ground is determined by the intensity of the sound, the duration of exposure to the sound, and the number of occurrences at different times of day and under various atmospheric conditions. As to frequency of exposure, four noisy flights per hour over a given location may be acceptable or tolerable but as the number of such flights increases per hour the total noise impact increases substantially and rapidly becomes intolerable. Therefore, air traffic volume as well as the kind of aircraft used is an important element in the aircraft noise problem.

The noise problem at major airports has become serious as the jet airplane is being used more and more by general aviation and has come to be the dominant kind of airline flight equipment and the amount of air traffic has risen. The total number of passengers, passenger-miles, mail, express, and freight ton-miles, and flight operations of airlines in the United States are shown in Table 1, along with the number of piston-engine, turbo-prop, and jet engine aircraft in the service of these carriers for the years 1950-1969. It can easily be seen why there is a noise problem today at major airports.

TABLE 1

Traffic and Equipment of United States Scheduled Airlines* 1950-1969

Year	Passengers (000)	Passenger-Miles (000)	Mail, Express, and Freight Ton-Miles (000)	Number of Flight Operations** (000)	Number of Piston Engine Aircraft	Number of Turbo-Prop Aircraft	Number of Jet Aircraft
1950	19,220	10,241,400	340,169	4,002	1,159	. . .	. . .
1953	31,625	18,244,683	458,190	5,384	1,367	. . .	. . .
1956	45,943	27,612,000	656,473	6,553	1,649	54	. . .
1959	55,999	36,371,800	846,427	7,353	1,531	212	84
1962	62,549	43,760,400	1,308,023	7,060	1,164	251	396
1965	94,662	68,676,500	2,303,131	7,819	875	288	712
1968	150,151	113,958,300	4,167,082	10,377	202	379	1,700
1969	159,188	125,414,200	4,690,326	10,929	120	310	1,973

*Includes domestic and international U.S. scheduled airlines except for the number of flight operations which includes non-scheduled airlines as well.
**A flight operation is one takeoff or one landing.
Sources: Civil Aeronautics Board, Federal Aviation Administration, and Air Transport Association of America.

In Table 2 are data showing the number of scheduled airline flight operations per year at the major airports in the United States in 1969. O'Hare Field in Chicago was the busiest airport with over 623,000 scheduled airline flight operations per year. Wold-Chamberlain Field in Minneapolis-St. Paul ranked nineteenth with about 137,000 operations.

TABLE 2

Number of Airline Flight Operations
at Major Airports,* 1969**

Airport	Number of Flight Operations***
O'Hare, Chicago	623,367
Los Angeles	430,413
John F. Kennedy, New York	385,529
Atlanta	335,006
San Francisco	305,284
National, Washington, D.C.	225,609
Miami	266,745
LaGuardia, New York	258,279
Dallas	251,279
Wayne, Detroit	201,941
Boston	210,217
Newark	208,079
Philadelphia	197,511
St. Louis	184,031
Pittsburgh	169,778
Denver	157,619
Cleveland	149,976
Kansas City	137,252
Minneapolis-St. Paul	137,151
Baltimore	129,093
Houston	113,978
New Orleans	110,761
Seattle	103,978
Dulles, Washington, D.C.	61,535
Midway, Chicago	30,376
City, Detroit	29,389
Willow Run, Detroit	14,660

*Includes scheduled and non-scheduled airline operations.
**Fiscal year.
***A flight operation is one takeoff or one landing.
Source: Federal Aviation Administration, *FAA Air Traffic Activity, Fiscal Year, 1969* (Washington, D.C.: U.S. Department of Transportation, Federal Aviation Administration, Office of Management Systems, 1969), pp. 33-39.

Measurement of aircraft noise

Just how much noise is necessary to create a noise problem is a matter of some dispute. It is clear that different people have different noise sensitivity and the effects on different people of a given noise level and frequency of noise varies. For some persons excessive noise can actually cause measurable medical effects[4] while for others extreme and frequent noise is no more than a minor irritation.[5]

Although there is no generally accepted definition of what constitutes excessive noise, the most common noise yardstick is the decibel (db) scale which is an expression of the sound pressure that moves the ear. The scale begins at one db, which is the weakest sound that can be picked up by a normal ear. Then the scale increases as the square of the change. The scale is in logarithmic form so that ten times the minimum is ten db and one thousand trillion the minimum is 150 db. This means that a twenty db change in aircraft noise from about 110 to 90 would be very noticeable.

The "Perceived Noise Decibel" (PNdb) scale, under which aircraft noise is frequently reported, has been widely adopted as the standard measure of the subjective loudness of noise. There is evidence that with aircraft noise below 90 PNdb there are almost no complaints. Between 90 and 105 PNdb there are some, but not many, complaints. Above 105 the volume of complaints increases rapidly with increasing PNdb levels.[6] New York, London, Oslo, and other cities have established airport noise maximums of 100 to 112 PNdb, but many experts believe that 100 PNdb is the maximum noise tolerable because, above that level, hostility to the noise source rises rapidly.[7]

As noted earlier, the aircraft noise problem increases with the frequency of takeoffs and landings and the average level of noise tolerated from each aircraft substantially decreases. One study has shown that with one occurrence per day, community noise tolerance will allow up to 115 PNdb before vigorous individual complaints and potential concerted community action appear. With 64 flights per day this drops to 97 PNdb, and with 128 flights per day the tolerability level falls to 94 PNdb.[8]

Landings represent the major noise problem for many airports. This is because landing approaches are generally less steep than climbouts after takeoffs and greater land area is exposed to low-altitude noise for a larger period of time.

Legal aspects of the aircraft noise problem

A common complaint of airport neighbors is that aircraft noise has made it difficult to sell their homes and that when they can sell their homes the price is below that which they would get if there were no noise problem. Because of the multitude of factors that determine the value of residential property, including such things as availability of public transportation, nearness to shopping facilities, accessibility to parks and other recreational facilities, the age of the house, the physical characteristics of the house, distance to schools, etc., it is always difficult to isolate the effects of one factor, such as aircraft noise.[9] Actually, while it is true that a major airport can have a negative effect on residential property value in the noise-sensitive area, it can also raise the value of commercial land in that same noise-sensitive area, and substantially raise the value of all real estate that is near the airport but not in the noise-sensitive area.

In any event, many law suits have been filed against major public airports by neighboring residents. A 1968 article reported that there were $200,000,000 in aircraft noise lawsuits outstanding in the United States.[10] "Willingness to go to court apparently varies with the increase in temperature or decrease in property values."[11] Most such suits are unsuccessful.

Injunctions

All courts agree that some residents aggrieved by substantial noise from nearby public airports should have a legal remedy but that the proper remedy is not an injunction preventing airport operations.[12] This is based on the reasoning that the general social need for public airport operations is a paramount interest. The remaining possibilities for the unhappy airport neighbor are relief on the basis of trespass or nuisance or inverse condemnation.

The trespass approach

Trespass has not been a satisfactory approach for the airport neighbor. If he sues on the basis of flights through the airspace above his land, he is thwarted by the Congressional doctrine that the landowner does not own the navigable airspace above his property. Also, since complaining property owners who reside up to several thousand feet from either side of takeoff or glide paths cannot allege any property rights in these paths, no trespass is committed against them.

The nuisance approach

The nuisance approach is also unsatisfactory. In most situations, public airports are considered to be of sufficient value to the general good to be regarded as legalized or privileged nuisances and this status provides immunity from both injunctions and some or all damage actions. The identity of the defendant, a public airport, has a lot to do with this. Such airports are generally created via statutory authorizations. They are publicly owned. The operations of the airlines using the airports are authorized and regulated by the federal government. For these reasons jet noise will not generally support a nuisance claim.[13] Thus the nuisance approach has had little success.

Inverse condemnation

The most successful legal approach has been that based on the theory of inverse condemnation or constitutional taking. Under this theory it is claimed that aircraft noise has resulted in the taking of a property right for a public use without paying just compensation and that this violates either the fourteenth or the fifth amendment of the federal constitution or a similar provision in a state constitution. The damages recoverable are limited in such cases to the loss in market value of the plaintiff's property.[14] Although many American courts agree that inverse condemnation is an appropriate theory upon which to proceed, they disagree as to whether all residents who are substantially injured should recover or whether a method of limiting the number who may recover should be used. In some courts the flights must be directly over the subject property to constitute taking. In others an overflight is not required.[15] All that is necessary is that the flights are close enough, whether or not directly overhead, to interfere substantially with the complainant's use and enjoyment of the property.[16] In any event, the number of actual damage awards and the money amount involved has been small.[17]

Responsibility for the aircraft noise problem

The responsibility for causing the aircraft noise problem at public airports rests with airport operators, the Federal Aviation Administration (FAA), the Civil Aeronautics Board (CAB), aircraft and engine manufacturers, airlines and other aircraft operators, local government, real estate developers, and property owners.

Airport operators

The first step toward creating the aircraft noise problem was unknowingly taken by airport operators when they made decisions as to where the major scheduled airline airports were to be located. Many of the major airports in the United States were located long before the jet age and the planners were unable to visualize the noise problem that would eventually develop. Consequently, airport location decisions were not made on the basis of noise pollution considerations of any major degree. A second step in creating the noise problem was the failure of airport management (and local and state government) to zone the land around major airports to control the use of land to prevent noise-sensitive land users from acquiring such land.

Whatever might have been airport management's role in creating the aircraft noise problem, it finds itself today as the chief target of anti-noise groups and the lawsuits involving the noise question are filed against the local airport.[18] The situation of the airport operators is a rather difficult one primarily because, although they are the target of the anti-noise sentiment, they cannot completely solve the noise problem themselves because much of the problem is beyond their control. Airport management does not decide what kinds of aircraft will be purchased by airlines, the number of airlines that will be authorized to serve a given airport (although airport operators often encourage additional air service to their airports), the number of flights scheduled to and from a given airport, the flight procedures followed by the airlines and the FAA, or, in many cases, the use of land around the airport. Airport operators do not have full control even over the configuration of their own airports. Runway layout is determined primarily by the direction of the prevailing winds since aircraft must land and take off into the wind for reasons of safety. A principal area of control that the airport operator does have is over the procedures followed by the airlines and others in operating their aircraft when on the ground. Unfortunately, noise-abatement procedures and regulations for ground operations can have only limited impact on the total noise problem.

Noise standards

It has been suggested that airport management can directly influence the aircraft noise problem by setting up noise standards for aircraft it will allow to use its facilities. This has been done to some degree in New York City where no jet aircraft may land or take off at any Port Authority airport without permission (adopted in 1951). Also, the Port Authority regulations permit a maximum of 112 PNdb on takeoffs from its airports. This is a liberal ceiling on noise since it is above the point (about 105 PNdb) where complaints are serious. The 112 PNdb was adopted to provide for a noise level that was no greater than the noise produced by 75.0 per cent of the four-engine large piston aircraft.[19] The fact that there have been lawsuits filed against the Port Authority since the noise limit was imposed indicates that 112 PNdb is unacceptable to a significant number of people. Should an airport operator decide to impose a PNdb limit of, say, 90, aside from the possible legal difficulties involved in such a move,[20] the single airport operator could not realistically be expected on its own to do this and thus bar certain aircraft entirely from its facilities. To do so would mean that all present jet aircraft used by airlines would be barred and would definitely discourage airlines from serving that airport. This would, in turn, reduce substantially the air service to the community and also reduce the economic and social benefits of the airport to the community. Barring certain aircraft by *all* major airports collectively and simultaneously could force the airlines, the aircraft and engine manufacturers, and the federal government to come up with solutions to the noise problem. However, such action would be drastic and has not been forthcoming.

Banning or limiting night flights

It has been suggested that airport management can and should ban or limit flights at night. Again, a single airport management would find it difficult to go it alone on such a move unless an alternate airport were available.[21] It would disrupt airline operations and harm the local economy where the airport is located. If, on the other hand, all major airports would collectively and simultaneously limit or ban night flights, then more success could be achieved in the sense that the night aircraft noise would be reduced or eliminated and at the same time the airlines and aircraft and engine manufacturers and the federal government would be encouraged to act faster in reducing aircraft noise.[22]

Airport operators have been hesitant to take steps to control the number and type of aircraft using their facilities. An executive of an airport operators' organization has said:

> Lawyers will differ as to the airport operators' authority to control or not control the numbers and types of aircraft that operate from the airport.
>
> Another aspect of the problem is that under certain circumstances some airports have contractual relations with some of the airline users that may also impose certain restrictions on what would otherwise be the basic landlord rights of the airport operator.
>
> However, even if the airport operators had complete and free powers to control the use of their airport by different types of aircraft, it probably wouldn't be the best answer . . . A solution on a national basis probably would be more useful for both the airports and the aircraft operators . . ."[23]

What airport operators can do

In a realistic sense, the individual airport operator can deal with the aircraft noise problem by (1) instituting ground operations regulations; (2) encouraging the airlines and the FAA to make use of noise-abatement flight procedures; (3) providing runway configurations and lengths that will minimize the noise problem; (4) encouraging and cooperating with noise-abatement organizations; (5) explaining to the neighboring public the causes of aircraft noise and what is being done about it by the airport, the airlines, the FAA, and others; (6) encouraging local government to control land use around the airport where it is still possible; (7) attempting to influence Congress, the airlines, the FAA, the CAB, and aircraft and engine manufacturers to work to reduce the problem; (8) discouraging the use of the airport for airline training flights; (9) giving high priority to the noise problem as a factor in determining the location of any new airports; (10) encouraging and/or participating in land-use studies in airport areas; and (11) encouraging the use of soundproofing and other construction improvements in noise-sensitive areas.

Thus, although airport management cannot by itself solve the aircraft noise problem and most airport operators have shown a lack of interest in doing anything about it, there are certain things that airport management can do in a positive way which can reduce it and help people to understand it. Examples are found of airport operators who have worked hard to alleviate the noise problem. The Los Angeles Department of Airports has actively participated in the Los Angeles Sound Abatement Coordinating Committee and is the fiscal sponsor of the programs the Committee proposes. Such projects have included a pilot project to determine if it is structurally and economically feasible to insulate dwellings against jet aircraft noise and an experiment to develop a glass fiber sound shield designed to lessen the roar of jet engines in ground test runups at night.[24] The Department of Airports has also spent millions of dollars "to help study and solve the problem of noise impact on several schools" near the major airport.[25] The Department has also issued regulations banning east takeoffs at night except under certain wind conditions, ordered flight procedures on west takeoffs, established rules for ground runups of jet engines at night, made runway improvements to reduce the noise problem, and has worked with the city of Los Angeles toward the goal of rezoning property around Van Nuys (general aviation) Airport.[26] The Los Angeles airport commissioners have recently adopted a new Los Angeles International Airport development plan that will create a freeway loop around its perimeter, improving vehicle access to terminal facilities and establishing a more effective noise buffer between runways and the neighboring residential community of Westchester.[27]

Although Los Angeles is more seriously affected by the noise problem than are most major airports and the pressure to do something about noise has been great in that city, the actions of the airport authorities there illustrate that airport operators can be activists in the campaign against excessive aircraft noise and that some meaningful results can be obtained.

The FAA

Authority to curb aircraft noise

As one of its several responsibilities under the Federal Aviation Act, the FAA has the authority to issue certificates for aircraft, aircraft engines, and propellers if it is found that such aircraft, aircraft engine, or propeller is of proper design, material specification, construction, and performance for safe operation. The FAA may also prescribe in the certificates issued any terms, conditions, and limitations as are required in the interest of safety.[28] The FAA also has the authority to certify the airworthiness of aircraft. Such certificate shall be issued by the FAA if the aircraft conforms to the type certificate applied for and the aircraft is in condition for safe operation. The FAA may also prescribe any terms, conditions, and limitations as are required in the interest of safety.[29]

It is clear that the Federal Aviation Act empowers the FAA to determine whether or not aircraft and aircraft engines shall be permitted to be used in the United States and that the objective of such control is safety. The FAA has felt that aircraft noise is not a safety factor and, therefore, it was not authorized under the Act to accept or reject aircraft and aircraft engines on the basis of noise considerations. Consequently, the noise factor was not part of FAA deliberations on any jet aircraft or engine that is now in use. This means that an important method of controlling aircraft noise was not used.[30] Certainly, if the FAA could have and would have used its certification power to require that aircraft and engines be relatively quiet, the aircraft and engine manufacturing industry and the airlines would have had incentive to try to come up with quieter aircraft than we have had. Instead of designing engines first and trying to silence them later, they would have been encouraged to design quieter engines first and then modify them upward in power. In the absence of such control by the FAA, however, there were no regulatory restrictions on noise and engines were designed and built on the basis of efficiency and economy with no important consideration of the noise problems they would bring about.

The question arises as to whether the FAA did or did not in fact have the power to consider the noise factor in its certification process. The FAA says it didn't think it had such power. It preferred to handle the noise problem through voluntary cooperation among the aircraft and engine manufacturing industry, airlines, and airport operators, and by conducting research. In 1967 the FAA created the Office of Noise Abatement to handle its noise-abatement program.

Certainly, the emphasis in the certification section of the Federal Aviation Act is on safety and not on nuisance factors such as noise. However, if there had been a genuine interest in the noise problem on the part of the FAA that agency might have at least tried to construe its powers to include noise abatement. The certification section of the Act could possibly be interpreted to include noise as a certification factor since noisy aircraft lead to use of "noise-abatement" flight procedures such as steeper glide paths on landings, sharp turns on takeoffs, and using crosswind runways on occasion, that many airline pilots claim are unsafe procedures. Therefore, could not the use of noise as a certification factor result in elimination of "unsafe" noise-abatement procedures and hence be interpreted to be in the interest of safety and thus a valid exercise of the powers given to the FAA under the certification provision of the Act?

Even if the FAA did not wish to use the certification section of the Act, it might have recognized that the part of the Act that deals with the general powers and duties of the FAA (Section 307 (c)) specifically states that the FAA is authorized and directed to prescribe air traffic rules and regulations governing the flight of aircraft for the protection of persons and property on the ground. "Protection of persons and property on the ground" can be interpreted to mean protection from excessive noise. Presumably, the FAA could have used this power to try to do something about aircraft noise when exercising its certification power.

Legislation of 1968

In the summer of 1968, to a great extent as a result of efforts by a study group established by President Lyndon B. Johnson,[31] Congress enacted into law legislation which specifically gives to the FAA the authority to consider noise as a certification factor.[32] The law gives to the FAA the authority to prescribe and amend standards for the measurement of aircraft noise and prescribe and amend such rules that it may find necessary to provide for the control and abatement of aircraft noise. The law specifically adds noise reduction as a criterion for issuance and revocation of certificates relating to aircraft. The law also contains a provision granting the FAA authority to require "retrofitting" of existing aircraft to bring them into conformity with new regulations but there is a requirement that the FAA weigh any proposed regulation on three main counts. These are (1) whether it is technically practicable, (2) whether it is consistent with the highest degree of safety, and (3) whether it is "economically reasonable." The National Transportation Safety Board also has review power over any FAA noise reduction rule.[33]

FAA regulations of 1969

In November, 1969, the FAA issued its first regulations under its new authority, to be effective December 1, 1969. Found to be generally disappointing to anti-noise groups, the FAA regulations apply only to the new "jumbo" jets—Boeing 747, Lockheed L-1011, and Douglas DC-10. Depending upon the size and type of aircraft a maximum of 93 to 108 "Effective Perceived Noise Decibels" (EPNdb)[34] will be allowed on takeoffs and landings. Since noise generation doubles with each additional ten EPNdb, the regulation can reduce the noise generated by one-half the current noise level produced by pre-jumbo jet aircraft of 110 to 120 EPNdb. However, the regulations will not be strictly applied to the Boeing 747A, an airplane that was already in production and the first issue of which appeared early in 1970, because Boeing applied for certification of the 747A one year before the FAA began drafting its noise rules and was too far along in production. The 747A will only have to meet a provision requiring that its noise output be reduced to the lowest levels that are "economically reasonable, technologically practical, and appropriate to the particular type of design." The stretched version of the 747, the 747B, will be required to meet the established standards by January 1, 1972.

Since the regulations do not apply to aircraft already in service on December 1, 1969, there will be no immediate noise reduction as a result of the FAA rules, although the 747A is significantly more quiet than its predecessors and the FAA may issue regulations for existing aircraft in the future. It will be some time before the FAA, the object of considerable pressure from aircraft manufacturers, airlines, airport operators, anti-noise enthusiasts, political figures, and others, effectively uses its power to control aircraft noise. A major barrier is the fact that the FAA must weigh any noise control requirement on the basis of whether it will be "economically reasonable." This factor had a lot to do with exempting the 747A from the current rules and the unwillingness of the FAA to as yet require retrofitting of pre-747 aircraft since the cost of doing so will be quite high. In the meantime the noise problem will continue. Had the FAA been able and willing to use its certification power or if Congress had specifically given it such power before the first jet aircraft were produced or at least before the second generation of jet aircraft were produced, the present crisis might have been much less severe.

The CAB

The CAB has responsibility for economic regulation of air transportation and, as part of that responsibility, certifies scheduled airlines to serve given cities in the United States.[35] Although the CAB may attach terms, conditions, and limitations to such certificates of public convenience as necessary that "the public interest may require," the Board has not done so in terms of noise abatement. The Act does not require that noise be part of the CAB's deliberations in certificate cases and the CAB has not felt that economic regulation of air transportation includes regulation of noise produced by the airlines certificated by the Board. The CAB has thus concluded that aircraft noise has to do mainly with the character of the aircraft, an FAA problem, rather than with whether or not a given airline should serve a given point.

The CAB, nevertheless, is partly responsible for the aircraft noise crisis that exists today. Leaving aside any further discussion of whether or not the CAB could or should impose compliance with noise-abatement requirements as a condition for the receiving of a CAB certificate, the Board, by having control over the number of air *carriers* serving an airport, also has control over the number of *flights* in and out of a given airport because the more carriers that serve a given point, the more flights there will be. Since the CAB and the FAA usually do not try to control the number of flights scheduled by the airlines certificated by the Board,[36] the carriers are free to schedule as they see fit. This means that, on multi-carrier routes, such as New York to Chicago or Chicago to the Twin Cities, each airline schedules to get the largest share of the available traffic and the philosophy tends to be that the more flights the better. The result is an excessive number of scheduled flights, more flight operations at the airports involved, lower load factors[37] for the carriers, and more noise than would be the case if fewer carriers served the route in question. Because the CAB has frequently authorized additional air carriers to serve routes already served by one or more carriers, the Board has added to the noise problem. If the CAB believes that multi-carrier service over a given route is desirable and in the public interest, it should be provided but, at the same time, some government control of the number of flights, either through the CAB or the FAA, should also be provided in order to ease the noise problem and also to assist in boosting airline load factors and reducing the amount of airport congestion.

In addition to the multi-carrier route problem created by the CAB, there is the general problem of the CAB certificating too much service to and from certain airports such as those at Chicago and New York. This is an involved problem and is not discussed further here.

Aircraft and engine manufacturers and airlines

Given the unwillingness of most airport operators to do much about aircraft noise and the unwillingness or inability of the FAA and the CAB to do much about it in a direct sense, the manufacturers of aircraft and engines have been left to emphasize cost, speed, and efficiency factors rather than environmental factors when developing new aircraft. The airlines and other operators had little incentive to insist on quiet aircraft and, as a result, purchased what was available and what was available was noisy.

One could argue that if the manufacturers and airlines were really interested in the welfare of the public they could have worked on the noise problem without the compulsion of legislation or regulation. The fact is that some of these companies have tried to develop quieter aircraft. Many others, however, have expressed interest in reducing aircraft noise but have neglected to do anything because technological change in aircraft engines to reduce noise would be too costly to them. This latter view demonstrates why the failure of the FAA to act on the noise question proved to be so important.

Other contributors to the
aircraft noise problem

Most major airports, when originally constructed, were located in sparsely settled areas and were without close neighbors in any important number. An opportunity was available to zone the land to prevent land use by noise-sensitive users such as schools, home owners, hospitals, rest homes, churches, and so on. The airport managers could have accomplished this zoning by acquiring the land in question and then restricting its use to non-noise-sensitive uses. This was not usually done so it was then up to local (and state) government to control the use of the land. This also was generally not done and the result was that houses, churches, schools, etc. were allowed to be built right up to the airport fences. One author reports that the projected high noise level around John F. Kennedy Airport in New York already includes about 35,000 dwelling units, at least twenty-two public schools, and several dozen churches and clubs. At Los Angeles International Airport the projected high noise level area includes 47,000 dwelling units, thirty-three public schools, and a score or more churches plus at least three hospitals and a college.[38]

Contributing to this were the real estate developers who were more interested in the sale of the land than in environmental questions. In addition, no attempt was usually made by them to provide special insulation or other soundproofing for the new buildings near airports. Perhaps it is too much to expect that real estate developers have any responsibility for such environmental questions.[39]

Lastly, the individual home owner, school district, church congregation, etc. is also at fault for not knowing better than to build or buy in a noise-sensitive area, although real estate developers and agents are partly at fault here, at least in the case of the residential problem, for falsely minimizing the noise problem in their sales messages and showing property only when the "other" runway was being used or on a particularly "quiet" day. In the words of one author:

"People seem to have a mysterious moth-flame attraction to noise centers. In the early days of railroads towns were strung out along the tracks as if everyone were trying to get his share of the soot and rattle. But Federal housing officials are convinced that for the most part people buy houses near airports either out of ignorance . . . or as victims of real-estate hucksters who show them the houses during the hours of least traffic and when the wind is blowing favorably.[40]

Solutions to the aircraft noise problem

Reducing or ending the aircraft noise problem is especially difficult to accomplish because of the fact that there is a multi-responsibility for its creation and also for its solution. The ideal solution could be reached faster if there were participation and cooperation by all those responsible for the problem in the first place. This would require participation and cooperation by airport operators, the FAA, the CAB, aircraft and engine manufacturers, airlines and other aircraft operators, local (and state) government, real estate developers, and present and future property owners. All of these people could contribute to solving the problem.

Noise-reduction technology

The simplest solution in terms of least disruption of existing ways of doing things is to make the aircraft quiet by somehow muffling the noise emitted by the jet engines. This would mean that aircraft still to be built would be built with quiet engines and aircraft now in use would be retrofitted by acoustic treatment of the engine nacelles or by nacelle redesign. The FAA may eventually require that these steps be taken. The primary obstacles to retrofitting at present are the high cost of retrofitting existing aircraft and the doubt expressed by some experts as to whether a satisfactory noise level can be attained at all through retrofitting.

Various retrofitting costs have been suggested by various authorities. The estimated cost of acoustical treatment of engine nacelles varies from about $500,000 to about $1,000,000 per aircraft (varying with the number of engines and the kind of aircraft). Total retrofitting cost for the nation's scheduled airline jet fleet has been estimated to be as high as $2,000,000,000. In addition to the retrofitting cost itself, there are possible additional operating costs caused by reduced aircraft range, higher maintenance costs, and increased fuel consumption. An important unanswered question is how the costs of retrofitting are to be paid and by whom—the airlines, the federal government, the airlines' customers?

As to the effectiveness of retrofitting existing aircraft, the only thing agreed upon seems to be that existing aircraft will never be made "quiet" but that they can be made "less noisy." The maximum expectation appears to be that retrofitting will reduce noise by about ten PNdb from the present average of about 118 or 120 PNdb. This reduction of ten PNdb can result in a 50.0 per cent reduction in noise. This would be of considerable help and still would leave the aircraft fairly noisy but perhaps tolerable. Actually, the noise reduction attained will vary as between landings and takeoffs. Tests made by McDonnell Douglas show the noise reduction on a short-duct DC-8 to be 10.5 to 12 EPNdb on landing approach, depending on weight, and reduced takeoff noise to be 3.5 EPNdb. Tests by Boeing on a full-length duct 707 showed landing noise cut by 15.5 EPNdb and takeoff noise cut by 3 EPNdb.[41]

Consequently, retrofitting may alleviate the problem to a considerable degree but it awaits a decision from the FAA to require its introduction and determine how it should be paid for. It also awaits the rather long time required to retrofit all existing jet aircraft used by scheduled airlines. It appears very unlikely that retrofitting of all or most of the noisy jets could be accomplished before the end of the 1970's. New aircraft will make their appearance in the 1970's but, even if they have relatively quiet engines, the predominant share of the aircraft fleet will still be excessively noisy through the decade. Beyond that time the combination of retrofitting, the new and presumably quiet large jet aircraft and the introduction of short-takeoff-and-landing (STOL) and vertical-takeoff-and-landing (VTOL) aircraft for short-range flights could conceivably solve the noise problem. Although aircraft and engine technology may be the ultimate solution to the aircraft noise problem, it must wait several more years before its impact can begin to be felt.

Noise-abatement flight procedures

While awaiting the elimination of the aircraft noise problems through technology, certain noise-abatement flight procedures can be followed to reduce the amount and frequency of noise although not eliminating it or even making it completely acceptable. Noise-abatement procedures are primarily the responsibility of the local FAA and the airlines but local airport management can encourage their institution as can anti-noise groups, property owners, etc.

Noise-abatement flight procedures include (1) using "preferred" or "preferential" runways—those that cause the least noise problem and the fewest complaints—whenever wind conditions permit, (2) requiring turns away from noise-sensitive neighborhoods after takeoff and/or sharp cutback in thrust during the climb, (3) requiring the steepest landing glide slopes that are consistent with safe operation to increase the altitude of aircraft over a given location, (4) reduction in gross weight which reduces the amount of power needed, (5) requiring pilots to use low power at low altitudes, and (6) the removal of airline flight training from noise-problem airports.

Such procedures can and do have some effect on aircraft noise but in themselves will not solve the noise problem. Airline pilots are not in agreement with some of the procedures because of their safety implications.[42] Such procedures are, of course, abandoned when weather or other conditions do not permit their safe use.

Local legislation

Some communities have attempted to deal with the aircraft noise problem by passing laws that limit or prohibit flights over a given area or limit or prohibit flights below a certain altitude over a given area. Sometimes maximum noise levels permitted have been established. Courts have found such local ordinances to be unenforceable, however, on the ground that the allocation of air space is within the jurisdiction of the federal government, not the local government.[43] If their legality were upheld, such legislation would seriously disrupt air traffic and be of serious economic and social consequence to the community involved. This would lead to great reluctance to actually enforce them.

Control of land use

A solution to the aircraft noise problem is to move the people away from the airport and the noise. For existing airports this means either zoning of unused land areas to prevent residential and other noise-sensitive uses or purchase of land already occupied by noise-sensitive users and turning the land over to non-sensitive use.

In the case of most existing major airports it is too late to zone most of the adjacent land area because it is already in use, and zoning cannot be made retroactive. However, where some unoccupied land does exist it can be taken over by the airport itself or can be zoned by local government to prevent noise-sensitive use. Unfortunately, local government has not shown much interest in this kind of zoning in the past.[44] Although most major airports were originally located in thinly-populated outskirts of metropolitan areas, the lack of land-use control, the geographical growth of cities, the movement to the suburbs, the tendency of airports to attract real estate developers, and the expansion of the size of the airports, have brought more and more residents into areas adjoining airports.

It is unfortunately true that efforts to date to persuade local authorities to refuse building permits for homes, or even apartment houses, under approach paths have frequently been futile—even where residents already living near the building site had suits pending against the airports for noise annoyance.[45]

The other land-use alternative is for the airport operator or the local government to purchase the occupied noise-sensitive land area adjacent to the airport and convert the land to non-sensitive use. This has been done to some degree in Los Angeles and several other cities. Unfortunately, the value of the land adjacent to airports is often quite high (some of the country's best residential neighborhoods are involved) and the amount of land involved is large—the noise-sensitive area extends from five to ten miles from the end of a runway and is several thousand feet wide. Consequently, the amount of money needed is great and airport operators and local governments ordinarily do not have access to funds of that kind for that purpose. However, it is conceivable that, if law suits against airports begin to be a serious cost burden, it may eventually be cheaper to buy up adjacent real estate.

In any event, land-use control at existing major airports can be accomplished to only a limited degree. The opportunity to do this on a significant scale has long since passed in most cases. Therefore, land-use control can be an important solution to the noise problem primarily at new major airports rather than at existing airports. In selecting the site for a new airport, care should be taken to consider carefully the noise consequences, to design the airport to minimize the noise problem, to locate the airport where land around it is not yet developed, and to provide for local government or airport management control over land use around the airport.

There is some question whether even at new airports local governments are willing to and are capable of providing adequate land-use planning. Zoning power is held by several government units in some cases and housing developers often carry considerable weight with local zoning authorities. If the FAA would require compatible land-use zoning as a condition for grants to airport operators under the Federal Airport Act, better zoning would be encouraged.[46]

Move the airport

One solution offered in desperation by anti-noise groups is to close down the airport and/or move the airline traffic to a new location. This can be done and has been done in some cases. However, the investment in most major airports is so great that it is deemed not wise to close down completely or to bar airline traffic if noise is the only problem. If the airport is obsolete and/or excessively congested, however, then the noise problem can add incentive to move to a new location and can, in fact, help considerably in getting such a decision made. Unfortunately, construction of a new major airport requires seven to ten years so that, even if a decision to move is made, noise relief is not immediate. In any event, the noise problem has become important in decisions as to whether existing airports should be further developed or closed down and also where new airports should be built.

Other solutions

Additional solutions that have been proposed are appropriate mainly for existing airports. One such proposed solution is soundproofing of existing and newly constructed buildings, including underground construction. This could be required by local ordinance or tax deductions could be offered to those who do it voluntarily.[47] Another suggestion is that shrubbery and trees around buildings can be used to muffle aircraft sound.

A third proposal is that the airport management lease the right to make noise for a stated period of time, perhaps two or three years. At the end of the period the property owner would be required to prove loss of value suffered from noise and payment would be made by the airport which, in turn, would pass the cost off to the airlines using that airport. The advantages of this plan are supposed to be that it would compensate all owners harmed by noise, it would encourage proper location of airports, and it would encourage the airlines and aircraft and engine manufacturers to develop quiet aircraft. The philosophy behind this interesting idea is that those who make noise should pay for the right to make noise.[48]

A fourth proposal is that the federal government through an act of Congress be made solely liable for takings due to jet noise at public airports.[49]

These proposals do not offer solutions to the noise problem but rather are an attempt to make aircraft noise more acceptable or to fairly compensate those who are injured by it.

A final comment

It is clear that the problem of aircraft noise is a very serious one which is likely to become much worse at most major airports before it becomes better. It is also clear that because there is multiple responsibility for causing the problem, there must be multiple responsibility for finding solutions to it. As far as airport operators are concerned, their attitude in most cases has been that they are neither responsible for causing the problem nor for solving it, and that one must look elsewhere, particularly to aircraft technology and to the federal government, for the solution. The failure of many airport operators to face up to the question of aircraft noise and to try to do something about it and to educate the public about the subject, has helped to not only worsen the problem but to contribute greatly to the lack of understanding of the problem by the general public and to the animosity felt by airport neighbors toward the local airport management.

NOTES

1. "The Racket That Won't Go Away," *Business Week*, March 16, 1968, p. 130.
2. Robert L. Parrish, "LA Girds for Jet-Noise Showdown," *American Aviation*, January 6, 1969, p. 23.
3. Jet Aircraft Noise Panel, *Alleviation of Jet Aircraft Noise Near Airports*, (Washington, D.C.: U.S. Government Printing Office, 1966), p. 5.
4. Among the medical consequences of excessive noise suggested are contraction of arteries, increase in heart beat, dilation of pupils of the eyes, heart disease, mental illness, stomach ulcers, allergies, enuresis (involuntary urination), spinal meningitis, excessive cholesterol in the arteries, indigestion, loss of equilibrium, and impaired vision. John H. Mecklin, "It's Time to Turn Off All that Noise," *Fortune*, October, 1969, p. 132.
5. For a discussion of how noise affects different people see Karl D. Kryter, "Evaluation of Psychological Reactions of People to Aircraft Noise," in Jet Aircraft Noise Panel, *op. cit.*
6. *Ibid.*, p. 5.
7. "Jet Noise in Airport Areas: A National Solution Required," *Minnesota Law Review*, May, 1967, footnote 59, p. 1098.
8. Karl D. Kryter, *op. cit.*, p. 22.
9. Such attempts have been made. See, for example, Frank C. Emerson, *The Determinants of Residential Value With Special Reference to the Effects of Aircraft Nuisance and Other Environmental Features*, Ph.D. Dissertation (Minneapolis: University of Minnesota, 1969) and Newell N. Nelson, *A Study of the Effect of Airports on the Value of Adjacent Real Estate for the Minneapolis-St. Paul Metropolitan Airports Commission*, April, 1968.
10. Charles M. Haar, "Airport Noise and the Urban Dweller," *The Appraisal Journal*, October, 1968, p. 551.
11. *Ibid.*
12. This discussion of the legal implications of aircraft noise is based in good part on that in "Jet Noise in Airport Areas: A National Solution Required," *op. cit.*, pp. 1088-1097; Charles M. Haar, *ibid.*; and Lyman M. Tondel, Jr., "Noise Litigation at Public Airports," in Jet Aircraft Noise Panel, *op. cit.*
13. Charles M. Haar, *ibid.*; p. 553.
14. Recovery has been allowed in the only two cases the United States Supreme Court has decided involving loss of property value due to aircraft noise. These are *United States v. Causby*, 328 U.S. 256 (1945) (noise from military overflights destroyed chicken busi-

ness) and *Griggs v. County of Allegheny,* 326 U.S. 84 (1962) (noise from commercial landings and takeoffs depreciated property value). The Griggs case also established that neither the airlines nor the federal government are liable but that liability rests with local government which picks the site of the airport.

15. In the two cases decided by the United States Supreme Court, overflights were involved. The issue of taking without overflights has never been presented to that Court.

16. There are several unanswered questions associated with inverse condemnation. One is whether or not a given property owner should be compensated more than once if aircraft noise damage continues for a certain length of time, or does a given damage award cover all future as well as past damage? What if the damage becomes more severe as a result of increased volume and frequency of air traffic?

17. Lyman M. Tondel, Jr. reports that between 1955 and 1965 damages were recovered in only six cases. In five of them a total of $71,584 was recovered against airport operators on a constitutional taking theory, and in one $12,500 was recovered against Lockheed Aircraft Corporation on a nuisance theory (test flights were involved). In addition, $690,670 was recovered in twenty-one cases brought against the United States government in situations involving military airports. Twenty of these were on a constitutional taking theory and one was on a negligence theory. There were many more cases in which there was no recovery. See Lyman M. Tondel, Jr., *op. cit.,* pp. 123-124. In a recent case in Los Angeles, a Superior Court awarded damages of $740,000 to owners of 632 parcels of land in amounts ranging from $400 to $6,000 each. *Aaron v. City of Los Angeles,* Number 837799 California Superior Court, Los Angeles County, February 5, 1970. The case is now under appeal.

18. Paul K. Dygert argues that the costs of airport noise should be paid by the local airport management and then be charged to those airport users for whose benefit the noise costs have been incurred. See "A Public Enterprise Approach to Jet Aircraft Noise Around Airports," in Jet Aircraft Noise Panel, *op. cit.*

19. The British Ministry of Aviation has adopted maximum levels of 110 PNdb for daytime aircraft operations and 100 PNdb at night.

20. The Port of New York Authority has successfully imposed its liberal noise level and other restrictions. According to a Port Authority spokesman, the legality of the restrictions is based on the right of a landowner to control the activities of those who use his facilities—activities for which the airport operator might be held liable to property owners in adjacent communities. See Sidney Goldstein, "A Problem in Federalism, Property Rights in Air Space and Technology," in Jet Aircraft Noise Panel, *op. cit.,* p. 136. Port Authority regulation of runway use was upheld in *Port of New York Authority v. Eastern Air Lines, Inc.,* 259 F. Supp. 745 (1966). Another factor is that Port Authority rules and regulations are expressly subordinate to FAA rules and regulations. If, however, a legal challenge were made specifically against the Port Authority's noise level ceiling, there is some doubt that the regulation would be upheld. Noise-abatement flight procedures have been worked out between the Port Authority, the FAA, and the airlines and hence no legal challenge has been made.

21. The Port Authority of New York has banned the use of certain runways at John F. Kennedy Airport by jet aircraft after 10:00 P.M. unless wind conditions make it necessary, but other runways are available. There is a night curfew on jet aircraft at the FAA's Washington National Airport but Dulles Airport is available for such night flights.

22. There is also the possible problem that banning or limiting night flight operations could be applied legally only against takeoffs and not landings because the former originate on airport property and the latter are originally executed off the airport premises and to regulate them would be undue interference with interstate commerce. See *American Airlines, Inc. et al., the Port of New York Authority et al., Charles Ruby et al. v. Town of Hempstead et al.,* 272 F. Supp. 226 (1966).

23. E. Thomas Burnard, Executive Vice President, Airport Operators Council International,

Inc. in *Hearings Before the Aviation Subcommittee of the Committee on Commerce,* United States Senate, 90th Congress, First Session (Washington, D.C.: U.S. Government Printing Office, 1968), pp. 75-76.

24. Fred S. Hunter, "LA Studies House Insulation as Way to Decrease Jet Noise," *American Aviation,* September 16, 1968, p. 28.

25. Robert L. Parrish, *op. cit.,* p. 24.

26. Francis T. Fox, "Consideration of the Problems Arising From the Effects of Jet Engine Sounds and Recommended Solutions," in Jet Aircraft Noise Panel, *op. it.* Because the airlines agreed to comply with the flight procedures required by the Department of Airports, no legal challenge has been made against them.

27. A five-year program outlined in the plan also includes land acquisition for buffer zones around the airport.

28. *Federal Aviation Act of 1958,* Section 603(a).

29. *Federal Aviation Act of 1958,* Section 603(c).

30. Federal officials, including those at the FAA and the CAB, have been aware of the seriousness of the aircraft noise problem for many years. They received a warning in the President's Airport Commission's report (Doolittle Report) of 1952 entitled *The Airport and Its Neighbors* (Washington, D.C.: U.S. Government Printing Office). However, most federal officials did not show much interest in the problem until recently. See Robert Sherrill, "The Jet Noise is Getting Awful," *The New York Times Magazine,* January 14, 1968. In 1969 the federal Department of Transportation signed a contract with a research firm for the latter to conduct a twenty-month study of the transportation noise-generation problem (all modes) and its potential abatement. See "Contract Awarded by DOT For Study of Transportation Noise-Generation Problem," *Traffic World,* May 31, 1969, p. 39.

31. See President Lyndon B. Johnson, *Message on Transportation to Congress,* (Washington, D.C.: U.S. Government Printing Office, March 2, 1966).

32. Public Law 90-411.

33. For a description of this law see "Aircraft Noise Abatement Bill Awaits LBJ Signature; 'Retrofit' to be Required," *Traffic World,* July 20, 1968, p. 84.

34. EPNdb is a computed value taking into account the actual sound pressure level on the human ear, plus the duration of the noise in pure tones, such as the screeching noises jet engines make.

35. *Federal Aviation Act of 1958,* Section 401.

36. Except at certain hours at New York, Washington, D.C., and Chicago airports since June, 1969.

37. Percentage of available seats occupied.

38. Charles M. Haar, *op. cit.,* p. 555. This problem has been of particular importance in New York. See, for example, "Airport Area Housing Criticized," *Aviation Week and Space Technology,* November 13, 1967, p. 55.

39. The federal Department of Housing and Urban Development has established a policy of not authorizing federal government-backed loans for construction of homes or federal grants for water and sewage projects in areas where noise exceeds certain levels.

40. Robert Sherrill, *op. cit.,* p. 77.

41. *Aviation Daily,* December 3, 1969, p. 191, and Michael L. Yaffee, "FAA Noise Certification Seen Inevitable," *Aviation Week and Space Technology,* November 25, 1968, p. 39.

42. See "FAA Fears Political Tug of War on Noise Abatement Programs," *Aviation Week and Space Technology,* December 5, 1966, p. 36. See also statement of Airline Pilots Association in *Hearings Before the Aviation Subcommittee of the Committee on Commerce, op. cit.,* pp. 157-159, and Charles H. Ruby, "Operational Procedures," in Jet Aircraft Noise Panel, *op. cit.*

43. Examples are *Allegheny Airlines et al., Port of New York Authority et al. v. Village of Cedarhurst,* 238 F. (2d) 812 (1956); *American Airlines et al., v. City of Audubon Park, Kentucky,* 407 F. (2) 1306 (1969); and *American Airlines et al., Port of New York*

Authority et al., Charles H. Ruby et al. v. Town of Hempstead et al., 272 F. Supp. 226 (1966).

44. The legal difficulties in zoning in airport areas are discussed in Marshall T. Bohannon, "Airport Easements," *Virginia Law Review,* February, 1968, and Robert L. Randall, "Possibilities of Achieving a Quiet Society," in Jet Aircraft Noise Panel, *op. cit.*

45. Lyman M. Tondel, Jr., *op. cit.,* p. 120.

46. "Jet Noise in Airport Areas: A National Solution Required," *op. cit.,* p. 1107. This was suggested in Jet Aircraft Noise Panel, *op. cit.,* pp. 6-7. Since 1964 the Federal Airport Act requires the FAA to require airport sponsors to satisfy it that "appropriate action" has been or will be taken, "to the extent reasonable," to restrict the use of land in the vicinity to "compatible uses," *Federal Airport Act,* Section 11 (4).

47. The federal Department of Housing and Urban Development estimates that it would cost $240,000,000 to soundproof and air condition houses in the worst noise areas around New York's John F. Kennedy Airport, Chicago's O'Hare Field, and Los Angeles' International Airport. See "The Racket That Won't Go Away," *op. cit.,* p. 122. A 1966 study for the Federal Housing Administration concluded that for ten to fifteen PNdb increases in noise insulation modification costs exclusive of changes in house ventilation or cooling would approximate $200 per PNdb per 1,000 square feet of floor space. U.S. Department of Housing and Urban Development, *A Study—Insulating Houses from Aircraft Noise,* (Washington, D.C.: U.S. Government Printing Office, 1966), pp. 58-59.

48. See Charles M. Haar, *op. cit.*

---

22   **The Potential for**
International Air Cargo
Robert W. Prescott
Flying Tiger Lines, Inc.

With the increasing popularity of multinational U.S. firms, air cargo on international routes becomes increasingly important. Further, the increase in the economies of many emerging nations of the world, particularly in the Far East, means more air cargo on an international basis. In this selection, the president of one of the "all cargo" air carriers looks to the potential for air cargo in the years ahead.

As someone once said, ".... the best thing about the future is that it comes only one day at a time." That used to be a handy axiom for the stereotyped airline operator accustomed to flying by the seat of his pants. Today, airline operations are too complex, too sensitive to a broad range of national and international events, too much a part of local and national economies, to survive a cavalier environment.

Operations today must be considered as a prelude to operations tomorrow, and "guesstimating" all the tomorrows involves far more than merely gazing into a crystal ball. Rather, it means being constantly alert to both major and minor

From Robert W. Prescott, "The Potential for International Air Cargo," *American Import and Export Bulletin,* May 1970, pp. 295-304. Used by permission.

shifts in policy and practice of nations and people throughout the world, and being geared to respond on short notice to these shifts.

Reduced to the finest of detail, the factors influencing the international air cargo business can become interminable. However, a relatively small number of indicators appear to be prerequisite clues from which trends may be determined—and revised as unanticipated shifts become clear.

Herman Kahn provides a handy base for interpolating what might be ahead for the next decade or so. He suggests that the one variable that can be expected to have the greatest impact on aviation is population. World population increased from 10 million in 8000 B.C. to 3.3 billion in 1965, an average growth rate per millennium of 80 per cent. Between 1965 and 2000, it is projected that the population will almost double—to 6.4 billion, an increase per millennium of 5600 per cent.

Of equal importance is what Kahn expects will happen to the world gross national product. In present dollars, it is expected to increase from $2.1 trillion in 1965 to $10.9 trillion in 2000. Per capita gross national product will rise from $650 to $1700, a significant boost in the buying power of individuals on a world-wide basis.

If the projections prove reasonably correct, airline passenger miles in the Free World will increase by a factor of 20 by the year 2000. And if the trends of the past few years have any validity, air freight business will be larger than passenger business by 2000. In fact, conservatively, the U.S. growth is estimated to increase by a factor of 120 in the next 30 years. If one examines the past history and projections of the economies in Japan, Korea, Malaysia, Hong Kong, China and much of Western Europe, the future for the world cargo market fairly boggles the mind.

International air cargo movement offers such great potential for a number of reasons:

1. International markets are long-haul by nature, and air freight is essentially a long-haul business.
2. Developing nations jump into the air age because of the prohibitive capital costs of rail, highway, and port facilities.
3. The high rate of technological improvement in aircraft permits absorption of increased costs in far greater proportion than in other modes of cargo transport. Hence, air freight rates will continue to decline relative to other rates, thus broadening the competitive overlap.
4. Air freight can fly direct courses, ignoring land and port barriers, a very important efficiency in international transportation denied to surface vessels and vehicles. For example, the air route from Tokyo to Chicago is 6326 miles. By water and rail, through the San Francisco gateway, it is 7393 miles—1000 miles or 17 per cent farther.

Aside from these reasons, the key to the business potential for the air cargo carrier is how well a nation turns its economy from an agricultural base to one highly industrialized. Perhaps the most striking example of such a transformation in recent times is the Far East. U.S. exports to this region over a five-year period showed an average gain of 10 per cent, larger than to any other part of the world. Imports, on the other hand, have been growing at an even faster pace—30 per cent in 1968, about 22 per cent in 1969, and a figure close to that for 1970. Thus, trade between the Orient and the U.S. probably is the most dynamic of that between any parts of the world.

The rising GNP of these Far Eastern nations—some as high as 16 per cent—leads to another interpretation for the cargo carrier. They are customers with a supermarket of goods that keeps changing in variety and size. No longer can the airline operator afford to disregard the contents of the boxes he carries in his airplane. He must become thoroughly customer oriented. He must have much more than a cursory understanding of the distribution processes in a growing number of industries.

The experience the Flying Tigers has had in recent times might serve to illustrate the point made here. A fair share of the cargo to and from the Far East was mail. However, there were also computers, aircraft parts, office machines, chemical products, and electronic components for Japan and Taipei. Making the return trip to the U.S. were radios, telecommunications equipment, tape recorders, power machinery, clothing and textile fabrics, optical instruments, television sets, and cameras. Hong Kong received fresh vegetables and fruits, electron tubes, motor vehicle and aircraft parts, electrical machinery and man-made fibers. From Hong Kong to other points along the route in the Orient and U.S. went fish, clothing, travel goods, handbags, children's toys, and costume jewelry.

Carrying this range of goods is probably not a new experience to most air cargo carriers, but detailed planning and implementation to meet the specialized demands of the customer may be alien. Experts knowledgeable in these specialized industries must be available to help prepare customer-by-customer, commodity-by-commodity and industry-by-industry total shipping packages. But this kind of help would be meaningless if it weren't for the development of more efficient and more economical systems for handling freight on the ground.

For example, the 18-pallet capacity of the DC8-63F stretch jet makes the unitized handling of freight and mechanized loading highly economical and remunerative. Cargo crews can off-load an entire aircraft in less than 30 minutes. Savings from such procedures, naturally, are passed along to the customer, making air freight that much more attractive. A substantial tariff discount can be offered shippers who containerize their merchandise to make possible loading aboard the aircraft directly from docks located some distance from the terminal complex.

Moreover, containerization is a stimulus for air freight business outside the immediate area of an airport large enough to handle the superjets. Freight forwarders in surrounding cities can package the containers much like they load single-destination trucks. The containers would then be shipped by rail or truck to the nearest jet air terminal for reloading onto a cargo jet. Furthermore, the containers can be designed with environmental controls to carry perishables or special fixtures for delicate instruments and equipment.

While on the subject of the DC8 stretch jet, one other point on operations might be made. Variety may be the spice of life, but when it comes to cargo airplanes, a mixed fleet is a formidable drain on profits. The Flying Tigers now operate a single airplane fleet and besides raising our capacity, the switch netted a significant reduction in operating costs. Among other economies, the move cut down on such operating inefficiencies as separate flight crews and maintenance forces, huge inventories of spare parts, and complicated accounting procedures. In light of these facts, it would seem that the future will see a movement to the more economic and efficient single airplane fleets for the air cargo airlines.

Returning to Kahn's estimates for the year 2000, we find that his are average figures and reflect the counterbalancing effects of the day-to-day and year-to-year variations upon which all trade flourishes or fails. Many factors influence these shifts and if an air cargo carrier is to plan on an annual 20 per cent increase in trade—at least in the Far East—his response time to these shifts often can determine the color of ink at the bottom of his P & L statement.

In a sense, most of the factors ultimately causing slides and jumps in the growth curve are outside the direct influence of the air freighter. Population, for instance, is a moral, religious, and national matter. One—but not the only one by far—clue to shifts in the trend line is national economy. A growing economy—even the promise of one—is a spur to export and import business. But recession, near recession, pause, or whatever the economists might label it, often as not focuses the sharpest attention on the outflow of the national currency. While this may appear to be purely an internal matter, it is a shift which the air cargo carrier must heed. His success depends on balance—for every ton of imported goods, he must fly a ton of export. Empty cargo space only helps set speed records, not profit levels.

The state of the world being what it is, the economies of all the larger, affluent nations are closely interdependent. A recession in the U.S., the largest exporter in the world, will certainly cause some belt tightening in all of the major exporting countries. Thus, the air cargo carrier will be getting it from both ends of his route. His real mission will be to weather this relatively short-term shift downward without disrupting (too much) the pattern of service he has established and without diluting the confidence and respect in him held by his customers, employees and shareholders.

Politics in the well-developed nations have a more subtle influence on international air freight. By and large, even though elected and appointed officials come and go, the wheels of government—at least those wheels affecting air transport—continue to be oiled by the same professional civil servants year after year. However, coups and military takeovers in the name of nationalism can quickly eliminate a country as a shipping point along the route. But, rarely do these major disruptions occur overnight. They foment for a long time, often for years, before they burst into life. Usually, the winds that fan this fire are well identified by the international air cargo carrier. His people on the scene often can identify the real—and not so real—cast of characters that will soon rise up and parade as the new government. In that knowledge resides survivability, also, the clues as to whether multi-nationality will be a protection or a hindrance.

In many respects, the international air transport company is multi-national. From the standpoint of each country in which he has facilities, he should appear to be a national. Most of his employees should be nationals, especially those who deal directly with the customer. The exception, of course, is at start up of service in a given country. When FTL, for example, began operations in various overseas areas, the makeup of the respective management teams included U.S. nationals to a considerable degree. But, as quickly as possible, highly competent and keenly-motivated nationals were hired and trained to replace the Americans to a maximum extent.

While the U.S. carrier may be able to keep his American managers behind the scenes, it is far more difficult to hide the U.S. flag painted on the fuselage of the airplanes. It becomes a target for all kinds of people, especially those political leaders who are fired with so high a degree of nationalism that it keeps them in a constant fever. Among the earliest purchases they push in a newly-formed government is airplanes for a nationalized airline. It appears that many of the evolving nations are side-stepping railroads and ship facilities for moving their products and jumping directly into the air age. After all, it is far less expensive to build a crude but serviceable airport than it is to build a network of modern roads, tracks and docks.

As every international trader knows too well, the jet age ushered in many dislocations——a few quite pleasurable. Now that we are entering the jumbo jet era and later the SST age, we may have to relive some of the more dramatic moments triggered by the conversion of the first DC-3 into a cargo transport. Then a means of transportation thought to be a luxury for a privileged few gradually became a matter of national policy and an integral part of the nation's balance of trade. In other words, the forecasts that the airline operators had been making for years were finally heard in Washington, D.C. Later, many of the listeners acted as though they never heard the forecasts before. Some even claimed themselves as the source of all this bounty and promise. It is so much like a merry-go-round. Haven't we seen that donkey and elephant before?

If nothing else, all international traders are keenly aware of the rules, regulations, opinions and counter-opinions emanating out of Washington. Air cargo carriers are in the same boat as any other international (and domestic) freighter, except the oars are a bit shorter for those who fly airplanes. Furthermore, the air carrier must cope with still another regulatory body, the International Air Transport Association—IATA. The current concern of this body is rate structures. It becomes a strange assembly of vested interests when airline operators wholly subsidized by their governments sit and discuss international rates with private enterprise operators. However, all members of IATA are in concert when it comes to the importance of air transportation to their national economies. With this in mind, it takes no superior form of ESP to predict that, in time, air freight rates will be much more equitable to both the transport operator and user.

While rates command immediate attention, another problem looms on the horizon that could have a negative effect on the air cargo business until it is solved. The problem is the air terminal itself.

Just as the Piper Cub airport had to be beefed up to accommodate the DC-4s, CL-44s and DC6s, many of today's air terminals had to be overhauled to handle the 707 jet series. Another remodeling is underway because of the 747, L-1011, DC-10, and, sooner or later, the SST. Not only will the terminal facilities have to be expanded (runways and buildings), but ingress to and egress from the terminal areas will have to be brought into the 20th century. Otherwise, the surface traffic to the terminal will have more of an influence on flights than weather, jumbo jets, and strikes by the teamsters and air controllers. And, aside from the strikes, this is another one of those problems common to every nation in the world that has an air transport economy.

Other than an avalanche of unanticipated shifts in the trends, the air terminal problem can have a frightening impact on the future of air transportation. Decisions on expanding and building air terminals for the jumbo jet age are being made with horse and buggy perspective. Further, most of the energy is being expended on problems associated with passenger service at the expense of freight service—which could surpass passenger ton-miles before this century closes.

To the U.S. airline operator who deals only in freight, his way is pretty clear and he can direct all of his arguments and influence on the decision-makers toward a single goal. The operators of passenger-first-and-freight-when-space-is-available service have a much more difficult path to tread. And, unhappily, the problem is much the same in most of the countries doing international air freight business. However, there is a glimmer of hope. One European air terminal refused to allow 747 traffic until it has worked out something more than a stop-gap solution to the problem of handling in one fell swoop such a quantity of people, baggage and cargo.

As severe as the airport problem may be, most air cargo carriers, being consummate optimists, know that there will be a solution. It may not be perfect, not the one they would prefer, but at least it will be workable.

To summarize: Both the political and economic climates are warm and, for the immediate future, are nourishing an unprecedented growth in international air cargo business. The idea of having Syracuse, New York, a day away from Hong Kong is intriguing to commodity buyers and sellers in both cities. Internationally-minded businessmen of the 20th century view the whole world as their sales region. Many are beginning to realize that the cost of shipping their products between countries by rail, truck, and ship is considerably higher than the bill of lading tells them. They are becoming "jet-age people," impatient with the old ways of doing business and constantly seeking new, innovative, and imaginative ways to reach their customer.

The world is in constant movement and eternal change. For the next decade, the Far East looks to be the testing ground for truly long-haul air cargo transportation. Unlike the Atlantic, the Pacific is an air ocean. The newly-evolving nations in and along it, looking hungrily for business in the West, will help create a new pattern for international trade—a pattern that once initiated, practiced and established would become the norm.

The pattern in the next decade or so could be adopted—and perhaps improved upon—by the industrially-minded and more stable nations in Africa and South America. It would have flexibility to bend to the changes in products, technologies and people's tastes and desires. Thus, we can conclude that, barring catastrophic unforeseens, we should see and enjoy in the years to come an upsurge in international air cargo transportation without precedent.

23　Little Airlines that Seek New Skies
Business Week

The "non-skeds" or "supplemental airlines" are a part of the air transportation industry little known until recently. Operating on a charter basis, originally to "affinity groups" or organizations, these airlines offer a tailor-made service at a relatively low price. The rise of the supplemental airlines has been controversial in transportation circles and continues to be bothersome to the regularly scheduled air carriers. This selection gives some of the interesting background on this rapidly growing segment of air transportation.

This summer was long and hot for the big national flag airlines. Profits have not kept pace with the purchase of jumbo jets, and hijackers have given them unwanted publicity. Worse, about seven out of every 10 passengers winging around the Continent on pleasure trips use chartered, nonscheduled airlines. As a result, there are signs that supplemental carriers are challenging the economic hegemony of the bigger airlines that are members of the International Air Travel Assn.

Armed with second-hand jet transports, the independent operators are doing battle with European flag airlines because the latter tried to cartelize their service. The IATA airlines dovetail their schedules, fix fares, and pool the revenues. Fares per passenger mile are much higher than rates in the U.S., a fact which scheduled airlines explain away by pointing out that most flights are short-haul, yet international and that fuel costs are higher in Europe. A 330-mi., one-way coach flight from New York to Montreal costs $30.24. A 260-mi. hop from London to Amsterdam costs $30.

Though the supplementals have resembled the tramp shipping of the early 1900s, they are eager to operate with more certainty. As jet aircraft seat more passengers than old prop planes, split charters that book more than one group

Reprinted from the October 3, 1970, issue of *Business Week*, by special permission. Copyright ©1971 by McGraw-Hill, Inc.

have become essential. Britain's Caledonian Airlines is fighting regulatory agencies at home and in North America to gain these rights.

The next step is to split manifests between regularly scheduled passengers and charter passengers. West Germany's Atlantic is currently trying out in the courts its right to split manifests on transatlantic flights. Such supplementals are irked that IATA rules were augmented allowing the scheduled airlines to make bulk seat sales similar to charter bookings. If the independents start to carry scheduled passengers, they could unsettle the iron-clad hold IATA airlines had over fares, especially transatlantically.

Affiliates

The bulk of charter traffic in Europe now runs between the North countries and the sunny Mediterranean. Some 1.6 million of 8-million Swedes traveled outside Scandinavia last year. A third of them went on charters that could take them to places such as Majorca, for a week of everything, for only $100.

Some European charter carriers operate as subsidiaries of the scheduled airlines. France's Air Charter International is wholly owned by Air France, West Germany's Condor is owned by Lufthansa, and Scanair is held by SAS. These IATA-affiliated carriers hauled 6 million passengers last year. But the more innovative independent air charterers are too individualistic to form an association.

Many of the independents started as packagers of tours rather than as aviators. Copenhagen-based Sterling Airways is the creation of a Danish Lutheran pastor named Eilif Krogager. His Tjaereborg tourist agency, named after the town where he preaches, began by buying buses. It now owns 33 aircraft, including 21 Caravelle jets. Sterling even offers a 30-day, round-the-world jaunt, with meals and lodging included, for $1,000. Sterling's cost for the inclusive eight-day tour from Copenhagen to Paris is $60. But a scheduled economy round-trip in an IATA carrier, such as SAS, between Paris and Copenhagen is $150. Sterling is seeking U.S. approval for a license to make more than its present limit of six flights a year to the U.S.

Says Ralph Cohen, assistant to the president of SAS (North America): "The supplementals have probably been loss-leading in hopes of getting a bigger foot in the market. The fare structure for supplementals and skeds has not kept pace with inflation."

Hot properties

Independent supplementals are fairly hot properties, especially for transportation companies which want to diversify into air travel. The U.S.'s Grace Lines offered $8.7-million in cash this year for Denmark's Conair. The charter airline attracted 180,000 passengers last year and reportedly is reluctant to sell out.

"There are still some places in the world," comments SAS's Cohen, "where airlines are glamour stocks." And some charter airlines are actively traded around. Transair of Sweden has changed hands in the past six years like a butter knife at a smorgasbord. Originally owned by a tour operator, it was bought by the Wallenberg banks, then Axel Johnson's industrial empire, then again by the tour operator, and finally by Svenska Handelsbanken. Now Transair merely operates and maintains its three Boeing 727s, which actually belong to a Gothenberg shipyard, Eriksberg, and leases the planes to SAS's subsidiary, Scanair.

Mixed bag

The supplementals are not a brand-new, fly-by-night phenomenon. Though Switzerland is known as the airbase of Swissair, an Alpine carrier named Balair dates back to 1925. Joining with Ad Astra of Zurich in 1930, it helped to found Swissair. In 1953, it was refounded with Swissair holding 40% of the shared capital. Last year, the reborn airline flew 371,000 passengers, increased its payload miles by 40% over 1969, and made $415,000 on $18-million in revenues.

By diligently chasing such mixed bags of cargo from bunches of soccer fans and Chinese social clubs to tons of eggs for the Bahamas, Caledonian Airways, which styles itself as the "Scottish international airline" right down to the mini-kilted stewardesses, has rocketed in less than 10 years to become Britain's largest supplemental. It has 40 salesmen around the world scrambling after payloads to keep aircraft full. The result is that it has a higher payload than even most scheduled airlines.

Last year, Caledonian racked up a net profit of $1.3-million on revenues of $29.2-million, doubling its previous performance. The company has come a long way from its beginnings on St. Andrew's day in 1961 when it made its first flight of immigrants from Barbados to Britain with a leased DC-7. "The nonsked business is good, but we're getting near a plateau," says John de la Haye, part owner of Caledonian. "As a supplemental, we get into seasonal ills, and having scheduled routes is some insurance against this."

Caledonian may get those routes. It is expected to make a formal bid next week for British United Airways which would put the Scottish carrier in the scheduled business. The new merged airline, if all goes according to plan, would acquire routes from BEA and BOAC. Despite resistance from those lines, the Caledonian plan has wide backing in Britain's Conservative government. The result would make Caledonian the second long-haul carrier to fly the Union Jack, and the first run by private enterprise.

24 The Rise of Third Level Air Carriers

Virgil D. Cover
University of Georgia

It is commonly said that there are three "levels" in the airline industry: the first level is the trunk airlines: the second level the regional or feeder carriers; and the third level, the air commuter-air taxi operations. Third level airlines have been growing rapidly both in the air commuter and air taxi classifications. In this selection, a noted transportation economist looks at some of the reasons for this growth and discusses the regulatory struggle over "substitute service."

It has been customary when viewing airline traffic growth to think of air travel as increasing at something like twelve per cent per year. This has been a good, comfortable, and reassuring figure and it was reasonable to plan for regular airline expansion on the basis of it. This prospect, however, did not mean that everything about the airline business was to be described with plus signs. Instead, airline managers lived with pockets of business which were conducted at a loss, and in some cases they faced the problem of eliminating the deficit-producing traffic.

Some points which airlines have served simply were not good traffic producers. The airlines were sometimes locked in to the service because the points appeared in their grandfather certificates, and when they petitioned for permission to withdraw from the deficit points, they were reminded that, as public servants, they could not expect to make money on all their business.

In some cases, points which were at one time valued revenue producers fell in the airlines' estimates because of changing conditions. With the railways, "changing conditions" sometimes arose from the economic decline of a community, or from the growth of competition by automobile or air transportation. With the airlines, the introduction of more expensive and larger equipment has often made the serving of rather important communities an uneconomic undertaking. Serving a community with a DC-3 might be quite appropriate—serving the same community with a 707, or even a DC-9 might be like killing a fly with an elephant gun.

Trunk line replacement by air taxis

Being "locked in" on a grandfather certificate point was the case with American Airlines at Douglas, Arizona, in 1953. American estimated that it would save $13,532 annually if it were permitted to suspend service, and it proposed that

From the *Transportation Journal*, Fall 1971, quarterly publication of the American Society of Traffic and Transportation, Inc. Used by permission.

Frontier Airlines assume the service. The Civil Aeronautics Board denied the request insisting that "the burden of providing the unprofitable service should not be shifted from American to the government in the form of a subsidized local-service obligation."[1]

The Civil Aeronautics Board was not opposed to a local-service carrier taking over at Douglas. Instead, Douglas could not be incorporated into the local-service routes in the area except at an excessive subsidy cost.

In 1963, American renewed its request, saying it would save $12,041 annually by eliminating Douglas. The Civil Aeronautics Board again disapproved, citing the 1953 decision and saying:

> The situation here is the same . . . An award to Bonanza, or to either of the other two applicants, would result in substantial subsidy costs to the Government. Clearly the transfer of American's authority to a local-service carrier is not in the public interest.[2]

American Airlines, consequently, continued service at Douglas. However, on September 21, 1964, the Civil Aeronautics Board approved a plan under which Apache Airlines assumed service to Douglas-Tucson-Phoenix, and American temporarily suspended at those points. American underwrote Apache Airlines by $26 per flight. The authority was extended for three years on July 17, 1967, and again on August 28, 1970.[3] In the latter case, the financial underwriting amounted to $7,970 per month if 98 per cent of schedules were completed. The American Airlines timetable shows "Douglas-Bisbee" as a point with the notation: "Connection to AA Flights at Tucson and Phoenix Via Apache Airlines."

Thus American Airlines continued to be responsible for service to a community by having a smaller carrier, classified as an air taxi, assume responsibility for the service but with American underwriting the service financially. The public service obligation was thereby recognized, but the larger carrier was permitted to limit its losses.

Eastern Air Lines in 1968 requested approval of an agreement under which a smaller air carrier, Pennsylvania Commuter Airlines, would replace Eastern at Lancaster, Pennsylvania.[4] Lancaster had been on the routes of Colonial Airlines which Eastern had acquired in 1956. Under the plan, beginning November 1, 1968, Pennsylvania Commuter Airlines offered three daily round trips, Lancaster to Washington via Baltimore, and Eastern discontinued its single round trip by Convair to Scranton, Reading, and Washington. Commuter Airlines was to use Beech 99 equipment, and Eastern was to provide assistance in communications, reservations, ticketing, and insurance, and was to guarantee Commuter Airlines a return not to exceed $55,000 annually for the first three years.[5]

Eastern has made similar plans with other air taxis, at other points. Its System Timetable effective January 21, 1971, page 74, showed "Air Commuter Service" to nineteen points, including four points in the Bahamas.

One of Eastern's early agreements was that with Air South at Waycross, Georgia, a city of 21,000 in the southeastern part of the state, 203 air miles from Atlanta. The C. A. B. approved of Eastern's suspension on June 12, 1969. Eastern had provided one daily round trip, Atlanta-Waycross, via Macon.

The Eastern-Air South agreement provided three round trips, Monday-Friday, and one round trip Saturday-Sunday and holidays. The agreement further provided:

> Air South will use modern, twin-engine turbo-prop aircraft with a gross take-off weight of less than 12,500 pounds, configured for 15-20 passengers, and with adequate capacity for baggage, mail, and express; Eastern and Air South will cooperate to provide communications, reservations, ticketing and other services for interline passengers moving beyond Atlanta; Air South will provide insurance at the minimums and covering the liabilities stated in the agreement in companies satisfactory to Eastern; and Eastern will underwrite Air South's replacement service at Waycross in a sum not exceeding $105,000 during the three-year period of the contract.[6]

Eastern Air Lines stated, and the Board agreed, that Eastern would gain from a reduction of its operating expenses. Waycross did not object to the proposal and the Board found

> . . . that service to the traveling public will be substantially improved by the agreement.

The Board, however,

> (retained) authority to withdraw (its) approval and authorization if circumstances (should dictate). Thus, if Air South's service to Waycross (should prove) to be unsatisfactory either in terms of quantity or quality, Eastern (would) be required to resume its service at Waycross.

After a year's experience with the replacement service, Eastern asked for an amendment which would increase "the total maximum payment" from $105,000 to $120,000. Air South was said to have "experienced a level of operating costs well in excess of that which had been forecast." During the year ending June 30, 1970, Air South had incurred a loss of $110,645 on its Waycross operation.[7]

A week after it filed its application in the above case Eastern asked for approval of Amendment No. 2 of the Air South agreement. Under this, the three round trips Monday-Friday would be reduced to two. The Board approved the request, noting that Waycross did not object to the reduction although Waycross was critical of the timing of the proposed schedules. The Board concurred in the criticism

> (noting) with concern Air South's failure to provide Waycross with an early morning flight to Atlanta and (trusting) that this situation would be remedied by appropriate schedule changes.[8]

The Board, in reaching its decision to approve the Amendment, took into consideration the 27 per cent load factor which had prevailed on the three round trips and concluded that

> ... the elimination of one round trip will result in savings to Air South while meeting the air service needs of Waycross.[9]

Eastern Air Lines has established a similar plan at Rome, Georgia, for Rome-Atlanta service, providing cooperation on the ground, and economic support of "up to $165,000" for three years.[10] Other points at which like arrangements have been made are Bowling Green, Kentucky,[11] Reading, Pennsylvania,[12] and Binghamton, New York.[13]

One other trunk line carrier, Northeast, has made a number of agreements with air taxis for replacement service. The first of them, with Cape and Islands Flight Service, Inc., and Winnipesaukee Aviation, Inc. (the Commuter Carriers),[14] provided for temporary suspension of Northeast's authority to provide seasonal service (summer service) at Laconia and Berlin, New Hampshire, and Boston, distances of 86 and 153 miles respectively. The agreement was for ten years, provided for a specified number of round trips, service by smaller aircraft, ground service cooperation, insurance, and financial underwriting "in a sum not exceeding $50,000 during the first two years of the contract."

A similar ten-year agreement with Northern Airways covered seasonal service at Newport, Vermont, the main variation being compensation which depended on gross revenues.[15]

Other agreements have covered Bar Harbor, Maine; Hyannis, Nantucket, and Martha's Vineyard, Massachusetts; Lebanon, New Hampshire; Montpelier, Vermont; Manchester, New Hampshire; Burlington, Vermont; Augusta/Waterville, and Lewiston/Auburn, Maine.[16] Two commuter airlines, and Mohawk Airlines replaced Northeast completely, or partially, at these points. A major reshuffling of routes was involved. No guarantee of income to the replacement carriers was provided. However, there were "services agreements" between Northeast and Mohawk, and between Mohawk and Executive Airlines, Inc., by which ground service was provided.

The Civil Aeronautics Board definitely felt the public interest would be served by these changes. *Aviation Week* interpreted the results of the Order as enabling each level of carrier—trunk, regional, and air taxi—"to operate more profitably on a single level."[17] The C. A. B. felt there would be "no significant adverse impact on other carriers or the traveling public." The C. A. B. was hopeful "that in the long run the proposed new pattern of service may result in substantially improved service to the public."[18]

The Board, however, cautioned Northeast and Mohawk

> not to place undue reliance on our temporary approvals and particularly to refrain from taking any steps which would preclude them from reinstating operations which they are now being permitted to suspend.

And the Board imposed a condition

requiring that the suspended carrier reinstate service if the replacement fails to provide a minimum number of frequencies in a market.

Regional carrier replacement by air taxis

The New England route realignment case thus involved three levels of carriers. A great number of the replacement agreements have involved instances of regional carriers withdrawing either partially or completely and leaving the route to be covered by a commuter-air taxi carrier.

The Civil Aeronautics Board's record of these agreements[19] shows the first of them as having been drawn by Allegheny Airlines and Henson Aviation, Inc.[20] This covered Allegheny's scheduled air service between Hagerstown and Baltimore, Maryland. Henson agreed to provide five flights during the week and two flights Saturday and Sunday. Allegheny agreed to guarantee breakeven operations for two years. Allegheny was able to withdraw from an unprofitable Convair 580 operation with service of an amount and at a time that was not best for the public. The air taxi provides more and better service with smaller equipment on routes with traffic characteristics that may lead to profit.[21]

Allegheny entered a number of similar agreements in the following months. These involved points served in nine states extending as far west as Danville, Illinois. In most cases, Allegheny underwrote the financial success of the air taxi "during the first two years," but in several cases there was no guarantee at all. The agreement might extend beyond the period of the financial guarantee. Allegheny would provide reservation and ground handling services, for which it might, or might not, be reimbursed by the air taxi. Where the air taxi compensated the larger carrier for these services, they were usually calculated at $1 or $2 per passenger. In the case of some Mohawk agreements, the air taxi paid as little as 50¢ "per passenger boarded."

Modifications were made in the original agreements as time passed. The original Allegheny-Henson plan was extended to Salisbury, Maryland, on May 8, 1969.[22] The term "Allegheny Commuter" came to be used by some of the air taxi lines, and was shown on the aircraft in some cases.[23]

Mohawk, Frontier, and North Central have also entered agreements under which air taxi operators would take over as replacements. Mohawk's agreements were both upward and downward, with Mohawk replacing Northeast at some New England points,[24] and with Executive Airlines replacing Mohawk at certain New England points, and with Command Airways and Air North replacing it at some points in New England and New York. The Executive Airlines and Command Airways contracts provided no financial guarantees. The Air North contract provided underwriting not exceeding $525,000 during the first three years of the contract.

Frontier's contracts have been of two sorts: (1) Frontier continued operating between Cody, Wyoming, and Billings, Montana, but reduced the number of its schedules, and Combs Airways provided service in place of Frontier. Frontier provided ground services and financial support to Combs. (2) Frontier also entered agreements with air taxi lines at points where the C.A.B. permitted temporary suspension of Frontier's service. The points covered were as widely separated as Montana and Texas. No financial support was provided. Although the C. A. B. was urged by some of the cities where suspension was being considered to require Frontier to extend a financial guarantee to the air taxi line, the Board rejected the suggestion in view of the requirement that Frontier should resume service if the air taxi should fail to provide satisfactory service.[25]

The North Central Airlines cases have involved suspension of North Central's service at Wisconsin-Minnesota-Illinois points. In one case, North Central asked to suspend at Land O'Lakes, Wisconsin, where the airport could not handle Convair 580 equipment. North Central proposed to dispose of its DC-3's, and Land O'Lakes being the only point with an airport not adequate to accommodate the CV-580, North Central would have been compelled to retain one DC-3 aircraft and crew if it were required to continue service.[26] Land O'Lakes had refused to improve its airport. The Board approved of North Central's suspension for a three-year period, but provided that North Central would have to reinstitute service if the replacement, Midstate Air Commuter Airlines, failed to provide satisfactory service. The Board said:

> The temporary suspension will enable North Central to retire all of its DC-3 equipment and to avoid the continued use of these aircraft solely in order to serve Land O'Lakes on a seasonal basis.

North Central did, indeed, proceed to dispose of its DC-3's. In June 1970 it had thirteen DC-9's and 34 CV-580's.[27] What aircraft it would use to service Land O'Lakes if it were compelled to resume service is thus a matter of speculation.[28]

The introduction of air taxi, commuter lines, and the withdrawal of the trunk and regional carriers have combined to create both benefits and disadvantages for the airlines and the communities involved.

For the airlines, trunk and regional carriers, there has been relief from the immediate obligation to continue performing a service which is uneconomic because circumstances have changed, and what was once a profitable market has ceased to be so. It may be that the potential has declined. It may be that advancing technology—larger and more powerful planes—makes continued service under conditions which have not changed greatly, inadvisable from the standpoint of the carrier, or from that of the traveling public.

The new aircraft are heavier and many runways are neither strong enough nor long enough to support them. The new aircraft are faster and should be used to move people between points which are more distant than the 67 miles between Baltimore and Hagerstown, Maryland, or the 88 miles between Massena and Watertown, New York.[29]

Both the trunk and regional carriers were anxious to increase the lengths of their hops because the equipment they were purchasing was more productive in the longer hauls and on routes of higher traffic density.[30] The Civil Aeronautics Board has been anxious to reduce the subsidy payments to the regional carriers, and the regional carriers have been anxious to concentrate on that business which would produce a profit without subsidy.

The Board has permitted regional carriers to enter a "standby" status so far as their duty of service is concerned. On occasion the carrier has been permitted to withdraw completely as in cases where the "use it or lose it" test has been applied and the community has not produced the minimum of five passengers per day which must be in prospect before subsidy will be considered. But, where the community was entitled to service which a regional carrier was reluctant to provide, the solution of having the service performed by a third level has had more advantages than disadvantages.

The regional carrier is permitted to suspend temporarily and cut its losses. Frontier Airlines is quoted as describing a Montana-North Dakota operation in the following words:

> For every passenger we carried who paid a $20 fare, the government was paying $20 in subsidy and it was costing us at least as much.[31]

The airline, however, is required to resume service if the air taxi service proves inadequate. The Board has regularly warned the suspending airline that it may be required to resume service and that it should not place itself in a position where resumption would impose substantial difficulties.

Such a warning may make clear the position of the Civil Aeronautics Board that the certificated carrier continues to have a duty of service to the community. But what is to be done when the airline, by virtue of the Board's permission to suspend does enter a position in which the problem of resumption of service would be so great that requiring resumption would be beyond reason? It may be that the problem will be happily solved by the presence of another air taxi which is ready to spring into the breach. This was the case with Eastern Air Lines at Bowling Green, Kentucky, mentioned above.[32] The original replacement, Air South, ceased operating on March 31, 1970, the agreement under which it replaced Eastern having been approved on August 4, 1969. Following Air South's withdrawal, Eastern first asked for approval of a new agreement with Northern Airlines, which airline was already providing more service to Bowling Green than had been contemplated under the Eastern-Air South agreement.

Before the C.A.B. could act on the Eastern-Northern agreement, the application was withdrawn. Eastern then asked approval of an agreement with Wright Air Lines, another air taxi which had been operating into Bowling Green. The C. A. B. did approve the Eastern-Wright agreement and service by Wright between Bowling Green and Louisville and Nashville is shown in Eastern's System Time-table under "Air Commuter Service." Although Louisville and Bowling Green asked that service by Eastern be reinstated, the C. A. B. thought that service by Wright,

... sponsored and sustained by Eastern, will satisfactorily fulfill Eastern's service obligations at Bowling Green and provide service to the traveling public which will be a substantial improvement over both the prior replacement service and the service which would be provided if (the C.A.B.) were now to require that carrier to resume operations.

For the legalistically minded, it is interesting that the C. A. B. observed that

Eastern has been in default of its certificate responsibilities and in violation of Board Order 69-8-10 ever since Air South ceased operations at the end of March 1970 ... We do not view Eastern's eleventh-hour request for an emergency exemption as having absolved the carrier of its obligation to reinstitute service promptly at Bowling Green once air service by Air South came to an end.

A need for a review of the common carrier duty of service

The situation at Bowling Green gives reason for a reconsideration of our policy in air transport. How sound or necessary is a policy under which we require our trunk or regional carriers with their expensive equipment to continue service to points which they have outgrown? And, in view of the growth in the number and activity of air taxi companies, how important is it to the community that it be protected by a requirement that service continue to be performed by the larger carriers, which are so often an unwilling servant? As it was put in a case in 1963 involving a trunk carrier which wished to withdraw:

Compelling an unwilling carrier to remain in Midland/Odessa in order to maintain a now fictional competitive trunkline service between Dallas and Midland/Odessa would be a useless gesture. The more realistic view is that expressed by Midland/Odessa witnesses. For example, the mayor of Midland said: "American Airlines in Midland is kind of like having a quit man on your payroll, you better get rid of him. They don't want to serve Midland. We need somebody that wants to serve Midland and wants to be aggressive and provide service." The president of the Midland Chamber of Commerce expressed the view ". . . the city would be better off with replacement of American by some other carrier, for we'd rather have the flights than the prestige."[33]

The common carrier duty of service may have been logically conceived but the duty has had to be performed by carriers under circumstances that defeat accomplishment of its ends.

Enforcing the duty of service has been taken to the extreme in railway passenger service. Bankrupt railways have been required to continue offering service where the prospects were for nothing other than deficits, and very substantial deficits. It is true that communities have sometimes subsidized the service, but this has been done reluctantly, and the subsidy has been given, then withheld, then given again.

The duty of service has been as clear in motor trucking as it has been in aviation or the railway business. The enforcement of the duty, however, has not been pushed often, and where it has been pushed, the enforcers have met with doubtful success. Trucking companies are quite different organisms than airlines and railways.

The airline picture is to be differentiated from that of the other agencies by the classification of the carriers into trunk lines, which must make ends meet out of revenues, and local-service or regional carriers, which pay what costs they can out of revenues, and receive a payment, possibly erroneously called "subsidy" to help them make ends meet. The "subsidy," provided by Section 406(b) of the Federal Aviation Act, and supported by federal appropriations, represents an admission that the communities which regional carriers serve do not produce enough business for normal support of the airlines. Thus, in judging the extent to which the duty of service should be enforced on an airline at a light traffic point, the Civil Aeronautics Board is necessarily also considering what service is "required for the commerce of the United States, the Postal Service, and the national defense."[34]

It is suggested here that conditions at the level of the light traffic points have changed so that the requirements of "the commerce of the United States, the Postal Service, and the national defense" no longer need subsidy support to anything like the extent it has been forthcoming in the past. Air commuter-air taxi[35] lines have multiplied in number and they serve many points. Anyone trying to determine how many there are can find just about any figure he wishes. The Civil Aeronautics Board concluded, from a study of the operations of scheduled air taxis as found in the Official Airline Guide, that "94 air taxi operators provided scheduled service to 384 points in 46 states, the District of Columbia, Puerto Rico, and the Virgin Islands."[36] Of the points served, 148 received their only air service from scheduled air taxis.

It is probable that a more realistic figure came from reports which the Civil Aeronautics Board required from air taxi operators operating as commuter air carriers. The reports were to show the situation as of September 30, 1969. Replies came from 177 commuter air carriers, all of whom operated regular schedules, only 13 of whom carried only mail.[37]

He who wishes a different figure may find it in material issued by the Federal Aviation Administration when it established rules applying to air taxi operators on April 1, 1970. According to *Aviation Week*:

The agency noted that over the past 15 years the overall number of air taxi operators has increased from approximately 2,000 to 4,000 and that the number of scheduled operators has gone from less than 80 in December, 1965, to 250 by the end of 1968.[38]

Whatever the true figures may be, those which are available indicate that the air commuter-air taxi population is substantial. These "third level carriers" are described as "fragmented" and "uncoordinated" and as indulging in a "highly localized level of activity that is neither profitable nor properly organized as an element of the total air transport industry."[39]

The aircraft used by these carriers range from small single engine equipment to turbine powered ships carrying twenty persons.

The existence of this flight potential gives a flavor of reasonableness to the requests of the trunk lines and regional carriers that they be permitted to withdraw from light traffic points. This seems particularly true in a time when business activity is at a low level and costs are rising, and the airlines are serving points where costs regularly outrun revenues.

How serious would be the withdrawal of the trunk or regional carriers from some points? In many cases, probably in most cases, the representatives of the small communities are willing that the larger carrier withdraw so long as there is assurance that the third level carrier will actually perform the service. Often the service will be improved. Instead of one round trip per day to the central city, the air taxi will perform three round trips. In all likelihood the equipment will be small and less comfortable than that of the regional carrier. Safety may be a consideration, but safety has received attention in the rules issued by the Federal Aviation Administration which became effective April 1, 1970. From the standpoint of the community the real question is: will the air taxi survive and continue to offer service? The comfort of the passenger, and even the convenience of the schedules is secondary. What can a small community expect?

The C. A. B. appears to subscribe to the position that the obligation of the withdrawing carrier remains, and while it may be more implied than actual, for it would be unrealistic to expect a carrier to purchase a DC-3 or a CV-240, or even a new, smaller airplane in order to reinstate service and to establish ground facilities, the possibility is present. In view of this, it seems reasonable to ask if it is sound policy to continue to apply the common carrier duty of service to a certificated carrier at many low density points where it now applies.

Free competition at low density points

These low traffic points need air service, but the need is limited. Neither the population nor the incentive to travel is there to support a regional air carrier. Air taxis commonly are already serving the points because the service the regional carrier renders is so limited and of such a low standard that anyone who offers service will receive some patronage. An economy of free competition prevails for there is no requirement that an air taxi ask public authority for permission to operate. The investment required to enter the air transport business is small, and it appears that if one or a few firms withdraw, others will enter. Competition will protect the public interest—there is no need to limit by certification, and no need to protect by rate regulation.

Some communities have not been altogether happy with the withdrawal of the regional carriers.[40] In some cases the entrance of the air taxi lines has improved the service, and the withdrawal of the regional carrier enlarged the opportunity for the air taxi. However, in areas where, at best, air traffic density is light and any sort of service would have light patronage, complete abandonment of air service may be the answer.[41] In these areas the air carrier meets competition from the private automobile and the telephone, with the bus company gaining business as well, as the traveler's choices deteriorate.

However, air service to many of these communities can hardly be self-sustaining even at the air taxi level. It was marginal at best even when business activity was at a high level, and regional carriers who served with subsidy support now find that the subsidy covers a small proportion of an increasing deficit. Some communities are simply condemned to doing without air service as the pressure on the Federal budget increases and the requirements for "the commerce of the United States, the Postal Service, and the national defense" are less compelling.

Such a reassessment of our needs may be quite in order, and although business recession brings more losses than gains, the shakedown which is occurring in short haul air service to communities of light traffic density will be one of the gains. The common carrier industry will be stronger and it may well be that the growth of the third level air carriers will contribute strength to our transport system sufficient to fill the vacuum caused by the retreat of the larger carriers.

NOTES

1. Frontier Route No. 93 Renewal Case, 16 C. A. B. 948 (1953) as quoted in Southern Rocky Mountain Area Local Service Case, 38 C. A. B. 301, 384 (1963).

2. 38 C. A. B. 301, 384-85 (1963). The Board was certainly not unsympathetic with American Airlines in its desire to withdraw from Douglas. In fact, it recommended that there be a study of the results of having American and Continental withdraw from Douglas and other points, and having local-service carriers assume the points, probably at a low subsidy cost.

3. C. A. B. Orders E. 25241 and 70-8-113 respectively.

4. C.A.B. Order 68-10-35, October 8, 1968.

5. It was later determined that two round trips were sufficient and one round trip was eliminated. The average load on 15 passenger aircraft had been two passengers and the load factor 13.6 per cent. The load factor on other flights had been 28 per cent. The Lancaster Airport Authority did not object to the amendment. In case the demand for service increased, "Pennsylvania Commuter stands ready to increase its schedule frequency." The elimination of the round trip was expected to save Pennsylvania Commuter $50,000 annually. See C. A. B. Order 70-2-63 of February 16, 1970.

6. C. A. B., Application of EASTERN AIRLINES, INC. for authority to suspend service temporarily at Waycross, Georgia, Docket 20762, Order 69-6-56, June 12, 1969, p. 2.

7. C. A. B. Docket 20762, Order 70-9-31, September 4, 1970.

8. Air South's System Schedule at the time (dated July 1, 1970) showed the first flight departure from Waycross was at 10:05 a.m. Its October 1, 1970 Schedule showed the departure at 10:35 a.m. This was still in effect in January, 1971. Thus the schedule became less satisfactory.

9. Although no statistics are issued by the Civil Aeronautics Board relative to the finances of air taxis or air commuter carriers, the Board is optimistic with regard to the financial success of the air taxis which have replaced other carriers. In a letter of December 8, 1970, the Bureau of Operating Rights stated: "The Form 41 Reports (Report of Financial and Operating Statistics for Certificated Air Carriers) show that the certificated carriers,

which have financial arrangements with the substituted carriers, are making financial payments to some of the commuter carriers. However, the smallness of these payments indicates that the substitute carriers, for the most part, have had financial success. As a consequence, the certificated carriers apparently have not been required to seek out funds to cover the deficits of the smaller commuter carriers."

10. C. A. B. Docket 20648, Order 69-6-176, June 30, 1969.

11. C. A. B. Docket 20964, Order 69-8-10, August 4, 1969. Air South, Inc., the replacement carrier suspended service on March 31, 1970, and in Docket 20964, Order 70-9-132, of September 24, 1970, the C. A. B. approved the substitution of Wright Air Lines for Eastern between Bowling Green and Louisville. The financial plan provided that Eastern would extend station and ground support and reimburse Wright for 110 per cent of its direct and indirect expenses. Eastern was to collect and retain all revenues.

12. C. A. B. Docket 20648, Order 69-8-76, August 13, 1969.

13. C. A. B. Order 69-12-39, December 8, 1969.

14. C. A. B. Docket 20940, Order 69-6-51, June 11, 1969.

15. C. A. B. Docket 21039, Order 69-6-57, June 12, 1969.

16. C. A. B. Docket 21334 and others, Order 69-12-73, December 16, 1969.

17. *Aviation Week and Space Technology*, January 12, 1970, p. 39.

18. An inquiry to the Civil Aeronautics Board with regard to the success of the replacement services brought the following response: "For the most part the substitution of commuter operations or air taxis for certificated carriers at the marginal traffic points has proven satisfactory. The cooperation of the certificated carrier, the commuter carrier, and the community involved have contributed to the success of these arrangements." Letter from Bureau of Operating Rights, Civil Aeronautics Board, December 8, 1970.

19. Civil Aeronautics Board, Supplemental and Replacement Air Taxi Service on Certificated Carrier Routes, September 30, 1970.

20. C. A. B. Order E-25834, October 13, 1967.

21. In approving of a later agreement between Allegheny and Crown Airways at DuBois, Pennsylvania, the C. A. B. noted that in the first year of the Hagerstown agreement, Henson served 11,313 passengers, or 108 per cent more than the 5,429 passengers Allegheny had served the previous year. See C. A. B. Order 69-2-157, February 28, 1969, p. 2.

22. C. A. B. Order 69-5-27, May 8, 1969.

23. See C. A. B. Order 69-3-42, March 11, 1969. Pocono Airlines used "Allegheny Commuter" markings on planes on its Wilkes-Barre/Scranton and Newark schedules. A competing air taxi line, Altair Airlines, protested that "the Allegheny Commuter operation (was) likely to cause public confusion." The C. A. B. directed that an informal study be made of the problem but took no position at once. One Board member dissented from the majority decision indicating he believed "public confusion" could result. The trade mark "Allegheny Commuter" was later referred to in C. A. B. Order 69-6-82 of June 16, 1969, in which Allegheny was authorized to suspend service temporarily at Mansfield, Ohio, in favor of Fischer Bros. Aviation, Inc. The C. A. B. noted without comment that "Fischer will use Allegheny's trade mark 'Allegheny Commuter Airlines' in its Mansfield services . . ." There were other references in other cases. The Board disposed of the problem in straightforward fashion in its Order 70-1-144, January 29, 1970, when it authorized Pocono Airlines to operate as "Allegheny Commuter." Ransome Airlines was likewise authorized to use the name under C. A. B. Order 70-6-83, June 12, 1970, and in this case Board Member Murphy dissented because he felt the public would be "misled into believing that the air taxi's services are those of the certificated carrier." His concern in this case arose because both Ransome and Allgeheny "operate(d) side by side in the same markets." Atlantic City Airlines was authorized to use "Allegheny Commuter" in service involving Atlantic City, Philadelphia, and Cape May. See C. A. B. Order 70-6-147, June 26, 1970. In sum, it does not appear that the C. A. B. viewed the confusion that would result as significant.

An article in *Air Transport World,* January, 1970, "Commuters Move Toward Closer Coordination with U.S. Trunk and Regional Air Carriers," spoke of the "Allegheny Commuter" concept as growing, and as including nine third-level airlines. *Air Transport World* of May 1970 spoke of the tendency of "several larger carriers . . . to organize commuter services 'in company'." *Aviation Week* of February 15, 1971, p. 37, reported that "Allegheny Airlines commuter service carried 250,477 passengers to 16 cities during 1970, accounting for 4% of Allegheny's total passenger boardings."

24. As discussed above in C. A. B. Docket 21334, Order 69-12-173, December 16, 1969.
25. See C. A. B. Dockets 22067 and 22124, Order 70-11-25, November 5, 1970, and the request of Muskogee, Oklahoma, that the Sedalia-Marshall-Boonville Stage Lines, the air taxi, be given an earnings guarantee.
26. C. A. B. Docket 20754, Order 69-5-139, May 29, 1969.
27. *Air Traffic World,* December, 1970, p. 40.
28. For other North Central cases, see C. A. B. Docket 20710, Order 69-10-12, October 24, 1969, and Docket 20519, Order 70-4-118, April 23, 1970.
29. Mileages from Civil Aeronautics Board, Air Taxi Activity, Six Months Ended Decmeber 31, 1969, Docket 21761, BOR-IR-4.
30. The replacement of regional and trunk carriers is only one of the reasons working toward an increase in flight length. The certifying of regional carriers on longer routes is another. Isolating cause and effect is not possible here. However, length of hop has increased, as shown by the statistical measure "Overall flight stage length (miles)" in the Civil Aeronautics Board's Traffic Statistics, for various months. "Overall flight stage length" is defined by the Board as "The average distance covered per aircraft hop in revenue services, from take-off to landing. Derived by dividing the total aircraft miles flown in revenue service by the number of aircraft revenue departures performed." The table below indicates how the length of hop has increased during four years which coincide with the time period in which air taxis have been introduced as replacements.

Overall Flight Stage Length (Miles)
October of Various Years

	1967	1968	1969	1970
Allegheny	142.9	153.0	176.3	190.4
Frontier	135.8	146.7	157.1	168.4
Mohawk	134.8	149.7	151.2	166.2
North Central	92.2	100.0	110.6	127.5
Eastern	333.3	371.2	432.1	455.2
Northeast	293.6	355.2	410.3	568.0

31. "Small Towns Isolated as Airlines Cut Service," *New York Times,* September 20, 1970.
32. C. A. B. Docket 20964, Order 70-9-132, September 24, 1970.
33. American Airlines, Service to Midland/Odessa Case, 37 C. A. B. 583, 601 (1963).
34. Federal Aviation Act of 1958, Section 406(b), p. 33.
35. As defined by the C. A. B., a commuter airline is one performing "five scheduled round trips per week between two or more points." *Air Traffic World,* May 1970, p. 100.
36. See *Aviation Week and Space Technology,* February 23, 1970, p. 27.
37. See "U.S. Commuter Turboprop Aircraft Almost Doubled Within 12 Months," *Air Traffic World,* May 1970, p. 99.
38. "FAA Adopts Air Taxi, Commuter Rules," *Aviation Week and Space Technology,* December 22, 1969, p. 32.
39. See "Consolidation Gains in Commuter Industry," *Aviation Week and Space Technology,* January 12, 1970, p. 39.
40. "Small Towns Left Isolated as Airlines Cut Service," *New York Times,* September 20, 1970.
41. In one case, Mohawk Airlines opposed the motion of Sullivan County, New York, which would require Mohawk to continue to offer service after October 26, 1970, when

Mohawk's authority expired. Mohawk estimated it was losing $26 for every passenger it carried. The C. A. B. suggested: "As a possible alternative Mohawk may wish to consider a replacement agreement with an air taxi, with Mohawk holding responsibility to resume service if the air taxi fails to provide a specified level of service. If this alternative is adopted it may be possible to resolve the problem of service to Liberty/Monticello without hearing procedures. However, by advancing this suggestion, we do not intend to foreclose the possibility that we would determine, on the basis of an evidentiary record, that Mohawk's authority should be unconditionally renewed or terminated." See Docket 22162, Order 70-7-77, July 16, 1970. In Docket 22162, Order 70-10-150, October 30, 1970, the Board refused to compel Mohawk to continue pending the final determination of Docket 22162, and Mohawk was thus given permission to suspend temporarily.

---

25 **As the Crow Flies**

Transportation & Distribution

Management

Airlines make extensive use of all sorts of modern instrumentation. Flying a plane is a far from simple task one—which is evident in the complexities of navigation, of the essentials of flying. This selection discusses new navigational methods which use on-board computers, as well as other new technological developments which are not apparent to the traveler.

The airliner of today frequently does not travel in a straight line—nor even along the highly publicized "Great Circle routes."

Instead, it zig-zags. It zig-zags because of limitations in the present system of aerial navigation, which on the average route add about 1 1/2 percent to the mileage that must be flown. But a new navigational technique, known as "area navigation," may soon allow the commercial air transportation industry to straighten out its routes, and thereby achieve an important reduction in its operating expense level.

Elimination of a 1 1/2-percent circuity factor might, at first glance, seem a rather minuscule economy. But it takes on a new dimension of importance for an industry where costs are routinely measured in megabucks—and where the influx of new and ever-more-expensive aircraft is shooting those costs still higher. For the fiscally troubled U.S. airlines—less than half of which showed profits during 1969—this 1 1/2-percent saving could be critical.

It costs somewhere around $400-500 per hour to keep the average jetliner in the air. [According to *Aviation Week*, September, 1969. Some typical per hour costs: Douglas DC-8, $504.40; Douglas DC-9, $487.70; Boeing 707, $471.30,

From *Transportation & Distribution Management*, October 1970, pp. 40-41. Used by permission.

Boeing 727, $402.70. Costs for "jumbos" such as the Boeing 747, of course, are proportionately much higher.] During that hour, the jetliner will travel about 450 miles, at a per-mile operating cost of about a dollar. In a single day, such a jetliner might well fly across the country and back again, a round trip of some 7,000 miles—1 1/2 percent of which is 105 miles, at $1 apiece. Over a year, this can add up to an astonishingly high figure.

Moreover, the same limitations imposed by present systems of navigation are partially responsible for congestion at many major airports. Some aircraft sit profitlessly on the ground, waiting their turn to take off; others mill around aimlessly in "holding patterns," awaiting landing instructions. Area navigation techniques have the potentiality to sharply reduce some of these waiting periods, for still further financial savings.

Back in the days of aviation pioneering, there were three basic navigational techniques: landmarks, star sights, and dead reckoning. In the first, the pilot looked at the ground and tried to orient himself by prominences below him. In the second, he "steered by the stars," just as did the sailors of old. In the third, he tried to compute his present position by figuring speed, heading and time elapsed from his last "known location"—usually his takeoff point. The first requires a very clear day or a very low flying altitude; the second and third are subject to varying degrees of error which could, over a long distance (especially with dead reckoning), become gross.

Establishment of "VOR" (Visual Omnidirectional Radio) stations spotted across the country, and development of sophisticated instruments to use them, produced a new era in navigation. VOR stations broadcast distinctive radio signals that are picked up by instruments aboard the aircraft; these can determine both distance and direction of the plane from the broadcast point. Since the station's position is known, the plane's own location can be computed with precision.

While this system eliminated the uncertainties associated with landmark, star-sight and dead-reckoning navigation, it also introduced some problems—notably, the element of circuity. In order to effectively utilize the VOR network until recently a pilot had to "home in" on the signal of each station (or "waypoint"); that is, he had to head his plane directly toward each such waypoint along his route.

It worked like this: leaving Los Angeles on a flight bound for Chicago (see illustration), the pilot would head—not for Chicago—but on a course toward his first waypoint (Ontario, Calif.). When his instruments showed him directly overhead of Ontario, he would then home in on waypoint No. 2 (Hector, Calif.) and fly straight there. There are 14 such waypoints along the Los Angeles-Chicago route; needless to say, not all are situated precisely along the shortest and most direct route between the two cities. Thus, in order to pass over the waypoints, the plane had to deviate from its "true" route to Chicago, adding extra mileage—and extra time—to the trip.

In point of fact, this is still the way air navigation is being performed. However, the innovative "area navigation" concept was recently approved by the Federal Aviation Administration, and several companies are in the process of developing the new avionic equipment necessary to make use of it. One such firm—Avian, a division of Avionic Products Engineering Corp., of Gaithersburg, Md.—will have the first prototypes ready for inflight testing by the end of the year.

Area navigation

The area navigation concept also makes use of the VOR stations—but, by a complex process of triangulation, avoids the requirement that the plane pass directly over each station en route to its destination. To accomplish this—a function which appears much easier to the layman than it is in actual electronic execution—a small computer is installed in the cockpit, making the necessary calculations and advising the pilot of his position on a moment-by-moment basis.

In area navigation, a series of *imaginary* waypoints are plotted along the most direct origin-to-destination route; each is located near (but no longer directly overhead of) a VOR station. The imaginary waypoint, the VOR station, and the (unknown) location of the plane at a given moment in time form the three points which geometrically define a triangle.

The distance and direction of the imaginary waypoint from the VOR station are pre-determined, known quantities. The distance and direction of the plane from the VOR station can be calculated through standard techniques by listening to the VOR signal. The plane's heading is also known. From these factors, it is a relatively simple mathematical exercise to compute the distance and direction of the plane from the imaginary waypoint—the third, and critical, leg of the hypothetical triangle.

If this were all there is to it, area navigation would already be in use. The problem of "vagrant" signals, however, can throw this geometric simplicity into vast confusion at the drop of a mountain range—or even a little bad weather.

"Vagrants"

Normally, radio signals travel in a straight line from transmitter to receiver. But they can also "bounce" off things like mountains, or even convolutions in the atmosphere—which is why a cheap transistor radio in Boston can suddenly burst forth with Grand Ole Opry from a Nashville broadcast station. Such "vagrant" signals can wreak havoc with a navigation system based on calculating the distance and direction of a given radio signal; all of a sudden, the vagrant makes it seem that the signal is coming from somewhere else altogether.

Avian has coped with this problem by building a little "fail-safe" logic into its cockpit computer. The computer recalculates the plane's position, on the basis of triangulation, some 20 times a second. So long as no vagrants intrude, everything runs smoothly; but the moment the first vagrant is received, it gives the appearance that (a) the plane, or (b) the VOR transmitter, has suddenly and drastically changed position.

As computers go, the Avian device isn't terribly bright—its limited size and circuitry inevitably restrict its "intelligence." But it's bright enough to realize that neither airplanes nor radio transmitters are likely to leap vast distances in milliseconds. It immediately does two things: (1) it advises the pilot that vagrants are being received (by a "trouble light"), and (2) it immediately stops using the VOR signal for navigational purposes. Instead, it shifts over to a back-up dead reckoning system and continues to calculate the plan's approximate position on this basis. (Some of the "deluxe" models even feature equipment to take star sights.)

The pilot can then "wait out" the vagrant, hoping that a true signal will come back soon. Or he can change the frequency of his navigational receiver to that of another VOR station (whose position with respect to the imaginary waypoint toward which he is heading is also known), in the hope of receiving a true signal from *that* transmitter. In either case, the computer—as soon as it begins receiving a signal which agrees closely with its dead-reckoning position—reverts to its radio-navigation function, and goes back to using dead reckoning only as a double-check.

Landing problems

A final value of the area-navigation system is demonstrated at major airports in adverse weather conditions. FAA rules require a minimum of a 300 foot ceiling, and half a mile of visibility, for visual landing; below this level and down to the minimum (below which the airport is considered "socked in," and must be closed), only instrument landings are permitted. These instrument landings work on about the same principle as the VOR navigational network, and require that extremely expensive radio-transmitter equipment be installed at the end of the runway.

For reasons of economy, most airports have so equipped only one runway. Since conventional radio navigation requires that the plane be headed directly toward the transmitter, all instrument-landing approaches must be made at that runway. If the wind direction and velocity is such that landing on that particular runway is undesirable, the plane nevertheless must make its approach *as if* it were going to land there until it breaks through the low cloud ceiling; only then does it abort the landing, circle around—all the while remaining below the cloud level—and land on the proper runway. All of this takes a great deal of time, and can "stack up" planes for an hour or more.

Area navigation techniques allow the aircraft to use the computer-directed triangulation method to approach any runway at the airport—even one not equipped with the necessary radio transmitters—directly. The computer simply listens to the transmitter's signal, calculates the proper approach path for whatever runway is to be used, and makes its landing without having to first execute the conventional low-level pass over the airport.

"Gadgetry"

The Avian device also features two additional innovations (both of which are also being marketed separately as "add-ons" to existing instrumentation, for

FOURTEEN WAYPOINTS interrupt the air route from Los Angeles to Chicago, each involving a deviation from the "true" direct course between the two cities. Area navigation techniques do away with the need for this kind of zig-zag routing.

companies unwilling to undertake full-scale conversion to area navigation). The first replaces the conventional dial-and-pointer instrument indicating the plane's distance from the next waypoint with a "digital read-out" viewer; the pilot need not read the clock-type dial, but may simply glance at the number displayed. The FAA has required this changeover for all aircraft in the interest of greater navigational ease.

A second improvement over conventional instrumentation is the radio receiver. Each time the pilot wants to receive a new navigational-aid radio signal—or, of course, talk or listen to a different station on his communications linkage—he must manually shift to the desired frequency. Where only a few stations are involved, the pilot has leisure in which to do this. But often there are many stations indeed—one short (one hour flying time) route has more than 60 navigational stations, each of which must be tuned in at the proper time, and at Newark Airport the takeoff alone involves 11 separate stations broadcasting on 11 different frequencies. At times like this, says Avian president William T. Bloodworth, "you have one guy flying the plane and the other (i.e., the co-pilot) just sitting there dialing the radio."

Avian's device works on the principle of the push-button automobile radio (although electronically it is a great deal more complicated); at least five (sometimes more on "deluxe" units) frequencies can be preset, and are available at the touch of a button. This greatly eases the pilot workload; although it is an integral part of Avian's area-navigation system, it, too, comes in a separate unit that can be added onto existing radio equipment.

Within the next few years, it is probable that virtually all commercial aircraft—and many private and corporate planes as well—will be equipped with some form of area navigation equipment. The savings, although small in percentage, should be large enough in terms of actual dollars to have a significant impact on the financial troubles being encountered by the industry.

D.

Freight Forwarders, Pipelines, and Inland Water Carriers

Here, we are concerned with three types of carriers whose importance is not obvious to the casual observer of the transportation scene. They are: domestic surface freight forwarders, petroleum pipelines, and inland water carriers. Each of these has been selected as representative of a whole class or group of similar carriers.

Of the "indirect" carriers, freight forwarders are the most important in terms of volume transported. "Direct" carriers are so called because they are in direct control of the operation of the vehicles with which they perform their service for the public. Indirect carriers may or may not operate vehicles in terminal service, but they purchase transportation service from a direct carrier for the line-haul or main part of the journey. This group includes REA Express (formerly Railway Express Agency), Parcel Post, and the air freight forwarders as well as the domestic forwarders. Indirect carriers are not considered to be a separate mode of transport but generally are treated as part of the mode from which they buy the majority of service. An idea of the importance of domestic surface freight forwarders can be gained from the fact that they originate some 4.5 million tons of freight a year as against about 1.6 million originated by the air freight industry.

As a mode of transportation, the pipeline has a characteristic which makes it unique. It is the only means of transport in which the vehicle is stationary and only the cargo moves. In the United States today there are several hundred thousand miles of pipelines which move various products, including water, natural gas, and many different chemicals. Of all these, only the petroleum pipelines are considered to be for-hire carriers which compete with other modes of transport. There are two types of oil pipelines, those which move crude oil and those which move refined oil products. Together, the oil pipeline companies operate about 210 thousand miles of line. Although this mode probably carries fewer products and has fewer individual customers than any other, in recent years it has generated more ton-miles of freight movement than the trucking industry.

Inland water carriers are only one of several "trades" which make up the water mode of transportation. The craft which ply our rivers and canals generate more ton-miles annually than do the Great Lakes trade, the coastal trade, or the ships that serve outlying states and territories. Like pipelines, inland water carriers specialize in carrying relatively few bulk commodities in large volume at slow speed. In terms of total volume of national cargo movement, inland water carriers rank fourth after railroads, pipelines, and trucking companies.

26

The Role of the Forwarder
in Efficient Transportation

Harry M. Baker
Coast Carloading Company

Richard J. Riddick
Freight Forwarders Institute

Until recently, the nation's railroads provided two basic freight services, one for less-than-carload (LCL) amounts, and one for full carloads (CL). Since the railroads loaded multiple consignments into an LCL car themselves, LCL service cost them more to perform than CL service, where the customer loaded the car, and its price was substantially higher. Around the turn of the century, some entrepreneurs discovered that they could consolidate different small shipments into a car more cheaply than the railroad could and thus profit from the "spread" between LCL and CL rates: the freight forwarder came into being. In the last few years, the railroads have quietly phased out LCL service and now handle principally carload shipments. In the future, therefore, the freight forwarder should become even more important.

Probably every shipper is aware of the fact that freight forwarders exist, and that they have an important place in domestic transportation. We have become so accustomed to the convenience of the freight forwarder that we give little thought to his origins. As a matter of fact, freight forwarders have been serving the shipping public for many years. They were in existence before there were airplanes or motor carriers. In a sense, they existed before our railroad system was fully developed.

No exhaustive study has as yet been written on the freight forwarder industry. However, many early writings tell of their existence in some form. Years ago they were active in the field of international commerce, arranging for the transportation of goods across international boundaries in Europe and from Europe to many destinations overseas. What was probably the first freight forwarders association was formed in Leipzig, Germany, in 1818. The London Shipping and Forwarding Agents' Conference was founded in January, 1897.

A special committee of the Ohio State Legislature, in 1867, stated that early forwarders issued through bills of lading, provided agencies at the points of delivery for the adjustment of losses, and supplied the great want of the mercantile community for prompt dispatch of freight and settlement of claims. They were held by the courts to have common carrier status because of their

From Harry M. Baker and Richard J. Riddick, "The Role of the Forwarder in Efficient Transportation," *Transportation and Tomorrow*, Stanford, California: Graduate School of Business, Stanford University, 1966, pp. 120-130. Copyright 1964, Stanford University. Used by permission of the copyright holders.

many points of similarity with common carriers. The courts, at that time, also held that to constitute a common carrier it is not essential that the person or corporation undertaking such service own the means of transportation.

The early dispatch companies and fast freight lines made varying arrangements to compensate the railroads. Later their operations came to be based on the payment of carload or volume rates and then charging a higher rate on the individual shipments. Railroads, at first, sought to prevent forwarders from combining shipments of different owners and paying the rate applicable to the consolidated lot, by adopting tariff or classification rules against such combining of freight. In 1908, the Interstate Commerce Commission rejected such rules saying, in effect, that the carrier (in this case the railroad) dealt with the shipment tendered, not with its ownership, nor with its ultimate use. In other words a carrier may not properly look beyond the transportation to the ownership of the shipment as a basis for determining the applicability of its rates. The Supreme Court upheld the I.C.C.

The pattern, thus established, of assembling shipments into volume lots and forwarding them at the carload or other volume rates to break-bulk points for distribution to the owners of the individual lots, has continued to the present time.

Until the trucks made their appearance as freight haulers in the 1920's forwarder operations were limited to points on rail or water routes. However, in the 20's forwarders began making extensive use of truck service for assembly and distribution and also for certain terminal-to-terminal movements. Off-line service was thus extended up to several hundred miles from rail centers.

At the time of motor carrier regulation in 1935, forwarders had contracts with thousands of truckers for assembly, distribution, and terminal-to-terminal movements of their freight. Forwarders filed tariffs under the Motor Carrier Act naming motor connections as participants under divisions. Some forwarders also filed applications for permits or certificates under the Act. The I.C.C. found that forwarders were common carriers at common law, but were not common carriers by motor vehicle within the meaning of the Motor Carrier Act. As to the tariffs, the Commission, by a supplementary report, also found that the joint forwarder-motor tariffs were unlawfully on file and ordered them stricken. However, that order was deferred from time to time until forwarders were regulated.

Proportional rates were established by certain motor carriers in 1937 and 1938, which were designed as a substitute for joint forwarder-motor rates. These were condemned as discriminatory.

The inability of forwarders to pay full published rates of motor carriers for assembly and distribution, and the blocking of all legal routes to divisional or proportional rates, caused the industry, its supporting carriers, and numerous shippers to press for regulation of the industry. The I.C.C. also recommended regulation of forwarders in many of its Annual Reports to Congress.

Congress commenced hearings and action to regulate freight forwarders beginning early in 1940 and continuing until Part IV of the Interstate Commerce Act was enacted on May 16, 1942.

In its report on the forwarder bill the House Committee significantly noted that forwarders perform a unique type of transportation service by means of coordinated use of the facilities of rail, motor, and water carriers in the transportation of freight and expressed the view that immediate legislation was the only effective means of preserving the freight-forwarding industry and retaining for the shipping public the inherent advantages of this mode of transportation.

A few of the things the Interstate Commerce Act did at that time were to designate by law that freight forwarders were common carriers, and it defined what they were and their relationship with the shipping public. The definition of a forwarder by the Act is:

The term 'Freight Forwarder' means any person which (otherwise than as a carrier subject to Part I, II or III of this Act) holds itself out to the general public as a common carrier to transport or provide transportation of property, or any class or classes of property, for compensation, in interstate commerce, and which, in the ordinary and usual course of its undertaking, (a) assembles and consolidates or provides for assembling and consolidating shipments of such property, and performs or provides for the performance of break-bulk and distributing operations with respect to such consolidated shipments, and (b) assumes responsibility for the transportation of such property from the point of receipt to the point of destination, and (c) utilizes, for the whole or any part of the transportation of such shipments, the services of a carrier or carriers subject to Part I, II or III of this Act.

A more easily understood definition came as a result of an I.C.C. investigation in the Howard Terminal Case:

... A Freight Forwarder is one who assembles shipments, consolidates them for shipment to destination, assumes responsibility in his bill of lading, fixing charges, serving the general public, not owner of goods shipped or act as shippers' agent, shipping tonnage in its own name, responsibility continuing until shipment is released at destination.

In effect, the forwarder acts as an arranger or broker for transportation, but unlike most other brokerage businesses, he assumes full responsibility for the merchandise from origin or pickup, the haul to destination terminal, and ultimate delivery at destination.

The rate charged was made up of the pure costs of pickup, loading, line-haul unloading, and delivery, plus overhead and a reasonable profit. Included in the overhead was, among other things, an assumption of loss and damage expense. This being the case, the forwarder was in a good position to charge a very refined rate in relation to the service performed. In addition to the assembly and distribution costs at origin and destination, the major factor in the establishment of rates was the basic rail carload rate, which is pretty well established from territory to territory on a mileage basis. With a complete understanding of these rates, it was possible to construct a freight forwarder's tariff.

Information in Exhibit 1 indicates the proportion of the freight forwarder's rate devoted to pick-up, loading, line-haul, unloading, delivery, overhead, loss and damage, and profit. Comparisons of freight forwarder, rail carload, and rail LCL for two commodities moving between selected city pairs is presented in Exhibit 2. In every case, freight forwarder rates can be seen to fall closer to rail LCL than rail carload rates but somewhere between the two.

The pickup service can be performed within the local terminal area by either the forwarder's own equipment, a separate cartage affiliate, or a contractual arrangement with a local cartage company. The same is true of the delivery service within the terminal zone. This terminal zone is prescribed by the Interstate Commerce Commission and is based upon the population of the main city in which the terminal is located. A city over 100,000 population, by the most recent census, would allow a terminal zone to reach five airline miles beyond the established city limits. This, incidentally, is the maximum size of a terminal zone. Beyond these areas the forwarder uses the services of short-haul carriers having I.C.C. authority for handling interstate traffic. It is the usual practice to publish point-to-point rates, with the forwarder absorbing the inbound charges or beyond charges.

Because freight forwarders are the only common carriers without a large, costly, and many times obsolete capital investment, they are in a better position to combine the various modes of transportation, innovate new ideas, and experiment with new methods to the almost immediate advantage of the shipping public.

The most dramatic of the recent innovations in co-ordinated transportation in which the freight forwarding industry has played such an important part has been the much talked-about piggyback developments. The idea is not new, but with the technological improvements in equipment and the demands of manufacturers and consumers for more rapid service, the transportation innovators

EXHIBIT 1

Basic Factors in Freight Forwarders' Rate Construction

	Door to Door	Dock to Dock	Door to Dock	Dock to Door
Pick-up	75	—		—
Loading	25			
Line haul	390	445	520	535
Unloading	30			
Delivery	90	—	—	
Pure transportation charges	610	445	520	535
Overhead, loss & damage, profit	150	150	150	150
Forwarder rates	760	595	670	685
	Rates in cents per hundred weight			

went to work. The volume of freight moving in this manner has increased by startling amounts, yet it is still in its infancy.

There are five (5) basic plans for freight moving in piggyback service.

Plan I is where the rail carriers, using their own flatcars, haul over the rails trailers owned by the motor carriers. The motor carriers solicit the traffic, perform the pickup and delivery, and bill the customer on the basis of their own motor carrier rates. In turn, they pay the railroads on a division or an agreed contract charge for performing the line-haul transportation. This, in effect, is a "substituted service" wherein a railroad substitutes rail for highway service. It does not constitute a true co-ordination of two or more services in a conjunctive sense. Such co-ordination is obtained when the one service is an extension of the other, rather than a mere substitution.

Under Plan II the railroads own all of the equipment and utilize the trailer-on-flatcar for the handling of their own freight which they have solicited, billed, and rated at published rail rates. These rates are frequently on a level with existing motor carrier rates.

In accordance with Plan III the railroads accept from the general public freight tendered by shippers in their own trailers for movement by the railroad on railroad flatcar equipment. Rates charged by the rail carrier are usually on an all-freight basis, subject to stated minimum weights and certain other restrictions.

Plan IV is different from the other plans outlined in one very important respect. Under this arrangement the shipper must furnish both the flatcar and the trailers. The freight loaded in the trailer is subject to certain maximum weights and other restrictions. A most unique aspect of this plan is that the rate charged by the railroad applies whether the trailers are loaded or empty. In other words, for the first time in transportation history, the rail carriers are assured of full revenue regardless of whether the equipment that they are hauling over the rails is loaded or empty.

EXHIBIT 2

Rail Carload—Rail L.C.L.—Forwarder Comparison

	Bangor, Maine	Boston, Mass.	Utica, N.Y.	New York City, N.Y.	Mari-etta, Ohio	Cleve-land, Ohio	Free-port, Ill.	Chi-cago, Ill.
Shoes								
C/L	6.63	6.63	6.63	6.63	6.44	6.44	3.69	3.69
L.C.L.	11.37	11.37	11.37	11.37	10.42	10.42	9.48	9.48
FWD.	9.79	9.55	9.79	9.55	10.28	10.28	9.37	7.48
Machinery								
C/L	3.90	3.90	3.90	3.90	3.90	3.90	3.71	3.71
L.C.L.	10.46	10.00	9.33	9.69	8.50	8.45	7.62	7.73
FWD.	9.76	7.99	8.85	6.92	8.25	7.53	7.21	6.12

All rates to Los Angeles, San Francisco, Portland, Seattle

Plan V traffic moves generally under joint railroad and truck rates or other combinations of co-ordinated service rates. Either mode may solicit traffic for through movement.

Piggyback Plans III and IV are the most recent and revolutionary developments in this mode of transportation. The co-ordination and integration of services and facilities has long been a major goal in the transportation policy of our country. Piggyback, particularly Plans III and IV, offers the most realistic answer to co-ordinated and integrated transportation that has yet appeared.

A further co-ordination can, and has, been achieved through a standardization of container equipment. Various sized standard containers can be used by shippers, consolidated to larger units, trucked to rail and/or docks and/or air terminals for complete co-ordination of all conceivable modes of transportation. Freight, as we know it, can be moved to any place in the world regardless of the medium through which it moves by this method, without costly damage and delay, in a very efficient and economical way. The enthusiasm of the railroads for Plan IV is readily understandable.

While the rate paid to the railroad is the same whether the trailers are loaded or empty, there is little doubt but that empty movements would be at a bare minimum. The transportation people of this country would co-ordinate efforts under Plan IV in such a way as to balance loadings. The resulting economy in our transportation system is obvious when we take into consideration the tremendous empty car mileage confronting the railroads today. The use of piggyback trailers with refrigerator units, collapsible containers for hauling liquids, and standard demountable bodies would all contribute to the ability to attain balanced loading. Of the Piggyback plans, it is Plans III and IV that are so dramatically different in concept. Here the railroads' service is stripped of the non-essential expensive terminal services and transit privileges and is reduced to pure transportation, furnishing the power and exclusive rights-of-way to haul shipper-owned flatcars and trailers from a consolidation point to a breakbulk or distribution point.

The Interstate Commerce Commission has on a number of occasions investigated the various plans with a thought to eliminating confusion and discrimination between various types of shippers and common carriers. To date, we still do not have a final determination on the various plans. This has, in a way, slowed the expansion of this new concept.

It is clear that the forwarding industry plays a very important role and one complementary to the railroad industry in furnishing a completely co-ordinated service to the shipping public. We do not perform any service that the railroads could not perform for themselves. However, over the years they have found that they could not profitably provide this consolidating and distributing service with the size of their organizations. The service to be performed today involves too much specialization and closer management attention to be done by rail executives concerned with other types of business. The individual forwarders provide this service from a smaller organizational unit, in a more efficient and economical manner. The overall service is better, the cost to the public is less, and there is ample room in the charge and cost differential for an efficient company to make a reasonable profit.

For many years, before the railroads had through service rates, freight forwarders were recognized as co-ordinators of transportation. Their function was to fit into their service each innovation and new development as it came along. Freight forwarders, therefore, are in a prime position to assist in developing the full potential of piggyback for the entire shipping public. As an independent, highly specialized carrier, the forwarder has the freedom of choice to select and co-ordinate the underlying media of transport that can best enable piggyback to be of the greatest value to the shipping public and a tremendous factor in our transport system. The forwarder is in a position to be the catalytic agent that can fuse the elements that are present in this new concept of transportation.

In summary, a few statistics will illustrate the size of the forwarding industry. In 1951, 94 forwarders, of which only 62 reported revenues over $100,000, reported total revenues of $338,500,000 and employed 12,724 persons. Ten years later, 88 forwarders, of which 64 reported revenues in excess of $100,000, reported a total of $448,900,000 and employed only 10,912 persons. It can be seen that many of our corporations today are larger than the entire forwarding industry by either gross revenues or number of employees. However, the job provided by this small segment of the transportation industry is a very important one and vital to the competitive way of our free enterprise system.

Under the National Transportation Policy, Congress is charged with the duty to provide for fair and impartial regulation of all modes of transportation so as to preserve the inherent advantages of each. Freight forwarders have definite inherent advantages which must be preserved, maintained, and expanded in order to give the benefit of these advantages to the public. Any discriminatory action to destroy or any failure on the part of Congress to rectify discriminations not only violates the National Transportation Policy but is injurious and costly to the shipping public.

Freight forwarders are firmly committed to rail operations. The revenues paid to the rail companies for power and exclusive rights-of-way to handle formerly unprofitable LCL traffic now amounts to in excess of 200 million dollars per year.

When one realizes that the freight forwarder is the only competitive voice offered to the motor carrier where the huge volume of LCL traffic is concerned, it is possible to appreciate its tremendous importance. As an example, just six years ago on the West Coast, between Southern California and the Pacific Northwest, the motor carrier rate was 15% higher than the freight forwarder rate for the same commodity from the same origin to the same destination. Through negotiations with one of the large railroads operating into this area, a forwarder was successful in reducing the rail transit time to compete with the fastest surface transportation. This healthy competitive service caused the motor carriers to reduce their LCL rates to the forwarder level in the face of increasing labor costs and higher equipment costs. In spite of this reduction through competitively influenced efficiencies, these same motor carriers have continued to show good profit margins. It can be left to your imagination to speculate on what would have happened to these rates had the forwarders' voices been silent. Remember one thing, if nothing else. The forwarder today is one of only two surface common carriers who hold themselves out to handle the increasing volume of LCL traffic.

27

Oil Pipelines' Place
in the Transportation Industry
J. L. Burke
Service Pipe Line Company

Since this selection was written, the oil pipeline industry's share of the total freight market has risen from 18 to 22 per cent. This is due, of course, to the increased use of petroleum as fuel by our expanding population and the increase of the pipeline net to meet the demand. The oil pipeline is our cheapest method of domestic freight transportation. The latest reliable estimate is that the average cost per ton-mile is .271 cents, far lower than the rail figure of 1.43 cents or the truck figure of 7.70 cents per ton-mile. This selection remains a near classic because of the succinct way in which it explains the economics, history, and operation of the pipeline industry.

Introduction

By rubbing his lamp, Aladdin brought forth the all-powerful genie. But no feat of the genie could have been more astounding than that of the modern pipeliner who, by pressing a button, produces wonders of which Aladdin never dreamed.

This modern-day genie calls forth not only oil, gas, and their products but also metallic ores, coal, limestone, gilsonite, borax, and paper mixtures, all in liquid suspension. Chemicals, alchohols, acids, and sulfur also move through steel or plastic pipelines at the command of today's genie.

When pipelines are discussed, the average consumer of this variety of products is likely to envision the gas or water lines that serve his home or business. He would be astonished to see the massive complex of large-diameter oil, natural gas, and products lines that span our country and are the nation's prime movers of energy.

Hidden beneath the surface of the ground, pipelines are rarely noticed. They

From J. L. Burke, "Oil Pipelines' Place in the Transportation Industry," *I.C.C. Practitioners' Journal,* April 1964. Copyright, Association of Interstate Commerce Commission Practitioners. Used by permission.

do not hold forth the glamour inherent in other more visual types of transportation. Much about them is little understood and often misunderstood. . .

The oil pipelines' ability to transport enormous volumes of crude oil and petroleum refined products daily from point to point at about the same cost to shippers as 20 years ago, is an achievement unparalleled by any other form of overland transportation. This economical transportation makes a dollars and cents contribution to the oil industry and to the consumer of petroleum products.

These pipelines have developed on sound private enterprise principles without government subsidies. With a comparative minimum but adequate degree of Federal regulation, they have become a network of transportation systems capable of serving all of the important producing and refining areas of the nation.

The nation's first successful oil pipeline was completed in 1865. Today, over 200,000 miles of oil pipelines are operating in the United States. In 1930, they carried 5 per cent of all intercity freight moving by all types of carriers, including truck, water, rail, and air. Currently, pipelines carry about 18 per cent of the nation's total intercity freight, both public and private.

The transportation of energy is the sole function of oil pipelines. A nation's economic growth is proportional to the constructive utilization of its energy and, in this, the United States leads the world.

Our abundant supply of energy has given our nation the highest standard of living and the strongest economy in the world. Through a competitive private enterprise system, fostered by a society that is greatly dependent upon energy industries, the supply and availability of low-cost energy is at an all-time high. Coupled with this growth is the growth of the oil pipeline industry.

It is estimated that we accomplish 99 per cent of our work through the use of machines. Oil and gas furnish approximately 74 per cent of the basic energy required to run these machines.

By the end of the next decade, our nation's consumption of energy is expected to double. Forecasts indicate that petroleum demand will concurrently rise two-thirds to seventeen million barrels per day.

These long-range forecasts also foretell that by 1980 more than half the nation's energy requirements will be met with petroleum transported by pipeline. In 1940, only 14 per cent of this supply of energy was moved by pipeline; after little more than 20 years, the figure has risen to over 40 per cent.

For at least the next 16 years, fossil fuels (oil, gas, coal) are expected to be our main energy sources. Nuclear power and hydroelectric power together are expected to generate an estimated 6 per cent of the nation's electric power by 1980 but are not anticipated to be direct competitors with fossil fuels.

This article will deal with crude oil and products pipelines only. In the Federal area, they are regulated by the Interstate Commerce Commission while the natural gas pipelines are under the jurisdiction of the Federal Power Commission. All are also subject to state regulation on intrastate operations.

The following three sections consider separately Oil Pipeline (1) Economics, (2) Operations, and (3) Regulation.

Economics

The principles discussed here are equally applicable to all conventional pipelines transporting liquids or liquified solids. This includes coal and other slurry pipelines as well as pipelines contemplated to transport solids in capsule form. A more recent development in the art of pipelining, the transportation of solids in capsules, is now being studied and field tested by a group of Canadian researchers.

Economic incentive for first oil pipelines

The first operationally successful oil pipeline was a 2-inch diameter 6-mile line laid in 1865 from the Pithole Oil Field in Western Pennsylvania to the Miller's Farm Station of the Oil Creek Railroad Company by Samuel Van Syckel, a promoter. At that time the crude oil was moved from the wells to the rail loading point by mules and wagons. The transportation charge was $1.50 per barrel; service was poor, being affected by mud, wagon breakdowns, teamster, and mule problems.

Prior to Van Syckel's successful promotion of this short line, several others had tried to lay oil pipelines. All had been unsuccessful, principally because of leaky pipes and mechanical problems. He solved the leak and pumping problems and began transporting oil to the rail point for $1.00 per barrel. The line returned its investment in a very few months.

In spite of its auspicious beginning, the company organized to own and operate the pipeline defaulted on its bank obligations two years later. Some of the economic factors which caused the bankruptcy then still confront the pipeline industry today. The first and most significant was the inexorable depletion of natural oil reservoirs as soon as they began to produce. In Van Syckel's time, when the law of capture prevailed, depletion of the reservoir and rapid decline in the rate of oil production was the order of the day.

Today, proration controls and scientifically planned production schedules result in a more predictable oil field development and decline. Orderly production practices have benefitted the pipeline substantially because the sizes of the lines required to connect new production are smaller and their economic life is longer.

Other factors contributing to the bankruptcy were overexpansion—Van Syckel added a second line as soon as the first proved successful—and a 50 cent reduction in the one dollar rate. The excessive profit achieved by Van Syckel attracted other entrepreneurs. Within relatively few months other pipelines were laid from the Pithole Field to rail and water loading points. Shortly thereafter the railroads, realizing that the fixed origin and destination pipeline operation guaranteed long-haul traffic for them whenever the pipeline terminated on their facility, became interested in the promotion and ownership of pipeline gathering systems.

Although today anyone is free to enter the oil pipeline business, the industry is stabilized as consumer demand and refinery requirements are met. The early tendency toward overexpansion caused by the lure of apparently unlimited demand and excessive rates is long past.

The first long distance oil pipeline was completed in 1879, fourteen years after the first gathering system. This 115-mile, 6-inch line which ran from Coryville, Pennsylvania, east to Williamsport and a junction with the Reading Railroad, was promoted by a group of producers who were looking for an adequate, suitably priced outlet for their oil. They were assisted by the Reading which wanted crude oil traffic.

The first long line was built in spite of vigorous opposition by the other railroads, and it proved highly successful.

The initial rates published for the pipeline-rail movement were lower than the current all-rail rates. The competition to supply the New York market resulted in a rate war during which the rates dropped so low that the New York Central, one of the all-rail carriers, concluded that it was not obtaining sufficient revenue to cover its out-of-pocket costs.

In 1881, the Standard Oil Trust completed its National Transit Pipe Line from Western Pennsylvania to New York City. During the same year, the Coryville-Williamsport line was extended to the Philadelphia refining area. The low cost of transporting crude oil via these and other new lines resulted in pipelines supplanting railroads as long distance transporters of crude oil just as pipelines had previously supplanted teams as a means of collecting oil in the fields.

Current costs and rates

The typical 1964 long-haul pipeline rate is 10-20 per cent of the rail rate as indicated by the examples in the following table, which are generally representative:

From	To	Commodity	Rate per Barrel Pipeline	Rail
West Texas Origins	Lima, Ohio	Crude Oil	38.5c[1]	285.9c[4]
Elk Basin, Wyoming	Wood River, Ill.	Crude Oil	34.0c[2]	153.7c[5]
Baton Rouge, Louisiana	Greensboro, N.C.	Petroleum Products	25.5c[3]	304.9c[6]

Pipelines are now the principal petroleum carriers, moving 75 per cent of the crude oil delivered to refineries and 45 per cent of the light petroleum products leaving refineries.

The moving of products from the refineries to market was, until the early 1930's, almost universally accomplished by rail, barge, or truck. Products pipelines then began their growth, and each year have increased their share of the traffic. This situation has occurred because, under today's technology, the cost for transport by pipeline decreases about 30 per cent each time the volume of oil moving through a pipeline doubles if the pipeline is properly designed for the larger volumes. Thus, the steady increase in petroleum product consumption, coupled with the trend toward population concentration, has made it possible to economically justify the construction of many more and larger pipelines from refineries to consuming points.

The per mile construction cost of an 8-inch pipeline is one-third less than that of a 12-inch pipeline. The larger 12-inch pipe can, when operating at its most economic throughput, transport three times as much oil as the 8-inch line, and the per barrel operating cost, ex capital charges, for moving oil through the larger 12-inch line is only one-third that of moving the same barrel through the smaller line. These cost relationships are equally applicable to both crude and products pipelines.

The rapidly increasing demand for long distance, cross-country pipelines with their lower transport costs resulted in the development by the steel industry of large diameter, high-strength pipe; that is, pipe with diameters greater than 10 or 12 inches and capable of withstanding 800 to 2,000 pounds per square inch pressure.

Development of nationwide pipeline network

Before the development of high-strength, big-inch, welded steel pipe in the 1930's, each pipeline company, when faced with the problem of increasing capacity, usually laid an additional line alongside the existing line. This is called looping the line. Until the early 1930's, 8-inch pipe was the largest pipeline which could be operated at the normal operating pressures of that period. Although 10- and 12-inch pipes were frequently used, they tended to split at the seam and required a lower-than-desirable operating pressure.

The economic capacity of each lapwelded, threaded, and coupled pipeline was about 20,000 barrels per day for each 8-inch pipeline and 60,000 barrels per day for each 12-inch pipeline. At the end of the 1920's, immediately before the development of high-strength, larger diameter pipelines, the major refineries processed 80,000-125,000 barrels per day, a volume exceeding the capacity of the largest diameter pipelines then available. With the pipeline the refiner had designed, financed and built to serve his own plant being used to capacity for his own traffic, there was no economic incentive to solicit nonproprietary volumes. Traffic for others would require the construction of additional pipelines which probably would not reduce, and might increase, the cost of transporting the owner's crude oil.

The successful development of high-strength, big-inch pipe provided an incentive for the solicitation of nonproprietary volumes since the increased volume moving through a single larger pipeline would, as pointed out earlier, reduce the cost of transporting the pipeline owner's crude oil. World War II added impetus to the change when curtailment of normal tanker movement from Texas to the East Coast required the pipeline industry, under government programming to reverse, interconnect, and maximize the utility of existing facilities. Under this program, an all-pipeline route from West Texas to the Philadelphia-New York refining area was developed. Also, many of the larger pipeline carriers commenced publishing joint tariffs naming through rates thereby adding to the refiners' choice of crude sources.

During and especially immediately after World War II, the oil refining industry underwent material changes which affected pipelines. Refineries which therefore had processed only sweet crude were compelled, by crude shortages incident to the demand for greatly increased amounts of products to carry on the war effort, to accept limited quantities of sour crude. Corrosion and product quality problems required these refiners to process the sour crude separately from the sweet. Also, the increasing postwar demand for varied products resulted in the development of new specialized refining processes which frequently required the pipelines to segregate crude with unusual characteristics for separate processing. This necessitated pipelines inaugurating a service called "batching" or segregating crudes by grades.

When the post World War II surge in petroleum demand developed, the pipeline industry was prepared to take advantage of the opportunities for economies which big inch pipe and interconnected pipeline systems presented. Large and small shippers who were interested in moving oil between common origin and destinations joined together in new big-inch pipelines sometimes on an undivided ownership interest basis, other times as stockholders in a separate pipeline company. These big, new pipelines ran from central junction points to refining centers or to other pipeline transfer points. The resulting economy has made it possible, as shown on the following chart, for the common carrier crude oil pipeline companies to publish rates during 1962 which were about 20 per cent lower than those published during 1945.

The average rate for all pipelines has remained almost constant since 1945, but products pipeline rates have increased about one-third. The average product line rate has increased because most product pipeline growth has occurred in short-

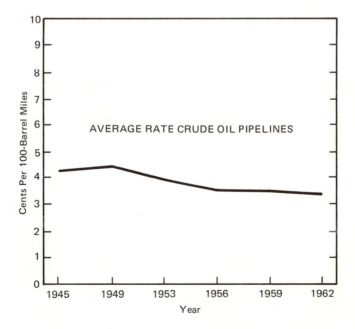

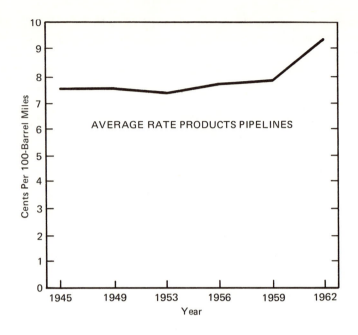

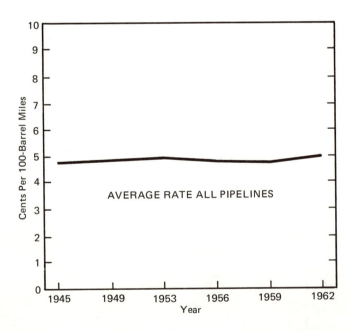

haul traffic through congested metropolitan areas. Pipelines, like other modes, have a higher per mile cost and rate for such traffic. Charges for long-haul product movements have declined.

The ability of pipeline companies to hold the line on rates has contributed to the oil industry's being able to maintain lower prices on gasoline and other pipelineable petroleum products in contrast to the steady upward trend in prices of other commodities.

The simultaneous decline of crude oil pipeline rates and increases in refinery operating costs were among the economic factors influencing refiners to discontinue the operation of small local plants and concentrate refining operations at fewer, larger refining centers. This trend in the oil industry has substantially increased the length and volume of pipeline traffic. Today, refiners routinely process crude transported more than 1,500 miles via pipeline. . .

Financial climate

The decline of pipeline rates in the face of steadily rising costs of construction and in operating material, supplies, and labor has been an unusual attainment. This is attributable primarily to three factors: (1) the industry's outstanding record of constant alertness to and adoption of cost reducing technical and operating improvements; (2) the steadily increasing volume of traffic; and (3) the partial isolation of pipeline costs from inflation.

Pipelines are protected from much of the technological obsolescence and inflation spiral which has plagued other industries. The technology of pipelining, i.e., the moving of liquid through a pipe, is so basic that it has not been appreciably affected by new technology. Buried pipe and right of way represent 80-90 per cent of a pipeline company's total investment. Approximately 70 per cent of operating revenue is needed to cover capital charges. Only 30 per cent of the pipeline rate is needed for labor, material, and other operating items. Thus, 70 per cent of an operating pipeline company's rate is isolated from the effect of inflation. New construction is, of course, subject to cost increases. But even here the industry has, by using bigger and higher strength pipe, reduced the quantity of steel needed per unit of capacity. This, combined with improved construction and operating practices, has enabled the industry to maintain an almost level cost for new capacity.

The risks in pipeline investments are limited to economic rather than technological factors. Pipelines have required longer than anticipated construction periods, have been slowed by weather problems and landowner resistance, but to date none has failed to operate because of technical problems. Pipelines still have economic problems when an oil field fails to develop as anticipated, a refinery shuts down, demand grows more slowly than anticipated, or a competitive pipeline is constructed.

Since the reserves in a proven oil field can be calculated reasonably well, and since refineries and population centers do not make major shifts or disappear, pipeline projects tend to be long-term, safe, stable investments. The financial promotion by pipeline is characterized by the following factors:

A. Investors, both public and private, consider pipeline equities and debt obligations to be attractive investments.

B. Many well conceived pipeline projects based on reasonably assured long range traffic may be financed with high debt-equity ratios.
C. Pipeline projects generate returns ranging usually from 4 to 8 per cent. These rates of return, reflecting competitive and regulatory influence, are relatively low compared to the earning potentialities of other industries but are long range and reliable.
D. Pipelines, to a greater extent than any other transportation mode, have a very high initial cost of entry. This has been a significant factor in the sound development of the United States pipeline industry. The necessity of committing large amounts of capital initially and then obtaining a low, but usually steadily increasing return on the capital over a long period of time, has tended to attract only responsible, courageous, patient, and financially strong entrepreneurs.

Ownership by refiners

The history of the development and growth of pipelines is substantially different from that of any other form of transportation. One of the major differentiating features lies in the ownership.

During the latter part of the nineteenth century, when the pipeline industry was developing, several lines were organized by private entrepreneurs whose only objective was a profit from the transportation.

These projects were unsuccessful because pipelines are immobile. They have no origin or destination flexibility. When the shipper for whose traffic the line was promoted decided to use another transporter, the pipeline, unlike other modes, could not solicit traffic from others, nor could it transfer its equipment to another route. Most of these early nonrefinery owned projects were ultimately taken over by the refiners who shipped through the line. The refiner became the "shipping public" of the pipelines because the refiner's crude supply and product market demand established a definite and reasonably assured volume of traffic to justify the ownership of the pipeline. This situation required the refiners to finance, build, own, and operate the pipelines upon which their refineries were dependent for a crude supply, because only through assuming the investment and risk of ownership of such pipelines could they be assured of a steady, uniform quality, low-cost supply of crude oil, their essential raw material. The nature of ownership and development of products pipelines were similar since refiners were reluctant to develop marketing outlets without an assured low-cost efficient products pipeline between their refinery and the marketing area.

Pipelines are suited to refinery operations because a refinery served by pipeline does not have to provide unloading terminal service nor return empty tank cars or trucks, and it has considerably more flexibility as to locations than a refinery dependent upon water routes.

A producer is not usually interested in providing capital for a pipeline. He prefers to convert his oil to cash and then to additional producing facilities as quickly as possible. He seldom has sufficient production of his own to justify the high investment required for a pipeline and has no long-term assurance of a continuing market at the final terminal. A similar result is that it has become necessary for the refiner to provide the capital to construct extensions to new producing areas. Since substantial production will not develop until after adequate pipeline transportation has been made available, the refiners have assumed the risk of relying on sufficient oil ultimately being produced to pay out the pipeline investment.

Developments in pipeline ownership by nonrefiners

Although some pipeline companies have survived from the early days without financial ties to refining companies, the number of such companies and the percentage of the industry they represented constantly declined until the early 1950's.

The typical nonrefiner-controlled pipeline gathered oil and transported it to small specialized local refiners in the same area. By the early 1950's, national defense demands and growth in petroleum consumption had created a nationwide refiner-owned pipeline network, which, like the U.S. rail system, included junctions where oil could be transferred from one pipeline company to another. Junctions developed at former major oil fields which were initially served by many pipelines and remained on the route when expansions and new lines were laid. Also, large refining complexes had developed at natural transportation and population centers, and the one-pipeline one-refinery situation of the pre-big-inch period had caused a concentration of pipelines at these key points.

There has gradually developed a continuing need for connections between these natural pipeline centers and between the major refining areas and population concentration points where the oil products are consumed. The pipeline network is the one transportation agency found by the House Armed Services Committee to be in sound condition with no question of its ability to expand capacity in the event of a national emergency.[7]

The nonrefiner-owned Buckeye Pipe Line Company was initially a part of and moved crude for the Standard Oil Trust. It gained considerable traffic and revenue during World War II, when some of its crude lines were reversed and joined into a cross-country continuous pipeline movement. In 1952, the company began transporting products by pipeline. Via independent financing, it built and operated a products system from the New York City refining area to consuming centers in upper New York State. The project worked out well, and the company has since then expanded its activities until in 1963 its total assets had increased 130 per cent over 1952. Its stock was listed on the New York Stock Exchange and was recommended as a growth issue by qualified investment services. The controlling ownership of the company has recently been purchased by the Pennsylvania Railroad which had earlier acquired one-third of the stock on the open market as a desirable long-term investment.

Other nonrefiner-owned systems are the Pipeline Division of the Southern Pacific Railroad, the Little Inch Division of the Texas Eastern Transmission Company and the Mid-America Pipeline Company.

The Southern Pacific has constructed an extensive product pipeline system principally along its railroad right-of-way. Texas Eastern transports petroleum products and liquefied-petroleum gas from the Texas Gulf Coast to Chicago, Cincinnati, and Cleveland. It has recently extended its lines to the Philadelphia area, and is now in the process of constructing an LPG line into upper New York State. Mid-America, promoted and organized by the Katy Railroad, was completed in 1960 and moves propane, butane, and natural gasoline from processing plants in the Southwest to consuming centers in Oklahoma, Kansas, Iowa, Illinois, Wisconsin, and Minnesota.

A pipeline system operating at less than maximum capacity has a strong incentive to solicit additional traffic because the fixed capital costs continue the same whether the line is full or only half full. Thus, the additional barrel which contributes a full unit of revenue increases only the variable operating costs. In the quest for this profitable additional barrel, individual pipeline companies are anxious to extend service to any likely customer. This situation in itself belies the occasional complaint that pipelines are not true common carriers. They are common carriers both by law and by business necessity. The potential shippers or "public" for almost 100 pipeline companies is 300 refineries. The industry by its nature and function is able to serve its potential "public" better than any other transport mode. Many refiners and marketers are located on water and transport their crude or products by barge or tanker. Those served by pipeline have a choice of several competitive pipeline routes and a wide selection of crude oil sources and product markets.

For example: Fifteen pipeline companies currently participate in tariffs to Clark Oil and Refining Company's Blue Island, Illinois, refinery. Clark does not own any crude oil pipelines, yet it can, through these published tariffs, originate crude oil shipments almost anywhere in the states of Texas, New Mexico, Oklahoma, Kansas, Colorado, Wyoming, Montana, Nebraska, and Illinois, for movement to its plant.

Great Lakes Pipeline, via its local and joint tariffs, serves 28 refineries making their products available to marketers throughout the upper mid-western section of the United States.

Pipelines are not only serving to help make America a great and progressive nation but are making essential and important contributions to the overall improvement of the world's standard of living. American pipeline technical and managerial know-how is now being extensively adapted to accommodate the construction and operation of pipelines for movement of oil from remote or underdeveloped areas of the world to market. In Europe, American pipeline personnel and equipment are helping to provide the energy for Europe's rapidly expanding economy.

Operations

The transportation of slurries, capsuled solids, and an array of liquids illustrates the versatility of pipelines, but the handling of petroleum and its derivatives represents the real substance of pipelining. In this country, oil pipelines transport a daily average of 6 million barrels of crude oil and 3 million barrels of petroleum products. Converted, this amounts to approximately 875,000 tons of crude and 375,000 tons of products.

The physical task of moving the commodity, be it petroleum or any other, from its source to its destination comprises that phase of pipelining called Operations. . .

Pipe

The great advantage of pipelines is that they remain immobile while the commodities they carry move. Thus, pipelines are not subjected to the interference with movement and attrition of equipment that attend the other forms of transportation. Pipelines also serve the dual purposes of being both the container and the conveyer of the materials they transport. They are naturally available for continuous and uninterrupted service; deadheading and carrybacks are not required; and they are almost immune to aboveground activities and buffeting from the elements. This last characteristic, plus invisibility, makes pipelines vital to national defense.

The pipe used is made from steel and is manufactured to standards established by the American Petroleum Institute (API). These standards provide for uniformity of dimensions, hydrostatic testing, and grading of pipe according to the strength of the steel used in its manufacture. In practice, pipelines, like most engineered structures, have a wide margin of safety and use only a portion of a pipe's full strength. This practice is in line with recommendations of codes issued by the American Standards Association (ASA). Adherence to these standards and codes has contributed to the dependable and safe operation characteristic of pipelines.

The dependability of operations is further enhanced in modern pipelines by protecting the lines from soil corrosion. This is accomplished by applying a protective coating material to the pipe surface. In addition, the line is placed under cathodic protection by creating a flow of electric current from the soil into the pipe to counteract the galvanic current associated with the corrosion of steel in soils. A good coating supplemented by cathodic protection essentially eliminates external corrosion.

Internal corrosion is effectively prevented by the use of chemical inhibitors and a regular maintenance program aimed at cleaning the pipe with swabs or scrapers. The inhibitors are added in minute quantities to the material being handled and inhibit corrosion by dispersing as a thin protective film on the internal surface of the pipe. Inhibitors are usually not required for crude oil lines but are regularly used in products lines.

Scrapers are run in most crude pipelines at regular intervals of a few months to sweep out deposits of water and to remove wax and asphalt which tend to accumulate on the walls of the lines. These contaminants, if not removed, would interfere with the efficient operation of a line and eventually could plug it. Product lines require less frequent cleaning.

Machinery

Energy is required to move a fluid through a pipeline. The energy required to sustain flow takes the form of differential fluid pressure. The amount of pressure required for a given rate of flow can be calculated quite accurately and depends upon changes in elevation along the line, diameter and length of line, roughness of the interior surface of the pipe, and density and viscosity (fluidity) of the flowing material. Reciprocating or centrifugal pumps driven by engines, electric motors, or gas turbines are used to pressurize the fluid. For short pipelines, all the pressure is imparted at the input end of the line; for long cross-country pipelines, the total pressure required to move the product is supplied in successive steps by pressuring stations placed at 30- to 100-mile intervals along the line. At these locations the pressure is increased to limits generally ranging from 500 to 1,500 pounds per square inch.

Pressuring stations moving liquids are called pump stations. The machinery in the stations may consist of one or several units comprising several thousand horsepower. In many cases, the station operation is automated so that no attendant manpower is required and the stations are controlled and monitored from a control center many miles away.

Generally, this supervisory control of remote stations takes place over company owned and operated communication facilities, either wire line or microwave. Leased wires are also being used to an increasing extent, although pipeline companies have traditionally owned their own communications much as have the railroads. The design of these remote controlled stations incorporates devices for failsafe operations and protection from all ordinary upsets and for continued operation in event of interruption in the remote control communication circuit.

Consignment of traffic

Pipelines obtain material for transport in a variety of ways. Products pipelines usually originate from storage concentrated at refineries and connect with and deliver to distribution terminals. Crude oil lines gather small volumes of oil from widely scattered producing areas for movement to the refineries.

The handling of crude oil from lease to refinery includes many pipeline operations. In connection with this, it should be noted that there are in the United States about 600,000 oil wells. These wells produce an average of only 12 barrels per day, a number of them producing one barrel or less per day. The advantages of pipeline transportation are so attractive to the producer that most of these wells have a pipeline connection for shipping the oil produced to markets even though it may be uneconomical to the pipelines.

Crude oil pipeline operations begin at the oil producer's lease storage tanks. There, a pipeline representative, called a gauger, measures the volume of oil in the tanks, its temperature and API gravity (unit weight as defined by the American Petroleum Institute). These last two measurements are essential because crude oil is measured by volume, which varies with temperature, and because the price structure of crude oil hinges on API gravity, a higher gravity usually meaning a higher price. A sample of the oil is tested to assay its content of basic sediment and water (BS&W). If these impurities are minimal (generally less than 1 per cent by volume), the pipeline accepts custody of the oil. Otherwise, it is refused, and the producer must treat it, using chemicals and heat, to remove the impurities and bring it up to the pipeline's standards.

When the gauger accepts custody of oil from a lease, he closes and seals a valve on the inlet to the producer's tanks and breaks a seal and opens a valve on the pipeline connection which will permit the oil to flow or be pumped into the pipeline gathering system. This system, in contrast to the trunk or main-line system, operates at low pressures and is generally made up of 2- to 8-inch pipe and small, low-volume pumping units ranging in size from 5 to 200 horsepower.

After the oil has been delivered from the producer's tank to the pipeline, the gauger returns and makes a closing measurement of volume and temperature of the oil remaining in the tank below the pipeline connection. He then completes and signs the run ticket and reverses the position and sealing of the valves. A representative of the shipper observes the gauger on both opening and closing measurements and validates the run ticket by countersigning it.

The run ticket may be compared to what might be a partial receipt copy of a bill of lading. The shipper tenders crude to the pipeline in large quantities using a tender form. The run ticket serves as a partial receipt, the volumes recorded being credited against the tender until the total amount is reached. The run ticket shows the gross volume, temperature, and gravity of oil taken by the pipeline for the account of a shipper and the credit of the producer. Thus the pipeline, servicing thousands of run tickets through its oil accounting department, performs a bookkeeping service for both shipper and producer.

The pipeline oil accounting group corrects the volume of $60°$ F., deducts the BS&W content, and arrives at a figure of net oil run. The pipeline company notifies the shipper how much oil he has bought from the producer for the shipper's account. In areas where production is prorated by law, the pipeline must also take care not to receive more oil than is allowed. The average pipeline rate for performing this whole gathering operation is approximately 5 cents per barrel which includes movement through the gathering system to the main line pump station.

Nearly 50 per cent of all oil run from leases is now being measured by Lease Automatic Custody Transfer methods (LACT). LACT, a recently developed cost reduction technique, provides an automatic, unattended measuring and recording device, which is either a meter or a small calibrated dump tank. In most cases, the volumes recorded are also adjusted to $60°$ F. automatically by a temperature compensating device.

There are generally at least two tanks at a LACT unit—a run tank and a "bad oil" tank. Raw crude oil is processed from the well through treaters and through gas and contaminant separators into the run tank. It is automatically pumped from the run tank through a BS&W monitoring device, the meter, and a back-pressure valve, and delivered to the pipeline. A sample, taken and stored automatically, is checked at least once a month, or each time the pipeline gauger writes a run ticket. In case the BS&W monitor detects oil with a BS&W content greater than that allowed by the pipeline's published rules, it will automatically change the position of valves so that the oil is diverted away from the meter back to a bad oil tank. This generally initiates an alarm which tells the producer's lease operator of the trouble.

Because of a normal amount of wear and slippage in a positive displacement type meter, a correction factor must be regularly determined and applied to the volume registered by the meter. This is done by using a special vessel, called a prover, of known capacity in series with the meter so that the metered volume can be accurately checked against the known volume of the prover. The ratio of the metered volume to the prover volume is called a meter factor and is determined as frequently as necessary—generally once a month—to provide an accurate measurement. The operators of pipelines handling liquids take extreme precautions to make accurate measurements of volumes, either in tanks or by meters, because they must account for the same amount they are recorded as receiving.

Delivering to consignees

Deliveries from the pipeline are made by the same method used in receiving the oil from the producer's lease; the only difference is in the size of deliveries. Where a pipeline gauger may take custody from a producer in a 200-barrel tank, a pipeline commonly delivers into refinery tanks as large as 150,000 barrels and gauges them with the same type of equipment used on the 200-barrel lease tank. Deliveries are also made automatically through meters which operate the same as LACT units in gathering systems. The principal difference is in the size of equipment and volumes handled since deliveries at rates of 300,000 barrels per day are not uncommon. The delivery ticket, comparable to the receipt copy of a freight bill, is essentially the same as a gauger's lease run ticket in that it shows volume, BS&W content, temperature, and gravity.

The pipeline's oil accounting group again does the book work of calculating the delivered volumes. This is used by the pipeline for determining the total transportation charges, and by the shipper and consignee for their purposes. The pipeline rates, like those of railroads and other carriers, are named in published tariffs filed with the Interstate Commerce Commission on interstate traffic and state commissions on intrastate traffic.

The usual terminus for crude oil pipelines is a refinery, but the oil may be moved by several interconnected pipelines before it is delivered to its final destination. In this manner, pipelines operate with interchanges of shipments similar to truck lines and railroads. A measurement of quantity and a test of quality are made at each pipeline junction where custody is transferred from one pipeline to another, and a delivery ticket is written to account for the oil and to be used in computing the division of the transportation charges between the connecting pipelines.

Deliveries from product lines are handled through similar measuring facilities and in much the same manner at final destination truck or rail loading terminals from which the products are moved to retail marketing outlets.

The pipeline bases its charges to the shipper on the volume of oil delivered at destination. Until recently, all pipelines subtracted from this volume a "tender deduction" ranging from one-half to one per cent for crude lines to several per cent for products lines to cover vaporization and shrinkage losses "inherent in the transportation by pipeline" of these fluids. Improved pipeline efficiency and the adoption of "closed-system" operation have so reduced losses that most major crude oil pipelines have now eliminated or greatly reduced the tender deduction requirement.

Scheduling consignments

Because of the complexity of refining operations and the many types of crude oil produced, it is necessary to segregate crude oil by grades so that it can be used to best advantage by the refinery. Two or more grades of crude quite often come from the same oil field but from different producing strata underground. When this occurs and the oil is to be segregated by grades, separate gathering systems must sometimes be built into the trunkline stations. There the crude is segregated in tanks and moved through the main trunk of the pipeline in batches of several thousand barrels each. Major pipelines may have as many as 15 separate grades of crude oil en route through their systems with as high as 100 batches moving currently through segments of the line.

The importance of batching operations is even greater for products pipelines. These lines often handle many batches of different products for different shippers. In both crude and products lines operations, constant attention is given to preserving the integrity of each shipment and to minimizing commingling between abutting batches as they pass in sequence through the line. It is common practice to condict a joint test of each batch whenever custody changes to confirm the quality of the product.

The problem of batching is handled by pipeline personnel called schedulers and dispatchers. They work with carefully prepared schedules which include both departure and arrival times of shipments. A batched product may require days or weeks of intransit time, be increased or decreased in volume as it passes through a pipeline system, and be one of many separate batches in the system. It is the duty of these personnel to track each batch and to advise the receiving consignees when their shipments will arrive.

The problem of scheduling traffic in modern pipelines is so related to a need for centralized control of operations that automation and remote control have become inevitable. Consequently, pipelines have made remarkable progress in this area and further experimentation and development are underway. Computer control of selected pipeline operations is being investigated by several companies, and it is only a matter of time until a computer or other techniques of automation will be programmed to control an entire pipeline operation.

Regulation

The Interstate Commerce Act

Interstate oil pipelines were made common carriers subject to what is now part I of the Interstate Commerce Act, 49, U. S. C. A. 1-27, by the Hepburn

Amendment of June 29, 1906, 34 Stat. at L. 584. For a few years thereafter, pipelines still operated mainly as private facilities with operators construing the Act (1) to apply only to those carriers desiring to offer pipeline transportation to the general public by publishing and filing tariffs with the Commission, or (2) as avoidable by their incorporating a different company in each state through which oil moved and transferring title to the oil at state borders.

The Interstate Commerce Commission instituted an investigation of pipeline transportation in 1911 and ordered interstate lines to file tariffs with the Commission on or before September 1, 1912. *In the Matter of Pipelines,* 24 I. C. C. 1 (1912). The Commission's order was appealed to the Commerce Court which enjoined its enforcement on the ground that opening up all private interstate pipelines to public use was a deprivation of private property without compensation. In other words the Hepburn Act as thus applied to pipelines was unconstitutional. *Prairie Oil and Gas Company, et al.* v. *U.S.A. et al.,* 204 Fed. 798 (1913).

The Interstate Commerce Commission appealed to the Supreme Court which reversed the Commerce Court and sustained the Commission's Order as valid as to all pipelines involved except the Uncle Sam Oil Company. *The Pipe Line Cases,* 234 U.S. 548, 34 S. Ct. 956 (1914). In deciding that the pipelines other than Uncle Sam were common carriers subject to the Interstate Commerce Act, the Court said:

> The only matter requiring much consideration is the constitutionality of the act. That the transportation is commerce among the states we think clear. That conception cannot be made wholly dependent upon technical questions of title, and the fact that the oils transported belonged to the owner of the pipeline is not conclusive against the transportation being such commerce. . . .
>
> The control of Congress over commerce among the states cannot be made a means of exercising powers not intrusted to it by the Constitution, but it may require those who are common carriers in substance to become so in form. So far as the statute contemplates future pipelines and prescribes the conditions upon which they may be established there can be no doubt that it is valid. So the objection is narrowed to the fact that it applies to lines already engaged in transportation. But, as we already have intimated, those lines that we are considering are common carriers now in everything but form. They carry everybody's oil to a market, although they compel outsiders to sell it before taking it into their pipes. The answer to their objection is not that they may give up the business, but that, as applied to them, the statute practically means no more than they must give up requiring a sale to themselves before carrying the oil that they now receive. The whole case is that the appellees, if they carry, must do it in a way that they do not like. There is no taking and it does not become necessary to consider how far Congress could subject them to pecuniary loss without compensation in order to accomplish the end in view.

In affirming the decree with respect to the Uncle Sam Oil Company and thus deciding it was not a common carrier subject to the Act, the Court said:

There remains to be considered only the Uncle Sam Oil Company. This company has a refinery in Kansas and oil wells in Oklahoma, with a pipe line connecting the two which it has used for the sole purpose of conducting oil from its own wells to its own refinery. It would be a perversion of language, considering the sense in which it is used in the statute, to say that a man was engaged in the transportation of water whenever he pumped a pail of water from his well to his house. So as to oil. When, as in this case, a company is simply drawing oil from its own wells across a state line to its own refinery, for its own use, and that is all, we do not regard it as falling within the description of the act, the transportation being merely an incident to use at the end.

The Uncle Sam decision is the legal basis for present-day privately owned products pipeline systems. Such systems conduct products from the owner's own refineries to their own distribution terminals and thus are like Uncle Sam's line "conducting oil from its own wells to its own refinery."

Following the Supreme Court's 1914 decision, pipeline carriers filed tariffs with the Interstate Commerce Commission, but further effort at regulation was limited. In 1922, the Commission considered the reasonableness of minimum tenders, commonly 100,000 barrels, which pipelines were publishing in their tariffs and thus requiring from shippers as a prerequisite to shipment. The Commission decided that tenders in excess of 10,000 barrels were unreasonable. *Brundred Brothers v. Prairie Pipe Line Co.*, 68 I. C. C. 458 (1922). This decision affected oil movements from points in Kansas, Oklahoma and Texas to points in Pennsylvania.

In 1934, the I. C. C. undertook an exhaustive investigation of the reasonableness of crude oil pipeline rates, gathering charges, regulations and practices. This investigation was the outgrowth of a complaint lodged with the Commission by a group of refiners asking for suspension of reductions in rates that had been made by Stanolind (now Service) Pipe Line Company. The suspensions were asked on the grounds that the reduced rates gave Stanolind's shipper-owner an advantage over the complainants who had only rail facilities available to them. The Commission refused to suspend the reduced rates and announced a general investigation on its own motion of all pipeline rates, charges and practices.

The investigation dragged out over a number of years. Meanwhile the Commission undertook to value pipeline property as of December 31, 1934. The valuations ultimately found for all pipelines in the period 1939-1943 provided a basis for judging the reasonableness of rates.

Late in 1940, the Commission rendered a decision in the rate investigation which had started in 1934, holding that crude oil pipeline rates yielding more than 8 per cent return on the value of carrier property were unreasonable, and reaffirming and extending the effect of the decision in the *Brundred Brothers* case that minimum tenders in excess of 10,000 barrels were unreasonable. *Reduced Pipeline Rates and Gathering Charges*, 243 I. C. C. 115 (1940). Most of the pipeline companies which had not already voluntarily reduced rates did so in 1940 and early 1941. The Commission's final order in the case was entered in 1948 directing a few companies which had not complied with the minimum tender requirement to do so, but finding that in the interim, rates had generally been voluntarily reduced to the 8 per cent return level. *Reduced Pipeline Rates and Gathering Charges*, 272 I. C. C. 375 (1948).

Meanwhile, attention had also turned to the rates of products pipelines. In *Petroleum Rail Shippers Ass'n* v. *Alton & Southern R. R.*, 243 I. C. C. 589 (1941), several rail carriers and two products pipelines, Great Lakes Pipe Lines Company and Phillips Pipe Line Company, were defendants. The Commission ordered reductions in the rates of Great Lakes and Phillips and established a minimum tender of 5,000 barrels of the same specifications from one shipper to one consignee, subject to delay until the carrier had accumulated 25,000 barrels of the same specifications. In this case, the Commission established the principle of a rate of return of 10 per cent as being reasonable for products pipelines. The distinction between the 10 per cent maximum return allowed for products lines and 8 per cent maximum permitted on crude lines was attributed to the greater hazards and risks involved in products line operations.

In the case of *Minnelusa Oil Corporation* v. *Continental Pipe Line Company, et al.*, 258 I. C. C. 41 (1944), the Commission reaffirmed the 8 per cent return on crude line valuations established in its earlier decision in *Reduced Pipeline Rates and Gathering Charges, supra.* The case involved the reasonableness of joint rates for the movement of crude oil from Wyoming origins to Salt Lake City. In addition to the decision that rates should not exceed an 8 per cent return, the complainant also was awarded reparation for the period after filing of the complaint when rates were found to be unreasonable. This was the first and only time a pipeline carrier had been ordered to pay reparation.

The most recent U.S. Supreme Court consideration of the application of the Interstate Commerce Act to pipelines involved Champlin Refining Company's private products line extending from its refinery at Enid, Oklahoma, across Kansas and Nebraska to a terminal in Iowa. In the first of two cases, Champlin was required to file valuation reports with the I. C. C. and to follow the I. C. C.'s uniform system of accounting with respect to its ownership of the line. *Champlin Refining Co.* v. *United States*, 329 U.S. 29, 67 S. Ct. 1 (1946). Thereafter, the Commission ordered Champlin to file tariffs and this order also was appealed ultimately to the Supreme Court. The court held that Congress did not intend for that section of the Interstate Commerce Act which imposes the duty of serving the public at regulated rates to apply to private products lines "whose services were unused, unsought after, and unneeded by independent producers." *Champlin Refining Co.* v. *United States*, 341 U.S. 290, 71 S. Ct. 715 (1951).

The present provisions of part I of the Interstate Commerce Act as applied to common carrier pipelines in most respects are the same as for railroads and are similar to those covering other modes. They require: that a tariff covering a particular movement of property, oil in this case, be filed with the Commission before transportation begins; that the rates and charges provided in the tariff be just and reasonable, that they be strictly observed, and that they not be greater for a short haul than for a longer haul which includes the short-haul route; that just and reasonable regulations and practices be established for the transporting and handling of property; that the carrier not give any unreasonable preference and not unduly discriminate in any way in connection with the services rendered; that the carrier provide and furnish transportation upon reasonable request therefor and establish reasonable through rates with other such carriers; that the carrier not pool traffic, service, or gross or net earnings with another carrier except with the specific approval of the Commission; and that the carrier keep its accounts and records in conformity with the uniform system of accounts for pipelines prescribed by the Commission.

Pursuant to the Act, the Commission requires carriers by pipelines to submit an annual report which becomes a matter of record available to the general public. The 58-page report form calls for full and detailed disclosure not only of accounting and statistical items relating to the common carrier activity, but also disclosure of information about such matters as "Corporate Control Over Respondent," including details about stock ownership, voting powers and elections; funded debt, debt to affiliated companies and notes payable; "Compensation of Officers and Directors," including names and amounts; and "Payments (of $20,000 or more) for Services Rendered by Other than Employees."

The Commission is given broad powers under the Act in connection with making of investigations, holding of hearings, and the issuance of orders to effectuate the purposes of the Act. Its agents are authorized at all times to inspect and copy any and all accounts, books, records, memoranda, correspondence, and other documents of the carrier, and the same type of records of any person controlling, controlled by, or under common control with any such carrier as the Commission deems relevant to such person's relation to or transactions with such carrier. Pursuant to this authority, the books of account are examined regularly by the Commission's auditors.

The Act makes it unlawful for any common carrier or any officer, agent, or employee of same, or for any other person or corporation lawfully authorized by the carrier to receive information therefrom, knowingly to disclose or to permit to be acquired by any person or corporation other than the shipper or consignee, without the consent of such shipper or consignee, any information concerning the nature, kind, quantity, destination, consignee, or routing of any property tendered or delivered to such common carrier for interstate transportation, which information may be used to the detriment or prejudice of such shipper or consignee or which may improperly disclose his business transactions to a competitor; and it is made unlawful for any person or corporation to solicit or knowingly receive such information which may be so used.

Severe penalties, including prison sentences in some cases, can be imposed for violations of the Interstate Commerce Act.

Clayton Antitrust Act

The Clayton Antitrust Act is brought into play mainly where a carrier has interlocking directors and officers with companies with which it has financial dealings. Section 10 of the Act, 15 U. S. C. A. 20, provides that carriers shall not have any dealings in securities, supplies, or other articles of commerce or any contracts for construction or maintenance in the amount of more than $50,000 in the aggregate in any one year with another company, when the carrier shall have upon its board of directors or as its president, manager, purchasing or selling officer, or agent in the particular transaction any person who at the same time is a director, manager, purchasing or selling officer or who has any substantial interest in the other company, unless such purchases or dealings shall be with the lowest bidder under bidding arrangements prescribed by the Interstate Commerce Commission.

Elkins Act and consent decree

The Elkins Act of 1903, 49 U. S. C. A. 41, was passed by Congress to strengthen certain provisions of the Interstate Commerce Act prohibiting rebates and concessions and to stop the discriminatory practices of the railroads between shippers. When pipelines were brought under the Interstate Commerce Act by the Hepburn Amendment of 1906, they automatically became subject to the Elkins Act.

In 1940, the Department of Justice began antitrust suits against virtually the whole oil industry, including actions against the oil pipelines, charging violations of the Elkins Act prohibiting the granting of rebates. It was the theory of the Justice Department that shipper-owned common carrier oil pipelines were granting rebates when they paid dividends to their shipper-owners. Among other things, the Justice Department sought to recover the penalty authorized by the Elkins Act of three times the amount of such rebates. The total amount of the possible penalties was stupendous, having been estimated to be as high as 2 billion dollars.

On December 23, 1941, the pipeline and oil company defendants agreed to a consent decree in settlement of this action. *U.S.* v. *Atlantic Refining Co., et al.,* Civil Action No. 14060 in U.S. District Court for District of Columbia. The substance of this decree was that no defendant pipeline company should pay to a shipper-owner dividends or other valuable considerations derived from transportation or other common carrier services which aggregate more than the shipper-owner's share of 7 per cent of the valuation of the carrier's property. If the decree is violated, the United States may recover three times the amount of excess payments from the shipper-owner.

This decree was entered into a full year after the Interstate Commerce Commission had established an 8 per cent return for crude lines and 10 per cent for products lines as a reasonable and permissible rate of return.

Transportation earnings in excess of 7 per cent of valuation must be retained by the carrier as a separate item in the surplus account and may be used only for: (1) extending existing or constructing or acquiring new common carrier facilities, in which case the value of such facilities must be deducted from the valuation used for determining permissible 7 per cent dividends; (2) maintaining normal and reasonable working capital requirements during the current calendar year; and (3) retiring of certain debts outstanding at the time of the entry of the decree.

Under the decree each carrier-defendant is required to make a yearly report to the Department of Justice showing the valuation used as the earnings basis for the year, total earnings available for distribution, dividends paid, and disposition of earnings in excess of 7 per cent, if any. These reports are checked with the carrier's records as to compliance with the decree on different occasions by the Federal Bureau of Investigation.

The decree was entered originally against 20 defendant oil companies and 59 affiliated pipeline carriers. It is by no means a perfect instrument. Numerous problems of interpretation have arisen, but except for one instance, neither the Government nor the defendant oil companies, parties to the decree, have sought court interpretation.

In March, 1958, the Department of Justice sought judicial interpretation of certain provisions of the decree. The most interesting and important question raised in these government actions was one having to do with inclusion in the valuation base of properties bought with debt capital. This came to be known as the *Arapahoe* case. The Department of Justice's contention was that the portion of the carrier property represented by debt capital should be excluded from the valuation base in establishing permissible dividends. The Supreme Court ruled against excluding debt capital in the valuation base pointing out that not only was the government urging a "strained construction" but had accepted the contrary construction for sixteen years. *U.S.* v. *Atlantic Refining Company*, 360 U.S. 19, 70 S. Ct. 944 (1959).

State regulation

Many of the pipeline carriers operate on both interstate and intrastate levels and are therefore subject not only to federal but also to state regulation. More than half the states have adopted some form of regulation pertaining to oil pipelines. Many of these follow generally the federal provisions requiring common carrier status of those lines operating on an intrastate basis. In other states, the common carrier status is imposed as a prerequisite to exercise of the right of eminent domain, an important element to the pipelines.

Conclusion

Oil pipelines have never been subsidized. They are adequately regulated by the Interstate Commerce Commission and definite remedy lies with that body and with state regulatory agencies for any of the rare complaints against common carrier pipelines. Oil pipelines are now recognized as an important segment of the nation's transportation industry the same as more visible types such as railroads, trucks, airplanes, and water carriers. The pipelines do not buy and sell oil for profit but merely transport it in competition with each other and with other modes. Anyone is free to enter into the oil pipeline business.

In setting forth this brief account of the economics affecting oil pipelines, their method of operation, and the regulations under which they operate, it has been our purpose by factual explanation with a minimum of editorializing to encourage a better understanding of this essential segment of our transport system, its place and importance in America's transportation industry. We hope this understanding by all interested in the welfare of our nation's transportation system will be of aid in oil pipelines industry relations with other carriers, with government representatives, and with the public.

NOTES

1. Sohio P. L. Co., I. C. C. No. 432, Joint with Atlantic, Mid-Valley, Shell, and West Texas Gulf P. L. Cos.
2. Service P. L. Co., 11-L, I. C. C. No. 501.
3. Plantation P. L. Co., I. C. C. No. 28.
4. Southwestern Lines, 133-I, I. C. C. No. 4530.
5. CB&QRR, 10799T, I. C. C. No. 20555.
6. Southern Freight Tariff Bureau, 16-E, I. C. C. No. 5-85.
7. From Statement by the Honorable John J. Allen, Jr., Under Secretary of Commerce for Transportation, Department of Commerce, Before the Subcommittee for Transportation, Committee on Armed Services, House of Representatives, July 15, 1969.

---

28   Big Load Afloat
American Waterways Operators, Inc.

Casual observers of domestic transportation often do not realize that it includes an extensive system of inland waterways. Rivers and canals handle about 9.9 per cent of all intercity ton-miles; Great Lakes traffic amounts to 6 per cent. In combination, then, the two trades carry almost 16 per cent of the ton-miles moved in the United States.

The inland water courses of America served as early routes of exploration and commerce. Today, in 38 of the 50 states, vessels provide commercial transportation services on rivers, canals, bays, sounds, or lakes. Eighty-three of our cities of over 100,000 population are located on commercially navigable waterways.

This rather practical selection shows the economic importance of inland water transport, presents a little of its history, and discusses in detail its operation and equipment.

From *Big Load Afloat*, Washington: American Waterways Operators, Inc., specially revised to 1971, pp. 1-38. Used by permission.

Water transport is a business builder

Most freight moving on U.S. inland waterways is carried in unmanned, non-self-propelled barges having drafts of 6 to 12 feet. Standard depth for inland navigation channels is 9 feet. A small part of inland waterways service is provided by shallow-draft self-propelled freighting vessels and tankers, but the normal freighting equipment is the barge.

The barges are moved in groups or strings by towing vessels, either a towboat which is designed and operated to push the barges ahead, or a tug which is designed primarily to pull the barges on a hawser. In some instances, however, the tug may push the barges ahead or carry them alongside.

Shallow-draft water carrier operations provide service principally for the transportation of bulk-loading commodities—both dry and liquid—moving usually in barge-load lots of 500 to 3,000 tons per barge. There are ocean-going barges of 33,000 tons capacity.

The commodities particularly attracted to inland water-borne transportation are raw materials, moving in large quantities from one stage of production and processing to the next stage of finishing. Petroleum products, chemicals, grains, and coal, for example, lend themselves especially well to barge transportation. Many heavy, bulky semifinished as well as finished products also move by barge. Barge transportation is an essential part of our mass production and marketing processes.

The economic value of this mode of transportation has been demonstrated and proven to many industries—mining, agriculture, petroleum, iron and steel, chemicals, aluminum, forest products, and the building trades in general. The Government's space program is dependent on barge service to transport the booster engines from production plants to test sites and launching sites.

Increasing demand for water transportation service has stimulated improvement of water channels as well as improvements in equipment and technology of operations. Barge service is safe and reliable. It is the lowest cost mode of transportation for the commodities for which it is adaptable. . .

The barge and towing vessel industry has kept pace with shippers' needs, both as to equipment and service. Navigation techniques and aids have been developed which permit around-the-clock operations of towing vessels in all kinds of weather. Origin-to-destination speed is at an average of about 6 miles per hour, with some high-speed integrated tows making 15 miles per hour. The development and construction of barge equipment is keyed to shipper needs.

Because of these service characteristics, barge transportation has become a primary business growth stimulator. It returns to the nation's business community and to the nation's consuming public benefits of measurable value from the nation's water resources. These water resources provide the base on which this mode of transportation operates and from which it derives its single great inherent characteristic—low cost of service.

A growing national resource

Barges—pushed by towboats or pulled by tugboats—and shallow-draft freighting vessels plying more than 25,000 miles of navigable inland channels carry almost 15 percent of the nation's domestic commerce.

A towboat or a tug may push or pull one barge or any multiple of barges ranging up to as many as 40 barges in push-towing operations or three or four in pull-towing operations, depending on the type of service and the characteristics of the waterway on which the tow is operating.

Cost of barge service to shippers averages 3 mills per ton-mile. For purposes of comparison: rail service costs the shipper almost five times as much— about 15 mills per ton-mile; truck service costs 21 times as much—65 mills or 6 1/2 cents per ton-mile; air freight service costs about 20 cents per ton-mile. Some shippers get rail service for 6 or 7 mills per ton-mile. Those who get it at this lower price do so not because of carrier generosity but because of competition and most often because of barge competition.

Low cost is the inherent advantage of water transportation.

To make inland water transportation publicly available the Federal Government, under Congressional authorizations dating back to the beginning of the Republic, provides, maintains, and operates a system of internal commercial navigation channels without charge to anyone for their use.

The Congress of the United States, as a part of national transportation policy, has declared that the inherent advantages of each mode of transportation shall be recognized and promoted "to the end of developing, coordinating, and preserving a national transportation system by water, highway, and rail, as well as other means. . ."

Approximately [For a listing of individual companies, vessels operated, and type of operation see *Transportation Series*, Volumes 3, 4 and 5, published by Corps of Engineers, U.S. Army, available from District Engineer, U.S. Army Engineer District, New Orleans, P.O. Box 60267] 1,700 companies are engaged in commercial operations on the inland water of the United States—[as of 1964] 113 companies certificated by the Interstate Commerce Commission to provide service as regular route common carriers; 32 companies holding ICC permits to provide services under contracts with shippers; 1,150 companies engaged in the transportation of commodities which are exempt from regulation under provisions of the Interstate Commerce Act; and about 400 companies engaged in private transportation of their own commodities.

The 1,700 companies operate 15,000 dry cargo barges and scows with a total cargo capacity in excess of 17,000,000 tons; 3,000 tank barges with a total cargo capacity of approximately 6,800,000 tons; and 4,250 towboats and tugs with a total aggregate power in excess of 3,707,531 horsepower.

The physical plant of the shallow-draft water carrier industry as a whole is in excellent condition. It is made up of modern equipment. Fleet growth since World War II has followed a consistent, steady pattern of additions, modernizations and replacements of equipment to meet customer requirements. The fleet keeps pace with requirements in every respect.

The total investment of all for-hire carriers operating on the inland waters (exclusive of the Great Lakes) in carrier equipment only is estimated at $1,650,000,000. This is exclusive of terminals and other shore-based equipment. The estimate also excludes the equipment of private carriers.

The industry is assured of a continuing source of investment funds, although it was not until recent years that the shallow-draft water carriers went to outside sources for financing. Because this has been a growth industry since the end of World War II, little difficulty has been experienced by carriers who have sought outside financing. They have found it through the normal channels of banks, other financial institutions and insurance companies. The loan departments of the more aggressive banking institutions are seeking opportunities to finance water carrier equipment. There is little investment-trust financing in the inland industry, although there has been evidence of interest on the part of financial institutions in this direction. . .

Approximately 80,000 persons are employed aboard the inland fleet. An estimated equal number of persons are employed in shore-based work directly connected with inland fleet operations—office personnel, terminal operators, service personnel, and shipbuilding and ship repair personnel.

This modern inland fleet operates around the clock in all kinds of weather with the assistance of radar, radio-telephone communications, searchlights, depth finders, swing-o-meters, and other aids to navigation.

An important over-all effect of water transportation is to hold down the delivered cost of commodities—both the commodities transported in water-borne commerce and those transported by other modes competing directly with water-borne commerce. . .

From keelboats to towboats and tugs

The first piece of transportation equipment to see service on our internal water courses was a canoe.

Then came the rafts—called flatboats or broad-horns. They were flat-bottomed and box-like, covered from bow to stern. They were one-way vessels for going downstream, propelled by the currents with little but guidance from their handlers.

The keelboat made its debut with the 19th century. It was a long, narrow vessel with graceful lines. It was a sturdily built two-way traveler—upstream as well as downstream. It carried as much as 80 tons of freight. For downstream hauls it needed only careful, skillful guidance. To propel it upstream men walked the river bank and pulled the keelboat with ropes or they stood aboard and pushed it by using iron-tipped poles that reached to the river bottom. One historian reported 500 keelboats on the Ohio River and its tributaries in 1819. The number on the Mississippi undoubtedly was far greater.

In 1811, just four years after the invention of the steamboat, the river steamer NEW ORLEANS was launched at Pittsburgh and went into service between there and New Orleans. By 1836, river steamboats were making calls at New Orleans at the rate of 1,000 per year. By 1852, the public landing at Cincinnati was reporting river steamboat calls at an annual rate of 8,000, about one per hour.

Traffic on the inland waterways expanded so rapidly with the development of the steamboat that Congress acted in 1824 to improve the rivers and harbors on a planned basis. The President was authorized to utilize the services of the Army Corps of Engineers for this work. Ever since that time, the Corps has had responsibility for the planning, improving, and maintaining of the nation's navigable waters, including harbors.

An Act of April 30, 1824, is of historic significance and reads in its entirety as follows:

AN ACT TO PROCURE THE NECESSARY SURVEYS, PLANS, AND ESTIMATES, UPON THE SUBJECT OF ROADS AND CANALS.
(Sect. 1.) Be it enacted by the Senate and House of Representatives of the United States of America, in Congress assembled, That the President of the United States is hereby authorized to cause the necessary surveys, plans, and estimates, to be made of the routes of such Roads and Canals as he may deem of national importance, in a commercial or military point of view, or necessary for the transportation of the public mail; designating, in the case of each canal, what parts may be made capable of sloop navigation: the surveys, plans, and estimates, for each, when completed, to be laid before Congress.
(Sect. 2.) And be it further enacted, That to carry into effect the objects of this act, the President be, and he is hereby authorized to employ two or more skillful civil engineers, and such officers of the Corps of Engineers, or who may be detailed to do duty with that Corps, as he may think proper; and the sum of thirty thousand dollars be, and the same is hereby appropriated, to be paid out of any moneys in the treasury, not otherwise appropriated.

Before 1824 river and harbor improvements were not coordinated and what was done was carried out by state and local agencies. Until that time the general practice was for the Treasury Department to make harbor surveys and coastal charts, and to erect lighthouses, public piers, beacons, and buoys.

Local governments and private interests benefiting from them usually executed local harbor improvements.

The first money appropriated by Congress for river improvements was made on May 24, 1824, in "An Act making appropriations for deepening the channel leading into the Harbor of Presque Isle and for repairing Plymouth Beach." Congress set aside $20,000 for each of these projects, one on Lake Erie and the other on the New England Coast.

The incredibly rapid spread of a rail network over the nation, particularly after the War Between the States, dampened interest in waterways, but they were of vital importance to the growing nation for the first half of the last century.

At the height of the packet boat era in the United States just before the War Between the States, the river fleet was reportedly carrying more tonnage than that handled by all the vessels of the British Empire.

During the War Between the States, there was a constant struggle for control of the rivers and coastal waters serving the areas of conflict. Traffic in these waters was brought to a virtual standstill. Hundreds of steamboats were burned.

For all practical purposes, river transportation became a casualty of war. The fleet was not rebuilt. One of the reasons was the emergence of the railroads as the dominant form of transportation. In 1850 there were only 9,000 miles of rail lines in the United States; by 1890 the trackage had increased to almost 164,000 miles. Of devastating significance was the railroads' entry into water transportation. They even bought some privately owned canals. Their purpose was not to promote water transportation, but to destroy it. The railroads used some water shipping lines as fighting ships to bleed competing water lines to death economically. Others were bought to let the vessels rot at their docks. And the docks and terminals rotted with them. Railroad-purchased canals were relegated to disuse. The railroads' tactics in this respect finally attracted the attention of Congress and in 1912 the Panama Canal Act was passed to divorce railroads from ownership of water carriers.

The early river fleet operated over completely natural channels. Although channel clearing was started with snagging operations on the Ohio River in 1824, little improvement was made until after the turn of the century.

Except for local operations inland water transportation was largely stagnant from the end of the War Between the States until after World War I. President Theodore Roosevelt appointed the Inland Waterways Commission in 1907 to study the status of waterways and water carriers. This Commission recommended in 1908 that Congress make more suitable provision for improving the inland waterways of the United States.

The Panama Canal Act followed four years later and is considered by historians as the legislative keystone of the revival of inland waterways transportation. This Act prohibits railroads from owning, controlling or operating a water carrier that operates through the Panama Canal or elsewhere, provided, however, that in the case of a water carrier not operating through the Panama Canal authority is conferred upon the Interstate Commerce Commission to make a determination as to whether such ownership or operation will be in the public interest and will not exclude, prevent or reduce competition on the route.

As might be expected, passage of the Act did not result in immediate divorcement of railroads from ownership of water carriers. The litigation that followed did however except in some cases where the water operations were considered auxiliary to rail services.

In 1959-1962 a major test of the Act was made. The Illinois Central and Southern Pacific Railroads in 1959 filed an application with the Interstate Commerce Commission seeking approval to acquire the John I. Hay Company barge line, a major common carrier operating on the Mississippi River system and the

Gulf Intracoastal Waterway. This was the first major effort by railroads to invade domestic water carrier operations since passage of the Panama Canal Act. The American Waterways Operators, Inc., opposed the application, as did other interests. In 1962, ICC denied the application in a decision reaffirming the established public policy of separation of ownership and operation of the various transport modes.

To help meet wartime demands in 1918 a Federal manager was appointed to commandeer and put into operation as soon as possible all available equipment capable of being used for the transportation of freight on the rivers and canals. The Transportation Act of 1920 declared the intent of Congress to promote, encourage, and develop water transportation. Four years later the Inland Waterways Corporation was incorporated by the Congress as a pioneering operation to demonstrate the transportation capabilities of modern towboats and barges. Historians generally date the beginnings of modern inland water carrier operations at about this period.

The vessels and the men aboard

What the vessels are not—they are not pretty in the esthetic sense. They are not picturesque as were the sternwheelers that Mark Twain glamorized. Neither do they have the glamorous bigness of ocean-going vessels.

What they are—they are the most efficient transporters of freight in existence.

The barges are unimpressive to look upon except for their austere bigness. But to a shipper who knows how safely, economically and smoothly they ride the waters to produce 3-mills-per-ton-mile transportation they have a kind of beauty all their own. The average barge can carry about five times its own weight. No other type of freight vehicle compares with it in this measure of efficiency.

The towboats which provide the power to move the barges have a business-like appearance in keeping with the stark efficiency of the barges.

Towboats are square on the bow and almost square on the stern with somewhat clumsy-looking uprights at the bow. They appear to squat low in the water, the water almost lapping the deck. But a towboat wears an air of power and authority. The clumsy-looking uprights at the bow are towing knees. They are pusher plates against which barges are snugged and securely lashed.

Tied together, barge on barge, and in turn lashed to the towing knees of the power unit, they form a tow that looks and acts like a single vessel. One towboat and one barge may make a tow. One towboat and 10 barges, or 20 barges, or 30, or even 40 barges may make a tow. And the snub-nosed, squat towboat translates its power and authority into action to move the tow, to steer it, to control it. In movement a tow becomes a thing of beauty—one kind of beauty to an observer, another to a skilled river pilot, still another to a shipper getting transportation at a cost which enables him to hold his markets, to broaden and expand them.

The tugboat resembles the towboat only in power and efficiency. It has a shaped bow, sits higher in the water, and has a racy look about it. It hauls barges astern on a hawser, or snugs them up against the hip, or slips its bow into a slot between two of them, or even slips its bow into a built-in V slot in the stern of a barge. And tugs shove ocean liners and freighters around in a working display of their power in harbor operations. The tugs do the open water towing of barges— on the intracoastal canals, in the Gulf of Mexico, off the Atlantic and Pacific Coasts, and in trade to and from Alaska and Hawaii. They are rugged, dependable, low-cost transporters like the towboats...

The tug in effect is an ocean-going vessel, used most extensively in open water service, whereas the towboat is used exclusively on the rivers and other protected, relatively calm water courses.

There is a wide variety of towboats plying the nation's waterways today. They range from vessels with single screws to vessels with four propellers with each screw driven by an individual diesel engine. Some come small in over-all dimensions approximating 36 feet long, 12 feet wide, 6 feet draft, with engines of about 100 horsepower. The largest towboat is 170 feet long, 58 feet wide, with draft of 10 feet 3 inches. This vessel has four screws with engines that develop up to 9,000 horsepower. Towboats of 6,000 horsepower and up are capable of pushing barges carrying as much as 40,000 to 50,000 tons of cargo. In comparison, a modern diesel freight locomotive of 6,000 horsepower can handle efficiently a train of 120 cars loaded to an average of 50 tons per car, a total of approximately 6,000 tons...

To push or to pull?

Generally the type of water determines which of two methods of towing is used—push-towing or pull-towing—and therefore the type of power unit, either towboat or tug.

On most of the inland systems where the water routes are protected by surrounding land masses and where the waters are relatively calm either in their natural state (as on the lower Mississippi and the Missouri Rivers), or where a system of locks and dams creates relative calmness, the towboat is used for push-towing operations. For push-towing the barges are tied rigidly together by steel cables or ropes to form a single unit, and this unit is then lashed solidly against the boat's towing knees. The power unit working at the rear of the tow can handle a greater number of barges at greater speed under more absolute control than can be handled in pull-towing operations. The relatively flat-bottomed towboat with massive power in its propellers also has a set of multiple rudders which afford maximum control for forward, backing, and flanking movements such as are required to navigate the restricted channels of the rivers and canals.

Character of the waterway, condition of the waterway, lockage conditions, size of tow, and horsepower of the towing vessel in relation to the size of tow all influence origin-to-destination running times of towboats.

Wind, wave, and tidal actions will break up a tow of vessels lashed rigidly together as is done for push-towing. Where these conditions exist, the pull-towing method is used in which a tug hauls barges behind on a hawser. These conditions exist on some portions of the navigable inland waterways, particularly sections of the Gulf Intracoastal Waterway and Atlantic Intracoastal Waterway. This method of operations naturally prevails in towing vessel operations which are being employed to an increasing extent on the Gulf of Mexico, along the Pacific Coast, to some extent along the Atlantic Coast, and between the Pacific Coast and Alaska and Hawaii.

There is a limit to the number of barges which may be pulled on a hawser, however, and it is obvious that a towing vessel can exercise little guidance control over barges being pulled except to provide propulsion power. Tugboats are rigged for this work.

Many towboats are now being placed in service rigged for both push-towing and pull-towing. To rig a towboat for pull-towing requires only the addition of a towing bitt located ahead of the steering rudders. However, towboats are limited as to the waters on which they can work. They are not built for sea duty.

Power and control

Practically the entire fleet of towboats and tugboats is powered by diesel engines. The steam-powered vessel is a relic of the past and only a very few of them are left in service. The complete shift from steam to diesel propulsion when once started in towboats and tugs took place very rapidly.

The diesel towboat which replaced the sternwheeler on the rivers and canals and in the harbors is responsible for bringing the barge and towing vessel industry to its place of national prominence on the transportation scene in the last 30 years.

The development of the diesel-powered towboat and tug has produced the most efficient application of power in any mode of transportation. The great service gain is the result of applying maximum usable power to the task of moving freight, applying it with the greatest possible efficiency, and keeping the power unit at work a greater per-entage of the time.

The adoption of the propeller as a replacement for the stern wheel or side wheel on river and canal boats immediately posed the problem of a limitation on the size of the propeller imposed by the small space between the bottom of the boat and the bottom of the channel. This problem has been met in two ways: the development of more efficient propellers; and the development and perfection in towboats of the tunnel stern. The tunnel stern is a design feature in which part of the propeller is actually above the level of the water surface in a spoon-shaped recess in the bottom of the hull which is filled with water by vacuum action when the propeller is turning. Another device has been introduced to river towboats to improve propeller efficiency. This is the Kort nozzle, a funnel-shaped structure built around the propeller to concentrate the flow of water to the propeller. Under certain favorable operating conditions the Kort nozzle is reported to add as much as 25 percent thrust to the propeller.

One of the most important gains in efficiency was the development, principally during World War II, of dependable reversing-reduction gears capable of transmitting high horsepower. Before these gears were available, the conflict between high engine efficiency at high RPM's and high propeller efficiency at low RPM's, usually resulted in a sacrifice of efficiency at both ends. Good reversing-reduction gears permit engine operation at the most efficient RPM. Propellers are designed for whatever RPM can use the horsepower most efficiently within the available diameter.

An added benefit of the improved power gains is the adaptability of such installations to the use of pilot house controls which permit faster and more accurate handling of the engines with resulting time-savings in maneuvering.

One of the greatest unsolved problems in gaining maximum efficiency from diesel propulsion on the inland waterways is the variation in load on the engine which is brought about by differences in size of tows, and by variations in the depth of water. Among the techniques which are being tried to cope with this problem are diesel-electric drive, controllable pitch propellers, and overload limiters.

In the continuing work to improve efficiency, hull design is receiving added attention through exhaustive tests of towed and self-propelled models in testing basins.

The exigencies of navigation in and out of the Chicago area with its multitude of very low bridges has produced the telescoping pilothouse design. The pilot, behind a tow of barges which themselves just clear the bridges, can lower his pilothouse to go under bridges and then immediately come up again to see ahead for navigation. This design, peculiar to the Chicago waterways, mounts the pilothouse and all the electrical and mechanical controls necessary to operate the boat on a hydraulic ram.

The telescoping pilothouse is an innovation dictated by the existence of low bridges which had been built over the waterways in the Chicago area before barge and towboat operations reached their present capacity. The telescoping pilothouse is not desirable for normal operations. It sacrifices working and living space, adds to construction and maintenance costs, and reduces both the efficiency and safety of the vessel.

In the pilothouse of a modern towboat the controls and aids to navigation reflect intensive application of modern science.

Electric steering controls which actuate huge hydraulic steering rams instantly align the two separate sets of rudders, one set forward and one set aft of the propellers. The setting of the steering levers by the pilot is a fingertip operation.

One thumb-size lever for each engine is a combination clutch, gear shift, and throttle, and instantly provides the engine speed, power output and direction the pilot wants.

Fingertip electrical controls direct the probing of the three-mile beam from each of two or three powerful arc lights.

Communications and navigation

A powerful directional bull horn on top of the pilothouse sends the pilot's voice to the deckhands working out on the tow or to a man on shore half a mile away.

The pilot is in instant communication with any part of the vessel through his intercom system and by direct line to the mate supervising work out on the tow. Walkie-talkie radio is coming into wide use for communications between the pilothouse and the deck crew, between vessels and movable bridges over the waterways, between vessels and locks, and from vessel to vessel.

The pilot talks to the office or to his home through the short-range radiophone connected into the land-line system. Where the short-range stations are too far from the river, he picks up the long-range phone and talks to a station a thousand miles away.

When he is not using his long-range radio, he keeps it tuned in on the intership channel. All other towboats do the same, and consequently long before two approaching boats are within sight of each other or close enough to exchange passing signals by whistle, the two pilots have made radio contact, discussed the navigating conditions involved in their passing, and have agreed how they will pass.

Efficient communications are an essential tool in inland water transportation. Dependable communications between company offices and towing vessels result in better dispatching of traffic as one ingredient of achieving greater shipper satisfaction; better utilization of equipment and therefore more economical operations; greater safety of vessel personnel, equipment and cargoes; and a measure of added personnel benefit to crews on long voyages away from their home port because it affords them a means of contact with their families when needed.

The radiotelephone is the communications lifeline of the shallow-draft industry. Most towing vessels are equipped with one or more radio sets operating on various frequency ranges assigned by the Federal Communications Commission. . .

When it is foggy or rainy or when the snow flies, the pilot of a river or canal towboat no longer has to tie up. Radar presents him with a constant map of the river showing his position with relation to the shape of the river and any object in it. So helpful is this radar reference map that most pilots use it for checks even on clear nights.

In doubtful waters and particularly in bad visibility the pilot leans heavily on radar. He also finds an indispensable aid in the depth-finder which, working through a transceiver suspended in the water from the head of the tow, continually records the depth of the water on a tape in the pilothouse.

When fog shuts out visibility entirely and the pilot is groping through narrow waters with the aid of radar and the depth-finder, he also has a swing indicator to tell him the second his tow starts to drop off course. Thus he can apply corrective rudder even before the deviation shows on radar.

The use of the automatic pilot is becoming popular as a more accurate steering device when visual steering ability is restricted. In clear weather the automatic pilot, carefully used, will steer the tow with less rudder angle—and consequently give more miles per hour.

Barges

Virtually any commodity can be shipped by water. The inland waterways industry has implemented this theory by developing a variety of types and sizes of barges for the efficient handling of products ranging from coal in open hopper barges to chemicals in "thermos bottle" barges, and from dredged rock in dump scows to railroad cars on carfloats. And barging is the only practical mode for long distance moving of out-sized machinery, tanks, kilns, and some of the space vehicles.

Speed is important to the barge line operator. So the underwater hull shapes and operating features of barges receive the same attention from the naval architect as does the modern high powered diesel towboat. Combined testing of towboat and barge models in experimental tanks in the United States and Europe often result in technological improvement of barge hull lines. Shipboard equipment is subject to the same theories of automation as any shoreside operation.

Thirty years ago most river barges were designed as single individual units, having a rake, or slope, on each end. For navigating singly, this form is still most efficient. However, model testing showed that the assembly of multiple units of this form in a single tow resulted in great loss of efficiency by the cumulative drag of many water-breaking rakes in the middle of the tow.

Some barges were designed to be assembled into integrated tows having an underwater shape that is nearly the equivalent of a single vessel. Such an integrated assembly made up of several vessels has a lead barge with an easy rake at the bow to minimize the resistance of the water. This lead barge has a square stern for joining with the square end of another barge, thus eliminating any underwater surface break. The trailing barge in an integrated assembly has a short rake on the stern. The bow of this barge will be square. Between the lead barge and the trailing barge, double square ended barges are inserted. The water resistance of such an integrated tow is nearly equivalent to the smooth underwater lines of a single vessel of equivalent total length. A premium benefit is the increase in capacity due to the added buoyancy of the square ends of the barges.

The integrated high speed tow is generally efficient for the carriage of a large volume of a single commodity over a long distance on a continuing basis. Identical draft of all barges comprising the tow is vital to the efficiency of the operation. They have 'been most successfully used for transporting petroleum and petroleum products, chemicals and other liquids where they can be continuously operated as a unit.

The fully integrated design concept, however, has the disadvantage that a single barge built for an intermediate position in such a tow, square on both ends, is extremely unwieldy to handle when separated from the other units of the tow, especially in a current. Such barges are difficult to move around in terminal areas. The water resistance of these barges if placed in a tow with other barges which do not have matching square ends makes such use of them prohibitive.

There is a useful and successful compromise with the concept of the fully integrated tow. This produces a barge with a well designed rake on one end and square on the other end. Two such barges assembled square-end to square-end provide about 8 per cent increased capacity over two similar barges having rakes at each end. At ordinary towing speeds they have about 18 percent less resistance. By assembling such semi-integrated barges into fleets the combined effect of added capacity and less resistance permits a typical boat moving a typical tow of such barges to make about 25 percent more cargo ton-miles per hour than the same boat with the same tow of barges having a rake on each end. At the same time, by having a rake on one end these semi-integrated barges can be handled singly without difficulty. . .

The men aboard

Skill, experience and a feel of the river are required to pilot a tow, some as long as the greatest ocean liners, through the inland waterways. . .

The size of a vessel's crew is determined by a number of factors, such as the size and power of the boat, the degree of its automation, the size of the tow (number of barges) which it is handling, and the waterway on which it is operating.

Vessel employees in line-haul operations work a 12-hour day, spending six hours on watch and six hours off, seven days per week, usually from the time the boat leaves its home port until it returns. There are instances, however, when crew changes are made en route. In general practice, the number of days crewmen work before they are given time off is determined by operating requirements. Crews normally work an 84-hour week. Vessel employees receive from one-third day off to a full day off at regular pay for each day worked. This practice is necessary to keep the boats in operation over long reaches of waterways where regularly scheduled crew replacements would be impractical.

Living conditions are recognized as important to operating efficiency. Four full meals are served every day. Laundry service is provided. Crew quarters are usually set apart from the noisier parts of the vessels, and in some cases are soundproofed. Working conditions aboard river boats have improved immeasurably in recent years. Many crews now enjoy the advantages of air-conditioning. Television and other recreational activities are provided aboard most boats.

Modern labor saving equipment with safety features for the protection of the crew have also made the work easier than in the era of the steamboat when the crew toiled endless hours at backbreaking work.

Wages in the industry have shown a steady increase. Actual pay varies for a variety of reasons. Some lines are unionized, others are not. Some vessel personnel hold Coast Guard licenses, others do not. Licenses are not required by law or by regulation for crewmen operating diesel-powered towing vessels except in the case of some ocean-going vessels. In some instances pay scales are based on the horsepower of the boat. . .

The 80,000 employees working aboard the shallow-draft water carrier fleet provide three or four crews for each vessel because of the nature of the working schedules. Operating on a six-hour-on and six-hour-off schedule requires that two working crews be aboard the vessel at all times with a third and sometimes a fourth crew ashore for relief.

In 1961, towing vessel employees were brought under provisions of the Fair Labor Standards Act for purposes of minimum wages but are still exempted from the provisions of maximum hours and overtime.

The job of the crew begins with the make-up of the tow, except in the case of the integrated tow in which the barges are specially built to form a single unit and are not broken up. In the case of some line-haul operations, the tows are made up prior to the towboat's arrival.

In the make-up of a general river tow, putting together barges of all types and sizes requires time, energy and skill.

Because the boat handling a general tow will pick up or set out loaded and unloaded barges at many points along its route, the positioning of any barge for discharge en route is very important.

A loudspeaker system or walkie-talkie radio keeps the captain in the pilot-house in direct communication with the mate out on the tow. The towboat has to be maneuvered without hitch in the difficult and frequently hazardous process of backing, turning and swinging barges in order to make up a tow as quickly as possible.

With rigging of wire cables and ropes the deckhands join the barges into an end-to-end formation. The job is eased by stationary ratchets and winches on each end of the barges, holding down the amount of loose rigging that must be carried. A good deckhand exercises as much dexterity as a cowboy in handling the heavy lines used to lash the barges.

Make-up of the tow in many operations is handled by a special crew using a small workboat. In many of the major ports this work—as well as the break-up of tows and distribution of barges to loading and unloading docks—is handled by harbor fleet operators. Thus line-haul towboats can arrive in port, cut loose from their tow of barges, take on another tow which is already made up and be on their way again in an hour or two.

Once under way with instructions from company traffic officials, the captain puts to work the latest technological advances that have eased the burden of river navigation. Neither night, fog nor snow delays him. With fingertip control of immense power, he can move thousands of tons of cargo safely and efficiently over thousands of miles of water highway.

Part
Two

Industrial Traffic and Distribution Management

Introduction

Every business firm pays for transportation service. In many companies it is the second or third largest expense item on the profit and loss statement. Nationally, our total freight transportation bill comes to 9 per cent of the Gross National Product. Expenses of this magnitude dictate that the purchase of transportation should be made wisely and systematically.

For perhaps a hundred years, the most efficient business firms have employed specialized purchasing agents whose job is to buy transportation—to deal with the demand side of transportation. Traditionally, these purchasing agents have been called traffic managers. Over time and from company to company their duties have ranged from the ridiculous to the sublime—from, as clerks, checking freight invoices to, as vice-presidents, overseeing large conglomerations of people, vehicles, and warehouses.

Prior to the beginning of serious transportation regulation in 1887, the traffic manager was a skilled negotiator who represented his firm in the jungle-like business environment of the early railroads. His success depended upon his skill at wresting rate or service concessions from the railroads, most of which were in a monopolistic or near-monopolistic position.

With the advent of public regulation, with its published rates and rules against discrimination or unequal treatment, the traffic function became an almost routine task. The skill of the traffic man became a matter of knowing alternative rates, routes, and services and of choosing the cheapest way to ship. Indeed, it is still common for a firm to hire a traffic consultant who routinizes these choices by designing a simple "route card" or "rate card" which is then prominently displayed in the firm's shipping department. From there, it takes very little "management" to decide on the best choice for each shipment or order.

After 1920, however, the growth of competition among modes of transportation made the matter of decision-making in traffic management important once again. New types of carriers released the shipper from dependence upon the railroads. Often the superiority of one carrier over another became a matter of service rather than price. The traffic man, through his choice of transportation firms, had an opportunity to create good will with customers, to reduce costs, to influence production and marketing, and to increase profits.

Today, instead of traffic management, we talk of physical distribution, and even rhochrematics (the science of material flows). Top management is beginning to integrate traffic activity with purchasing, inventory, production control, sales, and customer service.

Two developments seem to be responsible for this "new look." They are the total cost concept and the improved methods of analytical decision-making. The total cost idea is the recognition that distribution requires the combined efforts of several departments of the firm. It is more important for these departments to cooperate to produce the lowest total distribution cost than for one of them to minimize its costs at the expense of others.

Innovations in information systems and in methods of analysis have joined with the computer to expand available distribution alternatives. The transportation activity as part of the distribution or logistics function once more has become an important part of the management apparatus of the firm. Indeed, it represents one of the more dynamic areas of modern business management.

The first four selections of Part Two discuss various aspects of the "new look" in traffic management and distribution. The balance explains specific activities and problems which involve the traffic and distribution manager.

The Meaning of
Business Logistics

Paul T. McElhiney
California State University, Los Angeles

Charles L. Hilton
Tri-State College

"Business logistics" is a term which encompasses all of the supply and distribution activities of the modern business firm. Its comprehensiveness may recommend it over the alternative term "physical distribution management." This article discusses the concepts involved in a logistics or distribution system and stresses the fact that transportation is the largest element in such a system.

Business logistics is a new term in the vocabulary of the American businessman. It may be defined as *that phase of economic activity which concerns itself with assessing the needs of goods and services for time utility and place utility and providing them with these utilities.*[1] The objective of economic activity is the creation of goods and services which will satisfy human wants. People who produce goods and services, therefore, try to accomplish three things: (1) produce a useful product or service that people want to buy, (2) have it ready when it is wanted, (3) have it where it is wanted. In formal economic terms, these are referred to as utilities. Production changes raw materials into usable things and gives them *form utility.* Planning, storage and sometimes transportation assure the goods will be available at the right time and give them *time utility.* Transportation moves the goods to places where they are needed and gives them *place utility.* Recently, marketing men have been saying that advertising and selling (or demand creation) give ownership of the product to those who need it and thus create *possession utility.* Actually, possession utility is probably just another way of saying time utility plus place utility, but it is important to consider because it reveals some additional people involved in the logistic process.

What we have been talking about so far is really only the part of business logistics which takes the product from the production time to the customer. This is often called *physical distribution,* and people often treat this as the whole process. One expert manager, for instance, recently defined physical distribution as follows:

> Basically, physical distribution is the science of business logistics A formal definition would say that it's the addition of time and place utility to the form utility provided by manufacturing. Less formally, one could say that

From Paul T. McElhiney and Charles L. Hilton, *Introduction to Logistics and Traffic Management,* Dubuque: Wm. C. Brown Co., Publishers, 1968, pp. 1-7. Used by permission.

it's getting the proper amount of the right kind of product to the place where the customer wants it at the time that the customer wants it. . . . Physical distribution is the key link between manufacturing and demand creation . . . . it has a profound effect on the success of both, and consequently on the basic profitability of a business. . . .[2]

While this is very helpful definition, it provides an incomplete picture of business logistics because it leaves out *physical supply.* Just as every business has customers, it is also a customer and needs the right kind of products where it wants them when it wants them. This aspect of business logistics takes place on the *procurement* side of production while physical distribution takes place on the marketing side.

Altogether, we find that the solution of logistic problems includes many departments of the typical company. Among them are production control, purchasing, transportation, warehousing, inventory control, market research, advertising, sales and customer service. Traditionally, these things that have to be done to supply a business and distribute its product have been treated more or less as isolated and perhaps even competitive activities when really they are all steps in the same process. Today, businessmen are frequently dealing with these activities not as individual and separate processes but as the components of a *system.* Since, by definition, the parts of a system move in unison under one means of control, these parts of the logistic system are being placed under unified control in more and more modern business firms.

A collection of new terms

The application of the systems concept to the flow of materials into, through and out of our production machinery is new. There is still disagreement as to how broad the treatment ought to be and what it should be called. A recent article by a leading transportation educator gives an indication of this and presents definitions of some of the new terms which are being proposed.

Some advocates have chosen to lay stress upon the problem of optimizing the physical costs of marketing. The term Physical Distribution has come to be associated with this effort. Others have approached the issue from the purchasing agents' viewpoint. Some of this group have used the term Materials Management. Sometimes this term is used synonymously with another borrowed from the military, Business Logistics. This concept includes all problems of the firm relating to the transport, storage and supply of material. Some exponents treating the problem of refining the coordination of production and marketing have given us the term Industrial Dynamics. In all approaches the search for lowest total costs is implied; the concept of systems essential.

Now we have another term, Rhochrematics. . . . Professor Brewer of the University of Washington introduced the term in 1960. . . . It comes from the Greek word "rhoe" which means flow and "chremi" meaning materials or things. The suffix "ics" is added to denote a body of knowledge or science. As used by Brewer the term is used to mean the science for the management of material flows. It encompasses all areas of material management and physical distribution.[3]

Origin of business logistics

Of all the new terms set forth in the above quotation, *business logistics* possibly enjoys the best antecedents and conveys best the broad and systematic planning which is visualized in the systems concept. The derivation of the world *logistics* gives some interesting insight into the meaning of our new term *business logistics.* It comes from two different words which may be found in *Webster's New International Dictionary.* The first of these is *logistic* which comes from the Greek word *logistikos* which means "skilled in calculating." Our word *logistic,* therefore, means "pertaining to reasoning; logical. Pertaining to reckoning or calculating." In fact, at one time it meant "the art of arithmetical calculation."[4]

The second word from which business logistics is derived is shown in the dictionary as *logistics.* Although it has the same basic spelling as *logistic* it has an entirely different origin and meaning. The French have a verb *loger* meaning "to lodge" or "to quarter." Their word *logistique* (pertaining to lodging) is derived from it and translates into English as "logistics." Traditionally, the term has been used in European military science, and even today is defined as "that branch of the military art which embraces the details of the transport, quartering, and supply of troops in military operations." A logistician in the French Army, therefore, was a quartermaster. Subsequently, logistics became a very popular term with the supply forces of the American Army and became widely used in World War II. Finally, it was adopted in Army Regulations in 1949. Then it was taken to mean the handling of every phase of military materiel including procurement, production, movement, supply and construction and operation of military facilities.[5] Since the term has been widely used by our extensive military supply organization, businessmen have become quite familiar with it and have adopted it also.

Two important characteristics

That there are two words behind the meaning of "business logistics" makes it an even more useful term, for the modern practice of business logistics has two important characteristics. First, it is systematic and mathematical. Second, it is broad and embraces every phase of procurement, movement and supply. Business logistics employs the *total cost concept.* It seeks to optimize the total costs of supply and distribution by playing one factor off against another. For instance, air freight transportation is much more expensive than steamship. Yet one company uses it to supply dealers with foreign automobile parts because expensive warehouses can be eliminated and investment in goods stowed in the hold of a slow cargo ship avoided; a lower total storage and transportation bill is the result. In simpler applications, a purchasing agent may be asked to buy in large quantities or a marketing manager to push for higher individual sales in order to make savings on shipping in larger volumes. Such savings require interdepartmental cooperation and so the logistics system must be broad to cut across departmental lines. On the other hand, it must utilize mathematical techniques in order to measure the potential and actual savings of changing the combination of functions in the supply and distribution system of the firm.

Many of the articles and even some of the books which are appearing in traffic and transportation literature are devoted to specific mathematical techniques designed to solve specific distribution problems or specific types of distribution problems. Typical of these is the classic "transportation matrix" problem designed for the firm that has multiple plants or multiple warehouses and multiple markets; the solution answers questions for management such as the following: Which of our products should be made in which plants and in what quantities? Should an additional plant be built? Which plants should serve which warehouses? How many warehouses should the company have, where should they be? How big should the warehouses be? Which market should each warehouse ship to? Mathematical techniques are also widely used for inventory control to answer such questions as when inventories should be replenished to prevent stock outs, what commodity mix should be ordered to meet anticipated demand, the optimum amounts that should be ordered. These and other logistical questions which arise do not require intensively difficult mathematics in their solutions; however, they do require a large number of calculations and so the easiest way to work them is on the computer. Understandably, computer applications are also attracting much comment in the literature of physical distribution. Although a few standard-type computer programs are available which can be tailored to some of the distribution problems of the typical firm, the real need is for people who can deal with the unique problems of the individual business firm. The successful logistician of the future may be the one who can recognize problem areas in his firm's distribution system and program the computer to find solutions, giving his company the advantage over the competitor who cannot use the computer imaginatively.

Before a manager can deal imaginatively with logistics problems, however, he must understand the *organization* of the logistics system. This is the broad aspect of business logistics mentioned above. The solution of total-cost problems or optimum-cost problems, such as we have been discussing, requires the cooperation of many parts and departments of the business organization. Such cooperation may be obtained by reorganizing the departments of a firm which deal with logistics and distribution problems. An important aid to this reorganization is the *systems concept* which is, essentially, a new way of thinking about old problems. We are concerned mostly with the largest element of the logistics system, which is movement, and the man who specializes in it: the transportation and traffic manager. We are concerned further with the broad or integrative aspects of business logistics and how the traffic department can be fitted into the logistics system.

Importance of movement

One of the things which all of the operative departments of a business have in common is that they are busy moving things. Some move supplies, some move people, some transfer goods on the production line, some send papers around, some transmit ideas. Thus, transportation in one form or another is the largest component of a logistics system. Peter Drucker has emphasized this effectively:

> Physical distribution is perhaps the most neglected area of management to-day. It is also the most promising area, in which a fairly small amount of work can bring the largest dividends. The reason why physical distribution has been so badly neglected is that . . . until recently we never looked at it. We saw people moving materials into plants or shipping products out of warehouses, or moving them into the shipping room. But we never saw the industrial process consisted primarily of moving things around. And we never did anything with the old knowledge that nothing is more expensive than handling things—lifting them, moving them, sometimes dropping them, packing them. . . .[6]

A business logistics system is created to gain efficient control of this movement into, within and out of the industrial process. Because so much movement is involved, it is often the transport specialist, the traffic manager who becomes the logistician in the modern business firm. This represents a considerable challenge for the traditional transportation specialist for he must broaden his horizon and become a qualified decision maker on the management team. This new frame of reference does not mean the traditional, routine functions of traffic management are now less important. In fact, the purchase of transportation itself may be a more important activity then ever, for movement must now be coordinated carefully with all the other activities in the logistics system. Although logistics management requires a much broader problem-solving approach than traffic management perhaps does, there must still be someone in the firm who is highly trained in the specifics of purchasing transportation service.

Approach to the study of traffic management

Traditional approaches to the study of traffic management have, perhaps, stressed *traffic* somewhat more than *management*. This was because the traffic manager was essentially a technician who had to comply carefully with the rules of a carrier industry which tended to be monopolistic in nature and with the legal requirements of regulatory bodies. Today, of course, rules and laws must still be obeyed, but the transportation industry has become much more competitive and many alternatives are available to the shipper. Also, as emphasized, logistics is the new environment of traffic management, and tremendous amounts of creative thinking and managerial ability are required to operate logistics systems. However, the traffic manager must still be thoroughly grounded in a knowledge of transportation and traffic management . . . .

REFERENCES

1. J. L. Heskett, Robert M. Ivie and Nicholas A. Glaskowsky, Jr., *Business Logistics* (New York: The Ronald Press Company, 1964), pp. 6-9.
2. Wandell M. Stewart, "Never a Greater Need for Review of Distribution Systems," " *Handling and Shipping*, May, 1965, p. 45.
3. Walter Kramer, "Rhochrematics," *Delta Nu Alphian*, January, 1964, p. 7.
4. C. T. Onions, *The Oxford Universal Dictionary* (Oxford: The Clarendon Press, 1955), p. 1162.
5. Richard M. Leighton, "Military Logistics," *Encyclopedia Americana* Vol. 17, 1956, p. 574.
6. Peter F. Drucker, "Darkest Africa of the American Economy," *Handling and Shipping*, May, 1965, p. 47.

---

30   Managing Procurement and Transportation in the Physical Distribution System

Paul T. McElhiney

California State University, Los Angeles

Goods are moved through a business firm, as this selection shows, in what is called the "logistics cycle." This selection stresses the function of the purchasing agent as well as that of the traffic manager. One of its key concepts is "logistical integration"—the problem which logistics managers face when they try to secure the cooperation of outside firms such as suppliers and carriers in making their distribution systems work.

Introduction

Until recently, the procurement side of the logistics cycle has been somewhat slighted in physical distribution management. The original emphasis of this new field was upon creating efficiency in the flow of goods from production to the customer. Logically, many distribution experts soon recognized that purchasing or procurement is the backside of the mirror of sales and distribution and that efficiency may also be treated in the inbound flow of goods.

The purpose of this paper is to discuss fundamental developments in two parts of the procurement side of the physical distribution system—the part which purchases raw materials, fabricating materials, parts, and supplies: and the part which purchases transportation. In many companies this means the Purchasing

From Paul T. McElhiney, "Managing Procurement and Transportation in the Physical Distribution System," *How Marketing Works: Practical Readings*, Paul T. McElhiney and Henry S. Ang, editors. Dubuque: Kendall-Hunt Publishing Company, 1971. Used by permission.

Department and the Traffic Department. The Traffic Department is not restricted to dealing with inbound shipments, but this paper is oriented somewhat more toward the procurement side of the distribution structure than the marketing side. The approach of the paper is to reveal some broad management tendencies that are developing in procurement and transportation rather than to discuss specific techniques of managing the departments in question.

I. Horizontal flows in the business firm

An appropriate beginning is to view certain relationships between departments in a hypothetical business firm to identify elements of a physical distribution or, as it is sometimes called, logistics system.

Two charts are presented showing a schematic arrangement of departments in an assumed manufacturing organization. A feature of these charts is that they purport to show the functional relationship between departments rather than authority and responsibility relationships. Traditional organization charts are designed to show such managerial relationships and tend to stress the vertical relationships in a business firm. They are concerned with who reports to whom and focus attention on the "up-and-down" information and decision flow in a firm. Companies do not function in a vertical pattern, however. They function horizontally; departments in an organization have more end-to-end than up-and-down relationships when it comes to the flow of work and not the flow of authority.

Figure 1 illustrates the physical distribution or logistics flow in a hypothetical manufacturing company. On the chart, the term "physical distribution" is used in the narrow sense involving only distribution from the manufacturing operation to the customer or what is identified as the "marketing side" of the cycle. As can be seen, distribution on the "procurement side" from the vendor to the manufacturing operation is referred to as "physical supply" which is also frequently call "materials management." On this chart, the overall physical distribution activity has been labelled "logistics." Also of interest is that some departments have been labelled as "non-logistic functions" indicating that they have little to do with distribution. Others which deal directly with physical distribution have been identified as "logistic functions." The "flow of goods" level of the chart portrays the activities of the logistic departments in maintaining a horizontal flow of goods through the organization.

Figure 2 emphasizes the horizontal flow characteristics of a business more strongly than Figure 1. As one traces the flow of raw materials and supplies through the logistic departments on the chart, the end-to-end relationship of the activities becomes obvious. The chart also introduces the concept that the public is part of the flow system. More specifically the "public" with which the firm deals directly consists of two elements; these are customers who buy from the firm and vendors from whom the firm buys. The systems concept, which is discussed subsequently, is helping us to realize that these outside elements are

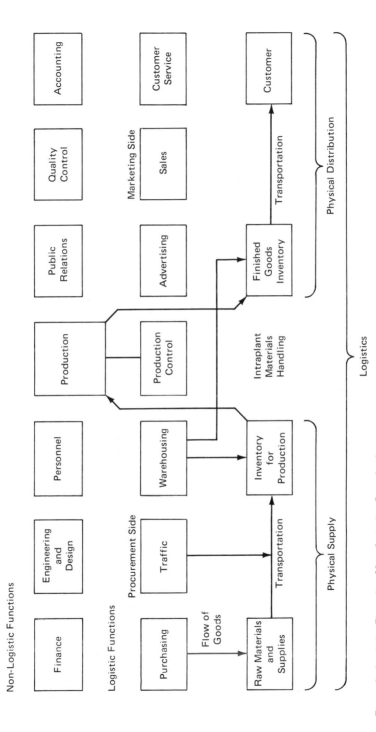

Figure 1. Logistics Flows in a Manufacturing Organization

just as much parts of a physical distribution system as any of the non-logistic or logistic departments shown on the charts as integral parts of the company.

New frames of reference

Currently, many new concepts of business organization and management are being discussed. Nearly every sub-discipline of business administration has its own "buzzword" concept. Among the most popular of these are the marketing concept, the total cost concept and the systems concept. These are all important to the efficient management of purchasing and of transportation. This importance lies not so much in their direct application as in the attitudes they create, for they are new frames of reference for business—new ways of looking at old problems.

Although most business men understand these concepts generally, it is helpful to set forth a definition of each of them. This is because these concepts have characteristics in common which reveal a principle to follow.

Marketing concept

The marketing concept is a business philosophy which holds that a firm should be so organized as to consider every marketing decision from the consumer point of view. Once the company discovers what the customer really wants it should be so managed as to fulfill these wants in a manner profitable to itself.[1] The marketing concept has been evolving for more than a few years. The idea that the consumer is worthy of primary consideration is opposed to what might be called the "production concept." Under the production concept, for the past hundred years business has produced whatever the engineer invented, secure in the knowledge that people would buy it in their never-ending struggle for a higher standard of living. Today, the consumer is surfeited by competitive and substitutable products adequate to his every want—it becomes important to find out if he wants something else before production of another new product is begun. The notion of consulting the consumer first is a refreshing innovation.

Total cost concept

The total cost concept is related to the truism that the whole is greater than the sum of its parts. Each step in a process should be appraised according to the effect it has on the total cost of the process, and no single step should be cheapened if that increases the total cost of the process. The total cost approach has been used widely to reduce the total cost of processes by examining individual steps and finding better ways to do them or by eliminating them entirely.

Systems concept

The systems concept recognizes the interdependence of the steps in a process to achieve a given objective.[2] The activity of one step is directly related to the activities of the steps on both sides of it in the chain. The application of this idea to business is extremely useful because it reveals that the typical business system is substantially larger than was traditionally recognized. Management theorists

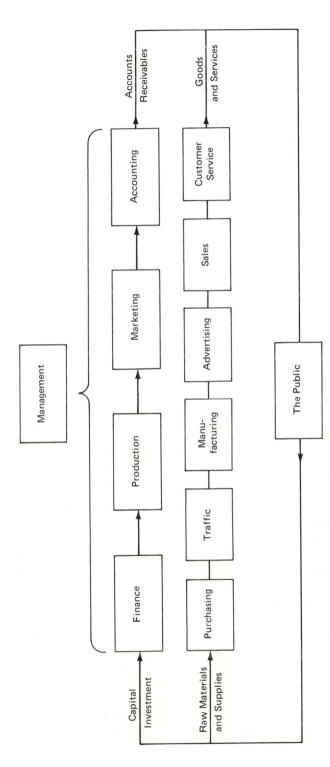

Figure 2. A Business Organization as a Horizontal Flow System

have tended to concentrate upon the problems of the individual firm without focussing on the fact that the welfare of the company is integrated with the welfare of other companies with which it has end-to-end work-flow relationships.

Common characteristic of the concepts

The statement was made above that the importance of these concepts (and they are essentially management concepts) lies not so much in their direct application as in the attitudes which they create. There is a great lesson they bring to the manager of a department in a logistic chain of departments or to the manager of a company in a logistic chain of companies. The lesson is that the manager should look beyond his own horizon to find all of the variables in his management problem.

Some systems theorists see three types of elements in a distribution system.[3] "Components" are the elements such as humans, machines, and buildings that make up the actual parts of the system. "Determiners" are outside elements such as inputs and environmental factors which constrain what the system can do. "Integrators" are the forces such as company policy and management techniques which make the components and the determiners work smoothly together.

Another writer on the subject, Dr. E. Grosvenor Plowman conveys the same idea in somewhat simpler language.[4]

> Business logistics involves acceptance of responsibility for the decisions and actions of insiders and outsiders, that is, of employees and non-employees. The common carrier by rail or truck or barge or air is an example of a separate enterprise that often fills a vital role in getting a product to a customer where and when he wants it. This acceptance of total or overall responsibility creates the third kind of integration, that is, *logistical integration.*

Thus, a manager must deal with "insiders" and "outsiders." When goods are moving in his own plant or own equipment they are in the hands of insiders and are under his direct control. When they are in the hands of a vendor, or a customer, or a carrier, however, they are in the hands of an outsider and are not under the direct control of the distribution manager. The manager must recognize that his distribution system contains many of these determiner or outsider elements. If he is to manage an efficient system he must learn to control these elements although they are not under his direct control. Dr. Plowman calls the art of doing this "logistical integration." One can assume that successful logistical integration must contain substantial portions of skillful human relations.

II. Entropy in distribution systems

Another useful management idea comes to us from systems theory. This is the concept of *entropy*. Technically, entropy is a mathematical measurement of the amount of unavailable energy in a thermodynamic system. As such it is a precisely determinable amount which changes as the system performs. The concept is related to the second law of thermodynamics which stated in its simplest form is that "heat always tends to pass from a hotter body to a colder one," "there are no conditions whatever under which heat will pass of its own natural tendency from a lower temperature to a higher one."[5] It is possible to reverse this process, of course, with a refrigeration machine, but this requires the expenditure of energy. This is similar to the natural tendency of water to run down hill; it will not run up again unless a pump is used and this requires the application of energy. The same concept can be applied to the decrease in efficiency of other systems such as business organizations. Norbert Wiener, the originator of the science of Cybernetics, characterized entropy as follows:[6]

> As entropy increases, the universe, and all closed systems in the universe, tend naturally to deteriorate and lose their distinctiveness, to move from the least to the most probable state, from a state of organization and differentiation . . . to a state of chaos . . . order is least probable, chaos most probable . . . But while the universe as a whole . . . tends to run down, there are local enclaves . . . in which there is a limited and temporary tendency for organization to increase. Life finds its home in some of these enclaves. . . .

There are two useful ideas in this statement which can be drawn from systems theory and applied in management practice. These are, first, that systems tend to run down and, second, that the application of energy can reverse this tendency. Particularly interesting is the exposition that the probable tends to overcome the improbable and that disorganization is probable and that organization is improbable.

The distribution manager is continually faced with systems which are running down and he must be continually expending energy to wind them up again. Let us examine an elementary illustration of how the probable overwhelms the improbable in distribution systems and makes them run down.

Suppose the Purchasing Department negotiates a contract under which a vendor shall deliver to the receiving and stores department ten cases of Product X each morning. The first day, since it is a new arrangement, the receiving personnel count and inspect the shipment thoroughly. However, on each succeeding day the arrival of the shipment is given less attention until on the tenth day the receiving clerk is in serious danger of being out-counted. This is particularly true if the shipment has checked out perfectly every time he has checked it thoroughly, because the subconscious assumption is that if it was all right last time, it will be again. Some note of improbability, therefore, must be injected into the situation to reverse the running down process or entropy which is taking place.

The manager usually cannot afford to concern himself with correcting isolated bits of entropy as in this simple example. He must introduce improbability on a wider scale so that disorganization is reversed in his whole operation. He must continually expend energy in reorganizing or innovating in order to stop his organization from running down. Since the beginning of the Physical Distribution Revolution, distribution managers have been doing this. They have been doing the improbable with regularity—they have been innovating on a wide scale. At first, innovations were often restricted to localized, interior improvements to the group of components directly controlled by the distribution manager. Recognition of the systems concept and the existence of "determiner" elements in the system is now increasingly causing the innovation to take the form of "logistical integration" which acts upon the outside parts of the system. A view of some of the new techniques being applied by procurement and traffic people demonstrates the surprising extent to which they are doing the improbable— going outside of their own companies and reshaping the activities of their vendors and their carriers.

III. Innovation and logistical integration

The problem of how to integrate the "determiners" or "outsiders" into a distribution system is one requiring a subtle management touch because an effective solution must often go "against the grain" of American business tradition. In a "free enterprise economy" where "competition is the life of trade" the unsatisfactory vendor or carrier is simply not patronized. Whenever possible, procurement and traffic people avoid the company who sells poor service for a high price; customarily they do not invade its organization and its privacy in an attempt to improve the situation. Today, however, purchasing agents and traffic managers are reversing their *laissez faire* attitudes in two ways. First, they are taking the initiative in going to the outsider instead of waiting for the outsider to come to them. Second, they are often giving him management and engineering consulting to help him improve his activities. Similar trends are visible in both the procurement of supplies and the procurement of transportation but purchasing agents possibly have developed more sophistication so far than have traffic managers.

"Do it yourself" is nothing new in procurement. Purchasing agents have long subjected equipment requirements to the "make or buy" decision. Often, careful analysis reveals that the firm can produce a needed good more efficiently than it can be obtained outside. Or perhaps the opportunity to use excess plant capacity tips the scale in favor of an in-plant procurement operation. In transportation, the decision to engage in private trucking of their own goods in their own vehicles is often made by traffic managers. These approaches should certainly always be considered as procurement alternatives, especially in last resort situations where vendors or carriers adopt a monopolistic attitude or refuse to become efficient. These are, in fact, techniques which allow the procurement man to reject competition when competition does not exist. Modern "do it yourself" is not so isolationist, however; it reaches out to involve the supplier or carrier and forces him to be progressive.

Searching for service

One of the most frustrating problems for the industrial salesman or the transportation salesman is finding out who has the authority to purchase or to specify routing. Salesmen wander from office to office calling on the wrong people. Efficient procurement agents recognize that the buyer cannot make a sensible purchasing decision until he has seen all of the wares or services on the market. He must see all of the salesmen and for this to happen they must know who he is.

Some companies have instituted seminars to deal with the problem. Lockheed Missiles and Space Company of Sunnyvale, California, has conducted such meetings to give orientation to industrial salesmen[7] and Walgreen Drug of Chicago has held annual seminars for transportation and distribution representatives. Such programs are used not only to explain company organization and objectives to salesmen but also to show them how to sell to company procurement people sometimes including even the kind of sales presentation which should be made.

Even companies who do not go to the length of conducting a seminar are taking the initiative in seeking out the supplier instead of waiting for his salesman to call. In some cases this may even include a "cold call" by the purchasing man on a vendor he thinks can make or supply the needed article.

Trends toward supplier development

In taking the initiative in helping the supplier do a better job, purchasing agents have significantly surpassed traffic managers. This is partly due to the different nature of what they are buying and partly because they started sooner. New purchasing techniques which have been developed range from Value Engineering, through Vendor Rating, Supplier Evaluation, Learning Curve Pricing, Contract Purchasing, to Supplier Development. An examination of each of these shows that the customer is tending to inject his own management more and more deeply into the vendor's business affairs. Sometimes this is purely selfish, sometimes it results in economies for both sides.

Value Engineering. Value Engineering has been characterized as the "biggest thing since mass production."[8] It is unique in that the Purchasing Department usurps some of the prerogatives of Engineering. Essentially, it causes the Purchasing Department to examine the product it is buying and ask three questions. "What does it do?" "What does it cost?" "What else would do the job better and/or cheaper?" If Engineering and Production can accept the "improvement" important savings often can be made. Admittedly this is primarily an internal technique not affecting the vendor directly, but it can be a step toward telling him how to manufacture his product.

Vendor Rating. More directly involving the supplier is the procedure known as Vendor Rating. In this case, the customer keeps score on the supplier, rating his performance against competitive firms. The rating is usually a composite derived from price, on-time deliveries, and rejects. It may be a straight or weighted average, and a high price vendor may earn a better rating than a low price one because his physical performance is better. Each month, suppliers are notified of their ratings and those which remain unsatisfactory are given increasingly smaller orders.

Supplier Evaluation. Supplier Evaluation proceeds a step further. In this technique, purchasing personnel or a team from Purchasing and Engineering visit and inspect the facilities of a possible new supply source. Production facilities, information flow, and transportation system are inspected, a form is prepared comparing the projected behavior of the new sources to existing suppliers.

Learning Curve Pricing. Although it is strictly limited as to situations in which it can be used correctly, Learning Curve Pricing recognizes that a new supplier's costs decrease as he learns more and more about producing the customer's item. Some customers even demand to see the vendor's records so that the proper learning curve to apply can be calculated from the cost figure. New suppliers are then granted higher prices during the prototype or learning period, but subsequently, contract price is progressively reduced until a realistic, long-term level is reached.

Contract Purchasing. Also known as "blanket order buying," Contract Purchasing has advantages for both the purchasing company and the seller. Bids are taken and orders place for homogeneous, continual use items only once a year. The proviso is made that deliveries will be made on a periodic basis. Thus, the customer gets the advantage of a volume price but does not have the expense of storage. The supplier can schedule production of the items more efficiently using excess capacity and slack time so long as he meets delivery dates.

Supplier Development. Under the systems concept, the Purchasing Department recognizes that the vendor is part of the distribution system and treats him as an external production department. Therefore, suppliers are worthy of careful cultivation and development. In the Supplier Development process, enlightened purchasing agents are not only going out to discover potential suppliers but are extending them consultation, machinery, and financing. Usually this cultivation is possible only with small suppliers and sometimes the buying company must be careful not to overwhelm the small vendor with too much business.

Parallel transportation trends

Traffic managers or transportation buyers have not influenced carrier management nearly so much as purchasing people have affected suppliers. Causing a transportation company to treat you favorably is more difficult because carriers serve the whole public and they are strictly regulated by the government to prevent them from showing undue favoritism to one shipper over another. However, alert buyers of transport service are realizing that there are ways in which they can take the initiative in improving transportation efficiency. Today we are in a buyers' market for transportation and there are various ways the customer can benefit from competition between carriers.[9] Some timely examples are reviewed in this section.

Scheduling receiving and delivery. A simple example is seen in pick up and delivery of shipments. Many companies experience severe congestion of their shipping and receiving facilities because of random arrival of transportation company vehicles. An easy solution is to plan and work out with the carriers a reasonable schedule of times for them to arrive and to enforce it. Close attention to trucking company arrivals is particularly appropriate when carriers calculate demurrage or equipment detention charges on a per-minute basis.

Small shipment problem. Another aggravating problem for today's shipper is that carriers are less interested in handling small shipments. A small shipment, especially a minimum shipment, can cost the transportation company more to handle than it brings in revenue. Since it is difficult to forecast which small shipment will be unprofitable, carriers tend to look unfavorably on all small shipments. Solving the problem calls for deliberate attention and action by the Traffic Department. Traffic flows must be analyzed so that big shipments can be matched with small ones. Carriers then must be advised and controls established to move a specified number of small shipments for each large and profitable one.

Outside expediter. A technique which might have been considered too expensive or even too bold a few years ago is that of using expediters or tracers who go out in the field to find out what is wrong. These people work on both the supplier and the carrier to find out why delivery dates are not being met. When an order is due to be shipped by a vendor, the customer's expediter shows up at the vendor's plant and asks to see it move from order picking, through packaging and across the loading dock. He then gets in his car and tails the carrier's truck to the terminal and further if necessary. The mere presence of the expediter may be enough to improve the delivery situation without direct action upon his part.

Synthetic freight rates. In the area of transportation pricing a computer applied technique is appearing which shows some promise of eventually improving our whole freight rate structure. This is referred to as "synthetic freight rates."[10] In this procedure, freight rates are simulated upon a computer. Either the relationships between the commodity rates for various regions and their parallel class rates, or the cost factors making up a rate can be placed in the computer memory. Then the computer can construct a synthetic freight rate; this can be compared to the rate the carrier is charging to indicate whether his rate is reasonable. So far, this is seen primarily as a negotiating tool, but in the future it could become a means of constructing usable freight rates.

Summarized conclusion

There are, of course, many other new management techniques being used by both purchasers of materials and purchasers of transportation. Those discussed are emphasized for the way in which they reveal the trends in modern procurement management. They are applications which illustrate the principles of logistical integration and of innovating to overcome entropy.

Part I of this paper shows that modern concepts—especially the systems concept—are revealing the true nature of the distribution system. Outsiders such as customers, vendors, and carriers are recognized as active parts of the system. Since they are outsiders, the problem of how to control them arises and the principle of logistical integration becomes important.

Part II of the paper reviews the idea that systems run down because entropy increases or that probable occurrences tend to outweigh improbable occurrences. Activity to establish the improbable or innovation to overcome entropy is suggested as a cure.

The procurement techniques discussed in Part II show the extent to which logistical integration is taking place in modern procurement management—particularly in the purchasing of goods. Purchasing, and to some extent traffic personnel are injecting their own management activity into the outside elements of the logistics system. In view of the traditions of free enterprise management isolationism, such integrative and innovative activities are indeed "improbable" activities and as such are reversing the growth of entropy.

NOTES

1. See William J. Stanton, *Fundamentals of Marketing* (New York: McGraw-Hill Book Company, 1967) pp. 11-12; and Charles F. Phillips and Delbert J. Duncan, *Marketing Principles and Methods* (Homewood Ill.: Richard D. Irwin, Inc., 1968) pp. 39-40.
2. See Donald J. Bowersox, Edward W. Smykay, and Bernard J. LaLonde, *Physical Distribution Management* (New York: The Macmillan Company, 1968) p. 103.
3. K. H. Schaeffer and A. Shapero as quoted in Frank H. Mossman and Newton Morton, *Logistics of Distribution Systems* (Boston: Allyn and Bacon, Inc., 1965) p. 15.
4. E. Grosvenor Plowman, *Lectures on Elements of Business Logistics* (Stanford: Stanford University Press, 1964) p. viii.
5. Allan D. Risteen, "Thermodynamics or the Mechanical Theory of Heat," *Encyclopedia Americana*, 1956, Vol. 26, p. 527.
6. Norbert Wiener, *The Human Use of Human Beings* (New York: Doubleday and Co., Inc., 1956) p. 12.
7. "A Break for Vendors," *Business Week*, May 19, 1962, pp. 94-98.
8. "Biggest Thing Since Mass Production," *Reader's Digest*, January 1964, pp. 107-110.
9. E. Grosvenor Plowman, "How Control of Transportation Contributes to Profitability," *Transportation Journal*, Winter 1962, pp. 13-18.
10. E. Grosvenor Plowman, "The Computer in Pricing and Billing—Synthetic Freight Rates," *The Computer's Role in Transportation and Distribution Management*, Seminar, The University of Wisconsin Management Institute, August 5, 1969.

Physical Distribution
        in Semi-Maturity
        Donald J. Bowersox
        Michigan State University

Here, a leader in the field of physical distribution management outlines the historical development of scientific distribution analysis. He describes the forces which made it a logical business development and calls for a realistic view of the function of traffic and transportation management in the overall logistics system.

It is my sincere belief that the Physical Distribution Concept represents one of the truly new developments to emerge in management philosophy during the past few decades. Unfortunately, it is also one of the most misunderstood concepts—particularly as it relates to traffic management.

At the outset a working definition of Physical Distribution Management is in order. To me, Physical Distribution is that portion of corporate management concerned with the design and administration of systems for control of raw material and finished inventory movement. In a broad sense, Physical Distribution includes the integrated planning and administration of traffic, inventory, warehousing, location, packaging, purchasing, communications and related functions.

Many different titles have been used to describe Physical Distribution: Business Logistics, Physical Supply, Materials Management, Market Supply, Logistics of Distribution, Total Distribution, and even Rhochrematics. While some details of treatment vary, all agree that the essence of distribution management is one of getting the correct mixture of raw materials or finished goods to the correct place at the correct time, and at the lowest *total* cost outlay. It makes very little difference whether we spend more or less for transportation, for example, as long as we accomplish our mission at the lowest total cost expenditure for the integration of all functions involved in Physical Distribution.

Like any basic concept, the doctrines of Physical Distribution are simple. The difficult part of Physical Distribution comes in measurement and implementation. The problem is complicated by the basic fact that all firms must in some way complete the physical distribution mission as a prerequisite to staying in business. The question is not one of do or not do. Rather the question is: How well and how cheap? How well in terms of profitable sales support? How cheap in terms of total cost outlay?

Turning to the historical development of Physical Distribution, we start with

From Donald J. Bowersox, "Physical Distribution in Semi-Maturity," *Air Transportation*, January 1966, pp. 9-11. Copyright Air Transportation, 1966. Used by permission.

acknowledgement that the basic functions are certainly not new, the tools of statistics and mathematics are certainly not new, the problem is not new, and most of all, awareness of a need is not new.

The need for adequate physical supply as a basic part of commerce was clearly noted as early as 1882 by Francis Wayland in his work, *The Elements of Political Economy*. Professor Wayland went so far as to conclude:

"The difficult problems of Political Economy pertain almost entirely to matters of Distribution and Exchange."

Arch W. Shaw in 1912 outlined the need for physical supply coordination. In his work, *Some Problems in Market Distribution,* he concluded:

"The essential element in any business activity is the application of motion to material."

Fred Clark in 1920 and Percival White in 1927 outlined the need for approaching logistics on a system-wide basis. White, in particular, viewed marketing as a process of moving from a conglomeration of goods on one hand to an assortment on the other. He stressed the need for balancing marketing effort and logistical support on a system basis. Fred Clark, to my knowledge, was the first to use the term Physical Distribution.

Thus, awareness of a need for integrated activity on both the practioner and scholar level has existed for many, many years. However, during the 1930s and 1940s, writers made great advances in description of the many functions of Physical Distribution, with no unified attempt to explain logistics as a system of total action—*and the hidden costs went on.* Consultants continued to assist individual firms to work out specific problems concerning a warehouse or a market—*and the hidden costs went on.* Accountants continued to keep score without cross-departmental cost analysis—*and the hidden costs went on.*

The new approach

After World War II, we were technologically ready to confront the complex problems of integrated management. Military logistics, systems analysis and applied mathematics had uncovered a new approach to the study of complex movement problems. However, we faced a new barrier. The postwar years were filled with unexpected economic boom. Management properly turned attention to the immediate task of filling pipelines.

It was not until the recessions of the 1950s that widespread management and research effort began to focus on the problems of logistics. By this time, several unrelated occurrences made a penetrating evaluation of Physical Distribution Systems timely:

Five forces

1. The postwar period had been characterized by rapid increases in freight rates. Traditional methods of distribution had become costly, margins had narrowed. The profit squeeze made reevaluation necessary.

2. A significant change in inventory stocking practice had occurred. At one time it had been common practice for inventory to be held about 50/50 between distributors and retailers, advances in inventory control methods by 1950 had made 90/10 ratios appear attainable. This switch in stocking philosophy, in turn, placed greater emphasis upon dependable movement capabilities.

3. By 1950, foreign competition became a reality. With strict price competition, more efficient physical distribution became necessary in order to maintain profitable operations.

4. Production stability had been realized. After many years of increasing production economies, it became apparent that the point of diminishing returns had been reached for several industries. Other methods of cost reduction had to be found.

5. As a nation we had begun to feel the initial impact of the Computer Age. While a few years earlier the first computers had been a novelty, their use by 1950 was rapidly becoming commonplace. The high-speed digital computer, coupled with advances in applied analytical tools, placed at the disposal of business an orderly way to cope with the millions of details of logistics management.

These five forces attracted managerial concern to Physical Distribution. In many ways, looking back, perhaps Physical Distribution emerged too fast and much too acclaimed as a cure-all. Managers were concerned, but lacked know-how. Many firms moved fast, made mistakes, and stopped—some to appraise prior to moving on, others to retreat.

From these first few years of the 1950s some interesting observations can be expected. First: leadership came from industry—primarily buyers and suppliers of transportation. In general, universities lagged, associations entrenched the traditional, and consultants continued to solve isolated problems. Second: despite failures, the groundwork had been established for a learning explosion which fortunately began to crystallize during the second five years of the 1950s.

Outdated successes

By 1955 successful case studies were available. Looking back, some of these "successful" cases look somewhat naive. However, at the time they stood as monuments of accomplishment. Given this start, trade associations began an active program in continued education. Formal education institutions also followed the lead of industry. In 1957 the first formal course for credit in Physical Distribution was offered at Michigan State University. Today, over 45 universities have courses. In addition to teaching, research work at various universities has made a vital contribution to our expanding knowledge of Physical Distribution.

A very important contribution to development during the late 1950s was the role played by several carrier advisory groups. While formed for the purpose of selling high-cost transportation, as a trade-off for other cost savings, these carrier groups opened many doors and convinced many managers of the need for reevaluation of their distribution systems.

Finally, by the early 1960s, it could safely be concluded that Physical Distribution had become a vital part of American business know-how. Several trade publications dealing with Physical Distribution topics were available, text books had been written, and finally, after several years of planning, a specialized association—The National Council of Physical Distribution Management—had been formed.

Semi-maturity

The present status of Physical Distribution can be characterized as one of semi-maturity. I like to draw the analogy to mass production techniques in the 1930s. There is little doubt it's here to stay. However, there's much to be done. We are sure Physical Distribution will continue to grow in importance for one very simple reason. Unlike some other concepts, such as marketing, we in Physical Distribution deal in the tangible facets of material, space and time. The potential for efficiently aligning these tangible facets of business is limited only by our resourcefulness and imagination.

It's difficult to speculate on the future of Physical Distribution. Perhaps the best way is to review a few problem areas we currently confront. How we ultimately solve these problems should provide considerable insight concerning future progress of Physical Distribution.

First, one of our most pressing problems centers around what I call the organizational bias. In the early days, it was assumed that a firm must establish a so-called Distribution Department. If they did, they were assumed to be enamored of the total distribution movement. The confusion stems from the fact that many companies have no Physical Distribution Department and still do an excellent job. Others have vice presidents of distribution and do an inferior job. Such contrasts are easy to observe. Many of the best Physical Distribution operations in the country operate without benefit of formal portfolio.

What seems to have happened somewhere along the line is confusion between organization structure and philosophy of operation. It is not important that a firm have a formal distribution organization. It is important that all levels of management in a firm think and act in terms of distribution capabilities and economies.

Organization by nature is a customized adjustment to accomplish mission with available capability. In one case complete reorganization may be in order, while in another situation none is required. Some multi-divisional firms elect to set up separate Physical Distribution companies, while others use staff coordinators.

It is not the organization, but rather the philosophy of operation, which is of critical importance.

A second problem area is one I refer to as the transportation bias. This total talk could very well have centered on the role of traffic management in Physical Distribution. In the early days, transportation came under heavy criticism for the simple reason that far too many firms made the mistake of considering Physical Distribution and Transportation synonymous. This was, and is, a mistake. *Physical Distribution is much more than transportation.* However, in reading much of the current literature, one gets the impression that a Physical Distribution system can operate without traffic management. This, also, is a mistake.

The truth of the matter is that a good physical distribution system must have a soundly run, fully integrated transportation effort. Traffic management is and always will be a function area of total distribution effort worthy of professional management. Given 10 firms that see fit to establish a formal distribution operation, it seems logical that a given number of traffic managers with advancement potential would be promoted to direct the new operation. Likewise, it is also logical to expect some financial, warehouse, computer, inventory and materials handling executives to also be promoted in the 10 hypothetical firms.

Exaggerated inference

I am somewhat amused by the inference that traffic management is a dead career field. Many years ago the famous humorist Mark Twain put to rest recurrent rumors about the state of his health by saying, "The report of my death is greatly exaggerated." The death of the traffic manager is also greatly exaggerated.

As long as we have physical distribution, we will need traffic management. As always, some will move up to corporate responsibilities and some will not. Currently, far too much effort is being expended on defense of the *status quo*. The world, however, is not static. Distribution is a complex business and change must be rapid and exacting for survival.

Today, and increasingly in the future, Physical Distribution advancements will be limited by the people gap. I would conclude, therefore, that we have little time for divided ranks. Our most serious problem is one of attracting high-quality people into transportation and physical distribution as career fields.

A world of promise

Finally, a few comments are in order concerning problems related to applied mathematics, computers, and so-called scientific management. The world of quantitative methods is exciting and holds a great deal of promise. Frankly, problems can be tackled using mathematical programming and computers which heretofore could not be defined.

However, no mathematical solution or computer is capable of managing a distribution organization. The tools for better management are no substitutes for better managers. Thus, we must keep the potential contributions of scientific management in proper perspective.

The problem is that we do not maintain proper perspective. Often it ends up with the blind leading the blind. On one hand, we find the mathematician who wants to simplify the situation to fit his model; on the other hand, we find the manager who either believes every mathematical conclusion or does not believe any.

Traffic managers, physical distribution managers, and other members of a firm's logistics team need not have advanced mathematical capabilities. We do not have to develop our skills to the point where we understand capabilities and limitations. We need to learn the language. We have to be able to ask for the help we need.

The field of physical distribution stands at a point where future developments may well depend on the experienced manager's ability to open the door for the application of new and powerful techniques. This is a responsibility that does not show on an organization chart. It is a responsibility which, in the final analysis, must rest upon the shoulders of line managers. Until line management support and experience are combined with computer capabilities, mathematical techniques have little real world value.

32　　　　　　　　　　　1984—What Then?

Karl M. Ruppenthal
University of British Columbia

Business logistics suggests total movement—for instance, inventory control, warehousing, and ordering, as well as transportation. Another new development is automation in the information function: punch cards, computer control, and other devices are coming to the fore.

In this selection, Dr. Ruppenthal combines the subjects of business logistics and automation in the information function—and he takes a look at the "crystal ball" of the future.

Virtually everyone is aware of some of the radical changes which are taking place in every sector of American life. Today we probably are witnessing the most significant social revolution that the world has ever seen. In every corner of the world there are evidences of it, and we are exposed to it in every aspect of human existence . . .

In the business world we see an entirely new face being drawn upon the surface of business life. The changes take place so fast, new inventions are developed so rapidly, and new devices come into being at such a prodigious rate, that they scarcely make the headlines any more. We are becoming accustomed to rapid and important changes, and we are almost numbed to the fact that they are taking place. As a matter of fact, the business executive himself is changing— and he is changing in an exceptional way.

A man who holds an important spot in business is no longer considered to be a little bit of a freak if he knows something about statistical probability and linear

From Karl M. Ruppenthal, "1984—What Then?," *Air Transportation*, December 1964, pp. 9-11. Copyright, Air Transportation, 1964. Used by permission.

programming. He may pick up matrix algebra and some other concepts, ideas, and terms which 20 years ago would have been completely foreign to business. Even though he may not know everything there is to know about the inner workings of the computer, he is curious to learn more about its applications and to learn more about where it fits into his own company, his industry, and the sociological scheme of things.

Executives today are probing new frontiers. They are becoming more interested in areas that formerly were completely foreign to their own particular domain. These new tools and techniques are so very important that the executive who chooses to ignore them faces personal obsolescence. Indeed, if he ignores them too long, he may find himself consigned to the executive scrap heap which is sometimes called early retirement.

I think that nowhere in American industry is this change more insistent—or more desirable—than in the area having to do with transportation, inventory, and supply—this area which is generally coming to be known as business logistics.

Throughout the land there is a growing awareness of the interdependence between the type of transportation, between inventory policy, and the amount of working capital needed by a company, and thus the amount of profit shown on its balance sheet. We are coming to recognize increasingly that business logistics is the essential link between production and marketing. And without the strong, well-organized link neither of these other functions can do very well.

In view of the rapidity of these changes taking place in this area, I think it is interesting to speculate what it may look like in 1984. What things can we expect two decades hence? How will the responsibilities of our successor differ from those which we have today? How is this whole area likely to change?

If I am to take the role of a forecaster, I would note that for many years forecasters have been careful to hedge their predictions, and to make certain that they were not caught with a statement which is too precise. It is generally considered that in all types of crystal ball gazing it is better to be partially correct than to be totally wrong. If you look at the old Indian Medicine man doing his marvelous rain dance and praying on the parched prairie for a little water from on high, he has always been careful to refrain from reporting that the rain is coming *tomorrow* or on any particular day. He will simply state that the rain is coming soon—thus he is almost always correct . . .

I am certain that many of my readers read George Orwell's amazing *1984*. In it Orwell predicted awesome, and some awful, devices, certain of them marvelous from the technological aspect. Almost all of the things which he envisioned just 15 years ago are reality, or very near to it, today—about 20 years before their time . . .

So my concern as a forecaster is not that the things about which I write will not happen, but that they will occur a lot sooner than we think. And this has been the case of almost all technological forecasting today. It is almost impossible for any human being to dream or conceive of an invention without having another human who can bring it into reality. We have the technical capability in the United States today, so that almost all of the new devices which one can imagine in transport and movement and communications can quite easily become true.

The only questions are: *Are they worth the cost? Will they perform the function that we want them to perform?*

Two years ago, Al Russell of Sears Roebuck, appearing at Stanford's first Business Logistics Forum, discussed a new distribution system which the company was putting into effect. Sears has a very large share of the market in white goods—ranges, refrigerators, stoves, and so forth—but a study indicated that it was not making much money on them. It was discovered that Sears could not reduce manufacturing costs significantly, although its factories were among the most efficient in the industry. It could not raise price; if they did, it would lose the market to some of the competition. As a result, Sears took a look at its distribution. It analyzed very carefully all of the elements of the company's distribution; it sought to determine exactly how much time every unit spent in each place that it sat, and how much it cost to have it sitting here.

Sears found that the average inventory on this type of merchandise was about four weeks, and that each piece of merchandise was handled and rehandled eight, 10 and sometimes even 15 times. The company had the paradoxical situation of being overstocked on many items and out of stock on others. Its cost of markdowns and damaged goods was entirely too high. The company was not making very much money. Since it could not effect economies in production or in the marketing function—at least, this is what Sears' studies indicated—it decided that the only area from which it could squeeze out water was in the logistics of the matter.

This Sears proceeded to do. It set up an entirely new distribution system consisting of distribution warehouses. Instead of having a full carload of eight-foot refrigerators move from the factory to six or seven stores, each taking a few of them, the firm assembled the products in a central warehouse. There, products from each of the central factories were mixed and a full carload shipped.

In this process, Sears was able to eliminate entire warehouses; it was able to cut the average inventory of the stores by 50%, and to effect fantastic savings in the amount of required working capital. In addition, Sears did a number of other things which probably were even more important: it almost entirely eliminated the out-of-stock problem as well as the problem of the "dog items" (these are the ones that sit on the floor for so long that you can hardly give them away to a customer). It established a smooth flow of these items so that they essentially are handled twice—the first time when they are placed on the pallet at the factory, and the second time when they are set at the consumer's door.

All of these savings came about because the company recognized the movement of white goods as really one big, continuous movement from the factory to the consumer, interrupted occasionally by certain short stops in warehouses and other places.

By 1984 it may be possible to make this process a lot more automatic. By that time the company will have a tremendous volume of information about what the American public is doing. It will know, for example, how many units of each type of refrigerator were sold last year; its forecasters will be able to predict the increase in the market. It will take into account the economic cycle, the number of families being formed, the number of babies being born, the impact of new types of consumer foods.

This information will permit a tremendous amount of planning. As a matter of fact, companies will be able to ascertain the probable quantities of each type of refrigerator that will be needed a year from next June, and to set up a near-automatic ordering system so that the factory will know immediately how many of each unit to produce. Automatically they will come into the mixing warehouse. Instead of, say a two-week supply, the total inventory can be cut down to about two days or, perhaps, even one day.

In the highly detailed Sears study it was discovered that for every dollar saved in transportion and distribution costs, it could increase profits twentyfold. This means that every savings made in the area of logistics can be particularly important.

If you can cut the average inventory from four weeks to two weeks, why can't you cut it even more? If you can cut it down to a one-day inventory, thereby achieving a perfect inventory, then, of course, you'd have a optimum system. If the forecasters were absolutely correct, and if one could tell exactly how many refrigerators of each type housewives were going to buy in every store next year, it would be possible to do away with many purchasing agents and many routing clerks. The whole system becomes almost completely automatic.

As a matter of fact, a single transaction card is all that would be required when the housewife comes into the store to buy a refrigerator. This one IBM-type punchcard could deplete the store's inventory records by one unit, automatically tell the factory to prepare shipment of another, charge the customer with the amount of the purchase, and even debit the latter's bank account with the amount of the purchase price. It could credit the salesman's commissions, add up the store's cumulative business for the day, and eliminate nearly all of the people now employed in computing these various transactions.

There is only one small risk—the forecasters may not always be entirely correct. The impact of a new variety of frozen food may be different from what we anticipate, and instead of wanting 10-foot refrigerators, the consumer may decide that she wants a 12-foot unit. And if we have a one-day supply only, we are faced with the same problem that we had before: *how do you make certain that you have in stock the items which the customer wants?*

But here again we have some alternatives. One will be to bypass the warehouse system; to bypass this highly efficient, smooth-running machine that we have, and to bring the refrigerator out by air freight, helicopter or rocket. Each of these has a certain cost assigned to it, but we can carefully evaluate the possibilities of our system being wrong and the magnitude of probable error, and equate the cost of error.

If it is not wrong too often, it will be far cheaper to bring out the occasional refrigerator by rocket at a fantastically high transportation cost than it would be to have excessive inventory in the pipeline. This is the direction that logistics will certainly be going by 1984.

I think there is a real problem in the systems which we will be developing (and there's no question that they will be developed). Every type of industry has peculiar logistic problems. Obviously one which worked well in the grain industry has very little application in electronics, toys, or in high-fashion goods. The problems in each one are individual, but there is no doubt that each one is susceptible to an analysis. Each system can be improved by careful attention to the specific problems of each individual industry. There is little doubt that increasingly we will have this systems approach in every industry that has something to move.

The only real question by 1984 will be whether or not the systems may become *too* good. The total cost of a particular system may be so great that we may be reluctant to make any change. Our industries may be so large, our systems so complex, that it will be extremely difficult for the innovator to come and say, "I have a better system. Why don't you put it to use?"

This, I think, is one of the most difficult and important problems which will face us in 1984.

---

33   Rate Sharks

Richard F. Janssen

In any firm, after the choice of route and carrier has been made, shipment completed, and charges paid, the traffic department still has an important role to play in the movement of goods. It has to audit the freight bill to ascertain whether or not the proper charges have been made.

Auditing may be internal and/or external—i.e., by the traffic department and/or by an independent firm. By law, the carrier must charge the legal rates as stated in the tariff. Any deviation will give rise to claims for recovery of overcharges.

Many shippers do not realize that external auditing firms exist and do not understand the type of service they offer. This selection illustrates the importance of the auditing function.

CHICAGO—A growing number of cost-conscious companies are finding windfall returns in a most unlikely place—their old freight bills.

They are turning these dry, and sometimes dusty, documents over to a flourishing group of firms that make a business of scrutinizing shippers' freight bills to ferret out unintentional overcharges by railroads, trucking lines, barge operators and air carriers.

What might seem like dull reading to most persons often proves quite profitable for both the shippers and the bill checkers, who are known by some in the trade as "rate sharks," although they prefer calling themselves traffic "analysts"

From Richard F. Janssen, "Rate Sharks," *The Wall Street Journal*, June 24, 1959. Used by permission.

or "consultants." For the shipper, a recovered overcharge means revenue that might have been lost forever if an eagle-eyed rate expert hadn't spotted an error. Because bill-checking firms work on a commission basis, usually getting 50% of recovered overcharges, shippers generally have everything to gain and little or nothing to lose.

$40,000 in five minutes

Riffling through a stock of trucking bills paid over a two year period by an Ohio glass container maker, rate expert Charles Butler of Chicago's Midwest Freight Traffic Service Bureau, Inc., illustrates how his special knowledge can save a client money. He notes the shipper has been paying a recently-posted higher rate. But Mr. Butler is aware of a tariff technicality which entitles the container concern to pay a lower special rate on its wares—a technicality that has gone unnoticed by both the shipper and the carrier.

"The overcharge in this case amounted to $40,000," says Mr. Butler, adding pridefully, "I found the error in just five minutes."

Through such recoveries, many of them smaller, to be sure, some 350 rate firms across the country are saving millions of dollars for shippers. The nation's freight bill is now about $32 billion a year and going higher with each rate increase and gain in national production, so the potential for the operators of these calculating hair-splitting service agencies in existence according to traffic authorities is constantly increasing; ten years ago there weren't more than 100 bill-checking agencies.

Bill-checking firms credit their post-war boom to a number of factors. With rail freight rates nearly doubled during this period, shippers are more anxious than ever to seek savings. More important, billing has become much more complex with the stepped-up use of motor carriers, barges and aircraft adding countless new tariffs to the many volumes of rate schedules already piled up by railroads. The span of new products turned out by industry also has meant many additional rates, all adding to the possibilities of error.

In hopes of wringing some extra cash from their freight bills, "probably 80% of the major industrial firms in the country now send their bills out for audit," estimates Fletcher Day, traffic consultant of Dickinson Traffic Service, Pasadena, California.

Recession helps the boom

The 1958 recession brought many new cost-conscious customers into the auditing fold, says James Ash, President of Detroit's Freight Traffic Service Co. "Among the 30 new clients I won last year are Ford Motor Co., and the Chrysler Corp.," he adds. Forwarded freight bills of these industrial giants offer something of a freight problem themselves. "When Ford sends bills for one month from its plants all over the country, they sometimes fill over 40 filing drawers," notes Mr. Ash.

Both Ford and Chrysler do their own audits first, then send the bills to Mr.

Ash "because they have nothing to lose," he says. This appealing feature spurs numerous companies to send their bills to two or more audit bureaus in turn, hoping each will find errors the others missed. Such zealousness, however, is not encouraged. "You waste your time on too many dry runs," complains one analyst.

One enthusiastic subscriber to the services of a number of audit bureaus is Chicago's Montgomery Ward & Co., big national mail order firm. "If we didn't do our own auditing first and then send the bills to outside firms, Ward's would be out over $140,000 a year," estimates G. R. Klaud, Midwest traffic manager. In his own territory alone, five Ward rate clerks recover over $35,000 a year, more than covering their salaries, and outside firms return another $18,000, he says.

"While this is peanuts in relation to the company's total purchases of $19 billion worth of transportation a year, it's large enough that you can't afford to overlook it," Mr. Klaud adds.

Swift saves thousands

Even after a careful audit by its own staff, Swift and Co. "saves several thousand dollars a year by outside audits," says E. F. Majeske, head of the meat packer's transportation department.

Some companies have given up their own bill auditing efforts and let outside auditors do all the work. International Harvester Co., a farm implement maker, had about seven rate experts of its own doing nothing but auditing a few years ago, reports A. C. Friedsam, general traffic manager. "But we just couldn't employ enough to handle the load, so we decided to send all the bills out," he says. Gross recoveries in the last few years made by Consolidated Freight Bureau in Chicago have ranged between $85,000 and $142,000 annually, Mr. Friedsam notes cheerfully.

In most cases, auditing firms follow through when they discover an error and see to it that their client gets a rebate from the carrier. In some instances, however, the rate analyst only points out errors to clients. International Harvester, for example, deals with the erring carrier itself, paying the outside auditing firm only 27.5% of the rebate instead of the usual 50%.

Freight bill auditors pride themselves on their detailed knowledge of highly complex and fast-changing tariffs. Rates published by rail and truck carriers are different for each route and type of shipment, and they number in the millions. In a recent year, the Interstate Commerce Commission, Federal rate-regulating agency, received from common carriers over 168,000 new tariffs and 12,000 changes.

Spotting an overcharge

For an idea of the complexity of this field, visit the office of Midwest Freight here in Chicago. Lining one long wall are cabinets filled with nothing but tariff books; a large storeroom to the rear holds the overflow. Slim Dale Morrissey, who studies traffic management at Milwaukee's Marquette University, pulls out one thick truck traffic volume at random and explains how easily a wrong rate may be paid:

"Say you're shipping blankets of wool, rayon and cotton from Sargent, Ga., to Indianapolis," he says, pointing out the rate for such a shipment. "You could well be paying $2.82 a hundred pounds and thinking nothing of it, since the rate is right here, but if the wool content by weight is not over 50% the rate drops to $1.93," he explains, flipping to another section of the bulky book.

Midwest audits about 10,000 bills each month, estimates its president, Joseph Heitzinger, who also is acting president of the newly formed trade group, the National Association of Transportation Consultants. "You can't look at every one, so you just check those your sixth sense tells you are most likely to be mis-rated," explains Mr. Morrissey.

Frequently "errors" arise from the shipper's own unwittingly wrong description of the product. Harry Scott, head of Scott Traffic Consultants, Pittsburgh, tells of this catch: "An East Coast firm was sending out its product under the heading of finished castings, at a rate of $4.84 a hundred pounds. I visited the plant and discovered they were really rough castings, and that he was entitled to a rate of only $1.69."

Result: "We got refunds of $2,000 to $4,000 a carload, and the company ships about 100 loads a year," Mr. Scott reports. What's more, the shipper hasn't made the same mistake again, so he continues to save several hundred thousand dollars a year.

While bill audits mean recovery of about $3,000 a year for his firm, "The auditors' suggestions on new routings and rates mean far greater savings that can't be measured," comments James Corcoran, general traffic manager of Wells Lamont Corp., a Chicago glove manufacturer. "If we didn't employ Midwest Freight, we'd have to have thousands and thousands of tariffs on file ourselves," he adds.

Webcor passes on savings

"We save our customers $75,000 a year in freight charges because of one find by Midwest Freight," reports John Ihrig, executive vice president of Webcor, Inc., a Chicago hi-fi phonograph manufacturer. One audit revealed that Webcor's customers were receiving record players at a rate set in the days when the instruments were much more fragile and bulky because of protruding hand cranks and horns. The bureau convinced the carriers that modern phonographs were more compact and entitled to a 15% lower rate.

Many traffic bureaus woo new accounts by offering to audit their old freight bills before going on a current basis. Since August, 1958, when a new Federal law went into effect, rebates have been collectible for as long as three years after an error has been made in billing; previously, the limitation was two years.

"We had rebate checks coming in for the next year and a half after Midwest

Freight audited old freight bills in Stineway-Ford Hopkins Drug Co.," relates L. W. Thomason, assistant treasurer of the Chicago-based drug store chain. Now the drug concern has its bills screened by Midwest before paying them, so rebates are not as frequent.

Sometimes a group of shippers of similar products benefit from a rate analyst's single find. Don Taylor, 31 year old president of Taylor-Anderson Co., Minneapolis, relates the tale of foul-smelling substance that wasn't being properly identified by about 20 companies. "They were shipping a packing-house waste which they called cracklings," he says, "but they should have called it dry rendered tankage, which travels at a 25% cheaper rate." The savings amounted to around $90 a carload, or about $54,000 a year for the group of shippers, he estimates.

Rate cuts boost business

The railroads' current drive to slash rates on agricultural products to meet competition from unregulated trucking firms is bringing added business to some auditors.

"Some rates are changing so fast that the railroad clerks can't keep up with them," reports Charles H. Wickman of Chicago's Wickman Traffic Service. One railroad lowered rates on potatoes moving south from Idaho to $400 a carload from $500, but a Wickman client continued to be billed at at the higher rate. "The railroads don't object to our efforts to collect the overcharges because in this way we're helping them keep their rates competitive," comments Mr. Wickman.

However, a check with some railroad officials indicates Mr. Wickman's statement may be a bit too sweeping.

"Don't quote me, but I think the rate sharks are a pain in the neck," says the claims official of a major railroad. "We would eventually discover the errors ourselves anyway and make refunds," he insists. An executive of the Illinois Central Railroad "highly respects" the rate analysts but complains about the "one-man firms that operate out of their vest pocket and even come to our office to use our tariff files to check their bills."

But many rate analysts counter that carriers make plenty of errors in billing, some of them purely mechanical or arithmetical.

Paying a bill twice

"I handled a case just the other day in which a Texas electrical manufacturer paid the same bill twice on a shipment to Philadelphia," reports Daniel E. Nugent, a partner of the New Century Freight Traffic Association in Chicago. A freight-bill payment agency had been slow in sending its check to the truck line, so the line independently billed the shipper. When the agency's bill finally came, it also was paid. Upshot: A $700 refund for the shipper and $700 for New Century.

"Many firms don't even check a bill's arithmetic," says Kenneth Abers, partner in a Kansas City, Mo., traffic counseling firm.

"I found one last year in which a clerk made a $400 overcharge by a mistake in adding freight charges."

Usually, however, it is the complexity of tariffs that makes it possible for rate men to make a comfortable living. For one thing, they contend, many shippers don't grasp the potential of a tariff technicality called "aggregate of intermediate rates." Occasionally, because of a rate adjustment, it becomes cheaper for a shipper to move goods through a number of intermediate points than to ship directly from origin to destination on a so-called through rate. By pointing out such rate irregularities, rate analysts can save shippers sizable sums.

A chemical firm was paying $1.27 a hundred pounds for shipment straight from a Texas factory to an Ohio customer, recalls Mr. Nugent. But by routing the cars first to the inbetween town of Carey, Ohio, and then on to the destination, the firm could save 15 cents on each 100 pounds. In many cases, the cars don't actually have to go to the intermediate point, the but the shipper still is entitled to the lower rate, Mr. Nugent says.

Costly meat error

An Eastern railroad rate official says one routing technically noted by a rate analyst has cost Eastern railroads about $1 million in rebates on overcharge for the shipment of fresh meat from the Midwest to Eastern cities.

Some rate structures are so tricky that carriers sometimes will differ sharply in the type of error they make on identical shipments. Edward M. Fisher, president of Columbus Freight Traffic Service Bureau, Inc., Columbus, Ohio, recalls one instance where refrigerators were moving to his town from Texas. "In one year, about half a dozen different carriers participated over several routes," he says "and they assessed nine different rates on the same item." Four were overcharges and five were undercharges, he says with a chuckle.

The tedious task of checking old freight bills often is used as a come on by traffic firms to get clients for their other services, such as performing routing and rate work on a retainer basis for small firms which don't have their own full-time traffic departments. But for many, it's their bread and butter.

"Auditing is perhaps our biggest source of revenue," says Mr. Nugent of New Century, whose staff of 40 rate experts last year recouped about $1 million from careless carriers.

What do the audit firms do when they find a client received a bill that's too small? "We turn our head," says a Windy City analyst.

34   The Small Shipment Problem

Gilbert L. Gifford

University of Arizona

One of the traffic problems facing business firms today is how to send a small shipment economically and satisfactorily. Because of ever-rising costs, carriers are becoming reluctant to handle the small, expensive-to-handle shipment. In this selection, a noted transportation educator defines and examines the problem, and suggests possible solutions to it.

Just what is the "Small Shipment Problem"? In a few words *High cost, poor service (or none at all)—high loss and damage.* There is a great deal of misunderstanding about the problem and it would seem that a few definitions are in order. What is a "small shipment"?

The motor carriers want to class anything under five thousand pounds as such. There is considerable difference in operational problems in shipments between one thousand pounds and five thousand pounds. When you stop to consider that a single piece as a shipment weighing one thousand pounds requires special handling, to say nothing of five thousand pounds, it is realized that there are different categories. The shipment under one thousand pounds, if broken down into ten one-hundred-pound shipments, can be handled quite easily.

Industry in general tends to consider any less-truckload shipment as a small shipment. The U.S. Post Office, United Parcel Service, and Greyhound have a maximum of fifty pounds, while REA Express will handle any shipment from less than one pound on up.

Let us consider the factors involved in this problem. The value of the shipment as well as the volume in which it moves are both important. The weight-space factor, i.e. the cube or density must be considered. The time element must also be considered a part of the problem since most of the small shipments are considered rush shipments. Pilferage makes loss claims high and damage claims are also important.

My recommendations:

Consolidation of small shipments
Reduction in costs of pick-up and delivery
Reduction in loss and damage
Concerted effort on the part of both shippers and carriers
Government standing by only as referee

There is another aspect of this problem that should be mentioned at this point, the difference between the large shipper who has a large number of small ship-

From the *Transportation Journal*, Fall 1970, quarterly publication of the American Society of Traffic and Transportation, Inc. Used by permission.

ments under one hundred pounds and the small shipper who frequently ships individual shipments of one hundred pounds or less at one time. The large shipper can consolidate his small shipments, making it more economical for the carrier to handle while the small shipper is not able to do this unless he teams up with someone else who has the same problem.

In January 1967, the chairman of the Interstate Commerce Commission (ICC) assigned the "small shipment problem" to a special ad hoc committee for study and recommendation of proposed solutions.[1] Although the service problems involved cut across modal lines, it was determined that the most crucial area related to the motor carrier industry, and the study was accordingly limited to that industry. This committee made no attempt to include the service of REA Express, United Parcel Service or Parcel Post. Attention was directed entirely to the problem of the motor carrier industry and no attempt was made to define a small shipment as such. However, the Interstate Commerce Commission Bureau of Economics, in a study entitled "The Role of Regulated Motor Carriers in the Handling of Small Shipments"[2] defined arbitrarily as less than truckload, shipments weighing less than ten thousand pounds, which moved by regulated motor carrier. It noted that these shipments move relatively short distances, are characterized by a variety of service demands and may include virtually any type of commodity. Shipments weighing less than fifty pounds were designated "small parcels" and are for the most part handled by specialized carriers.[3] It was noted also in this study that the "small shipment problem" related to the entire transportation industry, but it consists in the final analysis of a great many individual problems which arise in connection with the relationship between individual carriers and shippers. It was noted at that time, November 1967, that the data available were so incomplete as to preclude an accurate measurement of the impact of inefficient or unsatisfactory small shipments service in local or regional areas, on the national economy, or on segments of the transportation industry. Changes in small shipments tonnage handled by class I and class II common and contract motor carriers of general freight since 1950 compare *un*favorably with growth of the Gross National Product, indicating that regulated motor carriers have failed to participate fully in the general economic expansion, although all shipments tonnage handled by regulated for hire class I and II motor carriers has remained relatively constant since 1950.[4]

However, 1968 was a good year for the motor carriers since, with the GNP up 9 percent, ICC regulated trucking companies rose 12 percent.[5] Small shipments revenues have risen by more than 175 percent and despite the many deficiencies in data, it appears that Commission regulated general commodity, class I and class II motor carriers transport four times the small shipments tonnage and generate twice the intercity small shipments revenue of all other regulated carriers combined. Although regulated motor carriers enjoy certain competitive advantages, the domination in respect to LTL shipments is due to many factors, not the least of which are the numerous restrictions on the services of competitive carriers, many of which are self-imposed. Moreover, slow growth in the total amount of LTL freight, during a period of unprecedented economic expansion, and the spectacular growth of private carriage, shippers associations, parcel consolidators, and specialized carriers, indicate that for hire motor carriers operate in something less than a monopolistic environment. Truckers who were once extremely anxious to obtain all types of freight have become increasingly selective as to freight they are willing to handle. In increasing numbers they attempt to solicit only those cargos which yield relatively large unit profits, and avoid many types of small shipments which they consider unprofitable. It is evident that by these practices, some motor carriers seek to enjoy the benefits of regulation but to avoid the statutory obligations imposed upon them as common carriers.[6]

Interstate Commerce Commission Chairman Virginia Mae Brown in a speech said, "First, the public has a right to expect service. Second, the public has a right to expect reasonable delivery schedules and the assumption of liability. Finally, the public has a right to expect service from carriers at rates that are not only lawful, but also just and reasonable. These rights of the public are, of course, basic, elementary, and well known to each of us. But they do not need to be frequently recalled to our attention so that we do not lose sight of our first obligations—that of service to the public."[7]

A growing number of motor carriers seeking to avoid shipments they consider to be unprofitable, resort to the curtailment or abandonment of service by embargos, rate increases, insistence upon more expensive packaging, and/or by tariff restrictions. The most serious threat to maintenance of adequate small shipments service appears to be the increasing tendency of interlining carriers to cancel through route-joint rate agreements, and their refusal to participate in new agreements. The Commission is aware of the potential long term consequences of such service curtailments but lacks authority to compel the establishment of through route-joint rate agreements. It has sought to maintain essential small shipment service, first by granting new applications for authority to transport small shipments, and second, when appropriate by compelling authorized carriers to provide adequate LTL service. These approaches have not solved the problem and the Commission has requested statutory authority to establish through routes and joint rates among motor carriers and between motor carriers and carriers of other modes.

While there is a lack of definitive evidence as to the actual effects of the various small shipments rate increases, general economic principles and available data indicate that higher rates alone will not provide a permanent answer to the problems of how to offset rising unit costs of small shipments operations. Besides which, the loss of any sizable volume of traffic tends to stimulate requests for additional rate adjustments, thereby setting into motion a constantly escalating type of rate making.[8]

One of the keys to the solution in the small shipment problem would be more accurate answers to the question of just how much it really costs to handle this particular type of freight. Available cost data are not sufficiently precise to support a determination that a specific rate or rates generally are too low to cover costs. Cost data indicate that motor carrier terminal costs have increased faster than line haul costs. This could be particularly true in the case of small shipments.

While it is difficult to provide any long term forecast in respect to the motor carrier problems in handling small shipments, certain possibilities are evident:

1. As a result of the continued growth of piggy-back, containerization, and shipper associations, motor carriers may eventually handle most of their small shipments in relatively short-haul movements.
2. The increasing highway congestion will to some extent impede trucking service, particularly in the case of short-haul motor carriers operating in urbanized areas.
3. The growth and shift of urban populations will increase the cost of providing small shipment service within the metropolitan area for line-haul intercity carriers while, at the same time, creating additional demands for this service between subcenters of the main urban area.
4. Economy and efficiency of operations over the new interstate highway system will create pressures on regular route for-hire, common carriers to bypass small off-route communities.
5. The increasing number of motor carrier mergers may be an indication that a relatively few large carriers may be able to provide LTL service more economically and efficiently than an excessive number of smaller firms.
6. The evolution of the specialized motor carrier and the continued increase in private and exempt trucking may tend to reduce the future importance of the regulated motor common carriers, even though their services will continue to be an essential part of the total national transportation picture.[9]

There are several alternatives to which a shipper may turn, in trying to solve the small shipment problem, private carriage being one of the favorites. But in addition to this, such alternatives include nonprofit shipping associations, consolidations, use of pool-car services, drop shipping, and operating private and short-haul for-hire combinations. However, such alternatives are not generally available to smaller volume shippers or those shippers located in small isolated communities. The passage of through routes and joint rates legislation is a fundamental element in obtaining a better coordinated national transportation system.[10]

Many years ago the Interstate Commerce Commission for statistical purposes established a minimum weight of ten thousand pounds as a basis for separating carload traffic from less-carload traffic and subsequently utilized the same classification for less-truckload shipments. This is not a particularly satisfactory classification, since modern shipments very often, being lighter, more bulky, could easily fill a forty-foot trailer with a six-thousand-pound weight.

As mentioned before one of the misleading concepts in regard to small shipments is that individuals and small businesses represent the major shippers in this category, while larger corporations do not have this problem. The fact is that larger corporations are the principal users of small shipment services, and while some shippers may fall within several groupings, there appear to be at least three main categories of shippers, regardless of type that are concerned with this problem. *First* are the large volume shippers of single and multi-piece small-lot shipments. Here a definition should be set up. Single parcels are defined as single-piece shipments weighing up to fifty pounds. The multi-piece, small-lot shipments are considered to be primarily those small-lot shipments weighing something less than two thousand pounds, but also could include the larger shipments weighing between two thousand and ten thousand pounds. *Second,* the small volume shippers of single and multi-piece shipments, and *third,* individual shippers, either business or residential, of occasional single-piece shipments or parcels. These are the basic characteristics of shippers of small shipments.

On analysis it is found that the most distinguishing features are related to *weight, type of commodity, value of commodity, distance, cost,* and *type of service demanded.* In general, small parcels are those which weigh approximately fifty pounds or less. These are the type packages handled by the Post Office, United Parcel Service, REA Express, and the bus companies. In fact, a spokesman for REA Express has said that they are going to limit their shipments to those that one man can handle with a hand truck. The larger shipments could be divided into groups of fifty to one hundred, one hundred to two thousand pounds, and two thousand to ten thousand pound classes. It is to be noted here that the handling of shipments in the two major weight groups are extremely dissimilar and highly incompatible from an operational point of view.

In one study it was found that, out of about 4½ percent of the total motor common carrier freight bills in the territory of the Middle Atlantic Conference, 91.4 percent of the total shipments moved were under two thousand pounds. An additional special study was made of minimum charges shipments, distributed in twenty-five pound weight brackets, and the preponderance of these shipments was tendered in actual weights of less than one-hundred twenty-five pounds. Small parcel shipments consist of individual parcels, normally of low intrinsic value and generally of less density per cubic foot than the average freight shipment.

A comparison of the average weight per shipment of different types of intercity regulated carriers showed that the *parcel post average was 5.7 pounds; air parcel post, 2.2; air express, REA, 23.8, United Parcel Service, 11.0; bus express, 26.4; air freight forwarder, 42.0.* These are all in the small parcel carrier group. In the larger small shipment carrier group, average weight per shipment was *class I motor carriers, 591.1; class I railroads, 136.0; REA, 61.1;* and *freight forwarders, 510.0.*[11] A study made in 1964, showed that the small shipment traffic consisted of 12,891,711 shipments, bringing in a revenue of over $214 million, which indicates that this is a very important part of movement of goods in the United States, and there is no doubt that this has increased tremendously in the last five years.

Let us look at the economics involved in the small shipment problem; why so many small shipments? It is not easy to answer this question since there are so many different kinds of movements, different kinds of materials to be moved, as well as different kinds of shippers and receivers of these small shipments. There is the householder who orders from a mail order catalogue, or wants to ship a parcel to his son or daughter at college; there is the small businessman who buys in small quantities. Then there are many larger firms who have multiple outlets. Retailers operating as chains, although buying in large quantity very frequently have these shipments broken down to various destinations. This all means that many of these shipments are one hundred pounds or less, and thus become a problem to the carriers.

With the advent of the motor truck, our distribution system has changed, and many buyers buy on a hand-to-mouth basis, which means small shipments; in effect a storage system to assist in reducing stock. It is now possible to containerize and put shipments on pallets. There are consolidators available for this, there are shippers cooperatives, but still many of these shipments move individually and form the basis for the most serious part of this problem.

On the supply side it is evident that these small shipments are expensive to handle. It means hand labor, and labor is expensive. It means a greater possibility of loss and damage; pilferage is much greater with small shipments than it is with larger shipments since the opportunities are much more numerous. Pick-up and delivery in cities is getting more and more expensive, not only from a labor standpoint but from the standpoint of delays in traffic and cost of operating around the terminal. The actual cost of handling a small shipment is often greater than the value of the contents itself. Pick-up and delivery requires specialized facilities for handling and motor carriers in many instances are finding that they cannot cope with the high cost of pick-up and delivery. It has been suggested that they might consolidate or pool their services, but they are wary of doing this since they have been taught *not* to cooperate with those who are supposed to be their competitors.

The air carriers are not too concerned with this because someone else does the pick-up and delivery for them. The United Parcel Service is operating in some areas and handling the pick-up and delivery on a specialized basis and is one of the possibilities for solving this problem. The United States Post Office makes deliveries only and does not provide pick-up service, which means that the customer (the shipper) must provide pick-up service, and of course the intercity bus companies dodge the pick-up and delivery problem entirely by requiring that the shipper provide the pick-up service and the consignee provide the delivery service. Of all the carriers providing service in the small parcel category, the REA is best equipped to handle pick-up and delivery of small shipments, since it is the only organization that has rights to provide pick-up and delivery service in all fifty states.

Most of the August 1969 issue of *Traffic Management Magazine* was devoted to the small shipment problem, one part being a report on a special survey on this subject. *Traffic Management* in this survey, made of a representative cross section of transportation executives, solicited their opinions concerning certain questions asked on the subject of small shipments. A summary of the most important points will be helpful here.[12]

It was discovered that shippers have a tendency to avoid radical solutions, rather expecting the Interstate Commerce Commission to bear down with the weapons it already has to combat motor carrier service failures. In regard to new legislation, the majority felt that the joint-rate through-route amendments to the law would be the best means of solving part of the problem although the Interstate Commerce Commission and various shippers organizations have been trying for years to push this through Congress, and it is possible that the extra pressure being exerted at this time might bring this about this year.

Many of those responding to the questionnaire seem to be looking to various self-help projects such as cooperative distribution centers, and other joint shipper activities as the best and most controllable solution. That is, it appears that they are hoping to solve the problem by minimizing the number of small shipments tendered to the carriers. Of course, this is one of the best solutions of the problem if it is available to the individual shipper. Many shippers seem to believe that increased competition would help solve the problem by expanding authorities of small shipment specialists, such as REA, United Parcel and even Parcel Post. No mention was made of of what might be expected from a change in the national postal system; that is the setting up of a government corporation to handle the U.S. mail and Parcel Post. Even with this change, there may be limited improvements.

Curiously, a minority which is described as being quite vocal, including some of the biggest industrial shippers, is convinced that deregulating under five hundred pound shipments would go a long way towards solving the problem, while the majority feels that the idea has no merit at all. But *Traffic Management* found that shippers tend to be free from cynicism about carriers' intent, finding the ultimate solution, whatever it may be, as impossible of attainment without cooperation. Wide-scale coordination of pick-ups and deliveries is repeatedly mentioned as the ideal place for truckers and their customers to get together.

In the *Traffic Management* survey regarding the subject of deregulation of small shipment movements, "The consensus shaped up this way. Ninety respondents believed that deregulation would leave shippers in a kind of no-man's land with no recourse to regulatory agencies; seventy-nine felt it would produce generally uneven, unreliable service; seventy-four thought it would result in less availability of motor service; forty-seven saw it putting shippers in competition with each other for delivery service; thirty saw the rate seeking a level the traffic would bear; twenty-seven saw it encouraging competition to open-end motor carrier service; and only twenty thought it would improve service."[13] There is considerable controversy at the present time on both the national level and the state level concerning the subject of deregulation, and this applies to more than just the small shipment problem. It is true that the regulation of transportation has become so complicated that the whole fabric of laws needs to be overhauled and simplified, and it is quite likely that there will be some deregulation present in the overhaul that should take place before too long.

As can be expected, many of the respondents to the *Traffic Management* small shipment survey came up with variations of the same solution to the problem, and that is consolidation. Just raising rates won't solve the problem, several of them said. It was suggested that an LTL shipper should limit his shipments to one or two carriers and not use a larger number. It was suggested that more payload and higher revenues for trucking firms is the answer rather than raising the rates. Changing of certain regulations to permit larger sized equipment, wider use of doubles and so forth, to advance economical handling of shipments by motor carriers was also proposed. Another suggestion was that motor carriers should have air freight forwarding certificates, putting them in the position of being inter-modal consolidators; of course, this is a present trend that the Interstate Commerce Commission is following as it has already granted several of the long-haul motor carriers permits to operate this type of service.[14] Pooling shipper resources is one of the common suggestions which would be either in pool shipments or the organization of shippers cooperatives or at least the use of consolidators to help solve the high cost problem of pick-up and delivery. The use of distribution warehouses to collect or distribute small shipments in an area providing only large shipments for the line haul carriers between major points was one of the suggestions. Turning a mass of small shipments into a consolidated, scheduled enterprise would help solve the problem which could bring freight savings of 15 to 20 percent to the shippers through cutting of carrier's costs. "Judging from the survey the biggest point of shipper frustration over small shipments is this: continual freight rate increases without significant broad scale attempts by carriers to innovate elsewhere."[15] Carriers are accused of not conscientiously trying to cut handling costs or use ingenuity in developing modern techniques to increase efficiency and develop containerization and use of automated facilities. Some traffic managers thought that a rate structure should be devised that would disregard classification on shipments up to five hundred pounds by using flat charges, but increases should be more moderate than those proposed in the past which were beyond the level of reasonableness.

As an indication of the problems of a large shipper and receiver, the experience of S. S. Kresge Company provides an interesting insight. From an interview with H. E. Chapman, Kresge General Traffic Manager, it is reported that since his company is experiencing rapid growth, sales and profits have quadrupled in the past decade. Kresge is now operating about one thousand Kresge, K-Mart and Jupiter stores, and is opening K-Mart Discount Department stores at an average rate of more than one a week this year. It is expected that sales will comfortably exceed $2 billion in the year ending January 31, 1970, and will top $3 billion by 1972. One might think that this is all large shipments, but Kresge has six thousand vendors, five hundred shipping points, and over thirty thousand shipments moving daily to its stores. Of this merchandise, 85 percent goes directly from supplier to store without passing through its distribution centers, and most of this traffic falls into the small shipment category. "Probably 75 percent of our shipments are five hundred pounds or less," Mr. Chapman explained.[16] Following the practice of other big retail chains, Kresge has responded to the small shipment challenge by developing multiple consolidations to minimize transportation costs. Kresge moved two hundred million pounds of freight in consolidations in 1968; as a result, the company was able to hold its freight costs relatively stable, despite carriers' rate increases. Freight cost, as a percentage of the cost price of merchandise was 2.77 percent in 1968, as against 2.76 percent in 1967. Benefits from consolidation are: (1) it gets the goods delivered on schedule, whereas individual small shipments often are delayed in transit; (2) claims are reduced because of less handling; and, (3) better control of shipments.[17]

Another industry that is plagued with small shipment problems due to changing consumer tastes and a wide variety of stock is the phonograph record industry. CBS Records, Division of Columbia Broadcasting System, has solved its problem by combining an existing private truck service with a specialized common carrier and, in 1968, realized savings in excess of $265,000. This method of solving the small shipment problem is a good example of physical distribution at its very best, since it is an indication of knowledge of the needs of shippers and receivers, and the use of various kinds of transportation as well as specialized warehousing to solve the problem and not only get good service, but do it at a considerable saving.[18]

Another example of savings by use of all modern techniques of movement of goods is the Raytheon Company's new assembly by air called RAYAIR. It is said to resemble "an internal forwarder operation building weight for economy." This new Raytheon set-up is designed as a three phase operation. *First,* to funnel individual air freight, air express, air forwarder and some air parcel post shipments to and from more than sixty cities into one channel of distribution. *Second,* to bring into the program varied minimum shipments, moving by surface modes, such as REA express, truck and forwarder, and *finally,* to set up four to six key points in the United States from which the shipments could be distributed within a two hundred-three hundred mile area. "Over all cost savings resulting from the RAYAIR program were $152,500 in 1967 up to $199,400 in 1968, and during 1969 we expect the savings to increase again up to $233,400."[19]

Among other advantages are better control of freight, with more effective tracing and record keeping, improved billing controls, easier instructions for sales and purchasing personnel, and quicker response to emergency shipments.[20] This is another good example of what physical distribution can do to put together various forms of transportation, and storage, and make a savings in dollars and cents as well as considerable improvement in service.

These last examples are from large shippers who are able to gain these savings through remodeling their own transportation movements. Unfortunately such are not easily available to the small shipper or even the medium sized shipper, who has a great many LTL size shipments.

Probably the best solution to the problem is to organize a shipper's cooperative. This is particularly advantageous to retailers in a city or in an area such as Arizona where the Arizona Shipper's Association is now beginning to function, similar to organizations in other states. The receivers notify their shippers to deliver the freight to a certain consolidator, say in New York or in Chicago. This consolidator loads these many small shipments into freight cars or trailers which are then dispatched across the country as a single shipment, either piggy-back in the case of trailers or as a regular rail carload shipment. These shipments are received by the representative of the cooperative who has made arrangements with a local drayage firm to break bulk and do the distributing. Major savings are possible with this kind of movement for the simple reason that small shipments, anywhere from one hundred pounds on up can have the advantage of a carload rate, or at least a truck load of piggy-back rate which is considerably less than the small parcel rate or the LTL or LCL rate. The carriers prefer this because the truck load or carload shipment is one upon which they can make a return with a minimum of effort on their part, there is less loss and damage and thus fewer claims, and everybody is happy because the service is better and less expensive.

Now that REA is separated from the railroads and on its own, it is the writer's opinion that this organization should be given every support by the shipping public involved in small shipment. As mentioned before, it is the only carrier that is, at present, able to give pick-up and delivery service throughout the nation, all fifty states and including most small communities. If REA is able to utilize line haul motor carriers and rail as well as air, and if it will follow the practice of limiting itself to pick-up and delivery and emphasizing the real small shipments, it can satisfy a real need in the United States. It's true that REA has a serious problem of living down its past history, and many shippers will have to learn that REA is now a different firm and is, we hope, willing and able to give good service at a reasonable rate. It seems to have been a mistake to have refused Greyhound the right to buy out REA, since the combination of Greyhound and REA could have provided United States shippers with a real service that has been sorely need in recent years and has not been available to the shipping public.[21]

It is probably too late to think of reversing another trend but it seems that the railroads have missed a very good opportunity by almost completely phasing out the mail service. It is realized that the Post Office Department led the way in deserting the railroads, but it seems that the railroads could have very profitably gone to high speed multiple service trains that combine passenger service, express service, and rapid mail service on the railroads of the United States. They could use the same type of service that the Santa Fe offers with its "Super C" trains, using piggy-back cars, combined with mail cars, and passenger coaches and could have made a profitable operation. Many railroad people will not agree with this, but this has not been explored to any extent and it would have been a solution, in part, to the small shipment problem, because it would have handled parcel post as well as express and would have given the public a type of service that is not now available.

If REA is permitted to expand its service, provide good, speedy, dependable pick-up and delivery, along with the line haul service provided by truck, by rail, by air, depending upon the service required and the time limits, the solution of the small shipment problem could very well be found in this manner. If REA would concentrate its rates on its pick-up and delivery costs, linked with a fairly low, line haul cost, it should be able to give a service that is within the reach of all users. Ralph Nogg, Executive Vice President Operations REA said, "We are willing to be the cartage company on these small shipments all over the country for the trucking industry."[22]

When the United States Post Office Department is reorganized and put on a self-sustaining basis, it is possible that this will provide good competition for REA. If this does not develop, perhaps another organization such as United Parcel Service or American Delivery Systems should be expanded to provide such competition in the small parcel field.

It is noteworthy that Consolidated Freightways has started a small parcel service only between such major centers as Chicago, New York and the West Coast. This was set up as a separate subsidiary company to do the consolidating and then purchase the line haul service from its parent company. This is a step in the right direction and with its exceptionally wide geographic coverage of the United States perhaps this might be one solution to the problem.

Shippers of small shipments under one hundred pounds should review their own buying practices and see if it is not possible to order in larger quantities and to ship in larger quantities. At least they should try to cooperate with other shippers and receivers between the same points in an attempt to provide larger shipments for the carriers.

It is realized that small shipments are expensive to handle. If there is no way to cut the costs of handling small shipments, one might question whether these shipments should move at all. Many times some of the costs are hidden by providing private transportation such as in pick-up and/or delivery service. If the charging of rates for small shipments that would cover the costs would force some marginal shippers or receivers out of business, the question is whether they should be in this business. This is the function of a free market economy, i.e., to guide allocation of resources so perhaps this is one place where this should be allowed to work. Should a common carrier be required to perform unprofitable service in order to fulfill his common law duty as a common carrier? Is this not taxing other shippers to subsidize those who ship at the unprofitable rate? This can only lead to a further deterioration of the common carrier portion of our transport system and an increase in private carriage to the detriment of all concerned.

In summary, I recommend *first,* separation of "parcel" service and "small shipments" service. It is my feeling that this should be made a clear-cut legal separation on some weight basis such as fifty pounds or any other that may seem most feasible.

Second, consolidation of small shipments wherever possible.

Third, reduction of cost of pick-up and delivery.

Fourth, reduction in loss and damage.

Fifth, savings in handling and movement should be the goals of all concerned with small shipments—both shippers and carriers alike.

Sixth, the government should be standing by only as a referee to make sure that there is no discrimination, that services are performed promptly and at a reasonable price.

As it stands today there is considerable waste in the movement of small shipments as well as frustrations and disappointments due to high rates, poor service, and the difficulties of handling these shipments.

NOTES

1. *Small Shipments Problem,* Report of the Ad Hoc Committee of the Interstate Commerce Commission, November 30, 1967, pg. 1, U.S. Gov't. Printing Office.
2. Interstate Commerce Commission, Bureau of Economics, Statement No. 67-2, November, 1967, U.S. Gov't. Printing Office.
3. *Ibid.,* pg. 1.
4. *Ibid.*
5. John T. McCullough, "Service is the Name of the Game," *Distribution Manager,* Vol. 68, No. 4 (Philadelphia, Pennsylvania, April, 1969), pg. 22.
6. ICC Bureau of Economics, *op. cit.,* pg. 1, 2.
7. *Distribution Manager, op. cit.*
8. ICC Bureau of Economics, *op. cit.,* pg. 2.
9. *Ibid.,* pp. 2, 3.
10. *Ibid.,* pg. 3.
11. *Ibid.,* pg. 8.
12. Joseph S. Coyle, "Small Shipments and You," *Traffic Management,* Vol. 8, No. 8 (Chicago, Illinois, August, 1969), pp. 42-45.
13. *Ibid.,* pg. 43.
14. Pacific Intermountain Express Air Freight Forwarding, Inc. began operations October 29, 1969 between Oakland-San Francisco, Los Angeles, Chicago, Newark and New York.
15. *Traffic Management, op. cit.,* pg. 45.
16. *Ibid.,* as quoted on p. 49.
17. *Ibid.,* pp. 49, 50, and 52.
18. *Ibid.,* pp. 57, 58, 59, and 62.
19. *Ibid.,* pp. 67, 68, and 70.
20. *Ibid.,* p. 70.
21. *Traffic Management,* October, 1969, pg. 19 reports a new small shipments service, American Delivery Systems Inc., of Detroit as making a strong bid for this business. Their idea is to obtain forwarder rights throughout the U.S. to ship parcels up to one hundred pounds and shipments via other common carriers up to five hundred pounds. This system involves the use of special materials handling techniques in their terminals.
22. As quoted in *Distribution Manager,* July, 1969, pg. 49.

---

35   **Freight Fracas**
                            Donald Moffitt

Another answer to the small shipments problem is the shipper cooperative. In recent years a number of shippers have joined together in associations to consolidate their freight movements and to secure lower rates for larger movements. Railroads, for years, have offered "pool car" service. And other carriers have worked to promote this type of traffic.

The shipper cooperative illustrates various arrangements aimed at lowering

From Donald Moffitt, "Freight Fracas," *The Wall Street Journal,* April 16, 1964. Used by permission.

transportation costs. Some of these arrangements are legal; others are not—a fact which gives us a glimpse into the complexity of transportation law.

SAN FRANCISCO—An increasingly popular shipping method that allows companies to cut transportation costs is raising the ire of many truck lines and freight forwarding concerns.

Under attack are shipper cooperatives—nonprofit groups which pool members' shipments so they can be moved at volume rates rather than at the higher tariffs assessed on small loads. The groups, which often slice 20% or more from freight bills, are being formed at a fast-growing rate under a Federal law aimed at helping small businessmen compete with big-volume shippers. The Interstate Commerce Commission says there now are about 300 such shipper co-op groups, more than triple the 85 in existence as recently as 1957.

This growth hasn't gone unnoticed by the transportation industry—particularly the longhaul truck lines and freight forwarders; forwarders are firms which consolidate small shipments into carload lots, profiting from the service. Because operations of the shipper groups are especially suited to piggybacking—the hauling of trailers on flatcars—the railroads have been beneficiaries of the co-op trend while the truckers and forwarders have suffered. Their traffic loss has become so substantial, in fact, that the truckers and forwarders have launched a major effort to contain co-op activities. They charge, among other things, that many of the co-ops are either operating illegally or are at least violating the spirit of the law.

A spreading controversy

As a measure of their mood, the truckers and forwarders have had a number of the co-op associations brought into ICC hearing rooms to answer complaints of law violations. And they've gone so far as to hire undercover sleuths to investigate their customers' ties with some associations. Such efforts have fired a controversy which has carried to the halls of Congress.

Like freight forwarders, shipper associations consolidate small shipments from a number of firms to obtain less costly carload rates. The associations, however, offer an incentive the forwarders can't match. Instead of pocketing a portion of the rate savings as a profit, the shipper groups distribute the savings among their members. The truckers and forwarders, of course, aren't entirely at a disadvantage because they usually offer more frequent and faster service than do the associations. Association members, in fact, say they still hand over much of their freight to the truckers and forwarders.

Nonetheless, when shippers are mainly interested in cutting costs, truckers and forwarders find it tough to compete. They have to quote published rates, which can't be changed at will because of tight control by the ICC. Bona fide shipper groups, on the other hand, are excluded from all Government regulation.

Truckers and forwarders insist they have no quarrel with legitimate shipper associations, but they're convinced many are merely freight forwarders disguised as non-profit associations to evade regulation. "There are some good, honest associations," says a San Francisco forwarder. "The people we're after are shady promoters who set up an association, solicit our customers and go about their merry way raking in the cash until somebody blows the whistle."

35 complaints filed

Since the truckers and freight forwarders started their legal drive against the shipper associations in 1961, they've filed 35 complaints with the ICC against individual groups. Fourteen cases have so far been argued before ICC examiners, and reports on seven have been issued. Six of the reports recommended "cease-and-desist" orders against individual associations for allegedly engaging in the freight forwarding business without authority of the ICC. Nine more associations closed voluntarily after complaints against them were filed, according to the Committee on Transportation Practices, a trade group formed by the truckers and forwarders to handle their case.

Still, hardly anybody argues this drive has made more than a small dent in the activities of shipper associations—many of which are unquestionably legal, reputable groups. "The publicity actually has alerted even more shippers to the advantages of cooperative efforts," says J. William Harrell, president of the American Institute for Shippers Associations, Inc. a three-year-old trade organization.

In some cases, associations restrict themselves to consolidating small shipments for businessmen in the same field. Shippers Cooperative, Inc., Los Angeles, a typical association of this nature, serves a group of Georgia textile makers and their Los Angeles distributors, making up carload carpet lots to reduce costs of small shipments by an average of 20%.

But others get big

But other associations have placed no such limitations on themselves. Some of the largest have hundreds of members and do millions of dollars of business yearly. Associated Shippers, Inc., a St. Louis-based association, provides 186 members service to and from such far-distant points as Boston, Detroit, New Orleans and Los Angeles. Last year Associated's revenues rose to $2.5 million, up from $25,000 in 1958, its first full year of operation. Patrick M. Browne, manager, says Associated leases as many as 40 trailers a day to meet its needs.

Though the associations were originally designed to help small shippers get carload and truckload rate breaks, some of the country's largest companies have joined the groups—a point the truckers and forwarders are quick to note. International Trailer-on-Flatcar Associates, Inc. (ITOFCA), a Chicago-based association, started with only eight corporate members late in 1959 and now counts 82, including such companies as Minnesota Mining & Manufacturing Co., Union Carbide Corp., Du Pont Co., Swift & Co., Inland Steel Co., and Time, Inc. The association handles some 20,000 trailer loads of freight annually.

ICC rules on piggyback rates have helped promote the growth of the shipper groups. For instance, in one widely used form of piggybacking, shippers or their associations can lease trailers and then pay railroads a flat rate for hauling the loaded trailers atop flatcars, usually at a low cost of 50 cents a mile. But to restrain shippers from completely abandoning more costly truck and boxcar service, this plan limits to a single commodity 60% of the total load in two trailers atop a flatcar. So ordinarily, even with his own trailer a shipper of a single commodity wouldn't be able to qualify for the low rate.

But an association enables such a shipper to obtain the lowest cost anyway. ITOFCA, for example, "marries" one trailer load of polyethylene from Union Carbide's plant at Whiting, Ind., with another of steel from a nearby Inland Steel Co. subsidiary for hauling on a single flatcar from the Chicago area. Since neither load exceeds 60% of the total, each qualifies for the low hauling charge.

These arrangements help members reduce freight bills substantially. George C. Hillenbrand, assistant traffic manager for Time, says ITOFCA enables his company to send a trailer load of magazine sections printed in Chicago to a processing plant at Old Saybrook, Conn., for only $1.05 a hundred pounds, about 20% below the $1.32 rate quoted by truckers and freight forwarders. Union Carbide says savings on its polyethylene shipments can run as high as 50 cents a hundred pounds, or $175 a full trailer load.

To escape ICC regulation as commercial freight forwarders or truckers, shipper associations are supposed to adhere to a rigid set of rules. They aren't allowed to solicit members, offer any kind of service for compensation, or operate trucks that actually do hauling, though they can own or lease trailers and rail flatcars. "But it's easy to deviate from some of the rules," says Mr. Hillenbrand, president of ITOFCA, "and some associations—not ours—do."

Freight forwarders charge that some associations have been profit-making competitors in disguise. A case in point is that of Continental Shippers Association, Inc., once one of the country's largest. Continental this year went bankrupt, leaving a stack of bills totaling more than $400,000.

A group of Philadelphia manufacturers formed Continental late in 1959 to take advantage of low-cost piggyback service to the West Coast. Evidence developed by ICC investigators showed that an officer of Shulman, Inc., a regulated freight forwarder, helped him start the "non-profit" association. By 1961 Continental—managed by a Shulman subsidiary under a contract—had under lease 25 rail flatcars and 90 trailers for carrying 100 million pounds of freight a year for 582 "members" all over the country. Its rates were 10% to 15% below those quoted by regulated freight forwarders and truckers.

To all appearances, Continental was indeed a non-profit outfit. In 1960, for example, with revenues of $1.4 million, it ran in the red to the amount of $33,000. But according to testimony given the ICC, Continental's piggyback equipment was being leased from a Shulman subsidiary, Ardmore Leasing Corp., at a rate of $18 a day for each flatcar and $10 a day for each trailer. Yet, an ICC examiner says, Ardmore was obtaining the flatcars from another leasing company for only $8 a day and the trailers for only $5 a day. Thus, he calculates,

Ardmore siphoned off as much as $700 a day from the association in "excessive charges." The examiner ruled Continental was in violation of the law.

A team of investigators for the truckers and forwarders now is busy trying to obtain evidence that other shipper associations are breaking the law. In Los Angeles, for example, a tough-talking ex-trucker currently is posing as a traffic consultant and contacting shippers in the area to try and determine how and why they joined associations. He's hoping to come up with enough evidence to convince the ICC that some groups are illegally soliciting members.

Though buffeted by opposition, shipper associations early this year won an important legal skirmish. In a case involving Atlanta Shippers Association, Inc., an ICC division panel had ruled an association could not incorporate and still be considered a cooperative group excluded from ICC freight-forwarder regulation. But the full commission reversed this ruling in a 4—3 vote in January.

Too, shipper associations have so far been cheered by the fate of attempts to require them to secure "certificates of exemption" from the ICC before setting up shop. Twice in recent years bills have been introduced in Congress to establish such a requirement. But the bills didn't pass. As it stands now, shippers can freely organize an association for pooling their freight, and it's up to the ICC or transportation industry groups to prove any are operating illegally.

---

36 A Systematic Approach to a Perplexing Shipping Problem

Robert E. Swindle
Arizona State University

When possible, the modern science of physical distribution makes use of mathematical problem-solving techniques. This author reviews briefly some of the applications of linear programming to transportation and distribution problems. He cites their limitations and gives an example of a nonlinear problem. All in all, he provides traffic managers with a method by which they can determine the optimum way of combining shipments and so build the volume necessary to secure the lowest freight charges.

Since the headings in this article immediately reveal a discussion of popular mathematical models in operations research, it may be wise to advise the reader that he *is not* being presented with an extensive reiteration of materials which he may have encountered previously. The purpose of this article, instead, is to survey briefly the available decision tools in operations research and to demon-

From the *Transportation Journal*, Summer 1971, quarterly publication of the American Society of Traffic and Transportation, Inc. Used by permission.

strate their inapplicability to a very real problem in the physical distribution process.

Tools of operations research

Several linear programs have become standardized tools for decision making, with detailed procedures appearing in a proliferation of text books for the rapidly growing discipline of operations research.[1] Among these programs are:

Waiting-time or Queuing Models, which balance the costs of providing specific levels of service against alternative costs of not providing the service. An example would be the determination of the optimum number of cashiers at a supermarket, wherein the cost of additional cashiers would be compared with lost sales which might result with fewer cashiers and longer waiting lines.

Inventory Models enable management to establish optimal reordering quantities and periods. These models employ probability theory, with respect to sales levels, and incorporate a trade-off between the cost of carrying excess inventory and the cost of lost sales resulting from depleted stocks.

Allocation Models are applicable when two or more processes or outlets are competing for an insufficient amount of resources. The scarce resources, in this instance, may range from the unavailability of sufficient manpower to limited machine time, to imbalanced inventories of raw materials or finished goods.

Replacement Models generally are utilized in connection with items which have a fairly constant useful life. In managing huge signs with many light bulbs, for example, replacement models make it possible to minimize costs through determination of the optimal time for replacing all the bulbs, rather than enduring the expense of replacing them individually as they fail.

Transportation and Assignment Models are used in connection with the transfer of single commodities from various origins to various destinations. With transportation models, the number of origins may vary from the number of destinations, and inequalities may exist with respect to the amount of a product to be produced or shipped and the quantities required. In contrast, use of assignment models dictates that the number of origins and destinations be equal, i.e., that there be a one-to-one relationship.[2]

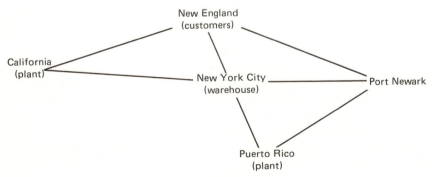

Figure 1. A hypothetical problem in physical distribution.

Other OR Models are placed in various categories, such as sequencing, routing, competitive, and search models, although the distinction between some of these categories often is obscure. Simulation is a widely used tool in decision-making also, particularly where a problem is too complex to fit a mathematical model.

Historical data or randomly generated events are utilized to replicate (simulate) a real process or system. A compression of time is effected also, with the use of electronic digital computers, enabling numerous experimental runs and observations of a system or process, until the relationships of the relevant variables are identified, interpreted, and (hopefully) improved.[3]

Limitations of OR models

The major deficiency of linear programming models is that, as the name denotes, they require that the variables under consideration have a significant degree of linearity, i.e., that the dependent variables change in predictable patterns in response to changes in independent variables. In a real-life process or system, of course, this convenient relationship often does not exist.

Linear programs are applicable to many physical distribution problems, as indicated previously, and numerous case histories substantiate their utility. When a model does fit a particular problem, however, its usefulness often is restricted, in that limiting factors or managerial policy may dictate the course of action to be taken. To illustrate, consider the hypothetical situation in Figure 1.

One objective function of the company represented in Figure 1 is to minimize the cost of packing and distributing canned tuna to customers in the New England area. No model is required to solve the initial decision; all shipments possible would be effected from Puerto Rico, where the cost of labor is considerably lower than that paid at the California plant.

Whether to ship Puerto Rican product to New England from stocks stored in the New York City warehouse or directly from Puerto Rico also is evident, in that competitive service to New England would prohibit the extra week required to accomplish the combination water-surface shipment from Puerto Rico (steamship service is not available from Puerto Rico to Boston).

Industry patterns also dictate the mode of transportation to be used. Only in an extreme situation, such as a national railroad strike, would truck service be utilized from the West Coast, since the rates are considered prohibitively high. For shorter distances, as from New York City to points in New England, rail rates are not sufficiently lower than truck rates to justify the additional intransit time required via rail. To vary from these industry patterns would be to give competition an advantage, with respect to either time or expense incurred.

Statement of the problem

A relevant and recurring problem in physical distribution, and one for which no solution model exists, is that of combining customer orders in an optimal manner for the minimization of freight costs. The following schedule of rates will help to state the problem more clearly.

If customer orders totaled 6,000 pounds for Hartford and 16,000 pounds for Portland, it might be tempting to ship them separately, since the Hartford weight would appear to match exactly the minimum-weight requirement for that point. To do so, however, would result in the following freight charges:

$$\text{Hartford } 6,000 \text{ lbs. @ } .95 = \$ 57.00$$
$$\text{Portland } 16,000 \text{ lbs.}$$
$$\text{as}$$
$$20,000 \text{ lbs. @ } 1.12 = 224.00 \; \$281.00$$

By combining tonnage for the two points, a cost reduction of $19.60 could be realized:

$$22,000 \text{ lbs. @ } 1.12 = \$246.40$$
$$\text{stop charge} \qquad 15.00 \; \$261.40$$

Lower freight costs can be effected in this manner due to what is termed the weight-break-point. Between each set of minimum weights in Table I is a weight-break-point (k). To determine k between 6,000 and 20,000 pounds to Portland, for example, would require the following computation:

$$1.58k = 1.12(20,000), k = 14,177 \text{ lbs.}$$

If orders for Portland equal or exceed k—14,177 pounds in this instance—it becomes more economical to effect shipment at the next higher minimum weight, or 20,000 lbs at 1.12 per cwt.

In the first example, therefore, where the two points were shipped separately, the shipper would have been paying for 4,000 pounds (20,000—16,000) of what has been termed "phantom" tonnage, or air. This is the reason that inclusion of the 6,000 pounds for Hartford with the Portland shipment, albeit at a higher rate, would result in lower total freight costs.

Notice too that a stop charge of $15 was assessed in the second example, where merchandise for the two points was combined into a single shipment. This is a fixed charge which is applicable when a shipment is stopped intransit for partial unloading (or loading) at locations which are intermediate to the final destination. The formula for assessing stop charges, therefore, could be stated as: the number of points (locations) for which merchandise is included in a single shipment, less one, times the stop charge.

TABLE I

Motor Carrier Rates per cwt. from New York City

Pounds	Hartford	Providence	Boston	Portland
6,000	.95	1.10	1.19	1.58
20,000	.59	.71	.81	1.12
32,000	.42	.58	.57	.87
36,000	.40	.55	.55	.78

Stop Charge is $15.00

With this information, the previously stated rate schedules (Table I) may be modified as shown in Table II.

With r being the applicable rate per cwt. and k being the weight-break-point, and s standing for stop-in-transit assume the accumulation of customer orders in the following array, for shipment from New York City:

Hartford	6,000 lbs.
Providence	12,000 lbs.
Boston	12,000 lbs.
Portland	18,000 lbs.

The problem still may appear fundamental to the decision maker, and this is why the difficulty is experienced. Such transportation decisions are left to line employees within the respective distribution departments, and the complexity of the problem is not always comprehended. For when several points are considered simultaneously, the number of possible combinations are numerous.

Specifically, the number of combinations (C) are $C = 2^n - 1$, with n being the number of points involved in the particular decision. Considering only Hartford and Portland, as was done previously, the number of possible combinations are just three (i.e., $C = 2^2 - 1$, When three, four, or five points are considered at one time, however, the number of possible combinations increases to seven, fifteen, and thirty-one, respectively; and accurate insight from a visual inspection of the rate schedules becomes impossible.

Systematic approach to the problem

With the last four letters of the alphabet representing the locations being considered, as specified in Table II, the following formulas may be developed as guidelines for rate determination of the fifteen possible combinations:

1. $(w)wr+(x+y+z)zr+2s$
2. $(w+x)xr+s+(y+z)zr+s$
3. $(w+y)yr+s+(x+z)zr+s$
4. $(w+z)zr+s+(x+y)yr+s$

TABLE II

Motor Carrier Rates per cwt. from New York City

Minimum Weight	Hartford (w)		Providence (x)		Boston (y)		Portland (z)	
	r	k	r	k	r	k	r	k
6,000	.95	12,425	1.10	12,909	1.19	13,613	1.58	14,177
20,000	.59	22,781	.71	26,132	.81	22,526	1.12	24,858
32,000	.42	34,285	.58	34,135	.57	34,729	.87	32,264
36,000	.40		.55		.55		.78	

Add stop charge(s) of $15.00 for total number of points combined in a single shipment, less one.

5. (w+x+y)yr+2s+(z)zr
6. (w+y+z)zr+2s+(x)xr
7. (w+x+z)zr+2s+(y)yr
8. (w+x+y+z)zr+3s
9. (w)wr+(x)xr+(y)yr+(z)zr
10. (w)wr+(x)xr+(y+z)zr+s
11. (w)wr+(y)yr+(x+z)zr+s
12. (w)wr+(z)zr+(x+y)yr+s
13. (x)xr+(y)yr+(w+z)zr+s
14. (x)xr+(z)zr+(w+y)yr+s
15. (y)yr+(z)zr+(w+x)xr+s

With the data in Table II, the above formulas and a calculator, the following information may be computed:

1. (6000).95+(42000).78+(15)2=414.60
2. (18000).71+15+(30000).87+15=418.80
3. (18000 as 20000).81+15+(30000 as 32000).87+15=470.40
4. (24000)1.12+15+(24000 as 32000).57+15=481.20
5. (30000 as (32000).57+(15)2+(18000 as 20000)1.12=436.40
6. (36000).78+(15)2+(12000)1.10=442.80
7. (36000).78+(15)2+(12000)1.19=453.60
8. (48000).78+(15)3=419.40
9. (6000).95+(12000)1.10+(12000)1.19+(18000 as 20000)1.12=555.80
10. (6000).95+(12000)1.10+(30000) as 32000).87+15=482.40
11. (6000).95+(12000)1.19+(30000 as 32000).87+15=493.20
12. (6000).95+(18000 as 20000)1.12+(24000 as 32000).57+15 =478.40
13. (12000).95+(12000)1.19+(24000)1.12+15=540.60
14. (12000).95+(18000 as 20000)1.12+(18000 as 20000).81+15 =515.00
15. (12000)1.19+(18000 as 20000)1.12+(18000 as 20000).71+15 =523.80

The optimal arrangement is revealed immediately as being No. 1, where the Providence, Boston, and Portland tonnage is combined, with that for Hartford being shipped separately. Although two other combinations, No. 2 and No. 8, result in only slightly higher freight charges, the range for all combinations is from a low of $414.60 to a high of $555.80. This represents a difference of $141.20, which emphasizes the importance of determining the optimal combination of shipments.

Compared with programs which may be computerized, the above procedure may be considered laborious—but consider the alternatives. First, a computer program could be written for this type problem. However, this still would involve the punching of data cards each time, valuable computer time would be utilized, and the decision lag often would be too great to be useful. Also, periodic changes in rates by the trucking companies would require that the program be rewritten.

The second and only other apparent alternative is to leave the selection to the discretion of the decision maker. As has already been demonstrated, however, such an approach can be costly. Line personnel charged with making the determination may be incapable of or disinterested in the minimization of costs. Moreover, the distribution manager may not be in a position to ascertain that optimal solutions are being derived for such problems.

The schema proposed here is not considered to be a final solution to the stated problem, far from it. Until a more sophisticated program is developed, however, it is offered as a systematic procedure for the minimization of freight costs, in replacement for the decision-making void which presently exists.

NOTES

1. Recommended as relatively nontechnical books in this area are the following: Enrick, Norbert Lloyd, *Management Operations Research* (New York: Holt, Rinehart and Winston, 1965); Moore, P. G., *Basic Operational Research* (London: Sir Isaac Pitman & Sons Ltd., 1968); and Theil, Henry and others, *Operations Research and Quantitative Economics* (New York: McGraw-Hill Book Company, 1965).
2. The most straightforward explanation of these models, perhaps, is presented in Loomba, Paul N., *Linear Programming* (New York: McGraw-Hill Book Company, 1964).
3. A concise explanation of simulation is presented in Philippakis, Andreas S., "Simulation: Basic Concepts of a Computer Oriented Technique," *Arizona Business Bulletin*, June-July, 1968. Also, for a demonstration of a specific application of simulation, see: McKenney, James L., *Simulation Gaming for Management Development* (Boston: Graduate School of Business Administration, Harvard University, 1967).

---

37   Truckers, Railroads Push Drives to Trim Freight Claims
Richard Martin

The shipper is basically interested in having his goods transported safely, on time, and to the proper receiver. His choice of carrier may hinge on the carrier's reliability and prevention of claims. While the shipper wants to be adequately compensated in case of loss or damage, he would prefer to avoid claims altogether.

Carriers are becoming increasingly aware of the shippers' position and of the fact that a low claims ratio means a more satisfied shipper—as we see in the following selection.

From Richard Martin, "Truckers, Railroads Push Drives to Trim Freight Claims," *The Wall Street Journal*, January 25, 1965. Used by permission.

DALLAS—"I'm looking for three wood crates of import freight from a Norfolk, Va., company," Jim Thomas, a claim agent for Roadway Express, Inc., recently told a luncheon meeting here of agents from other trucking companies.

A few hours after Mr. Thomas finished his lunch he got a phone call from the official of a rival trucking company, who had spotted the missing crates on his loading dock. Except for his lunchtime plea Mr. Thomas might never have found the crates, worth about $1,500 because they were marked only "WHW-Norfolk" and "Made in Hong Kong."

In the past two years the monthly meetings of trucking agents in Dallas have turned up about 10,000 pieces of stray freight valued at more than $700,000. This cooporation between rivals in a fiercely competitive industry reflects the increasing efforts of rail and highway carriers to trim their mounting freight claim bills.

In 1963, the latest year for which figures are available, U.S. trucking companies and railroads paid $226.6 million in claims on lost and damaged merchandise they had carried, up from $199.6 million in 1961. To carriers worried about profits being squeezed by rising costs, the claims figure seems a likely target for trimming.

Improving service

"Other costs, such as payroll and fuel expenses, can't be drastically reduced without affecting our ability to serve the shipping public," said W. F. Carroll, director of terminal operations of Eastern Express, Inc., Terre Haute, Ind. "But claims prevention improves service while reducing costs."

While meetings of local associations, such as the Dallas sessions, help truckers locate shipments at other firms' terminals, conference phone calls aid some truckers in rounding up stray freight at their own terminals. Olson Transportation Co., Green Bay, Wis., which connects its 16 terminals with long-distance conference calls twice daily, says such calls help find about 30% of its stray shipments before claims are filed on them.

Many carriers have started photographing poorly loaded shipments they receive to show a terminal manager when his employes are to blame. Strickland Transportation Co., Dallas, largely credits the Polaroid photos it began taking in 1963, along with conference phone calls, with chopping claims 14% that year while revenues rose 4%.

New equipment is helping trim claims bills by assuring freight a smoother, safer ride. Aero Mayflower Transit Co., Indianapolis, attributes most of its 4% reduction in claims payments in 1963 to air suspension systems which replaced steel springs on about 350 vans, and soon plans to have 85% of its 1,500 vans equipped with air suspension springs.

Softer ride

Nearly all railroads are buying softer-riding freight cars which have cushioned couplings and underframes. Hydra-Cushion, Inc., Chicago, a major producer of such devices, equipped 5,708 cars with them in the first nine months of 1964, up from 4,888 in all of 1963 and only 1,532 in 1961.

Some roads are building automated freight yards where electronic devices reduce damage by feeding into computers data on such things as weather conditions, car weight and speed. The computers activate long steel jaws on the tracks which grip car wheels and slow cars to safe coupling speed.

To get full benefit from their new equipment, many carriers are placing increasing stress on employe education programs. Union Pacific Railroad Co. and Southern Pacific Co. use demonstration boxcars with Plexiglass sides to show yard personnel how freight is shifted and smashed when careless couplings slam cars together at speeds above four miles an hour. The Atchison, Topeka & Santa Fe Railway Co. pushes claims prevention at company picnics and sponsors slogan contests for workers' wives.

Employes of some trucking lines frequently find messages urging greater care of freight, or cartoons exposing careless handling attached to their pay checks. "Personnel are interested in anything that appears in their pay envelopes," says J. L. Boies, vice president of Carolina Freight Carriers Corp., Cherryville, N.C. "This gives us an excellent opportunity to sneak in a claim prevention message."

More intensive investigations of claims are reducing damage payments for some carriers. If scientific analyses reveal, for example that weakness in a container caused damage, a carrier often can cancel the shipper's claim and even hold him responsible for other merchandise ruined by the leaking container.

Yale Express System, Inc., processes its claims through computers to speed settlement and detect causes of damage. "We can analyze 10,000 claims in minutes to spot trends and see what commodities, terminals and workers are causing us problems," says G. G. Weinstock, director of insurance.

Industry sources estimate that thievery accounts for about 4% of the claims trucking companies pay. To discourage pilferage, Yale has installed closed circuit TV cameras to scan loading docks at its New York terminals. Other carriers sprinkle some shipments with invisible powder; the powder shows up when employes' hands are exposed to ultra violet lights as they leave work, so the carriers can tell if unauthorized workers have been tampering with shipments.

Despite the saving achieved in claim losses by special programs, some men in the industry take a skeptical view. "Claims prevention is a rather tangible field," says A. E. Hocklander, manager of cargo claims for Merchants Fast Motor Lines, Inc., Abilene, Texas. "You can get some pretty elaborate schemes that just aren't worth the trouble. Our people make 6½ cents a minute. Crash prevention programs, with all their double checking, increased paperwork and time lost listening to lectures, would cost us more than we would recover from reduced claims."

A few shippers are pushing programs of their own to reduce damage to freight. Minnesota Mining & Manufacturing Co. claim specialists recently devised a stacking arrangement that prevents scuffing and tearing of its giant rolls of masking paper in shipping. The new arrangement also drastically cuts time needed to unload the rolls from a freight car, 3M says.

But carriers complain that many shippers still aren't sufficiently concerned with the problem. They contend that shippers' attempts to minimize packaging costs too often result in use of cheap containers which won't withstand normal handling, or in re-use of worn-out containers.

"The big shippers are concerned and trying to improve their practices," says Emmett Morris, general claims manager of Interstate Motor Lines, Inc., Salt Lake City. "But I don't think some of the small manufacturers who depend on volume to keep their production costs low care whether they sell their merchandise to a customer or the carrier."

---

38 **Transit Insurance:**
Should You Have It?
Handling & Shipping

Common carrier liability is not unlimited. Some firms take out inland marine insurance, a highly specialized type of insurance, to protect themselves against the risks of loss. Inland marine insurance plays a vital, though little known, role in protecting shipments—a role which this selection helps to make better known.

A shipper has several truck loads of expensive freight waiting at a truck terminal for interline pickups. The terminal is struck by lightning, catches fire, and burns to the ground with the shipper's goods still in it. Is the carrier liable for the shipper's loss?

Almost certainly not. The contract on the back of the standard bill of lading follows the common law practice of classifying lightning, floods, hurricanes, and earthquakes as Acts of God. No matter how much the carrier may have neglected his celestial insurance, the shipper must establish that he was negligent down here. This means proving that the carrier had enough warning to avoid catastrophe, or that he did not act to minimize loss and damage.

The common carrier's liability for freight in his possession does in fact have a number of common law and other kinds of loopholes. Traffic managers should know of these to decide if their particular freight needs coverage against the risks involved.

To find out what protection transit insurance does offer a shipper, H&S recently interviewed two Insurance Consultants, Jason Crain and David A. Langner, of Cleveland, Ohio. Both are Chartered Property and Casualty Underwriters, and members of the Insurance Consultants Society. Members of I.C.S. are forbidden to participate in commissions on the sale of insurance.

H&S's reporter led off by asking Crain if transit insurance was something unusual in the insurance business:

CRAIN: No, there's nothing unusual about it. Transportation insurance—or inland marine transportation insurance as it's somewhat paradoxically called—is an extension of marine insurance. When goods leave the custody of the owner for an ocean crossing, the carrier has absolute control of them. The owner insures his interest against the possibility that the carrier may never return, by paying a premium to an underwriter. If the ship is totally lost, the underwriter reimburses the owner. Today, in inland marine transportation insurance, the insurance company reimburses the shipper for his loss. However, most inland marine claims are for damage or partial losses. Since the carrier is usually liable for damage, the insurance company pays the loss to the shipper, and takes over his claim against the carrier. If the claim is contested and goes into court, the case could take years to settle. But the shipper has long since been paid and the legal intricacies of the claim become the insurance company's problem.

H&S: What are the other advantages of a transit policy?

CRAIN: The insurance company promptly makes up the shipper's loss even if it's impossible to collect from the carrier. This comes about when the carrier is specifically excused for loss or damage. According to the bill of lading, which serves as a contract between shipper and carrier, the carrier is not responsible for Acts of God, such as flood, wind, lightning, and earthquakes. Also if the carrier goes bankrupt and many other people have claims against him, the shipper would have a very tough time trying to recover his losses. But even in these instances, the insurance company reimburses the shipper first, then considers whether to take proceedings against the carrier.

LANGNER: Another point—the shipper may have wanted a released rate on his bill of lading. This makes it a contract between shipper and carrier to limit the carrier's liability. In a catastrophic loss which exceeds the carrier's liability the shipper may call on the insurance company to make good the loss in excess of the released value.

H&S: Is there a standard transit insurance policy?

CRAIN: Generally speaking, the policies are tailored to the individual shipper. But he has a choice between the two main types of transit insurance. He can decide to insure against "named perils"—fire, windstorm, collision, or any other specific danger. Or our shipper can opt for an "all-risk" policy where, with certain exclusions, the insurance company virtually takes on the entire risk of transporting the goods. But the programs a shipper can get vary with deductibles, franchises, the nature of the shipments and so on. The rates can run from a few mills to 10 cents per $100 of value of goods shipped.

Certain insurance companies have banded together to put out a standard transit insurance form. But generally these companies will modify the form if the shipper requests it.

H&S: What limitations do insurance companies place on their transit policies?

CRAIN: Companies will normally not insure certain types of shipments—

freight of extraordinary value, such as money, accounts, bills, etc. Then there are other exclusions—risks which the insurance company will not accept. War, delay, loss of markets, and inherent vice in the goods themselves—these are some of the exclusions. (*Inherent vice does not mean a truckful of pornography. It's insurance language for goods which shrink, decay, ferment, or in some way tend to destroy themselves—Ed.*) Or in some policies, the insurance company limits its liability to a stipulated dollar amount which is the limit of recovery.

H&S: How do insurance companies recover from carriers?

LANGNER: In much the same way as the shipper who does his own claim work. For the small routine loss, the shipper is in a much better position to negotiate with the carrier for a settlement. As we said earlier on, the advantage of transit insurance is that it reimburses the insured for a severe loss where he is not likely to recover fully and promptly from the carrier.

Now a carrier may attempt to settle a claim with a shipper for manufacturer's cost of the goods. The shipper can recover from his insurance company at the invoice value of the goods he has lost. In this way, he doesn't lose his profit.

When an insurance company processes small, routine claims, it is in effect performing a service. The cost of that service is built into the insurance premium. The more claims, the more service, the higher the rates.

H&S: What differences are there between policies covering shipments by motor carrier, air, rail, and water?

CRAIN: One policy will cover shipments by all modes. The policy will many times carry varying limits of liability for different modes. Air freight generally has lower liability limits than surface freight for example.

H&S: What sets the premium level?

CRAIN: Largely the loss record of the shipper. The shipper who has astutely used good packaging to keep his losses down, and followed up his routine claims against carriers promptly would seldom call on his insurance company. In his case, the premium might amount to a few hundred dollars a year, depending on the commodity.

On the other hand, the shipper who uses the insurance company as his claims service department must expect to pay more. You would have to include these factors in setting premium rates: volume of business; kinds of goods shipped; modes of transportation used; packing; loss limits; the kind of territory through which the shipments move; how much of the freight is shipped under a released bill of lading; and as we were saying earlier, past loss experience.

An easy method of determining premiums is to apply a rate ranging from .01 to .10 per $100 valuation of the total shipments. Alternatively, you could apply a rate to the total sales for the year.

H&S: Don't shippers find the cost of extra insurance too high when added to their freight costs?

LANGNER: If a shipper buys transportation insurance in the same way as a business buys fire insurance—that is, for catastrophe loss only—he would hardly notice the additional cost. For example, a policy with a limit of $100,000 on any one conveyance, and $200,000 on any one catastrophe, with $500 deductible and assuming no previous losses, would command a rate of about .01 per $100 of valuation. The deductible rules out the small loss which the shipper is better advised to collect from the carrier, or absorb if the carrier is not liable.

Of course, a series of insured losses over a short period of time might send up the rate, but the shipper has had insurance protection in the meantime.

H&S: How much is transit insurance used today?

CRAIN: Any organization which uses a lot of transport needs this type of insurance. When a large motor carrier went bankrupt recently, it came out that the company had unsatisfied claims far exceeding its liquidated assets. Without insurance, a shipper using that company would have had to swallow part or all of any loss.

The policy should also cover the interest of the shipper in goods which may not be at his risk in the ordinary course of business. For instance, a shipper f.o.b. his own plant could collect from his own insurance company if he didn't succeed in collecting from the purchaser.

The shipper with a back-stop transit insurance policy with a high limit can protect himself from that catastrophic loss where he has no recourse to collect anywhere else.

The most important part of any insurance program is loss prevention. Insurance companies as a rule are very willing to give shippers information and help on proper loading, package design, and all kinds of safety techniques.

---

39   Containerization: The Long Revolution

Kenneth Marshall

Containerization is a transportation innovation which can aid the traffic manager in several ways: for instance, by providing another answer to the small shipment problem; and by reducing materially loss and damage, thus lessening the freight claim problem. In addition, it makes intermodal shipment possible without excessive cost and delay at each transfer point. In the last respect, the "long revolution" still has a long way to go but, as this article indicates, significant progress has been made.

From Kenneth Marshall, "Containerization: The Long Revolution," *Transportation & Distribution Management*, November 1970, pp. 21-23. Used by permission.

Nothing, runs a hallowed historical maxim, can block the progress of a revolutionary idea whose time has come.

The trick is to recognize when the time has come. Quite often, the idea and the means to put it into practice have been around for years before someone gives the ingredients one more shake, and it all suddenly starts to happen.

The container revolution is a good example of this process at work. The idea of moving goods from the shipper's door to the receiver's place of delivery in a packing box which is also a vehicle seems to date from the first flush of the railway age. Loaded wagons were carried on flat cars regularly in the 1820's in England and wooden containers were commonly used in the 1830's to avoid breaking bulk between ship and train. In the U.S., a container service was established between Boston and New York City as early as 1847; the containers were carried on flat cars from Boston to Fall River, Mass., then transferred to ships to complete the trip. Railroads serving New York also did good business hauling wagons of food and produce on flat cars into the city in the early morning. At the stations, the wagons were hitched to horses and dispersed through the streets, returning empty to be deadheaded back to nearby farms at night.

But after such a promising start, containerization on the railroads fell into abeyance, except for a few small-scale experiments, until the 1950's. The reason would seem to be that, as the railroads became the dominant form of transportation in the U.S., they concentrated on station-to-station service; shippers and receivers were responsible for moving their own freight to and from the stations. What were called "merchandise" containers were used on some roads for LCL freight, but again only for the station-to-station haul; the customer unpacked his goods at the station. According to Dr. Ernest W. Williams, who has written extensively on the history of coordinated transportation, when the railroads first began offering pickup and delivery service in the 1930's "little use was made of containers in the through handling of freight on a door-to-door basis, although . . . some use was made of bulk containers, especially in the construction trades."

It was through the development of piggyback (a term abhorred by many editors when it was first used) that the railroads again took up the idea of door-to-door service. To begin with, at any rate, their main motive was to release box cars from LCL service for the more profitable carload business.

Piggyback service, using truck trailers for pickup and delivery under rail rates and billing, was begun by the Chicago, North Shore & Milwaukee in 1926. The service attracted little attention, and continued in desultory fashion until 1947, when it was discontinued. Other railroads also experimented with piggyback on a small scale. The Chicago Great Western started such a service in 1936, followed by the New Haven in 1937. Surprisingly, in view of its subsequent history, it was the success of the New Haven with piggyback which prompted other railroads to eventually adopt the system in the mid-1950's.

Regulatory problems

One explanation for the railroads' 30 years of indifference to containerization in piggyback or other forms may have been the inevitable regulatory complications.

The Interstate Commerce Commission, in its decision *Container Service* in 1931 (173 ICC 377), required that container rates be related to the class rate structure and imposed a number of other restrictions designed to ensure that no traffic would move in containers at less than the carload rate of the time. This snuffed out the hope of any simple container rate structure.

However, to quote Dr. Williams again, "doubtless more rapid progress could have been made had the interest of the carriers been focused upon (coordinated container services) as a desirable goal. It took the force of competition, felt through the diversion of vast tonnage of high-grade general freight from rail and domestic water carriers to truck, to provide the impetus for a major effort to develop coordinated services."

The impetus was provided in the post-World War II period. From the mid-30's onwards, the railroads had been turning over their less profitable LCL freight to the infant trucking industry for transportation—a sort of substituted service. It was all perfectly legal according to the ICC, for a common carrier to provide this type of service, so long as both carriers were authorized to serve the two points that the freight would move between.

By the early 1950's, the infant had grown into a giant, and the system was working the other way, with independent motor carriers using piggyback for all or parts of long line hauls. A study of traffic movement between New York and Chicago for May 1953 led the eastern railroads to conclude that millions in freight revenues would be diverted from box cars to motor carrier trailers by this "new" concept. At this juncture the now-defunct New Haven presented the ICC with 20 questions concerning the legal relations, limitations and obligations incident to the movement of highway trailers on flat cars (TOFC). In its reply, the commission resolved a number of legal arguments and ruled among other things that a railroad did not need operating authority to perform TOFC service for its own freight or to pick up and deliver such freight in rail terminal areas; nor was it obliged to offer TOFC services to all motor carrier comers.

Expansion of piggyback

Immediately after the New Haven decision, a number of railroads established or expanded TOFC operation, and within a few years, it was one of the healthiest sectors of the rail freight business. Starting out as "a hodgepodge of converted flat cars, cut-down gondolas, and other jerry-built systems," according to one expert, piggyback rapidly evolved into a variety of sophisticated systems and hardware. The pace of development was hectic. Eugene F. Ryan, a pioneer designer of piggyback equipment, recalls that the universal stanchion used to secure the trailer to the flat car in most present-day systems was drawn on the back of a napkin at lunch, after it was discovered the system about to go into production would require four men and several hours to install.

The piggyback car was a tremendous improvement over the railroads' conventional break-bulk cargo handling systems, earning about seven times a year more in gross revenues than the average box car. Some railroads, however, were prepared to follow the logic of the system and remove the wheels from the trailer and even the decking from the flat car, leaving the bare box fastened to the center sill of the car.

The former New York Central railroad began developing such a system in the late '50's. The more conservative elements in the railroad industry said it wouldn't work. According to R. L. Milbourne, one of NYC's directors at the time, the plans for the system had to be given to engineers outside the rail industry "who did not know that equipment of this nature could not be designed," and who therefore had no inhibitions about attempting the task—and succeeding.

The system in fact worked so well that when New York Central (which was operating both systems in the early '60's) came to compare them, it found "that the container with detachable road wheels was ten times more efficient than the piggyback system," according to Mr. Milbourne.

Meanwhile, the merchant shipping industry, faced with the same inexorable rise of handling and labor costs, had arrived at similar conclusions about the potential of the container.

Techniques for unitizing ships' cargo are, of course, as old as marine commerce itself. The ancient Greeks are said to have used giant two-man amphorae for handling general cargo as well as wheat and other bulk; and hogsheads, crates and boxes were as necessary as rope and tar in the sailing ship era.

Containerization in the modern sense of integrating the packing box into the transportation system first began in the early years of this century. At that time, van containers in the form of huge wooden boxes which could be lifted on and off a wheeled chassis were used to ship household goods overseas.

Efforts to work out international and intermodal standards for cargo containers date from this period, too. In 1905, the World Chamber of Commerce, headquartered in Rome, established a body "to investigate and to formulate packaging for intermodal use throughout the world." But apart from a few high-minded resolutions, nothing came of it.

The first attempt to set up a marine container service is generally credited to Seatrain, which tried to sell the merits of the system to the American shipping public in 1927. The service met with what is described as "only limited success," and Seatrain concentrated its efforts on ships designed to move loaded box cars. The first of these services was established in 1929 to run loaded freight cars between New Orleans and Havana, Cuba. In 1932, the service was expanded to include Hoboken, N.J. The freight cars were stowed on deck and in the hold in cells—the origin of the modern cellular container ship. Not until 1957 did Seatrain begin using its train ships to ship van containers in the spaces not occupied by box cars.

Sea-land

One year earlier, however, in 1956, Sea-Land Service had begun operating a container service, using a tanker which had been modified to carry sixty 32-foot highway trailers in addition to its cargo of oil. The demountable containers had been specially designed for the service and were loaded on the ship with a conventional shoreside crane.

Containerization was something more than an interesting experiment for Sea-Land at the time, according to A. Jack Mayor, one of the most ardent advocates of the system within the company. It was close to being the line's last chance.

Sea-Land was in those days what today would be termed a break-bulk coastwise shipping company, competing desperately with aggressive overland carriers. With stevedoring costs running at 60 to 70 cents out of every dollar, there was very little left for line haul, overhead, claims and other costs of doing business.

As Mr. Mayor diagnosed the problem, the high cost of handling freight was only a symptom; multiple handling was the real seat of the disease that was killing not only Sea-Land, but all the other domestic steamship operators. "We were losing touch with our customers, who had grown accustomed to the convenience of trucking, with its door-to-door service. Turnaround time had become one of the important clues to survival for the break-bulk operators. We knew (with containerization) we could improve ship utilization by at least 30 percent and reduce stevedoring costs by about 75 percent."

Sea-Land's expectations of its container system showed every sign of being confirmed, and in 1957 the company started full-scale operation of trailerships carrying 226 trailers. By 1966, 10 years after its first trials with a modified tanker, the company was operating 29 trailerships, with services to all the principal U.S. ports and to Europe, South America, and Puerto Rico.

Matson

On the west coast, meanwhile, Matson Navigation Co. had embarked on an experimental container program aimed at improving its freight operations to Hawaii. The service began in August 1958 with six conventional freighters, each outfitted to carry 40 van containers as deck loads only. The containers, grossing up to 25 tons were lifted off their road wheels by conventional dock-mounted whirley cranes and positioned on small deck-mounted cones which mated with four corner fittings in the container bottom and served to lock the load in place. The number of containers per ship was increased to 100 over the next two years, but they remained on deck.

These "deck only" container ships, according to Matson's Foster L. Weldon, who headed the company's 1956 research program into containerization, "represented the lowest level of container operations that would provide a useful test of the service; at the same time it was the highest level we could afford, considering the risk involved if the longshore union refused to cooperate. Nevertheless, the cost reduction was high, and the potential of the experiment as a vehicle for working out labor policy was very great indeed. It helped shape the rather revolutionary longshore agreement whereby the union has limited its membership and waived its objections to mechanization and methods changes in return for a fixed annual sum used for welfare items relating to technological unemployment."

With its labor problems arranged, Matson introduced in 1960 an all-container ship on its Hawaii run in which the containers were stacked six high in vertical slots below deck. The ship, again a converted freighter, could carry 296 containers in its hold and another 140 on deck, giving a total capacity of 436. At the same time the ship was put in service, Matson introduced a specially designed dock-mounted gantry crane which was fast enough to allow the ship to make a one-day turnaround.

Close upon the first below-deck container ship, in the late months of 1960 the company introduced two "convertibles" for the sugar trade which is the key-stone of Matson's operations to Hawaii. Each ship carried 390 loaded containers outbound and returned with 16,000 tons of bulk sugar in the hold with the empty containers stacked entirely on deck; the sugar provided the "ballast" for high-stacking the light containers.

Matson can also lay claim to the first fully automated container ship equipped with its own gantry crane which went into service in 1965 between Honolulu and other ports in the Hawaiian Islands.

"The promise of containerization," said Matson's Weldon at the start of the company's pilot run, "is that with relatively simple equipment, and without subsidies, an uneconomical transportation system can be converted in a rela-tively short time into a competitive and profitable one."

Just why the promise should have taken so long to become a reality has been analyzed variously by the pioneers of modern containerization themselves: "One of the basic reasons for the delay," says A. Jack Mayor, "is the transportation industry's penchant for intramural squabbling and its opposition to new tech-nology."

A more general explanation was offered by A. Scheffer Lang, former Railroad Administrator: "The really crucial element in economic progress is not invention *per se* (since so-called 'new technology' is usually based on old science) but innovation—which is the process whereby new ideas (inventions) are put to work. And the important obstacles to innovations are institutional, not tech-nical."

---

40   Captive Carriers
James R. MacDonald

One of the duties of the industrial traffic manager is to discover all of the transportation alternatives available to his company. Often, when competition between public carriers does not result in the price level or service needed, a

From James R. MacDonald, "Captive Carriers," *The Wall Street Journal,* November 11, 1964. Used by permission.

company can provide this competition by using its own private transportation. Although the examples in this selection are limited to motor and rail transport, private carriage is becoming increasingly common in all modes of transportation.

While the nation's railroads and truck lines wage a fierce battle for the hand of the shipper, the object of their affection is finding it increasingly easier to do without either one.

In an effort to beat rising transportation costs or gain better service, a growing number of shippers are spurning for-hire carriers and hauling the goods themselves. The Interstate Commerce Commission estimates that private carriage now accounts for nearly 15% of all intercity freight transport. That's a sharp gain from the 5% share it held at the end of World War II.

The shipper inroads into the transportation business are most apparent in trucking. Today, 12 out of every 13 trucks on streets and highways are shipper-owned and they account for two-thirds of all intercity truck tonnage. Customer demands for faster deliveries and a steady increase in common carrier truck rates—an average of 2% a year for the past five years—are mainly behind the surge toward do-it-yourself trucking. With James R. Hoffa's Teamsters Union possessing a new labor contract that will boost trucker costs roughly $200 million a year for the next two years, truck lines see little chance the trend to higher rates will be halted anytime soon.

A chance to cut costs

The chance to cut costs is probably the biggest attraction of private carriage and the savings which a company can achieve are sometimes dramatic.

For example, Container Corp. of America estimates the annual cost of moving paperboard between its Chicago mill and a carton manufacturing plant in Wheaton, Ill., will drop 65%, or about $20,000, because of a changeover to its own trucks made early this year.

Altogether, Container Corps'. fleet of 242 tractors and 503 trailers has cut the firm's annual transportation bill by "close to $800,000 compared with what the same service would cost using for-hire truck service," says D. W. Ryan, manager of materials handling and trucking.

Container's saving comes partly from the use of its trucks as mobile ware-houses. "The big advantage is being able to work directly from production lines right into the truck trailers," explains Mr. Ryan. The Wheaton operation, for instance, uses three tractors and 30 trailers with the surplus trailers spotted at loading docks and loaded as the paperboard rolls off production lines. When one is filled, a tractor hooks on and hauls it out to the Wheaton plant. Normally, there's a trailer-load of scrap paper waiting at Wheaton so the tractor simply drops off its load of paperboard, picks up the load of scrap paper and returns to Chicago where the process starts all over again.

Saves warehousing expense

"This saves both the time and expense of having to warehouse the paperboard and waste paper," Mr. Ryan says. "A common carrier couldn't afford to tie up his equipment like that."

Often, however, it's the need for faster deliveries rather than the possibility of cutting costs which prompts a company to operate its own trucks. Such was the case when Sears, Roebuck & Co. decided recently to begin trucking merchandise between its Memphis catalog distribution center and three catalog sales offices ranging up to 350 miles away.

"The big reason we switched to our own trucks was because we found we could cut delivery time to only 12 hours from the average 48 hours it took the common carrier," declares William L. Robinson, Sears' general traffic manager. "The cost of using our own trucks wasn't much different from the common carrier rate but we needed the faster service."

For the same reason, Brunswick Corp., diversified maker of bowling lanes, medical supplies and school equipment, is building up its own trucking operation.

Delays can be costly

"Service is the main reason we lease and operate a fleet of trucks," says Harold Hansen, Brunswick transportation manager. "When we ship bowling equipment from our Marion, Va., plant to a new bowling alley, we've got to be sure it arrives right on schedule." He explains that the company makes arrangements for an installation crew to be on hand at a specific time and if the equipment isn't there the crew gets paid anyway. The crew's pay is no small consideration: It ranges from $250 to $350 a day. "On top of this, if a late delivery delays the opening of the alley, the proprietor loses $800 to $1,000 a day in revenues," Mr. Hansen adds.

Brunswick currently operates a fleet of 16 trucks, 10 of them in intercity movement. But the company is beginning a study of its entire transportation-distribution program "which will probably lead to expansion of our trucking operations," says Mr. Hansen.

For many companies, problems with shipping goods in less-than-carload volume via common carriers has led to private carriage.

Thus, the traffic manager for a major plastic products company reports it switched to its own trucks because "we just couldn't pound it into the trucking company that what we needed was fast service. What would often happen was that the trucker would pick up 75% of a truckload at our plant but before the truck would leave his terminal he would try to fill it up completely. Sometimes this would take a week or more. While we can understand his desire for a full load, we just couldn't live with that in today's competitive market. All things considered, we're not saving anything in freight costs, but service to our customers is much improved," he says.

While private carriage is expanding rapidly, it probably would be growing still faster except for one major problem—finding a load for a return trip. One shipper estimates that it costs 40 to 45 cents a mile to operate an empty truck over the road, a price stiff enough in many instances to more than wipe out any saving a company might otherwise make in hauling its own goods. Some companies, such as Container Corp., solve the backhaul headache by carrying supplies for its plants on the return trip.

But often such an arrangement can't be worked out. Hormel & Co., Austin, Minn., meat packer, cites an insurmountable backhaul problem as the reason it finally gave up on an attempt to establish its own transport system. "Up to roughly five years ago, we leased a fleet of 20 trucks that we used to haul various meat products from our Midwest packing plants to other parts of the country," says Robert Propf, general traffic manager. "But we just couldn't fill those trucks on the return trip, so we gave the business back to the truck lines."

An apparently obvious solution—hauling freight for someone else on the return trip—is prohibited by ICC rules (unless the cargo is on the Agriculture Department's list of 100 or so farm commodities that are exempt from regulation). But truck line executives charge many companies have taken to hauling freight for others as the solution, anyway. "I'll wager that if the truth were known close to half the private carriage in the country would be either outright illegal or questionable," says a Chicago trucker. He suspects numerous instances of illegal haulage by shippers who operate their own fleets.

But he, and other common carrier truckers, are often reluctant to complain to Federal and state officials about this breach of the law—for perhaps good reason. "It just so happens that some of this is being done by our own customers," the trucker says. "So how long do you think I'd have that business if I were to blow the whistle on them?"

Up to now, shipper efforts to haul their own goods have been almost exclusively confined to trucking operations. But there are signs that companies soon may be expanding their do-it-yourself operations to the railroads.

This year, for instance, Pennsylvania Power & Light Co. invested $1 million in the purchase of 74 railroad hopper cars to haul coal from a mine near Pittsburgh to its Brunner Island generating plant near Harrisburg, Pa. The cars are run together as a "unit train" on the tracks of the Pennsylvania Railroad with the Pennsy also providing the motive power.

Because of the efficiencies of this unit train, officials of the railroad and the utility say it will cut coal hauling costs by 40%. The new rate for hauling coal on the shipper-owned train over the 219-mile run is $2.42 a ton, compared with the conventional rate of $4.17 a ton.

Another utility, Commonwealth Edison Co., of Chicago, last month began using a 70-car unit train to haul coal between a mine at Belleville, Ill., and its Joliet, Ill., generating plant. The utility owns all the cars, with the Gulf, Mobile & Ohio Railroad supplying the tracks and motive power.

This is just the first instalment of what will ultimately be two 126-car unit trains operating between Belleville and Joliet. When complete, sometime in

1966, the two trains will haul four million tons of coal annually between those two points.

Commonwealth Edison estimates that when both trains are in operation it will save $5 million annually over what it was paying to move the coal. The new rate is $1.30 per ton in the utility-owned unit trains, compared with $2.50 per ton before.

---

41   The Logistical Mathematics of Private Carriage . . .

E. Grosvenor Plowman

Formerly Vice-President—Traffic,

United States Steel Corporation

Formerly Undersecretary of Commerce

for Transportation

In this final selection in Part Two, the "dean" of transportation economists discusses some of the methodology which a firm may use in deciding whether or not to enter private carriage—a far from easy decision. And he brings us back, once more, to the concept of logistics.

. . . It is probable that most business ventures into private carriage have been initiated without knowledge of all the costs involved. Determination of cost, either before going into private carriage, or after operation has commenced is a task for trained accountants. Failure to obtain and to rely on carefully prepared accounting reports is a common reason for incorrect conclusions about cost.

Usually the initial estimates of the cost of private carriage are on the low side. For example, the enthusiastic proponent of private carriage often overlooks such elements as the cost of services such as light and heat, because obtained within the company. Also often forgotten is that fact that, if the capital investment was employed in buying a new production machine it would be expected to earn its share of administrative overhead and a profit as well as interest on investment. Costing techniques for evaluating private use of transportation equipment can be useful also in developing estimates of for-hire costs.

Lease versus purchase

An important decision preceding use of private carriage is as to the desirability of leasing or buying the equipment. By "lease" is meant not a legal instrument, but any financing procedure that provides for regular payments from current earnings, with the gradually declining unpaid balance guaranteed chiefly by the resale value of the particular equipment. The problem of an automobile for a salesman is a simple example of the choice that must be made in obtaining any kind of transportation equipment for private operation. The lease cost must be compared with the purchase costs of the car:

1. the price of the car,
2. interest on this money,
3. cost of supervision,
4. cost of maintenance,
5. *less* the net resale value.

Assume that net purchase *price* of an automobile delivered to a company salesman is $2400, that *supervision and clerical cost* incurred by the company during the life of this vehicle is $8, that the car is run 40,000 miles before turn-in at a cost for *fuel, tires,* and *repairs* of $1600, and that the car is sold after 24 months' use for a yet yield of $800. The total cost, including interest at 4 per cent on the $2400 purchase price, is $3400.

Cost + Interest + Supervision + Operation and Maintanance−Resale Value
$2400+ $192 +   8   + $1600   − $800

Alternatively, the car may be leased. If 6 per cent interest is paid on the declining balance, with one thirty-sixth of the principal paid each month, interest will also be $192. $1600 of the original purchase price will have been paid out in two years. The sale price of $800 at the end of the two-year period equals the balance due so no adjustment is needed here. Cost of leasing the car, including $8 for supervision and clerical cost, and $1600 for fuel, tires and repairs would be $3400, the same as if it had been purchased. Whether the car is purchased or leased the cost would be 8.5 cents per mile of use.

The examples of ownership versus leasing of a salesman's car have been equated by using a lower interest rate of 4 per cent for the company's total investment, and an interest rate of 6 per cent on the declining balance in the case of the leased car. This was done to illustrate that, often, the advantage of ownership versus leasing is dependent on assumptions that are deliberately favorable to ownership. In the case of interest, the fact that the company considered use of its own money was worth only 4 per cent does not justify purchase. The real question is what this money would return if it had been invested in a cost-reducing new machine for the company's factory. If the latter return is 10 per cent or even more, clearly the company's money should have gone into the new factory equipment and the salesman's car should have been leased.

There is an intangible value arising from leasing equipment for use in private transportation of either passengers or freight. This is that both lessor and lessee are interested in maintaining the leased automobiles or trucks or barges or railroad tank cars in good condition. There is less tendency to keep on using old equipment by making "makeshift repairs." The factor of clean, good looking and well-maintained vehicles can be valuable as a contribution to safety morale, public relations and advertising. Of great importance is its effect in encouraging careful and efficient use of the equipment.

This intangible factor can become an offset to the fact that leasing, by introducing a second corporation which must be paid for its services, tends to cost slightly more than direct ownership. Of course such a comparison that is slightly adverse to leasing is valid only if one assumes that both lessor and lessee can obtain funds for their equipment capital requirements at the same interest rate. Even if this is the case it is not valid if the money used for purchase could have earned a substantially higher return, for example, by being invested in additional production facilities or in a new or more efficient warehouse.

The effect of the estimated load factor

The key question that determines whether to undertake private carriage of one's own freight is whether operating efficiency can be developed and maintained by the private operator. If the load factor is inadequate, for example, the unit cost will be high. There will be little or no justification for private carriage, unless positively required because of the favorable effect on other logistical factors.

Assume the capacity of one tractor-trailer is 17 tons per trip. It can make 250 round trips (or 500 one-way trips) per year between the factory and a warehouse located 200 miles away. From plant to warehouse it is known that the load will vary from 10 tons minimum to 17 tons maximum and will average 12 tons. On the return trip, the average is to be 2 tons. The annual lift will be 3500 tons, while the annual capacity is 8500 tons. Thus the load factor is 41 per cent.

Whether use of a company-operated private truck with over half of its capacity unused is justified depends on part on the tangible and intangible advantages of having full control of operation. One tangible advantage may be reduction in the cost of packaging, since the truck body can be designed to protect unpackaged or lightly packaged products. Another is the ability to schedule the truck so as to eliminate the need to hold reserve inventory at the warehouse. These small savings can be measured by skilled accountants, and their dollar value estimated.

Of greater importance may be the intangible service feature that the private truck can make deliveries under emergency conditions direct to the customer, thus by-passing the warehouse. Or the truck may take part of its freight in a container which is transferred to a local truck at an intermediate point for delivery to customers. While such service may be duplicated by common carriers, its additional cost must be paid for. The company's truck can perform much of this type of special customer service with little or no addition to its cost, provided use of private carriage has already been found desirable and justified by the regular movements and despite the low load factor.

There is an obvious relation between the degree of decentralization of production and consumption and the need for private carriage of freight. Viewing the century that has elapsed since mechanized transportation by railroad, steamboat, and pipeline became an important *agent of industrialization,* decentralization has shown rapid and continuing growth. At the time of the American Civil War, Great Britain was the major industrial nation. Raw materials flowing toward

England and industrial products moving in the opposite direction helped to shape the East-West pattern for American common carriers by railroad.

The industrial New England and North Atlantic states gradually supplanted the formerly dominant British manufacturers. This shortened the raw material and finished products hauls, and became the first step toward decentralization.

Today's industry of all types is established in all the numerous economic regions within the United States. The national market has thus been subdivided into numerous smaller markets. As a result inbound and outbound hauls are, on the average, much shorter than a century ago. This reduction in length of haul has been a major factor that has stimulated and justified much of the great increase in private carriage, particularly by truck. The higher per-mile charges made by common carriers for short distances combined with the service flexibility of private carriage by truck, usually offset the low load factor.

Despite the obvious relation between decentralization and private carriage, there is no single pattern that will automatically guide decision. To treat this relationship as a generalization applicable to all situations is unsound and will only lead to costly errors. Each private carriage situation must be tested and evaluated in its own environment. Furthermore, the old adage that "one man's meat may be another man's poison" aptly describes the fact that competing users of transportation may need private carriage in different ways.

One petroleum refiner may rely on common carrier pipelines. Another may own and operate a fleet of private barges. One chain store concern may have its own private trucks deliver to stores in one direction, then haul products from a factory to a central distributing warehouse in the reverse direction. A competing chain store enterprise may use railroad common carriers to deliver products from factories to numerous local warehouses from which distribution to the retail stores is accomplished by contract truck. In these examples the average load factor is one of the basic determinants as to whether or not to engage in private carriage.

Computing average transit time

Private carriage is most useful and low in cost when circumstances permit a high-average load factor. Equally important is ability to keep all of the equipment in constant use. The natural tendency of private carriage is to accumulate more equipment than is desirable from the standpoint of both optimum service and cost. This problem of determining the best relation between equipment and tonnage ready for shipment can be approached from two different angles. Both require a survey to determine the over-all time required for an average round trip, including the loading and unloading intervals.

Assume that the trips made by one truck in a week average out at five hours, broken down into 45 minutes for loading, an equal time for unloading, and 210 minutes time in transit on the round trip. The five-hour period required for the average trip means that only one trip can be accomplished per 8-hour day. This is a practical or empirical estimate based on the fact that an average is composed of actual situations, some of which will greatly exceed or fall short of the five-hour average. The cost of overtime operates as a penalty against any effort to make two trips in one 8-hour shift. Another factor is that, in making deliveries either to a customer or to one's own warehouse or plant, it is undesirable to arrive at destination less than two hours before the end of the normal work day. This is to avoid imposing overtime costs upon the receiver of the truck shipment. This consideration also immobilizes both for-hire, and private carriage delivery by truck on Saturdays, Sundays, and holidays.

If the average time of five hours is divided into 40 hours, the theoretical number of trips in a normal work week would be eight. As shown, the minimum that can be estimated realistically is five trips per week. On the five-trip basis the utilization is 62½ per cent of the theoretical maximum. Combined with a load factor of say 25 per cent (average one-way load using half the capacity of the truck, returning empty), there may be little or no cost-saving justification for use of private carriage.

Determining equipment requirements

Many transportation situations require use of more than one truck, or barge, or airplane, or freight car. Cost competitiveness of private carriage requires favorable utilization of equipment capacity. Achievement of low cost of private transportation requires decision as to the optimum number of vehicles needed for a particular movement.

Assume a situation such as

Volume to move:	500 tons per day, 50 weeks per year, 5 hours round-trip time, 5-day week
Capacity of each truck:	20 tons per one-way trip
Investment and operating cost per truck:	$ 8,500 to $10,000 per year according to use
Driver earnings and related costs:	$10,000 per year
Loading and unloading helper, cost per man:	$ 6,000 per year

There are three possible ways to supply 500 tons per day by truck with intransit time, including loading and unloading time, of five hours per round trip. The entire 500 tons can be moved in a single 8-hour shift. This will require 25 trucks and the same number of drivers, but only two loading-unloading helpers. On a two-shift basis, by careful scheduling, three trips by nine trucks can be made in 16 hours without overtime penalties, requiring four helpers. On a three-shift basis it becomes possible to schedule four trips by seven trucks, using six helpers.

The single shift operation would require:

25 trucks costing $8,500 each...$212,500
25 drivers costing $10,000 each 250,000
2 helpers costing $6,000 each.. 12,000
$474,500

average cost per ton: 474,500 ÷ 125,000 = $3.796

A two-shift operation, with three trips per day per truck would require:

9 trucks costing $9,500 each...$ 85,500
18 drivers costing $10,000 each 180,000
4 helpers costing $6,000 each.. 24,000
$289,500

average cost per ton: 289,500 ÷ 125,000 = $2.316

A three-shift operation with four trips per day per truck would take:

7 trucks costing $10,000 each..$ 70,000
21 drivers costing $10,000 each 210,000
6 helpers costing $6,000 each.. 36,000
$316,000

average cost per ton: 316,000 ÷ 125,000 = $2.528

In this example the most desirable operation plan appears to be the two-shift arrangement, requiring nine trucks, 18 drivers, and four helpers for loading and unloading. (It should be noted that this example has been greatly simplified to bring out the fundamental factors.)

The complexity of private carriage logistics

These simple examples may seem to belabor the obvious. In fact, they represent the type of analysis that is essential to sound decision-making but that is often omitted. Furthermore, such analysis should be repeated at intervals if the enterprise is to remain in an optimum position in its use of private carriage, and in its evaluation of existing or proposed freight rates.

It must also be borne in mind that these examples all deal with transportation as the major factor to be considered. As has been shown in other chapters, this is rarely the case. Other factors such as warehouse location and operation and convenience in delivery to customers also must be incorporated into the logistical analysis. The mathematics required for decision then becomes complex indeed.

> Cost analysis as a tool of transportation management is not as impervious to change as it may at times appear to be. . . . Recently, for instance, containerization has generated increased interest . . . in the relationship of "number of pieces" to handling costs. . . . Contrary to some current thought, a great share of so-called constant and joint costs are neither unfathomable nor indivisible and may be reasonably and effectively traced, measured and managed . . . the increased willingness on the part of management and policy makers to accept a greater degree of sophistication and complexity in cost analysis may be described as one beneficial side effect of the "computer age." [Quoted from article by Dr. K. P. Rahbany, *Traffic World Magazine*, October 6, 1962, Washington, D.C., pages 60 and 72.]

Part
Three

Transportation Rates and Costs

Introduction

Part One of this book looked at the supply of transportation furnished by the carriers. Part Two considered the demand side of transportation evidenced by the shippers and their representatives. Logically, the next step is to consider the results of the interaction of these two sides of the transportation equation: the price of transportation.

Transportation pricing or rate making is an extremely complex subject. There are over two million different kinds of commodities shipped to several thousand different origination and destination points in the United States. Each commodity carried between points of origination and destination may travel over a multitude of possible routes and in many possible combinations of carriers; and each commodity has a price or a rate. Therefore, an almost astronomical number of prices is involved.

By law the rates or prices must be published and made available to the interested shippers, public officials, and competing carriers. Also by law, the carrier cannot charge nor the shipper pay other than the published rate. It follows that these price lists are of crucial importance to everyone involved.

Rates are published in books called "tariffs" and these are on file with the public bodies charged with the task of regulating transportation. Tariffs may be as small as a single page or as large as several hundred pages. The number of these tariffs is prodigious: in 1962 it was estimated that 205,275 active tariffs were on file with the Interstate Commerce Commission in Washington, D.C., and occupied over a mile of shelf space; over 800,000 pages of new tariffs are filed annually with the I.C.C.

It is impossible here to cover the subject of rates and tariffs. The interested reader is referred to a standard transportation text for a discussion of the process of rate making, the kinds of rates and the distinctions between them, and the theory of rate classification.

However, we can say that rates, like all prices, must be based at least partially on costs—on which costs and how these costs are to be allocated among the various commodities moved are matters of long-standing debate. Likewise, the degree of cost-oriented rate making, as compared with value- or demand-oriented rate making is also a matter of debate. Since these matters are the basis of the process of rate making, several of the selections in this part consider them.

Complexity and confusion challenge man's ingenuity and make him essay simplifications. Since transportation rates are regulated prices, the whole complex process of rate regulation or control becomes important. The Interstate Commerce Commission is charged with regulating rates for all modes except air and private transportation. Therefore, rates will be affected by its considerations concerning transportation costs, levels of comparative rates, compensation for the carriers, reasonableness, and discrimination. In view of this fact, one of our selections is by an outstanding I.C.C. Commissioner who adds further depth to the discussion of transportation pricing.

Part Three can sample only a portion of the vast literature on the matter of transportation rates and costs. As a "sampler," it is aimed at complementing existing textual material, which, as we noted in the Preface, is one of the main purposes of this volume.

42 The Role of Cost
in the Minimum Pricing
of Railroad Services
Association of American Railroads

The problem of transportation pricing is comprehensive. It affects the location of industry and the economic health of towns, states, and regions. Value of service or demand pricing was developed while railroads had a near monopoly on transportation and remains with us today, even though the economic conditions which fostered it changed long ago. More relevant than value of service or demand pricing to today's competitive transport world is cost pricing. But the problem of what degree of cost pricing is adopted, and, in particular, of "what cost," is hotly debated.

In this selection, prepared by the Association of American Railroads with the advice and help of ten outstanding theoretical economists, the problem of "what cost" is well stated and a solution to the problem is proposed.

Introduction

Increasing competitiveness in transportation has stimulated debate regarding the principles which should guide the determination of any floor below which particular railroad rates will not be permitted to fall. A central issue in this debate is whether particular rates should be cost or market oriented. This statement examines the issue—bringing to bear accepted principles of economics that apply throughout the economy. It sets forth the role of cost in pricing and in so doing shows that prices must be *both cost and market* oriented.

Examining first the basic cost concepts and then the nature of railroad costs, the analysis concludes that incremental costs provide the valid cost guide for minimum pricing and that "fully distributed" costs must be rejected as an economic test of any particular price or rate. These conclusions are reached by reference to the interest both of the pricing carrier and of society as a whole, and they have the same force and relevance for pricing within modes of transport as among modes.

Underlying cost principles

The increase in total costs resulting from an expansion in a firm's volume of business is commonly referred to as *incremental cost*. This cost is of vital eco-

From the Association of American Railroads, "The Role of Cost in the Minimum Pricing of Railroad Services," *The Journal of Business of the University of Chicago,* October 1962, pp. 1-10. Copyright, The University of Chicago Press. Used by permission. Prepared with the advice and help of William J. Baumol, Burton N. Behling, James C. Bonbright, Yale Brozen, Joel Dean, Ford K. Edwards, Calvin B. Hoover, Dudley F. Pegrum, Merrill J. Roberts, and Ernest W. Williams, Jr.

nomic significance. For the businessman it provides an essential guide to his production and pricing policy. If he is considering a reduction in price, he needs to know whether the increase in total revenues from greater volume will more than cover the additional costs that will be incurred. For the whole economy it is incremental (not fully distributed) cost that is the relevant cost guide of how much of what shall be produced and how much should be invested in various lines of production. This cost, which is measured by the value of the additional resources that will be used up when more of anything is produced, represents the real cost to society.[1] Incremental costs indicate (by comparison with the incremental revenues they will bring) whether additional outputs of any commodity are worth producing and (by incremental cost comparisons) which of the alternative ways of satisfying wants or requirements is the most efficient.[2]

But not all costs can be identified causally with specific quantities of production. Much of the controversy over cost concepts stems from the false notion that all costs can be traced and attributed to specific blocks of output. Although many costs are *traceable,* there are also *non-traceable* costs which simply do not lend themselves to this method of identification:

a) Fixed costs.—Some costs, called *fixed costs,* do not change in magnitude when the quantity of output for a given plant varies. Hence, it is impossible to assign any specific portion of these costs to a particular unit of output (e.g., to a particular ton-mile of traffic. Rather, a fixed cost must be imputed to the entire supply of the type or types of service with which it is associated.

b) Joint costs. —Different services may sometimes share their costs, as, for example, when the same roadbed is employed to transport both food products and lumber.

Such common and joint cost conditions are frequently encountered in the railroad industry as well as elsewhere. *Common costs* are outlays devoted to either of two or more classes of services which may be variably proportioned at the discretion of management, with the result that it is, in principle at least, possible to trace them to individual services. *Joint costs,* in contrast, are costs for which the proportions of output are not variable, so that supplying one class of service in a given amount results automatically in making available another class of service in some unalterable amount. The practical consequence is that incremental joint costs are not traceable to individual railroad services and can be allocated only arbitrarily. In contrast, those common costs which are incremental are traceable in principle, although it may be impossible over a considerable range to do so in practice.

For any business or industry there is no rigid division between variable costs and fixed costs. Some cost elements which are fixed in the very short term or with small changes in output may over a somewhat longer period or a broad range of output become incremental if additional investments or other inputs are required. However, an indefinitely long-term view of incremental costs is not appropriate, for some fixed costs may be expected to remain fixed over any time period and range of output that is reasonable to consider in setting a price floor. Depending on the particular circumstances, incremental costs might contemplate a range of short terms. The only general rule for deciding which measure of incremental cost to use as a *cost* guide for minimum pricing is that the choice of incremental cost functions must be geared to the duration of the expected revenue change.[3]

Each particular situation requires its particular cost analysis by management. For example, a cost structure will be affected significantly by the extent of unused capacity in the production factors involved. Where unused capacity is substantial and persistent, the fixed cost elements per unit of output are correspondingly greater and more enduring, and the incremental costs proportionally smaller.

Arbitrary apportionments of nontraceable costs among particular kinds of outputs must be employed in the calculation of "fully distributed costs." This measure will be further considered later in particular reference to railroad rate-making. However, it is apparent from what has been said that fully distributed costs have no true economic content because their derivation falsely assumes that all costs can be traced to particular kinds or quantities of output and can rationally enter directly into pricing decisions. The greater the degree of nontraceable costs, the more inappropriate is the use of fully distributed costs as a guide to minimum prices.

Nature of railroad costs

Fixed costs, which are independent of volume and are not attributable to specific amounts of traffic, are an important characteristic of railroad cost structures. Large portions of railroad investment costs represent expenditures for long-lived facilities that have been "sunk" in the enterprise at various times in the past. The facilities involved are of such specialized nature that they are not generally transferable to other pursuits without great loss. Fixed costs associated with sunk physical investments, as well as organizational or other cost factors which are underutilized, are irretrievably committed to an essential public service unless disinvestment, organizational shrinkage, or, as a last resort, abandonment occurs.

Because of the long but varied lives of their facilities and the inherent uncertainties of forecasting, adjustment of railroad capacity to changing requirements is difficult. Unutilized railroad capacity is a chronic problem which demands effective steps to retain existing traffic and to attract additional traffic. Moreover, railroad investments in recent years which were intended for modernization and greater efficiency have in many instances also increased capacity, although this has not usually been the purpose. Significant technological improvements include heavier rail and track structures, electronic yards, centralized traffic control, and better communications, as well as improved locomotive power and higher-capacity freight cars. Realization of the potential economies of these and other interrelated improvements depends on large and increasing traffic volumes.

The railroads own, and hence must fully pay for, the costly plant facilities they use. In contrast, highway, water, and air carriers use publicly owned rights of way and facilities. To the extent that they repay the economic costs of these facilities furnished to them, their payments are mainly through use charges which make their costs of this sort predominantly variable. For these and other reasons, these rival carriers can adjust their capacities to fluctuating demand more promptly and precisely than can the railroads.

The rapid growth of electrical utility volume has been due to a steady reduction of real prices on average and to promotional pricing designed to utilize capacity effectively and to expand sectors of demand that are price-elastic. These achievements have been made possible, on the cost side, by sustained technological progress and economies of scale in the generation and transmission of electricity and, on the demand side, by strong markets and commendable regulatory insight. This kind of economic performance, generally regarded as serving the public interest, is no less socially desirable for the railroads. And even though it is more difficult to attain because of their highly competitive environment, such performance is at least equally urgent because of the railroads' financial plight.

The public interest requires maximum economic utilization of the vast capacity of the railroads' plant and operating organization. To this end it is essential that the burden of fixed costs be spread over as large a volume of traffic as can be developed with attractive rates in excess of the relevant incremental costs. This mode of operation is desirable not only for the railroads in providing them with the opportunity for reasonable investment returns. It may also be advantageous to the shippers in lower shipping costs. Above all, it is in the public interest because it provides the maximum amount of transportation service for the resources which are employed for this purpose.

Relevant incremental costs

In determining incremental costs, it is necessary to distinguish between sunk and prospective investments. Sometimes the pertinent incremental costs involve making added investment (e.g., cars or locomotives). In that event all the added costs to be incurred (including use-depreciation and cost of capital) should be recognized as incremental. Sometimes capacity is so excessive that the traffic at issue can be handled without added investment. The investment costs then are sunk and may become fixed for long periods. Once the commitment has been made, and if a plethora of capacity subsequently develops, the recovery of anything more than incremental cost is better than nothing.

Prudent railroad management should certainly be aware of the threat to long-term profitability, and even survival, from fixing rates on a substantial proportion of traffic near strictly short-term incremental costs. Nevertheless, in the complex and varied circumstances of the railroads, there will be some situations where pricing of particular services on the basis of short-term considerations will improve utilization and will yield accretions to net income not otherwise obtainable. In view of their primary responsibility to make effective use of their vast facilities through volume retention and development, railroad managements require considerable latitude in estimating relevant costs as well as in pricing decisions. There is no single cost formula which will always and automatically be appropriate.

In rapidly expanding industries operating with short-lived facilities and highly flexible organization, recognition of the transitory nature of fixed costs and their tendency to be transformed rather quickly into incremental costs is an essential costing precept for pricing purposes. But railroad costs cannot be cast in such a simple mold. The reality of their fixed costs cannot be made to disappear with a general assumption of variability with traffic volumes if the time period is stretched out long enough. With the persistent and serious under-utilization of capacity which is characteristic of the railroads' basic plant and organization, large amounts of fixed costs remain fixed indefinitely. The least effective way to cope with unutilized railroad capacity would be to include its fixed costs in floors for pricing. For the high prices which would result could only discourage utilization of these facilities and aggravate the condition.

Neither extremely short-run nor extremely long-run incremental cost is an economic concept of general applicability to all minimum pricing problems encountered in the railroad industry. The determination of the relevant incremental costs appropriate for a particular pricing decision is not simple[4] but must reflect complex railroad cost conditions that arise from persistent excess capacity, irrelevant fixed-cost elements, and such interrelated dynamic factors as changing volume, changing labor and material costs, technological innovations, and improved operating techniques. Where such dynamic forces are at work the incremental costs of additional traffic, which may be induced by a reduced rate, may be quite different from those indicated by past experience.

More pentrating analysis of specific cost elements is needed for a better understanding of their relationship to traffic volumes. Such analysis, which is beyond the scope of this statement on cost concepts, should be intensified by the railroads. Particularly urgent is the need for cost determinations which are "tailored" to specific situations instead of the commonly used general measures which are vitiated by excessive averaging.

Costs and pricing

Forward-looking costs are essential because the pricing decisions they must guide necessarily look to the future. The estimation of such costs must reckon with changes in operating techniques which may result from expanded volume and associated or unassociated technological innovations. Because of these factors, historical experience provides no sure basis for determining those future incremental costs which alone are relevant in setting price floors.

As a general rule, any rate below incremental costs is both unprofitable and socially wasteful of resources because the additional (incremental) revenue obtained is less than the additional cost incurred.[5] However, this does not mean that the railroads should set rates *at* that cost level or that they should be required to do so. On the contrary, this cost reference is uniquely important as a guide in determining the specific rates which will provide the maximum contribution to the overhead burden and thus to net income. The margin above incremental costs which maximizes this contribution depends upon the price sensitivity of demand, determined primarily by the alternatives available to shippers. The judgment of management should be relied upon to make this determination, subject to limitations imposed by regulation of maximum rates and discrimination. Thus, while incremental costs should not *determine* prices or rates, they set the lower boundary (and demand conditions and regulation of the upper boundary) within which pricing decisions should be made.

Railroads produce a multiplicity of different services in many markets with dissimilar demand characteristics. For example, the demand for the transportation of coal for three hundred miles eastbound may be entirely different from the demand for the transportation of the same commodity three hundred miles westbound because of competitive or market influences. Basing rates on demand (as well as on incremental costs) to attain the maximum contribution means, therefore, that rates for all services will not be the same either absolutely, or in relation to cost, or in contributions to the net income of the carriers.

Since demands for rail services have become increasingly elastic as alternative means of transportation (both for hire and private) have become ever more available, the greatest total contribution to net income will for many items and hauls result from a low unit margin above incremental cost and a large volume. Estimating the volume of traffic which might move at different levels of rates and the effect on net income is a key aspect of pricing. This vital function is a primary management responsibility which should be performed on the basis of managerial and not regulatory judgment. Rates so determined, however, can legitimately continue to be subject to regulation of maximum rates and to legal rules against unjust discrimination.[6]

Differential pricing is consistent with the public interest in the economical utilization of resources. It can yield significant benefits to the users of rail services by encouraging the retention of traffic and the development of greater traffic volumes and improved profits, thus fostering the adoption of improved technology and service, as well as lower rates.

Pricing designed to achieve such results should not be condemned as "destructive" or "unfair" competition. Rather it is necessary for constructive competition and maximal economy and efficiency in the utilization of resources. By the very nature of competition some are hurt by it. It may well be that realistic assessments of incremental costs as a pricing guide would encourage rate reductions where carrier or regulatory policies have stressed preservation of historic rate structures or keeping rates high enough to maintain "fair" market sharing. Indeed, reductions designed directly to improve profits may do so mainly by shifting traffic away from firms operating by other modes, which are thereby hurt or even destroyed. But this does not constitute predatory competition. Predatory practices must be taken to refer to temporary price reductions designed to eliminate competition in order to clear the way for high and monopolistic rates in the future. Ease and low costs of re-entry of trucks and other modes make predatory competition by the railroads unprofitable and hence unlikely. Moreover, such undesirable practices constitute a legitimate concern of the regulatory authorities. Regulatory powers should not, however, be used to prevent price reductions which are designed to improve or maintain profits by increasing or retaining traffic volume. Such prevention is particularly undesirable socially, because of the low rates of utilization of the large property investments of the railroads.

"Fully distributed" cost an invalid basis for minimum pricing

The relevant incremental costs constitute all the cost information pertinent to the determination of floors in the pricing of particular railroad services. "Fully distributed" cost, measured by some kind of arbitrary statistical apportionment of the unallocable costs among the various units or classes of traffic, is an economically invalid criterion for setting minimum rates, from both a managerial and a regulatory standpoint. No particular category of traffic can be held economically responsible for any given share of the unallocable costs. Whether any particular rate is above or below some fully distributed cost is without real economic significance for minimum pricing.

Stated differently, the appropriate aim of the railroads is to determine that margin above incremental costs, traffic volume considered, at which a rate produces the maximum total contribution toward fixed costs and net income. Fully distributed costs cannot serve this vital economic purpose. They present an entirely false picture of traffic profitability. Their use would drive away great quantities of profitable, volume-moving traffic now handled at rates below fully distributed costs.

Another misconception is the view that if some railroad rates are below fully distributed costs a burden is imposed on other traffic which must pay more to make up the "deficiency." But, when the true significance of unallocable costs is understood, it becomes apparent that a particular rate which maximizes the contribution to such costs over and above the relevant incremental costs cannot possibly burden other traffic even though rates on the latter may be higher. If such contributions from lower-paying traffic were lost because of unattractive rates, railroad earnings and expenditures for improvements would suffer, and the ability to provide good service would be impaired. Traffic which is not moved cannot possibly help to bear the unallocable costs. It is the fully distributed cost doctrine which, by pegging minimum rates on a false economic premise, would burden not only railroad shippers but the economy as a whole and would tend to bankrupt the railroad system by artifically restricting the economic use of railroad facilities and services.

Especially in competitive industries, no cost system can really assure that all costs will be covered and a "normal" profit earned, for sales volume will play a significant role. If guaranteed coverage of all costs and a normal profit are the objectives of fully distributed cost pricing, it cannot succeed. For that matter, neither can pricing based on relevant incremental costs plus a maximum contribution to fixed costs and net income, as determined by conditions of market demand, provide such a guarantee. But if these contributions are maximized throughout the pricing structure, the best result has been achieved and no further improvement is possible under prevailing market conditions.

Thus, the fully distributed cost doctrine does not reflect valid principles of pricing, where fixed costs are significant. Application of this false criterion in the railroads' present competitive environment would bring about prices which (for much traffic) would shrink volume. If the same total constant costs were then distributed on the shrunken traffic volume, even greater fully distributed unit costs would result, and if this should cause the railroads to raise rates still higher relative to the price of other modes of transport, then rail traffic volume would probably be still further reduced. A costing procedure which can inaugurate such a destructive cost-price spiral is not qualified to serve as a basis for pricing in the railroad business or in any other with unallocable costs and unused capacity.

The social costs of such a pricing method could be enormous. The railroads could not function economically and quite possibly could not survive the use of this misguided basis of pricing. Under it, much traffic either would not move at all or would be moved only by modes of transportation with higher actual economic costs. The end result would be a greater total transportation cost borne by the whole economy in return for a reduced total volume of transportation service.

"Full cost of low-cost carrier" also a false standard

An offshoot of the fully distributed cost fallacy is the contention that rail rates should not be permitted to go below the "full cost of the low-cost carrier" (such carrier being determined on the basis of comparative fully distributed cost), whether it be that of a railroad or a different mode of transport. This contention, also, has no validity as a measure of "inherent advantage" or relative economy in the utilization of economic resources of the nation. For the reasons pointed out above, the low-cost carrier is properly identified by incremental cost, not by so-called "full" cost.

Only a railroad's own incremental costs are of any significance as a guide in establishing its minimum rates; and this same principle applies as well to other modes of transport and other industries. Imposing a different and higher *cost* standard deprives railroads of traffic which they can transport more economically, artificially stimulates the growth of uneconomic transportation by other means including private transportation, deprives the shipping public of the benefits of low-cost service, and imposes higher commodity prices on the consuming public. However computed, the use of fully distributed costs would be wasteful of economic resources by misdirecting their use and by keeping them idle or underutilized.

In addition to its inherent defect, this specious "cost" proposal has another deficiency. To whatever extent carriers which operate on public facilities may not have to meet full economic costs in conducting their business, their "fully distributed costs" are not consistent with those computed for the railroads. For the railroads a fully distributed cost computation embraces the entire costs. The effect of the use of the "full cost of the low-cost carrier" doctrine is to obstruct the railroads in pricing their services in competition with other modes to the extent that they may be subsidized. Thus, this proposal constitutes umbrella rate-making to protect any subsidized modes of transportation from legitimate competition by the railroads.

Summary

1. In the determination of cost floors as a guide to the pricing of particular railroad services, or the services of any other transport mode, incremental costs of each particular service are the only relevant costs.

2. Rates for particular railroad services should be set at such amounts (subject to regulation of maximum rates and to legal rules against unjust discrimination) as will make the greatest total contribution to net income. Clearly, such maximizing rates would never fall below incremental costs.

3. Pricing which is not restricted by any minimum other than incremental cost can foster more efficient use of railroad resources and capacity and can therefore encourage lower costs and rates. This same principle applies to other modes of transportation.

4. The presence of large amounts of fixed costs and unused capacity in railroad facilities makes it especially important that railroad rates encourage a large volume of traffic.

5. Reduced rates which more than cover incremental costs and are designed by management to maximize contribution to net income do not constitute proof of predatory competition.

6. "Fully distributed" costs derived by apportioning unallocable costs have no economic significance in determining rate floors for particular railroad services. The application of such a criterion would arbitrarily force the railroads to maintain rates above the level which would yield maximum contribution to net income and would deprive them of much traffic for which they can compete economically. For similar reasons, restriction of railroad minimum rates according to the "full cost of the low-cost carrier" is economically unsound.

NOTES

1. Social costs which are escaped by the enterprise must also be included in the calculation.

2. In addition to those costs which vary with rate of output for a given investment level, incremental costs include cost increments associated with new investment. For example, if special equipment is acquired in order to handle certain additional traffic, the costs are incremental to that traffic.

3. More specifically, the decision is governed by such revenue dimensions as the nature and amount of the contemplated change in volume, the length of the commitment to carry the traffic, the duration and geographic scope of the changed rate, the alterations of the service that might require added investments, and the time period in which changes may legally or practically take place.

4. The relevant incremental costs are a function principally of the prospective volume in relation to present volume and unutilized capacity in existing plant and organization. The rate over time at which the prospective volume is likely to be achieved, the prospects for its continuance over the longer term, and its distribution over stated time periods (for example, seasonality and peaking characteristics) are all relevant to the determination of appropriate incremental costs. From consideration of the prospective volume and its characteristics it may be feasible to estimate those elements of plant and organization which will require ultimate replacement, allowances for the use of which should figure currently in costs. If volume promises to build up substantially over time, the likelihood and cost of the required expansion in capacity must be recognized in the computation of the price floor.

5. The application of this principle in particular situations may require special care in estimating the pertinent incremental costs and incremental revenue. Especially in the short run they may be different from what they superficially appear. Example: the hidden incremental costs of dismissing and later reassembling a key work-force; and the hidden, foregone incremental revenue that may result in losing a profitable customer by refusing to take an occasional order below incremental cost.

6. The railroads also are subject to the limitation of a reasonable over-all "return," but this regulatory limitation has not for many years of low earnings been a matter of real concern. If excessive profits were ever achieved, it would be the lawful responsibility of the regulatory authorities to apply the appropriate restraints.

---

43   The Case for Full Cost Ratemaking

Roy J. Sampson
University of Oregon

This selection analyzes further the "what cost" problem. Its author disagrees, in part, with the authors of the previous selection and argues for a special type of full cost in ratemaking.

The controversy between advocates of so-called full cost and incremental cost pricing of transportation services is of great practical and theoretical significance. The transportation industry itself is divided on this controversy, to some extent

From Roy J. Sampson, "The Case for Full Cost Ratemaking," *I.C.C. Practitioners' Journal*, March 1966, pp. 490-495. Copyright held by Association of Interstate Commerce Commission Practitioners. Used by permission.

along modal lines. Economists in general favor incremental cost pricing. Those economists favoring full cost pricing, therefore, are more likely to receive brick-bats than bouquets from their fellow professionals, and to be accused of partisanship for some mode of transport by some other mode.

Full cost, or fully distributed cost, as used herein, refers to the total of all direct or variable costs associated with the output of any particular transport service, *plus* all indirect or fixed costs to be incurred *in the future* as a result of the continuation of the service (including as an indirect cost whatever "profits" are necessary to retain or attract the capital necessary for continuing the service). Also, for those carriers using publicly supplied facilities, full cost would necessarily include a so-called user charge at least sufficient to recoup future public expenditures for these facilities. User charges, however, are a different topic, and thus, to avoid unduly complicating the present discussion, will be arbitrarily excluded from consideration here.

Note that so-called sunk investments, or fixed costs arising from already-made investments, are not included as a part of this definition of full cost. There is no economic necessity for recovering past expenditures, except that failure to do so may make it more difficult or expensive to raise necessary funds in the future. The pertinent investment cost to be recovered is the *replacement* cost of the facilities necessary to carry on the business rather than the original cost of presently-used facilities. The pertinent fixed costs, then, are those which will enable replacement of facilities to be made if, as, and when needed—or which, in the language of the U.S. Supreme Court in the *Hope Natural Gas Case,* will enable a firm "to maintain its financial integrity."

Incremental costs, sometimes referred to as out-of-pocket costs, added-traffic costs, or marginal costs, may be defined in various ways. The Interstate Commerce Commission, for example, has described these costs as "the costs which could have been avoided if the traffic were not handled." The Doyle Report has referred to them as "the added cost of producing an additional unit of service neglecting all fixed costs and indirect costs which cannot be specifically attributed as being incurred because of the extra unit of production." Economists generally define marginal costs as that additional cost necessary to produce an additional output. These different definitions all are various ways of saying the same thing. Rather than getting bogged down in terminology, therefore, we may consider that incremental cost, as used here, is any cost less than full cost as that term has been defined above.

To consider pricing policies or systems in a rational manner, it is necessary to understand that there is nothing sacred, or "right" or "wrong" as such about any pricing policy or system. Price policies are made by particular individuals or groups of individuals (as owners, corporate managers, regulators) attempting to use pricing as a tool in achieving particular objectives. Prices, and objectives, are established within a particular economic and philosophical environment. The economic environment may be pure competition, monopolistic competition, pure or differentiated oligopoly, monopoly, government regulation, inflation, depression, a growing or declining industry, or some combination of these and other factors. The philosophical environment may vary from the "just price" of Medieval times to the "profit-maximizing" price of Adam Smith's "economic man" or to Karl Marx's philosophy of "To each according to his need." The proper or "right" price tool to be used, then, depends upon the environment and the objectives sought.

We may properly ask, then, (1) What is the nature of our present transportation environment?; (2) What are our transportation objectives?; and (3) How do the alternate pricing policies under consideration here fit into the present environment and objectives? In answering these questions, a brief review of the history of transport pricing, especially railroad pricing, is in order.

Incremental cost pricing in transportation, whatever its first origin, has long been used by the railroad industry. This industry has the necessary permissible characteristics for such pricing; that is, it has a large sunk investment, substantial fixed or indirect costs, long-lived capital assets, and often short-term excess capacity (at least in some of its resources).

During the era of almost complete dominance of railroads in long-haul inland transport, roughly from the Civil War until the Post-World-War I period, incremental cost pricing and its companion value-of-service pricing became almost articles of faith for railroad managers and transportation economists. The railroad industry, like industry in general, was expanding rapidly. There was little or no effective intermodal long-haul transport competition. Low incremental cost rates on low-valued goods allowed such goods to move freely, while rates considerably higher than full costs could be levied against other goods. Although some persons objected to the principle of charging what the traffic will bear, or at least to that portion of the principle which led to higher rates on some commodities than appeared justified by particular costs, it would be difficult to establish that the system's disadvantages during that period outweighed its advantages.

Today, however, the transportation environment is different. New technology has brought keen intermodal for-hire competition to the transportation industry, and even permits the alternative of private transport. Value-of-service, therefore, has a lower ceiling than it formerly had under non-competitive conditions. Carriers no longer have such golden opportunities to recoup the differences between full cost pricing and incremental cost pricing on portions of their traffic by charging prices considerably higher than full costs on other portions. Value-of-service pricing, formerly a railroad monopolistic tool, now has been turned against the rails.

Now for the objectives. Almost everyone is interested in a free private-enterprise competitive profits-motivated economy, including the transportation portion of the economy. But what do we want specifically from transportation?

The primary social objective of transportation is *not* necessarily to move the greatest volume of traffic, or to move traffic by an particular mode, or to move any particular traffic between any given points, or to preserve any carrier or mode. Rather, the objective is to make the most efficient use of our limited available resources in satisfying our wants. This means that the costs of using transportation resources, or any resources for that matter, must be measured against the benefits received. That is, we must look for the most favorable overall cost-benefit ratio. We cannot obtain the most favorable cost-benefit ratio, and cannot efficiently allocate resources between various transport modes, or between transport and non-transport uses, by measuring benefits against costs, some of which are higher and some of which are lower than full costs, or against costs which are varying percentages of full costs.

What are the ultimate effects of incremental cost pricing in the context of our environment and objective?

No elaborate economic reasoning is necessary to demonstrate that any privately owned business must at least recover its full costs on its aggregate business if it is to continue long-term operations. The alternatives are bankruptcy or some form of subsidy or government ownership. Likewise, simple arithmetic indicates that if a business does not recover full costs on some portion of its sales, it must recover *more* than its full costs on some other portions if it is to continue in long-term unsubsidized private operation. Further, if it is correct that for competitive or other reasons carriers cannot charge prices *above* full costs on some portions of their traffic, they cannot charge prices *less* than full costs on some other portions if they are to continue in their present form of ownership and operation.

If one agrees, therefore, that today's alternate transport opportunities or competitive factors do effectively prohibit most carriers from pricing some of their services higher than full costs, one cannot advocate incremental cost pricing without at the same time advocating long-term carrier bankruptcy, subsidization, or government ownership. Even if one believes that value-of-service pricing will permit some carriers to charge considerably more than full costs on some substantial portion of their traffic, one cannot advocate incremental cost pricing without also advocating that those users of carrier services who are so unfortunate as to have no competitive alternatives be forced to subsidize those more fortunate users who do not have to pay for the full costs of their services.

In addition, incremental cost pricing by one mode of carriage does have an economic effect upon competing modes, and thus upon resource allocation in the economy as a whole. The nature of this effect is so obvious that no discussion of this point is necessary. How one feels about the result, however, will be determined by one's ethical or philosophical concepts, just as will one's attitude toward government ownership, governmental subsidy, or subsidy of one group of users by another group.

To summarize, aside from the effects of incremental cost pricing upon competitors and whatever this involves for allocation and efficiency in the economy as a whole, this pricing system is not economically sound as a long-term policy even from the individual carrier's viewpoint unless (1) the carrier is willing to accept government ownership, subsidy, or eventual bankruptcy, or unless (2) the carrier is willing to admit that it actually does retain enough monopoly power over some portion of its traffic that it can force this traffic to pay more than its full cost of movement in order that traffic not subject to such monopoly can move at less than its full cost of movement. It is difficult to reconcile either of these situations with the concept of a free-enterprise competitive economy.

Various arguments have been used against full cost pricing. Every elementary economics textbook correctly affirms that profits are maximized or losses minimized at the point where marginal cost equals marginal price; that is, that it pays a firm to seek new business on an incremental cost basis. No economist would dispute this as a short-term proposition. If a firm has excess capacity, certainly any use of this capacity which covers the direct costs of its use and contributes something to overhead is preferable to non-use. This, however, is strictly a short-term proposition.

The catch to incremental cost pricing insofar as regulated for-hire transportation is concerned is that traffic cannot be turned off and on to fit into varying short-term capacities, nor can prices be readily adjusted as the ratio of incremental costs to full costs changes. Once a particular movement is attracted to a common carrier at a certain rate, for example, the common carrier obligation to serve, government regulation, and economic stability in the shipping industry or region concerned may require that the carrier continue to handle this traffic at rates not drastically higher than the original incremental cost rates. But eventually long-term forces take over.

The carrier capacity being used to move goods at incremental cost prices eventually must be replaced, but at *full* costs to the carrier. Suppliers of transportation capital equipment will not reduce their own selling prices to an incremental cost level merely because a carrier is stuck with low rates. In effect, carriers must replace expired capacity at full cost even though their return on its use has been and will continue to be at a lower incremental cost pricing level. This factor, combined with the inability to recoup incremental cost pricing losses through high value-of-service pricing, has contributed substantially to carrier financial problems, especially railroad problems during recent years. Strictly short-term pricing policies, even though attractive during periods of temporary excess capacity, do not necessarily make economic sense for regulated carriers in the long-term. Unfortunately, the long-term has caught up with some carriers.

Perhaps the most persuasive economic argument in favor of incremental cost pricing is that the carriage of low value-of-service traffic at rates which cover direct costs and produce at least some revenue contributions to fixed costs may allow other traffic to move at lower rates than would otherwise be charged. This may be true, although substantiation might be difficult in view of ratemaking techniques and carrier profit motivations. But, even if true, this does not reduce the real costs of carrying the allegedly benefiting traffic; instead, it merely disguises and perpetuates inefficient resource allocation rather than eliminating it. Particular traffic movements which cannot occur without a contribution from other incrementally priced traffic, from the viewpoint of economic efficiency, should move by some other lower-cost mode or not at all.

It is often said that the full costs of a particular movement or type of traffic cannot be determined due to the unallocable nature of joint and common costs. The specific allocation of costs, however, falls into the realm of the cost accountant or the engineer rather than that of the economist. If economists and traffic experts can give accountants and engineers proper concepts to work with, at least they may be able to do a much better job of cost allocation than is now being done. If we can induce electronic computors to tell us how to put a man on the moon, cannot we induce them to tell us the approximate full costs of shipping a batch of widgets from A to B?

It is possible too, of course, that true common or joint costs may be a much lower proportion of full costs of transportation than is commonly thought. Further, it should be noted that common and joint costs are not unique to the transportation industry; instead, almost every major industry or firm has similar if not greater elements of commonness and jointness. Certainly no economist would argue that true common or joint costs can be allocated on any economically scientific basis, but neither would any knowledgeable person argue that practicable and workable allocations are not made constantly in all industries, including transportation. For that matter, incremental costs probably can seldom be perfectly ascertained either. Perfection in cost allocation, or in anything else, may not be completely attainable, but this does not mean that we should not try to achieve it.

In conclusion, then, in considering alternate competitive carriers from the viewpoint of economic efficiency, long-term efficiency is best measured by comparing alternative full costs. This concept is equally essential for long-term economic resource allocation and for long-term survival of particular modes and firms. Applied to the question of incremental cost versus full cost ratemaking, it supports the latter. Anything less is economically unreasonable, even if not legally so.

Certainly full cost pricing can never be perfect, and its immediate application to all transport services might be highly disruptive to established patterns of traffic movement and industrial location. Our goal, however, should be to work gradually toward such a pricing system. The first step in that direction would be for carriers not to undertake any additional substantial and permanent traffic obligations on an incremental cost basis.

As long as substantial excess transportation capacity exists, long-term optimization over short-term expediency will be painful and difficult to sell. Full cost ratemaking will meet strong practical and theoretical opposition. But in the long-term full cost pricing will be in the best interests of the transportation industry itself, including *all* its modes, as well as the interest of the shipping public and the overall economy. The present road of incremental cost pricing can only lead to even greater chaos in the realm of transportation rates.

44   Competitive Pricing in Railroad Freight Rates

Joel Dean
Joel Dean Associates, Inc.
Columbia University

This selection on transport pricing discusses pricing in railroads—and in other modes too. Its point of view is different from those of the two previous articles, being at once more general and more applied. Mr. Dean, let us note, is also one of the ten authors of Selection 42.

During the past twenty years the railroads' share of intercity freight traffic has declined from more than two-thirds to about one-third. Most of the lost business is now carried by trucks. Why is this?

The four factors

Four major factors have contributed to the truckers' success in taking traffic away from the railroads:

1. Decentralization of economic activity.
2. Improvements in trucking efficiency relative to railroads.
3. Inattention to service by railroads.
4. Faulty railroad pricing.

Decentralization of economic activity

The decentralization of economic activity, partly to eliminate long transport hauls, has resulted in permanent loss of some rail traffic. Growing regional markets and modern profit-center management techniques are likely to foster further decentralization, which will hurt rails more than trucks.

Despite the fact that rail costs are frequently lower than truck costs even down to hauls shorter than 100 miles, as transport distance shrinks the cost differential narrows and the importance of better truck service looms larger.

Improvements in trucking efficiency

In the long run, freight traffic will inevitably gravitate to the mode of transport that serves shippers' needs most economically. Efficiency advances during the past several decades have been more rapid in the trucking than in the railroad industry.

From the *Transportation Journal,* Spring 1962, quarterly publication of the American Society of Traffic and Transportation, Inc. Used by permission.

Much of the relative improvement in trucking costs was due to extension of the highway system by new and greatly improved construction techniques, and to development of larger, faster, more efficient trucks. However, the era of most rapid improvement in trucking technology seems behind us. Although the Federal Highway Program will permit further increase in average truck weights and speeds, the resulting rate of reduction of costs and delivery time will be much slower than in the past. From now on, efficiency improvements due to new railroad technology (piggy back, for example) should match improvements by truckers. In short, trucking is now a mature mode of transportation.

Truckers also have outstripped railroads importantly in the area of labor costs per hour of effective work. While much of the improvement in speed and weight of freight trains has been dissipated by union feather-bedding, truck-driver demands were policed by competition from owner-drivers, always ready and anxious to take over.

Inattention to service by railroads

Railroads have often been accused of neglecting their customers' service needs. Railroad operating management today is taking belated but important steps to speed up and regularize service, to keep customers better informed on the whereabouts of their goods, to provide specialized equipment suited to the needs of important shippers, and generally to tailor railroad service to meet the traffic flow requirements of customers. But in many instances railroads probably should not try to match truckers' service fully.

Elimination of the service inferiority should be attempted only when service improvement is clearly worth more to a shipper than such improvement costs the railroad. However, the railroads' financial management can and should provide better guides than are now available about the economic value to shippers of various aspects of service, such as speed, reliability, and convenience.

Faulty railroad pricing

Four factors account for the declining railroad share of total freight business: relatively rapid improvement in trucking efficiency; decentralization of economic activity; poor service; and faulty pricing.

The fact that railroads have any profitable traffic left is a real tribute to the inherent efficiency of this form of transport. Several characteristics of the rail rate structure push traffic into truckers' hands: (1) many unrealistically high rates: (2) rates higher for high-value commodities than for low-value commodities; (3) inadequate incentives for heavy loading; (4) excessive discounts for long hauls.

Unrealistically high rates

Most class rates, and many related exception rates, are so far above trucking costs as to move virtually no traffic. The aggregate transport volume of items now classified only under these "paper" rates is very substantial. Virtually all of this traffic has been diverted from the rails to the trucks by non-competitive pricing, without opportunity for relative costs of the two modes of transport to exert any influence at all.

Rates related to value of commodities

The railroads' heritage from past monopoly power is a rate structure characterized by a higher railroad freight rate for commodities with high value per pound than for commodities of lower per pound value.

If the value of commodities should be recognized by the rate structure at all, exactly the opposite treatment would be most effective in competition with trucks. This is because trucks reduce the time merchandise is tied up in transit. The higher the value of the merchandise, the larger is the inventory cost saving from fast delivery. Hence, to compensate for the railroads' slower and more erratic service, rail rates per hundred pounds should be lower relative to trucks on high-value than low-value commodities.

"Across-the board" postwar price increases aggravated the distortion between high-value and low-value commodities. On balance, the rate increases were greater for previously high-rated than for previously low-rated commodities, even though during this period truckers increased their service superiority over the railroads. There has been no cost justification for this widened commodity-value disparity in rates, because cost changes have been unrelated to the value of commodity carried. Thus, rail freight rates were set further below truck costs on bulky low-value commodities for which truckers have never competed, while rail rates have increased relative to truck costs on high-value commodities for which trucks were already most competitive.

Inadequate incentives for heavy loading

The railroads' greatest comparative advantage is on shipments too heavy or bulky to fit in a single truck van. Yet the typical tariff throws away this advantage by charging the minimum average rate per hundred-weight for a "carload" which is roughly the same size as a truckload.

At most, the shipper is offered one or two alternative minimums, which encourage loading at such minimums but not beyond. The railroads could increase their profit even on the traffic they already carry, by sharing with shippers in the form of continuous incentives the cost savings of heavier loading per car and of multiple-car shipments.

Excessive discounts for long hauls

Existing tariffs usually allow discounts per ton-mile on longer hauls which exceed the distance cost-saving to the railroads. This pattern of pricing tends to increase the rail rate relative to trucks on short hauls, thereby increasing the length of haul for which trucks can compete successfully.

Costs and competition in railroad pricing

Why should such obvious errors in competitive pricing persist? One reason is the appalling complexity of the existing railroad rate structure, which hides the effects of the rate characteristics. A more important reason is that the existing rate structure was not built up under today's competitive conditions. Most of the rate structure is a carry-over from an era when truck competition was nonexistent or unimportant.

All profitable freight rates are set between two limits. The lower limit is the railroad's cost of providing the service. The upper limit is the cost to shippers of equivalent service from some alternative mode of transport.

This does not mean that financial analysts are able to make rate decisions. In those cases in which the pricing decision will have greatest impact on earnings, there is considerable room for discretion and judgment between the floor and the ceiling. In all cases, the purpose of an estimate of the floor and the ceiling is to orient the rate-maker. Knowledge of the ceiling helps him to anticipate the effect of a proposed rate change on the volume of traffic. Knowledge of the floor is needed to compute the contribution profit from any proposed rate change in conjunction with the traffic change anticipated therefrom.

Costs that set the rate ceiling

The ceiling on a railroad rate that will move traffic is the shippers' cost of obtaining equivalent service from another mode of transport. This opportunity-cost rule has universal application in the railroad industry, because, even in the case of commodities and routes where no other public carrier operates, any substantial shipper has the alternative of providing his own trucking.

For many years most railroads did not feel much pricing restraint, because their ceiling was very high. This was because alternative modes of transport were poor substitutes for rail transport, and because price competition within the railroad industry has been effectively restrained by rate bureaus and government regulation. Hence, customers' alternatives took the form of not shipping or not producing the commodity. But the development of highway networks destroyed this early railroad monopoly position.

Transport alternatives available to shippers differ in two dimensions—price and service. To be competitive, railroad rates must take account of both.

Costs that determine the price of truck transport

The rate ceiling set by alternative transport is established by the costs of an efficient truck operation. The fact that truckers now competing on any given route may have higher than optimum costs does not matter; truckers' costs will be driven to an efficient level promptly by other truckers. Nor should any attention be given to the published rates of truck common carriers. If these rates are materially higher than trucking costs, shippers always have the alternative of providing their own trucks.

The important factors determining optimum trucking costs per ton-mile for any given traffic are:

a. Mileage utilization of equipment and empty return ratio.

b. State highway weight limits, or weight of a full truck load if restricted by light density of the commodity.
c. Length of haul (measured by road—not rail—mileage).
d. Degree of metropolitan concentration and other terminal characteristics.
e. Type of equipment required.

Conspicuous by its absence from this list is any mention of the value or other characteristics of the commodity carried, aside from its density and form (which may influence weight per truck load and equipment requirements). To convert data on the preceding five factors into an estimate of the trucking cost relevant to a specific railroad rate-making decision calls for specialized analysis.

Costs that determine value to shippers of the service differential

To specify accurately the ceiling rate at which traffic will move over the rails, we must know the value to shippers of any enduring service disparity between truck and railroad. In most (but not all) cases, railroad service is inferior to trucking service. Railroads should either eliminate the service inferiority, or make allowance for it in their rates. It is often not possible or desirable to provide rail service identical with truck service. Hence, rail rates must usually make concessions for a service disparity, and rate-makers need the best estimate they can get of the dollar value of this disparity to the shipper.

The service disparity between railroad and truck is made up of two parts: (1) differentials in loading cost, drayage, breakage, and other direct costs to the shipper; and (2) differential transit time, including not only a longer average time in transit for rails but greater unreliability in railroad delivery time.

The first part of the service disparity, differential direct costs incurred by shippers, usually can be estimated satisfactorily by careful evaluation of facts obtained from interviews with shippers' and receivers' traffic managers. The second part, translating differential transit time and uncertainty into dollar value to the shipper, requires more imaginative analysis and considerable judgment. This value is determined primarily by the investment in the shipment, the cost-of-capital to the receiver and/or shipper, and how the commodity fits into the receiver's production process.

Costs that set the rate floor

The rate floor is not a level to which rates should be permitted to fall, but rather a base above which revenue contributions should be maximized. One can easily get agreement that this floor should be the rails' cost of carrying freight, but agreement often ends when one tries to define the appropriate concept of cost. Proponents can be found for everything from ICC "fully distributed" cost to the obvious avoidable cost of the particular haul. Many misunderstandings arise out of attempts to use a single cost concept to serve several disparate purposes, and one of the hardest lessons for most sale managers to learn is that there is no such thing as the cost.

And there really is no such thing as the incremental cost—even for commodities of the same form and density. The relevant incremental cost for a particular rate decision depends, for example, upon the duration of the commitment to carry traffic. For temporary or reversible pricing decisions that utilize otherwise idle capacity, the rate floor need include only the added direct line-haul and terminal costs and the physical wear and tear on rolling stock and facilities.

In the more common case, due to contractual or political inflexibility, commitments to carry freight at a given rate are long lasting. Hence, the appropriate measure of the rate floor is usually long-run incremental cost, which must include an allowance for the eventual expansion of capacity if existing capacity will be inadequate. In addition, the relevant incremental cost varies not only with duration of the traffic commitment but also with a particular rate's geographic scope, because incremental cost of carrying the same load for the same distance can vary widely from one road to another.

In the past, the ICC has placed road-blocks in the paths of railroads when they tried to base rates upon the principle of maximizing contribution profit over incremental cost. However, measuring contribution from a rate floor set by incremental cost not only maximizes railroad earnings, but also usually brings about the most efficient use of economic resources devoted to transport.

Pricing between the ceiling and the floor

Wherever there is room for discretionary pricing between the rate ceiling and floor—as there almost always is for some length of haul and some weight of shipment—the objective should be to set rates that will maximize total dollar contribution over incremental cost. This objective is often served by a rate structure going below that needed to merely undercut costs of alternative modes of transport.

Such opportunities arise under two kinds of circumstance. The first is when rates can be set which give shippers incentives to change their utilization of railroad equipment in a way which reduces the railroad's cost—for example, incentives for loading cars more fully or for using equipment during off-peak periods. The second is when rates can be set which increase the aggregate amount of traffic (as opposed to increasing the rails' share of the same traffic) because of transport demand highly responsive to rate changes.

Reducing rail costs by increasing utilization of equipment

To provide incentives for heavier loading, freight rates should be a continuously decreasing average charge per ton-mile, all the way to the capacity of the car. Alternate minimum charges do not accomplish this objective, unless there are so many alternative minimums as to approximate a continuous incentive.

The railroads can profitably share with shippers as much of the cost saving from heavier loading as is necessary to induce such heavier loading. Although some shippers may at first be unreceptive to incentives disrupting traditional ways of thinking or threatening to increase competition within the shipper's industry, the economic pressure of greater efficiency will eventually cause most shippers to welcome such incentives.

Special rates or discounts should similarly be allowed for multiple-car shipments, with the average charge per ton-mile decreasing continuously all the way up to a full train.

To even out seasonal peaks and valleys, some sort of standby charge or penalty for peak season use of facilities is essential. Alternatively, off-season discounts can be offered on commodities which utilize seasonally idle facilities.

Increasing the aggregate traffic

Rail rates far below the ceiling of truck costs are needed to move some commodities in volume. The primary consideration in setting rates on such commodities, however, should be maximization of profit—not maximization of traffic flow. There are now many low-rated commodities, especially farm products, carried at rates below the level that would maximize rail profits.

Discounts for long hauls are desirable if the amount of long-haul traffic is highly responsive to railroad freight rates. However, just the fact that long hauls provide railroads with cost savings is not sufficient reason to pass these savings on to the customer. Concessions should be made only when they are expected to increase contribution profits.

Systematic pricing for railroads

These competitive rate making principles are really quite simple, certainly far simpler than the present maze of rates with little rationale. Indeed, a simple comprehensive rate structure that could profitably replace the entire class rate system can be constructed, using as determinants of the charges only (1) form and density of the commodity, (2) weight loaded in the car, (3) length of the haul, and (4) speed and reliability of delivery.

In conjunction with such a simplified basic rate structure, there would be many opportunities to discriminate profitably by selective rate reductions. Once the principles of selective pricing have been thought out, the cost-behavior measurement needed to apply those principles to a large number of separate rate decisions would be no barrier to systematic pricing in this era of electronic computers.

Compared with many industries, the railroads are admirably situated for applying systematic economic analysis to their pricing problems. The service being priced is relatively standardized and has only a small number of close substitutes. Competitive reactions of the most important substitute, trucking service, are highly predictable. Competitive reactions among railroads are restrained by a long-standing tradition of pricing co-operation. Finally, a wealth of relevant statistical data is available for forecasting cost behavior.

In this speech, an outstanding regulatory commissioner discusses, from an applied viewpoint, transportation costs and their uses. The student will gain an appreciation of the difficult role of the administrative commission and an appreciation too of the practical application of economic concepts.

The importance of transportation to the national economy is well understood by the general public. The importance of rate regulation to the economy of the transportation industry and hence to the well-being of the general public is not so well understood. All too often rate regulation is held by the general public to be synonymous with higher charges. Little consideration is given to the fact that the principal statutory standards of lawfulness of rates, fares, and charges prescribed by Congress and administered by the Commission are designed to protect the general public. Rates must be just and reasonable, they must not create any unjust discrimination, undue preference, or undue prejudice and they must be published so that all may ascertain what they are.

It may be said that the ultimate objective of the existing body of regulatory law is to develop, coordinate, and preserve a national transportation system under private ownership and operation capable of meeting the expanding needs of the commerce of the country, of the postal service and of the national defense, with the general burden of expense or cost necessary to support such a system fairly and reasonably distributed among all the users of the services. The attainment of these objectives is the real problem of rate regulation entrusted to the Interstate Commerce Commission.

Rates are established by the carriers in the first instance. Consequently, rate-making always has been, and no doubt always will be, a process depending largely upon the exercise of judgment by the carriers. However, in the exercise of this judgment, carriers are subject to the overriding authority of the Commission to prevent the maintenance of any rates that are in any way unlawful. As times change so also do the considerations which guide carriers and the Commission in making rates.

Before competition between modes of carriage became vigorous, rates were made largely on a theory of value of service. Often it was said that rates were based on what the traffic would bear. These methods were followed and subscribed to by carriers, shippers, and regulatory bodies alike, and were regarded by students of transportation as proper and in the public interest. Since the

From Howard Freas, "Rate Regulation Today," *I.C.C. Practitioners' Journal,* June 1966, pp. 777-782. Copyright held by Association of Interstate Commerce Commission Practitioners. Used by permission.

primary concern at that time was with maximum reasonable rates, there was little urgency for the development of transportation costs. With the growth of extensive and intense competition, the cost of rendering a particular service has become of vital importance. This called for the change in emphasis which has occurred gradually in the application of principles of ratemaking. Today in competitive ratemaking carriers consider costs in order that they may hold or secure competitive business on a profitable basis and this Commission considers them in order that destructive competition may be avoided and the advantages of low-cost transportation may be realized by the public. As interagency competition has intensified, the Commission has allowed greater latitude to the managerial discretion of carriers in competitive ratemaking—particularly that involving different modes of transportation.

Because of the growing importance of transportation costs in carrier ratemaking, there is great need for determination of accurate formulae for their ascertainment. In 1939 the Commission formally organized a separate section to deal with this matter. Since then, methods have been improved and the use of costs has become the foundation of transportation pricing. Among the instances in which such data have been useful are the following:

1. To determine if rates are compensatory,
2. To determine if they are excessive,
3. To determine if they are unduly prejudicial,
4. To ascertain the most economical mode of transportation,
5. To determine fairness of divisions of joint rates, and
6. To disclose the extent of passenger deficits.

With regard to compensativeness it is now well settled that a rate, to be found reasonably compensatory, must ordinarily exceed out-of-pocket costs and make a contribution to the transportation burden. The maintenance of rates below out-of-pocket costs normally constitutes an unjust and unreasonable practice and casts an unfair burden on other traffic, usually bringing about unfair and destructive competition and fostering unsound conditions in the transportation industry. Failure of the carriers to produce evidence sufficient to show that proposed reduced rates are compensatory is one of the most frequent reasons for the Commission's disapproval.

However, it should be noted that even a rate returning more than out-of-pocket costs is not necessarily reasonably compensatory. If it is not required by the needs of commerce or compelled by competitive necessity, it is not reasonably compensatory unless it bears its share of the transportation burden. If all rates were permitted as a matter of course to fall to a level barely above the out-of-pocket level, the financial deterioration of the carriers in contravention of the National Transportation Policy would result. Full costs plus a reasonable profit must be returned in the aggregate if the transportation industry is to meet the needs of commerce and the national defense.

Clearly, fully distributed as well as out-of-pocket costs have their proper place in ratemaking. Where issues of intermodal competition are involved, full costs should be the test in determining the most economical mode of transportation. This does not mean, however, that all rates should return full costs under all circumstances.

The important role of costs in ratemaking is illustrated by the increasing number of suspension cases in which data are provided by the Cost Section. In 1949, that Section provided the Board of Suspension with costs in only 472 cases. By 1963, this number had increased to 2,879 and in fiscal 1965 to more than 3,000. In spite of the number of cases which come before the Suspension Board, there are relatively few instances where the proponents offer costs which can be used in evaluating the reasonableness of the proposed rates.

Some rates disclose almost on sight that they are unreasonable. We have had cases in which the one-way line-haul cost alone approximates twice the total revenue yield. Sometimes this occurs because the carriers do not know the cost of performing a particular service. In other instances noncompensatory rates have been published to satisfy shippers—the carriers have frankly admitted that they hoped for suspension.

The problem of obtaining adequate data is not limited to the suspension level. The Commission constantly strives to find ways to secure better evidence in contested rate cases. Many cases go to formal hearing before the Commission either without any costs or with data which do not adequately reflect the transportation characteristics of the traffic involved.

I might mention here two types of evidence frequently resorted to by the parties which by themselves are ordinarily of little value in determining compensativeness. The first is system average expense per vehicle- or car-mile. This figure is obtained by dividing total expenses by the total intercity vehicle-miles operated. The parties then compare the resulting expense per vehicle-mile with the revenue per vehicle-mile produced by the proposed rate at the proposed minimum weight. This method assumes that all expenses are caused by miles operated. However, in addition to distance there are many other factors which affect costs. Weight of shipment, density, terminal services performed, whether the traffic is single-line or interline, special services such as refrigeration—all these factors must be considered in designing rates that will produce adequate revenues for carriers handling a wide variety of commodities in different quantities.

The second type is based on the added-traffic theory. Some carriers faced with the prospect of an empty vehicle coming back to the terminal feel that any revenue they can get will be profit. Rates based on this theory almost invariably ignore joint costs. In motor carriage consideration is at times limited to loading and unloading expense and to the extra expense of fuel required in returning the equipment loaded rather than empty.

Making rates on the back-haul principle has ordinarily been condemned, not only because it is to the disadvantage of particular competing carriers, but because public interest requires a broader approach. Public interest is not determined by the financial welfare of a particular carrier, but by the adequacy of over-all service. It presumes an adequate, stable, and dependable transportation service for the people generally. While reduced back-haul rates may be of benefit to certain barriers and to shippers they would favor, they are incompatible, in my opinion, with an adequate transportation service. Rates for comparable services should not vary as between shippers solely because one has access to a carrier with an unbalanced load in the right direction whereas the other has not. Probably more important is the fact that unbalanced loads are not always experienced and when they are, one carrier's back-haul may be a competitor's heavy movement.

There are, of course, some carriers and shippers who would like to make rates on the added-traffic theory. If this principle is to be recognized as justification for reduced rates, it should be recognized uniformly. The validity of incremental costs is one of the many questions presently under consideration in Docket No. 34013, *Rules to Govern the Assembling and Presentation of Cost Evidence.* The record in this important case is now closed, and a recommended report and order is being prepared by the hearing examiner. It is to be hoped that this proceeding will produce methods for improving the quality and reducing the quantity of cost evidence.

Useful cost data are developed by the utilization of recognized formulae. Two of the most used are Rail Form A and Highway Form B, issued by our staff. These formulae distribute expenses according to service groups such as line-haul service, switching service, station clerical service, and general overhead. They follow generally accepted accounting and other principles similar to those used in manufacturing and other industries where it is necessary to assign or apportion expenses to products or services. Since this subject will be discussed by a panel, there is no need for me to analyze these formulae in more detail.

One example of our efforts to refine cost data is the institution of probability sampling procedures in Docket No. 34540. Sample plans have been sent to motor carriers and other interested parties, and it appears that the sampling program will be operational in the near future. The proposed plan is advanced as a means of securing better statistical data for developing motor carrier costs. If adopted, it will provide the carriers with more accurate and representative traffic information which, in turn, will provide more reliable data to support general rate proposals. The sampling plan, intended for use in our studies of motor carrier regional costs, is similar to the Deming Plan in which certain carriers are already participating.

Today we accept as commonplace major innovations in ratemaking which but a few years ago were considered revolutionary. Railroads have published trainload, unit train, and piggyback rates which have found wide public acceptance. Motor carriers are also developing new concepts in transportation. Reduced rates are offered through the elimination of such services as loading and unloading. More specialized equipment is being used. Modernization and automation are contributing to coordination and reduction of charges. Yet with all of these improvements two old problems, the governmental subsidy problem and the small shipment problem, remain unsolved.

In my opinion the cost of performing a given service is the true economic cost, no matter by whom it is satisfied. This is not to suggest that, because the Government furnishes a facility, common carriers should not use it. Nor do I mean to imply that carriers should charge rates that would in all instances reflect the true economic cost and pocket the difference between the rates charged and the expense sustained. But it is to say that the charges which these carriers now avoid should be considered in computing their cost for purposes of determining the most economical mode in intermodal competitive situations.

It should be needless to point out that the costs discussed are not the total expense to the Government for providing the facility, but only a proper prorate of so much thereof as is of direct benefit to the favored carrier. How this proper prorated amount is to be determined is a question I am not prepared to detail at this time. It may be that it can be determined by the same formulae now used to determine the share of the expense of maintaining the rail right-of-way that is assigned to out-of-pocket cost. Or conversely it may be determined by omitting from the computation of the non-subsidized carrier factors such as maintenance of right-of-way or taxes on the right-of-way. User charges present another approach to this problem.

User charges are much discussed these days. President Johnson in January of this year in his Fiscal Budget Message to Congress recommended user charges because said charges are

. . . in keeping with the policy that a greater share of the cost of certain programs which provide special benefit or privileges should be borne by identifiable beneficiaries.

He went on, expanding on these remarks, by stating:

In fairness to the taxpayers and to encourage efficient use of government-financed transportation facilities, the substantial benefits received by travelers and shippers from federal expenditures on highways, airways, and waterways should be paid for by the users of these facilities in larger measure than is now the case . . .

The imposition of user charges is for the Congress. If and when reasonable charges are imposed (nominal user charges as suggested by the President's Council of Economic Advisers will not be sufficient), the problem will disappear. Meanwhile, it is beyond the power of the Commission to determine compensativeness as though such charges existed, nor would it be proper to do so. However, it is neither beyond the Commission's power nor inappropriate for it to take this into account in determining the relative economy of two modes of transportation. In fact, I am convinced (and I am speaking only for myself) that it is the Commission's duty to do so in appropriate proceedings. The general public will be better served when the true low-cost carrier is permitted to compete on a fair and equitable basis for the available traffic.

Faced with increasing labor and other costs motor carriers have attempted to increase their charges on small shipments. The Commission has recently disapproved several proposed general increases on such shipments. Although mindful of the fact that shippers require transportation prices which will permit them to remain competitive, the increased rates were not disapproved on this basis. They were disapproved because reliable data relating to cost and revenue needs of the carriers were not presented to justify the proposed increases.

Some motor carriers are attempting to alleviate their problems and at the same time aid the smaller shipper by establishing reduced rates which apply when a shipper tenders a volume quantity of less-than-truck-load shipments at one time. Generally, the reductions are related to reduced cost of performing pickup service. Another innovation is the publication of reduced all-freight proposals at relatively low minima. The Commission has for some years recognized price discounting in cases dealing with large volume movements. I think it likely that both large and smaller volume reduced rate proposals will increase. Sound innovations are beneficial to the public, and the Commission stands ready to encourage any lawful proposals. On the other hand, as competitive pricing looks more and more to volume movements, small and scattered communities as well as carriers with limited operating rights may be adversely affected. These matters present broad questions of public policy. However, it does appear that some progress is being made toward the solution of the so-called "small shipment" problem.

In the face of these problems and the new concepts and developments in the field of ratemaking, we strive to maintain a flexible attitude. No rigid formula can be devised for determining the many problems involved in developing, coordinating, and preserving a sound national transportation system. Under the procedural guidelines set for by Congress, the Commission attempts to meet the practical needs of individual situations from both carrier and shipper standpoints. And in line with this question of practical needs, let me say that we are continuing our efforts to shorten the time involved in the processing of formal cases.

The first Commissioners recognized the importance of transportation when they stated, in 1887, "the regulation of no other business would concern so many or such diversified interests or would affect in so many ways the results of enterprise, the prosperity of commercial and manufacturing ventures, the intellectual and social intercourse of the people, or the general comfort and convenience of the citizen in his every-day life." There have been great changes in the transportation industry since 1887. However, the overall regulatory objective of providing adequately for the Nation's transportation needs has never changed. There is little doubt concerning the healthy condition of our national transportation system today. Total revenues and ton-miles are at an all-time high. I feel that all of us are fortunate to be a part of transportation during this important period of innovation and economic expansion.

Part
Four

Transportation Problems and Issues

Introduction

In an industry as important as transportation, there is no lack of problems and issues. Indeed, they abound. Since our aim in this volume is to complement and supplement textual material, and to do this within a limited space, we have included in Part Four only a sampling of the transportation problem areas (and only a few of many possible articles within each area.) The first of our 10 selections gives a general overview of the transportation system and of its problems and issues in the present decade. The remaining selections take off, in broad categories, from there.

Urban transportation is a multifaceted problem. Solutions to it—both present and proposed—are controversial and far-reaching in their effects. Each passing day, with its time-consuming, energy-dissipating, and frustrating traffic jams calls attention to the blighted central city, "urban sprawl," air pollution, commuter financial responsibility.

Transportation in general is constantly changing, growing, evolving. Although the American transportation system is one of the finest in the world, it is basically a disconnected and uncoordinated one. As we saw in Part One, the five transporation modes are in themselves separate industries. Can they be organized into a single system? If such organization is desirable, how can it be implemented? Is a single "Transportation Company" the answer?

Government's function in transportation has been a subject of debate for many decades. What is the proper government function, given that transportation is the "life-blood" of the economy? To essay an answer to that question, we must consider government's function in the "old days" of transportation, its policies and administrative practices in the present, and its specific changes in approach—for instance, its creation of the Department of Transportation.

The reader should consider Part Four as no more than an introduction to the field of transportation problems and issues—an exciting field which, we hope, the student will pursue further on his own.

Transportation's
Troubled Abundance
Gilbert Burck

*As an overview of the whole area of transportation problems and issues, this
selection does a remarkable job of surveying the many facets of today's transportation world. While the examples are all in terms of 1971, the point remains that
there exists a real transportation conundrum: a hugely abundant transportation
system with equally abundant problems.*

If colossal volume were all that mattered, the American transportation system
would be the envy of the world. During the past twenty years the U.S. has spent
an almost incomprehensible $2.3 trillion moving people and goods around. Last
year alone the figure came to nearly $200 billion, an outlay equivalent to nearly
a fifth of the country's G.N.P., and almost as much as the G.N.P. of Japan. Yet
the U.S. transportation system is mired in trouble. Taken together, *Fortune*'s
fifty largest transportation companies lost money in 1970. While the motorcar
chokes the big cities, transit companies go broke by the dozen. While some
truckers are rolling in money, a great deal of the rail mileage is bankrupt, and
much of the rest is deteriorating physically and financially.

Few domestic problems of our time have been worried over more than the
Transportation Problem. During the past decade thousands of books and pam-
phlets have been dedicated to diagnosing and prescribing for it. Forums of
experts regularly assemble to discharge sagacities on the subject. Every few years
some congressional committee publishes thick volumes defining and discussing
it. Each succeeding Administration in Washington issues some pronouncements
about it. And Congress itself, as crisis follows crisis, solemnly deliberates measures for dealing with the problem. This time, however, something more than
palliatives may lie ahead. The Nixon Administration's program looks like the
boldest and soundest government plan for transportation in a long while. A
special interagency task force worked out a legislative package that among other
things would provide more freedom for new competitors to get trucking, for
railroads to abandon uneconomic facilities, and for all carriers to make their own
rates.

What the automobile wrought

Transportation in the U.S. suffers from overabundance; indeed, it is so abundant
that some of it isn't used efficiently or effectively. To a lopsided degree, automobiles and trucks do the transporting. Of the money Americans spend on

Reprinted from the July 1971 issue of *Fortune magazine* by special permission; © 1971
Time, Inc.

moving people and goods about, 83 percent goes for highway transportation. Of the $109-billion outlay for passenger transportation last year, only $13 billion went to public transport—airlines, buses, trains, and transit lines. In addition, some $2.5 billion went to private planes. Americans spent all the rest, or $93.5 billion, in buying, fueling, cleaning, insuring, repairing, and parking their cars, and providing roads for them.

This overwhelming automotive preference has shaped and colored all of the nation's transportation. Automobile owners' taxes have paid for most of the highways on which commercial trucks and buses roll so swiftly; and the highways and trucks in turn have radically changed the country's industrial geography. Private cars have been a large factor in the decline of the long-distance passenger train, even as they now provide the chief competition for the airliner. And the congestion and air pollution attributable to automobiles are responsible for the revival of interest in mass transportation in big cities and in the densely populated corridors between them.

The great freight cartel

The country's freight service, which cost $87 billion last year, also suffers from badly distributed abundance. If there is one thing critics of U.S. transportation policy agree on, it is that there is a lot of waste in the freight business. There is less agreement on precisely where the waste occurs, and precisely how much it costs. But most economists believe that freight traffic is often allocated uneconomically. Trucks, for example, haul quite a bit that railroads could handle more cheaply, and vice versa. Professor James C. Nelson of Washington State University, a long-time specialist in transportation economics, estimates that the annual cost of misallocation runs to a few billion. What's more, there is a lot of excess capacity. Rail haulage involves large amounts of uneconomic standby facilities. Many of the vehicles adding to traffic congestion are trucks making return trips with little or no freight. Professor George Hilton of U.C.L.A. reckons that rails and trucks use only 50 percent of their capacity. He estimates the annual waste at several billion.

The underlying trouble with the freight business, more and more economists think, is that it is dominated by a great freight cartel, which governs all railroad traffic, about a third of truck traffic, and close to 10 percent of inland-waterway traffic—roughly half the country's intercity ton-miles. A cartel is an association of producers trying to improve profits by fixing prices in collusion, and the U.S. freight cartel, administered by the venerable Interstate Commerce Commission, fits this description. The ICC adjudicates the rates members make, passes on their issues of securities, and controls entry into and exit from the industry. For their part, cartel members must behave as common carriers—they must provide service on demand, assure safe delivery, treat all customers alike, and charge "reasonable" rates. In return they are allowed to get together to make rates. Most still follow the old railroad practice of pricing their product according to the value of service: freight worth more per pound pays more per pound. This, ironically, has been hard on the railroads. Regulated truckers, protected against one another, have continued to take high-value, high-rated freight away from the rails.

How the public pays

The transportation cartel has also been costly to the public. Partly because the cartel is incomplete, leaving out many truckers and most barge lines, there is more competition than cartel members like. Moreover, there is competition within the cartel, between truckers and railroads. Nevertheless, cartel membership makes for waste. In return for their common-carrier franchises, railroads are obliged to maintain unprofitable lines, yards, cattle pens, and other services, and to post money-losing rates to politically powerful shippers. Exempt and private truck carriers, because they often run empty on the return trip, waste a lot of their capacity. Regulated truckers must handle money-losing traffic, and must go back empty rather than solicit traffic at reduced rates.

The cartel setup, moreover, is made to order for the extortions of organized labor. The pioneers in extortion were the railroad brotherhoods, which like all unions in monopolistic industries found it relatively easy to get what they wanted because their employers could easily pass the added costs along to the public in the form of higher rates. The Teamsters Union has learned the lesson. It avoids the kind of featherbedding and the anti-innovation bias that have made the brotherhoods notorious, but it has been merciless in its wage demands. Significantly, the *average* annual earnings of regulated-carrier employees exceed those of all other major industry groups. And that is why the unions are against any change in the status quo.

The freight cartel has also discouraged railroad technology. The ICC is required by law to protect the "inherent" advantages of all forms of transportation. So it has been driven to look on innovation such as unit trains and lower rates for multicar shipments as unfair competition. Just recently the ICC said nay to an arrangement under which the Illinois Central leased entire trains to customers on an extended basis. The ICC has even prevented railroads from making special rates for container shipments.

No wonder, then, that the movement to give carriers more freedom has gathered a good deal of headway. Some reformers would abolish the function of common carriage. Others argue compellingly that the ICC should be abolished altogether, and the freight business made subject to the Sherman Antitrust Act. Columbia University's thirty-ninth American Assembly, held last April, dealt with the Future of American Transportation and included representatives of trucking companies, airlines, railroads, and barge lines. It recommended—not everyone there wholly agreed—that a regulated carrier be permitted considerable leeway in adjusting rates. The assembly, organized by Professor Ernest Williams of the Columbia Graduate School of Business, also recommended that control of entry into the transportation business be relaxed. Williams says it was the first time in history that so diverse a group agreed on so many controversial transportation issues. If Congress heeds such expressions of informed opinion, 1971 may go down as the year in which U.S. transportation began its journey into the free-enterprise system.

All ton-miles aren't equal

For the hard-pressed railroads, relief from overregulation cannot come too soon. At least 35 percent of their traffic is being hauled at a loss, not so much because of competitive as because of political pressures. Much if not most of the money-losing traffic consists of stuff nobody else will handle, such as wood pulp and agricultural products—as common carriers the rails have no choice. Given the freedom to change these prices, the railroads could go on to rationalize the rest of their rate structure. Moreover, railroads roll up 90 percent of their ton-miles on only 10 percent of their track. Of their 206,000 miles of main lines, at least 40,000 and possibly 60,000, located mainly in the East and Midwest, are down-right unprofitable. But abandoning large amounts of track under current state and federal regulation would be so expensive and time consuming that most railroads are discouraged from even trying. Given the right to take the initiative, they would be in a better position to put the rest of their property on a paying basis.

But freedom itself would not be much of a remedy unless the railroads did something with it. The notion that they can use rate-making freedom to recapture mountains of freight handled by other modes does not seem quite so valid in reality. To get a lot of inland-waterway traffic, railroads would probably have to cut rates so much they would net very little on the additional business. Anyway, revenues of inland waterways total about $525 million, or less than 5 percent of railroad-freight revenues.

Also doubtful is the railroads' ability to capture very much long-distance truck freight. Railroad ton-mile costs, which average around 1 cent, are about a sixth of truck ton-mile costs, and it is easy to conclude that trucks are handling a lot of freight that railroads would be handling if their rate structure were more "cost-oriented" than it is. But railroads are burdened with some special disadvantages. Largely because they maintain their own roadbed, they need about six times as much capital to generate a dollar of revenue as trucks need. This is one reason why many authorities, including Paul Cherington, professor of transportation at the Harvard Graduate School of Business Administration, think that heavy trucks should be taxed more than they are.

But some doubt that railroads, as operated today, could capture more than 10 percent of truck traffic, no matter how they price their product or how much, within reason, trucks are taxed. Most of the freight carried so profitably by long-distance trucks is shipped in less-than-truckload lots, which only one or two railroads handle any more. Much of this freight, thanks to the industrial dispersion made possible by expansion of the highway system, either originates or terminates (or both) in places not served by rail. To ship by rail or by piggyback, an off-rail customer must first load the shipment on a truck. Most important, shippers do not usually buy ton-miles alone: more and more, they buy speed and service. So they often pay more to ship by truck because the truck is faster and less likely to damage their goods. The world's fastest freight train, the Santa Fe Super C, often covers the 2,228 miles from Chicago to Los Angeles in thirty-eight hours, *averaging* sixty miles an hour, a speed trucks cannot match. But the train runs only once a day, so missing it means a day's wait. Also, the freight must be trucked to and from the train. From door to door, a fast truck can still match the Super C. Compared to slower trains, the truck shows up even better.

More and more railroad men are coming to understand that they must radically improve their technology if they are to realize the inherent advantage of the flanged wheel and steel rail. For most kinds of freight, mile-long trains are an abomination. Each car must be strong enough to be put at the head of the train. The slack between cars amounts to about a foot a car. Thus a locomotive starting a 100-car train travels about 100 feet before the caboose begins to move, and the cargo takes a ferocious beating. Long trains are hard to run fast, but even when they are run fast, the time they save is more than offset by the time they waste in classification yards, where they are taken apart and put together.

Ideally, most trains should be short enough to run swiftly from origin to destination, with few stops. The main reason mile-long trains are operated is that union rules compel railroads to carry five or six men on a train. Sooner or later the carriers have got to fight it out with the unions, or automate their trains, or both. Automation is already working fine on some passenger trains. It can work just as well on freight. Moreover, the Santa Fe has developed a prototype model of a container train with electric motors on wheels four feet apart, powered by a diesel-electric generator car. The train comes in continuous sections that can be hooked together tightly. Since there is no slack between sections, the train can accelerate and decelerate swiftly, and run more than 100 miles an hour on well-maintained track. And since it carries only containers, the train itself does not have to be broken up in classification yards.

Their own rescue plan

But such innovations will take money to develop, and right now the railroads haven't even got the money to buy the cars, locomotives, track, and yards they need. That is why many farsighted railroad men who used to sniff at government help now believe it is an urgent necessity. Last year alone, they point out, the federal government spent $5.5 billion on highways, $360 million on waterways, $1.3 billion on airways, airlines, and airports. State and local governments spent $15.8 billion, mostly on roads. As for the railroads, all they got was part of the $16 million the government laid out for high-speed ground transportation. To cap it all, railroads must spend 18 percent of their operating expenses just to maintain their rights-of-way.

The Association of American Railroads has sponsored a rescue plan called ASTRO (for America's Sound Transportation Review Organization). It estimates that modernizing the railroads will cost about $3.3 billion a year over eleven years. Since the industry itself can be counted on to raise only $1.9 billion a year out of cash flow, the plan argues that $1.4 billion a year should be forthcoming in the way of government loans, subsidies, tax relief, and a research program. It is possible that the carriers will be able to raise more than $1.9 billion a year. But there is little doubt that $3.3 billion a year is a conservative estimate of what they will need to make up for years of subnormal earnings and to use their new rate-making freedom (if they get it) to become what they must become to survive: aggressive merchandisers of freight service.

U.S. passenger transportation, by contrast, needs not more freedom but better balance. Exercising free choice in a free market, consumers are buying enough autos to make passenger transportation overwhelmingly a do-it-yourself activity. At the same time, they are spending $5 billion or a little more than 5 percent of their total passenger-transportation outlays on commercial ground transportation—taxis, local buses, mass transit, and intercity buses and trains.

But this $5-billion sector of passenger transportation, small and shrinking as it is, contains part of the solution to the problem of traffic congestion in the big cities and metropolitan areas. The number of autos in use has grown 50 percent in ten years. Although city roads and streets account for only 18 percent of all paved roadways, about half of all vehicle-miles are driven within city limits. Thus traffic congestion is reaching a point where something must be done.

It is easy to indict the motorcar. Some argue that it costs the country about $13 billion a year more than the $94 billion people are spending directly on it. Air pollution may cost the nation more than $11 billion, and cars cause half the pollution. Automobile accidents not covered by insurance cost about $6 billion a year, and free parking on streets may represent a subsidy of several billions to car owners. So, the argument goes, let's tax automobiles for using city streets as well as for parking on them—and perhaps even bar automobiles from some areas of cities. And let's subsidize rapid transit, buses, commutation, and trains in the heavily populated corridors. Although the rush to mass transportation got its start in the academic world, politicians are beginning to realize its potentialities. The Urban Mass Transportation Assistance Act of 1970, which provides subsidies of as much as $10 billion over twelve years, may be just the beginning.

But the movement needs to be tempered by an awareness of the comparative economics of mass transportation and the private car. The motorcar has by now almost completely altered city travel patterns, which used to follow the inflexible lines created by railroads, trolley cars and buses. At least two-thirds of the inhabitants of metropolitan areas drive to work. Furthermore, automobiles account for 86 percent of all travel between cities, and for more than half of all trips of more than 1,000 miles. Annual travel per capita, which came to 400 miles in 1916 and 2,400 miles in 1940, mounted to 7,000 miles last year. The private car, not the airplane, has been responsible for most of the increase.

Perhaps most important, the automobile has become the country's cheapest form of passenger transportation. True, a standard sedan averaging 10,000 miles a year costs 11 or 12 cents a mile when all expenses such as depreciation and repairs are counted. But since the owner needs the car anyway, he counts only variable or out-of-pocket costs, and the variable costs of making a trip are about 2 cents a mile (more, of course, if the trip involves heavy doses of tolls and parking fees). Two people can usually make a trip by car more cheaply than by public transportation even when the owner reckons his costs, as economic jargon has it, on a fully distributed basis. On this basis, today's small car costs only 5 to 6 cents a mile, or less than public transportation.

Escalation forever

The car as transportation has still another advantage that is commonly underestimated because it seems so obvious: the car owner does his own driving and thereby avoids laying out money for public mass transportation, whose costs are rising faster than other costs. Most mass transportation is a prime example of the Baumol-Bowen effect, advanced by Professors William J. Baumol and William G. Bowen of Princeton University: although productivity rises faster in some sectors of the economy than in others (in some industries it is stagnant or declining), wages generally rise at the same rate everywhere. This means that relative costs in the low-productivity industries rise *cumulatively and without limit.* Suppose, for example, that both productivity and the general wage level were increasing at only 3 percent, which these days is an optimistic supposition. Average wage costs will then not rise at all. But in industries with little or no productivity increase, wage costs will increase 35 percent in a decade. Thus either the demand for the products made by the industries with little or no productivity increase will soften and the industries will decline, or these industries will claim an ever increasing percentage of the labor force and will slow the growth rate of the economy. Examples of industries with little or no productivity increase are education, the performing arts, and municipal governments and their services. Wages paid by the New York subway, for example, have been rising faster than national productivity. So the subway system, which used to get by on a nickel fare, now loses money on a 30-cent fare and needs 40 to 60 cents just to meet variable costs. If wages continue to rise as they have, the subway must be subsidized more or fares will rise high enough to kill most of the demand.

Another example of the Baumol-Bowen phenomenon is the conventional long-distance passenger train, with its expensive lounge and bar cars and its seventy-ton dining cars. Back in the early 1920's, when railroads made a little money on passengers, the average fare was around 3.4 cents a mile. Last year it came to 4 cents. But in fifty years hourly wage costs have risen almost sixfold. Equipment costs, reflecting expensive amenities like air conditioning, have risen about as much as labor costs. If conventional passenger trains were to do as well as they did fifty years ago, fares would have to approach 20 cents a mile, a rate that would virtually eliminate paying passengers. A trip between New York and the Pacific coast would cost more than $600.

For more than twenty years, railroads tried to make a go of the passenger business on a cut-rate basis, charging between 2 and 2.8 cents. All they got for their troubles, except in the booming war years when passengers were standing in the aisles, were mounting deficits. By 1955 only a few passenger trains were covering their variable costs. Since World War II, Professor Hilton reckons, railroads have lost $10 billion on passengers—"probably the most uneconomic activity ever carried on by private firms for a long period."

The overhead problem

Intercity passenger service, greatly reduced, is now in the hands of the Amtrak organization (formerly Railpax), set up by the federal government to relieve the railroads of the passenger burden The railroads still foot part of passenger-train costs however; their Amtrak contracts compensate them only for "avoidable" costs. Even with this break, Amtrak will be lucky to avoid huge and mounting deficits on all runs expect Boston—New York—Washington and New York—Florida. Some critics argue that the government should have appeased those who must travel long distances overland by making intercity bus service better. Long-distance bus service does not just survive, it makes money. For a fraction of the long-distance passenger-train deficit, the government could upgrade a lot of bus service to a high-speed, luxury level, with hostesses serving free cocktails and meals.

A considerable school of thought holds that high-speed trains in the densely populated corridors can relieve congestion at an economic cost. Just recently the Geo-Transport Foundation of New England published a glowing prospectus for rehabilitating passenger service between New York and Boston. G.T.F. proposes to upgrade some of the line and to build a brand-new ninety-two-mile track between New Haven and Providence. Capital costs of $565 million would be financed by 7 percent government-guaranteed bonds. Total revenues would pay all costs and leave a net income after debt service.

The prospect sounds wonderful, perhaps a little too wonderful, particularly when one turns to the performance of the Metroliners between New York and Washington. It is hard to nail down the economics of the Metroliners, but they are expensive to buy and operate. Each car, purchased in quantity today, would bear a tag of at least $500,000. Thus annual interest, depreciation, and insurance would come to at least $90,000 a car. Each train carries a four-man operating crew costing around $1 a mile, or $223 for the three-hour trip—not counting bartenders and porters.

With a New York—Washington coach fare of $17 (7.5 cents a mile), parlor-car fare of $27 (12 cents a mile), and a load factor of 65 percent, the Metroliners have covered variable costs by a good margin. But they and a few other passenger trains account for most through trains on that line, so any realistic bookkeeping must eventually assign them their pro rata share of total overhead. On this basis, the Metroliners are not making money, and are not likely ever to make money at tolerable fare levels. And they are no more immune from the Baumol-Bowen effect than the New York City subway system. Their costs are bound to rise much faster than average. This means either cumulatively higher fares or cumulatively larger deficits, or both. The former would tend to dry up demand for the service, and the latter would become progressively harder to pass on to taxpayers.

Such projects, to be sure, should not be analyzed too narrowly. The classical principle of opportunity costs can be interpreted as saying that resources should be allocated where they are used least inefficiently. If corridor trains prove to be more efficient for the economy as a whole than a new highway built at, say, $7 million a mile, then subsidization can be economic. But the cost of operating a motorcar is not subject to the Baumol-Bowen effect, and so grows relatively cheaper. The airplane is much less in hock to the Baumol-Bowen effect than the train. As for ground transportation, the bus uses relatively little manpower, can be made as comfortable as a train, and in restricted lanes can be operated at very high speeds. Since it shares highways already built, it enjoys very low costs. The bus may not be the most economic way of moving people between Boston and Washington, where existing rail lines can be upgraded to a high standard of service. But elsewhere buses should be considered before billions are poured into high-speed rail lines.

The case against rails

Since no two cities or metropolitan areas are alike, the problem of urban congestion varies from city to city, and its solution depends on what kind of city its citizens want. In general, there are several ways of relieving traffic congestion in big cities and densely populated metropolitan areas. One is to keep down the influx of suburban cars by building commutation lines so attractive that suburbanites will want to ride them. Another is to install modern electronic traffic controls. Still another is to devise new, or improve old, ways of getting around.

What to do about commutation is probably the most controversial subject in the transportation world. Several economists look upon a sizable revival of rail transit for commuters with unconcealed scorn. Investment in rail transit, they argue, was economic between 1897 and 1908, when cities were gridded with streetcar tracks and connected to the suburbs by interurban lines. Owing to them, people traveled between well-defined residential areas and well-defined central business districts. Owing to the car, they do so no longer.

Others argue that rail transit cannot be depended on to relieve congestion and pollution. New rail lines in Chicago and Toronto, they note, drew nine-tenths or so of their passengers from bus lines and only about one-tenth from automobiles. Such lines, moreover, stimulate a lot of construction in the central cities, and so attract more autos and cause more congestion than ever. It is also argued that most of the proposed rail-transit systems subsidize well-to-do commuters. The poor, the aged, and the handicapped need public transportation the worst, maintains Martin Wohl, director of transportation studies at the Urban Institute, but they are not helped at all.

Nevertheless, new rail commuting lines are being put into service. The fifteen-mile Philadelphia-Lindenwold commuting line, subsidized by automobile bridge tolls, can certainly be regarded as successful. It has drawn a lot of riders who used to drive back and forth, and so has achieved its prime aim of reducing the flow of automobiles into congested downtown Philadelphia.

Encouraged by the Lindenwold Line's performance, the transit industry is waiting anxiously for the inauguration of the seventy-five-mile, $1.4-billion Bay Area Rapid Transit line early next year. BART has already been responsible for a lot of new construction near its Oakland and San Francisco stations, but its managers confidently expect it to relieve more congestion than it causes. They will run their elegant automated trains so fast that people will leave their cars in trackside parking lots. "We're going to make a partner of the automobile," says General Manager B. R. Stokes. "If a man is willing to drive to the freeway, he will be more than willing to drive to the nearest BART station." If Stokes is right, expensive rapid transit may yet establish a place for itself as an alternative to expensive highway construction.

But improved commutation will at best relieve only a small part of urban congestion. The big cities are starting to revive public transportation and to experiment with curbing the private car. Municipalities of around 500,000, which as a rule are pleasantly free of congestion, are thinking ahead to the day when they, too, will be choked with traffic. By 1980, if current plans are realized, at least 500 miles of new subway and rapid-transit lines will be built. But rail rapid transit makes economic sense only in cities with densely populated downtown business districts. Looking for cheaper and more flexible ways to move city dwellers, the experts have come up with a wide variety of ideas, several of which are being promoted in a wide-ranging transportation policy paper now making the rounds in high Administration circles. Some of the more practical ideas:

● The bus with priority. In several metropolitan areas, buses have been assigned exclusive lanes during rush hours, and the result has been a dramatic acceleration of service. Under experimentation is the idea of monitoring traffic electronically in order to keep it moving fast so that buses will not have to be assigned part of the road.

● The dial-a-bus, a cross between a taxi and a bus. You call and state your destination, and a computer using a mathematical routing formula picks the appropriate bus and sends it to you. You may have to wait longer than for a taxi, and take a more roundabout route, but the bus will cost less.

● The jitney. Back during World War I, impecunious but enterprising individuals went into the transportation business by making a down payment on a flivver, laying in a stock of cardboard placards bearing place names, and running up and down looking for passengers. This highly elastic mode filled a need in central cities in the U.S. until the early 1930's. Then the taxi, transit, and union interests ganged up on it. But jitneys continued to flourish elsewhere in the world. Now they are on the rise again in the U.S., both legally and illegally. They operate like buses in that they stick to fixed routes, run on a schedule of sorts, and charge 25 to 40 cents. The Urban Mass Transportation Administration is thinking of sponsoring an experimental service in black neighborhoods.

• The ordinary taxi, which some argue has not been used economically, either because its fares are too high or it is run as a monopoly or both. Given freedom of entry and competitive fares, taxis could achieve a much higher load factor. New York City taxis are burdened with a monopolistic fare structure and tolerate no freedom of entry, yet they carry more than twice as many people as the city's commutation trains and nearly one-quarter as many as the subways.

• The so-called dual-mode system, which promises to provide much better service than any transit system, and at much lower cost. The system will consist of small mass-produced vehicles seating anywhere from four to twenty people; they will operate automatically on guideways, but can be driven on ordinary streets. When adequately tested, says A. Scheffer Lang, head of the Transportation Systems Division at M.I.T., this system "will probably displace all further rail rapid-transit construction, and substitute for additional expressways in most metropolitan areas."

But such innovations will not be enough. Some cities may find themselves forced to levy user charges on the private automobile, varying with traffic and time of day, and even ban it in certain areas. Most cities also need more financial help. Although the metropolitan areas account for half the country's vehicle-miles and for practically all congestion, they get only a small share of the billions that federal, state, and local governments are plowing into transportation. Provided the cities use resources with discretion and refrain from squandering them on grandiose and wasteful projects, they are certainly entitled to more.

---

47   The Metropolitan Transportation Dilemma
Wilfred Owen
The Brookings Institution

Perhaps the most pressing and, at the same time, the most frustrating of today's transportation problems is urban transportation. Transportation is both the cause and the effect of urban concentration. As such, it is the key to the problem and to the problem's solutions. The solutions are not simple. Indeed, there is little assurance that they have been found.

The following selection does an excellent job of setting the problem forth in its historical, economic, and social context. And, since it creates more questions than it answers, it serves to illustrate the complexities of its subject.

From Wilfred Owen, *The Metropolitan Transportation Problem,* Rev. Ed., Ch. 1, Washington, D.C., The Brookings Institution, 1966. Used by permission.

American cities have become increasingly difficult to live in and to work in largely because they are difficult to move around in. Inability to overcome congestion and to remove obstacles to mobility threaten to make the big city an economic liability rather than an asset.

The crisis in transportation is largely the result of the growing concentration of population and economic activity. In 1960 more than 125 million people were living in the cities and suburbs of the United States. Each year urban America is spreading at the rate of a million acres—an area as large as the state of Rhode Island. In the past decade and a half, the growth of urbanization has been equivalent to duplicating the populations of metropolitan New York, Detroit, Los Angeles, Chicago, and Philadelphia.

This concentration of people and resources in urban areas would have been impossible without the mobility and supply lines afforded by transportation. The capacity of the transport system and the low cost and dependability of transport services have enabled an increasing number of people to seek the economic, social, and cultural opportunities that urban living ideally provides. But paradoxically, metropolitan cities have now grown to the point where they threaten to strangle the transportation that made them possible.

The paradox is particularly striking because the past several decades have seen more revolutionary changes in transportation than all previous history. With the technical ability to solve its transportation problems well in hand, the modern city is confronted by a transportation problem more complex than ever before. Despite all the methods of movement, the problem in cities is how to move.

One reason for this dilemma is the fact that urban areas have been unable to adjust to the changing conditions brought about so rapidly by the technological revolution in transportation. The older urban centers, with physical characteristics that were fixed in less mobile times, have been staggered by the impacts of recent innovation. And the newer suburbs have compounded the transportation problem by duplicating the errors of downtown and by creating problems of public administration and finance that traditional governmental organization was not designed to meet.

The problem and its impact

Every metropolitan area in the United States is confronted by a transportation problem that seems destined to become more aggravated in the years ahead. Growth of population and expansion of the urban area, combined with rising national product and higher incomes, are continually increasing the volume of passenger and freight movement. At the same time, shifts from rail to road and from public to private transportation have added tremendous burdens to highway and street facilities. They have created what appear to be insuperable terminal and packing problems. Continuing economic growth and the certainty of further transport innovation threaten to widen the gap between present systems of transportation and satisfactory standards of service.

Manifestations of the transportation problem in urban areas include the mass movement between work and home and the cost that it represents in money, time, and wasted energy. The transit industry is experiencing rising costs and financial difficulties, while the rider is the victim of antiquated equipment and poor service. Obsolescence and inadequate capacity have become characteristic of the highway network, and terminal problems mean high costs and delays for all forms of transportation. The speed of traffic in central business districts during so-called "rush hours" is frequently as low as six to ten miles an hour, and the problem is finding not only the room to move but a place to stop. The scattered location and obsolete design of freight terminals and the absence of satisfactory physical relationships among the several methods of transportation create a heavy volume of unnecessary traffic as well as delays and high costs that penalize business, the consumer, and the community.

For a nation with 85 million motor vehicles, relatively little has been accomplished toward adapting the city to the automotive age. A limited mileage of urban highways has been built to adequate standards, but for the most part traffic still moves on an antiquated gridiron of streets laid out long before the needs of the automobile were known. These streets were designed principally for convenient real estate platting and access to property rather than for mechanized transportation. Despite the congestion of city thoroughfares, the automobile and truck have been left to park haphazardly along the curb and to load and unload in the street where space is so badly needed for movement.

Highway standards are generally in inverse relation to the needs of traffic. The modern highway in open rural areas often degenerates in urbanized areas to an obsolete right-of-way crowded on both sides with commercial activities strung out in unsightly array to create what has been aptly called America's longest slums. In the city, the concentration of traffic on narrow streets with their numerous crossings means that the speed and service potentials of the motor vehicle cannot be realized. The accident toll is outrageous. Since the turn of the century, half a million people have been killed in motor vehicle accidents on city streets and millions of pedestrians have been injured.

The greatest transportation difficulties are experienced while commuting between home and work. The separation of housing facilities from employment centers together with the rapid expansion of the urban area have created a pendulum movement from home to work that accounts for a larger volume of passenger traffic than any other type of weekday travel. This movement is frequently accomplished with the most antiquated facilities and under the most frustrating conditions. The trip to work often cancels the gain from shorter hours on the job, and the daily battle with congestion is in sharp contrast to other improvements in modern working conditions.

Half a century of neglect has meant a long-term deterioration of transit service and failure to keep pace with technological change. Rising cost and declining patronage have led to a succession of fare increases and further reductions in service. In many cases, it has been impossible to set aside necessary allowances for depreciation of equipment, and the industry as a whole has been unable to attract sufficient capital to renew, modernize, or extend its services for the nearly eight billion riders per year who depend on public carriers.[1]

The cost of providing the physical facilities required to meet urban traffic requirements has reached astronomical levels. High costs of land and damage incident to construction and the tremendous capacity and complicated design of the facilities required in built-up urban areas have thus far combined to make a full-scale attack impossible. Fifty-two billion dollars spent for urban streets during the past four decades has been grossly inadequate to achieve a reasonable quality of transportation service. The cost and complexity of highway construction is indicated by the fact that some expressways cost from $10 million to $30 million per mile.

The contrast between these needs and the financial possibilities of meeting them is not indicative of easy solution. Many metropolitan cities in the United States are suffering from a chronic shortage of funds. Today nine tenths of the mounting expenses of city governments are for services that did not exist at the turn of the century—traffic engineering, airports, parking facilities, health clinics, and a long list of others. At the same time, every city is being overwhelmed with demands for better schools, housing, recreation facilities, and other public services along with improved transportation.

City governments burdened by the heavy outlays required to accommodate ever-growing volumes of city traffic frequently find that attempts to relieve congestion serve only to move the critical point somewhere else. Expressways or parking facilities established to meet the demand attract further use and magnify the need. Moreover, new facilities mean not only heavy capital outlays but the loss of large areas of land from the tax rolls, reducing receipts at the same time that added revenues are being sought.

Historical nature of urban congestion

The urban transportation problem, although often thought of as relatively new and associated with the automobile and the United States, is both global and historic. All over the world the trend from agricultural economics to urban industrialization continues, and cities in every part of the globe are struggling with similar problems of achieving acceptable standards of urban mobility. Even where automobiles are few, the bus and truck and bicycle combine with less modern methods of movement to create a degree of chaos comparable to the least penetrable crosstown streets of New York.

The big city and its transportation problems were confounding the experts over a century ago, long before the complications of internal combustion. When the population of London increased from approximately one million in 1831 to over four million 60 years later, the poorer inhabitants of the city were forced to abandon the high-rent districts to commercial uses and the city was practically abandoned at night. Out of the resulting tide of traffic that ebbed and flowed from home to work came the commuter, or as he was more appropriately called in early times, the journeyman. One hundred years ago his oppression was experienced on foot, and a daily spectacle was "the streams of walkers two, three and four miles long, converging on the city."[2] But with the continued spread of the suburbs, the possibility of so solving the home-to-work problem became impractical and an ambitious program of railroad construction and bus operation was undertaken to cope with it. By the early 1890's a thousand London horse buses were carrying over 100 million passengers per year, and 400,000 daily commuters were carried into the city by rail.

Meanwhile American cities sought to relieve traffic congestion by constructing elevated and subway facilities. Surface transit vehicles were usurping so much street space in Boston more than 60 years ago that a subway was constructed to clear the way for other vehicles using the streets.[3] In 1905 congested traffic at rush hours was described as the number one problem of large cities in the United States, and pictures of urban traffic jams in the days of horse-drawn vehicles and electric cars attest to the fact that congestion was bad long before the motor vehicle made it worse. As early as 1902, the question was whether better results could be obtained "by starting on a bold plan on comparatively virgin soil than by attempting to adapt our old cities to our newer and higher needs."[4]

Although the urban transportation problem is both longstanding and worldwide, its characteristics are not everywhere alike. The problem varies widely among cities of different sizes, types, ages, and locations. Problems of a large metropolitan city are very different from those of a smaller town, and large cities themselves differ widely according to their history, topography, wealth, and function. But the long-standing nature of urban traffic congestion and its world-wide scope suggest, despite a variety of forms, that underlying factors may be universal and only partially related to modern methods of transport. Basic causes appear to be excessive crowding of population and economic activity into small areas of land and the disorderly arrangement of land uses that has maximized transport requirements. The great bulk and density of urban buildings and the concentration of employment in the downtown area have created a volume of passenger and freight movement that has become increasingly difficult to accommodate effectively regardless of transportation method. The congestion of people, horses, and street cars before the appearance of motorized transport, the rush-hour madness of the New York subways, and the lines of automobiles inching their way through the traffic circles of Washington are all manifestations of a continuing imbalance between transportation demand and available transport capacity.

Transportation and urban growth

Transportation has played a leading role in the congestion of cities. At an earlier time, heavy densities of population developed because the urban radius was limited to distances that could be covered on foot, or at best by horse. As lines of intercity communication were developed to serve the urban cores of the industrial age, they solved the problems of long-distance transportation that made it possible for greater centers of production and employment to supply and support themselves.

But within the urban area, transport innovations were less successful in providing a better distribution of population and economic activity. Innovation itself could not assure the mobility that economic interdependence in an urban complex requires. Transportation facilities were designed primarily to carry people and goods into the center of the city where there were already too many people and an over-concentration of economic activity. Lack of transportation in the early stages of urban growth combined with the recent development of mechanical transport have created an urban environment in which "each great capital sits like a spider in the midst of its transportation web."[5]

The proportion of the population of the United States in urban places of all sizes has increased from 6 per cent in 1800 to 70 per cent in 1960. During the past decade, the spectacular growth of urban population has placed tremendous additional burdens on transportation in a short period of time.

From 1950 to 1960, when the population increased by 28 millions, 84 per cent of this growth took place in the nation's 212 metropolitan areas. The population of these areas increased by 26 per cent. The largest growth took place in suburban areas, which registered an increase of 49 per cent compared to the 11 per cent increase in central cities.[6] (See Chart 1.)

From 1960 to 1963, when there was a gain of 7.4 millions in the total population, 80 per cent of this took place in metropolitan areas. Population in these areas rose to 119 millions in 1963, and the growth rate of the suburbs was more than three times that of the central cities.[7]

The result of these trends has been to concentrate transportation problems in a relatively small number of metropolitan areas. From 1950 to 1960, the population of metropolitan areas increased 53 per cent in Los Angeles and Houston, 45 per cent in Dallas, 35 per cent in Washington, D.C., 30 per cent in Seattle, 28 per

Chart I • Population Increase, 1950-1960

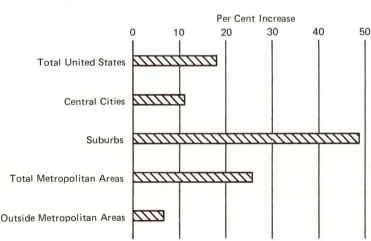

cent in Minneapolis-St. Paul, and 25 per cent in Detroit.[8] In 1960 five metropolitan cities had more than three million people, 19 had between one million and three million, and 29 had between 500,000 and a million. The 24 most populous urban areas contained more than 60 million people.

The intensity of the transportation requirements in these urban places and the importance of urban transportation systems are indicated by relating the magnitude of city population to the postage-stamp areas that they encompass. Sixty per cent of the nation's people are located in 1 per cent of the nation's land. Thirty-three per cent of the population is concentrated in one-tenth of 1 per cent of the area of the country. The metropolitan area of New York City contains more people than the combined populations of Arizona, Delaware, Idaho, Maine, Montana, Nevada, New Hampshire, New Mexico, North and South Dakota, Rhode Island, Utah, Vermont, and Wyoming.

The high proportion of the population in the urban category and the small amount of land devoted to urban uses mean that the density of urban population is very high and consequently that the load on transportation facilities is very heavy. In 1960, there were 24,697 persons per square mile in New York City, and in Manhattan the figure was 77,000 per square mile. This compares with about 50 people per square mile for the country as a whole. In Chicago there were 12,959 persons per square mile, and in Philadelphia 15,743. There were 11 cities in the United States that had a population density of more than 11,000 per square mile . . .

Population figures do not measure the full magnitude of the transportation problem, for in addition to those who live in the city a large number of people come into the city during the daytime to work. This problem is indicated in Chart 2, which shows the resident and daytime populations of major cities in 1950. In 57 cities the daily flow of workers added another ten million people to the congestion at the center.[9] The daytime population of Boston, for example, was 34 per cent above the census figures of resident population, Pittsburgh had to accommodate 49 per cent more people during the day than at night, and in Newark, New Jersey, the population doubled during daylight hours.

The intensification of urban crowding that results from the daily influx of commuters is measured by the fact that whereas in 1950 only 4 per cent of the population in the five largest cities of the United States resided within a radius of one mile from the central business district, the estimated daytime population within a mile of the center amounted to 30 per cent of the total population in each city. Less than 15 per cent of the residents of these largest cities lived within a two-mile radius from the centers, but estimated daytime population in that area amounted to half the resident population of each city.

To accommodate the heavy concentrations of people in urban centers, and to supply the factories and stores of the city with materials and good requires a tremendous volume of movement under the most difficult space limitations. Supplying 100 million urban residents calls for the transportation of 2,000 million tons of materials per year. For every urban dweller an average of some 18 tons of materials is consumed annually.[10] How much the final consumer

Chart 2 • Increase of Daytime Over Resident Population

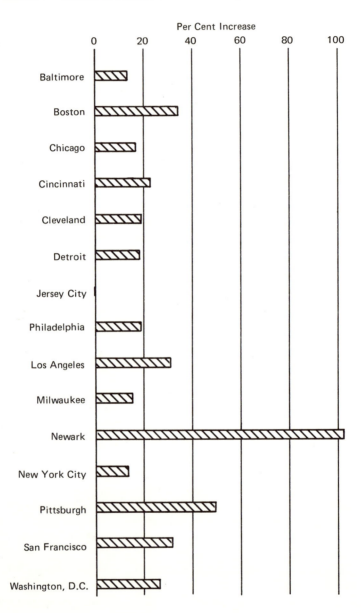

Per Cent Increase

must pay to have the essential channels of mobility and supply kept open is not known, but the marvel is that the biggest cities are rarely inconvenienced by any visible break in the life lines on which they depend. The principal problems of which the average urban resident is aware are the inconveniences, discomforts, and exasperation of coping with the mounting obstacles to personal mobility.

City vs. suburb

Relatively low-cost, reliable, and high-capacity transportation services have made possible these heavy concentrations of population and economic activity in the big city. The railroad lines to downtown, the subways, and the radial highways have supported congestion by creating the center and leading to it, and by making possible the furnishings of supplies, the marketing of urban products, and the maintenance of minimum standards of mobility.

But more recently transportation has become an agent of dispersal as well, making possible the avoidance of concentration and promoting a diffused pattern of industrial and residential development. Symbolic of the new role of transport are the two-car family, the truck and bus, and the circumferential highway. The trend will continue with the impetus of vertical take-off aircraft, the heliport, and private travel by air. The problems of overcoming transportation difficulties are giving way to the possibilities of exploiting the advantages of transportation. The relative force of these two opposite aspects of transportation development will continue to play an important part in determining the character of urbanization in the future.

Currently, the most notable characteristic of urban change is the rapid growth of the fringes and the loss of population in central core areas. But there has been little evidence that declines in population or economic activity will be sufficient to diminish transport problems in the heart of the city in the near future. In New York City, for example, the population of Manhattan reached its peak in 1910 and declined thereafter until 1930. By 1950, there was an increase of 100,000 above the 1930 figure but between 1950 and 1960 population gradually declined by one quarter million. However, during this period Manhattan's loss was offset by an equal population increase in Queens.[11] The effect has not been to diminish the intensity of development close in but only to reduce the relative importance of New York City in the metropolitan area. Thus the fringe counties that contained only 8 per cent of the metropolitan population in 1910 accounted for 38 per cent in 1960, while the population of Manhattan declined in relative importance from 31 per cent of the metropolitan total in 1910 to 11 per cent in 1960.[12]

Similar trends in Chicago indicate that the high-intensity areas of the city are losing population very gradually. The resident population of Chicago within two miles of the center reached a peak in 1910, after which it declined sharply until 1940, then rose again.[13] The same pattern of change took place in the zone two to four miles from the center. Beyond the four-mile zone population has been increasing over a long period of time. The maximum rate of growth is taking place in the areas eight miles out and beyond. (See Chart 3.)[14]

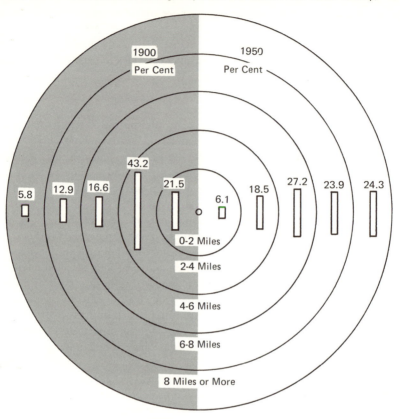

In Philadelphia a century of population movement has not greatly reduced the high density of population within the city itself. In 1950, the number of people in the one- to two-mile zone was still 175 times greater than in the 18-25 mile zone. Within three miles of the city center there were almost a million people in 1950, the same as in 1900. The only difference was that with the spreading of the metropolitan area, total population within two miles of the center was a much smaller percentage of the metropolitan total compared to sixty years ago.[15] Urban redevelopment may be expected to result in further reductions in population density. The close-in areas of Philadelphia three to five miles from City Hall are expected to lose one fifth of their population by 1980.[16] Yet even with substantial losses there will still be a heavy concentration of people and economic activity.

For the majority of American cities, there will continue to be density reductions close in. These reductions plus the growth of the suburbs will further reduce the relative importance of the city itself, but substantial loosening up of the older congested areas will still leave heavy concentrations of urban population. Thus the urban area as a whole faces continuing problems of traffic congestion near the center along with the additional demands for suburban mobility and commutation service between suburb and center.

Employment trends parallel population trends. In New York City, for example, it is estimated that the decrease in the total number of jobs will be 64,000 in 1965 compared to the 1956 figure, while in the metropolitan area as a whole there will be an increase of 457,000 jobs. The proportion of total regional employment accounted for by New York City declined from 66 per cent in 1946 to 56 per cent in 1965, and thousands of people are now commuting from the city outward to get to work.[17] But there has been no visible decline in the magnitude of daily movement to the center.

Despite the spreading industrial growth in the suburbs, the city proper still retains a major share of the manufacturing activity in metropolitan areas. From the standpoint of the transportation problem of the city, growth trends have not diminished the factors contributing to traffic congestion. The kinds of industrial establishments moving out of the city are those with a relatively low number of employees per unit of area, whereas office work centering in the downtown area involves a high density of employment and the type of employment that creates the greatest peak-hour traffic.

As population and industry have grown in the suburbs, retail business has expanded rapidly outside the city limits, and the percentage of metropolitan area sales being transacted in the city has declined. Again, however, the new stores have been necessary to accommodate the growth of population and income, and for the most part retail trade in the central city still flourishes.

Building permits for the year 1954 showed that half of the nation's construction took place in the suburbs of metropolitan areas and 31 per cent in central cities. The remainder was accounted for by nonmetropolitan areas.[18] These figures indicate that suburban growth has not destroyed the economic vitality in the central city. The tremendous suburban expansion has not appreciably altered the concentration of urban activity nor diminished the underlying causes of traffic congestion. What looked like dispersion a short while ago has been largely new growth, and this growth has of necessity taken place in the outer fringes where room for expansion is still available.

The outlook for urbanization

Despite the patterns of urban growth to date, and the presumption that centrifugal forces will gain rather than lose strength in the future, there is still no clear indication of the extent to which present trends in urban growth will continue. We do not know to what degree economic changes and development in technology will alter the process of urbanization. Future growth may mean that existing densities in central cities will be substantially maintained or again increased; that conversely the downtown area and much of the central city will continue to give way before the onrush to the suburbs. Changes are also being introduced through planned cities of very different design that are making their appearance in many parts of the country.

Congestion and blight have multiplied the difficulties and frustrations of urban life, and in many places the growth of concentrated living seems to have passed the point of diminishing returns. Further vertical growth and urban sprawl both promise to compound the difficulties of providing transportation and other community facilities in the second half of the century. The threat of greater congestion has raised the question whether a nation born of farms is destined to die of cities.[19]

The belief that this could in fact be the case has been reinforced by a growing realization that until world peace can be guaranteed, the closely-packed city is particularly vulnerable to nuclear destruction. "A nation which keeps its wealth, its productive capacity, its population, and its administration huddled together in a few metropolitan areas, invites blackmail and courts disaster."[20] We are told on the one hand that "all the long-range dangers and disadvantages of our situation can be mitigated—even if none of them can be entirely eliminated—by judicious dispersal of our basic industries and productive population."[21] On the other hand, it is contended that the dangers of fall-out threaten to devastate so wide an area that to flee has become futile.

According to Frank Lloyd Wright, the deadline for decentralization has been so shortened by the threat of nuclear warfare that the urbanite must either be willing to get out of the city or be resigned to blowing up with it. Protection against enemy attack is no longer to be found in banding together in cities, and the possibilities of arriving at a more even distribution of the population over the unused areas of the country have been vastly increased by recent innovations. This is especially true of developments in transportation. In the light of these considerations alone, it may be that "further centralizations of any American city are only postponements of the city's end."[22]

Many of the economic advantages of urban living have in any event already been neutralized. The city has become the victim of diseconomies that are reflected in high costs of living, including high costs of moving. Distribution costs and the difficulties of personal mobility often cancel other attractions of urban life. The theoretical benefits of urban location are frequently submerged in the rising discomforts and declining satisfactions of much that the city has to offer. The growing distances that must be covered from home to work, from one place of business to another, and from one friend to another tend to overcome the advantages of propinquity that the city is supposed to afford.

But more serious charges can be leveled at the urban area today. Blight and slums render large sections of the big city unfit for living. Although the wealth of the United States can be expressed in glowing statistics, about 20 per cent of the residential areas of its cities are slums. These slum areas contain one third of the urban population. To support them takes 45 per cent of the costs of municipal government, yet the same areas contribute only 6 per cent of total property tax revenues.[23] In New York City a quarter of a million dwellings lack toilet or bath, recreation facilities and open space are grossly inadequate, and even sunlight and air are at a premium.

Can we, then, provide a more satisfactory urban environment in new locations as transport technology enables us to move out and begin anew? The assumption that we can is often shaken by the newer suburbs. They have taken on many of the most objectionable aspects of the older blighted sections.[24] In attempting to flee from the undesirable conditions of the downtown area, frequently we have succeeded only in taking our mistakes with us.[25]

The idea of moving out to seek the health and enjoyment of air and sunlight has been a natural reaction to the noise and dirt of the city, but the endless spreading of cities has resulted in pushing the country farther and farther away. As a result, those who seek the restfulness or beauty of the countryside must constantly move outward to avoid the progressive waves of those who continue the escape from older blighted districts. This unplanned suburban development has resulted in the sprawl of large cities, the lengthening journey to work, and the growing difficulty of moving around.

Transportation has contributed in other ways to the diminishing desirability of urban living. The hazards and congestion of the highways, the noise and fumes of the motor vehicle, and the unsightliness of the gas station and used car lot have all added to the run-down character of the urban region. Transportation has created many of the conditions that people strive to escape, but it has also provided the means of escaping them and therefore the means of avoiding solution. And it has transported slums to the suburbs.

The solution is not to abandon the city, therefore, but to assure that the inadequacies of the close-in urban area are corrected and that new suburban developments avoid the mistakes of the past. In some cities the congestion of the central city seems to have reached the saturation point, but we may also be arriving at an economic limit to the outward spread of the metropolis made possible by improved methods of transportation. As the increasing radius of travel resulting from modern transport permits us to move farther from the center, the cost of community facilities of all kinds increases. The higher densities of more compact urban areas of lesser size may offer a more economical alternative.

It can hardly be contended, however, that the degree of metropolitan concentration reached today is necessary for the success of either business or the arts and sciences. Many of the activities that were necessarily located in the center of the city before the development of better means of transport and communications now could be decentralized and dispersed. The fact that some degree of concentration is an economic advantage does not lead to the conclusion that maximum concentration is the ultimate goal.

On the other hand, the big city can be defended on economic, social, and cultural grounds. The phenomenon of the metropolitan city derives from the fact that co-operative action makes possible greater productivity and higher standards of living, and it permits public services and amenities to be supplied more effectively and often at lower cost. A large labor force makes feasible the specialization required by large-scale industry and provides the skills needed for today's highly technical production processes. Even the availability of sufficient numbers of consumers to enjoy the fruits of modern production is predicated on the profitable markets afforded by concentrations of population. Advantages likewise stem from the variety of contacts and educational opportunities afforded by a larger population.

In any event, those who like the country have thus far been outnumbered by those who prefer a crowd, and the view that the city is bound to disappear has not as yet been borne out by events. More people are being attracted to cities and their urbanized surroundings than desire to remain rural, and at the center there continues to be a struggle between horizontal and vertical growth that has seen both sides of claiming victory.

Alternative transportation solutions

What the future of the city will be or what the city of tomorrow ought to be like are questions closely related to the provision of transportation. Transport innovation will to a large degree dictate what is possible, and the extent to which transport policy is directed to achieving urban goals will help determine what is feasible. Many observers believe that a continuing downward trend in mass transportation is inevitable as car ownership expands and as highway and parking facilities are further developed to cope with traffic congestion. This would presumably hasten the decline of the center. Others take the view that in the relatively dense areas of the central city the attempt to accommodate the continuing trend toward private automobile transportation is a costly mistake that can end only in the ruination of downtown and the frustration of urban dwellers. The greater efficiency of mass transportation must be exploited, it is contended, by devoting more attention and money to the modernization and expansion of public conveyance, which in turn will preserve the downtown area.

One of the basic questions, then, concerns the relative emphasis to be placed on expressways and parking facilities to accommodate automobile use as compared to the modernization of mass transportation facilities aimed at restoring lost patronage and reducing the number of vehicles entering the city. If the latter course were followed, would it be possible to promote greater use of transit or would the urban resident either insist on using his private car or go elsewhere to work or shop or to do business? The correct decision is of basic importance to the future of the city and its people. The costs of transport modernization will be very high regardless where the emphasis is placed. But the cost of doing the wrong things or of simply doing nothing could be higher. For the ability to provide a circulatory system of acceptable standards will be an important factor in the economic survival of the urban economy.

The view that better mass transportation is the way out of the current situation is based on the contention that attempts to use the motor vehicle in an environment established before motoring needs were known are bound to be unsuccessful. Failure will be in the form of either downtown congestion or desertion. Mass transportation is capable of moving many times more people than automobiles can move, and under restricted space conditions should provide a more effective method of transportation. The problem of urban congestion has become so great that many communities are coming to the conclusion that there could never be sufficient highway and parking capacity to permit the movement of all people in private cars.

The opinion is frequently expressed that cities are suffering from "automobile blight"; that if the automobile were banned from downtown areas and satisfactory mass transportation provided instead, congestion would be relieved and greater freedom of movement would assure economic survival for the city. "The cities just cannot resign themselves to automobiles and let mass transportation slide to ruin and extinction. They must preserve mass transportation or stagnate."[26] Downtown is doomed to die, it is contended, unless cities stress movement of people rather than movement of vehicles. With this sentiment there appears to be widespread agreement. "Eventually cities will be places few people will want to live in, work in, or even visit unless they act to restrict private transportation."[27]

The mass transportation solution does not stimulate universal admiration, however. According to Mumford, while congestion originally provided the excuse for the subway, the subway has now become the further excuse for congestion. Small cities where people walked and rode bicycles were in a better position to take advantage of motor transport than cities that invested heavily in trolleys and rapid transit.[28]

If mass transportation is not the answer, what of the possibilities of modern highways to relieve the city of the congestion that inadequate transportation once made necessary? Critics insist that elaborate urban expressways are futile because of the tremendous reservoir of traffic waiting to absorb any new street capacity. According to this view, expressways and parking facilities not only will not solve the problem of congestion but will actually make it worse. The traffic engineer who tries to accommodate the private automobile "is doomed to inevitable failure . . . the better he does his job the greater will be his failure."[29]

But the position is also taken that the automobile, far from being a cause of urban congestion, has in fact made possible a necessary deconcentration of population through the decentralization of urban living and working. The endless streams of traffic that choke today's downtown streets make it natural to suppose that the private car has been responsible for the congestion of our cities, but it can be argued that the opposite is actually the case. "The only relief from congestion has been possible because of the motor vehicle."[30]

Still another view is that neither automobiles nor mass transportation nor any other mechanical contrivance can solve the problems of urban congestion. "As a solution of the traffic problem these devices are pure deception."[31] Putting the emphasis on supplying transportation facilities rather than controlling the demand, it is maintained, serves only to aggravate congestion. "As long as nothing is done fundamentally to rehabilitate the cities themselves, the quicker will people forsake them" and the greater the problems for those left behind to cope with.[32]

We have the assurance, therefore, that the problem of congestion in urban areas has been precipitated by the automobile; that the automobile, on the contrary, has been our escape from congestion; that the automobile and mass transportation are both guilty of promoting congestion; and finally that neither is the primary culprit, but rather a host of other factors that have resulted, thanks to modern technology, in the successful attempt to crowd too many people and too much economic activity into too little space. And of the city itself we are told that preservation of the vast investment in urban America will assure both economic salvation and nuclear annihilation.

Metropolitan areas thus face the difficult task of arriving at decisions that will determine to a major degree the physical and financial future of tomorrow's city. Should they emphasize expressways and parking facilities to accommodate automobile use, or modernize mass transportation facilities in the hope of restoring lost patronage and reducing the number of vehicles entering the city? Or will solutions depend instead on the extensive replanning and rebuilding of the American city? . . .

NOTES

1. The terms "transit" or "mass transportation" are synonymous and include surface street car, bus, or trolley bus in local urban service as well as rail rapid transit operating on exclusive rights-of-way, generally subway or elevated. The term "public transportation" includes transit or mass transportation plus rail commuter services and taxis.
2. C. H. Holden, *The City of London, A Record of Destruction and Survival* (1951), p. 166. For a memorable picture of congestion at Ludgate Circus in 1870, see p. 67.
3. Edward Dana, "Reflections on Urban Transit." An address before the Canadian Club, Montreal, April 21, 1947.
4. Ebenezer Howard, *Garden Cities of Tomorrow* (1902), p. 134.
5. Lewis Mumford, *The Culture of Cities* (1938), p. 323.
6. The rate of population growth for the United States from 1950 to 1960 was 1.7 per cent per year for the country as a whole, less than 1 per cent outside metropolitan areas, and 2.3 per cent within these areas. Growth of the metropolitan areas themselves was 1 per cent in central cities and 4 per cent in the outlying areas. U.S. Bureau of the Census, "Growth of Metropolitan Areas in the United States: 1960 to 1963," *Population Characteristics*, Series P-20, No. 131, September 4, 1964, Table A.
8. U.S. Bureau of the Census, *Census of Population: 1950* and *Census of Population: 1960*.
9. Associated Universities, Inc., *Reduction of Urban Vulnerability, Report of Project East River*, Pt. V (July 1952), p. 14.
10. The President's Materials Policy Commission, *Resources for Freedom*, Summary of Vol. I (June 1952), p. 7. The task of feeding the city is illustrated by the collective appetite of New York City, whose daily diet consists of 2.5 million loaves of bread, 5 million quarts of milk, 15 million pounds of fresh fruits and vegetables, 4 million pounds of meat, and close to 30,000 gallons of wine. Every day 36,000 tons of refuse must be trucked away. Gilbert Millstein, "Statistics: Most of Them Superlatives," *New York Times Magazine* (February 1, 1953), p. 29.
11. The Port of New York Authority, *Metropolitan Transportation—1980*, New York, 1963, p. 347.

12. The same, p. 348. Most of this shift had already taken place by 1930, however, when the figure was down to 16 per cent.

13. It may be assumed, however, that the growth recorded by the close-in areas during the decade of the 1940's was not a reversal of the long-run trend but was occasioned by the wartime shortage of housing, which resulted in doubling up as well as the use of previously vacant dwellings.

14. As a result of these trends, the proportion of the population of Chicago living within two miles of the center declined from 17 per cent in 1910 to 6 per cent in 1950; and the proportion living eight miles out or beyond rose from 9 per cent to 24 per cent. . . . Actually the number of people in the close-in zone was the same in 1930 and 1950, and the only substantial change from 1930 to 1950 was in the outer zone. *Growth and Redistribution of the Resident Population in the Chicago Standard Metropolitan Area,* A Report by the Chicago Community Inventory to the Office of the Housing and Redevelopment Coordinator and the Chicago Plan Commission (1954), p. 18.

15. In 1950, 11 per cent of the total metropolitan population lived within two miles of the center compared to 24 per cent in 1900. Hans Blumenfeld, "The Tidal Wave of Metropolitan Expansion," *Journal of the American Institute of Planners,* Vol. 20 (Winter 1954), p. 13. . . .

16. Information from the Philadelphia Urban Traffic and Transportation Board.

17. Regional Plan Association, Inc., *Population 1954-1975 in the New Jersey—New York—Connecticut Metropolitan Region,* Bulletin 85, p. 25. Also, Port of New York Authority, *Metropolitan Transportation—1980,* 1963, pp. 349—50.

18. *Washington Post and Times Herald* (June 29, 1955).

19. Elmer T. Peterson, ed., *Cities Are Abnormal* (1946), p. v.

20. "Must Millions March?", *Bulletin of the Atomic Scientists,* Editorial (June 1954), p. 194.

21. The same, p. 195.

22. Frank Lloyd Wright, "The Future of the City," *Saturday Review of Literature* (May 21, 1955), p. 12.

23. National Association of Home Builders, *A New Face for America* (1953), p. 6. Data from Federal Works Agency, Public Buildings Administration.

24. For a view of what is happening to "prosperous" suburbs see "Blight—Suburban Style," *Urban Land* (May 1955).

25. "The far-flung metropolitan city of the motor age contains suburban slums and blighted commercial areas which are as appalling in their way as the old tight-packed city slums of the railway age." C. McKim Norton, "Metropolitan Transportation," *An Approach to Urban Planning,* Gerald Breese and Dorothy E. Whitman, eds. (1953), p. 82.

26. John Bauer, "The Crisis in Urban Transit," *Public Management* (August 1952), p. 176.

27. W. H. Spears, quoting Joseph W. Lund in "Transit Is Dynamic," *Mass Transportation* (September 1954), p. 40.

28. Mumford, *The Culture of Cities,* pp. 243, 441.

29. Walter Blucher, "Moving People—Planning Aspects of Urban Traffic Problems," *Virginia Law Review,* Vol. 36 (November 1950), p. 849.

30. Arthur B. Gallion and Simon Eisner, *The Urban Pattern* (1950), p. 193.

31. Mumford, *The Culture of Cities,* p. 296.

32. Charles M. Nelson, "Expressways and the Planning of Tomorrow's Cities," in *Proceedings* of the Annual National Planning Conference, American Society of Planning Officials, Los Angeles, August 13—16, 1950 (1951), p. 121.

The Streetcar:

Shaper of American Cities

George M. Smerk

Indiana University

In an earlier era, the horsecar and the streetcar answered the need for urban transportation. But beyond fulfilling a need, they exerted a positive influence on the way in which many cities developed.

By focusing on the past, this selection provides an interesting perspective on urban transportation. Many of the urban transportation problems of today turn on the physical structure of the central business district and on the particular way in which a city is laid out. While the streetcar is little more than a museum piece, its influence on the structure of American cities confronts us daily.

The streetcar and the street railway on which it ran, once among the most familiar pieces of urban street furniture, have almost disappeared from the American scene. As is the situation today with airport facilities, fifty years ago no town or city worthy of the name could consider itself within the circle of modern urbanized life if it was not served by a street railway. At the time of the First World War, the streetcar prevailed from shore to shore in towns and cities of all sizes. Indeed, the streets of some major cities had hundreds of miles of street railway track laid in them, and some had over a thousand cars clanging their way about as an integral part of the vital woof and warp of daily life.

The world has changed. No longer is the streetcar to be found in Chicago, Baltimore, Syracuse, Kansas City, Peoria, or any of a hundred other places where they had once been commonplace. Only in a few holdouts like Boston, Philadelphia, Pittsburgh, New Orleans, and San Francisco can cars be found operating in revenue service. Of this demise the streetcar buffs—of which there are large numbers—lament loudly, and the sentimental brush away a tear at the disappearance of another part of those safe old days which in retrospect seem so good. If you want to go by trolley, you can't get there any more.

But the streetcar was more than just a way of going places. In its clanging comings and goings on the thoroughfares of American urban places, from its humble horsedrawn origins in the first half of the nineteenth century to about 1920, the streetcar acted as an inexorable force in molding American cities. In an age innocent of private transportation for the masses, the distribution of population within a metropolitan area of any note was determined largely by the location of streetcar lines. The site of economic activity, too, was markedly determined and its particular form set by the streetcar. And all this was done

From George M. Smerk, "The Streetcar: Shaper of American Cities," *Traffic Quarterly*, October 1967, pp. 569-584. Used by special permission of the Eno Foundation for Transportation, Inc.

with what seems today to be a remarkably compact form and neatness, especially in contrast with the sprawling, auto-dominated, present-day metropolis, which possesses all the form and order of a large bread pudding.

All this came about with the advent of the Industrial Revolution and the economic need for population concentration in urban centers. The rush of population to the cities as the industrial age got under way forced the horizontal expansion of urbanized areas; technology was insufficiently developed to permit the construction of large buildings in the vertical dimension. Moreover, the factory system and increased specialization of all tasks, whether industrial or not, made necessary the separation of home and workplace. The limiting factor in this separation was how far one could walk in a reasonable time, say, thirty minutes. Moreover, in larger cities, such as London and Paris, except for those who could afford to own a coach or hire a cab, difficulty in traveling about within town tended to concentrate life in various neighborhoods or quarters of the city. In many ways, therefore, the new industrial cities of Europe were not a unified whole. They tended to be overlaid upon the existing medieval cities and towns which had existed prior to industrialization. In any case, travel difficulty meant that industrial populations clustered about the "dark satanic mills" in equally dark satanic dwellings. Clearly, some means of public transport was needed to make urban life more livable.

London was the first industrial-age city in which an attempt was made to meet the challenge of developing urban public transport. George Shillabeer, an enterprising coachbuilder, began to operate a line of omnibuses in 1829. Prior to that, there had been some efforts to provide service with vehicles similar to the stagecoaches used on intercity journeys, but limited carrying capacity had somewhat tempered their success as urban haulers. Shillabeer's vehicle was, in contrast, aimed strictly at the urban passenger traveling relatively short distances. It seated sixteen to eighteen passengers facing each other on two long seats attached to the sides of the body. A door and a step at the rear permitted relatively easy entrance and exit. The roughness of the streets made wheels of large diameter necessary to reduce as much as possible the effort required to move the brightly painted "buses." While the omnibus fitted well with the need for improved urban transport and was soon adopted in other cities on both sides of the Atlantic, as long as streets were poorly paved it was a slow and often bone-shattering mode of travel, as teams of horses struggled to pull them over the rough roadway, urged on by the bellowed curses of the drivers.

Advent of the street railway

The real breakthrough in improved public transport, however, came in the form of the street railway, an American invention with a most notable effect on United States cities.

It all began in November of 1832 when the New York and Harlem Railroad Company put a service into operation along Fourth Avenue in New York City. It was almost accidental that the railroad was used for urban transport service, since it had been built as a connection for a proposed steam railway linking New York City with Albany. In the true entrepreneurial spirit, however, the promoters of the railway saw an economic opportunity in offering local service, and extended the line of small horse-drawn cars well into the built-up part of the city on the southern portion of Manhattan Island. In addition to providing a valuable service, the horsecars immediately proved to be popular with the customers. For one thing, metal wheels on metal rails provided a more comfortable ride than omnibus wheels thumping and crashing over cobblestones.

The new mode of transport was also a source of joy to management. The reduction in the friction of the vehicle with the road surface made it possible for a horse to move faster and pull a greater weight than was the case with the omnibus.

Not everyone was overjoyed, however. Due to the reluctance of the city fathers in many urban areas to permit a railway on the city streets, little encouragement was given to street railway proposals. However, by the late 1840's and 1850's, as the horsecar proved its worth and citizens demanded a street railway as a sign of progress, if nothing else, construction was taken up with increasing rapidity until most of the world's major cities enjoyed at least the beginnings of street railway service.

Since the street railway grew up with the American city, it helped to shape it and give it form and order. This was generally not true in Europe and in other places where cities were originally shaped by the medieval necessity for walls or were centered around the church or castle, or in Renaissance times designed to prove and magnify the power of a great prince or planned to embellish the capital of a kingly despot. In the United States, cities as a developed entity were typically not a given factor when the industrial age got under way. Only in the oldest and largest eastern cities, where urban development was already well in hand by the beginning of the nineteenth century, were the street railways added after substantial growth had occurred.

A key factor in urban expansion, as well as its reasonable limit, was the distance one could travel in approximately thirty minutes. Since the average speed of a horsecar was about four miles an hour, the practical radius from the core of a city to its outermost built-up point was about two miles during the reign of the horsecar.

During the second half of the nineteenth century, changing technology lengthened the thirty-minute stride of public transport and widened urban horizons. The cable car, which typically moved at about eight or nine miles an hour, was too expensive to be utilized on any but the most heavily traveled lines in already extensively developed parts of the city. As a result, cable railways played but a negligible role in the extensive development of American cities, although they did tend to intensify development in certain already highly urbanized sections. The electric car, however, relatively inexpensive to build and operate, with an average speed of about ten miles an hour, permitted expansion out to a distance of about five miles from the city core. At the floodtide of urban expansion, prior to the age of the automobile, it was the electric streetcar that proved to be the most potent force of all in determining the shape, quality, and direction of American city growth.

One of the major contributions of the streetcar and the street railway was in creating a focus for the whole city in a central business district—the "downtown" of American cities. Older cities, like Philadelphia, Baltimore, and Boston, formed before the age of public transport, already had the beginnings of a downtown core in the form of a cluster of shops, business houses, and various cultural and civic edifices. The site of this core was often determined by a harbor—the transportation window to the world of the eighteenth and nineteenth centuries. As the country expanded to the west, the urban seed was often planted near the intersection of transport arteries—where two railroads crossed, or where road or railroad touched a navigable waterway.

The advent of mass transportation on the American urban scene emphasized the embryonic urban centerpoint, for the developing street railway network focused upon the core made it the easiest single place in the city to reach. Customers from all over the urban area could gather together easily in a relatively short time and at relatively low cost. As a result, stores and specialized service undertakings that could lead only the most precarious existence in outlying neighborhoods, with their relatively constrained accessibility, could thrive on the customer volume in the central business district. A gaggle of specialty shops catering to the whims of the ladies in particular—and their seemingly natural bent to shop endlessly for items of clothing or adornment—was possible. Department stores, with a startling array and variety of goods, also depended upon a large volume of customers. In short, all of the needs for customer volume were met in the shopping city which grew at the major hub of the streetcar lines.

Not only was downtown a market for goods, but also a market for jobs. The ease of reaching the central point made it possible to gather together a labor force from all the city and thereby concentrate a variety of skills in one place at low cost to worker and employer. Whether his operations depended upon highly paid specialists or sweated labor, the employer could look to the whole urban area as a source from which to choose those he would hire. Moreover, the competition between workers for jobs usually meant lower wages, an ideal situation for budding capitalists.

The centralization of jobs was also a boon to workers, since it allowed greater choice of opportunities. Furthermore, the mobility afforded by the streetcar also meant that the worker was not forced to reside close to his workplace. This mobility was a product not only of the availability of transportation but also of the almost universal nickel fare levied for any journey, regardless of its length. A worker with modest wages could live in pleasanter, more suburban surroundings rather than in the more closely built-up sections near the downtown area; his extra transport cost involved a longer riding time rather than a higher fare. Moreover, since real wages for labor increased slowly but steadily during the period following the Civil War, the fares charged actually became less of a burden on income.

As the most easily accessible point in town, the central business district became the focus for cultural facilities—libraries, museums, concert halls, and lyceums. Culture and social activity require a mass market just as much as does a department store. So, along with the workers and the shoppers, the streetcars brought crowds of music and theater lovers to their artistic feasts, and scholars were transported to the point where they could be served with the greatest variety of cultural goods most economically.

In the course of serving the public, the street railways at first followed the people. As private enterprise seeking profit, the streetcar companies looked initially toward developed areas for fares. Services were extended only where there seemed to be a good opportunity for revenue; development of new neighborhoods was not in the cards for the street railway companies in antebellum days and for a time thereafter. The relatively slender resources of the companies were partly the cause of this conservative policy, but the lack of strong population pressure outward—so significant in the latter decades of the nineteenth century—was another reason.

However, with the rush of rural and foreign-born peoples to the city in the aftermath of the Civil War, the streetcar often led in the development of new neighborhoods beginning in the decade following Appomattox, reaching its zenith during the heyday of the electric car in the twenty years following 1890. Developmental activities by the street railway companies capitalized on the pressure by the immigrants, for living space near the core, and the desire of an increasingly large part of the middle-class population for more spacious living.

The house with a garden sited in the balmy glens of suburbia is not a new ideal for Americans or, indeed, for English-speaking people as a group. It has long been a symbol of moving up to better living. Moreover, as lower-cost land was available on the outskirts of the growing cities, suburban living was not necessarily an expensive affair. Real estate developers and street railway companies soon forged close ties. Indeed, many street railway companies went into the real estate business, profiting from the sale of land and houses and at the same time building new markets and new revenues for their transport operations.

When a streetcar line pushed out into new territory, housing typically sprang up to a distance of from two to four blocks on either side of the route. The form of a given neighborhood, in terms of lot size and type of house, depended upon who did the development and what features other than transport availability added or detracted from the potential quality of the neighborhood. Small lots generally meant small houses for families with more modest incomes, whereas large lots were usually the sites of larger houses for more well-to-do folk. In other places, depending upon the demand and fashion prevalent in a given city, apartment houses of varying quality might spring up.

As might be expected, residential development of an area began along the street served by the streetcars. During horsecar days, this street was initially the most attractive location because of convenience. When the electric car came into use, this ceased to be true. Poles and wires were an adjunct of the electric car; their erection undoubtedly caused more than one conniption when proud householders saw their view spoiled by the necessities of the new technology. The cars were noisy, particularly in the early days of electrification, and proceeded on their way with an accompaniment of gear-grinding and motor whine. The heavier electric cars also produced loud thumps when passing over bad rail joints or poor trackage. And trackage of less than desirable quality was often a feature of the early days of electrification when many firms used the original horsecar track to bear cars of considerably greater heft than it had been designed for. As a result, property immediately along the streetcar route became less desirable for residential purposes by those who could afford a choice in the matter.

The clank and grind of the electric cars may have driven householders away, but the "abandoned" property and the access afforded by the street railway made the "trolley street" attractive to commercial development. Often the property could be purchased for a most reasonable price and houses cheaply converted into stores and shops. As a result of conversion of residences or purposeful store building, the streets along which the streetcars ran became shopping areas of a long, strung-out nature, dubbed disdainfully by planners of today the "strip shopping street." The market area tapped by these establishments extended along the streetcar line for some distance and included as well the three- or four-block residential area on either side of the transport route. In general, shops on such streets supplied necessities; the purchase of more exotic goods or shopping around in connection with a costly purchase demanded a ride downtown.

Eventually, however, expanding streetcar service developed some commercial competition for the core area. The junction points of major car lines outside the downtown area often became the site of shopping centers of considerable size. Service by several car lines meant that a much larger market area was accessible to a given location. What happened, in effect, was that two strip shopping streets collided with one another to produce a miniature downtown. Another spot ripe for the development of subshopping centers was at terminal points where the car lines or several carriers came together and passengers were often forced to wait: an excellent opportunity for whiling away the time shopping, and an equally excellent opportunity for businessmen.

The location of housing and jobs and the availability of public transportation had an obvious relationship. Those whose jobs were located downtown—in the earliest days of urban development, when cities were small by today's standards, most jobs would fall into this category—would naturally choose to dwell along streetcar lines going directly downtown. Downtown-oriented jobs eventually came to be more and more white-collar office-type jobs, sales personnel who staffed department stores and specialty shops, and those engaged in the sweated trades—garment workers, for example—when the sweatshops were located downtown.

As the nineteenth century progressed, factory districts grew up within certain parts of the cities. These districts tended to develop small public transport systems within the overall system of transport for the whole city to meet the needs of the blue-collar workers. These lines were generally not too well integrated into the rest of the public transport system. Over time, certain parts of town came to be dominated by people working in certain trades close to their homes. Choice in dwelling place was limited by accessibility of the factory area to the rest of the city. As factories came to be located farther and farther from the downtown, the general accessibility tended to be more limited and workers became, in large part, captives of their occupation. In Chicago, during the first two decades of this century, for example, the stockyards area and the territory around the South Chicago steel mills fitted this pattern of industry-dominated urban transport.

The construction of crosstown lines, beginning in the 1870's and 1880's in the larger cities, came as one of the by-products of the merger or consolidation of streetcar companies, and gave added flexibility to the street railway system as a whole. It also proved to be an advantage to those who may be classified as day laborers—those persons hired on a day-to-day basis and whose work location may vary considerably throughout the course of a week or month. These generally unskilled, low-income workers were often forced to live close to downtown in order to be able either to walk to a work site or have the greatest choice of streetcar service available to them. This was most true when the arterial lines belonged to different and rival street railway companies. Without the free transfer privilege, using several car lines necessitated the payment of more than one fare, a factor which loomed large in the budget of low-paid workers.

Older areas along radial street railway lines could be the site of low-income housing development once the crosstown lines were established. Since the electrification of systems was one of the reasons for consolidation (elimination of competition was, of course, a principal reason), and consolidation part of the background of the construction of crosstown lines, the old neighborhood had several transport-related forces at work upon it. As noted previously, electrified lines tended to be less pleasant to live along because of the noise factor; thus, opening areas devoted originally only to single-family dwellings developed to other uses, especially commercial. The crosstown lines and transfer privilege permitted the day workers a greater choice of dwelling place, since all parts of the city were accessible at low cost in reasonable travel time. Conversion of older housing, in what were at one time relatively high-class residential districts, was a logical outcome resulting in overcrowding and a general lowering of neighborhood tone. In places where land had been divided into relatively small lots, rising incomes of the early inhabitants, coupled with available property farther from the core that better fitted their aspirations, led to their movement out of the original neighborhoods. Again, high-density housing often replaced single-family dwellings as the housing demand of low-income groups became more acute. Squalor and slums were often the ultimate product of these conditions.

A more cheerful aspect of the streetcar-shaped city was development of the suburbs. Indeed, the growth of outlying sections of the city dates from the earliest days of the street railways. While suburbs today are often conceptualized as the essence of worthwhile life, the first suburban residents of most American cities were the dead. As cities and towns began to grow to more substantial size during the middle of the nineteenth century, burial grounds came to be located away from the downtown area in places that offered abundant land at reasonable cost. Since antebellum United States towns were frequently bereft of parks and other open space for recreation, the few parklike places in many urban areas were the cemeteries. Visiting them on Sundays became a popular pastime. Beyond the opportunity of paying respect to the dead, it gave residents of crowded or unpleasant cities an opportunity to enjoy fresh air and sunshine. After the Civil War, a conflict that did much to populate the cemeteries as well as increase the population of the living in the rapidly developing industrial cities of the north, there was pressure from the public for outlying parks and picnic groves for recreational purposes. Whether it was to a cemetery or a site of a more light-hearted nature, streetcar service was soon offered, since it provided street railway companies with a means to balance traffic and revenues throughout the week. So popular were the weekend recreational spots served by streetcars that often Sunday was the busiest day of the week for the streetcar companies.

The coming of electrically powered street railways had a most buoyant effect on the development of the suburbs. Electricity not only provided power for the streetcars, but also served to power an adjunct of the street railways that bloomed in the 1880's: the amusement park. Usually, the pleasure domes were owned by the streetcar company for the particular purpose of generating weekend traffic during the summer.

Young couples—and not so young couples—had the attractions of the suburbs exposed to them as a by-product of their weekend car rides. As the land along the extended streetcar lines and the interurban lines was ripe for development, many families gave up the old, built-up city for the proverbial vine-covered home in the suburbs.

As a result of the ubiquitous electric car pushing into outlying places, aided and abetted by steam railway commuter lines in some cities, a definite overall pattern of urban development was observable by the beginning of the twentieth century. As the lines of transport radiated from the downtown area, an urban configuration developed resembling the outlines of a starfish. Between the starfish arms, the land remained unurbanized. Indeed, in some midwestern cities it was possible to find land still used for farming relatively close to the core and between highly urbanized arms of the city.

Along the commuter railroads, the technology and economics of the steam locomotive made it impractical to space stops closer than two or three miles. Around the railway stations, small villages and towns developed, unattached to the city by continuous urbanization. Because the technical and economic capabilities of the electric car permitted more frequent stops and rapid acceleration at modest cost in comparison to locomotive-hauled trains, the electric interurban railways were able to space their stops more closely together. In either case, satellite developments—eventually bound to grow together—developed along the lines of public transport like so many beads upon a string, augmenting the starfish pattern.

As the United States entered the second decade of the twentieth century, a consistent pattern of urban development was recognizable based on the public transportation provided principally by the streetcar. Cities were compact and, despite their other faults, coherent forms, united by the strong thread of public transport and centered upon a vigorous downtown core. Transport technology, principally in the form of the electric car, provided the means of moving large numbers of people with a most modest use of scarce and valuable street space. Indeed, the increasing efficiency of service and parsimony in land use necessary for transport purposes had created cities of a size and population that would have been unthinkable before the age of public transport.

Decisive role of the automobile

But a new technology arose. The decisive role in shaping our cities played by the streetcar ended shortly after the First World War with the advent of the reliable and inexpensive motorcar as the common man's private magic carpet. While a small role continued to be played by public transportation for a decade or two following the First World War, the dominant force in shaping our cities for almost the last fifty years has been the automobile.

The automobile proved to be ideal in serving those areas where population density was too low to warrant investment in track, power supply, and equipment. In providing this service, the automobile was not only benefited by the wonders and economies of mass production, but also by the substantial public investment made in improving roads and highways. Public pressure for the improvement of roads was initiated in an organized manner by the bicycle enthusiasts of the 1880's. The efforts of the cyclists were soon augmented by farmers and early automobile owners. The greatest success of highway enthusiasts was reached with the beginning of federal participation in highway expansion in 1916. All levels of government were soon busily engaged in developing and improving highways. In urban regions, the area between the starfish arms unserved by public transportation was soon provided with improved roads, and new housing developments sprang up as this territory became readily accessible. Population rushed out into the suburban areas with little regard to the existence of public transportation. The end of the streetcar line once marked the end of the urbanized area; now such a terminus was left in the backwash of explosive suburban development. In the excitement over the new freedom of circulation afforded by the family car, few noted at first that the automobile-borne traveler required an amount of street space far in excess of that needed by the streetcar passenger.

For the electric railway industry, the automobile was merely one of many straws to bear, but its competition was the one that finally broke the back of the majority of street railway firms. Since the days when fast-talking promoters had pushed the building of the first horsecar lines, the street railways had been burdened by overcapitalization—that is, the capital represented by shares of stock and bonded indebtedness was far in excess of the assets, and hence the earning power of the firm.

The problem was compounded when, in an orgy of promotional and monopolistic zeal, fancy prices were paid to join street railway companies together into citywide traction systems. Even worse, a large part of the capital of the merged firms was in the form of bonded debt, which meant that interest charges had to be met annually, regardless of the business fortunes of the firm. Moreover, in return for the franchise to use the public streets for their track, certain obligations were placed upon the street railway firms. Among these were the limitation of the fare to five cents; the duty of sweeping, watering, and plowing streets; maintaining the streets; maintaining bridges; and other tasks that grew more burdensome as the years went by. Rising costs for manpower, equipment, and supplies, coupled with the five-cent fare, spelled trouble after the turn of the century. By the time of the sharp general price rise during the First World War, it spelled bankruptcy for many transit firms. In the face of rising automotive competition, the unkindest cut of all was delivered upon those streetcar companies with the obligation to maintain the streets; in some places, they were forced to pave the whole of the roadway for the convenience of their rival.

The great depression proved to be a more serious thorn in the side. Many companies had barely weathered the shaky days of the 1920's, when passengers began to desert the streetcars for the automobile in increasingly large numbers. A considerable number of transit firms had stayed in business only by cutting back sharply on maintenance of tracks and equipment. With the industrial collapse of the nation, there was a consequent falloff in the bread-and-butter rush-hour traffic, and a sharp drop in off-peak riding as tight consumer budgets cut into the downtown shopping habit.

As maintenance was cut to the bone, an air of decrepitude settled over the street railways of the nation, and rust and rotting window frames replaced the brave liveries and gold striping of the good times. The motor bus, originally used by some firms as a feeder to their streetcar lines, began to take over some lightly traveled streetcar lines in the 1920's; eventually, with the wholesale abandonment of street railways in the depression, the bus became the mainstay. Only in the larger cities did the streetcar remain in any large numbers. In an effort to bolster the tarnished image in the mid-thirties, the street railway industry promoted the modern streamlined streetcar which gained some acceptance. Again, during the Second World War, the whole public transit industry received a vast shot in the arm both from the return to prosperity and the rationing of gasoline. It was, however, the last stand of the streetcar.

At war's end, the rush to the suburban areas began again; this time it was a human movement of tidal wave proportions. At the same time, equipment and track were in dire need of replacement because of the pounding given by wartime traffic and the headache of wartime shortages added to earlier deferred maintenance. Cost of such work skyrocketed in the postwar inflation. In any case, the new urban development was far beyond the reach of most streetcar lines; extending them was too costly and, in any event, unthinkable in the automobile age. By the fifth decade of the twentieth century, the streetcar had become an embarrassing anachronism in most American cities, and—horror of horrors—one that impeded the smooth movement of the automobiling public. As a result, by the 1950's most American cities handled their transportation on rubber tires on the public streets.

The prime shaper of the city today is the automobile. New urban and suburban developments cluster around the freeway exits just as they once did along the interurban lines. The entire older part of the city is frequently in an advanced state of decay, fit perhaps to drive through, but not to dwell in for those who can afford choice.

If the automobile is triumphant as the basis of urban transport in most places, its triumph is fast becoming a rather hollow one. The great boon of the automobile is the freedom and flexibility it provides to its user who is not obliged to follow any particular route or adhere to the timetable set by a public transport firm. But when persons in great numbers crowd themselves and their cars into the same place at the same time, the end result is not freedom but that antithesis of freedom, the traffic jam.

What is left of urban mass transportation today is dominated by the motor bus except in a handful of cities where there is rapid transit service or some small vestige of the streetcar. Sights and sounds are missing that were once so common. Gone is the clang of the streetcar bell, the clatter of the wheels over the track of an intersecting line, the rumble of the steel wheel upon the steel rail. The cars, with their often colorful liveries of red or green and cream, of traction orange, and of gold striping, are almost gone. No longer does the motorman nudge over a switch point with a switch iron, or a small boy flatten a penny on the track.

In many cities once boasting large systems, few vestiges of the physical presence of the street railway or streetcar remain. Youngsters automobiling by wonder why there is track in a street so far from the railroad; a roadside eating place bears a remarkable resemblance to something to which a passing motorist once went downtown for his first pair of long pants. The more subtle imprint is still there: the strip shopping street, the highly developed shopping district, the odd way the houses appear to be much older near certain streets, the location of slums and the downtown, and the now dowdy older suburbs.

The streetcar is today literally a museum piece. Bands of enthusiasts sparked by nostalgia, or perhaps by a passion like that of the academician to delve into the esoteric, have, with great patience and sizable expenditure of funds, constructed operating museums. Here cars of all vintages are on display and often in operation on short stretches of track. The inevitable tourist, forever thirsty for something to dispel his ennui, finds a bit of the past in the museum for himself, and something startlingly different for his children.

There are places in the world where those who formulate transport policy have not been completely overwhelmed by the internal combustion engine. Particularly in Europe, Japan, and the United States, enthusiasm has been growing for mass transportation by rail in cities growing increasingly paralyzed by automotive traffic. In the United States, most of the interest has been in connection with the development of rapid transit subway lines. While there is need for such developments in places of large population and large demand, their construction can hardly be justified where the need for transport is more modest. In Western Europe—particularly in West Germany—the situation has been met by the development of a concept called light rapid transit. Vehicles that are suspiciously like streetcars, sometimes operating in short trains, are to be found running on reserved rights-of-way and in short subway tunnels, offering a quality of service competitive with the automobile at a fraction of the cost of building a full-scale rapid transit line. Such a means of transport may have a significant future role to play in medium-size urban areas in the United States.

Who knows but that in the general revival of mass transportation currently beginning in the United States, it may once again be fashionable to live along the streetcar line. Besides proving the adage that there is in truth nothing new under the sun, the modernized version of the street railway might prove itself a vital force in reshaping the cities forged by its ancestors so long ago.

---

49 The Evolution of the Motor Bus as a Transport Mode

John B. Rae
Harvey Mudd College

The motor bus serves two transportation markets: the intercity and the intracity. In both of these markets, it is a very important factor in moving people. This selection traces the history of the motor bus, describes the development of the vehicle and of the highway-street system, and reviews some of the current and proposed uses of the motor bus in solving passenger transportation problems.

The motor bus is the largest single public passenger carrier in the world today. In the United States buses carry almost half of all inter-city passengers using public transportation, although, because the typical bus trip is short, the airlines come out well ahead in passenger-miles. About twice as many passengers travel inter-city by bus as by air, but air travel accounts for three times as many passenger miles (1). These figures apply only to a third of all bus passenger mileage. The rest is intraurban travel. Here the bus at present has no serious rival as a commercial passenger carrier; and barring some new transport technology not yet in prospect, it will retain its commanding position—and this without considering school bus transportation, which uses three times as many vehicles as the commercial bus services and carries about half the pupils in the country to and from school (2).

From John B. Rae, "The Evolution of the Motor Bus as a Transport Mode," *High Speed Ground Transportation Journal*, Vol. 5, Summer 1971, pp. 221-235. Used by permission.

Besides being the most widely used, the motor bus can also claim to be one of the oldest modes of passenger transportation currently in service. The first mechanical road vehicle designed and actually used for carrying passengers was Richard Trevithick's steam carriage of 1801 (3). Its career on the streets of London was brief, but it was definitely a motor bus in the sense of being a self-propelled highway vehicle for the public carriage of passengers. The steam railway passenger train made its first appearance in 1825. Trevithick's carriage was the forerunner of a succession of experiments with steam omnibuses, some of them showing considerable promise, until the whole development was smothered in Britain by discriminatory tolls and adverse legislation promoted by both stagecoach and railway interests (4). The culmination was the famous (or notorious) Locomotives on Highways Act of 1865, better known as the "Red Flag Law," which provided that any self-propelled vehicle on a public highway must be limited to speed not exceeding four miles an hour and preceded by a man on foot carrying a red flag. The historian now can only speculate on what might have happened to highway transportation if technology had been left with a free hand.

Modern bus transportation as we now know it dates from the beginning of the present century, when the motor vehicle emerged from the experimental stage to become a practical operating device. The early buses were improvisations. At first they were usually ordinary touring cars, sometimes elongated to give additional seating capacity, or on intracity lines horse buses were converted by installing motors (5). Few carried over ten passengers. Routes were short and disconnected, restricted largely to areas that lacked rail service, either railroad or streetcar. As patronage grew, larger buses were constructed by putting passenger-carrying bodies on truck chassis. Such a vehicle went into service in 1914 between Hibbing and Alice, Minnesota (four miles), for a fare of fifteen cents one way and twenty-five cents round trip—an operation that in due course grew into the Greyhound System (6).

It was technically possible to build larger vehicles and to design them for their intended purpose. As one example, the double-decker, in the form of the Milnes-Daimler bus, appeared in London as early as 1905 and came into widespread use for local service, although it never gained acceptance in the United States. A double-decker bus has the advantage of being able to carry a big payload for the square feet of street space it occupies. However, unless there is a conductor to collect fares while the bus is moving, loading or discharging passengers in peak load situations may require an inordinate amount of time. Given the shoestring character of early American bus operations and the generally higher labor cost in the United States as compared to Europe, a second member of the bus crew was a luxury to be dispensed with if possible. There were more compelling reasons inhibiting the adoption of big buses in the United States at this period. The wretched condition of American roads before the First World War is difficult to comprehend in these days of super-highways; in 1900 there were less than two hundred miles of hard-surfaced road in the entire country outside the larger cities. The pneumatic tire for large highway vehicles did not become available until 1916. On unpaved roads and with solid rubber tires a large bus would shake itself and its passengers to pieces if it tried to move faster than a crawl, apart from the fact that neither road surfaces nor bridges could support heavy self-propelled vehicles. Under these conditions bus transportation could be little more than a minor supplement to rail transport.

It was therefore quite understandable that in the United States the bus should have come into its own as a transportation mode along with the highway building boom of the 1920's, including the adoption of a federal program providing support for the present primary road system (the routes marked "U.S."). The Association of American Railroads gives 1922 as the year when vehicle manufacturers began to design chassis and bodies specifically for buses, rather than to modify truck, automobile, or streetcar designs. The Association noted (this was 1945) that the change occurred with intercity buses first:

"Merchandising ideas have been applied to a greater extent in connection with intercity than with city bus business. Competition with rail carriers as well as with the private automobile has made intercity companies more dependent for ride-selling reasons on the appearance of their equipment. Special considerations of comfort, safety, convenience, and economy were necessary to help create a demand.

"The consequence was rapid growth in the popularity of the "De Luxe" intercity sedan type which turned producers' attention from the street car body in 1924. From experience it was quickly found that the street car type of body, when used for interurban or intercity service, did not offer the necessary attractiveness and comfort which were instrumental in determining whether or not the prospective traveler would travel by rail, bus, or auto.

"Just as the development of the pleasure automobile was largely influenced by the popularity of certain models, so also the popularity of certain features of bus body design has largely determined the lines of development. Out of the keen competition, long runs, and good roads came the vehicle of the long, low-hung body with cross seats, high speed, quiet motor and lighter but more sturdy construction" (7).

The most spectacular example of efforts to develop the bus to a level of acceptability competitive with other carriers was the introduction of sleeper bus service on the Pacific Coast. The first such route opened in 1928 between Seattle and Portland (8). Others followed, ranging as far south as Los Angeles, and services were maintained intermittently through the 1930's. The vehicles used, based on a design by Dwight E. Austin, engineer for Pickwick Stages, had surprisingly modern features. They accommodated twenty-five passengers in Pullman-type compartments, and they had lavatories and small kitchens equipped to provide sandwich meals. Their dimensions, compared with a 1968 single-level intercity bus, were: (9)

	1928 bus	1968 bus
Overall length	34 ft. 4 in.	35 ft.
Overall width	— 96 in.	— 96 in.
Overall height	10 ft. 3 in.	10 ft.
Weight	14,000 lbs.	28,733 lbs.

Bus service of this type was exceptional; its failure to survive is evidence that the bus continued to have limitations as a long-distance carrier. It was cheaper to travel by bus than by train, but it was likely to be slower and less comfortable. The American highway network was considerably better in 1940 than it had been twenty or even ten years before, but the only express highways (except for 160 miles of the Pennsylvania Turnpike opened late in 1940) were a few parkways from which commercial vehicles were excluded. The regular main roads still routed traffic through the center of every city, town, and village, making it impossible to maintain high-speed schedules over long distances. The bus had its greatest advantage on relatively short routes of low-density traffic where rail service either did not exist or could not be profitably operated. This feature appears in figures showing that in 1939 buses carried 37.5 per cent (132.7 million) of all intercity passengers using public transportation compared with 62 per cent (219.9 million) going by rail (10)—air travel was minor—whereas in passenger-miles the bus share was 27 per cent (9.5 billion) against 66 per cent (23.7 billion) for rail.

In intracity transportation bus travel grew with astonishing rapidity before there was any major technological change in the vehicle itself. In 1906 the electric streetcar carried 90 per cent of all intraurban transit passengers (11). Table 1 demonstrates what happened after that. By 1940 the trolley car could be found only in the very large cities; it is now a museum piece. Spartanburg, South Carolina, was the first American city to adopt all-bus public transportation (1923); in 1931 Canton, Ohio, became the first city of over 100,000 to do so (12).

The paramount factor in this process was the private automobile, but this is a large and elaborate story in itself. All that needs to be said here is that, as the use of public transportation declined and as city streets became increasingly occupied by automobiles, the advantages of even the ungainly buses of the early '20's

TABLE 1

Trends in Methods of Transit, 1919-68 (in billions of total passengers)*

Year	Street Car Passengers	Per Cent	Rapid Transit Passengers	Per Cent	Trolley Coach Passengers	Per Cent	Motor Bus Passengers	Per Cent	Total Passengers
1919	13.4	90	1.5	10	–	–	–	–	14.9
1924	13.1	80	2.2	13	–	–	1.0	6	16.3
1929	11.8	70	2.6	15	.005	–	2.6	15	17.0
1934	7.4	61	2.2	18	.07	.6	2.4	20	12.0
1939	6.2	48	2.4	19	.4	3.0	3.9	30	12.8
1944	9.5	41	2.6	11	1.2	5.0	9.6	42	23.0
1949	4.9	26	2.3	12	1.7	9.0	10.2	53	19.0
1954	1.5	12	1.9	15	1.4	11.0	7.6	61	12.4
1959	.5	5.3	1.8	18.9	.7	7.4	6.5	68.4	9.5
1964	.3	3.6	1.9	22.9	.3	3.6	5.8	69.9	8.3
1968	.3	3.8	1.9	23.7	.2	2.5	5.6	70.0	8.0

*Data supplied by the American Transit Association.

were accentuated. A bus was cheaper to operate than a streetcar, it was not bound to a track but could maneuver in traffic, and routes could be changed to accommodate to shifts of population. The one asset the trolley car retained was its greater capacity, which accounts for its longer survival in large cities with high-density travel corridors. Until 1940 the average seating capacity of buses used in both intracity and intercity service was below thirty (13), while a streetcar could seat between forty and fifty and had much more room for standees.

Competition with the streetcar gave little incentive for technical improvement of the bus. Loss of business to the private automobile was another matter, which made it essential for transit companies to improve the efficiency, economy, and, if possible, the popularity of their operations. The first major step in this direction was the introduction of the Fageol Twin Coach in 1927, the prototype of the bus design that has become virtually universal. This vehicle had two engines placed underneath, so that the whole street space occupied by the bus was available for passengers (14). This design, like the alternative rear-engined design, also puts the driver in the optimum position to handle the vehicle in traffic.

By the 1930's, to quote the historian of British bus services, "the motor bus had become an established form of service; the railway age was ended" (15). It is significant that this could be said in conditions where passenger rail transport was more readily available than in the United States. British bus development followed a somewhat different pattern from American. Under-floor engined buses were not used until the 1950's; the British counterpart in the 1930's had the engines mounted on the side of the vehicle. The uncomfortable charabanc of the early days, wherein passengers were completely exposed to the weather, disappeared. Britain was somewhat ahead in the introduction of diesel power— 1930 compared to 1934 for the United States (16). By the Second World War, therefore, the fundamentals of the modern bus were practically all in existence: engine moved out of the way so that the vehicle's capacity was optimally used and the driver had maximum vision; diesel power, requiring greater initial investment than gasoline engines but offering lower operating cost; double wheels and multiple axles. The one major future improvement, apart from enlarging the vehicles, was the addition of air conditioning. Toilets were not a common feature even of long-distance buses in that era, but they were used, as we have seen, on special runs.

What was lacking most then, and is still conspicuously lacking, was an understanding of the bus as a part of a transportation system. It was a great advantage that the bus could operate on ordinary roads and streets, free to maneuver and without the requirement of being constrained to a fixed right-of-way. It was in fact too easy. Buses were mingled indiscriminately with the rest of the traffic, subject to the same obstructions and delays in congested areas, and with no allowance for their function as mass carriers. Street space was cheap; it was and is used for bus stops and even for downtown terminals in the '20's and '30's. It is certainly preferable for a bus to pull up at the curb to load and unload than for a trolley car to stop in the middle of the street for the same purpose, but on crowded streets traffic is still held up.

How, at this point, do we judge "acceptability"? By 1940 the bus appeared to be on its way to ascendancy as a local carrier. It accounted for only about a third of intraurban transit travel but this represented a rapid rise from practically nothing in twenty years, with the declining volume of rail-borne passengers increasingly confined to the larger urban centers. For small towns and cities the bus provided whatever public transportation there was. Transportation studies during the Second World War, made in the hope of finding ways to conserve rubber and gasoline, brought out the startling fact that 17 per cent of the urban population of the United States, some 13 million people, lived in 2,320 towns and cities that had no mass transportation of any kind (17)! For the most part these were communities of less than 10,000 population, but many of them were suburbs in metropolitan areas.

Since the Second World War there have been several important developments in bus transportation. The vehicles themselves have not fundamentally changed, but in general they have become larger, more powerful, more attractively designed, and more comfortable to ride in. Seating capacities for both intercity and urban buses rose to an average of forty; then in the 1960's standard bus lengths increased from thirty-five to forty feet and capacities for intercity buses from forty-three to forty-six, including the deck-and-a-half Greyhound Scenicruisers, which were introduced in 1953 and redesigned in 1961 and 1962 (18). Current computations on urban bus transit allow for a passenger capacity of fifty per vehicle, because urban buses do not need to use space for baggage or toilets.

Legislation and practical considerations of operating conditions impose limits on further increases in size. The increases that occurred were possible because of striking developments in the highway system. The decade from 1946 to 1956 saw the building of most of the present network of toll roads and the beginning of California's freeways. The Interstate Highway Act of 1956 provided for the national system of express highways that is now approaching completion. The result has been that buses can operate between points served by express highways at speeds competitive with passenger trains and at considerably less cost. Given modern vehicles with air conditioning and rest rooms, the bus could offer as much in comfort and convenience as the railroad coach—more, indeed, in view of the steady deterioration of railroad passenger service.

In these conditions a marked increase in bus travel could have been anticipated, but it has not materialized. On the contrary, since 1945 there has been a steady decline in the number of intercity passengers carried by bus (excluding commuter and local or suburban service), as well as in passenger miles, with some sign of an upswing in the late 1960's. The peak of intercity bus travel was reached in 1950, when buses carried three-fifths of the intercity passengers using public transportation. The proportion has since fallen to just under half, although the number of passenger miles has increased from its lowest postwar level in 1962.

Long-distance bus travel, like railroad passenger travel, has had to compete with the private automobile, but this is not the principal reason for the failure of intercity bus travel to show sustained growth. Despite the great increase in the number of cars registered in the United States and in the passenger miles of automobile travel, the proportion of intercity passenger mileage represented by the private automobile has not changed significantly in thirty years, and in twenty years the average annual mileage recorded by the family car has risen only from about 9,000 to 9,600 miles (19).

The vital factor has been the rapid growth of air travel—less than a billion passenger miles in 1939; 76 billion in 1967. For trips of over 400 miles, perhaps 500, the ground transportation media are definitely out of the running in speed, and increasingly so in cost.

In local, specifically intraurban transportation, the bus has achieved almost complete ascendancy during the last quarter century. The demise of the trolley car has been noted. At this moment rail-borne transit systems exist in five United States and two Canadian cities (New York, Boston, Philadelphia, Chicago, Cleveland, Montreal, and Toronto), and New York City alone accounts for over four-fifths of all rail rapid transit passengers in the United States (Table 2). A new rapid transit system is under construction in the San Francisco Bay area and others are contemplated. Yet even if all the rail transit systems now under consideration should be built, they will include only a very small proportion of the more than two hundred Standard Metropolitan Statistical Areas listed by the Bureau of the Census for the United States. The others, for the foreseeable future, will rely on bus transit.

The evolution of the vehicle itself has been a major contributor to this development. The high-speed, large-capacity, comfortable bus that functioned so effectively on short-distance intercity runs was even better adapted to service between central city and suburb. No other form of mass transit could compete in either economy or convenience. The only serious threat to bus patronage, indeed, has been the private automobile, and it has been serious enough so that over one hundred fifty of the smaller American cities have lost bus systems since 1945 (20). There has to be a limit to this process. Any city of appreciable size must have a system of public transportation to serve those, perhaps a third of the total population, who for one reason or another cannot travel by car—de-

TABLE 2

Local Transit Patronage by Type of Service. All U.S. Operations — 1966

Transit Revenue Passengers (millions)

TYPE OF SERVICE	New York City*		All Other Cities		Total U.S.	
	Number	Per Cent	Number	Per Cent	Number	Per Cent
Motor Bus	838	39.4	3,864	85.0	4,702	70.5
Rail Rapid Transit	1,288	60.6	296	6.5	1,584	23.7
Street Car	—	—	211	4.7	211	3.2
Trolley Bus	—	—	174	3.8	174	2.6
TOTAL	2,126	100.0	4,545	100.0	6,671	100.0
Per Cent	31.9		68.1		100.0	

*Includes New York Transit Authority and affiliated Manhattan and Bronx Surface Bus Operating Authority and PATH rapid transit operation.
Source: American Transit Association. *Transit Fact Book*, 1967, and New York Transit Authority reports.

fined by the Department of Housing and Urban Development as "the poor, the handicapped, the secondary workers (where the family car is used by another member), the elderly, and the young" (21).

The increasing resort to the bus as the principal medium of urban public transportation has occurred under conditions substantially short of optimum utilization. The fact that buses could operate on ordinary roads and streets and did not require a private right-of-way was a great asset in terms of cheapness and flexibility, but it also subjected bus transportation to the improvisations and half measures that have passed for traffic control in practically every city in the world that has a traffic problem—which means every city that has traffic. Much of the potential of the bus as a mode of urban transportation was frittered away because vehicles capable of carrying large numbers of passengers at high speeds had to share street space indiscriminately with passenger cars and trucks, subject to congestion and delay.

The capacities of bus systems are known. A single lane on an ordinary street, with other traffic excluded, would accommodate 150-175 buses an hour, or 7,500-9,000 passengers on the basis of fifty passengers per bus. On high-speed highways a single lane could take 500-600 buses an hour if they operated non-stop; with stops at one-mile intervals and a thirty-second headway, the capacity is 120 buses an hour at a speed of 45 m.p.h. (22). Tests made by General Motors in 1963 indicated that a single lane of buses on an exclusive roadway and under manual control by their own drivers has a maximum flow of 1,450 vehicles an hour at 33 m.p.h. (23).

Even at forty rather than fifty passengers to a bus, any of these computations shows ample capacity for the transit needs of all but a few extremely high-density urban travel corridors, and the development of urban freeway systems stimulated by the Interstate Highway Act has made the bus an instrument of rapid as well as of mass transit, although so far this opportunity has been largely ignored. St. Louis offers an outstanding example of what can be done. When the twenty-four mile Mark Twain Expressway was opened in 1961, the St. Louis Public Service Company was ready with a "Rapid" bus service whose record has been as follows:

> The eight rush-hour lines make a total of 75 to 80 daily trips in each direction involving over 1,000 miles per day on the expressway. The shopper lines make about 20 daily trips in each direction involving some 200 daily miles on the expressway. The direction that each route operates on the expressway varies from 3.8 to 11.9 miles, with an average of 7.4 miles.
>
> The overall terminal-to-terminal speeds of the rapid lines range from 15.6 to 20.8 m.p.h. On the expressway itself, the buses travel with the general traffic at speeds of from 40 to 50 m.p.h. (24).

Some cities have contemplated more elaborate systems of bus rapid transit in the form of exclusive "busways." Proposals of this kind have been advanced and studies made in Los Angeles, St. Louis, Milwaukee, Atlanta, Pittsburgh, and Portland, Oregon, although no such system is yet in operation (25).

In effect, the bus is to be given a private right-of-way, an interesting development for a transport mode which had as one of its initial advantages the ability to operate on the public highways. The change is a reflection of the greatly increased complexity of all urban transportation. Bus transportation is a subsystem of the total urban transportation system, and its methods of operation have to adapt to accommodate to new conditions.

The busway idea does not diminish the flexibility of this mode of transport. It simply avoids the anomaly of a vehicle capable of carrying forty to fifty passengers expeditiously being held up needlessly in a mass of other traffic. The busway is an adjunct to and not a substitute for the highway. The St. Louis plan provides for eight express bus routes totaling 86 miles, of which 44 will be on freeways and the rest on busways. The bus, that is, can operate both on a private way and a public street. At the same time, a busway could be converted to rail transit if the traffic volume justified it; the choice is an economic rather than a technical consideration. The Atlanta study suggests that when peak-hour traffic volume on a given corridor exceeds 12,000 passengers per hour on public transportation, rail transit may become economically justifiable. At present there are only half a dozen such corridors in North America: four in New York City, one in Toronto, and one in Chicago (26).

On a less ambitious scale, a number of cities have tried to facilitate bus movement in the hope of making bus transit more attractive, as well as more economical. On the latter point, the Cleveland Transit System has estimated that every increase of one mile an hour in bus travel speed would mean a saving for the system of $1 million a year in operating costs (27). The most common technique is to provide exclusive bus lanes on busy streets, usually at rush hours; alternatively parking may be prohibited on such streets, and the effect is to make the curb lane an exclusive bus lane because motorists will avoid a lane full of buses loading and discharging. Good traffic engineering can also help by proper location of bus stops to minimize interference with the flow of traffic. Some examples of such measures are:

Occasionally, the number of buses on a given street will justify the marking of lanes for bus use only. The justification for such a lane is determined by such factors as number and width of lanes, number of buses and number of passengers. Several cities are using exclusive bus lanes advantageously. Results in a few of them:

Peoria, Illinois. Adams and Jefferson Streets, adjacent one-way major streets, have exclusive bus lanes during evening rush hours only. The city reports 25 percent speedup in transit service; 10 percent for other vehicles.

Rochester, New York. A two-block exclusive bus lane is used during evening rush hours only, with 30-minute saving in loading time during the peak two hours.

Birmingham, Alabama. Eight blocks on Third Avenue, morning and evening, showed 40 percent decline in accidents involving transit vehicles, nearly 28 percent decrease in bus travel time and 29 percent cut in auto travel time.

Baltimore. On one-way Cathedral Street, an eight-block stretch has an exclusive bus lane during both morning and evening rush periods. Benefits are a 17 to 22 percent speedup of transit travel and a 39 percent speedup of other traffic.

The possible benefits may not always justify the expense of lane-control signs, pavement markings, the continuing enforcement necessary, possible difficulties with turning maneuvers and the loss of a lane to other traffic.

Washington, D.C. An effective alternative to the exclusive lane was instituted on a stretch of Pennsylvania Avenue which has heavy rush hour bus movement. The transit company wanted an exclusive bus lane. Instead, rush period parking prohibition was established. Result: the heavy loading operation, in itself, made the curb lane in effect an exclusive bus lane. Drivers tend to avoid a lane having substantial bus operation. Congestion was reduced by 30 percent, delays from stopping and idling by 54 percent, and peak-hour travel time by 23 percent for automobiles and 10 percent for buses.

Recessed bus bays are proving their worth in several cities, including Phoenix and Washington, D.C. The latter uses 10- to 12-foot wide bays on the far side of intersections. The bays are 150 to 200 feet long, and are identified by different pavement. Their location beyond the signal point permits a bus to pull into the moving traffic stream during the red phase. Street capacity has been increased substantially (28).

Less has been done with reserved bus lanes on freeways, although this would appear to be an easy and economical way to get rapid transit. One objection is that at rush hours other traffic would be more congested by being restricted to the remaining lanes, but if one purpose of improving bus service is to encourage the use of public transit, having buses go through while private cars are delayed ought to have a persuasive effect. The reserved bus lane is of course justified only if the volume of bus traffic is great enough to utilize its full capacity.

Other technical methods for expediting bus movement are in the experimental stage. These include selective traffic control systems to give preference to buses over other vehicles at traffic lights and permitting them to have priority of access to freeways at metered on-ramps.

In short, during at least the last ten years, and for practical purposes the last twenty, the major advances in bus transportation have not come in the vehicle itself but in other parts of the system—that is, in the construction of highways permitting high-speed operation and the adaptation of existing street networks and techniques of traffic control to improve bus service. For urban transit the gains so achieved seem unimpressive. The proportion of transit passengers traveling by bus has continued to increase, but at negligible rate since 1960, and meanwhile the aggregate number of bus passengers has declined (see Table 1, Trends in Methods of Transit). This is a worldwide and not an exclusively American phenomenon. The Office of Economic Cooperation and Development observes:

Most cities in OECD countries are entirely dependent on them (buses) for public mass transport. Even in the large cities which have rapid rail transit, buses continue to be an indispensable complement to rail systems.

Nevertheless, bus service has been falling increasingly short of the expectations of the modern traveller and patronage is declining sharply—in 80 per cent of the cities surveyed (36 in all), bus ridership has declined, in some cases by as much as 30-40 per cent (29).

In short, the acceptability level of bus transportation as measured by public patronage has definitely not risen in twenty years. In intercity transportation the bus is not a serious competitor of the airplane for long-distance travel; its greatest utility is in the short and possibly medium distance runs, especially on routes of low-density volume. The term "possibly" is used purposely, because on high-volume medium distance runs, such as the Boston-New York-Washington corridor or between Los Angeles and San Francisco, air travel has become the dominant mode of public transportation and is likely to remain so unless an effective and economically viable mode of high-speed ground transportation should be developed.

The crucial area, however, is urban transit. For a very few metropolitan areas with highly concentrated populations and extremely high-density travel corridors, rail-borne rapid transit is feasible, indeed necessary, even though no American city has succeeded in making it pay its way. For all others the bus must be the medium of public passenger transportation, and we are barely on the threshold of adapting either vehicles or street systems to this purpose. For service between central business districts and suburbs, and also for intersuburban service, the conditions are comparable to short intercity runs and, therefore, the same type of bus is suitable. In downtown sections these vehicles share the same problems as buses engaged in local service, i.e., the need to have traffic controls and street arrangements designed to facilitate bus movement.

The greatest need as well as the greatest opportunity lies in local bus operations in central cities. These operations must use ordinary streets if they are to perform the function of providing public transportation for city residents, and this function may become more vital if cities choose to meet their problems of congestion and pollution by discouraging private automobile traffic in core areas. For this type of service one great improvement would be a bus designed for fast loading and unloading of passengers. This would require new ways of collecting fares, but such changes are certainly possible. The exact-fare procedures adopted in some cities, which require that proper coins be secured or tokens bought before boarding the bus, indicate that the usual time-honored and laborious techniques of fare collecting are alterable. The urban bus, after all, has undergone little substantial change since the 1930's, except in the dubious matter of becoming bigger. It is arguable that larger numbers of smaller, more maneuverable buses would provide higher quality service, although probably at higher cost as well. The OECD study just quoted comments thus on bus technology:

Buses possess a degree of flexibility no other public transportation can match: with proper innovation they could be equally adept at serving the transportation needs of central business districts, the needs of the commuters and the needs of travellers within outlying low-density areas.

Unfortunately, while other public transportation systems have benefited from evolutionary advances in technology, the bus has been largely untouched by technological innovation. While other modes have evolved to meet new needs, little effort has been made to adapt the bus to changing urban conditions or to make it responsive to the shifting patterns of travel demand—in many ways the bus is a paradox of technological obsolescence in the midst of rapidly evolving technology (30).

Some potential developments in bus technology that are feasible and promising rather than speculative are:

1. Dual-mode buses, capable of operating on both streets and rail transit tracks. This concept is of long standing, but so far it has not been possible to design a satisfactory vehicle. New designs, e.g., the rubber-tired subway cars used in Montreal, suggest that the problem can now be solved.

2. Computer-assisted scheduling. Test projects indicate that service can be made more flexible and demand-responsive.

3. Dial-a-bus, also termed Demand Activated Road Transit (DART). This is an elaboration of computer control into a system which, as the Department of Housing and Urban Development expresses it, "would pick up passengers at their doors or at a nearby bus stop shortly after they have telephoned for service. The computer would know the location of its vehicles, how many passengers were on them, and where they were heading. It would select the right vehicle and dispatch it by some optimal routing which had been devised for the system. Thus, the system could readily link many origins to many destinations" (31).

DART would thus combine the features of the bus and the taxi, and since it could offer something resembling door-to-door service, it might attract off-peak patronage far more than existing mass transit modes.

A recent excellent study of urban rail transportation has stated the principle that "The ultimate test of a transportation system lies not in any technoeconomic indices of efficiency but in the extent to which it finds acceptance within the total value scheme of the community it serves" (32). By this standard the bus has not quite arrived. In intercity transportation it expedited the decline of rail passenger service, but it never challenged the private automobile nor has it matched the phenomenal growth of air passenger travel. In the more promising field of local and intraurban transit, the bus has outclassed its competing modes of public transportation, but it has had no appreciable impact on travel by private automobile. A survey of Pittsburgh's predominantly bus-based public transportation showed that 85 per cent of its patrons either had no driver's license or no car, while in Chicago half the users of rapid transit and 65 per cent of all public transportation patrons were in these categories (33). Where rail rapid transit has been introduced, it has drawn from the bus passengers, not from people using their own cars. On the Congress Street rapid transit line in Chicago, which operates on the median of the Eisenhower Expressway, an inquiry among patrons produced the information that 88 per cent would travel by bus if the rail transit service was not available; the comparable percentage on the Yonge Street subway in Toronto was 90 (34).

The authors who made the statement about technoeconomic indices of efficiency have also pointed out: "As the automobile has increasingly become a symbol of social status, the social acceptability of public transit has declined; and, "The physical deterioration and aesthetic obsolescence of their facilities have contributed further to the growing market disadvantage of many transit systems" (35). This observation applies as emphatically to intercity rail passenger travel as to intraurban travel; it equally emphatically does not apply to air travel.

Consequently, in evaluating the status that bus transportation has reached in the United States—or its acceptability level—we are faced with a complex of technical, economical, and sociological factors, no one of them sufficient in itself as an explanation. While the bus is, as stated in the opening paragraph, the largest single public passenger carrier in the world, in the United States at least it has reached this position by becoming the leading second-choice mode of passenger transport—to the airplane for long distances, to the private automobile for short. The bus has never dominated passenger travel as rail transport (steam railroad, interurban, street railway) did in the decade before the First World War.

But while "technoeconomic efficiency" may be inadequate as a criterion for measuring the acceptability of a system of public transportation, a higher level of such efficiency would undoubtedly raise the level of acceptability. In other words, improvements in the speed, comfort, or convenience of bus service, or a reduction in cost reflected in lower fares, would encourage increased use of bus services in preference to private transportation on local trips and make the bus more competitive over longer distances. It is not the function of this paper to speculate on possible new technologies, but it is relevant to point out that insufficient use has been made of the technologies at our disposal. If the time and effort that American communities, especially the larger cities, have put into preserving obsolete systems of rail-borne transit had been expended on highway and street networks and traffic control techniques designed for optimal bus movement, and on improved functional design of the vehicles, they would be less burdened today with ailing transit systems and traffic congestion.

NOTES

1. Transportation Association of America, *Transportation. Facts and Trends,* 5th ed. (Washington, D.C. 1968), pp. 13-14.
2. *Automobile Facts and Figures,* 1969, p. 23; *Motor Truck Facts,* 1968, p. 42.
3. C. St. C. B. Davison, *Steam Road Vehicles* (Science Museum, London, England, 1953), pp. 6-7.

4. See John Hibbs, *The History of British Bus Services* (reprinted, New York, 1968), pp. 20-22.
5. *Ibid.*, pp. 127-128; "Development of Intercity Bus Transportation," p. 47, article published 1962 by National Association of Motor Bus Owners.
6. Association of American Railroads, *Highway Motor Transportation* (Washington, D.C. 1945), p. 67.
7. *Ibid.*, p. 133.
8. *Ibid.*
9. Data supplied by National Association of Motor Bus Owners.
10. *Transportation, Facts and Trends*, pp. 13-14.
11. G. W. Hilton, "Rail Transit and the Pattern of Modern Cities: The California Case," *Traffic Quarterly*, vol. XXI, no. 3 (July 1967), p. 380; Wilfred Owen, *The Metropolitan Transportation Problem*, 2nd ed. (Washington, D.C. 1960), p. 282.
12. *Highway Motor Transportation*, p. 145.
13. *Ibid.*, p. 131; "Development of Intercity Bus Transportation," p. 47.
14. "Chronological History of F. R. Fageol and his Achievements," by H. C. Arnot, Twin Coach Co., Kent, Ohio, May 28, 1948.
15. Hibbs, *History of British Bus Services*, p. 142.
16. *Ibid.*, pp. 147, 155.
17. C. L. Dearing, *Automobile Transportation in the War Effort* (Washington, D.C. 1942), pp. 7-8.
18. This information was provided by courtesy of Mr. Frederick H. Mueller of the National Association of Motor Bus Owners.
19. Ibid., p. 13; *Automobile Facts and Figures*, 1969, p. 51.
20. G. W. Hilton, "Rail Transit and the Pattern of Modern Cities: The California Case," *Traffic Quarterly*, vol. XXI, no. 3 (July 1967), p. 282.
21. *Tomorrow's Transportation* (Washington, D.C. 1968), p. 15.
22. Port of New York Authority, *Metropolitan Transportation-1980* (New York, 1963), pp. 298-299; W. R. McConochie, "Exclusive Lanes for Express Bus Operation in Cities of One to Three Million," *Urban Land*, vol. 22, no. 11 (Dec., 1963), p. 5.
23. J. W. Scheel and J. E. Foote, *Bus Operation in Single Lane Platoons and Their Ventilation Needs for Operation in Tunnels* (Warren, Mich., 1968).
24. G. W. Anderson, "Rail and Bus Rapid Transit for Downtown Access," *Dynamics of Urban Transportation*, report of symposium sponsored by Automobile Manufacturers Association, Oct. 23-24, 1962, pp. 7-10, 7-11.
25. W. R. Maynard, "The Busway to Make Rapid Transit Work—Now," *Traffic Quarterly*, vol. 23, no. 3 (July 1969), pp. 353-365; Wilbur Smith and Associates, *Transportation and Parking for Tomorrow's Cities* (New Haven, Conn., 1966), p. 182; and *The Potential for Bus Rapid Transit* (Detroit, Mich., 1970), pp. 58-62.
26. *Dynamics of Urban Transportation*, pp. 7-15.
27. Highway Research Board, *Getting the Most from City Streets* (Washington, D.C. 1967), p. 31.
28. *Ibid.* p. 32.
29. C. K. Orski, "The New Technology of Bus Transportation," *The OECD Observer*, June 1969, p. 38.
30. *Ibid.*, pp. 38-39.
31. *Tomorrow's Transportation. New Systems for the Urban Future* (Washington, D.C., 1968), p. 58.
32. A. S. Lang and R. M. Soberman, *Urban Rail Transit: Its Economics and Technology* (Cambridge, Mass., 1964), p. 90.
33. *Ibid.*, p. 88. The Pittsburgh survey was made in 1961 and the Chicago one in 1959.
34. Hilton, "Rail Transit and the Pattern of Modern Cities," p. 389.
35. Lang and Soberman, p. 4.

50

The Transportation Company:
An Economic Argument for
Intermodal Ownership

James E. Suelflow
Indiana University

Stanley J. Hille
University of Maryland

Traditionally, ownership of one means of transportation by a competitive mode has been restricted or forbidden by public regulation. Thus, as we noted in Part One, there are, in effect, five separate transportation industries. This separation of ownership has been based in part on the fear that one mode might be in a position to use its economic power to the detriment of the public or that one mode might dominate another and so impede the growth of a competitive mode. However, in recent times a number of scholars have found this "conventional wisdom" to be obsolete. Interest in intermodal ownership, principally the Transportation Company concept, has been renewed. This selection reviews the advantages and disadvantages of the Transportation Company concept and argues strongly that intermodal ownership is a superior form of organization for transportation firms.

Introduction

One of the few remaining frontiers available for cost reduction in the production process is in the area of product distribution.[1] At the same time, it is obvious that the principal cost element of distribution is transportation.[2] Thus if the possibility exists to reduce transportation costs through greater utilization and efficiencies within the transportation system, every avenue must be explored to achieve the desired effect.

The purpose of this article is to illustrate the economic benefits that might be gained through the existence of transportation companies. Transportation companies are defined as for-hire, common carriers which own and have the right to utilize any or all modes of transportation for the intercity movement of freight. Thus, any mode or combination of modes could be used for a particular shipment if they were the least costly alternative at a desired level of service. *Price* and *quality* of service must be considered together as the transportation offering where quality of the service is a function of the landed condition of the goods as

From James E. Suelflow and Stanley J. Hille, "The Transportation Company: An Economic Argument for Intermodal Ownership," *Land Economics*, August 1970, pp. 275-286. Used by permission.

well as the time involved for the goods to reach their destination. Furthermore, the measurement of time is probably best interpreted as the probability of a shipment being delivered "on time" or according to the transportation company's schedules as opposed to the probability of the shipment arriving either late or early.

Because transportation is one of many production factors, this factor might often be substituted for another. Such substitution should, in an economic sense, reduce total costs of production. Herein lie the economic arguments favoring a transportation company from the user's viewpoint. For example, a manufacturer could transfer his production process to a labor intense region where wage rates are lower than those at the current production site. In this instance, the manufacturer is substituting increased transportation costs and lower wages for higher current wage scales and lower transportation charges. For the substitution to be successful, the firm must produce a product at lower total cost.

When transportation is thus utilized, an increase in its demand is evident and leads to better utilization of excess facilities in the short run but, more importantly, economies of scale in the longer run. If we accept the fact that present-day transportation firms generally face declining average cost curves, and this will be the case under normal conditions when a company has excess capacity and/or heavy amounts of fixed costs, then the result of the increased demand will be to lower average unit costs.[3] As transportation costs decline through greater utilization and efficiency, substitution of transport for other production factors should continue, with transport becoming a greater portion of a user's total costs. This effect could be expected to continue as long as more efficient producers are brought into competition with one another through reductions in spatial cost. If a saturation point is reached and the most efficient producers are already included—allowing for substitutability of products—then future entrants will continue to reduce prices only if transportation becomes a smaller portion of total production cost. Thus, increased competition leads to a reduction in consumer prices even though transportation costs occupy a greater portion of the producer's total cost.

Advantages and disadvantages of intermodal ownership

Dialogue on the disadvantages as well as the advantages of the transportation company has been exchanged among transportation economists, regulatory personnel, managers of firms offering transport services, and shippers who utilize these facilities. At times the discussions have become somewhat emotional so that a reasonable conclusion based on these arguments alone is rather difficult.

Disadvantages

Those opposed to the transportation company and in favor of maintaining precedence argue that one should base decisions on past performance. As such, independent modes are both desirable and required in order to provide a full complement of different methods of transportation service.[4] Since the only transport industry advocates are the railroads,[5] they would dominate the new system because of their interest in promoting that form of transportation due to their heavy sunk investment.[6] Consequently, the railroads would direct traffic to their facilities and phase other modes out of existence. Allowing common ownership would thus stifle price competition and in the long run would lead to poor services which would prove more expensive to the shipper and society at large.[7] At the same time, destructive competition between the transport companies and the small independents of various modes would result in elimination of the independents.[8]

Management, it is argued, would find it difficult to operate all modes due to differences in economic structure.[9] As a result, each mode would undoubtedly be organized as a separate operating entity and there would be little opportunity to spread overhead costs. Moreover, the competitive nature of motor, water, and air transport and their low profit margin would make it impossible to absorb any significant amount of the railroad's burden. Thus, the only possible aid available would result if the railroads owned other modes and reduced competition. This would, however, lead to increased monopoly, a stifling of growth,[10] a reduction of new services by modes other than rail,[11] and would not be in the public interest.[12]

A recent poll soliciting comments from shippers, disclosed that a number of respondents expressed fears of the lessening of competition leading to even greater monopolies in the transport field and the subsequent increase of monopolistic abuses.[13] Some shippers believed that railroads rather than promoting multi-modal ownerships should concentrate their efforts on making themselves more efficient to compete with other already more efficient modes. Other shippers expressed the fear that the extent of regulation, together with its attendant rulemaking, and above all rates would skyrocket.

Locklin probably expresses the view of a number of opponents to the transportation company, who while they oppose the concept of a multi-modal company, would concede, "[we] are inclined to the view, however, that non-rail operations of railroads need not be restricted or limited to the degree that they frequently have been under existing legislation."[14]

Advantages

Those individuals more sympathetic toward the common ownership concept also put forth some rather convincing arguments of the advantages of transportation companies. General Doyle comments that "essential to this structure (the transportation company) is the idea that a single corporate entity, in competition with other similar entities, owns and operates several different forms of transportation. There would be a single sales force, one home office, a single corporate stock, one president, one board of directors and, more important, a *single pricing policy.*"[15] (Emphasis added.) The concept of a single pricing policy is more clearly illustrated by Hugh S. Norton. "In essence, the various modes are merely *different processes or methods* of producing the same service, viz., transportation, in the same manner as the Bell System's using various technological means, e.g., voice phone or teletype to provide communications service."[16] (Emphasis added.)

Therefore, on an economic basis, one might argue that the separation of our transport facilities into separate compartments according to type of vehicle is indefensible and leads to inflexibility.[17] As a result, private carriage is introduced in an effort to lower distribution costs.

Buland and Furhman summarize the views of many transportation company supporters when they state, "Today's common carriers, functioning under existing regulations, are losing ground because a large segment of the nation's industry provides its own non-regulated transportation and uses the common carrier only as a standby service. Private carriage has gained in popularity because it provides adaptable service for shippers *at attractive cost.*"[18] (Emphasis added.)

Others feel that the transport company would not only strengthen the nation's common carrier system by making the maximum use of each mode, but they go so far as to suggest this approach as one way for the common carrier system to survive.[19] There would also be the tendency to remove handicaps or inequalities which now exist among modes, including user charges and subsidies.[20]

Finally, the shipper would find it advantageous to have his transport needs filled by one company.[21] Thus, the shipper would have available from one source the "right" mode for each shipment:[22] the same carrier would also be responsible for any loss and damage claims.[23] Many shippers feel that increased competition, cost economies, lower and more stable rates and more expeditious handling of LCL shipments would result.[24] Phillips sums up these arguments by stressing that the transportation company's justification for existence must rest on long-run economies of scale.[25]

The above illustrate the most common arguments which have been advanced on the disadvantages and advantages of transportation companies. Endeavoring to reach a sound and reasonable conclusion as to the economic appropriateness of intermodal combinations, the following model is suggested.

The model

The theory of the multiple product firm, an extension of price discrimination already practiced by the single-mode transportation firm, seems to be most applicable to the multi-modal transportation company. The model of the multiple product firm was first presented by Chamberlin and Joan Robinson in the early 1930's. Professor Clemens, however, developed and refined the model in the early 1950's and it is this latter version which is the suggested analysis.[26] Clemens' model basically assumes that a firm has idle capacity, not only in physical facilities but in technical knowledge and/or organizational resources as well. Since that which a firm sells is not a product or even a line of products but rather its capacity to produce different items, the economic enterpriser will seek new markets which will be interested in using this capacity or, as might be the case, management know-how. Thus, the firm may well be producing a number of products or services which may belong to the same general class of economic activity but may be quite dissimilar physically. Furthermore, the model assumes that multiple product firms will enter new markets on the basis of profitability which also means that profit margins will probably be different in each market. As the firm penetrates these new markets, the degree to which prices exceed costs will tend to decline. The firm will continue to enter new markets until the price in the last one approaches the firm's marginal cost. At the same time, it is anticipated that prior outputs, prices and marginal revenues in preceding markets may have to be adjusted. The ultimate solution, shown in Figure 1, like the traditional price-discriminating model, is characterized by the equating of marginal revenue in all markets with marginal cost of the firm. Each of the products or services will have a specific market and the equilibrium price or prices for each good or service will be based on the item's demand elasticity. Total output of the Firm shown in Figure 1 is at q_4; however, the output for specific products is as follows: Product 1, $O-q_1$; Product 2, q_1-q_2; Product 3, q_2-q_3; and Product 4, q_3-q_4. Furthermore, the price and output for profit maximization for each is determined by equating MR of each product with the MC for the entire firm. Thus items with more elastic demands will have prices which come closer to marginal cost. As a result, a firm with any idle piece of equipment or capacity, any unused technical knowledge, or organizational resources represents a challenge to the sales or marketing manager. Further, if a market reasonably accessible to the firm exists in which potential price for a good or service exceeds potential marginal cost, this is an invitation of the firm to invade. The company's economic objective may be expressed as:

$$\pi = R_1(q_1) + R_2(q_2) + R_3(q_3) + R_4(q_4) - TC(q_1 + q_2 + q_3 + q_4),$$

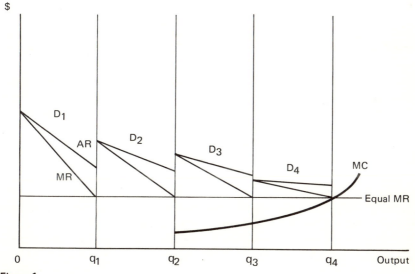

Figure 1

where π is profit; R is revenue; q is the quantity of service sold in each market; and TC is the total cost for the Company. In order to identify the profit maximizing position for each good or service, the partial derivatives of the above equation, set equal to zero, will satisfy the requirement, thus:

$$\frac{\delta\pi}{\delta q_1} = R_1'(q_1) - TC'(q_1 + q_2 + q_3 + q_4) = 0$$

$$\frac{\delta\pi}{\delta q_2} = R_2'(q_2) - TC'(q_1 + q_2 + q_3 + q_4) = 0$$

$$\frac{\delta\pi}{\delta q_3} = R_3'(q_3) - TC'(q_1 + q_2 + q_3 + q_4) = 0$$

$$\frac{\delta\pi}{\delta q_4} = R_4'(q_4) - TC'(q_1 + q_2 + q_3 + q_4) = 0$$

Fulfilling the above, the marginal revenue of each service is equated with marginal cost for the entire firm and profits are maximized.

Obviously Figure 1 represents an equilibrium position. With a firm in this condition, one might logically ask whether the interpretation is a short-run or long-run position. Reviewing the Clemens thesis, it is rather unclear what the time horizon might be. However, we note that discussion tends to evolve around capacity. If one is talking about idle capacity and the utilization of same, the implication is a short-run analysis. On the other hand, a long-run analysis would undoubtedly assume that a firm was operating under its most ideal conditions and capacity would be adjusted to fit current demand. Then, unused capacity would be nonexistent. Since, however, the model seems to allow for "some adjustment" in providing an extension of usable capacity, one might conclude that the time period to which Clemens refers is intermediate to either the long- or short-run conditions. For example, one might interpret excess capacity to be an excess of technical or managerial know-how referred to previously and certain new stocks or facilities might be acquired to take advantage of this excess managerial talent. Thus, while all factors of production do not vary, certain factors may be changed.

Applying the above model to the transportation company, one would find a firm selling a number of different services based on various qualities of transport offered both within and among the several modes. Thus, certain services will be faster, others slower, some better for bulk products, others better for smaller and perhaps more fragile items while still others might be better suited for low-value products and other types of services more suited to higher value items. The proper service offered to specific markets will depend on the quality of service demanded with respect to the price being charged. This is not to say that different modes of service might offer similar qualities of service at different prices or different qualities of service at very similar prices. Utilization of each service, however, will be determined by the elasticity of demand for that service at the price it is being offered.

Thus, if it could be argued that, because a transportation company is really selling capacity and expertise in the movement of goods (a service), the combination of these two attributes should favor the multi-modal transportation firm. This condition might be modified to recognize available capacity of a versatile nature in which the number of services offered by several modes are of comparable quality. The ability to offer the shipper a variety of services best suited to his needs will also allow for transport company utilization of excess capacity in the form of idle equipment or management know-how.

The transportation company would then seek to increase its profits by moving into new markets—a necessary condition for maximizing equilibrium of total firm marginal cost equal to the various services' individual marginal revenues. This solution was illustrated in Figure 1. If one applies this diagram to the transportation company, one could view q_1, q_2, q_3, and q_4 as different qualities of service being offered by the firm both within and between modes. Allowing time for proper adjustment, the transportation company's economic objective could be realized. Fulfilling the above requirements, the marginal revenue of each service would be equated with marginal cost for the entire firm and, consequently, profits would be maximized.

One might well question the extent to which product factors within a transportation company could be transferred from the production of one service to that of another. Obviously, in any industry total transfer is very unlikely and, as Clemens pointed out, it is necessary only that there be certain factors which can be utilized for or transferred to other uses. In the transportation field, it is obvious that the railroad right-of-way, one of the factors of production, certainly could not be converted easily into the right-of-way, or a factor of production, for supplying motor carrier service. Likewise, special equipment would be more difficult to convert to other uses. Certainly, however, within modes one might visualize a somewhat easier production factor transfer. However, it appears that there is still a substantial transferability available between modes. For example, idle capacity (one of the primary factors for multiple product or service utilization) in a particular mode might be readily available to users which have normally used a different mode. This excess capacity could be offered to the potential user at a lower price than that which he had been paying and the combination of the lower price with a somewhat different quality of service might well be equated by the potential user with the former higher price which he paid for a different quality of service.

Likewise, within ranges or what one might call the "margins" between modes of transportation, it might well be possible for a transportation company to utilize excess capacity in one mode having similar qualities as a service offered by another mode. This assumes that the supplier has full knowledge if excess capacity exists and it is here that the multi-modal firm under a single management would gain one of its fullest advantages.

From the user's point of view, it would, in effect, mean "one-stop transportation shopping;" or, more specifically, the shipper's ability to merely instruct the multi-modal transportation company that he desires a certain quality of service.

The transportation company could then quote him the various prices for this quality of service via different modes and the user could then express his demand for the service by stating the price which he is willing to pay. This would then eliminate the need for users to "shop" for many of their transport needs.

Within the context of the model, one might now review the arguments presented earlier in opposing the transportation company. Assuming a firm practices reasonable economic behavior, it is doubtful that there will be a stifling of competition, which would lead to poorer service and increased cost to the shipper. In fact, quality of service should be improved and costs related to this quality should diminish. This would result from a better utilization of excess production factors which, when unemployed, would force prices of already offered services up to a higher level. One often hears arguments with respect to the high fixed/variable cost conditions in the railroad sector. To some extent, this is also true in the other forms of transportation, airlines and trucking notwithstanding. Certain costs are always less variable than others and the more units of output over which these fixed costs can be spread, the lower will be the unit cost for a particular service. This is particularly true in firms whose capacity is underutilized.

Further, the arguments that railroads will dominate is not at all clear. Each segment or mode will seek profit maximization based on production costs and, even if it were true that the railroads would practice cutthroat competition, the barriers to re-entry of other modes are less monumental and new independent firms would be encouraged to enter the market. Moreover, a high fixed/variable cost ratio which might exist in the rail sector in a market with few firms is conducive to restraining price competition in the presence of excess capacity,[27] further belying any rail threat suggested above.

The mere acquaintance of different qualities of transportation and different prices to the shipper should, in fact, increase the potential growth of output rather than stifle it. Thus, a company operating under one management, with a coordinated staff, and utilizing a single pricing policy for different qualities of transportation service, would very likely lead to the economies of scale suggested earlier by Phillips.

Financial aspects of rail, air, and motor transportation

While the model may withstand theoretical criticism, nonetheless it is important to make a financial comparison of the different modes of transportation in order to substantiate the theory.

Opposition to multi-modal transportation companies implies that railroads which have the heaviest fixed investment would not act in a profit-maximizing manner and thus would negate the very assumptions underlying the previous profit-maximizing model. These opponents believe that the railroads, if allowed, would purchase other forms of transport and then proceed to operate only the railroad sector to the demise of other modes, despite the fact that their operation, in conjunction with the railroads, might provide more efficient means of transportation. The prerequisite for such behavior would require the railroads to possess the financial strength to take over and dominate the largest companies of the competing modes and then to provide all of the qualities of customer service demanded through rail operation only. However, statistics show that this strong financial power often attributed to the railroads may not, in fact, be as powerful as suspected.

Table I shows the top ten railroads, motor common carriers, and airlines in the United States indicated in *Fortune*'s 500 largest corporations and ranked by their 1967 operating revenues. Operating revenues were used for ranking as well as size comparisons since the varying cost structures of the different modes make it virtually impossible to use other data for such purposes. Furthermore, operating revenues are a good indicator of a company's worth, especially in situations involving purchases and sales—an important consideration if transportation companies would be allowed to exist.

With the exception of the Penn Central Railroad, airlines compare favorably in size with other railroads.[28] Moreover, of the five largest carriers, three are airlines. And the top ten companies include one motor carrier, five railroads, and four airlines. Of the top 20 carriers, two are motor carriers (Greyhound and Consolidated Freightways), eight are airlines, and ten are railroads. Thus, even though the motor carriers are considerably smaller than the other two modes' largest firms, they are, nevertheless, quite powerful and would not fall easy prey to the other modes. In fact, some of these motor carriers should be able to buy into other modes, e.g., Greyhound's attempt to merge with REA Express. Table II displays the same firms' aggregate average growth rates for the periods 1957 to 1962, 1962 to 1967, and the ten-year period from 1957 to 1967. Note that over the past ten years the top ten airlines have grown about three times as fast as the same railroads. If this growth rate is maintained, it is very likely that the larger airlines would dominate intermodal transportation companies far more than would the railroads. In addition, if the growth rate of the past ten years continues for motor common carriage, one would expect the largest motor carriers to rival all but the Penn Central Railroad in size in the next ten years. There would be little chance, however, that motor common carriers will ever be comparable to the largest airlines in size, if present airline entry controls are continued.

A look at the profitability of the three modes (based on a ratio of net income to operating revenue for the year 1967) shows that the top ten airlines are the most profitable with a 7.46 per cent return; the top ten motor carriers had a 5.10 per cent return; and the railroad's top ten had a 3.85 per cent return. This indicator would also suggest that railroads will not dominate a multi-modal transportation company because they will not have the financial wherewithal to do so.

Two other measures often considered in the analysis of financial strength include net operating income as well as the somewhat broader cash flow. The latter, however, must be used with extreme caution and, as most analysts will

TABLE 1

Fortune's Ten Top Railroads, Motor Carriers, and Airlines in the United States
(Ranked by 1967 Operating Revenues)

	Operating Revenues (000)	Percentage Growth Rate in Operating Revenues (1957-67) ('57 = 100)	Net Income 1967 (000)	Cash Flow (000)
Penn Central Railroad[a]	$2,074,276	108.09	$ 71,433[g]	$234,353
United Airlines[b]	1,098,938	292.00	72,819	185,852
Southern Pacific Railroad	909,298	154.48	90,332	158,815
Trans-World Airlines	873,219	332.06	40,770	152,080
American Airlines	841,531	275.05	48,085	144,752
C&O — B&O Railroad[c]	809,023	93.10	55,308	105,072
A.T. & S. Fe Railroad (Santa Fe)	663,494	120.80	53,585	117,160
Eastern Airlines	657,804	250.61	24,114	82,859
Norfolk and Western Railroad[d]	594,178	140.25	72,607	129,689
Greyhound	574,056	217.02	45,449	68,016
Union Pacific Railroad	574,020	117.53	102,133	169,005
Southern Railway[e]	469,583	119.66	39,945	72,161
Seaboard Coastline Railroad[f]	417,396	127.86	27,289	59,470
Delta Airlines	397,836	508.19	49,190	91,765
Northwest Airlines	384,088	460.23	58,716	117,482
Missouri Pacific Railroad	318,329	141.63	32,473	55,353
Consolidated Freight-ways — Trucking	311,872	405.82	10,689	27,529
Chicago, Burlington & Quincy Railroad	277,084	126.88	14,251	36,392
Braniff Airlines	256,377	407.67	4,702	31,116
Continental Airlines	188,168	808.52	17,307	44,880

agree, cash flow analysis is in no way designed to preempt a net-income analysis. However, if a firm is financially profitable, cash flow will be a valuable consideration in analyzing the firm's ability to meet its debt obligations as well as provide for capital replacements and expansions. Since depreciation in many companies is the most significant addition to net income in arriving at a company's cash flow, it is implied that large depreciation charges are advantageous because of their contribution to the cash flow.[29] The analysis of either of these factors does little to alter our previous conclusions, although the ranking of the 30 listed transportation companies changes somewhat from company to company. The major exception is the ranking of Union Pacific Railroad, which is number one in net income and number three in cash flow, although it ranked eleventh in operating revenues.

	Operating Revenues (000)	Percentage Growth Rate in Operating Revenues (1957-67) ('57 — 100)	Net Income 1967 (000)	Cash Flow (000)
Western Airlines	183,508	455.91	12,185	37,020
National Airlines	179,927	371.34	17,057	37,511
Pacific-Intermountain Express	150,419	288.95	2,010	8,943
Roadway Express	150,124	319.43	7,160	15,161
Transcontinental Bus	130,753	586.60	8,396	20,410
Associated Transport	105,266	195.30	943	6,357
Yellow Transit	104,196	579.61	4,501	10,528
McLean Trucking	91,673	382.56	3,658	7,979
Transcon Lines	77,985	582.67	3,146	7,959
U.S. Truck Lines	67,657	169.60	4,045	10,588

Source: *Moody's Transportation Manual*, September 1968; also, *Fortune Magazine*, August 1968.
aGrowth for years prior to 1967 include Operating Revenues of New York Central and Pennsylvania Railroads.
bGrowth for years prior to 1967 include Operating Revenues of United and Capital Airlines.
cGrowth for all years include both C & O and B & O Operating Revenues.
dGrowth for years priot to 1967 include Operating Revenues of New York, Chicago and St. Louis Railroad.
eSouthern Railway figures are not comparable prior to 1967 since consolidated statements were not available prior to that time. Therefore, growth figures include only Southern Railroad's revenues.
fGrowth for years prior to 1967 include Operating Revenues for both Atlantic Coast Line and Seaboard Air Line Railroads.
gBefore extraordinary item of $275,422,000 of costs and losses resulting from merger.

Grouping the carriers by both cash flow and net income, one notes that in the top ten companies there were six railroads, four airlines, and no motor carriers. The top 20 cash flow companies show ten railroads, nine airlines, and one motor carrier; an analysis of net income shows ten railroads, nine airlines, and one motor carrier.

A final but significant analysis of the various modes' financial strength is illustrated in Table III. This is a comparative balance sheet of Class I Railroads, Class I and II Motor Carriers, and Domestic Trunk Airlines developed on a percentage basis. Differences are noted in both current assets and Net Operating Property. In the former case, current assets are substantially greater for Motor Carriers and Airlines than for Railroads, whereas Net Operating Property, as a percentage of invested assets, ranges from approximately 50 per cent for Motor

TABLE II

Average Rates of Growth Ten Top Railroads, Motor Carriers and Airlines in the United States; 1957-1967

	Average Percentage Growth Rate in Operating Revenues		
	1957-62 ('57 = 100)	1962-67 ('62 = 100)	1957-67 ('57 = 100)
Ten Top Railroads	96.47	123.53	119.17
Ten Top Motor Carriers	164.51	175.37	288.50
Ten Top Airlines	154.61	212.11	327.96

Source: *Moody's Transportation Manual*, September 1968, and *Fortune Magazine*, August 1968.

Carriers to 60.9 per cent for Airlines and 76.9 per cent for Railroads. A review of liabilities also shows differences between modes. Comparing Capital Structures evidences the greater leverage of motor carriers and airlines. Railroads, on the other hand, have less of their capital structure in long-term debt. Aggregate equity financing by the several modes is the antithesis of debt capital with railroads having the greatest amount of this type of securities.

Conclusions

From the above analysis it is our conclusion that the present regulatory system should be changed to allow intermodal mergers and the resulting formation of transportation companies. To do so would best serve the public interest. Shippers would receive equal or improved service if they could deal with only one for-hire carrier for all of their transportation needs. The benefits of one-stop transportation purchasing would be further amplified as containerization use increases. At the present time, containers are often handled or required to be handled by more than one mode and, as the number of modes handling these containers increases, the number of different managers handling the goods also increases. Thus, the shipper's control over his freight declines, thereby reducing the benefits this technological improvement should achieve from multi-modal container movements. The transportation company would allow responsibility for movements to be held to fewer firms, thus providing greater coordination and efficiency.

Competition among carriers should increase. Transportation companies could extend into one another's territory through intermodal merger. Long-haul airlines might compete with trucks and rail through new coordinated movements. Moreover, restrictions on operating rights and their attendant monopoly powers

TABLE III

Comparative Balance Sheets for Class I Railroads, Motor Carriers (Class I and II)
and Domestic Trunk Airlines

	Railroads		Motor Carriers		Airlines	
Assets:						
Total Current						
Assets		9.5%		34.9%		25.6%
Operating Property						
(gross)	105.2		N.A.		92.6	
Less Accumulated						
Depreciation	28.3		N.A.		31.7	
Net Operating Property		76.9		49.3		60.9
Other Property (net)		1.7		-0-		2.5
Total Property (net)	78.6		49.3	63.4		
Other Assets		11.9		15.8		11.0
Total Assets		100.0%		100.0%		100.0%
Liabilities:						
Total Current Liabilities		7.2		29.7		15.6
Other Liabilities and						
Reserves		4.1		1.2		8.5
Capital Structure						
Long Term Debt		33.1		24.8		43.3
Capital Stock	18.7		15.9	15.4		
Retained Earnings	36.9		28.4	17.2		
Total Equity		55.6		44.3		32.6
Total Liabilities		100.0%		100.0%		100.0%

Sources: *Moody's Transportation Manual*, 1968; *Air Transportation Facts and Figures*,
1968; and *American Trucking Trends*, 1968.

could be reduced to accommodate the combinations. Railroads could then compete with one another where previously they were held to exclusive territories.

The authors would envision a controlling agency to prevent monopoly abuses
and to promote increased competition. This control could be minimized through
the use of antitrust legislation with regard to mergers and entry and exit and
current rate regulation could be reduced to minimum price controls. The latter
would prevent any possibilities of cut-throat competition.

It is highly unlikely that railroads would dominate the transportation company. The profit-maximizing model illustrated above indicates a course of action
equating the various marginal revenues of service qualities with the total firm's
marginal cost, regardless of a particular mode's cost structure. While there are
limitations to the use of the multiproduct model, it appears likely that the
transportation company adequately fulfills the requirements allowing for its use.
In fact, the primary excess capacity discussed above with reference to the multi-
modal transportation company might well be financial capabilities and management know-how. To date railroads have shown that they cannot produce profit-

able results in many segments of their transport service whether caused by current regulation or outside competition. This means other modes are essential to an integrated transportation firm.

To argue that railroads will phase out other types of carriers is economically naive.[30] The railroads may possess certain "excess" capabilities, but they need the other modes to provide an economically sound and healthy organization. Furthermore, barriers to entry in other modes are less stringent, precluding rail dominance for rail's sake. In the final analysis, the true measure of economic success is profit on investment and the combinations of railroads with other modes can aid in this economic pursuit.

NOTES

1. Donald J. Bowersox, Edward W. Smykay and Bernard J. LeLonde, *Physical Distribution Management* (New York, New York: The Macmillan Company, 1968), p. 13.

2. Charles A. Taff, *Management of Traffic and Physical Distribution* (Homewood, Illinois: Richard D. Irwin, Inc., 1968), p. 7.

3. See for example, John R. Meyer, *et al., The Economics of Competition in the Transportation Industries* (Cambridge, Massachusetts: Harvard University Press, 1959), pp. 86-101; also Bureau of Accounts and Cost Finding, Interstate Commerce Commission, *Explanation of Rail Cost Finding Principles and Procedures,* Statement No. 2-48 (Washington, D.C., 1948), p. 88. It is generally agreed the motor carriers have a fixed/variable cost ratio of approximately 10 per cent. Alan C. Flott, "Economics of Scale in Trucking," *Transportation Research Forum,* Papers, Sixth Annual Meeting, 1965 (Oxford, Indiana: Richard B. Cross Co.), pp. 13-15. Mr. Flott points out an often forgotten long-run scale economy in the motor carrier industry—customer service. This service, he says, increases with motor-carrier size and, as more points are served, is a great aid to the user. Meyer cites the fact that 5 per cent of airline costs are indirect and this introduces scale economies due to lower costs of operation with increased plane size and longer hops (pp. 135-140). *Rail Freight Costs in the Various Rate Territories of the United States,* Senate Document No. 63, 78th Congress, 1st Session (Washington, D.C.: United States Government Printing Office, 1943), p. 75. Figures are cited showing that fixed costs are 20 per cent to 30 per cent of operating costs, excluding investment costs in the long run. Dudley F. Pegrum, *Transportation: Economics and Public Policy,* rev. ed. (Homewood, Illinois: Richard D. Irwin, Inc., 1968), pp. 180-181. Professor Pegrum quotes Senate Document No. 63, above, and also states that fixed costs are usually calculated to be about two-thirds of total cost with 50 per cent of costs being variable in the short run. One can thus conclude that all modes have some fixed costs and thus enjoy certain economies of utilization in the short run. Moreover, all have long-run scale economies evidenced in fixed facilities and/or financial and management know-how.

4. Peter P. Beardsley, "Integrated Ownership of Transportation Companies in the Public Interest," *George Washington Law Review,* 31, 1962, pp. 85-105.

5. See for example, Senate Committee on Commerce, *National Transportation Policy* (The Doyle Report), 87th Congress, 1st Session, Senate Report No. 445 (1961), pp. 213-229.

6. D. Phillip Locklin, *Economics of Transportation,* 6th ed. (Homewood, Illinois: Richard D. Irwin, Inc., 1966), pp. 845-853.

7. Gayton E. Germane, N. A. Glaskowsky, Jr., and J. L. Heskett, *Highway Transportation Management* (New York, New York: McGraw-Hill Book Co., Inc., 1963), pp. 403-404.

8. Locklin, *op. cit.*
9. Germane, *et al., op. cit.*
10. Locklin, *op. cit.*
11. Germane, *et al., op. cit.*, and Locklin, *ibid.*
12. Dudley F. Pegrum, *Transportation: Economics and Public Policy* (Homewood, Illinois: Richard D. Irwin, Inc., 1963), p. 429.
13. *Railway Age,* October 30, 1967, pp. 32-34.
14. Locklin, *op. cit.*, p. 853.
15. Doyle Report, p. 221, *op. cit.*
16. Hugh S. Norton, *Modern Transportation Economics* (Columbus, Ohio: Charles E. Merrill Books, Inc., 1963), p. 376.
17. George L. Buland and F. E. Furhman, "Integrated Ownership: The Case for Removing Restrictions on Common Ownership of Several Forms of Transportation," *George Washington Law Review,* 1962, p. 185.
18. *Ibid.,* p. 184.
19. See for example, Doyle, Locklin, and Germane, *et al., op. cit.*
20. Doyle, *op. cit.*
21. *Ibid.*
22. Germane, *et al.,* and Doyle, *op. cit.,* Charles F. Phillips, Jr., *The Economics of Regulation* (Homewood, Illinois: Richard D. Irwin, Inc.), p. 551.
23. Germane, *et al.,* and *Railway Age, op. cit.*
24. *Railway Age, op. cit.,* p. 33.
25. Phillips, *op. cit.,* p. 553.
26. Eli W. Clemens, "Price Discrimination and the Multiple-Produce Firm," *The Review of Economic Studies,* Vol. XIX, pp. 1-11. Reprinted with corrections in, Heflebower and Stocking, *Readings in Industrial Organization and Public Policy* (Homewood, Illinois: Richard D. Irwin, Inc., 1958), pp. 262-276.
27. J. R. Felton, "Comment on Market Structure, Regulation, and Dynamic Change," *Performance Under Regulation,* Harry M. Trebing, Ed. (East Lansing, Michigan: Michigan State University, 1968), p. 147.
28. When comparing 1967, 1962, and 1957 operating revenues, companies which were later merged were included in the earlier operating revenue figures for both airlines and railroads. Since motor carriers typically buy out smaller companies as a means of achieving growth, these merged companies were not included in the 1962 and 1957 operating revenues. Railroad merger objectives were different. Those mergers were consummated to reduce excess capacity—not for growth. Only one airline merged during the ten-year period is included in the study. United Airlines merged with Capital to prevent the latter from pleading bankruptcy.
29. The cash flow analysis indicated in column 4 of Table I was arrived at as the summation of net earnings before common dividends, plus depreciation, depletion, amortization, net deferred income taxes, and net investment tax credits less any interest charged to construction as might be applicable.
30. Witness, for example, the Southern Pacific and its substantial motor carriers operations retained through grandfather rights; the Canadian National and its operations of motor carriers, airlines, and pipelines.

51

Government's Role
Toward Transportation

James C. Nelson
Washington State University

It is important in domestic transportation to assess the proper role of government. While government actions in many areas affect transportation the two pivotal areas are government subsidy and government regulation.

Both subsidy and regulation are subject to analysis in depth and the following selection does an excellent job of deepening our understanding of them and of outlining the issues involved. The reader should be alert to the excellent references cited by Dr. Nelson—any one of which can be pursued with profit.

The voluminous recent studies of regulatory agencies and public policy in transport attest eloquently to the continuing public interest in the long-standing issue of the appropriate role for government in the transport sector of the economy.[1] While little legislative action has been taken in recent years, these studies and the urgency of emerging transport issues have stimulated wide public discussion of the central question of public transport policy—the question of the proper role of the government in the allocation of traffic and resources in transport. Hence, a general review and evaluation of the major areas of government activity— transport promotion and transport regulation—is in order.

The past role: promotion

In the United States, government shares with private enterprise the risks and costs of providing transport in a mixed system of public and private enterprise. Government usually participates by furnishing the basic ways (and some terminals) while private enterprise conducts carrier operations over public facilities. Mixed enterprise is characteristic of air, highway and water transport but not of pipeline and railway transport. As most countries operate railways under public enterprise, this country's mix of private and public enterprise is unique.

Except for the pipelines, all domestic transport agencies, and the U.S. shipping lines and airlines in international commerce, have received subsidies from government at some time during their development.[2] During the 19th Century certain western and southern railroads were awarded federal land grants (and other state and federal aids) to encourage construction of lines into areas without efficient transport; in return, land-grant roads had to quote land-grant rate reductions on mail, troops and government property (until October 1, 1946).[3] Earlier, canals

From the *Transportation Journal*, Summer 1962, quarterly publication of the American Society of Traffic and Transportation, Inc. Used by permission.

had been constructed by state agencies and operated with tolls recovering capital and operating costs; however, since about 1880, by which time the railroads had largely superseded the canals, the federal and state governments have provided improved waterways entirely free of user charges except on the St. Lawrence Seaway. Even earlier, private turnpikes furnished main highways on a commercial basis; but, since 1850, highways have been provided by state and local governments, with ever-increasing federal aid (since 1916) for construction of limited federal-aid systems and with user fee support in the modern period. Finally, the federal government early undertook to provide the civil airways and still furnishes them without explicit user fees (although a federal excise tax of two cents a gallon on aviation gasoline is assessed). And federal air-mail subsidies have been awarded the scheduled airlines, although the domestic trunk lines no longer receive those subsidies. Local governments, with federal aid, furnish airport facilities, assessing user charges that generally have not been sufficient, with other airport revenues, to make public airports self-supporting.[4]

Over the years, tremendous sums have been spent by government in making way and terminal facilities available for use by private carriers; in giving direct subsidies to certain classes of carriers; and in engaging in expensive scientific research, and development for national security, making as a by-product much valuable technology available to the air carriers without charge to them.[5]

The national purposes for giving financial assistance to transport development are relevant to evaluation. Clearly, railroad grants had the unique national objective of stimulating initial settlement of undeveloped lands in the West by rapid development of a new transport technique, greatly reducing long-distance costs and increasing service speeds. Air transport aids sought improved postal communication, rapid introduction of a new technology, adequate equipment, aircraft manufacturing facilities and skilled personnel for national defense. Federal highway aid had improvement of rural postal services and stimulation of interstate commerce as its principal purposes; in addition, an underlying national defense interest has existed in a highly developed system of interstate highways adequate for the needs of commerce and the military. State highway investment largely has been in response to the *way-service demands* of a rapidly multiplying ownership of motor vehicles. The principal objectives for inland waterway improvement, including the no-toll policy, have been to give landlocked areas lower freight rates and to furnish additional competition for the railroads.[6]

The overall historical record indicates that perhaps the strongest motive for federal transport subsidies has been to bring about, more rapidly than otherwise would occur, the economic and social benefits of improvements in transport service and of lowered transport costs *when entirely new transport technology became available.* This was true of federal aids for highway and air transport development. That motive also stimulated the land grants to railroads, but with the significant difference that a century ago far greater emphasis was necessarily placed on land settlement and resource development in pioneering areas. The introduction of modern air, highway and waterway transport came long after the railroads had already opened up most of the remote and underdeveloped regions of this country. The grant of subsidies to those modes was intended to exploit their technologies at a faster rate than market demand could accomplish so that the economy might earlier have the new types of services and competitive transport.

As a broad generalization, the American system of mixed enterprise in transport has worked tolerably well. It has produced a fully-developed, large-scale, multiservice and essentially competitive transport system that is the envy of most countries. In general, the promotional policies accomplished their purposes and the government has made a truly important contribution to the American transport system. But as government promotion also has created excess facilities and inefficient transport, this by no means implies that the best and most efficient system has resulted. Nor does it mean that past policies necessarily should be continued indefinitely.

Looking objectively at the justification for continuing subsidies to domestic transport, it seems clear the most historical reasons for subsidies have disappeared long ago. There is no present need for land grants to stimulate initial development of railways. Motor transport is now a mature and thriving industry, operating over highways with high-type surfaces throughout the land. Although expanding traffic and urban congestion obviously require highway expansion, plainly there is no longer any need for public subsidies to introduce the advantages of motor transport to the American economy! Very likely, most needed highway development would come as rapidly as can be economically justified in response to *effective demand* on the basis of appropriate user fees and tools. The quick additions of modern highways in congested areas by state-owned toll road authorities suggest that the required facilities would come sooner on a full commercial basis than under existing so-called free-road policies.

Air transport, too, can no longer be regarded as an infant industry in need of developmental subsidies, except for non-economic subsidization of local and metropolitan airlines to give rural and urban communities more advantages of the air age. The rapid introduction of airline technology did not cease, nor even slacken, with cessation of air-mail subsidies to the trunk lines. Witness the 1958-59 introduction of pure jet transports! Placing user fees on the civil airways over a period of time would not seriously impede beneficial innovations. The traffic growth experienced by barge lines on well-located waterways suggests that free channel and lock services are no longer essential to intensive use of inland waterways. As the traffic on marginal waterways does not rise to efficient levels without user fees, serious questions can be asked concerning the economic justification of continued investment in such waterways.

The beneficial general results of this country's policy of stimulating economic development through encouraging adequate, efficient and competitive transport with subsidies have long ago been achieved. Today, the problem of transport policy is radically different than during the 1830-1930 period. Insufficient attention has been given to this fact in formulating transport policies in recent years.

The transport problem today, and in the foreseeable future, is to promote the right economic development of each of the five contending agencies, including coordinated services by two or more modes.[7] The primary aim of policy can no longer be to foster initial economic development of the western regions, nor even to hasten the introduction of new transport industries by means of subsidies. This is not to say that transport modes now not visualized will never be invented. Rather, present-day policymakers face well-defined and critical questions growing out of the existing relations among carriers, the current promotional and regulatory policies, and the competitive structure of transport. Thus, it would seem wholly unreasonable to leave the question of what subsidies may be desirable for promoting rapid development of a new transport mode until someone invents it and operations appear to be practicable.

The past role: regulation

The remaining general problem of government relations to transport is how best to promote adequate and efficient transport by self-sustaining modes, all paying appropriately adjusted user fees or providing their own ways. Can this best be done by increasing entry control to include private and exempt carriers and by using the suspension and minimum rate powers as allocators of traffic? Or can it best be done by lessening or abandoning such regulation and by allowing competitive forces to allocate the traffic?

All modern regulation of economic phases of transport has been modeled on railroad regulation. Railroad regulation came here and abroad because the markets for railroad service were monopolistic or oligopolistic, with group decisions on rates characteristic of market action. In the 19th Century, the public groups urging regulation by strong commissions (unwanted by the railroads) sought equitable treatment of shippers, travelers and of producing and market areas; in addition, they sought cooperation on joint rates and physical connections to maintain a continuing opportunity for water carriers to be competitive with railroads. At least until 1920, a national policy encouraged as competitive an organization of railroading as seemed feasible and as much intermodal competition as possible. The original regulatory structure therefore largely consisted of control of maximum rates and of the most obnoxious rate and service discriminations. Even the Transportation Act of 1920 did not greatly alter that concept of regulation, although it emphasized monopoly organization and carrier welfare more than previous legislation.[8]

Implicit, however, was the idea that the railroads would also be more *socially efficient* under that control scheme. As they carried almost all intercity traffic, no one conceived of regulation as a general tool for bringing about an efficient intermodal division of traffic. Efficient transport meant efficient railroading and controlled monopoly pricing, yielding (in theory, at least) lower rates for all and distributing the overhead cost burdens on demand factors, modified according to regulatory standards of equitable treatment. While it is doubtful that full efficiency in rail operations was ever achieved as inefficient routes were not eliminated, the regulated value-of-service rate structure worked tolerably well in terms of general economic development, shipper demands for low rates to extend markets, and carrier requirements for adequate returns.

Fundamental changes in the general regulatory task came with the legislation of the depression era. The Motor Carrier Act of 1935 and the Transportation Act of 1940 emphasized control of what was popularly regarded as excessive and "destructive" competition among carriers in the motor and water fields and between those carriers and the railroads. The chief regulatory tools now became the entry controls (certificate and permit requirements) and minimum rate powers. Limiting maximum rates and unjust discriminations was not the primary objective of motor and water carrier regulation. Implicit in the new scheme was the assumption that competitive forces could not insure that traffic would move by the agencies with the lowest resource costs or otherwise best fitted for particular traffic. To the original monopoly-limiting task and emphasis on protection of shippers and travelers was added the complex and extremely difficult task of using entry and minimum rate controls to produce a more efficient traffic division.[9]

The competition-limiting scheme of regulation beginning in 1935 has greatly increased the role of the Interstate Commerce Commission as market allocator. In many cases, minimum rate orders have not permitted the traffic to be allocated the way it would have been under market competition alone, or even as it would have been under competition if *minimum* rates had been set at the level of minimum economic cost of service instead of a level higher than that on a value-of-service basis. Because high-cost modes sponsor minimum rates that will give them a "fair" opportunity to compete on value-of-service rates rather than a full opportunity to compete on the basis of relative costs of service, the allocative role of the Commission has come to be known as regulatory "fair sharing" of the traffic. In many entry cases, individual motor carriers have not been permitted to share markets as they would under free entry or under controls devoid of protective purposes. Thus, this regulation has increased monopoly in regulated transport in an attempt to validate the value-of-service rate structure long after competitive conditions in transport destroyed its traditional validity.

Administrative and regulatory attempts to maintain the historic value-of-service rate structure and all established rate relationships for these decades have caused an inefficient division of traffic.[10] The efforts to validate value-of-service rates through rate-bureau and regulatory administration of prices have meant rail rates on high-valued commodities above the cost of service when alternative, but not necessarily less costly, services were available from other modes and private carriers.[11] Thus, shippers of high-grade traffic have been motivated to substitute those services for rail service, even though the alternatives have often been produced at higher economic and social costs than the rail service not used. A result is that billions of intercity ton-miles have been induced to move over high-cost rather than low-cost agencies. However profitable this may be to the high resource-cost modes, it leads to large-scale economic waste both in transport and other areas of the economy.

This total-cost-increasing division of traffic takes place even though shippers have made rational decisions in allocating traffic, or in deciding to use private carriage, *in terms of their own business* interest. Unfortunately, it has almost escaped official and industry notice that shipper choice cannot be effective for society, in influencing traffic to flow over the low-cost mode in given situations, unless the rates for the services of the different agencies, as well as those for the different services of each agency, are appropriately related to the long-run marginal or average costs of service.[12] But while it has been widely recognized that failure to charge user fees for public transport facilities may prevent free shipper choice from dividing traffic efficiently, there has been widespread neglect of the fact that the same result occurs, and probably in a very much larger volume, when carrier rates do not closely reflect the corresponding costs of service.

The general economic effects of regulatory "fair-sharing" are the same as those of the protective tariff. High resource-cost transport industries are motivated to over-expand facilities and services; low resource-cost transport industries are under-developed; the cost of transportation and goods to shippers and consumers is higher than need be; and since scarce resources are used inefficiently, real gross national product is below otherwise obtainable levels because of failure to attain the maximum contribution of transport to productivity and regional specialization.

The amount and kind of regulatory relaxation consistent with fostering overall economy in transport must do more than to permit rational rate competition to take place on the basis of the costs of the low-cost agency. Also needed is an adjustment of entry controls and of the scope of operating authorities (certificates and permits) so that the force of potential competition will always press carriers toward efficient operations, better services and creative pricing and management. A particularly needed reform is the abolition of all certificate and permit restrictions on commodities, points, territories, routes, return-haul opportunities and services that have unnecessary cost-increasing and excess capacity inducing effects and keep energetic firms from exerting competitive pressure on protected firms.[13] Only in this manner can the public enjoy the full economy of the forms of transport dependent on public facilities.

Conclusions

Drawing together the foregoing comments, how, then, can the role of government in transport be adjusted to serve a more economic purpose? It is assumed that government's role is ideal when it encourages provision of essential transport at the least total costs, including social costs.

Over the long run, the role of government can become more economic only to the extent that promotional and regulatory policies are designed to be fully consistent with achieving maximum overall economy in transport and high standards of efficiency in each of the several modes. The national transport problem of today is not to stimulate an initial supply of efficient techniques of transport nor to encourage development of vast underdeveloped land resources, but rather it consists of facilitating the right economic development of each mode of transport, including the essential public way and terminal facilities. Consequently, in the promotional sphere government should not continue subsidy after its economically valid purposes have been accomplished. And so much of the nation's capital is involved in public transport investments that they should be limited by fully economic investment criteria and by universal user fees, properly adjusted to the conditions of utilization and to require all transport alternatives and resource costs involved to be considered in expanding public transport facilities. In the regulatory sphere, legislation and policies must not seriously retard achievement of efficient divisions of traffic and allocations of resources in transport as in the recent past. Rather, they must allow market forces to motivate transport firms to take price, service, operating and investment actions required for adequate and efficient service as well as for maximum profitability of the firms under competitive standards for all modes and carriers. Thus, regulation must promote workable competition, as this will necessarily have to be the primary force toward achievement of these economy and efficiency ends for the public. Beyond this, a worthwhile role of regulation, as in the past, is to control monopolistic discrimination in rates and service and to limit maximum rates in traffic areas where intermodal and intramodal competition may still be inadequate.

The most direct, and perhaps effective, way to accomplish adjustment of regulation to a more economic role would be to abolish the controls and legislative policy that have brought the questionable results.[14] If reducing the scope of regulation cannot be legislated, then at least the standards in the Interstate Commerce Act that have led to uneconomic administrative and regulatory policies can be eliminated and new ones substituted to make the legislative policies of the Congress clear and consistent. This would occur if the Congress would indicate unequivocally to the regulatory agency that it wants to promote maximum economy and efficiency consistent with maintenance of competitive organization wherever economically feasible as the principal objective of regulation; that it wants "fair-sharing" of traffic in protection of high-cost carriers and modes totally eliminated; and that it recognizes that certain long-standing rate relationships and rate and service policies may have to be modified to the extent necessary to achieve these ends.

Having always been committed to stimulating a competitive organization for transport and to maintaining competition, even in the days when tolerably workable competition in this field was not possible without regulation of monopoly abuses, and having tried regulatory allocations of traffic and public transport investment policies that clearly have resulted in excessive transport costs and the threat of loss of essential transport facilities, the $64-question is: Is the nation now ready to face up to allowing the competitive markets that present-day transport technology makes feasible to divide the traffic efficiently and to influence the relative growth of alternative techniques as in other fields of enterprise?

NOTES

1. Among the most recent are the so-called Doyle Report on *National Transportation Policy*, Report by the Special Study Group on Transportation Policies in the United

States to the Senate Committee on Interstate and Foreign Commerce (Pursuant to S. Res. 29, 151 and 244 of the 86th Congress) Committee Print, 87 Cong. 1 sess., January 3, 1961; and *Federal Transportation Policy and Program,* U.S. Department of Commerce (March 1960); and *Rationale of Federal Transportation Policy,* the same (April 1960). For a list of the underlying staff reports, see pp. 32 and 71 of the latter reports, respectively.

2. See Federal Coordinator of Transportation, *Public Aids to Transportation* Vols. I-IV (1938-1940); Board of Investigation and Research, *Public Aids to Domestic Transportation,* H. Doc. No. 159, 79 Cong. I sess. (1945), and *Carrier Taxation,* H. Doc. No. 160, 79 Cong. I sess. (1945). The terms "subsidy" and "public aid" are used interchangeably to mean both the grant of money and the provision of facilities or services by government without requiring fully compensatory payments. Public expenditures for transport facilities do not necessarily result in public aids or subsidies; they do to the extent that uncompensated costs result from a complete lack of user fees, from inadequate user charges, or from grants of money or land that are not repayable. See *Public Aids to Domestic Transportation,* cited above, pp. 52-55.

3. For a brief review of state and federal aids to the railroads, including federal land grants during 1850-71, see D. Philip Locklin, *Economics of Transportation,* Irwin (1954), pp. 100-19; and Robert S. Henry, "The Railroad Land Grant Legend in American History Texts," *Mississippi Valley Historical Review,* Vol. XXXII, No. 2, September 1945, pp. 171-94. The reduced rate obligation continued until it was repealed by the Congress in 1946; by that action, the Congress recognized that more than full compensation had been made for the federal grants of land to certain railroads. The total of all land-grant rate reductions (including voluntary equilization of rates by competing roads) to June 30, 1943, was estimated to be $580 million, a sum several times the value of the granted land at the time land grants were awarded and in excess of the sums derived by the railroads from the grants.

4. James C. Nelson, *Railroad Transportation and Public Policy,* The Banking Institution (1959), pp. 93-107.

5. *Ibid.,* pp. 67-73; and statement of Burton N. Behling on public aids to civil aviation in *Railroad Passenger Train Deficit,* ICC Docket No. 31954 (February 1958), pp. 7-16. According to Behling in his statement on highway transportation and expenditures, *op. cit.,* from 1921 through 1956 total expenditures for highways and streets by all units of government amounted to more than $100 billion ($107 billion including disbursements for obligations retired), of which $57.3 billion was for capital outlays and almost $31 billion for maintenance.

6. Charles L. Dearing and Wilfred Owen, *National Transportation Policy,* The Brookings Institution (1949), pp. 12, 81-94, and 236-65.

7. See, for example, John R. Meyer, Merton J. Peck, John Stenason and Charles Zwick, *The Economics of Competition in the Transportation Industries,* Harvard University Press (1959); Nelson, *Railroad Transportation and Public Policy, op. cit.;* and J. R. Sargent, *British Transport Policy,* Oxford University Press (1958).

8. See James C. Nelson, "New Concepts in Transportation Regulation," *Transportation and National Policy,* National Resources Planning Board (May 1942), pp. 197-237, especially pp. 193-201. Also see Meyer and Associates, *op cit.,* Chap. I.

9. Nelson, "New Concepts in Transportation Regulation," *op. cit.,* pp. 201-16.

10. Meyer and Associates, *op. cit.,* Chaps. VI and VII; and Nelson, *Railroad Transportation and Public Policy, op. cit.,* Chaps. 6 and 10.

11. See Ernest W. Williams, Jr., *The Regulation of Rail-Motor Rate Competition,* Harper (1958), pp. 210-12 and 221-22. Williams assesses much blame on the railroads for accepting and continuing rate parity with truckers on value-of-service rates; but he also criticizes the ICC for regulatory actions and decisions perpetuating this policy and for often depriving the low-cost carrier of its cost advantage and a full opportunity to compete for traffic.

12. See Sargent, *op. cit.*, Chap. I.
13. Such as was recommended by the Board of Investigation and Research and its staff director in *Federal Regulatory Restrictions upon Motor and Water Carriers,* S. Doc. No. 78, 79 Cong. 1 sess. (1945), pp. 302-03. See also same title, H. Doc. No. 637, 78 Cong. 2 sess. (1944), *A Summary of a Report on Federal Regulatory Restrictions upon Motor and Water Carriers,* pp. 22-24; *ICC Administration of the Motor Carrier Act,* Hearings before the Senate Select Committee on Small Business, 84 Cong. 1 sess. (November-December 1955); and *Competition, Regulation, and the Public Interest in the Motor Carrier Industry,* Report of the same Committee, S. Rept. No. 1693, 84 Cong. 2 sess. (1956). See also James C. Nelson, *Controls of Entry into Domestic Surface Transportation Under the Interstate Commerce Act,* U.S. Department of Commerce (October 1959), available only in reproduced manuscript in the Library of Congress and Department of Commerce Library, Washington, D.C.; and *Rationale of Federal Transportation Policy, op. cit.,* pp. 10-19.
14. Meyer and Associates, *op. cit.,* take the position that most present-day economic regulation of transport is no longer required as "the existing market structures (and hence the possibility of workable competition) in transportation lie within the range of market structures observed in nonregulated sectors of the economy" and regulation, however useful in the past, has contributed to an irrational allocation of resources in transport. See Chaps. VIII and IX; compare with "New Concepts in Transportation Regulation," *op. cit.,* pp. 236-37.

52

National Transportation Policy:
Fact or Fiction?

Martin T. Farris
Arizona State University

In addition to noting the historic role of government in transportation policy, the serious student also should evaluate current transportation policy. National policy statements are not always easy to evaluate—or indeed to find—although in recent times the making of them has become something of a national pastime. This selection presents an analysis of national transportation policy, stressing its deficiencies as well as its positive aspects.

Transportation in the American economy affects practically every sector of society and almost all economic undertakings. Almost all things and almost all people require some form of transportation. It follows, therefore, that the transportation policy of the nation is an extremely important matter. The object of this article is to review the present state of national transportation policy with a view to assisting in the continuing discussion of how transportation policy might be modified or improved.

Reprinted from *Quarterly Review of Economics and Business*, Vol. 10, No. 2, Summer 1970, pp. 7-14. Used by permission.

Importance

One of the interesting modern-day developments is the establishment of policy guidelines, goals, and national priorities. Transportation policy guidelines, however, have existed for a long time. Indeed, policy guidelines in transportation were probably first established internally with the passage of the Northwest Ordinance in 1787.[1]

The reason for such guidelines, historically and in the present-day economy, stems from the importance of the transportation sector to business and economic development. Policy guidelines assist Congress, the regulatory agencies, the courts, the executive branch, and interested citizens in their plannings and action programs. Given the huge investment in transportation facilities, the large portion of the labor force involved, and the dependence of commerce and national defense on transportation, such guidelines can be extremely useful.

Establishment and identification of policy

The transportation policy of this nation is initially promulgated by the Congress. How the various parts of the industry are regulated, taxed, subsidized, or encouraged is accomplished through congressional action in appropriating funds, in delegating authority to commissions and boards, and in setting policy guidelines. The executive branch also influences national transportation policy by its power of appointment and of recommendation. Given the new Department of Transportation, it may be that in the future the executive branch will assume a larger and more forceful role than in the past. Finally, the judiciary influences transportation policy through the power of interpretation. Some might say that the courts actually establish policy but, theoretically at least, the role of the courts is only interpretive. Nevertheless, the power of the "purse strings" is persuasive and hence it is really the Congress which sets or establishes national transportation policy.

Even though transportation policy is highly important, it is not easy to identify its exact nature. There are at least two types of policy: the informal institutional policy and the formal statutory policy. The informal institutional policy is not very explicit and appears in congressional enactments and in statements of general "beliefs" and "philosophies." Examples of this type of policy are the private ownership concept, the public investment concept, the common carrier preference concept, and the concept of exemption.

The formal statutory policy, on the other hand, consists of explicit statements in the statutes in which Congress has enunciated national goals, aims, and guidelines. Sometimes these appear as preambles, as in the Transportation Act of 1940.

The "Declaration of National Transportation Policy," contained as a preamble to the 1940 act, is the most comprehensive and formal statutory statement of policy today. It reads:

It is hereby declared to be the National Transportation Policy of the Congress to provide for fair and impartial regulation of all modes of transportation subject to the provisions of the Act, so administered as to recognize and preserve the inherent advantages of each; to promote safe, adequate, economical, and efficient service and foster sound economic conditions in transportation and among the several carriers; to encourage the establishment and maintenance of reasonable charges for transportation service, without unjust discriminations, undue preferences or advantages, or unfair or destructive competitive practices; to cooperate with the several States and the duly authorized officials thereof; and to encourage fair wages and equitable working conditions;—all to the end of developing, coordinating, and preserving a national transportation system by water, highway, and rail as well as other means, adequate to meet the needs of commerce of the United States, of the Postal Service, and of the national defense. All of the provisions of this Act shall be administered and enforced with a view to carrying out the above declaration of policy.[2]

My concern here is limited to this statutory statement of national transportation policy.

Analysis of national transportation policy

The declaration can be broken down basically into two categories, each with several subparts. These are (1) carrier-oriented policy pronouncements, and (2) public-oriented policy statements.

Three ideas are involved in the carrier-oriented pronouncements. These are, first, the goal of promotion of "safe, adequate, economical, and efficient service and . . . sound economic conditions in transportation and among the several carriers" and second, "to encourage the establishment and maintenance of reasonable charges for transportation service, without unjust discriminations, undue preferences or advantages, or unfair or destructive competitive practices." Obviously, a price-regulation goal is established here. Finally, the goal of encouraging "fair wages and equitable working conditions" is carrier-oriented.

The public policy goals may also be divided into three subgroups. First, the goal of "developing, coordinating, and preserving a national transportation system . . . adequate to meet the needs of commerce . . . , of the Postal Service and of the national defense" is perhaps the broadest and most important of the public-oriented goals. Second, Congress pledged to "cooperate with the several States and the duly authorized officials thereof." Finally, it is the national goal "to provide for fair and impartial regulation of all modes . . . , so administered as to recognize and preserve the inherent advantages of each."

The general thrust of the 1940 statement was to emphasize transportation as a *system.* Prior to that time, transportation policy and rail policy had been almost synonymous. However, in the 1930s new modes of transportation had become important enough to be regulated by the federal government. Motor transportation was regulated in 1935, air transportation in 1938, and inland water transportation in 1940 by the same act containing this declaration. Therefore, the key words are "all modes" and "developing, coordinating, and preserving a national transportation *system.*"[3] This concept of an integrated system of transportation was based on the idea that each mode had a role to play and thus a statement on "inherent advantages of each [mode] " was included.

Additionally, the system was to be based on the idea of controlled competition. This is apparent by the inclusion of the traditional policy pronouncements about unjust and discriminatory rates and the inclusion of a new idea that competition should not be destructive. The general philosophy enunciated by the declaration of policy recognized that the former problem of regulation of transportation monopoly had given way to the problem of regulation of transportation competition.

Policy deficiencies

In spite of these admirable goals and in spite of the belated recognition of transportation competition as a national problem, the declaration was sadly deficient in a number of ways. Perhaps the major disappointment has been the inability to attain in the real world of transportation operation the goals set forth in the policy. This matter of the transportation system falling short of the policy goals has been well detailed and repeatedly analyzed in a series of governmental studies and reports in the post-World War II era.[4]

The typical approach has been to accept the policy pronouncement of Congress and show how performance has fallen short. Rarely have the deficiencies of the policy itself been analyzed.[5] I suggest that these deficiencies may be the important matter and that they may be summarized by three words: incomplete, inconsistent, and indefinable.

Incomplete

Even though the declaration purports to be a total national policy, it obviously covers only a portion of transportation. Basically the declaration applies only to those modes regulated by the Interstate Commerce Commission (ICC). Therefore, at least three modes of transportation are omitted. These omissions are air transportation, water transportation, and private transportation.

Air transportation has its own declaration of policy contained in the Civil Aeronautics Act of 1938 and subsequent acts. Maritime transportation is regulated, promoted, and subsidized by a series of congressional enactments over the years and in effect is a portion of US foreign policy. Both modes are regulated by agencies other than the ICC.

The provision of shipper-owned transportation, commonly known as private transportation, has become an increasingly important factor in the years since the act of 1940. The Interstate Commerce Commission estimates that over 60 percent of truck transportation and over 80 percent of inland water transportation is in shipper-owned vehicles and hence is exempt from economic regulations.[6] Although no one suggests that the shipper's right to provide his own transportation for his own goods should be denied, there is increasing concern with the competitive aspects of this development. Additionally, a number of enforcement problems such as illegal trucking, fraudulent "buy-sell" arrangements, and others are involved.

If it is indeed desirable to conceive of transportation as a "system," then the omission of air, water, and private transportation detracts considerably from the attainment of a *national* transportation policy.

Finally it is evident that the declaration deals principally with *regulation* of transportation. To be sure, the public-oriented parts mention "developing, coordinating, and preserving a national transportation system" and the act did establish the Bureau of Investigation and Research (BIR). However, the contexts of both the declaration and the BIR provisions, and of the act itself (as an amendment to previous regulatory acts) were regulatory in nature. A truly *national* transportation policy would have to deal with the promotion of various transportation modes, public investment criteria in transportation facilities, and the establishment of priorities and goals in attaining a "transportation system . . . adequate to meet the needs of the commerce of the United States, of the Postal Service, and of the national defense."

Therefore, it is possible to say that the 1940 declaration was not only incomplete in its coverage of the various modes and that it omitted important parts of the system but that it was also incomplete and less than "national" in its scope and direction because it was oriented solely toward regulation.

Inconsistent

Careful analysis of the carrier-oriented declarations discloses some definitional inconsistencies.[7] Likewise, the carrier-oriented statements seem inconsistent with the public-oriented policy statements. Finally, the public policy statements may be internally inconsistent.

The carrier-oriented statements call for "safe, adequate, economical, and efficient service and . . . sound economic conditions" in one part of the declaration. The word "economical" probably means, to most persons, the least expensive. "Efficient" could be defined in terms of the correct allocation of resources (capacity) of the carriers to handle the average needs of the transportation sector. However, "safe . . . conditions" cost money and the least expensive carrier is often not the safest. Likewise commerce and traffic vary seasonally and what is efficient in one time period is hardly efficient in another. Also "adequate" here could refer to "financially adequate" (as it did in the Transportation Act of 1920)[8] or to a system which is physically adequate. In the case of financial adequacy, the least expensive carrier (that is, "economical") may have very poor financial reserves. Likewise a physically adequate system may not possess the needed excess capacity for seasonal variations. Finally, "sound economic conditions" is not necessarily consistent with least cost or average capacity. Indeed, "sound economic conditions" can mean almost anything, depending on whose economic condition is involved (what is "sound" economically to the shipper is usually not "sound" economically to the carrier), what time period is involved ("sound economic conditions" during a depression can be very different from "sound economic conditions" during inflation), and the frame of reference considered ("sound economic conditions" for the carriers may not be the same as "sound economic conditions" for the entire economy).

The second part of the carrier-oriented declaration concerns rate regulation and contains the familiar minimax approach of prohibiting unreasonable and discriminatory charges while preventing "unfair or destructive competitive practices." Although such price-regulatory policy might be questioned in general, the matter of consistency with "economical" (that is, least-cost) transportation in such a framework is doubtful. It is likewise doubtful that such a price policy necessarily leads to the most "efficient" system in terms of allocation of resources. However, the goals of safety and adequacy are undoubtedly served by such price control approaches.

The final part of the carrier-oriented declaration calls for "fair wages and equitable working conditions." Aside from what is meant by "fair," it is readily apparent that this conflicts with the desire for the most "economical" (least-cost) system.

The public-oriented policy statements may also be internally inconsistent. In one part, the declaration calls for "developing, coordinating, and preserving a national transportation system . . . adequate to meet the needs of the commerce of the United States, of the Postal Service, and the national defense." "Developing" implies growth and change of economic relationships. "Preserving" means maintaining or protecting the existing carriers and economic relationships. It is hard to understand how Congress can both preserve and maintain while at the same time changing, causing growth, and finally "coordinating" the whole system.

In another part of the public-oriented policy, Congress pledges to provide "fair and impartial regulation of all modes . . . so administered as to recognize and preserve the inherent advantages of each." This certainly implies that each mode will maintain its relative position and economic role. Yet if the system needs "developing" and "coordinating" in order to meet the needs of commerce, the postal service, and national defense, how can these purposes be accomplished without endangering the 1940 position of some modes? Although it is laudable to try to preserve and maintain modes of transportation, it is fairly difficult to develop a system adequate for the various needs without conflicting with such preservation.

Finally, there is an internal inconsistency among the goals of "adequate to meet the needs of the commerce of the United States, of the Postal Service, and of the national defense." For purposes of national defense, considerable excess capacity should be more than enough to cover the usual seasonal variations found in commerce and the needs of the postal system. What is adequate capacity for commerce is not necessarily adequate for the postal system and neither is it adequate capacity for national defense. These goals, then, seem somewhat inconsistent. Likewise, one wonders how the needs of commerce, the postal system, and national defense can be met adequately while at the same time each mode is preserved and maintained.

When these public policy goals are compared with the carrier-oriented goals, more inconsistency and doubt arise. Is it possible to have an "economical" (least-cost) transportation system which continues to preserve and maintain each mode? A system "adequate to meet the needs of national defense" implies excess capacity for emergencies but is this most "efficient" (perfectly allocated)? Or is a system designed with national defense in mind necessarily the most "economical"? Many other inconsistencies between the carrier-oriented goals and the public-oriented goals are apparent.

My point is that the declaration is internally inconsistent in many ways in both of its parts and is also inconsistent in many ways between its parts.

Indefinable and undefined

The final deficiency in the declaration involves definition and measurement. Inherent in the foregoing discussion of inconsistency is the matter of definition. The phrases and terms used in the declaration are not formally defined in the act. The meaning of the words is left to interpretation. Indeed, it is questionable whether some of the terms can be defined at all given the circumstances under which transportation operates. Not only are the phrases and terms left undefined but they also may be indefinable.

If the terms cannot be defined, can they be measured? If the concepts cannot be measured, can they be applied? Lack of definition hinders greatly the administrative application of the policy declaration. Two examples will suffice to illustrate the point:

(1) The price regulation section provides that "unfair and destructive competitive practices" should not be fostered by regulation. This could mean that no mode should be allowed to price below its fully allocated cost. The Interstate Commerce Commission has sometimes held up this standard of "reasonableness" and justified its action by applying the "unfair and destructive competitive practices" criterion. However, there is a strong opinion among economists that the proper measure for pricing in transportation is marginal cost.[9] Is incremental or marginal-cost pricing an "unfair and destructive competitive practice" even though it is economically sound? Likewise, how can a cost criterion be used to define the level of minimum price controls when all modes do not pay the full costs of production of the service? It is common knowledge that some modes own their own "way," maintain and operate it (the railways) whereas other modes have their "way" provided by nature or public investment and pay nothing for its use (the inland waterways). When one mode has part of its costs paid by public investment and its competitor must pay for the same type of input, can fully allocated costs be applied at all?[10]

(2) The act is to be administered in such a way as to "recognize and preserve the inherent advantages of each [mode]." No definition of what is meant by "inherent advantages" is given and the term can be and is defined to fit almost any circumstance. One might ask: what are the "inherent advantages" of rail-

roads or of trucklines or of barge lines? How are "inherent advantages" measured? If it is to be recognized, it must be defined. If it is to be preserved, one should be able to measure it so as to test whether it is being diminished or being preserved. If transportation were a competitive industry with all modes providing all their own costs, then the carrier or mode able to provide a specific service at the lowest price would have the "inherent advantages" for that traffic. But competition is not allowed to allocate traffic, not all costs are covered by all carriers, minimum rates are regulated so as to prevent "unfair and destructive competitive practices," and "inherent advantages" becomes a meaningless phrase. It is not only undefined but it is indefinable in present circumstances.

Positive policy aspects

If the declaration of national transportation policy is deficient because it is incomplete, inconsistent, and indefinable, are there any positive aspects to it? Surprisingly, the answer is in the affirmative from two points of view: of ideas and of what is ideal.

The declaration does encompass the "right ideas." Almost everyone would agree that transportation should be considered as a system in which each of the parts has a distinctive role to fulfill. The idea of a system with many parts which are coordinated and treated as a whole *national* transportation system is contained in the declaration. Regardless of the debate as to the meaning of "inherent advantages of each [mode]," the idea that the separate parts are distinctive in some way, yet contribute to the whole system, is the correct one. The idea of a "safe, adequate, economical and efficient" carrier structure is acceptable generally even though the concepts may not be definitionally consistent. The idea of "fair and impartial regulation" would probably be accepted as proper even though "fair and impartial" may be indefinable. The analogy could continue on through nearly all the separate phrases in the declaration but the point is that generally almost everyone would agree that the ideas involved should be found in a general policy guideline for transportation.

The second positive policy aspect is that the declaration does establish an ideal. Nothing is perfect and everything is subject to change. Yet this does not keep us from having ideals or goals. The goal of a system adequate for the needs of commerce, of the postal system, and of national defense may be indefinable but it is still a valid goal. The ideal of "fair wages and equitable working conditions" may be inconsistent with the goal of an "economical" system yet it is a valid ideal. The goal of rate regulation which prevents monopoly abuses at the same time that it discourages the excesses of competition may seem unattainable and inconsistent but it is still a valid ideal. Much the same could be said for the other goals set forth in the declaration. My point is that the declaration does point the way, and moves in the right direction; it does set up goals and ideals no matter how unattainable they may be. In that sense there is indeed a national transportation policy.

Conclusion

Undoubtedly the national transportation policy is a *fiction*. As stated in the declaration, it has many shortcomings. It is incomplete, inconsistent, and indefinable. From the point of view of containing generally acceptable ideas, the declaration of national transportation policy is a *fact*. It does contain acceptable goals and it does establish ideals to be sought. Although one may be critical of the goals and ideals, it is a fact that they are indeed present in the declaration. In a word, national transportation policy is both a fact *and* a fiction.

NOTES

1. Some writers indicate that the Treaty of Paris of 1763, guaranteeing that the Mississippi River would be "free and open" without discrimination as to nationality and hence allowing early colonists access to the sea, was the first American national transportation policy. See Roy J. Sampson and Martin T. Farris, *Domestic Transportation: Practice, Theory and Policy* (Boston: Houghton, 1966), p. 354.
2. 54 Stat. 898.
3. Italics mine. The significance of this coordinated approach to all modes was pointed out early by Robert W. Harbeson in "The Transportation Act of 1940," *Journal of Public Utility and Land Economics* (now *Land Economics*), Vol. 17 (August 1941), pp. 291-302. However, the idea of a system is somewhat broader than that of a coordinated approach.
4. The "Sawyer report," of the US Department of Commerce, *Issues Involved in a Unified and Coordinated Federal Program for Transportation* (Washington: US Government Printing Office, 1949); the "Weeks report" (sometimes called the Cabinet Committee Report), Presidential Advisory Committee on Transportation Policy and Organization, *A Report to the President on Revision of Federal Transportation Policy* (Washington: US Government Printing Office, 1955); the "Mueller report," US Department of Commerce, *Federal Transportation Policy and Program* (March 1960); and the "Doyle report," prepared for the US Senate, Committee on Interstate and Foreign Commerce, 87th Cong., 1st Sess., by the Special Study Group on Transportation Policies in the United States, *National Transportation Policy* (Washington: US Government Printing Office, 1961).
5. Both the Weeks report and the Doyle report do contain suggested drafts of a "rewritten" policy declaration. Further, the Doyle report does contain some elementary analysis of policy deficiencies and inconsistencies of transportation law.
6. Interstate Commerce Commission, *Annual Report, 1967*.
7. For a more detailed analysis of this point, see Martin T. Farris, "Definitional Inconsistencies of the National Transportation Policy," *ICC Practitioners' Journal*, Vol. 35 (November-December 1967), pp. 25-33.
8. Sampson and Farris, pp. 253-56.
9. William J. Baumol, and others, "The Role of Cost in the Minimum Pricing of Railroad Services," *Journal of Business*, Vol. 35 (October 1962), pp. 357-66.
10. This difficulty with a definition of "unfair or destructive competitive practices" was pointed out early by Ralph L. Dewey, "The Transportation Act of 1940," *American Economic Review*, Vol. 31 (March 1941), p. 20.

53

The Compatibility of the
Rule of Ratemaking and the
National Transportation Policy

John J. Coyle
Pennsylvania State University

A pivotal aspect of transportation policy is the matter of regulation of rates or prices, officially regularized in the so-called "Rule of Ratemaking." Congress establishes transportation policy but the Interstate Commerce Commission administers or implements this policy.

This selection contains excellent background on this rule, its legislative origin, and, most important, the administration of the rule of ratemaking by the I.C.C. The important question posed here is: Has administration of the rule of ratemaking been in line with congressional intent?

Complaints regarding Interstate Commerce Commission[1] Decisions in intermodal rate cases seem to be increasing in frequency and intensity in recent years. While there is probably some basis for complaint in certain instances, it would appear that the Commission has become a convenient scapegoat in intermodal rate cases. The contention of this paper is that the major blame for problems which currently exist in administering intermodal rates is the result of an inconsistency between the rule of ratemaking and the national transportation policy. The former attempts to set an economic perspective on ratemaking whereas the latter adds certain social and political considerations.[2] The consequences of this difference between the two will be explicated in other sections of the paper. A separate but related contention is that the most recent amendment to the rule of ratemaking made in 1958 was not a substantive change in the law. Evidence to support the statements made above will be garnered by reviewing and analyzing the development of the rule of ratemaking along with related decisions and important congressional hearings. The National Transportation Policy will also be analyzed. The treatment will be in two epochs. First, attention will focus on the period from 1920 to 1958. The rule of ratemaking was originally fashioned under the Transportation Act of 1920 and was amended in 1933 and 1940. The second section will treat the latest amendment to the rule of ratemaking which was made in 1958. A major change was supposedly made at this time and a number of controversial cases have ensued.

Rule of ratemaking—1920 to 1958

The original rule of ratemaking was contained in the Transportation Act of 1920 and was one of the manifestations of a change in regulatory philosophy con-

From John J. Coyle, "The Compatibility of the Rule of Ratemaking and the National Transportation Policy," *I.C.C. Practitioners' Journal*, March-April 1971, pp. 340-353. Copyright, Association of Interstate Commerce Commission Practitioners. Used by permission.

tained in that Act. The rule of ratemaking directed Commission attention to the earnings of the railroads in order that an adequate transportation system could be provided. It indicated that railroads were entitled to a fair return upon a fair value of their property. This was not conceptually new since the Supreme Court had enunciated a similar view in 1898.[3] However, the original rule of ratemaking was different in its approach since it focused attention upon aggregate rail properties, not individual situations. In other words, the 1920 version of the rule of ratemaking represented an attempt to stabilize earnings of the railroad industry on a group basis.

The record of the Commission following the Act of 1920 demonstrates that revenue stabilization was not achieved. It became apparent that: (1) the mere raising of the level of rates did not necessarily augment carrier revenues since these across-the-board increases ignored differences in demand elasticities, i.e., not all commodities had the same elasticity of demand for transport purposes; (2) the cross-elasticity of demand or substitutability of carrier service was greater than anticipated, i.e., motor carrier carriers and others quickly capitalized on higher rail rates; and (3) administration of the provisions of the rule of rate-making and the related recapture clause proved difficult and entailed vast expenditures of time and money. For these and other reasons, a change was made in the rule of ratemaking under the auspices of the Emergency Transportation Act of 1933.

The 1933 version of the rule of ratemaking reads as follows:

> In the exercise of its power to prescribe just and reasonable rates the Commission shall give due consideration, among other factors, to the effect of rates on the movement of traffic, to the need in the public interest, of adequate and efficient railway transportation service at the lowest cost consistent with the furnishing of such service; and to the need of revenues sufficient to enable the carriers, under honest, economical, and efficient management to provide such service.

The changes made above made the rule of ratemaking more flexible. Attention was still devoted to revenue needs and adequate service but this was not tied to a fair return standard. Also, attention was directed toward demand elasticity by the words, "effect of the rate on the movement of traffic." Furthermore, its application was no longer restricted to general rate level cases but could now also apply in other rate proceedings especially intermodal rate cases where only a limited number of rates were likely to be affected.

The latter aspect received very little attention in the period immediately following the 1933 amendment. However, it did raise an interesting question that was brought out by Commissioner Joseph B. Eastman in the hearings preceding the Transportation Act of 1940, *viz.*, whose traffic was to be considered in a competitive rate case. Consequently, a phrase was added by the Transportation Act of 1940—"by the carrier or carriers for which the rates are prescribed."[4]

We should note at this point that when the Motor Carrier Act was passed in

1935, a rule of ratemaking was made applicable to the motor carrier industry under the new Part II of the Act, but an additional stipulation was added, *viz.*, that the Commission should preserve the inherent advantages of the motor carrier. This stipulation was made somewhat redundant by the National Transportation Policy which was added in 1940. But the stipulation was left intact although no corresponding addition was made for railroads in Part I nor was it included under Part III which was added for water carriers in 1940. In one of the early cases following the Act of 1940 the Commission stated that although this directive was not contained in the rule as pertained to railroads, it should be considered in all fairness to the railroads.[5] As we shall see, the question of inherent advantages becomes an important issue in later cases.

At this point the stage was set, the Interstate Commerce Act contained separate rules of ratemaking in each Part. The rules were basically the same with the exception noted above. It appeared then that in intermodal rate cases, proposed changes were to be viewed from the perspective of the proposing carrier, i.e., was such a change "economic" according to some criterion of reasonableness from his vantage point.

The National Transportation Policy was added as indicated previously in 1940, and its purpose was to provide the Commission with some guidelines for regulation of competing forms of transport. In reading the hearings which preceded the Motor Carrier Act of 1935 and the Transportation Act of 1940, one detects a concern in some quarters about regulation of motor carriers and water carriers by the Commission, i.e., would it tend to be protective towards the railroads. The concern for impartial regulation and the protection of the newer agencies was such that a national policy was added as follows:

> It is hereby declared to be the national transportation policy of the Congress to provide for fair and impartial regulation of all modes of transportation subject to the provisions of the Act, so administered as to recognize and preserve the inherent advantages of each; to promote safe, adequate, economical, and efficient service and foster sound economic conditions in transportation and among the several carriers, to encourage the establishment and maintenance of reasonable charges for transportation services, without unjust discriminations, undue preferences, or advantages, or unfair or destructive competitive practices to cooperate with the several States and the duly authorized officials thereof; and to encourage fair wages and equitable working conditions; all to the end of developing, coordinating, and preserving a national transportation system by water, highways, and rail, as well as other means, adequate to meet the needs of the commerce of the United States, of the Postal Service, and of the national defense. All of the provisions of this Act shall be administered and enforced with a view to carrying out the above declaration of policy.

From the above one can see that the National Transportation Policy is in effect superimposed over all other provisions. Also that it introduces "noneconomic" considerations such as national defense[6] which might require, for example, protecting an inefficient agency in case of national emergencies. Furthermore, it uses some nebulous terms like destructive competition which are difficult to define. In fact, competition by its very nature may be considered destructive since inefficient firms may be driven out of business and new technologies will replace old ones.

Finally, the concept of preserving inherent advantages has tended to be viewed by the ICC on the demand or user side which makes the quality of service of carriers a relevant consideration. If the focus was on the supply or carrier side, then only carrier cost would be relevant. In other words, if you view transportation from the user's viewpoint (demand) then decisions are made based upon the rate charged by the carrier and the quality of his service in relation to your requirements. So in some instances, air service may be purchased at very high rates compared to surface modes but the shipper offsets this by decreased inventory costs or warehousing cost. On the supply or carrier side, the concept of inherent advantage would refer to the carrier's cost of providing the service.[7] If the former perspective is taken then the Commission can get trapped into becoming an allocator of traffic, i.e., setting differentials on carrier's rates to offset service disadvantages. But the National Transportation Policy appears to lean in this direction and, in fact, inherent advantage was defined as cost and service in the congressional hearings.[8]

Before proceeding to an analysis of selected commission decisions following the Transportation Act of 1940, an additional point should be made about the rule of ratemaking. The rule of ratemaking is a legislative directive to the ICC. Unlike Sections 1, 2, 3, and 4, it does not lay down a rule of action for carriers subject to ICC jurisdiction. It directs the ICC to consider certain factors in the exercise of its power to prescribe just and reasonable rates. Theoretically, the rule of ratemaking could come into play in all rate cases where the reasonableness of rates is in question which covers almost all rate cases. However, there are many rate cases including intermodal cases where no reference is made to the rule of ratemaking.

As one would expect, the activity level during World War II in terms of rate proceedings was low. The first major case of interest to come before the ICC in the postwar period was the so-called *New Automobile case*[9] that attracted much attention a decade later in congressional hearings.[10] The case was a general investigation into rates, charges, rules, regulations, and practices in the United States applying to the interstate transportation of new automobiles. An important issue was the question of inherent advantage of the railroads and motor carriers.

The railroads involved felt that they were at a disadvantage and a "service differential" was necessary to enable them to compete. The Commission appeared hesitant to establish such a differential:

The effect on the relative advantages and disadvantages of rail versus other modes of transportation is the controlling factor in attempts by carriers to make their rates according to competitive necessity. Where regulated and dependable motor carrier service is available, its completeness, expedition, and flexibility unquestionably give it a certain advantage over rail service. It is impossible to determine exactly what this amounts to per 100 pounds. A figure adopted to represent the average situation would be insufficient to obtain traffic in some instances and an unnecessary inducement or waste in others. Only long experience under stable rates and normal conditions could demonstrate whether the present rates are so related to provide equality of opportunity.

In spite of their refusal to establish minimum rates for the carriers which would allow differentials, the ICC did appear to equivocate a little with the words, "equality of opportunity." It is very easy to read something into this that was not intended but one could argue that these words might imply sharing traffic. In a later comment discussing reasonable minimum rates, it was stated:

What constitutes a minimum reasonable rate is a matter to be determined in light of the facts of record in each individual case, avoiding arbitrary action and keeping within statutory and constitutional limitations. . . . Whether a rate is below a reasonable minimum depends on whether it yields a proper return; whether the carriers would be better off from a net revenue standpoint with it than without it; whether it represents competition that is unduly destructive to a reasonable rate structure and the carriers; and whether it otherwise conforms to the national transportation policy and the rules of ratemaking declared in the Act of 1940.

The subjectivity involved in determining a reasonable minimum rate is indicated by this statement. In other words, one could argue that the ICC could go from this definition to a policy of protecting carriers. This would appear to be particularly true in light of the references to the National Transportation Policy and also destructive competition.

As implied previously this decision has been hailed as the correct interpretation of the rule of ratemaking. The reason for this feeling is that the Commission concluded that the rates for each agency were to be determined in each case according to the facts and circumstances attending the movement of traffic by that agency since Congress had enunciated separate ratemaking rules for each agency, the major qualification being that proposed rates could not be below a reasonable minimum. One could argue that there is a clear rejection of umbrella or protective ratemaking, and such was done in later congressional hearings. However, one could also argue that the definition of reasonable minimum rates is so general that the ICC could protect carriers and not violate what they stated as policy in the case. Also, the carriers involved did not want minimum rates established. The ICC judged the existing rates to be compensatory, and therefore, did not prescribe minimum rates.

Beginning in the early 1950's in a series of cases the ICC appeared to be clearly involved in trying to determine service differentials and thereby establish a pattern of rates which would allow carriers to compete for the traffic. One example is a case decided in 1951 where a group of railroads sought reduced rates on petroleum products to meet motor carrier competition.[11] The railroads proposed an average reduction of three cents in their rates. The ICC stated that both types of carriage were a vital part of the transport system and should be afforded an opportunity to compete. The proposed rates of the railroad were rejected on the basis that they were lower than necessary to meet the competition. This approach is indicative of what transpired in a series of other cases. One very clear example was a decision in 1952 where once again certain railroads had proposed reduced rates to meet motor competition.[12] Here the Commission stated that the proposed rates would cover substantially more than the direct costs involved. However, they stated cost was not the sole criterion, and the rates should not be lower than necessary to meet the competition. There was no justification, according to the Commission, for the establishment of levels of rates lower than the total expenses to the shippers incurred in the transportation over the competitive mode.

That the Commission should espouse such a policy which seemed to contradict earlier decisions and what Congress had in mind when they established separate ratemaking rules, was mystifying to some and annoying to others. Actually, the Commission was just trying to live with the National Transportation Policy and its requirements to preserve inherent advantages as well as prevent destructive competition. In supporting the need for regulation of other modes and a national policy, the Honorable Joseph B. Eastman made the following comment:

> It is evident that the entire transportation industry, . . . is in need of . . . government control if a threatening chaos is to be transformed into order; . . . The object of such control is not the protection of the railroads only but the proper protection of every form of transportation. They all have their parts to play, for each one can do certain things better than others. The problem is to find their appropriate functions, protect them in the performance of such functions, prevent wasteful duplication of service without eliminating such competition as is economically sound. . . .[13]

Mr. Eastman helped to shape some of the legislation of this era and his above statement probably explains the philosophy of Congress with respect to inherent advantages and the transportation system in general. One can quickly detect the idea that each mode has a "slot" in the system and such must be protected. The problem is that there is an implicit assumption that transportation's output is fairly homogeneous but heterogeneity is more the case.[14] When it comes to making the "Eastman approach" operational, you have to go to the demand side, i.e., view service requirements. If shippers can use both agencies at slightly different prices then one should allow such rate spreads to permit everybody to compete.

The next section will treat the 1958 version of the rule of ratemaking and the hearings preceding same as well as some of the cases which followed. The amendment made in 1958 was hailed by some as a major overhaul of the rule of ratemaking. In actuality as shall be delineated, the amendment only acts as an admonishment to the Commission.

Rule of ratemaking—1958

In 1958 a series of Congressional hearings were held to discuss the problems of the railroad industry. One of the central issues was the policy of the Commission in intermodal ratemaking. The following amendment was proposed by the railroads and was commonly called the "three shall nots."[15]

In determining what is less than a reasonable minimum rate, the Commission: (1) shall not consider the effect of the rate on the traffic of other carriers; (2) shall not consider the relation of the rate to the rate of any other carrier; and (3) shall not consider whether the rate is lower than necessary to meet the competition of other carriers.

The suggested amendment was quite explicit and one can discern the intent of the railroads. They wanted Congress to lay down a clear directive to the Commission that rate adjustments should not hinge on preserving the competitive balance among the modes, i.e., rates should be judged strictly on whether they were compensatory.

Other interested parties protested that railroad proposal. The following statement is typical of those protesting:[16]

Under the railroads' proposal the Commission would be shorn of any real power as a referee in the competitive rate struggle between different modes of transportation. No longer would the ICC be able to control competitive ratemaking so as to preserve rate levels reflecting the value of the transportation service provided and a fair distribution of the overhead burden.

It was decided that the question of amending the rule of ratemaking merited separate hearings since it was such a controversial issue. The amendment proposed by the Senate Committee was the addition of a new paragraph to the rule of ratemaking which was to read as follows:

In a proceeding involving competition with another mode of transportation, the Commission, in determining whether a rate is lower than a reasonable minimum rate, shall consider the facts and circumstances attending the movement of the traffic by railroad and not by such other mode.[17]

The first person to appear before the Committee was former Senator Wheeler who had played a primary role in the passage of the Transportation Act of 1940. Senator Wheeler was invited to discuss Congressional intent:

Senator Smathers. Was there ever, at any time, an intention expressed on the part of any members of the committee, or of the Senate, that the Interstate Commerce Commission should, in effect, set rates so that one mode of transportation would be protected against another mode?

Mr. Wheeler. Definitely not. There was never any such intention. We thought we were making it perfectly clear that there was no way in which water carriers' rates could be raised so as to protect the railroads, and nothing to protect the motor carriers, and nothing to protect the railroads. . . .

Senator Schoeppel. Of course, all of that was tied to one cardinal factor; namely, that those rates when they were established, should be compensatory, was it not?

Mr. Wheeler. Exactly. As long as they were compensatory, then they could reduce their rates. The water carriers could reduce their rates as long as they were compensatory to take business away, or the motor carriers could reduce their rate to a compensatory level to take business away from the railroads, and the railroads could reduce their rates to meet the competition as long as their rates were compensatory.[18]

The following statement of the Chairman of the Senate Subcommittee clearly indicated the intent of the proposed amendment:

Senator Smathers. May I ask you this question: On behalf of the subcommittee I will say that is exactly what we have attempted to do, to write languages into this statute which, in fact, would carry out the intention of the Congress when it first put this ratemaking provision in in 1940, with respect to all.

Mr. Wheeler. Yes, I understand. . . .

Senator Smathers. We say, in a proceeding involving competition with another mode of transportation, the Commission, in determining whether a rail rate is lower than a reasonable minimum rate, shall consider the facts and circumstances attending the movement of the traffic by railroad, and not by such other mode.

Mr. Wheeler. Yes.

Senator Smathers. Now, in your opinion, does that expression there coincide with the Members of Congress in 1940.

Mr. Wheeler. Very definitely. . . .[19]

The intent here then is no different than what it was in 1940. In effect, it was reaffirmation and an admonishment to the Commission.

The Commission was not in favor of a change, and they contended that the proposed amendment added nothing to the law. Furthermore, the Commission criticized the specific mention of rail rates in the amendment and felt there was inconsistency with the controlling objectives of the national transportation policy.

The Commission felt that if an amendment was desired it should read as follows:

> In a proceeding involving competition between carriers, the Commission in determining whether a proposed rate is lower than a reasonable minimum rate, shall consider the facts and circumstances attending the movement of the traffic. Rates of a carrier shall not be held up to a particular level to protect the traffic of a less economic carrier, giving due consideration to the inherent cost and service advantages of the respective carriers.[20]

The amendment finally made was similar to that proposed by the ICC and read as follows:

> In a proceeding involving competition between carriers of different modes of transportation subject to this Act, the Commission, in determining whether a rate is lower than a reasonable minimum rate, shall consider the facts and circumstances attending the movement of the traffic by the carrier or carriers to which the rate is applicable. Rates of a carrier shall not be held up to a particular level to protect the traffic of any other mode of transportation, giving due consideration to the objectives of the national transportation policy declared in this Act.

The final Senate Committee report included some comments about the amendment which are relevant.[21] The Committee felt that each form of transportation should have the opportunity to set rates reflecting inherent advantages of that particular mode in order that the public could exercise its choice among carriers but unfair and destructive ratemaking practices were to be prevented. The Committee believed that the Commission had not been consistent in allowing the various modes to assert their inherent advantages in the form of rates. The recommendation was that the Commission consistently follow the principles laid down in the *New Automobiles* case. It should be clear from the latter statement and the discussion presented of the Congressional hearings that the 1958 amendment was not intended to be a substantive change in the letter of the law. Rather, it was more in the form of a "scolding" to the Commission. The following statement contained in the report clearly substantiates this:

> The subcommittee therefore believes it necessary to amend the Act only so as, in effect, to admonish the Commission to be consistent in following the policy enunciated in the Automobile case thus assuring reasonable freedom in making of competitive rates.

The report of the Senate Committee seems to indicate that the phrase, "giving due consideration to the objectives of the national transportation policy de-

clared in this Act," gives reference to prevention of unfair or destructive competitive practices. However, another of the objectives of this policy is the preservation of the inherent advantages of the respective situations. In the *New Automobiles* case, the Commission said that they could not measure the value of these
inherent advantages. In later cases as we saw, they used rate differentials to
resolve this problem. This practice gave rise to criticism which led to the 1958
amendment. However, the Commission is still faced with the same problem even
with the amendment. The next section will treat selected cases since the amendment of 1958 which will hopefully demonstrate that no major change will be
forthcoming under the present situation.

Recent cases

There have been quite a number of intermodal cases since 1958 where the
current version of the rule of ratemaking has implicitly or explicitly affected the
decision. As is customary, Commission policy in interpreting statutes evolves
over time when changes are made in important parts of transportation legislation. It would be possible to show the development of the Commission's policy
in interpreting the 1958 edition of the rule of ratemaking. However, the purposes of this paper could be best served by discussing the major cases that point
up the inconsistency between the rule of ratemaking and the national transportation policy. There are three cases that would appear to service this cause, *viz.*,
the *New Haven* case, the *Southern Grain* case and the *Ingot Molds* case. In all
three instances, the cases were handled in the three formal levels of hearings
within the Commission[22] and then treated by the courts. The cases will be
considered chronologically as they first appeared with the Commission, and no
attempt will be made to detail all levels of the hearings.

The first of the above cited cases to come before the Commission was the *New
Haven* case.[23] The case arose out of competition between certain railroads and
Sealand and SeaTrain companies. The railroads had proposed rates on a parity
with the coordinated water services and the water carriers asked for a differen-
tially lower rate because of inferior service. So the Commission was faced with
the same dilemma again. The Commission allowed a differential for the water
services. It was stated that although they had been directed by the 1958 amendment not to hold up rates of carriers, the national transportation policy required
national defense be considered. The Commission felt that equal rates would be
detrimental to the water carriers' ability to compete for traffic.

We can clearly see in this case the contradictory aspects of the rule of ratemaking and the national transportation policy. It should be noted as the Supreme Court did when they overruled the Commission that the proposed rail
rates were for the most part equal to or above fully allocated cost. Therefore, if
the rates were viewed from an economic perspective then they should have been
allowed. However, the Commission clearly has an obligation to follow the direc-
tives of the national policy which imposes other criteria. If the Commission had

originally allowed the rail reductions then they would have been subject to criticism for not observing the national policy.

The next major case was the *Southern Grain* case[24] which involved the Southern Railroad's proposal to substantially reduce rates on grain in certain areas predicated upon new technology and reduced services.[25] The rates did not purport to cover fully allocated costs rather they were based on out-of-pocket cost. When a decision was finally made by the Full Commission, the rates were raised but they were still below fully allocated cost. The Commission justified the rather low level of the rates because of unregulated motor carrier competition. The decision rendered in this decision raised hopes in some quarters that the ICC would abandon the fully allocated cost standard in intermodal rate cases and focus less attention on the national transportation policy.

It should be noted, however, that this decision was not inconsistent with previous ICC policy to any great extent. First, the Commission was definitely concerned with the national policy's criterion of destructive competition since minimum rates were established above those proposed.[26] This was done in deference to water carriers operating in the area. Second, the Commission was apparently concerned over protecting the proposing railroad from competition since unregulated motor carriers had been attracting an increasing share of the traffic. In other words, one could argue that the ICC was permitting the railroad a rate differential below unregulated motor rates which would enable them to compete for the traffic. In that vein, there is nothing basically inconsistent between this decision and what the Commission tried to do in the *New Haven* case, i.e., allow carriers to compete for traffic.[27]

The last of the three cases to come before the Commission was the *Ingot Molds* case[28] which involved proposed rail rate reductions which were to be on a par with a competitive water-motor service. The proposed rate was below fully allocated cost but above out-of-pocket cost.[29] After the examiner and Division 2 approved the proposed rate, the Full Commission rejected it on the grounds that the railroads did not possess an inherent cost advantage within the context of the national transportation policy. The Commission indicated that the class of traffic involved herein was very important to the water carrier.[30] The following comment seems particularly apropos,[31]

> In short, an inherent cost advantage under the national transportation policy reasonably could not embrace a concept that would impair the ability of a carrier not only to compete but to exist.

The evidence seems clear that the ICC feels compelled to use the fully allocated costs standard where the competing carriers are both regulated. Usually this is done to protect one mode of transport. This is most apparent here where the railroads proposed a rate on a par with the water rate but their better service would attract much of the traffic. It will be recalled that the ICC used an out-of-pocket cost approach in the *Southern Grain* case where the major competitor (unregulated motor carriage) was not subject to the national policy. So once again the Commission was influenced by the criteria imposed by the national transportation policy.

Conclusions

At the outset it was stated the major objective of this paper was to prove that the rule of ratemaking and the national transportation policy are inconsistent in that they emphasize different standards or criteria. The former appears to focus attention upon an economic criterion, i.e., rational allocation of resources, while the latter imposes social and political standards such as national defense.

There is no intent to implicate that the criteria of the national transportation policy are not legitimate and do not need to be taken into consideration. However, when the responsibility rests with one agency, then the social and political considerations are given predominant weight. The results will be inefficient use of existing resources with internal subsidies and high rates to shippers.[32] The analysis herein substantiated the dilemma of the Commission in spite of what some people regarded as a rather specific directive under the 1958 version of the rule of ratemaking.

The decision in the *Ingot Molds* case by the Commission and the substantiation by the Supreme Court seems to offer clear evidence that no major change will be forthcoming without major change. The Supreme Court raised the hopes of some people by instructing the ICC that cost criteria should be considered in the general investigation of cost that the Commission had conducted.[33] Apparently following the dictates of the Supreme Court, the ICC issued a notice on February 14, 1969 to reopen Docket No. 34013 to specifically consider cost standards in intermodal rate proceedings.

The reopening of the investigation will probably do little more than fill up lots of pages of testimony. Without political or social considerations, there is no logical support for an average cost or fully allocated cost standard. However, the Commission will be forced to use this criterion in intermodal rate cases because of the national policy. Some simple changes may be forthcoming in terms of measurement techniques but one can hardly expect any fundamental change.

The solution to the dilemma lies in giving some other agency such as the Department of Transportation the responsibility for the social and political considerations. In other words, if a particular transport service is deemed desirable for, let us say, national defense then a subsidy should be paid to maintain such services. The same criteria for evaluation to allocate funds could be used as in other similar situations such as missile requirements and moonshots which are felt necessary for national defense. The ICC would render its decisions on the basis of standards in keeping with rational allocation of resources. There would not be any inconsistency and better decisions would be made on both sides with no need to compromise standards.

A separate but related view was stated at the outset that the 1958 amendment to the rule of ratemaking was not a major change but rather an admonishment to the Commission. Evidence was offered from the Congressional hearings to support this hypothesis. The fact that the 1958 version was an admonishment to the Commission would appear to support the major contention of this paper that there is an inconsistency between the rule of ratemaking and the national policy.

NOTES

1. Hereafter referred to as the Commission or the ICC.
2. One might argue that the rule of ratemaking indicates certain considerations but the emphasis appears to be upon economic considerations.
3. Smyth vs. Ames, 169 U.S. 466 (1898).
4. It might be noted that a more extensive revision to the rule of ratemaking was proposed by the so-called "Committee of Six" appointed by President Roosevelt.
5. Petroleum and Petroleum Products to Ariz., 241 I.C.C. 21 (1940).
6. This is not meant to imply that such considerations have no validity but rather that they set the stage for different criteria to be applied.
7. There are differences of opinion, of course, on what should be the proper cost standard, i.e., out-of-pocket or fully-allocated.
8. U.S. Congress, Committee on Interstate Commerce, Senate Hearings, Transportation Act of 1939, 76th Cong., 1st Sess., 1939, pp. 1-3.
9. New Automobiles in Interstate Commerce, 259 I.C.C. 475 (1945).
10. These hearings will be analyzed subsequently.
11. Petroleum Products in Illinois Territory, 280 I.C.C. 681 (1951).
12. Petroleum Products in California and Oregon, 284 I.C.C. 369.
13. U.S. Congress, Senate, Regulation of Transportation Agencies, 73rd Cong., 2nd Sess., 1934, p. 96.
14. For further discussion, see: George W. Wilson, *Essays on Some Unsettled Questions in the Economics of Transportation,* Bloomington, Ind., 1962, pp. 14-23.
15. U.S. Congress, Hearings, Problems of the Railroads, 85th Cong., 2nd Sess., 1958, pp. 21-25.
16. Id., at p. 812, Statement of John R. Turney and John C. McWilliams.
17. U.S. Congress, Senate, Hearings, Ratemaking Rule, 85th Cong., 2nd Sess., 1958, p. 3.
18. Id., at pp. 9-10.
19. Id., at p. 14.
20. Id., at p. 169.
21. U.S. Congress, Senate, Transportation Act of 1958, 85th Cong., 2nd Sess., 1958, Rept. 1647.
22. Examiner, Division, and Full Commission.
23. Commodities—Pan Atlantic Steamship Corporation, 313 I.C.C. 23.
24. Grain in Multiple Car Shipments—River Crossings to the South, 321 I.C.C. 582 (1963).
25. The rates were proposed at 66 2/3 percent below existing rates and new jumbo cars were to be used with intransit services eliminated.
26. The Commission allowed rates which were 56 percent lower than the then existing rates instead of 66 2/3 percent.
27. It should be noted that the Supreme Court overruled the ICC and the Southern Railroad was eventually allowed to reduce these rates by 66 2/3 percent.
28. Ingot Molds, Penna. to Steelton, Kentucky, 323 I.C.C. (1963).

29. This case appears to represent a test of the out-of-pocket standard used in the Southern Grain case, i.e., would the ICC allow its use between two regulated carriers.
30. It should be noted that the railroads were not moving much traffic at their old rate.
31. Ingot Molds, Penna. to Steelton, Kentucky, 326 I.C.C. 82.
32. See: A. M. Milne and J. C. Laight, *The Economics of Inland Transport,* London, England, 1963, pp. 105-194.
33. Rules to Govern the Assembly and Presenting of Cost Evidence, ICC Docket No. 34013.

---

54   **Significant Changes Derived from Establishing the U.S. Department of Transportation: An Evaluation**

Grant M. Davis
University of Arkansas

In 1966, Congress established the Department of Transportation as the twelfth cabinet office in the executive branch of the U.S. Government. A rather broad grant of authority was vested in DOT, representing a marked change in national transportation policy. What advantages were foreseen from this move? What preliminary evaluation can be made of the effects of DOT? This selection attempts to answer these questions.

For a multitude of socio-economic and political reasons, the Federal government has financially promoted transportation. Historically, however, this promotional effort was basically ineffective and inequitable, and it prevented any rational approach to problem solving because of a total lack of integrated (1) program coordination, (2) planning, (3) priorities, (4) goals, and (5) managerial direction.[1] That is to say, executive agencies, departments, commissions, and bureaus responsible for promotional functions were organizationally dispersed throughout the executive branch and did not pursue consistent goals and objectives.

The major purpose underlying the Department of Transportation Act of 1966 was to correct certain inherent problems present in the Federal government's institutional approach to assisting and encouraging the several modes of transportation. The Department of Transportation has been operational since 1967, and it is now feasible to evaluate the organization's progress in correcting historical transportation deficiencies brought about by Federal promotional activities. The purpose of this paper is, therefore, to examine these problem areas that the

Reprinted by permission from the *Nebraska Journal of Economics and Business,* Vol. 9, No. 3, Summer 1970, pp. 53-68.

Department was established to correct and to evaluate the agency's efforts in eliminating those significant deficiencies.

Organizational evolution of Federal promotional agencies

The Federal government has historically displayed an inordinate interest in the purely modal aspects of transportation. In other words, the means of transportation—waterways, highways, airways, and railroads—were narrowly perceived as heterogeneous, unrelated media, not as vital components of a continuous domestic transportation system.[2] Federal agencies promoting transportation evolved along modal lines, and numerous organizations actively assisted transportation media. Even though these agencies were recognized from time to time, their efforts were relatively ineffective because diverse goals and objectives were pursued, priorities were absent, programs were not coordinated, intermodal planning was not practiced, and central management was not possible.[3] In short, each organization, together with accompanying programs and functions, was managed autonomously.[4]

In 1949 the Hoover Commission released its distinguished report concerning transportation organization in the executive branch. Specifically, the Commission proposed consolidating dispersed executive transportation agencies and bureaus into the Department of Commerce because of the necessity for grouping "activities according to their major purpose."[5]

The position of Undersecretary of Commerce for Transportation was created in 1950, when Congress enacted certain recommendations of the Hoover Commission, to provide transportation interests with a spokesman in the "upper echelon of government,"[6] and to coordinate Federal transportation programs and activities. Although the Undersecretary of Commerce for Transportation was responsible for administering transportation promotional programs through the Maritime Administration, Bureau of Public Roads, Great Lakes Pilotage Administration, St. Lawrence Seaway Development Corporation, and several minor offices, many significant transportation programs and agencies were not under his jurisdiction. The position appeared to be equal in importance to that of the Undersecretary of Commerce, but such was not the case. In fact, the office of the Undersecretary of Commerce for Transportation was not successful inasmuch as the official was basically placed in a line position, and his scope of authority was limited.

Subsequent reports concerned with transportation promotion criticized the organizational results brought about by executive implementation of recommendations proposed by the Hoover Commission. Two studies, one by Dearing and Owen in 1949, and the other the Doyle Report in 1961, recommended establishing a Department of Transportation rather than merely partially reorganizing promotional agencies into one department not solely concerned with transportation. Both reports, in fact, proposed similar recommendations and can be treated as a unit since program and agency consolidation was the predominant theme.

The fundamental logic underlying the Hoover Report's proposal for consolidating executive promotional organizations clearly adumbrated a Department of Transportation. Dearing and Owen specifically advocated establishing such a Department as an organizational vehicle for solving prodigious transportation problems, and insisted that representation of all modes of transportation was essential because efficient administration required that control functions "must be organically related."[7] Significantly, a unified independent regulatory commission was likewise proposed. General Doyle's comprehensive report, released in 1961, advocated proposals similar to those suggested by Dearing and Owen. Doyle succinctly pointed out that Congress was modally aligned, however, and suggested a reorganization of the legislative branch of government in an attempt to ameliorate government's institutional relationship to transportation promotion.[8]

It is clear, in retropect, that dispersed agencies, uncoordinated program administration, and internal preoccupation constituted the major deficiencies associated with executive transportation functions. A department concerned solely with transportation could conceivably eliminate or reduce these deficiencies and subsequently direct its total efforts toward the development of an integrated national transportation system.

Changes made by the Department of Transportation

In an aggregate sense, the Department of Transportation Act of 1966 merely provided for the consolidation and reorganization of dispersed executive agencies enforcing promotional statutes into one cohesive organization.[9] Nevertheless, by law the agency is vested with the responsibility of identifying national transportation problems, coordinating transportation activities and programs on an inter- and intra-government basis, developing investment standards based on economic criteria, and proposing rational transportation policies; all recommendations, of course, must be submitted to Congress for its approval or denial. The Department represents a new, reorganized approach to transportation promotion. It has restructured existing programs and directs them toward consistent, uniform goals and objectives, has developed and assigned program priorities, and is currently managing its activities on an intermodal basis.

Executive implementation of the Department of Transportation Act has, in essence, eliminated or diminished many of the significant deficiencies traditionally associated with executive transportation activities. These major changes have occurred in seven areas: (1) investment standards, (2) planning, (3) program coordination, (4) priorities, (5) goals and objectives, (6) research and development, and (7) public interest. Each of these areas will now be examined.

Federal investment standards

Public investment in transportation facilities and equipment has reached enormous sums. Combined state and Federal expenditures for airways, airports, airline cash subsidies, highways, and waterways, increased from $3,528,102,370 in fiscal year 1947 to $19,808,689,000 during the fiscal year 1968.[10] Table I illustrates total governmental outlays for transportation by category of carriers through fiscal year 1968. When considering the domestic transportation network as an interrelated, continuous system, these outlays emphasize the cardinal financial inequities existing among the several types of carriers relative to public investments. An examination of Table I indicates dichotomous reasons for these inequities, that is, fluctuating investment standards and investment standards not always based on sound economic criteria.[11] It is evident from Table I that government did not always consider national transportation requirements when investing in transportation projects, thereby inevitably creating modal imbalances and consequently misallocating resources.

Waterway projects were not atypical of "pork barrel"[12] investment decisions. Even though the U.S. Department of Commerce supplied project data to the Corps of Engineers on waterway projects, Congress was the ultimate decision maker with respect to a given project. Unfortunately, most of these decisions were not based on pragmatic cost-benefit analysis, and aggregate transportation requirements were not always recognized.[13]

TABLE I

Government Expenditures for Domestic Transportation,
by Type of Carrier, through Fiscal Year 1968*

Industry	Expenditures (billions of dollars)		
	Federal	State and Local	Total
Highway	$56.9[a]	$209.0[b]	$265.0
Air	12.5	6.9[c]	19.4[c]
Waterway[d]	8.0	4.9[c]	12.4[c]
Railroad[e]	1.4	0.2[f]	1.6
Totals	$78.8	$221.0	$299.8

*Data for 1968 are estimated.
[a]Of this total, $39.4 billion was covered by receipts of the Federal Highway Trust Fund from user charges in the period 1956-68.
[b]Of this total, $123.4 billion was covered by state and local highway user imposts and toll receipts in the period 1921-68.
[c]Partially estimated.
[d]Includes inland waterways, intercoastal waterways, Great Lakes and coastal harbors. Excludes expenditures for navigation on the Tennessee River ($321 million through fiscal 1967), the United States part of construction costs for the St. Lawrence Seaway ($132 million through fiscal 1968), the merchant marine ($21.5 billion through fiscal 1968), and the Coast Guard ($8.0 billion through fiscal 1968).
[e]Excludes government programs for research and development in local mass transportation and high-speed ground transportation.
[f]State only.
Source: Charles F. Phillips, Jr., *The Economics of Regulation: Theory and Practice in the Transportation and Public Utility Industries* (2d ed.; Homewood, Illinois: Richard D. Irwin, Inc., 1969), p. 14.

When cost-benefit analysis was utilized to ascertain the desirability of investing in a certain project, its purpose and applicability were often perverted. For example, before 1964 the Corps of Engineers applied "current freight rates" in estimating cost-benefits. This criterion, of course, augmented benefits directly attributable to water transportation. In 1964, however, the Bureau of the Budget prescribed usage of "water-compelled freight rates" when computing cost-benefits. Nevertheless, in 1966 Congress prescribed by statute "current freight rates" as a normal criterion upon which cost-benefits are to be determined.[14]

Investment decisions not based upon economic factors inevitably result in a misallocation of resources and produce other inequitable conditions. One result of the Department of Transportation Act, however, has been the development of a nascent movement toward uniform investment standards based on sound economic criteria. These standards, to be implemented in decisions relating to transportation equipment and facilities, must, of course, be submitted to Congress for its approval or rejection. The Secretary of Transportation's authority to promulgate effective standards is seriously attenuated as waterway projects, for all practical purposes, are excluded from his jurisdictional purview. More ominous, however, is the prohibition upon the Secretary not to prescribe investment standards for other Federal agencies. That is to say, investment standards apply only to departmental projects.[15]

Although its investment authority is narrowly restricted, the Department is currently developing standards, predicated upon rational economic criteria, to ascertain the desirability and feasibility of investing in highways, airways, navigational aids, and other major projects that have domestic and international ramifications. Significantly, future or incremental investments will also be based on economic criteria that entail national requirements, not the expedient need of some specific mode of transportation or political region.[16] In this regard, the historical deficiencies associated with public investment in transportation facilities and equipment are in the initial stage of being corrected.

National transportation goals and objectives

Diverse, varying, and unrelated goals and objectives were pursued by executive bureaus, agencies, commissions, and departments promoting transportation before 1966. In fact, no two agencies had similar objectives even though all organizations were concerned with some vital aspect of transportation. For example, the independent Federal Aviation Agency's principal goal was to maximize safety in flight, and the organization was eminently successful in achieving this objective. On the other hand, the Interstate Commerce Commission, also an independent agency, was responsible for enforcing motor carrier, railroad, and oil pipeline safety laws, but its major objective was impartial and effective economic regulation, not safety.[17] Surface safety was not maximized by the agency. In summary, goals, objectives, and national transportation policies were heterogeneous and varied among the several agencies promoting transportation.

By consolidating dispersed agencies and functions into one cohesive organization, the Department of Transportation was able to develop one single, yet realistic, set of goals and objectives. These objectives represent statutory changes and include:

1. *Economic Efficiency in Transportation:* to provide that mix of transportation alternatives, including modal system, related facilities and manpower, research and development, and so on, which results in maximum benefits such as service, convenience, comfort, capacity, and speed for a given cost.
2. *Optimal Use of Environmental Resources:* to increase the benefits derived from the preservation and enhancement of the environmental, aesthetic, and social factors of transportation.
3. *Safety:* to minimize the loss of human life, property, and human suffering through injury from transportation-related accidents.
4. *Support of Other National Interests:* to further all other objectives of the Federal government whenever they are affected by transportation, or when the Department of Transportation can perform a particular task more effectively and efficiently.[18]

These goals are the macro-objectives of the Department, and all programs and activities are directed toward attaining them. Only since the Department of Transportation was established has a majority of executive promotional programs been directed to one consistent and meaningful set of objectives.

Transportation planning

Federal planning for future transportation requirements commenced in 1920, with the enactment of the National Transportation Act.[19] This initial planning effort, however, was inadequate for two major reasons. First, an independent regulatory agency, the Interstate Commerce Commission, was the planning agency. Second, planning was undertaken only for a single mode of transportation, the interstate railroad industry. Although this original planning effort was ineffective,[20] it did establish the institutional framework for subsequent transportation planning agencies and activities.

Planning for future transportation programs and activities was intensively engaged in by executive agencies before 1966. The planning function was intramodal in nature, however, as each agency planned only for its particular mode of transportation. The Federal Aviation Agency, for instance, forecast future demands upon the Federal airway system and planned programs and activities accordingly. Future highway requirements were planned for by the Bureau of Public Roads. Even though highway and airway systems have similar features, interrelationships, and interfaces, highway and airway planning was conducted by two distinct Federal agencies[21] that failed to coordinate their planning efforts.

Another example of inadequacies brought about by the planning of dispersed Federal organizations for separate modes of transportation concerned highway planning in urban areas. Interstate highway systems connect congested areas. The Bureau of Public Roads planned for future interstate routes in conjunction with the state highway departments. The Department of Housing and Urban

Development, however, was responsible for planning detailed urban transportation systems under certain conditions. Interstate and urban highway planning functions were interrelated but were not coordinated until 1966, when it became evident that administration of urban mass transportation laws would be transferred to the Department of Transportation.[22] This is but one example of deficiencies brought about by the failure to coordinate activities. There are numerous other examples of waste, duplication, and inefficiency produced from not pursuing intermodal planning.

Congress established the executive office of Planning and Program Review to insure adequate, efficient, intermodal planning for national transportation needs. Not only does this executive office plan for future departmental functions, but it also coordinates and structures all planning conducted at the operating administration level of the Department.[23] Furthermore, planning is now primarily intermodal in nature and emphasizes coordination with other Federal, state, and local government bodies, in addition to private organizations. In this regard, the Department has corrected the historical problems associated with intramodal planning.

Program coordination

Since the domestic transportation network forms a continuous system, it is imperative that executive promotional activities be minutely coordinated and simply structured.[24] This, perforce, is a prerequisite to the attainment of national goals and objectives. Before the Department of Transportation was established, however, most Federal transportation programs were permeated with three discernible problems: (1) managing agencies were organizationally dispersed and were aligned by modes of transportation; (2) the absolute magnitude of programs precluded efficient administration;[25] and, (3) programs were directed toward varying goals and objectives.[26]

The Department of Transportation has moved to ameliorate these prodigious deficiencies in two basic ways. First, the Department's organizational structure encourages program coordination. That is to say, the agency is modally aligned at the operating administration level and functionally organized at the Assistant Secretary level. This innovative organizational alignment makes possible adequate representation for the several modes of transportation at the operating administration level and effective program coordination at the Assistant Secretarial level.[27] The operating Administrators, moreover, are prohibited from developing policy,[28] and the internal alignment of the Assistant Secretaries encourages cross-fertilization of ideas and concepts and minimization of modal influences, in addition to program coordination.

Second, in an attempt to simplify its program structure in order more readily to attain national objectives, the Department has restructured and reclassified hundreds of programs into a limited number of categories. These simplified categories, each encompassing hundreds of subprograms, are (1) Urban Transportation, (2) Interurban Transportation, (3) International Transportation, and (4) National Interests.[29] This simplified structure enables the organization to manage its programs meaningfully toward attaining stated goals and objectives.

Research

If transportation is to advance technologically and national problems are to be identified and solved, "software" and "hardware" research activities are essential. Needless to say, Federal transportation research endeavors are confronted with two momentous constraints—limited resources and limited manpower.

In the past sizable research expenditures were allocated to specific aspects of transportation with little or no consideration given to national needs, priorities, or the possibility of duplicate efforts. These Federal outlays failed to produce optimum results, inasmuch as managerial control and direction were vested in dispersed executive agencies.[30] An example of this lack of coordination and duplication involved research concerning the hydroplaning effect of pneumatic tires on wet pavement. Simultaneously, this phenomenon was separately investigated by the Bureau of Public Roads, the Federal Aviation Agency, and the National Space Administration. Nearly every phase of these endeavors was interrelated and obviously duplicative.[31]

Legislation establishing the Department of Transportation provides for and encourages research. In fact, the Act directs the Secretary of Transportation to identify and recommend solutions to national transportation problems. Currently, the organization not only carefully coordinates, controls, and directs its diverse research and development activities, but it also assigns research priorities in addition to identifying intermodal relationships involved in a given problem area.

PPBS (Planning-Programing-Budgeting-Systems)[32] is used to ascertain intermodal relationships and assign research priorities. Problem areas requiring research are, in rank order: (1) mass transportation, (2) safety, (3) the environmental aspects of transportation, (4) terminal and port congestion, (5) high speed ground transportation, and (6) marine science.[33] This ranking process, attainable by utilization of PPBS processes, facilitates allocating resources efficiently and effectively toward solving significant transportation dilemmas. Furthermore, all departmental research activities are coordinated and controlled through the office of the Assistant Secretary for Research and Technology. This organizational alignment alone avoids duplications and centralizes research efforts.[34]

National program priorities

If uniform and consistent national transportation objectives are to be achieved, realistic program priorities must be established and adhered to. Priorities, of course, are essential if resources are to be allocated optimally and economic waste is to be avoided.[35] Before establishment of the Department of Transportation, program priorities relating to transportation promotion varied from agency to agency. This variation occurred because priorities, for the most part, were determined through political channels,[36] with only minimal attention directed to authentic national transportation needs.

Transportation safety illustrates how program priorities varied extensively among Federal agencies. For example, the Civil Aeronautics Board emphasized aviation safety and consequently allocated over fifty percent of its annual appropriations to this cardinal activity.[37] On the other hand, the Interstate Commerce Commission, another independent regulatory agency, allocated only ten percent of its limited appropriations each year in a futile attempt to enforce surface transportation safety statutes.[38] National goals could not be achieved with limited resources so long as interagency program priorities were determined independently of one another. That is to say, safety is important in all of the modes of transportation and should not be emphasized to different degrees among enforcing agencies.

Confronted with strict constraints—funding and manpower—the Department of Transportation has commenced developing national program priorities. The genesis of this movement involves uniform and consistent goals and objectives. Four comprehensive categories of programs are now directed toward attaining the agency's goals. PPBS is now utilized to reevaluate existing programs and to provide a decision-making framework for evaluating new and proposed programs, with cost-benefit analysis forming the major criterion. By ranking problems and programs on a priority basis the Department has developed an analytical framework for rational transportation decision making.

Public interest

In many instances excessive social costs have been inadvertently produced by many segments of the domestic transportation system. Many highway routes, airports, and airways have disrupted neighborhood and community tranquility and have threatened or eliminated historical sites, aesthetic values, and natural resources. In other words, the detrimental aspects of transportation were not minimized before 1966.[39]

The general public has been excluded from initial transportation decisions that historically have affected its socio-economic welfare. That is, Congressionally established independent regulatory agencies "protected the public interest, but no Federal agency "represented the public interest." One major goal pursued by the Department of Transportation concerns maximizing the environmental aspects of transportation; the organization attempts to minimize social costs associated with any departmental function or activity.[40] Although experiencing only limited success in representing the public interest before regulatory agencies, the Department has accomplished significant gains in the field of highway route location.[41]

The agency is striving to increase public participation in initial government decisions regarding highway route location and design. Section 4(f) of the Act authorizes the Secretary to withhold highway construction funds from projects that threaten to disrupt neighborhoods, communities, natural resources, historic sites, or aesthetic values. Feasible alternatives, however, must be available. Nevertheless, the Department has experienced only limited success in implementing section 4(f) and representing the public interest because it is constrained by limited resources and Congressional opposition to many of its activities in this area.[42]

Conclusions and recommendations

During the course of the past three years the Department of Transportation has taken impressive strides in correcting or moving to correct many significant deficiencies traditionally associated with the Federal Government's institutional approach to transportation promotion. These improvements have occurred in the area of investment standards, planning, program coordination, research, national priorities, and representation of the public interest.

The organization is not a panacea for our national transportation dilemma, but by restructuring programs, developing investment standards, providing intermodal planning and program coordination, and assigning national priorities, it has developed a rational approach to transportation decision making; hence, it has achieved more effective promotion.

Even though the Department has been relatively successful in achieving its stated statutory objectives, several recommendations are in order. First, if the agency is to provide adequate and effective executive leadership in transportation, its jurisdictional authority must be plenary. For this reason the Federal Maritime Administration should be transferred from the Department of Commerce to Transportation.[43] Exclusion of the Administration's vital subsidy and leadership function means that maritime decisions, together with promotion, continue to be determined through the political process, with attendant problems and resource misallocation.

Second, public outlays in waterway facilities represent major financial expenditures that are, for all practical purposes, exempt from the Secretary of Transportation's investment authority. Efficient and equitable resource allocation demands uniform, consistent investment standards. These standards, moreover, must be based on rational economic criteria and applied to all modes of transportation impartially. Therefore, with the exception of national defense features of transportation activities conducted by the Department of Defense, all Federal investments in transportation facilities and equipment should be incorporated within the Secretary's investment authority.

Finally, the Department must be more pragmatic when representing the public interest. During the final months of the Johnson Administration the agency issued an administrative ruling designed to increase public participation in initial decisions concerning the location and design features of interstate highways. An adjunct to this ruling was a simplified appellate procedure that would have permitted any affected individual to appeal an adverse decision directly to the Federal Highway Administrator, who in turn could halt a multi-million dollar construction project.[44] The general public unfortunately lacks the engineering expertise necessary to evaluate the design features of sophisticated highways. This controversial rule was rescinded by Secretary Volpe in 1969. The Department must exert every effort to balance economic reality and social cost when representing the public interest.

To date the Department of Transportation's principal contribution has resided with its method of problem solving together with its concurrent effort to correct historical deficiencies traditionally associated with executive transportation programs. If continued, the Department's methodological approach to problem solving should provide government with an enlightened institutional relationship to transportation promotion. From this relationship there should evolve a domestic transportation system in which economic efficiency, safety, social benefits, and national interests are maximized.

NOTES

1. For a detailed discussion of Federal transportation deficiences, consult U.S. Congress, House, *H. Doc. 399*, 89th Cong., 2d sess., 1966, pp. 38-39; and David I. Mackie, "The Necessity for a Federal Department of Transportation," *Journal of Public Law* (Spring, 1959), 1:21-22.

2. Federal preoccupation with the purely modal aspects of transportation is best illustrated by examining the alignment of agencies enforcing Federal transportation laws before 1966. For instance, the Federal Aviation Agency, together with the Civil Aeronautics Board, was concerned with aviation. On the other hand, the Interstate Commerce Commission enforced laws relating to motor carriers, railroads, oil pipelines, freight forwarders, brokers, and some types of water carriers. The Coast Guard, however, was concerned only with one mode of transportation. The Department of Commerce was an organizational conglomerate concerned with several facets of transportation. Each agency, as noted above, was formed to administer laws pertaining to specific modes of transportation.

3. U.S. Department of Commerce, *Issues Involved in a Unified and Coordinated Federal Program for Transportation* (Washington: U.S. Government Printing Office, December 1, 1949), p. 1.

4. See U.S. Congress, Senate, Committee on Interstate and Foreign Commerce, *Report of the Special Study Group on Transportation Policies in the United States: National Transportation Policy*, Pur. to S. Res. 27 and 261 of the 85th Cong., 87th Cong., 1st sess., 1961.

5. U.S. Department of Commerce, *A Report to the Congress by the Commission on Organization of the Executive Branch of Government* (Washington: U.S. Government Printing Office, March, 1949), p. 3.

6. *Ibid.*, p. 7.

7. Charles L. Dearing and Wilfred Owen, *National Transportation Policy* (Washington: The Brookings Institution, 1949), p. 389.

8. U.S. Congress, Senate, *National Transportation Policy, op. cit.*, p. 103.

9. Legislation creating the Department of Transportation was heard by the House and Senate Committees on Government Operations, not by the Committee on Interstate and Foreign Commerce.

10. Charles F. Phillips, Jr., *The Economics of Regulation: Theory and Practice in the Transportation and Public Utility Industries* (2d ed.; Homewood, Ill.: Richard D. Irwin, Inc., 1969), p. 13.

11. Because of indirect consumption benefits associated with most Federal transportation investments, marginal social costs and marginal social benefits must be broadly estimated: hence, the possibility does exist for excess investment in some areas. For an excellent discussion of public policy and objectives as they relate to publicly provided facilities and equipment, consult D. Philip Locklin, *Economics of Transportation* (6th ed.; Homewood, Ill.: Richard D. Irwin, Inc., 1966), pp. 840-843.

12. For an apropos description of "pork barrel" investments, and the resulting decision-making process, consult "They All Want to Call the Shots," *Business Week,* vol. 78, No. 1917 (May 28, 1966), p. 80.

13. Testimony of Major General John P. Doyle, *Creating a Department of Transportation, Hearings, Before the Committee on Government Operations, Senate,* on S. 3010, 89th Cong., 2d sess., 1966, pp. 343-344.

14. U.S. Congress, House, *Department of Transportation Act,* H. Rept. 2236, 89th Cong., 2d sess., 1966, pp. 13-15.

15. The original section 7 of S. 3010 and H.R. 13200 authorized the Secretary of Transportation to develop investment standards based upon economic criteria for all modes. The maritime industry, however, used opposition to section 7 as a delaying technique, and ultimately Congress emasculated the section by exempting waterway projects from its jurisdiction. See U.S. Congress, House, *Creating a Department of Transportation, Hearings, Before a Subcommittee of the Committee on Government Operations, House of Representatives,* on H.R. 13200, 89th Cong., 2d sess., 1966, p. 475, for the typical opposition to section 7.

16. The Department of Transportation is now in the process of gathering data to be used in ascertaining sound economic criteria. Nevertheless, little has actually been done with respect to implementing section 7 of Public Law 89-640. See Grant M. Davis, "Policy Challenges and Objectives of the Department of Transportation—a Comment," *Quarterly Review of Economics and Business* (Spring, 1970), for a detailed discussion of section 7 activities.

17. The ICC demonstrated its inability to enforce satisfactory surface transportation safety laws when it combined its Bureau of Motor Carriers with the Bureau of Operations and Compliance, where enforcement, not safety, was emphasized. For an extended discussion of the rationale underlying this action, consult: U.S. Interstate Commerce Commission, *79th Annual Report* (Washington: U.S. Government Printing Office, 1965), p. 9.

18. U.S. Department of Transportation, *Department of Transportation: Goals and Objectives, Problems, Programs, and Priorities* (Washington: U.S. Department of Transportation, March 20, 1968), pp. 3-9.

19. U.S. Congress, *Public Law 152-91,* 66th Cong., 1st sess., 1920.

20. National planning for voluntary railroad consolidation was discontinued with the passage of the National Transportation Act of 1940.

21. A small degree of coordinated planning was conducted between the Bureau of Public Roads and the Federal Aviation Agency. This was, however, an atypical situation and was not intensively engaged in before 1966. Consult the Annual Reports of the U.S. Department of Commerce and the Federal Aviation Agency for the period 1960-1966.

22. Public Law 89-640 directed the Secretaries of Transportation and of Housing and Urban Development to undertake joint studies to determine the optimal organizational location for the administration of the Urban Mass Transportation Act of 1964. Reorganization Plan No. 2 of 1968 transferred management of Urban Mass Transportation functions to the Department of Transportation but specified that coordinated planning efforts between the two executive agencies be continued.

23. U.S. National Archives and Records Service, *United States Government Organizational Manual: 1966-1967* (Washington: U.S. Government Printing Office, 1966), pp. 376-425.

24. *Ibid.*

25. The cumbersome program structure of the Federal Aviation Agency was typical of most government transportation agencies before PL 89-640. Primarily concerned with aviation safety, major program categories included: operations, facilities and equipment, grants-in-aid for airports, research and development, operation, maintenance, and construction of Washington National and Dulles International Airports, and Civil Supersonic Transport development.

26. *Issues Involved in a Unified and Coordinated Federal Program, op. cit.,* p. 20.

27. S. 3010 and H.R. 13200, the original Department of Transportation bills, provided only for functionally aligned Assistant Secretaries of Transportation. No provisions existed for operating administrations. This was, moreover, the organizational structure advocated by General Doyle in his 1961 Report. Congressional and industry pressure, however, resulted in modally aligned operating administrations and functionally aligned Assistant Secretaries. Also, see U.S. Department of Transportation, *The United States Department of Transportation: Its Organization and Function* (Washington: U.S. Government Printing Office, 1967), p. 4.

28. "Department of Transportation and the Railways," *Railway Age,* vol. CLXII, No. 20 (May 22, 1967), p. 18.

29. U.S. Department of Transportation, *Department of Transportation Program Structure* (Washington: U.S. Department of Transportation, January 11, 1968), pp. 1-9, where programs and subprograms are examined in detail.

30. Although research findings were widely disseminated throughout the public and private sectors of the economy, no central control, direction, or coordination was present in Federal Research activities. See Grant M. Davis, *The Department of Transportation* (Lexington, Massachusetts: D. C. Heath and Company, 1970), Ch. 5.

31. The endeavors were undertaken and funded separately, but research data and results were shared between the three agencies.

32. For an excellent analysis of PPBS, consult David I. Cleland and William R. King, *Systems Analysis and Project Management* (New York: McGraw-Hill, 1968), p. 118. Essentially PPBS is a mechanism to institutionalize rational economic analysis of government programs.

33. *Department of Transportation: Goals and Objectives; Problems, Programs, and Priorities, op. cit.,* p. 16.

34. With the exception of the St. Lawrence Seaway Development Corporation, all operating agencies of the Department are engaged in research. All activities are coordinated and directed, however, by the Assistant Secretary for Research and Technology.

35. When the pricing mechanism is not applicable in the public sector, limited resources cannot be efficiently allocated without realistic priorities. Because most Federal transportation projects contain indirect consumption benefits, the pricing mechanism is not appropriate in most instances.

36. Financing for the Supersonic Transport illustrates how appropriations vacillate. See also U.S. Federal Aviation Agency, *Annual Report for the Fiscal Year Ended June 30, 1966* (Washington: U.S. Government Printing Office, 1966), p. 73.

37. U.S. Bureau of the Budget, *Appendix to the Budget of the United States Government for the Fiscal Year Ending June 30, 1966* (Washington: U.S. Government Printing Office, 1965), p. 889.

38. *Ibid.,* p. 935.

39. "Highway Law Deals Sharp Blow to Conservation," *The Birmingham News,* July 30, 1968, p. 23.

40. *Department of Transportation: Goals and Objectives, Problems, Programs, and Priorities, loc. cit.*

41. The Secretary of Transportation has implemented a "Design Concept" to urban area highway route location planning. This concept entails assembling a team of sociologists, urbanologists, and engineers in an attempt to locate highways in such way that social cost is minimized. See U.S. Department of Transportation, *First Annual Report: Part I* (Washington: U.S. Government Printing Office, 1968), p. 10, for an in-depth discussion of "Design Concept."

42. "Agriculture Urges Striking of Rail Boosts: DOT Decides Not to Fight Increases; Pleads That It Lacks Staff for Opposing Raise," *Transport Topics,* No. 1711 (May 27, 1968), p. 1.

43. Currently maritime groups are pressing for a separate executive Maritime Department. The same proposal was advocated by Maritime representatives during the Congressional hearings on S. 3010 and H.R. 13200, the Department of Transportation bills.

44. Grant M. Davis, "Proposed Federal Changes in Interstate Highway Route Selection and Design," *Alabama Business,* Graduate School of Business, vol. XXXIX, No. 9 (May 15, 1969), pp. 1-3.

---

55   The Case Against Common Carriage

Richard N. Farmer
Indiana University

To a considerable degree, the role of government in transportation is based upon the assumption that the common carrier system is desirable and worth protecting. While this assumption underlies most policy questions, it is rarely stated.

In this selection, Dr. Farmer addresses himself to this assumption: his "case"— questioning common carriage—has created a good deal of discussion in transportation circles and has led to some interesting speculation about government's role if the common carrier type of regulation were to be abandoned.

In much of the present protracted debate over the future of the American transportation system and the direction national transportation policy should take, it is taken for granted that any policy should have at its base the principle of common carriage. The desirability of common carriage is often simply stated as the ultimate desideratum, subject to no criticism.[1] To be against common carriage is ranked with being against motherhood, in the view of many persons concerned with transportation problems.

In spite of this presumed desirability, common carriage has steadily lost ground in the past decade to other forms of carriage. Regulated common carriage in particular has been hard hit by competition from both the private and the unregulated for-hire transportation sectors.[2] This shift from common carriage has been viewed with alarm by officials and persons connected with transportation firms, and there is no shortage of ideas and proposals which would lead common carriage back to its proper position of importance.[3]

However, it is possible that various structural shifts in technology and markets which have occurred in recent years have made common carriage much less relevant to the welfare of the nation than in the past. This paper is intended to state the case against common carriage as forcefully as possible, both to show that such a case does exist, and to suggest to proponents of common carriage the nature of the problem they face. If underlying economic factors steadily work against the common carriers, the price to be paid to maintain this type of transportation system may be more than the country is willing to pay. The entire elaborate structure of transportation policy, control, and direction may collapse, and no one will care enough to maintain it. Common carriage may not be worth saving in the long run, at least in its present regulated form.

The case for common carriage

Rather curiously, the case for common carriage is taken so much for granted that it is difficult to find a statement summarizing the major arguments in favor of such a policy.[4] However, the general argument is contained, by implication, in various statements of national transportation policy in acts to regulate transportation. The argument can be summarized as follows:[5]

1. Common carriage will provide a transportation system free of unjust discriminations, undue preferences, or advantage. Implicit here is some sort of control system which will guarantee such results. The most notable part of the control system in this sense is the price powers of the regulatory commissions.

2. The defense needs of the country will be better met with common carriage than with any other system. Implicit in this notion is that wars and crises will occur which will require transportation capacity, among other things. Common carriers should have such capacity and be in a position to provide capacity when needed.

3. Common carriage will best meet the needs of commerce of the United States.

4. Common carriage will promote the inherent advantages of the various transportation technologies.

5. Common carriage will best provide safe, adequate, economical and efficient services.

6. Common carriage will provide better working conditions for employees.

7. Common carriage will best meet the needs of the postal service.

These advantages are taken from the various statements of transportation policy in the transportation acts. The idea that common carriage will be best is implicit, since the acts deal largely with the regulation and promotion of such carriage. The general consensus, at least among transportation men, seems to be that common carriage is the best form of transportation organization to bear the main brunt of transportation requirements in the United States.

Such statements that common carriage is critical in American transportation are supported by analysis which suggests that presently occurring declines in common carriage will have disastrous social results, including the following:[6]

1. Increased social investment in transportation. If carriage is done privately, total investment in transportation facilities will necessarily increase.

2. Growing excess capacity in transportation.

3. Declining net income of common carriers.

4. Undermaintenance and reduced service capacity of common carriers.

5. Reduction of common carrier services offered.

6. High financing costs for common carriers.

7. Higher transportation costs.

8. A growing competitive struggle, with possibly disastrous results for the nation.

Also noted is the fact that regulated common carriers, with their obligation to serve, necessarily are superior to private carriers or exempt common carriers, who may be able to evade serving expensive customers. "Expensive" in this sense means customers who presumably are not able or willing to pay full cost prices for their services—or possibly even out-of-pocket prices.

Having accepted the hypothesis that common carriage is the ideal form of carriage, the typical argument notes that regulated common carriage in the U.S. has been declining for a decade, losing to unregulated for-hire firms and to private operations. Following this hypothesis, all of transportation is in peril, and recommendations for reform should consider ways and means of restoring common carriage to its historic place in the sun.

The case against common carriage

The major case which can be made against common carriage is that it costs too much, given alternatives open to numerous shippers. Shippers are not typically an irrational group, and their decisions to abandon common carriage shipping to move to other forms of carriage reflects careful calculation in most cases. The simple fact underlying much of the common carriers' difficulties in recent years is that shippers have been able to move their goods cheaper than the for-hire carriers can.

The reasons for the higher prices in common carriage deserve careful examination. If these pressures toward overpricing are irresistable, the future of common carriage is very much in doubt. However, if they are essentially correctable problems, it would be possible to revitalize common carriage with relatively little difficulty.

A major reason for higher costs and prices in regulated common carriage is that the carriers are required to perform services which are unrelated to the commercial market, yet which cost money. The bulk of these requirements are related to the obligation of service and with defense.[7] Thus if a small firm on a lightly travelled branch railway line needs rail service, he should get it under present policy, even if the cost to the carrier is more than it receives in revenues for performing this service. In theory, and far too often in practice, a group of users underpaying for service are given it, and the deficits have to be made up from other shippers.[8] The other shippers logically object to paying the subsidy and seek out alternatives, with the usual dismal results for the common carriers. Similarly, if defense requires that carriers perform certain duties, or make available certain equipment or terminal facilities, shippers as a whole must pay the bill—and the bill is correspondingly higher.

Unregulated for-hire and private carriers have no such obligation to serve, and their costs are lower as a result. The basic problem here is to decide whether or not policy is correct in insisting that internal transportation subsidies are useful, and that defense costs should be placed on shippers, rather than on the general taxpaying public. The issue has deep philosophical implications which are seldom explored adequately. Why should any given shipper be entitled to support any other shipper? What is the ethic here? Why should shippers pay for defense facilities, rather than all of us? This logic of obligation assumes that somehow the total public will gain by this policy, but it is not at all clear that the policy itself is meaningful.

A second major reason for higher common carrier costs to shippers is that the present rate structure in the United States is completely illogical. Some shippers pay far too little for what they get, while others are literally faced with extortion. The reasons for this are relatively clear: the long history of railroad value of service pricing, taken over intact (or almost so) by truckers and other technologies, without much thought as to the economics of the situation is the major cause. Failure to see that value of service pricing is completely illogical in a competitive situation has caused all common carriers serious trouble.[9] In recent years, many carriers have seen the fallacy of this structure, and have attempted to develop new techniques of price quotation, but inertia and inability to change quickly have cost the carriers dearly. Commission reluctance to allow destruction of a laboriously constructed price system has also inhibited rapid change, and in spite of innumerable single price changes, the old discriminatory structure still stands—to the detriment of regulated common carriers. The erratic system of price change now in effect virtually guarantees confusion, illogical pricing, and consumer resistance to use of common carriage.

The present institutional system of pricemaking also causes decline. In effect, regulated common carriers follow a cartel system virtually unique in the modern United States. Cartels have the advantage of protecting almost everybody in the cartel—in transportation, prices within a technology usually are set by common agreement among affected parties,[10] and rarely does a price get set which is objected to strenuously by any carrier. Cartels also have the disadvantage of giving open invitations to buyers to find a way around the cartel prices—which clearly is happening at an accelerating rate in the United States today. If a cartel is to work well, there can be no meaningful alternative outside the cartel for buyers. Unfortunately, in transportation the alternatives are numerous.

In theory, the commissions are responsible for determining that the prices set by carrier agreement are not too high. In practice, such control is exercised by compiling and studying the average cost (average total, out-of-pocket, or marginal) which is relevant in a given situation.[11] The difficulty here comes when the average cost of performing a given transportation service shows substantial variation between the high-cost and low-cost carriers. If a price is set to reflect, say, the average out-of-pocket cost of ten carriers, it will probably be true that some of the ten will have costs well below the average. The price for them will be more than adequate, while for higher-cost carriers, it may barely cover their costs. Forgotten here is that outsiders are perfectly capable of being as efficient as the best common carriers—that is, their costs will be substantially below what is firmly believed to be the typical out-of-pocket expense for the haul. The result, as might be expected, is traffic diversion to unregulated or private carriage, since the price set, even for efficient common carriers, is above cost by too substantial a margin.[12] As traffic is diverted, some common carriers may press for lower rates, but they may well be overruled by competitors who are higher-cost operators.

Commission notions about fairness of rates also inhibits common carriage. The prevention of price reductions proposed by carriers is a familiar story, the argument here being that traffic should somehow be shared by various types of competitors.[15] Where a given group of carriers are forced to charge prices higher than their managements (presumably perceptive businessmen) would like, and above costs which exist for nonregulated competition, diversion of traffic is inevitable. All common carriers lose in this sort of situation.

Finally, the abandonment of price as a weapon among carriers in the same technology has the effect of stifling much of the more competitive aspects of private enterprise. Firms can get somewhat careless in their marketing policies, since they know that their competitors are unable to do any effective price cutting. This type of relaxation has been eliminated to a considerable extent by inter-technological competition, but it is still present in some types of non-competitive traffic.[14] The railroads in particular have suffered badly as a result of this attitude, as they historically were in the position of having virtual monopolies of many sorts of traffic.

As shippers search for alternatives to avoid the overpriced regulated common carriage, the reaction of commissions and regulated carriers follows a path familiar to those who have studied cartel behavior. The suggestions follow two major lines: first, to force firms who could never be in the cartel (private carriers) to have higher costs; and second, to force firms who could be, but are not in the cartel, to join. In the former case, it is proposed that private carriage be further restricted and that present regulations concerning backhauls and similar situations, be more firmly enforced. In the latter case, it is suggested that presently exempt carriers be brought under regulation.[15] The difficulty in both cases is that the nature of motor trucking tends to make really effective enforcement of any common carrier system extremely difficult.[16]

There is a second group of reasons why regulated common carriers are losing traffic to unregulated and private carriage. These might be termed physical distribution problems, and in the long run they may turn out to be much more serious for common carriage than mere overpricing.

The concept of physical distribution for a firm involves the analysis of all physical flows through the firm, including the various stops of flows (ware-housing and inventory) in the course of production. Using this analysis, it is clear that any activity dealing with movement or storage of goods should be handled by a single executive responsible for physical distribution.[17]

Common carriers are able to provide only a fraction of the total physical distribution service for a firm—the portion relating to movement. This may in fact be the least important part of the process for a company, since warehousing costs run as high as 25 percent of the value of the goods annually.[18] Firms may be able to save money by concentrating on inventory reduction rather than transport cost reduction. But such calculations involve total control of movement and storage—which is another way of indicating why private carriage is so popular. The familiar problems of loss and damage, plus delays often attributed to common carriage, may prove intolerable here for many firms, and they may well prefer private carriage even though overall transport costs are higher.[19]

This type of physical distribution management, as compared to the more traditional traffic management, becomes extremely important in the sector where value of service pricing provides the most revenue for common carriers—namely, in high value per pound goods movements. Interest, inventory, and storage costs are highest in areas where goods moved are most valuable, and shippers are more willing to pay premiums for transportation control in these sectors.

This may appear paradoxical, since it has earlier been noted that common carriers tend to overprice their services. Clearly, if shippers use common carriage, they will press for the lowest possible prices. What is occurring here is a split in the kinds of services desired from common carriers. In some instances, shippers are quite satisfied with bare transportation services, stripped of frills. In others, they demand extremely complex services, which common carriers may be unable to supply.[20] The former situations are generally common in raw materials flows, such as agricultural products and ores. The latter are common when high value goods are shipped. But high value is a relative term—what is important to one shipper may be irrelevant to another. In effect, shippers demand a tailoring of transportation service to their own needs, and the regulated common carriers, with their complex and cumbersome tariffs and rules of carriage, are in a poor position to tailor their services in this way. Indeed, such adjustments may be illegal discrimination under present law. A major advantage of private carriage is not so much price as the ability to pay for exactly what is wanted. The relative inflexibility of common carrier services results in dissatisfaction among shippers and searches for more realistic alternatives. Present commission policy encouraging trucking mergers is certain to make this problem more serious as time passes. Railroads have often been accused of being too monolithic to meet the needs of shippers; if common carriers in trucking also become huge, we can dismally and confidently predict even more rapid increases in private carriage—particularly if smaller and more flexible common carrier truckers are wiped out in the process.

Conclusion

The frequently stated opinion that regulated common carriage is eminently desirable misses the key point that many shippers obviously do not agree. Traffic trends in the past decade suggest that common carriage has been declining relative to private and unregulated carriage, and that if relaxation of present rules covering exemptions and private operations were made, regulated common carriage would decline still faster. Hence the argument runs that we must restrict still further unregulated carriers. Central to this argument are the various reasons for the desirability for common carriage noted earlier. If in fact common carriage offers something which unregulated carriage does not, support for regulated carriage will be strong and continuous. If common carriage advantages can be obtained in cheaper and easier ways, such arguments, as well as carriers, will be swept aside.

NOTES

1. See, for example, Rupert L. Murphy, "Reliance on 'Self-Help' in Solving the Common Carrier Problem," 30 ICC Pract J 449-451.
2. The recent decline of common carriage has been summarized by Edmund A. Nightingale, "A Critique of American Transportation Policy Developments," 30 ICC Pract J 891-905 and 1004-1020; also Reprint.
3. See, for example, *76th Annual Report of the Interstate Commerce Commission, Fiscal Year Ended June 30, 1962.* Washington, D.C.: U.S. Govt. Printing Office, 1962, pp. 198-210.
4. One may search, for example, such documents as Special Study Group on Transportation Policies in the United States, *National Transportation Policy: Preliminary Draft of a Report Prepared for the Committee on Interstate and Foreign Commerce, U.S. Senate.* Washington, D.C.: U.S. Govt. Printing Office, 1961, 732 pp., for such a justification without avail. It is implicit here that regulated common carriage is critical, but the reasons why it is are not explicitly stated.
5. These are taken from various transportation acts, summarized in Stuart Daggett, *Principles of Inland Transportation.* New York: Harper & Brothers, 1955, pp. 639-735.
6. Special Study Group on Transportation Policies, *op. cit.,* pp. 70-81.
7. The duty of service with its corresponding cost implications is treated in Daggett, *op. cit.,* pp. 229-243.
8. A classic case of this type of internal subsidy is the commuter deficit. See the statement of James M. Symes in *Problems of the Railroads: Hearings Before the Subcommittee on Surface Transportation of the Committee on Interstate and Foreign Commerce, U.S. Senate, 85th Congress, 2nd Session, Part 1.* Washington, D.C.: U.S. Govt. Printing Office, 1958, pp. 82-85, to see what this one item has cost a single railroad.
9. E. W. Williams and D. W. Bluestone, *Rationale of Federal Transportation Policy.* Washington: U.S. Department of Commerce, 1960, pp. 24-28.
10. See C. A. Taff, *Commercial Motor Transportation, Third Ed.* Homewood, Ill.: Richard D. Irwin, Inc., 1961, pp. 430-475, for a description of the ratemaking process.
11. See I.C.C., *Cost of Transporting Freight by Class I and Class II Motor Common Carriers of General Commodities: Middle Atlantic Region, 1960.* Washington, D.C.: U.S. Govt. Printing Office, 1960, for an example of this technique.
12. Those curious about this point might check various class rates for motor common carriers and compare such rates with regional operating costs for heavy trucks (usually in the 30-50 cent per truck mile range). In a surprisingly large number of cases, the rate runs 150 to 190 percent of the total one-way truck operating cost, including depreciation and interest.
13. Special Study Group on Transportation Policies, *op. cit.,* pp. 398-407.
14. This is particularly true where the cost of handling a type of traffic by one mode is below marginal cost of other modes. Such railroad hauls as coal and long distance refrigerated traffic are cases in point.
15. See footnote 3 for the I.C.C.'s ideas on this point. A second suggestion is less regulation and increased exemptions per the late President Kennedy's requests. See D. F. Pegrum,

Transportation: Economics and Public Policy. Homewood, Ill.: Richard D. Irwin, Inc., 1963, pp. 585-600, for the full text of his 1962 message to Congress.

16. The enforcement difficulty is emphasized by Commissioner Everett Hutchinson of the I.C.C. in testimony in *Decline of Regulated Common Carriage: Hearings Before the Surface Transportation Subcommittee of the Committee on Commerce, U.S. Senate, 87th Congress, 1st Session*, Washington, D.C.: U.S. Government Printing Office, 1962, pp. 250-252.

17. See S. H. Brewer and James Rosenzweig, "Rhochrematics and Organization," *California Management Review*, Vol. III, No. 3, Spring 1961, pp. 52-71.

18. E. W. Smykay, D. J. Bowersox, and F. H. Mossman, *Physical Distribution Management*. New York: The Macmillan Company, 1961, pp. 92-93.

19. J. R. Meyer, M. J. Peck, J. Stenason, and C. Zwick, *The Economics of Competition in the Transportation Industries*. Cambridge: Harvard University Press, 1960, pp. 100-101.

20. One example of highly specialized transportation requirements is described by the National Fisheries Institute, Inc., in *Decline of Regulated Common Carriage, op. cit.*, pp. 250-252.